JOSEPHUS DANIELS

JOSEPHUS

HIS LIFE & TIMES

DANIELS

Lee A. Craig

THE UNIVERSITY OF NORTH CAROLINA PRESS   *Chapel Hill*

This book was published with the assistance of the
William R. Kenan Jr. Fund of the University of North Carolina Press.

© 2013 THE UNIVERSITY OF NORTH CAROLINA PRESS

All rights reserved. Designed by Sally Fry.
Set in Calluna by Tseng Information Systems, Inc.
Manufactured in the United States of America.

———

The paper in this book meets the guidelines for permanence
and durability of the Committee on Production Guidelines for
Book Longevity of the Council on Library Resources.

The University of North Carolina Press has been a
member of the Green Press Initiative since 2003.

Library of Congress Cataloging-in-Publication Data
Craig, Lee A. (Lee Allan), 1960–
Josephus Daniels : his life and times / by Lee A. Craig.
pages cm
Includes bibliographical references and index.
ISBN 978-1-4696-0695-8 (alk. paper)
1. Daniels, Josephus, 1862–1948. 2. Cabinet officers—United States—
Biography. 3. Ambassadors—United States—Biography. 4. United States—Dept.
of the Navy—Biography. 5. Press and politics—United States—History.
6. United States—Politics and government—1901–1953. 7. Publishers
and publishing—North Carolina—Biography. 8. Newspaper
publishing—North Carolina—History. I. Title.
E748.D19C73 2013
973.9092—dc23
[B]
2012041235

17 16 15 14 13 5 4 3 2 1

To Gabie & Ellee

Contents

Preface

For nearly thirty-five years, from the election campaign of 1898 until he became U.S. ambassador to Mexico in 1933, Josephus Daniels was the most powerful man in North Carolina. Governors came and went, but Daniels and his flagship newspaper, the Raleigh *News and Observer* (*N&O*), stayed. During President Woodrow Wilson's two terms in office (1913–21), Daniels served as secretary of the navy. No one ever held the position longer than he did. In that capacity, and as one of Wilson's closest confidants, Daniels was one of the most powerful men in the country. Once the United States entered World War I in 1917, Daniels became one of the most important men in the world.

Daniels earned his initial fame and made a fortune in the newspaper business. A self-made man, he owned his first newspaper at age eighteen. Before his twenty-first birthday, he owned three. Daniels revolutionized the newspaper business and, with other newspapermen of his generation, changed the relationship between politics and the news media. Before Daniels entered the business, except for the owners of the big-city papers, newspapermen could not survive financially on subscriptions and advertising alone. At the time, governments did not generally maintain their own printing shops; thus political patronage, in the form of government printing contracts, provided local newspapers with the margin between profit and loss. The price of that profit was effective control of the newspaper's content. The holder of the government contracts became a wholly owned subsidiary of the majority wing of the majority party granting the contracts. Daniels recognized that an expansion of subscriptions would allow a local newspaper to be profitable without government contracts. Advertising would follow where subscriptions led. But a broad subscription base required newspapers to be sold for their news content, not their political opinions. As a teenage newspaper entrepreneur, Daniels surmised that if he could create a news organization that generated a sufficient circulation and advertising revenues, then the politicians would come to his newspaper with their hats in hand rather than the other way around. It took many years, but Daniels succeeded in this quest, creating a publishing dynasty that would last a century.

Daniels grew up in a world with no radio, no television, and no Internet. News came from two sources, newspapers and gossip, and most of the important gossip came from something in the newspaper. Daniels supplied newspapers. When Daniels was born, "news gathering was considered a lowly occupation, its practitioners on a par with actors and acrobats. Not yet a profession or even a dignified craft, it was the 'haven of shipwrecked ambitions,' sought by men who had failed in other endeavors."[1] Daniels was among the handful of men who changed that situation, creating the modern newspaper, with international, national, and local news sections, including features, sports, comics, and editorials, all interspersed with advertisements and supplemented by classified ads.

A few of Daniels's contemporaries, such as William Randolph Hearst and Joseph Pulitzer, could make a living selling independent newspapers in a small number of densely packed cities, but America was a nation of farms and small towns. Daniels figured out how to turn a profit in places like Wilson, Kinston, Rocky Mount, and Raleigh, North Carolina. In the late nineteenth and early twentieth centuries the U.S. economy grew, on average, a bit more than 3 percent a year. The circulation of Daniels's newspapers grew five times as fast.[2]

While Daniels was amassing his own fortune, he served as one of his generation's most articulate and persistent critics of unregulated capitalism, never failing to call for government control, or outright ownership, of various private enterprises—including the era's greatest industry, the railroads. His newspapers pushed for the passage of the nation's landmark antitrust laws and the hard-nosed prosecution of other capitalists. Daniels foresaw the concentration of great wealth in the hands of men like James Buchanan Duke, founder of the American Tobacco Company. Arguing that the Dukes of the world would not use their wealth for society's betterment, Daniels did not hesitate to call upon the coercive powers of the state to constrain such men.

Daniels leveraged his success as a businessman into political clout, and he leveraged his political clout into an unlikely position: head of the U.S. Navy. A devout Christian and a near-pacifist, Daniels created one of history's greatest war machines, which helped win World War I. Having won the war, the Allies then lost the peace. Daniels was one of the few men Wilson held in high regard and consulted throughout his eight years in the White House. He disagreed with Wilson's neutrality policies before the United States entered the war, and he questioned many of Wilson's prescriptions for the postwar world. Yet Daniels failed to steer Wilson from either course. The former led to the country's entry into the war, and the latter led to the disaster that was the Versailles Treaty. World War II was a result of that failure.

A staunch anti-imperialist, as secretary of the navy, Daniels nonetheless oversaw an aggressive extension of U.S. military power, including the invasion or occupation of Nicaragua, Mexico, Haiti, the Dominican Republic, and Cuba. By default he became the receiver of several what today would be called "failed states." By the time he stepped down as head of the navy, he personally oversaw a gunboat empire. However, having once ordered the invasion of Mexico, later in life, as U.S. ambassador to that country (1933–41), Daniels would help steer it and the United States toward a long-term peace that benefited both countries.

Daniels proved to be a good judge of political talent. He saw something in a staid Presbyterian professor named Woodrow Wilson that many party leaders missed. And before anyone else, Daniels imagined the great potential in a man others considered a pampered, arrogant Harvard twit, and he gave that man, Franklin Delano Roosevelt (FDR), his start on the world's greatest political stage. Young FDR's career at the national level began as assistant secretary of the navy under Daniels's tutelage. "You have taught me so wisely," Roosevelt wrote to Daniels toward the end of their long service together at the Navy Department. As one of Roosevelt's biographers notes, Daniels was the only man under whom Roosevelt ever served in any capacity.[3] Henceforth, even after becoming president, FDR called Daniels "Chief." Later in life, Roosevelt paid homage to Daniels as tutor par excellence in the political arts. FDR might well have gone on to great things without Daniels's patronage, but he owed his start to Daniels.

In all of these roles, Daniels maintained his era's quest for progress, at least as he defined it. But progress came slowly to his home state. At the time of Daniels's birth in 1862, North Carolina's small farms and plantations employed the vast majority of the state's labor force—free and slave. Industrialization, sweeping across the northern states, had yet to spread to the South. The implements on most of the state's farms and plantations differed little from those used by the ancient Israelites. By the time Daniels died in 1948, the old ways were gone. Mechanization and industrialization had freed millions of workers from the farm.

Agriculture was not the only sector of the economy destined for revolution during Daniels's life. At the time of his birth, sail still dominated shipping on the high seas. Ship masts loomed over the dockyards of the state's ports in New Bern, Beaufort, Morehead City, and Wilmington. Travel from one of those ports to Liverpool could still take weeks. Other than the rudimentary processing of the state's agricultural and timber products, there was little manufacturing of which one could speak. Less than 5 percent of North Carolina's residents lived in an urban area, and "urban" in this context was not very urban in any contemporary sense of the word, meaning at the time a town of 2,500 or more residents. The residents of such "cities" maintained livestock and gardens, and the unpaved roads turned to muddy quagmires with even a small amount of rain. Typically, there was no electricity and no running water or sewage system.

Similarly, the South's financial resources were primitive at best. Bank deposits per person in the region were only one-fifth the value of those in the rest of the country.[4] In Wilson County, where Daniels grew up, as late as 1880 there was only one commercial bank. When he sought a loan to purchase his first newspaper, he borrowed money from a wealthy acquaintance, on the collateral of a friend. There was no financial institution from which he could receive a loan. At the time, Wilson's only bank would not have considered making an unsecured commercial loan to a young newspaper entrepreneur.

Education was a prerequisite of progress. Yet during Daniels's boyhood, North Carolina maintained no public school system. Although the state had developed a school system on the eve of the Civil War, that system had been completely abandoned during the war and Reconstruction. Until he went to the University of North Carolina to study law as a young man, Daniels never set foot in a public school. Perhaps because of this, he became the state's strongest voice for publicly supported education, another pillar of his progressivism.

Hardly any factories, few banks, and no public school system: This was the world into which Josephus Daniels was born. It was all about to change. By the time he died, the state's economy, though still heavily agricultural, had turned into a manufacturing juggernaut. North Carolina's burgeoning industrial sector largely revolved around the textile and tobacco industries. From virtually zero, the state leaped to three thousand textile employees in 1880, and after that the figure exploded, approaching a quarter of a million around the time of Daniels's death nearly seventy years later. The growth of manufacturing marked the beginning of the shift of economic activity from farm to town, a shift with profound social manifestations. It was called the New South. The rise of the state's towns and industry, "the sudden quickening of life in commerce and investment in certain areas of the South,"[5] accompanied a related change, this one in the countryside itself. At the time

Daniels died, the region's large planters were in the process of mechanizing the cotton harvest. This technological change accelerated the migration from farm to town, as well as the great African American migration from the rural South to the urban North. The South's own urbanization rates, while below those of the North, began to increase rapidly. As the region experienced economic progress, the quest for more became a "public zeal that . . . converted an economic development into a civic crusade."[6] Daniels became one of the New South's most outspoken crusaders.

Southern notions of progress took a dark turn regarding matters of race. When Daniels was born, slavery was still legal in the United States. Although Daniels's parents were too poor to have owned slaves, his maternal grandparents had been prominent slaveholders in eastern North Carolina. Emancipation by proclamation came during the Civil War but to little effect in the areas of the South that remained in Confederate hands. After the war the Thirteenth Amendment to the U.S. Constitution formally abolished slavery; but for the newly freed, there was neither forty acres nor a mule, and the majority of African Americans remained on southern plantations as laborers and sharecroppers.

The years immediately following emancipation were ones of social turmoil and some violence, as the newly freed African Americans and their northern white supporters tried to "reconstruct" the Old South into a new one. More than a few white southerners rebelled at these efforts. The Ku Klux Klan and other violent organizations, including the so-called red shirts, maintained a running war with the occupying Union army. When the northerners finally gave up and withdrew their military forces, the new social order was nothing like what any side—northern or southern, white or black—might have chosen on its own if given the opportunity. However, with southern whites once again securing control of state and local governments throughout the region, blacks got the worst of it. The immediate post-Reconstruction era saw the emergence of a new social order in the South; the conditions were oppressive by any reasonable standard, but the open warfare waged by groups such as the Klan subsided considerably.

Although African Americans were not equal in any meaningful economic, social, or legal sense, the days of mass state-enforced disenfranchisement and Jim Crow laws were still decades in the future. Following Reconstruction, the average annual number of lynchings, which serves as a crude barometer of white reaction to black independence, was a fraction of levels reached later in the century.[7] It was only *after* black voters began to exercise their political power, in the 1890s, in conjunction with white Republicans and dissident Democrats—a process Daniels and others referred to as "Fusion"—that the mainstream of the Democratic Party moved to eliminate the black vote and impose a southern form of apartheid. In North Carolina, Daniels led this movement. To Daniels, progress in race relations meant taking blacks out of the political equation. He thus led North Carolina's white supremacist movement and, more than any other individual, was responsible for the disenfranchisement of the state's African American citizens.

In a nation of laws, for blacks, being stripped of the franchise served as a kind of political death sentence, and the result was Jim Crow, the complete segregation of southern society, a society that was separate and unequal. At the time of Daniels's death, this aspect of the world he helped create had not changed. In the summer before Daniels died, Jackie Robinson first appeared on the field for the Brooklyn Dodgers professional baseball team, but in most of the South, Robinson could not eat, drink, or share a hotel room, a water fountain, a bus seat, or toilet facilities with his white teammates. Only a little more than a decade after Daniels's death, George Wallace could still run for governor of Alabama with the cry of "Segregation now! Segregation tomorrow! Segregation forever!" This was the South Daniels helped create.

———

In telling Daniels's story, I have focused on three aspects of his life: his career as a newspaper owner; his role as a leading progressive-era politico, including his leadership of North Carolina's white supremacy movement; and his three stints in public service. Chapter 1 looks at Daniels's family background and his boyhood in Wilson. Chapter 2 explores his early career as a newspaper publisher. Chapter 3 covers his first tour of duty in Washington, D.C., as the number two man in the Interior Department, as well as his subsequent takeover of the Raleigh *News and Observer*. Chapters 4 and 5 focus on Daniels's early management of the *N&O* and his success in turning it into one of the region's most important newspapers. In addition, those chapters review Daniels's role in North Carolina's white supremacy campaigns and, ultimately, the disenfranchisement of the state's African American voters. Chapters 6 through 9 focus on Daniels's years as secretary of the navy, including his oversight of Wilson's version of gunboat diplomacy in the Caribbean and as head of the navy during World War I, as well as his role in the postwar settlement, including the Versailles Treaty. Finally, Chapter 10 reviews his family life after he left the Wilson administration and examines the political battles in North Carolina during the 1920s; it concludes with his experience as U.S. ambassador to Mexico during the 1930s and early 1940s.

In addition to the vast body of source material touching Daniels's life and several careers, I have relied on a number of primary and secondary sources directly related to him. Six of these either are in his hand or were written directly to him. These include his memoirs, books, speeches, diaries, personal correspondence, and editorials. In addition, I was able to interview several family members and former employees. In doing this, I have had to wrestle with what one critic of biographical history calls "the private truth versus the public facade,"[8] which is to ask, When the sources contradict one another, what is the biographer to do? Space constraints prohibit elaboration on every possible scenario. Ultimately, the biographer must identify the "true" person and convey that truth to the reader.

In conducting the research on Daniels's life, I was both served and hindered by his voluminous written record. In addition to his memoirs, which ran to five volumes and thousands of pages, and many books and speeches, more than 400,000 pieces of individual correspondence have survived in the Wilson Library at the University of North Carolina in Chapel Hill, the Rubenstein Library at Duke University, and the Library of Congress. After reviewing these materials, I better understood the comment of one writer, who noted, "The biographer of a copious self-chronicler has a particular burden: the feeling that he might be serving leftovers."[9] On personal matters, when not contradicted by other sources, I have taken Daniels at his word. When skepticism seemed merited based on other information, I have supplied it. This is particularly true in respect to the use of his memoirs for tracing the early years of his life. During those years, the other paper trails, such as his speeches and correspondence, are less voluminous, and so his memoirs must carry more weight than perhaps I would have liked; but they do provide a firsthand account of the world in which he lived, and they give us a glimpse of the people in it and how he saw them.

As a capitalist, progressive muckraker, white supremacist, and imperialist, Daniels filled a number of roles that will not endear him to many modern readers. In telling his story, I have kept in mind a renowned historian's admonition: "It is easy to condemn the villains of the past and hard to understand the world that made them."[10] My objective is to help the reader understand Daniels's world and his actions. I will leave the condemnation to others. I have attempted to make this volume a true life *and* times, using my training as a historian to educate the modern reader about the great issues of Daniels's day. In this effort, I fear my formal training, which was in economic and business history, betrays me. The reader will be excused for thinking I have focused too much on Daniels the businessman, the economics of war, and the economics of race.

Emerson is credited with telling us there is no history, only biography. I would not make such a claim. I have benefited immensely from the literatures on the progressive movement, the postbellum south, and naval history, all areas of research in which Daniels's name appears frequently. He had his thumb in so many pies and turned up in so much of American history—even if often as the puppeteer offstage, hidden by the curtain—that to do justice to his life required incursions into literatures in which I can claim no expertise. To borrow the disclaimer of another historian, "The subject is too big. There is barely time for me to be approximately fair to the defendant's case. The book is heavily footnoted precisely because of my inexpertise. . . . I will often irritate you, mistake facts out of ignorance, misunderstand the texts I am citing, choose the wrong grounds on which to argue, miss important texts and statistics and writers, and fail to address all of your very reasonable doubts."[11] For this I apologize and accept all blame.

———

This volume has benefited greatly from the assistance of many people. My administrative assistants at North Carolina State University—Lovie Santaniello, Carolyn Smith, and David Strickland—have efficiently handled so many of the everyday chores of academic life that, were it not for them, this work would have taken another ten years to complete. Similarly, my research assistants—Dana L. Etheridge, Amy Bailey, Margaret Jarocki, Katherine Merrick, Jeff Horn, Lindsey Briggs, Brett Danforth, Andrew Copland, Rachael Huntley, and Victoria Schuch—deserve more credit for the final product than I can convey on these pages, and I consider their acquaintance and friendship to be one of the rewards of the effort.

I was also greatly assisted by the librarians, too numerous to name individually, at the following institutions: the Library of Congress, Washington, D.C.; David M. Rubenstein Rare Book and Manuscript Library, Duke University, Durham, N.C.; Southern Historical Collection at Wilson Library, University of North Carolina at Chapel Hill; Special Collections Research Center, D. H. Hill Library, North Carolina State University, Raleigh; and North Carolina Division of Archives and History, Raleigh. I extend special thanks to those who helped collect the photographs: Kim Andersen Cumber at the North Carolina State Archives, Amy McDonald at Duke, Mary-ellen Tinsley at Wilson Library, Julie Wood on behalf of Frank Daniels Jr., and my colleague and friend John Lapp.

Workshop and seminar participants provided valuable questions, comments, and criticism at the following venues: Alfred Chandler Lecture in Southern Business History, Department of History and the Center for the Study of the American South, University of North Carolina at Chapel Hill; the Triangle Universities Economic History Workshop; and the Shaftesbury Society Lecture, John Locke Foundation, Raleigh, N.C. In addition, several members of the Daniels family were generous with their time and memories during interviews. They are listed individually in the References section at the end of the volume.

Ask college professors to identify the frustrations of academic life, and they will invariably place obstructionist administrators and difficult colleagues on the list. This has not been my experience, at least not with respect to this project. My department heads, Steve Margolis and Douglas Pearce, as well as deans, Ira Weiss and John Bartley, have been supportive, and Steve Margolis also provided financial support for the project through his direction of the N.C. State Foundation of Free Societies Fund. Robert Whaples, John Milton Cooper, Ferrel Guillory, and an anonymous reviewer read the entire manuscript and provided valuable comments on just about every topic. The final product is greatly improved as a result of their diligence. In addition, Stephanie Ladniak Wenzel, my copyeditor at UNC Press, did an outstanding job, and I owe much to Chuck Grench, the acquisitions editor, who showed more patience than I deserved. He also read the entire manuscript and provided the right amounts of encouragement and authority in the right quantities at the right times.

I am also grateful to my wife, Jacquelyn, and other friends and colleagues—again, too numerous to name individually, in fact, much too numerous—who have patiently listened to me tell "Daniels stories" as the project developed over the past several years. I tried to stop myself when I thought their countenances reflected boredom, but I don't think I was very successful at this. I also owe a special thanks to my friend John Bennett and my colleague Michael Walden, both of whom have prodded me over the past few years by asking, every time I see them, "When will the book be finished?" Finally, I dedicate this volume to my daughters, Gabrielle Marie and Elizabeth Lee, who have given me the most precious gift the young can offer the old: hope for the future.

JOSEPHUS DANIELS

1. The Loveliest Village of the Plain

In the early eighties Wilson was strictly a cotton town. . . .
People depended almost solely on cotton, though some small
farmers raised their "hog and hominy," and the large planters grew
watermelons and some vegetables. But King Cotton ruled.

—JOSEPHUS DANIELS

Throughout his life, Josephus Daniels emphasized his humble roots in the sandy soils of North Carolina's coastal plain. Those roots were never quite as humble as Daniels insisted, but they were humble enough. Daniels's father, also named Josephus, was a first-generation American. Father and son were named for the first-century historian Flavius Josephus, whose eyewitness account of the Jewish Revolt and subsequent Roman sack of Jerusalem could be found in the libraries of the more literate early American families. (It was said of that time and place that "beyond the good book were very few other books," but the works of Josephus were among those few other books.)[1] The elder Josephus Daniels, later nicknamed "Jody," was born on January 21, 1828, in the little town of Bayboro, North Carolina, near Pamlico Sound. He was one of six sons born to Clifford and Susan Carraway Daniels.[2]

In the early 1780s, Clifford's widowed father, Thomas Daniels, had migrated from Northern Ireland, with Clifford and three other sons, to Roanoke Island, North Carolina.[3] Thomas and his sons were fishermen. Sitting at the confluence of Albemarle and Pamlico Sounds, tucked within North Carolina's Outer Banks, Roanoke Island proved an excellent location to practice their trade in the New World. There, and in the surrounding tidal areas, the first two American generations of Josephus Daniels's family fished, farmed, and became shipwrights. An Ulsterman of Scottish decent, Thomas came from a clan that was rapidly claiming territory across Virginia and the Carolinas. These Scots-Irish (Scots who had done England's dirty work in Ireland) established a reputation for hardscrabble frugality: "Wherever they settled, they gained a reputation for practical piety and aggressive independence. A saying among their neighbors held that the Scotch-Irish kept the Sabbath and anything else they could lay hands on."[4]

After reaching adulthood, Clifford moved from Roanoke Island to the mainland town of Bayboro, along the Bay River inlet. There he settled and started his large family with Susan Carraway. After Susan's early death, Clifford married Millie Jones, and with her he had six more children (four girls and two boys).[5] To earn a living, Clifford fished, as his father, Thomas, had. But he also engaged in some small-scale farming, which seems practical if for no other reason than because of the number of mouths he had to feed, and as his boys from his first marriage matured, he developed a modest business constructing and repairing small schooners, which were employed in the local and coastal shipping trade.

Several of Clifford's eight sons, including the senior Josephus, joined the small but growing family shipbuilding business. For reasons lost to time, in his early twenties, Josephus left Bayboro and the little family shop forever. Most likely young Daniels simply left a small backwater town to seek his fortune in the wider world, as countless ambitious youngsters have done before and since. First, he ventured north across the Pamlico River to the town of Washington in Beaufort County, where there were more and larger shipyards. A few years later, around 1850, he migrated to Rhode Island, where for some time he worked in still larger yards. Putting a strictly economic spin on Daniels's move, we can surmise that a skilled wage-worker in the shipyards of Washington or Rhode Island could earn more than would have been possible in the small, and increasingly overcrowded, family shop in Bayboro.

The general economic conditions of the late antebellum era drove the market for shipwrights in eastern North Carolina. During these years, the southern economy grew rapidly, as the Atlantic trade, in which cotton played no small part, boomed. Larger shipyards bustled with activity, and good hands could be hard to find. Little Washington, as it was known, was a thriving port compared with Bayboro. There, Josephus Daniels, with the basic skills he had picked up in his father's shop, quickly became an employee of the Farrow shipyard. William Farrow, or Captain Farrow as he was known locally, had been a successful merchant captain who, with age, saw more profit and less risk in leaving the rigors of the sea and settling onshore in the shipbuilding business. In addition to offering Daniels a steady job at a decent wage, Captain and Mrs. Farrow were the custodians of an orphaned girl from a once-prominent local family. Her name was Mary Cleaves Seabrook.

According to family lore, Daniels was smitten by Mary Cleaves from their earliest acquaintance. She gave him the nickname Jody. A mutual affection eventually blossomed between them, but Mary Cleaves was only fourteen or at most fifteen when they met. Although marriage at such an age was not unheard of at the time, by the consent of at least some of the parties involved, it was agreed that Mary Cleaves was too young to wed. Economic opportunity interrupted Jody's subsequent courtship of the young orphan, as both Daniels and Farrow thought the expansion of the local shipping and shipbuilding businesses warranted a move into larger ships. Although Farrow was too old to learn those new tricks, he thought Daniels might be up to it, but since he lacked formal schooling in marine architecture, Daniels would need some on-site training to learn how to construct the larger ships. Farrow encouraged, and perhaps even funded, Daniels's decision to make an educational tour of the northern shipyards. There the younger man could study the construction of those larger vessels, a turn of events that led him to Rhode Island, where he stayed for more than two years.

Of Jody Daniels's time in New England practically nothing is known. Eventually, however, now in his mid-twenties, he returned to Washington, again settling into life as a shipwright in Farrow's shipyard. Soon, displaying an entrepreneurial bent that he passed on to his son Josephus, Jody began some small-scale shipbuilding on his own. He had other business pursuits as well. Although the long-run trend in the coastal trade was without question positive, the industry was highly cyclical, and during the occasional downturn Jody Daniels worked in the retail store of John A. Arthur, who had become his closest personal friend outside the Farrow household.

Also, after returning from New England, Jody renewed his courtship of Mary Cleaves, and on New Year's Day 1856, twenty-seven-year-old Jody Daniels married twenty-year-old Mary Cleaves Seabrook. Mary Cleaves, as she was usually known to friends and family, came from a higher rung on the socioeconomic ladder than Jody Daniels. Born into a relatively prosperous slave-owning family, Mary Cleaves grew up on a plantation in Hyde County, which lies to the east of Washington along the northern bank of the Pamlico River at the point at which the river flows into the Pamlico Sound. Although the area was largely marshland, the rich soil along the creeks that drained into the Pamlico could yield profits to those who had the initiative (and slave capital) to levee, drain, and cultivate it. But farming there proved to be a hard life. Visiting long after the area had been tamed, Josephus Daniels lamented the oppressive heat and mosquitoes that blackened the sails of the vessel on which he toured the county, which despite the state's subsequent growth would remain lightly settled.[6] Heat, humidity, hurricanes, black bears, swarms of mosquitoes in the air, and snakes underfoot made carving an economic niche in this soggy wilderness an insurmountable challenge to all but a few. Mary Cleaves's father, James Seabrook, was one of those few, as had been both of her grandfathers.

James Seabrook, whose birthdate remains in dispute, was a farmer who also dabbled in medicine. After reaching adulthood, he established a farm on Smith Creek within eyesight of his parents' place and slowly but steadily built a modestly prosperous operation. Wishing to share his good fortune with a wife, in 1827, after a brief but formal courtship, James Seabrook proposed to nineteen-year-old Lois Davis, who was descended on her mother's side from a prominent family of land- and slave-owners, their name variously spelled Cleves or Cleaves. Lois received the proposal with enthusiasm. Her parents did not, for there was another suitor, a Mr. John Bell. Much older than James Seabrook, Bell had more property, and perhaps more importantly, the Bell name was older and more renowned among locals than that of Seabrook. The Davises had no intention of seeing Lois marry down either socially or economically, so they chose old Mr. Bell for their daughter. Lois, however, chose young Seabrook and eloped—"ran off," in the vernacular of an earlier time—with him. Though the Davises were horrified, no doubt, the exact sanctions they imposed on their daughter remain unrecorded. For his part, Bell held no grudge and remained on good, though understandably distant, terms with the newlyweds.

The marriage of James Seabrook and Lois Davis proved to be a happy one. Among the sources of this happiness was economic success; the modest farm James had established by the time of their marriage subsequently grew and prospered. By the early 1830s it produced "Wheat, corn, and cotton" as well as "fowl, sheep, hogs, and cattle"; there was a vegetable garden, an orchard, and an abundance of other fruits. Fish and oysters were plentiful in the nearby waterways. Surplus crops were sold up the Pamlico River in Washington or down the Pamlico Sound and then up the Neuse River in New Bern. The labor demands of such an operation were met by "a number of negro slaves."[7] Although the exact number of slaves is unrecorded, at the time only one-third of all southern families owned even a single slave.[8] To own "a number of slaves" and enough land to feed and keep them fully employed indicates the Seabrooks possessed considerable wealth, much more than, for example, Jody Daniels's family, which included twelve children, owned little land, and held no slaves.

The Seabrook–Davis marriage was more than a corporate venture. Spiritually, it appears that through Lois, James converted from a rather ill-defined Jeffersonian Deism to formal Methodism, a commitment which they successfully passed to subsequent generations of the family. In addition to a prosperous plantation and a devotion to the Methodist Church, the union of Thomas and Lois Seabrook produced three daughters, one of whom died in infancy, and two, Elizabeth Porter and Mary Cleaves (called "Polly" as a child, though the name did not stick), who lived to old age. Unfortunately, neither Thomas nor Lois Seabrook enjoyed a similarly long life. Thomas died in 1836, less than a year after the birth of his youngest daughter, Mary Cleaves, and Lois died twelve years later at age forty. Although the cause of death in each case is unknown, the fact that Thomas lingered and was treated by local physicians suggests disease as the proximate cause—perhaps yellow fever, which was not uncommon in the area at the time.

Though widowed at a young age, Lois Seabrook did not succumb to despair. Life without a spouse was hard, but the physical labor was still left to slaves. In the years following her husband's death, Lois managed the family plantation with the help of an African American slave who served as overseer. Young Mary Cleaves undoubtedly learned a thing or two about feminine independence from her mother. Whatever she learned from the experience, it would serve her well in the hard years to come. The Danielses knew backbreaking manual labor; the Seabrooks did not.

At the time of Lois Seabrook's death, her daughters were still minors. Her estate entered probate, and its dissolution was overseen by a court-appointed executor. Initially, the disposition of the estate followed a fairly common path. Family papers and surviving legal documents refer to two separate transactions, one involving tangible (that is, non–real estate) assets and one involving land. At the time the will was executed, all tangible assets, including furniture, slaves, farm equipment, and so forth, were liquidated, a not uncommon practice at the time. The region's agricultural economy was based on credit. Farmers borrowed to get the crop in the field with the expectation (and hope) that at harvest, the combination of yield and price would be enough to pay off the debt, with something left over for store-bought necessities and luxuries. In that economy, the primary difference between large farmers and small ones was the size of their debts. Thus the monies from Lois Seabrook's tangible assets (and some of her real estate) settled outstanding debts and property tax liabilities, with the remainder going to compensate the executor and the guardians of Elizabeth and Mary Cleaves. The girls themselves received nothing directly from the liquidation of these assets. As for the real estate, a portion of the land remained in trust for the girls until they reached adulthood, and thus they ultimately derived some wealth from their parents' economic success. However, each sister's share of the net proceeds would turn out to be only a little more than $1,000, a substantial sum at the time to be sure, but because of subsequent events, it would be nearly twenty years before they took possession of these monies, and they would face many hard times before that day arrived.

Despite the family's earlier prosperity, other than the land held in trust, the amount left after the estate was settled could not have been much, because the only cash with which the girls left Hyde County was $500 each, which, in an act of great charity, had been willed to them by their mother's old suitor, John Bell, who died the same year as their mother. With this generous endowment, more than twice per capita national income at the time, the girls were shipped to the home of their new guardian, Captain William Farrow, a family acquaintance who lived in Washington farther up the Pamlico River in Beaufort County. It appears the Farrows took control of the endowment that Bell left the Seabrook girls as well as the (net) cash flow from the rent on the Hyde County land held in trust in the girls' names. It follows that most if not all of that income went toward the upbringing of the girls. Whether in the end the girls actually received the full value of their mother's estate is doubtful, though it should be noted that in the years that followed, Mary Cleaves remained close to the Farrows, and there was never any hint that they misappropriated any funds from the estate. However, the same could not be said of the estate's executor. After reaching adulthood, Mary Cleaves's sister, Elizabeth, sued the executor over monies from the liquidation of Lois Seabrook's tangible assets, and although the exact terms of the settlement of the case have not survived, the formal charge was misfeasance.[9] In the end, other than the land in Hyde County, the value of which would not grow appreciably over the years, as farming moved inland with the state's population and economic activity, neither Elizabeth nor Mary Cleaves entered adulthood and then marriage with much more than her good name, a relatively genteel upbringing, and the clothes on her back.

After the move to Washington, through a mutual acquaintance Elizabeth soon met George Griffin, an up-and-coming merchant in the town of Wilson further inland on the coastal plain. They subsequently married in the early 1850s, and Elizabeth moved to Wilson, where Griffin's downtown livery stable, among his other small business ventures, grew if not prospered. Mary Cleaves, who had grown into an angular young woman of above-average height, remained in the Farrow home for almost eight years. Sometime early in her stay there, she met Farrow's young protégé, Jody Daniels. Love followed, and after Jody's return from Rhode Island, the couple married at the beginning of 1856.

By all accounts, the marriage was a happy one. If Tolstoy is correct and all happy families resemble one another, then at least part of that happiness derives from the important ways in which husbands and wives complement each other. Such was the case with Mary Cleaves and Jody Daniels. Although decidedly working class, from a family of no renown in a time and place in which such things mattered, Jody had a few assets to recommend him. He was bright enough, kind, handsome, hardworking, and entrepreneurial, and he possessed a valuable trade. Although he would have little chance to grow rich working with his hands, he had been ambitious enough to leave the backwater of Bayboro and establish himself in a successful business in a more bustling provincial town. Perhaps most importantly to his orphaned bride, any summary of his character would note that he was reliable.

Mary Cleaves, on the other hand, came from a well-regarded, albeit downwardly mobile, family. She too was bright, and although not beautiful in any classical sense, she possessed a pleasant countenance that locals might generously call pretty—certainly on the pretty side of plain. Possessing a good sense of humor, and generally more outgoing than her husband, she had a tremendous physical and mental energy, which had been honed during those years when she and her sister helped their widowed mother manage the family estate. This drive, which is easy to recognize in those who possess it but otherwise difficult to characterize, she passed on to her own children. Whatever it is and wherever it comes from, Mary Cleaves had it. She would remain an anchor in the Daniels family until she left this world in her eighty-eighth year.

One source of contention did emerge during the couple's courtship. Mary Cleaves, like her mother, was and would remain to her dying day a devout Methodist, whereas Jody's family had little commitment to a church beyond their claim to being "Ulster Protestants," which in those days contained no more information than saying they were not "Irish Catholics." One source claims that Mary Cleaves, stubbornly, would not marry Jody until he formally became a Methodist. The Methodists, originally followers of the Anglican theologian John Wesley, mixed high-church tenets with low-church evangelizing, a combination that proved to be popular in rural and small-town America. The church maintained features of Anglicanism, including an episcopacy and formal articles of faith, but it combined them with less ceremonial Sunday services, fervent preaching, and a strong emphasis on individual faith and responsibility. On North Carolina's socioeconomic ladder, the Methodists tended to occupy the middle rungs, lower than the Episcopalians but higher than the state's Baptists. Popular though the church might have been, given that Mary Cleaves had to insist that her betrothed join it, one assumes Jody joined with some reluctance. Still he joined. Years later, one of their sons described both parents as members of the church, even noting that Jody became a "member of the Board of Stewards." Perhaps his enthusiasm for Methodism increased with age.[10]

Despite their happy home, the young couple's life was not without travail. They lost their first child, a boy, during infancy. This was not uncommon at the time. Intestinal tract and respiratory infections yielded infant mortality rates more than twenty times higher than today's rates.[11] Neither the germ theory of disease nor the efficacy of public sanitation was well established at the time. Dysentery, often simply recorded as "diarrhea," when it was recorded at all, was a big killer. Town dwellers were particularly susceptible. A second child, another son, was born on September 9, 1858. Although named Franklin Arthur, after founding father Benjamin Franklin and John Arthur, Jody's close friend and sometime employer, the boy would be known simply as Frank. As for the family's dwelling, between Jody's return from New England and his marriage to Mary Cleaves, he had constructed with his own hands a small house in Washington, and here the little family lived quietly and in the relative comfort of a stable and happy home. All of that was about to be swept away with the winds of war.

By the time of Frank's birth, the political dispute between the states—encompassing slavery, the tariff, western settlement, and a host of related issues—had already resulted in bloodshed on the plains of Kansas. A little more than two years later, that conflict broadened into the Civil War. Southern radicals proposed secession as the only answer to the (threatened) tyranny of abolition. Jody Daniels maintained an unambiguous position on these developments. Though his wife had grown up in a slaveholding family, and although he could not be described as an abolitionist, he had no attachment to the institution of slavery. Furthermore, an ardent Whig, he openly opposed secession, and he remained, even during the Civil War, a Unionist. The Whig Party, once a national party, had split over slavery and abolition. In 1856, at Ripon, Wisconsin, a group of northern Whigs, abolitionists, nativists, a few antislavery Democrats, and members of various other splinter groups formed the Republican Party. In the late 1850s no party could straddle the growing political chasm between slavery and abolition. Men like Jody Daniels could continue to call themselves Whigs, and here and there one could find a group of locals who operated politically under the old name; but after the emergence of the Republicans there was no longer a national Whig Party.

In his objection to secession, Jody Daniels was not alone and perhaps at the time not even in the minority in his state. Secession never achieved the same sanctified status in North Carolina that it reached in the more "barn burning" regions of the South, such as South Carolina, which had left the Union shortly after Abraham Lincoln's election in the fall of 1860. Early in 1861, six other states (Alabama, Florida, Georgia, Louisiana, Mississippi, and Texas) joined South Carolina in secession and the formation of the Confederate States of America. After the attack on Fort Sumter in Charleston harbor (April 12, 1861), the recently inaugurated Lincoln called for 75,000 federal troops from the states remaining in the Union. Refusing to comply, the Virginia legislature seceded on April 17. Arkansas followed on May 6, and the next day the Tennessee legislature approved a military alliance with the Confederacy. With its neighbors to the north, south, and west now aligned with the Confederacy, and the Union demanding troops, North Carolina could not remain aloof from the impending hostilities. In May a special session of the state legislature called a convention to address the issue, and on May 20 the convention adopted an ordinance that repealed North Carolina's ratification of the U.S. Constitution.

Jody Daniels would serve the Confederate States of America, but not ardently. His war record remains a bit foggy even after much investigation by several parties, including his two oldest sons. In the years following Reconstruction, when such things mattered a great deal in North Carolina, his sons maintained that he volunteered for service with the Confederate navy. This was not quite accurate. Jody managed to avoid service in a Confederate army regiment, as he and his employer, Captain Farrow, ended up working in the Confederate naval yard in Wilmington, North Carolina, where Jody performed wage work for the Confederate navy. He was primarily employed repairing privateers and blockade-runners. Although Jody never actually served *in* the Confederate navy, as the war intensified, the difference narrowed between workers in strategic industries, such as shipbuilding and repair, and uniformed personnel. By the last year of the war, the Confederate government subjected, at least nominally, nearly all prime-age, able-bodied men to conscription of one form or another. It will never be known whether Jody served the Confederate navy out of a sense of duty to his state, or because it allowed him to avoid service in an army regiment or because he was nominally conscripted, or because he simply needed the money after the Union blockade had drastically reduced commercial shipping in the area. The question turned out to be important in the lives of his sons. After the war, having a distinguished record in a Confederate uniform, or having a father with a distinguished record, gave one a leg up in southern politics, and anyone without such a record was subject to questioning at best and possibly open condemnation. As the elder Daniels was never formally a member of the Confederate armed forces, his sons would be subject to the charge that he was a shirker or, worse, a Yankee sympathizer.

With Captain Farrow, Jody reported for work in Wilmington in the early summer of 1861. He contracted yellow fever soon after he arrived, but he recovered enough to enjoy a brief leave during which he continued to convalesce. He returned to Wilmington sometime in the late summer or early autumn. Over the next three years, he would only see his family on four more occasions, though at least two of these visits lasted several weeks. The Confederate States of America began formally conscripting able-bodied men into the army in 1862. As a worker with a skill deemed essential to the war effort, Jody was technically exempt from the draft, as long as he employed his craft in the service of the Confederate government. However, a second conscription act in 1864 allowed previously exempt workers to be drafted while remaining employed—in essence they became conscripted labor.[12] Jody Daniels avoided this fate as well. Although he was never in uniform, his service to the Confederacy was clearly of a military nature, and for much of the war he was not entirely free to come and go as he pleased. In any case, to abandon his employment as a shipwright would have formally exposed him to the military draft. He chose inglorious wage work over service in a regiment of the line.

There can be no doubting that Jody's young family suffered during his wartime absences. The uncertainties of war, reduction in income, separation for many months on end punctuated by the few intervals when Jody secured leave—all of these things must have been a challenge for Mary Cleaves and her soon-to-be growing family. As for Jody, among the emotional hardships that he endured was his absence when Mary Cleaves gave birth to their son Josephus on May 18, 1862. Given the timing of the boy's birth, it is likely he was conceived during his father's convalescence leave late the previous summer. Interestingly, on two of Jody's four subsequent leaves, he and Mary Cleaves conceived children. A daughter, Florence, was born in 1863, and died a short time later, though no cause of death was given, and another son, Charles Cleaves, was born in September 1864.

On one of his later leaves, Jody approached Union authorities in eastern North Carolina and received permission to ship goods, largely foodstuffs, from Union-held Hyde County into nearby, but Confederate-held, Little Washington in exchange for cotton.[13] Such trade across lines was not uncommon in areas that avoided the worst of the fighting. Knowing the area well, with personal connections on both sides of the shifting no-man's-land that separated the Union and Confederate forces, Jody was well positioned to facilitate this trade. However, he had neither the financial capital nor the mercantile connections to have arranged these transactions without help. At least part of the time he worked on behalf of a merchant named Hume, who operated out of Union-held New Bern, and in conjunction with a murky character named Kitcham. It is likely that he also dealt with his old friend John Arthur, or Arthur's business associates, at the Washington end of the trade, and it is likely that Hume and Kitcham had traded with Arthur before the war.

To legally trade across military lines, which is to say in order to avoid having his goods confiscated and getting himself hanged or shot as a spy, Jody had to have written approval from the Union army. To obtain this approval he had to post a bond of $500, which he could not have secured without financial backing. What was subsequently more important for his sons' postwar reputations, he had to formally swear and sign an oath of allegiance to the Union, an act about which he had no moral qualms. All of this guaranteed him the protection of the Union army, but it did nothing for him once he crossed into Confederate-held territory. Indeed, on at least one occasion he was taken into custody as a spy, an offense for which he most likely would have been executed if local residents had not intervened on his behalf. Given that he had officially renounced his allegiance to the Confederacy in order to trade under his Union bond, he was running a tremendous risk of being charged with desertion or even sedition by Confederate authorities. At the very least he exposed himself to conscription into a Confederate regiment.

On one of his trading excursions, during a leave in early 1864, Jody returned to Little Washington and moved his family to Ocracoke Island on North Carolina's Outer Banks. Although Ocracoke would become a popular vacation spot a century later, in the winter of 1864 it was a spit of barrier sand beyond the wilderness of North Carolina's far eastern coast. With no suitable port nearby and little commerce to speak of, primarily inhabited by fishermen, Ocracoke was primitive even compared to nearby Hyde County, where Mary Cleaves had grown up. Mary Cleaves had just lost a child; she had a six-year-old and a two-year-old in tow; and she was soon to realize she was pregnant with yet another child. To send her off to Ocracoke may seem curious in retrospect, but Jody had not spent the war isolated in a frontier outpost. Living in the most thriving and soon-to-be-last open port of the Confederacy, and currently trading with parties on both sides, he was well informed and well positioned to recognize that the combination of the increasingly constricting Union blockade and the pincer movement of Union forces in Virginia and Georgia would in time strangle what remained of the Confederate States of America. With some prescience he foresaw that those forces would eventually converge in eastern North Carolina, and he did not want his wife and sons to be in the path of the conquering forces.

Decades later, in his memoirs, Josephus Daniels claimed that his mother had twice been burned out of her home in Washington. This could not have been literally true, because the home Jody built survived the war and was sold by Mary Cleaves a few years after Jody's death.[14] Washington did, in fact, suffer from two major fires, one when the Union army pulled out and one shortly thereafter when the Confederates moved in. Mary Cleaves stayed with friends during this time, and so it is possible that the homes in which she resided were in fact burned to the ground. It is also possible that her son embellished or spoke metaphorically when, years later, he referred to these events and their impact on his mother. In either case, by 1864, Jody felt his family had seen enough of the war, and thus he decided that the certain hardships of Ocracoke would be easier to bear than the uncertain ones imposed by the victorious Yankees.

After moving his family to Ocracoke, Jody made one last visit there in the late summer of 1864, bringing supplies from the mainland. His oldest son, Frank, remembered that this was the last time he saw his father alive.[15] Josephus, barely two at the time, had no memory of his father, and Charles was yet to be born. Because of the shifting control between Union and Confederate forces in the towns of the coastal plain, the trading business in which Jody was engaged became too dangerous, and after he had provisioned his family on Ocracoke, he returned to work in the Wilmington naval yard sometime in the late summer or early autumn of 1864. He remained there until the Union navy began its final assault on Fort Fisher at the mouth of the Cape Fear River south of Wilmington. Once the fort fell on January 15, 1865, Wilmington ceased to be a valuable Confederate naval resource. Shortly before the fort was taken, Jody left Wilmington for good. Either he received his formal release from labor service, which was unlikely, or he simply left without receiving a furlough. He headed north toward home, crossing Union lines near New Bern. There he again worked with the local merchant, Hume, with whom he had traded across Confederate lines the previous year.[16]

With the war winding down, all might have worked out for Jody and his family had it not been for the fact that Captain Farrow had died earlier in the war, leaving no children. Jody felt responsible for Mrs. Farrow, who had once taken into her household both Jody and Mary Cleaves, and he attempted to look after the widow, even though she remained in Washington while he was in New Bern. Troops from both armies now roamed the area, often with no clear line between them. Thus there was little commerce passing through Washington in late 1864 and early 1865. (It was exactly the fear of these conditions that had driven Jody to move his family to Ocracoke.) However, succumbing to the appeals for supplies from local citizens, the Union commander at New Bern, General Innis Palmer, allowed a river steamer to be loaded with goods that were to be exchanged for cotton in Washington. Jody was familiar with the trade across no-man's-land from his earlier dealings with Arthur, Hume, and Kitcham, and hoping to pick up some cash by trading and to look in on Mrs. Farrow, he offered to join the expedition. Palmer allowed him to do so under the terms of his earlier bond and oath of allegiance, and the steamer departed New Bern on January 21.

Supposedly, a truce had been worked out between Palmer's representatives and a captain of the Georgia troops stationed near Washington. In the event, when the steamer arrived in Washington, the Union officers onboard found no Confederate officer with whom they could treat. After anchoring downriver, they returned the next day. What they met on their return was a hailstorm of Confederate fire from the banks of the Pamlico. Among those wounded onboard was Jody Daniels. No trade was consummated, and the steamer returned to New Bern that same day. Jody lingered for several more days but died on January 28 as a result of his wounds. Because he was shot by Confederate troops while onboard what was essentially a Union army vessel, not a few of his sons' future political enemies suggested that Jody had been a Yankee sympathizer. While he certainly did possess antisecessionist and antislave sentiments, and while he had traded across Union lines, there is no record suggesting he gave material aid or service to the Union army. He traded with the army's permission, not on its behalf.

Between the time the steamer docked in New Bern and Jody's death, word was sent to Mary Cleaves on Ocracoke. Given travel times and the uncertain state of military affairs in eastern North Carolina at the time, in all likelihood Jody died before Mary Cleaves even heard about his wounds. She nonetheless left the three boys in the care of friends, probably the McDaniels, another Washington family that had retreated to Ocracoke to wait out the end of the war. According to her oldest son, Frank, Mary Cleaves found her husband's death "so overwhelming that for months she was incapacitated to plan for her future. But for her children she would not have cared to live."[17] She would live for another fifty-eight years, would never think of marrying another man, and would always keep green the memory of her beloved Jody; but at the time, one could have forgiven her if she grieved more for the predicament in which she found herself than for her dead husband. Other than the small house in Washington, which contained nothing but a mahogany table and Jody's hand tools; the few possessions she had managed to transfer to the shack on Ocracoke; and the deed to the property she shared with her sister in Hyde County (which at the moment was about as illiquid as an asset could be), she had nothing but three young mouths to feed.

After seeing to the burial of her husband, Mary Cleaves returned to Ocracoke, as the war wound down in the spring of 1865. With no spouse, no job, and no prospects, she was nearly destitute. She seems to have gotten hold of a small amount of cash either from Jody's late trading operations or from loans secured by or from friends on Ocracoke. (Given her stubbornly self-sufficient nature, it was most likely the former.) With this money and no small amount of determination, she confronted her precarious situation. Her first goal was to find long-term accommodations, and to this end, in the late summer or early autumn of 1865, she moved with her three young sons—Frank, now seven; three-year-old Josephus; and the infant Charles—from Ocracoke to Wilson, North Carolina, where her sister, Elizabeth, had lived for more than a decade.

WILSON

The town of Wilson, which Josephus Daniels always called the "loveliest village of the plain," lies in the eastern North Carolina plain between the watersheds of the Tar and Neuse Rivers. The coastal plain stretches for roughly 200 miles inland, running from northeast to southwest, parallel to the Atlantic coast. The table-flat fields spread to the horizon, broken only by the occasional river, stream, or piney wood. Daniels evocatively and lovingly described the scene of his childhood. "There were no hills," he wrote, "only the wide sweep of flat land, lush with vegetation. Boundless aisles of corn, the emerald blades and tassels bending to the quiet breeze which rippled over the countless acres, stood on either side of the road. . . . Across the road, the blooms of the cotton plant stretched out in beauty in long rows as far as the eye could see. The yellowing leaves and flowers of tobacco contrasted with the varied colors of corn and cotton. Back of these, and often in long stretches, the pines lifted their needles and the stately oak gave grateful shade."[18] That description fits much of the region to this day. On either side of Wilson the plain is disrupted by the Toisnot and Contentnea Creeks. The former lies on the northeast side of town and the latter on the southwest side. The two creeks meet southeast of Wilson and there are joined by other small waterways, which ultimately flow into the Neuse River.[19]

Neither the Toisnot nor the Contentnea was navigable in any meaning-ful economic sense, and the area that became the town of Wilson was, ini-tially, nothing more than a crossroads long traversed by natives. Among the local economic resources were the excellent fishing prospects offered by the shad migrations up the Toisnot and, especially, the Contentnea. When whites first moved into the area in the early eighteenth century, the Tus-carora Indians, part of the Iroquois federation, maintained a town they called "Tosneoc," which local whites, largely of Celtic and Anglo-Saxon de-scent, variously turned into "Toisnot," "Tosneot," or "Tossnot," depending upon their particular linguistic take on the native term. The first church, Tosneot Primitive Baptist Church, was built in 1756. A general store was established in 1808, and in 1839 the Wilmington and Raleigh Railroad (later the Wilmington and Weldon) laid tracks through the area and opened a depot near the little settlement most commonly called Toisnot. In the next year the settlement received its first post office, officially called Tossnot Depot. Having a railroad stop nearby increased the economic importance of Toisnot, and subsequently the town itself became known as Toisnot Depot. The town served as an entrepôt for local economic activity, with farmers bringing commodities to the railhead and purchasing manufac-tured goods brought in via rail from more exotic places like Wilmington and the wider world beyond. By 1850, there were roughly 250 residents in the immediate vicinity of the crossroads.[20]

During this period the area around Toisnot Depot was part of the much larger Edgecombe County, which itself dated from colonial times.[21] Typically, as local population density increased in rural hamlets like Toisnot Depot, there emerged a demand for locally provided public services, such as roads, courts, tax assessment, law enforcement, and so forth. Accompanying this demand was a perception, not always mistaken, that distant county officials were more likely to see the hinterlands as sources of tax revenues, which were in turn spent on infrastructure (and patronage) in or near the county seat. Between 1787 and 1855 such motivations led to no fewer than nine unsuccessful attempts in the state legislature to create, in the western parts of Edgecombe County, a new county surrounding Toisnot Depot.[22] Before these efforts yielded fruit, the town of Toisnot Depot and a nearby village of Hickory Grove became jointly incorporated, through an act of the state legislature, as the village of Wilson in 1849.

The town was named for Louis Dicken Wilson, a member of the local gentry who had served five years as a state representative and seventeen as a state senator. Wilson raised a local company for service in the Mexican War, and his troops joined Winfield Scott's army as it marched victoriously from the sea to Mexico City. Alas, Wilson never basked in the glory of Scott's victories, having died from "fever" on the road to Chapultepec.[23] Wilson's name lived on, however, when the twin towns of Toisnot Depot and Hickory Grove became Wilson in honor of his memory. Finally, six years later, after three-quarters of a century of local political effort, in 1855 a county of the same name was carved out of the surrounding counties of Edgecombe, Nash, Wayne, and Johnston, and the village of Wilson became the seat of Wilson County.

At the time the state legislature formally chartered the town of Wilson, the tobacco boom had not yet hit eastern North Carolina, and on the eve of the Civil War, cotton was by far the most valuable cash crop that passed through the town. The primary economic activity besides farming was, as it had been since the eighteenth century, the processing of naval stores, especially tar and turpentine, from the local pine forests. With the rise of the steam engine and the ironclad ship, tar, which was used as caulking in wooden ships and a general weatherproofing agent, was not as sought after as it once had been, but the other major store, turpentine, had other uses and remained the most prominent of the locally manufactured goods. During the 1850s, when the town had only a few hundred residents, it had no fewer than five turpentine-distilling operations, making Wilson possibly, at least on a per capita basis, the turpentine capital of the world.[24]

Still, cotton dominated the pine tree in the local economy, and where there was cotton in the Old South, there were slaves. In 1860 roughly one-third of Wilson County's population and nearly 40 percent of the population of the village of Wilson itself consisted of slaves. In addition, 3 percent of Wilson's prewar population consisted of free blacks. How harmoniously the three groups—white, free black, and slave—got along would be subject to some degree of interpretation. Whites throughout the antebellum South, and indeed into the postbellum era, had a tendency to confuse black passivity and servility with contentment and even happiness. Josephus Daniels suffered from this view. "I never heard of any charges of cruelty to slaves," he wrote. "Humane feelings were united with self-interest in the protection of valuable slave property. Slaves received sufficient food and clothing and medical attention from the same doctors who attended their owners. After emancipation they regarded their former owners as friends who would and did aid them in need."[25] Other accounts of the period would dispute this interpretation, but whatever the true relationship among the various classes and races of Wilson, the Civil War would alter it forever.

After learning of Jody Daniels's death, Mary Cleaves's sister, Elizabeth, and her husband, George H. Griffin, encouraged Mary Cleaves to move to Wilson. The Griffins promised to house the family, and they reasoned that in terms of educational and economic opportunity, Wilson would be a better place to raise the boys than the remote Outer Banks. They were without question correct in this reasoning. Since Ocracoke was isolated geographically, culturally, and economically, for a single mother of three young boys to prosper there in 1865 would have been unlikely. Mary Cleaves must have realized as much after spending a few months there at the end of the war. While always guarded about receiving charity, even from a sister and her kindly husband, Mary Cleaves recognized that Wilson would be a much better location for the boys than Ocracoke. As for the family she was joining, in financial terms at least, Elizabeth had married somewhat better than Mary Cleaves, and by 1865 George Griffin—Uncle Griffin to Josephus Daniels and his brothers—had a successful buggy repair and manufacturing shop and livery stables in Wilson.[26] If nothing else, Uncle Griffin had managed to survive the war, keep a good roof over his family's head, and maintain a strong cash flow from his expanding businesses, all things Jody Daniels, no matter how kind and well intentioned he might have been, had failed to do.

Although Elizabeth insisted that Mary Cleaves move in with her and Uncle Griffin, upon arriving in Wilson, Mary Cleaves just as firmly insisted on renting a home. Unfortunately, her bad luck continued, and soon after she and her sons moved into the rental house, it burned to the ground.

She managed to save only a few personal items that had survived the war in Washington. Everything else was lost. After being burned out of her home, Mary Cleaves surrendered to her sister's wishes, and she and the boys moved in with the Griffins, who lived near Uncle Griffin's buggy shop on Goldsboro Street just off the town's main intersection. Despite the Griffins' charity, the proud Mary Cleaves "resolved to be self-supporting."[27]

In those days, for a widow with no work experience outside the home to make a living was quite difficult. However, given that so much of the clothing of the day was made and repaired within the home, nearly every woman below the loftiest rung on the socioeconomic ladder could make a modest living at millinery and dressmaking. Furthermore, it was one of the few forms of employment that was generally perceived as respectable for women at the time. Thus this was the business to which Mary Cleaves turned in the fall of 1865. For the next fifteen months, except on Sundays, she worked constantly at the job. Though a dedicated worker, Mary Cleaves had never sewed professionally, and so she put in long hours doing the same work that a more experienced seamstress could perform in considerably less time. The tedium must have taken its toll, because late in 1866 she accepted a position that she had previously turned down—that of Wilson's postmistress.

At the time, patronage appointments made up the vast majority of federal government jobs, and the post office was no exception. In a Republican-dominated era, such a position would have normally gone to a local Republican. However, as Josephus Daniels later recalled, "When I was a boy there was only one white voter in the town of Wilson who voted any other than the full Democratic ticket."[28] This was Willie Daniel, an antisecessionist Whig who had followed the Whigs into the Republican Party. Despite his political heresy, Daniel remained on good terms with the town's other leading citizens, including George Griffin and, through the Griffins, Mary Cleaves. Out of a sense of charity—since Mary Cleaves, like the Griffins, was a Democrat—and out of respect for her brother-in-law's high standing in the town, Daniel agreed to support her for the post office position.[29] As one family member put it, she got the job "because she was the only literate white person [the Republicans] could find who hadn't given aid or comfort to the Confederacy."[30]

Willie Daniel's support was more than nominal. Since the postmasters and postmistresses handled federal monies with no direct oversight, they were required to post a bond to protect the post office against any financial loss resulting from their malfeasance. Wilson had no bonding companies at the time, so Daniel would also have to sign Mary Cleaves's bond, essentially agreeing to repay any monies lost through her mismanagement of the post office. He generously did so. With the town's subsequent growth, the job of postmistress would prove to be a remunerative one for Mary Cleaves. Among other things, it allowed her to move one block northeast of her sister's home into a rented house on Tarboro Street. There she kept the Wilson Post Office in the front room, where it stayed for the next sixteen years. It soon became a local gathering place, and the time young Josephus spent in the post office would influence him mightily for the rest of his life.

Mary Cleaves's sons always maintained that she was the most dutiful of mothers. Of her struggles during the family's Wilson days, Daniels wrote, "If I could worship at the shrine of any mortal, my devotions would be at an altar erected to my mother."[31] Given Mary Cleaves's long hours as a seamstress and, later, as postmistress, the boys' care would have undoubtedly suffered despite their mother's devotion were it not for the presence of Sallie Daniels, the younger half-sister of the deceased Jody Daniels. Over the years, Jody had remained in touch with, though not particularly close to, his family in Bayboro. Jody's oldest son, Frank, recalled visiting his relatives there on only one occasion during these years.[32] However, Sallie was the oldest child from Clifford Daniels's second marriage, and for whatever reason, she and Jody remained close. Thus when Mary Cleaves and the boys moved to the rented house on Tarboro Street, Sallie, who was unmarried, came to live with the family, taking care of its quotidian needs. Josephus Daniels and his brothers were absolutely devoted to their paternal aunt, but after several years of caring for them, Sallie married. The boys mourned that day, and her absence strained Mary Cleaves even further.[33]

Adding to Mary Cleaves's stress was the presence of the widowed Mrs. Farrow. Josephus Daniels referred to her as his foster grandmother, and she would live with the family for the rest of her life. In Sallie's absence Mary Cleaves was soon forced to hire a live-in cook, a former slave known only as Dora. Mrs. Farrow's arrival was not entirely without benefit; in return for Mary Cleaves's generosity, Mrs. Farrow turned over the deed to the remaining Farrow property in Washington. Through the sale of this land (for roughly $500), combined with the sale of Mary Cleaves's own home in Washington (for less than $250), and, finally, her family land in Hyde County (which yielded roughly $1,250), Mary Cleaves was able to purchase for $2,000 the home she had been renting on Tarboro Street.[34] That $2,000 proved to be all the money she had access to at the time, and so the house represented all of the family's wealth. Although only slightly above modest, the wood-framed, two-story house bordered what was rapidly becoming Wilson's fashionable residential neighborhood, and it stood just off the town's central intersection and business district. It proved to be a good location and a good investment.[35]

Wilson served as the county's economic hub. As such, it was typical of small towns all over America: "The buildings that lined the main streets of such places contained general stores, grocers, hardware dealers, dry goods merchants, and taverns, all selling their wares entirely to retail customers."[36] The post office served as the center of that hub.[37] Because Wilson was also the county seat, and because the courthouse was literally in Mary Cleaves's backyard, the post office also served as a political hub. In short, it was a combination of coffee shop, bourse, and general meeting place. Each day the town's leading citizens gathered to collect their personal and business correspondence, discuss any information they might have received via post or gossip, and generally conduct whatever business or social intercourse they had with one another. There was no residential postal delivery service in those days, and so those who owned agricultural land beyond the town's edge would take a buggy into town, often daily. Those who lived farther out might come to town once a week or so. The big-city newspapers, which for Wilson readers came primarily from Raleigh and Wilmington, arrived by train in the mid-morning, and they were distributed at the post office later in the morning. The early to mid-morning period, when the locals gathered in anticipation of the arrival of the mail, witnessed the peak of the day's activity. Except for the time that Josephus spent in school or working elsewhere, he tried to never miss a morning in the post office. For him it proved to be a vocational school.

Mary Cleaves served as Wilson's postmistress from December 1866 to early March 1883. The position paid reasonably well, though she certainly did not get rich. In those days, the local postmaster or postmistress received a strict piece rate in the form of a flat percentage of the stamps "canceled" in the office. In 1867, her first full year on the job, she earned $420. By 1881, with Wilson's growth, she earned $1,300 annually, a very good salary at the time. Josephus was the only one of her sons to work regularly in the post office, or at least he was the only one to be officially remunerated for such work. After he ended his formal education in Wilson at age eighteen, his mother carried him on the books as a postal clerk, and he earned $90 a year. Before that he had run a small retail book and sporting goods store out of one corner of the post office. Wilson had no bookstore at the time, and, displaying his father's entrepreneurial streak, Josephus attempted to capitalize on the opportunity. Apparently it was not much of a moneymaker. His own amateur baseball team, which he organized and captained, consumed most of the sporting goods, and he and his bookish brother Frank consumed most of the reading material.

Even though Josephus did not receive explicit compensation for his work in the post office until he was eighteen years old, he had worked there regularly since he was old enough to read, and the job of sorting the mail generally fell to him. He loved it. He especially enjoyed having a first look at the out-of-town newspapers when they arrived each morning. On a typical day, after waking before dawn, he would gather and split wood for the day's heating and cooking and then haul water from the community well, chores he shared with his brothers. He ate breakfast, and then, on the days he did not go to school or work picking strawberries (in the spring) or cotton (in the late summer or early fall), he helped his mother in the post office. From his Uncle Griffin, Josephus acquired the habit of reading the morning papers while sitting on the back step of his mother's house. He usually had to read quickly before the patrons came to collect their mail. As the local merchants, lawyers, planters, and politicos gathered in his mother's front room each morning, the curious boy observed their dress, habits, demeanor, and transactions. He could see who looked up to whom, and he tried to figure out why the hierarchy was as it was. He learned who had money to lend and who needed to borrow, who had cotton futures to buy or sell, and who had business or political connections beyond Wilson. As Daniels recalled, "The leading men gathered daily at the post office, and I listened and came to share the feeling and views of the best thought of the town."[38]

This professional crowd was overwhelmingly composed of white men who were almost all part of the Protestant mainstream—Baptists, Presbyterians, Methodists, and Episcopalians. As the product of a devout Methodist household, Daniels generally classified acquaintances by religious affiliation, and he made a point of noting his occasional association with a Catholic or a Jew, but these were conspicuous by their small numbers. Being an openly hard-core Methodist, Daniels had no place in his religious beliefs for predestination, popery, or Talmudic doctrine; but he was no proselytizer, and he more often displayed his faith in his actions than in his words. As one of his sons remembered, "There was no piety flung around our house."[39] Overall, Daniels took a generally good natured, if dismissive, view of other religious groups, but he always drew a well-defined line around them. To Daniels, the differences between Protestant sects rep-

21

resented important theological points. Years later, after he married into a prominent Raleigh Presbyterian family, Daniels remarked that he always "believed" wholeheartedly in his wife—"minus predestination."[40]

Although Daniels was destined for a life of commerce, his soon-to-be-chosen field—the newspaper business—was never far from politics, and he was always a politician even if he never ran for office. Thus, not surprisingly, the topics that he followed most closely at the post office were those surrounding the local political scene. After Reconstruction, the Democratic Party controlled Wilson, but there and elsewhere in the state, the party had at least two factions—a diehard unreconstructed or "Bourbon" wing and a more progressive or "New South" wing. Although the terms "Bourbon" and "New South" could mean different things to different observers, from Daniels's perspective, the Bourbons primarily represented what remained of the planter aristocracy of the Old South. In the Bourbon world, farmland and cheap docile labor (primarily, though not always, black labor) to work it were the keys to economic wealth. In contrast, progressives like Daniels envisioned a New South in which economic growth was town based and driven by industry. The creation of a New South industrial dynamo required two things: modernization in the agricultural sector to free farm labor for the factories and northern capital to build them. During Daniels's boyhood the South had little of either.

From a young age, Daniels felt equal parts respect and animosity for the Bourbons. Part of this was class consciousness. Despite his own protestations to the contrary, Daniels never rose above making well-defined class distinctions. As one historian put it, "The hostility to their betters among the bourgeoisie is sometimes matched by a contempt for their inferiors."[41] And so it was with Daniels, whose betters among the haughty Bourbons tended to look down on him, while at the same time he cultivated a well-honed sense of superiority over the poor whites further down the socioeconomic ladder. A later observer of the southern social scene explained: "Those who stand closest to the line on which a distinction is drawn are those who insist upon it most hotly."[42] Daniels drew such lines, and though he would never have admitted it, he condescended to those below him. But his condescension was for classes, not individuals. Daniels always treated individuals, whether they were black sharecroppers or wealthy white industrialists, with the same personal respect, as long as they obeyed the social customs of their class. At the same time, as the product of an aspiring, upwardly mobile professional class whose members earned their living from what they knew, not what they owned, Daniels did not like being looked down upon by anyone, and the fatherless boy who swept out the post office in his brother's hand-me-downs was looked down upon by local Bourbons on more than one occasion.

An example of the type of social slight that annoyed young Daniels involved a local member of the gentry, a Bourbon who remained nameless in Daniels's correspondence. The prominent gentleman came by the post office regularly, bringing with him large piles of outgoing mail. Placing a pile in front of Daniels, the Bourbon demanded that the boy place the postage on the letters. This required a good bit of stamp licking, which, in addition to being physically sickening, Daniels found personally demeaning. Daniels later wrote that he wanted to say, "Lick your own stamps," but fear of his mother's retribution prohibited him from doing so. He licked the stamps and his wounded pride, though after leaving the post office, he never licked another stamp again for the rest of his life. From such experiences, he maintained a proletarian grudge against the landed elite.[43] "He hated the rich," one family member recalled.[44] That animosity did not keep Daniels from envying them or from aspiring to join their ranks.

In addition to the Democrats who dominated the town's politics, there were a few prominent white Republicans. Some of these, like Willie Daniel, had been Whigs before the Civil War; others were carpetbaggers who did not leave the state after the Union forces pulled out following Reconstruction. Because they were a minority party usually tied to northern industrial or financial interests as well as the state's African American community, Republicans had to work hard to find votes among the state's poorer white elements. Many of the poor men from North Carolina who had fought in the Civil War returned home to the kind of destitution that only impoverished rural areas know. They blamed their plight on Republicans, carpetbaggers, and blacks. Without access to, or support within, this core poor white constituency, the Republican Party's leadership was concentrated in the hands of a small number of prosperous whites. As Daniels described it, in Wilson, "there were a few high-class white men, who had been Whigs and opponents of Secession, who were Republicans."[45] Although their power shriveled rapidly in the 1870s, they were often within striking distance in the state legislature, and their ranks included some savvy politicos who would prove to be worthy foes of Josephus Daniels when he took control of the state's Democratic forces a generation later.

Wilson County also had a large African American community, which largely resided in rural areas or just beyond the town's (gerrymandered) limits. The members of this community overwhelmingly supported the

Republican Party at that time. In Daniels's view the "newly enfranchised Negro was at first as much the political slave of the white Republican politicians . . . as he had been of his owner before emancipation. . . . In Wilson and most other places the saying was, 'You can tell a man's politics by the color of his skin.'"[46] Although not literally true—after all, Daniels himself noted that some upper-class whites voted Republican—the expression captured the essence of how the parties divided along racial lines. A bit of back-of-the-envelope calculation suggests that probably more than 90 percent of African Americans voted Republican during the postbellum period—though when Election Day came around the votes of many men, white and black, could be up for sale.[47] Daniels grew up despising, at least as a group, Republicans of both races. From the time he became a journalist in his late teens and began leaving a written record, he could be generous in his personal appraisal of individual political opponents, even as he savaged them in print, but he was seldom generous to either Republicans or African Americans as a group. He especially resented the elevation of blacks to positions of authority over whites. He could respect an African American political opponent (and future Raleigh neighbor), such as James Young, with whom Daniels battled for years and whom Daniels described as "very bright . . . as smart as he could be." Yet later, when Young was appointed to the board of the (white) School for the Blind, Daniels promoted "the sense of outrage that a Negro should be appointed as leading member of the board of an institution for white blind children."[48] The seeds of these complex emotions were sown in Reconstruction Wilson. Of course later, as a newspaperman, Daniels learned that his readers expected him to take a position on the political questions of the day, and he found his anti-Republicanism was good for business.

White Democrats of both wings of the party, Bourbon and progressive, disliked what they perceived to be the unjust application of federal power during Reconstruction; thus, North Carolina's road back into the United States was marked by strife between white Democrats and Republicans of both colors. Until the end of Reconstruction, the Republicans controlled the state government (and hence political patronage), protected carpetbaggers, and promoted African American political interests, all of which angered local Democrats. To be a white Democrat in Wilson County in the late 1860s and early 1870s was to nurture a grudge against the newly freed blacks and their Republican protectors. Daniels acquired such a grudge. The extent to which that feeling of resentment resulted from the blame he assigned for his father's death and his mother's near-destitution is impossible to determine but easy to guess. In one generation, his mother had fallen from being the belle of a prosperous slaveholding family to relying on the patronage of the political party dominated by ex-slaves. For the class-conscious Daniels, it hurt to fall so low. He was not so much grateful for the aid his family received in Wilson as he was resentful that it had been necessary. As if to eliminate the pain, in his memoirs he barely mentioned his generous aunt and uncle, the Griffins, and almost never referred to them in his subsequent correspondence.

———

Class and race were never very far from each other in the postbellum South. During Daniels's boyhood, cotton remained king in Wilson County. Immediately following the Civil War, many planters attempted to simply return to the plantation organization that had proved profitable before the war. African American (and some poor white) labor was employed in work gangs on white-owned plantations. At this, however, the former slaves balked. They had not cast off their chains only to put them back on again as hired labor. It took a season or two to reach a widely accepted new arrangement among the freedmen and the plantation owners. The new arrangement was sharecropping, and it dominated the countryside around Wilson during Daniels's boyhood.[49]

Sharecroppers were well down the socioeconomic ladder, the higher rungs of which were dominated by unreconstructed Bourbons. Typically large landowners, these men sometimes farmed their own land, but more often they rented their land to those further down the ladder. Democratic in politics, the Bourbon was just a slave owner in a world without slavery. Reactionary in most things social, economic, and political, the Bourbon saw little that was good in the New South. A leading spokesman for this group was an ex-Confederate officer, Captain Samuel Ashe, the owner of what would become the state's best-known newspaper, the Raleigh *News and Observer*. Among the group's most prominent members was Montford McGehee, scion of a once-prosperous Person County family. McGehee had inherited the family's vast landholdings and managed to lose all of it over time. McGehee's incompetence as a farmer propelled him to become the head of the North Carolina Department of Agriculture, an example of a political logic not unique to that place or time. Of McGehee a Daniels acquaintance said, "After the slaves were free, he was lost," and so were many of his Bourbon colleagues across the South, especially when it came to dealing with African Americans.[50]

Others at the top of the socioeconomic ladder could look much like the Bourbons, but with one major exception: In politics they were Republicans. This group included urban carpetbaggers like Hiram L. Grant of Goldsboro or old-time agrarian Whigs like Washington Duke of Durham. The primary difference between the Bourbons and their Republican rivals was in their views of African Americans. To the Bourbons, blacks represented farm labor. It was the natural order of things, which had only been disrupted by meddling Yankees. Bourbons saw their interests as perfectly aligned with those of their former slaves. As former Confederate general Wade Hampton put it, "The best friends of the colored men are the old slaveholders."[51] The Bourbons provided employment for the newly freed and protected them from the depredations of the poorer whites who resided further down the social ladder and whose well of loathing for blacks proved to be nearly bottomless. Thus the rural elites established a type of oppressive paternalism for their black sharecroppers. "Race relations were invariably paternalistic," writes one historian of the era, "and [they were] strained by an endemic violence."[52] That violence largely came at the hands of poor whites. White elites may have exploited the blacks who farmed their land, but they also offered a minimum level of protection from other social predators.

Socially, town dwellers like the Danielses were usually somewhere between the Bourbons and the sharecroppers, and despite the class and racial grudges Daniels nurtured during his boyhood, he came from a happy home. As the middle of three sons, Josephus performed a balancing act between his older and younger brothers. In retrospect, one sees from their earliest days in Wilson the emergence of key personality traits among the boys, traits they would display to varying degrees for the rest of their lives.[53] Both physically and emotionally they acquired a combination of their parents' qualities, despite the absence of their father, and although there were a few inevitable similarities, the three boys would evolve into very dissimilar men.

By the time Josephus reached adolescence, he had developed both the cupidlike countenance and fleshy frame that he would maintain until his dying day. Pictures of the young man show a warm smile and the soft lines of his face. Thick, wavy hair combined with his mother's almost translucent blue-gray eyes gave him a slightly feminine countenance closer to pretty rather than classically handsome. He was known as Joe during his Wilson days, but the diminutive nickname did not stick. For the rest of Daniels's life he would be Josephus to everyone except his brothers and a very small circle of old and intimate friends. From time to time other acquaintances would take the liberty of shortening his Christian name to Joe, but they did so without any encouragement from Daniels.

Gentle yet outgoing, Daniels possessed much personal warmth. He was well spoken though soft spoken, and the absence of any hard edges physically or emotionally made him attractive to women. As one of his granddaughters described him, "He just had a certain quiet charisma, a charm; you could see it and feel it when he walked in the room."[54] While one might discount the fond memories of a loved one, there is no question Daniels possessed a physical presence that others, at least other socially prominent whites, found attractive. Even his opponents admitted as much. Later, after he moved to Raleigh, one of his bitterest enemies, the Bourbon publisher Samuel Ashe, wrote that Daniels was "among the most popular and well known [members] of Raleigh society."[55] Partly, this popularity was the result of Daniels's ability to get on well with members of both sexes. Perhaps because he was raised by a devoted mother, Daniels always felt comfortable around women, particularly strong-willed women, and he enjoyed feminine company. Even as a schoolboy he had girlfriends, in the various meanings of that word, and wrote affectionately of and to them. His correspondence and memoirs are filled with references to "charming" ladies or "pretty" daughters of colleagues and acquaintances, and he made no attempt to hide his infatuation with them. When a skating rink became the local attraction in Wilson, he wrote, "I dropped in now and then, more to chat with the girls—or some particular girl—than to witness the skating."[56] Bright and fond of school, though as a student he was not as successful as either of his brothers, Josephus loved the social and recreational aspects of childhood and adolescence, especially baseball, girls, and church, the last of which was for him as much a social institution as it was a religious one. Although he had a bit of a temper and could be goaded into fisticuffs, he was generally good at controlling it and with age mastered it completely. Socially well adjusted by any standard, outgoing, but not overly gregarious, he made and kept friends easily. Even though he would never run for public office, he was a natural politician.

Never a chauvinist, at least not by the standards of his day, he enjoyed the company and opinions of women as much as those of men. Confident in his opinions and articulate in expressing them, he grew to love the give-and-take of animated conversation—whether it involved the rise and fall of nations, local politics, or the doctrines of the Methodist Church. At a dinner party he could command the attention of the entire table or quietly listen to another guest's discourse. On other social occasions—a church reception or a gathering of townsmen at a county fair—he could stand in the middle of a circle and speak if called upon, though he did not crave to be the center of attention at such functions. He could just as easily listen and consider the positions of other speakers. Surrounded by friends and colleagues, he liked the banter of the post office, the country store, the dinner table, and, later, the smoke-filled back rooms of politics. Generous and warmhearted, if given a choice he would prefer to remain on the good side of an acquaintance, but he never feared making an enemy. Indeed, his life was filled with former friends, and potential friends, with whom he ultimately fell out. Invariably, these quarrels followed something Daniels printed, which itself might have reflected some political dispute as small as a state government contract or as large as a world war. In short, Daniels became a bit of a social oddity: the friendliest and most easygoing of men who never backed away from a conflict. Indeed, he loved a good fight.

His older brother, Franklin Arthur, developed into a more sober, studious lad. Generally good natured, Frank, as he was universally known, possessed a sense of humor but typically revealed it in the appreciation rather than the telling of a good joke. Less outgoing than Josephus, Frank possessed his brother's gentleness in dealing with others—"mild and conciliatory in manner," was how Josephus described him.[57] Of the three boys, Frank looked the most like his father, though in his youth he had his mother's more angular, birdlike build. Frank took seriously the role of senior male in the household, and he fulfilled it well. A good son, student, citizen, and neighbor, he would go on to study the law and ultimately become a judge, serving for half a century as a pillar of (white) society in eastern North Carolina. One of Frank's professors at the University of North Carolina, George T. Winston, a future president of what later became North Carolina State University, was once asked to define a gentleman. His response was "Judge Frank Daniels."[58] As a boy, Josephus looked up to his older brother and, in adulthood, respected him, but from the time they were teens, Josephus had enough self-confidence that he would make his own way in the world without deferring to or consulting Frank in any important way. Frank was a good man in his brother's eyes, but the older boy's personality and success never cast a shadow over Josephus.

Physically, the youngest brother, Charles Cleaves, resembled Josephus in every way. Indeed, in photographs of the two taken in early adulthood, it is difficult to distinguish one from the other. In countenance, both boys favored their mother, but both acquired the full-figured Daniels physique rather than their mother's more Spartan frame. Like his older brothers,

Charles displayed academic talent, perhaps a bit more than Josephus but less than Frank, and he had a certain passion and physical energy, often manifest in anger, that more closely mimicked Josephus than Frank, but that was where the similarities ended. Charles never had the sense of humor that either of his older brothers possessed. Nor was he as gentle or good natured as either of them. Whereas Frank could play the role of social mixer if it were forced upon him, and Josephus relished mingling, Charles had a more difficult time fitting in socially. After Frank left home, Josephus often took a role in guiding Charles. Unfortunately, Charles possessed a bad temper and a resentful nature. Josephus always indulged Charles—as an older brother, business partner, and political patron—perhaps a bit too much. During childhood, Josephus found Charles's personal tendencies mildly annoying. In adulthood, they would prove more financially costly and emotionally painful.

SCHOOL DAYS

Although by his own admission Josephus was the least academically gifted of the Daniels boys, he was still a top student, and throughout his life he maintained a deep respect for formal education. Like many mainstream Protestants of his day, Daniels saw education as a form of social progress and thus as a moral imperative. He viewed education as a path to both individual and societal enlightenment, and he was always personally grateful for the education he received in Wilson and, later, at the University of North Carolina in Chapel Hill. "Universal education must be the basis of the State's prosperity," Daniels favorably quoted a contemporary, adding that an education must also fire "a young man with a desire to learn . . . to introduce [him] to knowledge along lines that [are] new and intriguing."[59] For the rest of his life he projected this affection onto the institutions at which he studied and, in particular, onto his teachers and professors. During Daniels's boyhood in Wilson, the state's public school system was nonexistent. He was educated in private schools, and in adulthood he became the state's most ardent proponent of publicly funded, universal education and mandatory attendance. Later, after these goals had been obtained, he continued to fight for an expansion of financial support for the state's school system.

The first North Carolina state constitution, written by the Provincial Congress during the American Revolution, required of subsequent legislatures the establishment of "a School or Schools."[60] Other than creating the University of North Carolina in 1789, which would come to serve a very small student body (often fewer than 100 students enrolled at any given time), the subsequent sessions of the General Assembly interpreted this obligation to mean that the state's counties and municipalities were free to establish such schools *if* the local elected leaders possessed the desire and will to assess and collect the requisite taxes. Few did so to any meaningful degree. In areas where locals did provide a school, an "old-field" school, built on land donated by a local farmer (hence the name), sufficed. By the 1830s, there were no more than a few hundred such primary schools scattered across the state.

In the absence of a public school system, for those who had obtained a primary-school education either in an old-field school or through private means, there emerged at the secondary level a set of local private "academies" or "institutes" that, because they were forced to charge tuition, typically educated the sons (though a few also admitted girls) of relatively prosperous families. There were more than 40 of these institutions by 1800, and by the time a state public school system emerged in the 1840s, there were roughly 200 academies scattered across the state. Some died quietly without leaving much, if any, record; however, many sought formal charters from the state legislature, and at least a few charters explicitly called for the schools to support children of the poor. The requisite funds came entirely from local sources or, in some cases, religious organizations. (Among the most prominent of these was Saint Mary's Episcopal School for girls in Raleigh, which would one day be patronized by members of Daniels's family.) The state supplied no public monies for these schools, and rather than from local tax dollars, the funds came from outright charity or a direct subsidy via a surcharge on the tuition of the more prosperous students.

The election of 1838 saw the rise of the state's Whig Party. More inclined to tax and spend than the Democrats, the Whigs managed to pass legislation that enabled a county-level referendum on public school funding. Counties that voted for a school system (sixty-one of the state's sixty-eight counties did so) received a per-pupil subsidy from the state. Subsequent reforms in the 1850s contributed to the rapid expansion of the system, which prospered relative to that of other states in the region. In 1840, North Carolina had the highest (white) illiteracy rate in the country at 28 percent. By 1860, the rate had been reduced to only 11 percent.[61] That year, with nearly 120,000 students and 3,000 licensed teachers, State Superintendent Calvin H. Wiley could write with confidence that "North-Carolina has the start of all her Southern sisters in educational matters."[62] The Civil War put an end to all that, and just as Josephus Daniels was coming into this world, the North Carolina public school system was leaving it. Together, the Civil War and Reconstruction destroyed North Carolina's burgeoning investment in a system of public education.

As a result of the political and financial turmoil associated with the war and defeat, and the subsequent recalcitrance of local whites to Reconstruction, not to mention their objections to both integrated schools and funding for segregated schools, the state's school system simply ceased to exist. Thus looking back on his Wilson days, Daniels wrote, "There was no public school in the town then, and, in fact, there was no real public school worth speaking of until the graded school was established in 1883."[63] With the state's once-promising school system gone, Daniels's first experience at formal education came in a private, one-room school. In Wilson the primary school was in a classroom over a farm implement shop on Green Street, around the corner from Mary Cleaves's house. There Annie Bowers ("a fine buxom maiden lady," according to Daniels) ran a private primary school for twenty to thirty children during the winter months. The tuition at the time the Daniels boys attended went unrecorded. Although he was an eager learner and personally fond of Bowers, young Josephus appears to have been unimpressed with the school. Little wonder. At best such schools supplied the young with basic numeracy, literacy, and perhaps a smattering of history and civic instruction colored by a low-church Protestant ethos.

Eyewitness descriptions of the one-room schoolhouse and the education offered there emphasize the Spartan nature of both. As one observer described it, "The children sat on benches that were no more than thick planks of wood, eight inches wide, eight feet long. Their desks were planks as well, fastened onto the wall, held in place by supports, on which children kept their copy books and an inkwell. Lessons were by rote; lessons were serious business. There was no discussion; there were no questions allowed. The teacher took the copy books in the morning, inscribed the day's lesson along the top, and returned them to [the] pupils, who spent the day 'striving to imitate' their instructor's hand."[64] Mary Cleaves had already seen to the literacy of her boys, and young Josephus, and probably his brothers as well, sought more of an intellectual challenge from school than Bowers supplied. When he got a little older, Daniels found that something extra.

In an agricultural community such as Wilson, boys could easily obtain seasonal work in the fields that began just beyond the town. Planting and gathering the harvest typically had to be done in narrow windows of time; otherwise the crop would mature too late in the year or spoil in the field, and farm labor was often in short supply during those seasons. Thus, in addition to his work around the Wilson Post Office, Daniels picked strawberries and planted various row crops in the spring, and he picked cotton in the late summer and early autumn. In those days when the agriculture cycle drove the calendar of schools throughout the country, it was not uncommon to have a summer term after the crops were in the field but before the harvest began.[65] At the time, the school year was much shorter than it later became after the economic importance of child labor dwindled. In Wilson, the regular school year did not begin until October, after the cotton crop was in, and it ended in the spring when the corn had to be sowed and the strawberries picked. Therefore, between planting and harvesting, there was often a summer term. During Daniels's boyhood, Edward Morse Nadal taught the Wilson summer school.

A prominent Wilsonian who had served in the Confederate Army and the Ku Klux Klan with equal ardor, Nadal proved to be the type of colorful lecturer who has inspired students since antiquity. For a few weeks each summer, "Cousin Ed," as he was called by the Daniels boys, though he was unrelated to the family, presided over what Daniels referred to as "the free school," which meant his mother paid no tuition. It was a charitable undertaking by Nadal, an act of noblesse oblige. For local children whose parents could not afford Bowers's primary school or a private secondary academy, Cousin Ed's summer school was the only formal education most would ever receive. And an education it was. In the absence of grades, students of various ages attended class together, and it was not uncommon in those days for older, physically mature boys to challenge the authority of the schoolteacher. Those who challenged Cousin Ed did so only once. A stern taskmaster who ruled by physical intimidation when necessary, Nadal possessed a mustached countenance that was as fierce as his temper. As Daniels wrote, Cousin Ed "used the rod with a vigor that was well deserved."[66] His rule established, Nadal drilled the large class, which was filled with (white) children of all ages and backgrounds, on grammar, mathematics, and history.

When it came to mathematics, Josephus Daniels was a failure, and he would never be good with numbers as either a student or a businessman. He had a good, indeed excellent, head for business, but Daniels remained essentially innumerate throughout his life. Someone else would always keep the accounts of his various business enterprises. However, Daniels devoured Cousin Ed's history lessons. History became his favorite subject. Later, Daniels found he had a gift for languages as well, and he became fluent in Latin and could read Greek. Despite this prowess in other areas, as hard as Nadal tried, he could never drill anything beyond basic arithmetic into the head of young Daniels. Still, the two possessed a mutual love for history, and according to Daniels, each summer Nadal enthralled his charges with his history lectures, particularly those covering the recent war and Reconstruction.

A bellicose, unreconstructed Confederate and die-hard Democrat, Nadal possessed many talents. His family owned a prosperous farm beyond the Wilson town limits, and in addition to running the free school in the summer, he was a partner in the Wilson pharmacy. During these years, the pharmacy stood at the corner of Nash and Tarboro Streets near the town's commercial center, just one block down Tarboro from the Daniels house. In addition to his pharmacy work, Nadal exploited his mastery of mathematics by maintaining a local surveying business. In the summer school, Daniels and Nadal struck up a close friendship, and Cousin Ed eventually hired the boy to work in the drugstore and help with his surveying business. In doing so, he provided Daniels with regular employment and allowed him to leave the cotton fields forever.

From just beyond the Wilson town limits, the Daniels brothers could see cotton rows that seemed to stretch from horizon to horizon. Every year, as summer turned to autumn, the boys left the summer school and handpicked cotton all day, six days a week, until the harvest was completed. Cousin Ed saw the promise in Josephus and rescued him from that drudgery. In old age Daniels reflected on the day he left the cotton fields to go to work for Nadal at the Wilson pharmacy.

> It was on a very hot day near noon when, as I was picking cotton, I noticed Cousin Ed walking toward me. He asked me how much I was earning as cotton picker. "About twenty-five cents a day," I told him. "Isn't it very hard and back-breaking work on this hot day?" [he asked.] I assented. He said, "I will give you thirty-five cents a day to clerk in the drugstore." . . . "Let me finish picking out this row and have my cotton weighed," I said, "and I will go to town with you." He waited. That was the last day I ever did hard work in the sun. I've worked long hours and had hard tasks and anxious times, but it has always been in the shade.[67]

Nadal's considerable impact on Daniels did not end there. During the winter term, in addition to all of Cousin Ed's other roles in town, he taught at the Wilson Collegiate Institute. It was at the institute that Daniels and his brothers received the bulk of their formal education. As the public school system foundered during Reconstruction, parents demanding something beyond a primary education for their children returned to the private academy system that existed earlier in the century, before the reforms of the 1840s and 1850s.

Sylvester Hassell, the product of a distinguished Martin County family and an alumnus of the University of North Carolina, founded the Wilson Collegiate Institute in 1870, just in time for Daniels to be educated there. The institute served as a model private secondary academy for eastern North Carolina. For its day, it possessed an excellent physical plant, full curriculum, and distinguished and dedicated faculty. In addition to a few small buildings and ample grounds, the campus, which had served as a Confederate hospital until 1865, included a large two-story building with forty rooms. More recently it had housed the Wilson Female Seminary, which had subsequently moved into a smaller facility closer to downtown. When Daniels matriculated in 1874, the institute's grounds marked the far southeastern side of town, across the Wilmington and Weldon Railroad tracks, an easy walk from the Daniels home. Beyond it was the town line and, beyond that, a largely African American community that had been gerrymandered out of the town's politics. The land on which the institute sat passed through several hands in the decades before Josephus and his brothers attended the school. In 1870 two brothers from a prominent local family, the Woodards, purchased the tract with the intention of establishing an academy under the sponsorship of the Primitive Baptist Church. They recruited Hassell, a devout Primitive, and allowed him a relatively free hand in running the institute. Out of the same sense of civic obligation that drove Cousin Ed Nadal to teach the town's summer school, the Woodards provided the structures and grounds gratis. Tuition only covered the school's operating costs. Hassell stayed on as president for seventeen years, and his name became inextricably linked to the school. A map of the town dated 1872 clearly marks the property as "Hassell's Seminary."[68]

The institute's curriculum was first-rate and included Latin, Greek, rhetoric, mathematics, physics, music, history, and literature. The classics, including Caesar and Virgil, dominated the humanities component of the curriculum, though Shakespeare seems to have been popular as well. The well-educated Tar Heel of that day could quote liberally from Homer, Pliny, and Virgil. For his part, Daniels loved the classics and studied them for the rest of his life. The characters he found there were not the remnants of a lost civilization but, rather, voices that characterized his own life. Like the Achaean boys who lost their fathers on the plains of Ilium, Daniels longed for the father, similarly lost to war, he never knew. Confederate veterans, like Cousin Ed Nadal, who acquainted Daniels with their heroic struggle against the Union, represented modern versions of Nestor and Menelaus, who, with tales of their exploits before the walls of Troy, enthralled the young Achaeans of the Heroic Age.

Despite Hassell's hard-core Primitive Baptist beliefs and those of the school's founders and trustees—during the six years Daniels attended the institute, there were no fewer than three Baptist Woodards on the Board of Trustees, including the secretary and treasurer—Hassell attempted to maintain a curriculum with a strong nondenominational Protestant ethos. He must have succeeded; otherwise, the equally hard-core Methodist Mary Cleaves Daniels would not have sent her sons to the school. Being ardent supporters of a denomination that adhered to infant baptism, Articles of Faith, and an Episcopal hierarchy, all of which were anathema to the Primitives, both Mary Cleaves and Josephus maintained lifelong suspicions of the independence of Baptist congregations.

Although Daniels would have been the last person to admit it, there was more than a hint of middle-class snobbery in his family's view of Baptists, eventually the state's largest denomination, but one that was dominated by the state's poorest citizens, black and white. One of his mother's favorite witticisms was that a Presbyterian was nothing more than a Baptist who had moved to town. Although the joke was aimed at Mary Cleaves's sister, whose husband was, in fact, a Presbyterian who lived in town, it was used to tar members of both denominations. The joke, which Daniels never tired of repeating, reflected both his and his mother's generally good-natured approach to religious differences, but it also revealed their prejudices. Church historians attribute the social hierarchy of the denominations to the conscious policies of the various mainstream Protestant churches. That is to say they developed and cultivated internal cultures that targeted different socioeconomic groups. In the late nineteenth century, the Methodists were making a conscious effort to move their membership up the socioeconomic ladder.[69]

According to Daniels, the quality of the instruction at the institute was universally excellent. Given the rigorous curriculum, and with a faculty of ten, including two members who held master's degrees, for roughly 200 students, one would have been hard pressed to find a better secondary school anywhere in eastern North Carolina, and perhaps anywhere in the Reconstruction South. Despite the presence of the word "Collegiate" in its title, the institute was more like an outstanding and accelerated high school, and the offerings of its highest grades were similar to the first year of a liberal arts curriculum at a four-year college. This quality did not come at a low price. In order to make the school accessible to a wide range of students, the trustees charged tuition based on a sliding scale, from about $35 to $125 annually. The Daniels boys were near the bottom of this scale.[70] Though Mary Cleaves never had more than two boys at the institute at a time, the tuition proved financially burdensome, roughly 10 to 20 percent of the annual income she received from the post office during the years her boys were in school. With per capita annual income in eastern North Carolina at no more than $150 or $200 at the time, tuition of this magnitude would have been prohibitive for the vast majority of families.[71] Both the faculty and the student body were coeducational, though overwhelmingly Protestant and exclusively white.

Overall, Daniels's education must be considered excellent. He and his brothers received a primary school education from Annie Bowers and Cousin Ed Nadal; they had been brought up by a highly literate mother; and they were surrounded by the burghers of downtown Wilson since their earliest memories. Thus they were already well educated, at least by the standards of their day, before they ever set foot in the Wilson Collegiate Institute. In addition, all three boys were voracious readers. Josephus caught the bug from Frank, and he passed it on to Charles. Although by Wilson standards Daniels's tastes in reading material were eclectic, by subsequent and more cosmopolitan standards they were not terribly so. In addition to the classics from antiquity, by Daniels's own account, his reading focused on eighteenth- and nineteenth-century British figures, including Dickens, Thackeray, Macaulay, Gibbon, and Hume, and he became especially interested in the works of Thomas Carlyle, the Sage of Craigenputtock, claiming to have "read and re-read his *Heroes and Hero Worship*, the *French Revolution* and *Sartor Resartus*."[72] Although Carlyle's views on political economy, which were dominated by his skepticism of the common man's wisdom, were antithetical to Daniels's, the Sage is credited as the first to refer to the press as the "fourth estate," an elevation that flattered Daniels, the future newspaperman. Moreover, Carlyle was an empiricist, one "interested in how personalities . . . could sway the course of events."[73] This was Daniels's view of history and the news. Like Carlyle, he thought the world was made by men, not by impersonal forces.

Despite the fact that Daniels and his brothers were well prepared to begin their formal education at the institute, the school lifted them and its other charges well beyond the basic literacy, numeracy, and civic veneration offered at secondary schools across the state and around the country at the time. For the rest of his life, Daniels had the fondest remembrances of his days at the school, and he and his brothers received an excellent, liberal education there. A successful student by most standards—by his own account, near the top of his class every year—Josephus was at best abysmal at mathematics, and despite his considerable intelligence, he was arguably the least academically gifted of the three Daniels boys. A standardized set of marks that would support such a conclusion does not exist, but Josephus himself conceded as much. Many years after the boys had completed their schooling, Josephus found an old tuition account from their days at the institute. Noticing that his tuition exceeded that of Frank—Charles had not yet matriculated—Josephus concluded, with only a touch of self-deprecating humor, that Frank "was a good student and didn't need as much tutoring as I required."[74] And later in life, although he would frequently question Charles's judgment on many matters, Josephus never doubted or questioned his younger brother's considerable intellectual power.

Josephus might not have been the most intellectually gifted member of the family, and he may or may not have been the most athletic, but he was certainly the most ardent athlete in the family. During his days at Wilson Collegiate Institute, the new sport of football was introduced. With Hassell strongly behind the football team, it soon became the rage, but Josephus never cared much for it. "I never liked [football] much," he wrote. "My passion was baseball, which I played from early dawn until night fall when not in school or at work." Daniels became captain of the local traveling team, and although its overall record has been lost, into old age he was known to recount the glories earned on the diamonds of his youth. In particular, showing a typically good-natured disapproval of the demon rum, he recalled a famous victory of which he was most proud because his team "won in spite of the fact that two of our best players became intoxicated at the dance the night before the game."[75] Loaded into mule-drawn wagons, the team traversed the towns of the coastal plain seeking to play the best of the local (white) opposition.

In addition to Josephus Daniels, two other schoolmates at the institute would go on to a certain amount of fame, or infamy, beyond the confines of eastern North Carolina. (Frank would become prominent locally but was virtually unknown outside the state.) One of these was Mary Lily Kenan, who, according to Daniels, had "a lovely voice" and who would one day become the wife of Henry Morrison Flagler.[76] Kenan's future husband had partnered with a young John D. Rockefeller in a Cleveland mercantile house, later launching what became the Standard Oil Trust. More than thirty years Flagler's junior, Kenan was the magnate's third wife, and the scandal surrounding their marriage followed her for the rest of her days. Flagler's second wife, Ida, was still alive in a Florida insane asylum when the state legislature passed an act admitting insanity as legal grounds for a divorce. The ink was hardly dry on the legislation before Flagler divorced Ida and married Daniels's old classmate. Rockefeller's wife, Laura, a devout Baptist, was so scandalized by these events that she ceased receiving the Flaglers socially.

Daniels's other schoolmate destined for an altogether different type of fame was future governor Charles Brantley Aycock. Born near the rural crossroads town of Fremont, just south of Wilson, Aycock was the youngest of ten children. Three years older than Josephus, Aycock came to the institute later than most pupils, and although he and one of his older brothers, Barden, were in Josephus's class, they became best friends with Daniels's older brother, Frank. This friendship would ultimately lead Charles Brantley Aycock and Frank Daniels to become law partners in nearby Goldsboro. Fremont was too far from Wilson for the Aycock boys to commute daily; so they boarded near town, and Mary Cleaves Daniels informally adopted them. Josephus Daniels ungrudgingly conceded that both Aycock boys "were smarter than I was and better students." After their deaths, Daniels would write, "We could not have loved more if we had been kin." Daniels admired Aycock as much as any man he ever knew, and in an age in which on-the-stump oratory was a much-valued skill, Daniels called him "the most gifted speaker I have ever heard," which was high praise from a man who had heard and admired William Jennings Bryan.[77] A fiercely partisan Democrat and staunch white supremacist, Aycock would one day help Daniels lead the state's white supremacy movement.

With the close of the spring term in 1880, eighteen-year-old Josephus Daniels left the Wilson Collegiate Institute for good. There he had received an outstanding formal education. By the time he left the institute, he had also received an education in the cotton, strawberry, and melon fields of Wilson County. In those fields Daniels had learned what it was like to perform backbreaking work from sunup to sundown one day after the next. The Wilson Post Office had given him an education of another kind. By observation, he had learned the life of a small-town professional in the postbellum South. It was a life to which he aspired. Years later, reflecting fondly on those days, Daniels wrote, "I look back now upon that time as a period of a full, good youth. It had been as rich as it had been poor, and I now know that life tasted sweet in it. Like all the rest of us, I was never young but once but I would not swap my own boyhood or young manhood for any other anywhere on the wide earth of which I was to see so much as I grew older. I saw a good deal more of life but nothing better, friendlier, more stirring than the people and days of my boyhood in Wilson."[78]

As Daniels entered his early manhood, his basic economic problem was that he lived in an agricultural region but did not possess any land, the key economic asset. Of course, economic success was not limited to the planter elite. Daniels had learned that the men without land who prospered in town possessed a profession; they were bankers, lawyers, doctors, or journalists. Daniels, however, had no profession either. But he was not without hope, for during his teen years he had cultivated a vision. That vision was that he would become a newspaper entrepreneur. In so doing, he would bring together three errant strands of his young life. One strand was political. At the time, the newspaper business was inextricably linked to politics. Daniels would enter politics through the newspaper business. Another strand was economic. He would anchor his, his mother's, and his younger brother's fortunes to the profits he hoped to earn in the newspaper business. The third strand was social. The fatherless boy, a nobody from the dusty side streets of downtown Wilson, North Carolina, would make a name for himself and climb the social ladder, returning his family to a higher rung from which his mother had fallen. Still a teenager, Josephus Daniels resolved to purchase his first newspaper.

2. A Member of the Fourth Estate

I assert that there is no such thing as a self-made man.

—JOSEPHUS DANIELS

Although Mary Cleaves Daniels was not poor by the standards of the post-bellum South, when she arrived in Wilson in the fall of 1865, she was close enough to poor that the wolf could be heard at the door. Her sons were exposed to the more prosperous elements of coastal plain society, however, as they grew up in the Wilson Post Office, in addition to being nurtured by Mary Cleaves's own genteel roots. Lawyers, merchants, financiers, planters, and clergymen all passed through downtown Wilson regularly and, in some cases, daily. At the post office they exchanged gossip, business information, and political opinions. Even as a boy, Josephus Daniels recognized that the interests of these men intersected on the pages of the local newspaper.

At the time, newspapers served as the primary source of information. Even town gossip, the other main source of information, was often the by-product of something someone had read in the newspaper. Most towns of any size had at least one paper that typically came out weekly. More than a few locals also subscribed to a daily or weekly paper from one of the region's larger cities. In Wilson the main big-city papers came from Raleigh, the state capital, roughly sixty miles to the west, where the coastal plain began to give way to the rolling hills of the piedmont. Wilmington, on the coast, also supplied the town with printed news, and some prominent locals even subscribed to a Charlotte paper or two. Although Mary Cleaves did not sub-scribe to the Raleigh papers, Josephus read them in the post office before the local subscribers collected their copies. In later years he would claim that his boyhood aspiration was to run a Raleigh newspaper.

Of course young Daniels also read the local newspaper. During Recon-struction, the town newspaper in Wilson was the *Plain-Dealer*. Owned and edited by a twice-wounded Confederate officer, Colonel R. W. Singeltary, the paper was a modest journalistic success but a business failure. Accord-ing to Daniels, Colonel Singeltary "wrote strong editorials, but he paid scant attention to local and personal news and less to advertising or soliciting new subscribers or collecting from the old."[1] In the early 1870s another Confederate veteran, Colonel Henry G. Williams, and his son James moved to Wilson from the small town of Battleboro, which was a few miles north, bringing their paper, the *Advance*, with them. In providing local news coverage and business practice, if not journalistic style, the *Advance* proved more successful than the *Plain-Dealer*, and the new paper soon became the most prominent in Wilson, eventually driving the older one out of business. Ten-year-old Daniels befriended James Williams, and when not in school, working at the post office, or picking strawberries or cotton, Daniels could be found hanging out at the *Advance*. Pitching in here and there, the boy tried, probably neither very hard nor very successfully, to stay out of the way.

After the younger Williams died suddenly in 1873, the old colonel focused more attention on Josephus, finding productive chores for him at the newspaper and generally looking after him. According to Daniels, "Colonel Henry G., as everyone called him, ate and slept and drank politics"; he was just the kind of man Daniels was growing to admire.[2] The fatherless Daniels appreciated the colonel's attention and affection and returned it by working in the evening at the *Advance*. Even before he became a teenager, Daniels held four part-time jobs, all intertwined with his school obligations and household chores. Although he had given up field work, he now worked in the post office in the morning, at Nadal's pharmacy in the afternoon, and at the *Advance* in the evening. In addition, he assisted Nadal in his surveying business. He would soon add a fifth job, as the local business agent for two out-of-town newspapers. It was a busy schedule that was about to get busier.

Daniels's first opportunity to use the skills he learned in his apprenticeship at the *Advance* came through connections made at the Wilson Collegiate Institute. In 1878, at age sixteen, with his younger brother, Charles, and a schoolmate, Edward Oldham, Daniels founded the *Cornucopia*, a free weekly newspaper. Its expenses were paid by local merchants who could purchase a rectangular space, or "tombstone," for 25 or 50 cents, depending on size, in the paper to advertise their business. Daniels adopted the paper's motto, *multum in parvo*—"much in little"—as a standard of good journalism, one he would maintain for the rest of his life. Although all three boys engaged in the production of the paper, Josephus alone took credit for the organization of the operation, and in his own words, "the paper was a financial success from the start."[3] Exactly what that meant in terms of cash flow or profits he did not record; however, within the next year or so, Daniels, in cooperation with another acquaintance, J. R. Griffin, began a similar paper, the curiously named *Our Free Blade*, in nearby Goldsboro. Using an antiquated hand-operated Washington printing press, the four teens published the two local weeklies for two years.

Although the boys did not pay themselves a regular salary, it is difficult to imagine that the papers were money-losers. Daniels's cash-strapped mother could not afford to have two of her boys taking time out of their schedules every week for two years to simply engage in a money-consuming hobby. Even if the enterprises just broke even, there was the cost of time to consider. A boy writing, editing, and printing a free newspaper was a boy not planting, hoeing, or picking cotton, melons, or strawberries—or in Daniels's case, a boy not working in Cousin Ed Nadal's pharmacy or surveying business. Josephus and Charles surely supplied Mary Cleaves with some cash from the enterprise. Daniels himself must have considered those days as neither purely fun nor purely work but, rather, as an educational investment in his future. He was learning a trade. Indeed, in old age, Daniels described his years hanging out at the *Advance* and running the *Cornucopia* and *Our Free Blade* as "a good school [that] opened the door through which I entered the profession of journalism."[4]

In addition to performing odd jobs at the *Advance* and publishing two free papers, Daniels gained valuable experience as the local business agent for two Raleigh newspapers, the *Observer*, a daily which was on its way to becoming the state's leading newspaper, and *Hale's Weekly*. Daniels served as the subscription and collection agent for these papers, and it appears that on occasion he also supplied them with local news items. Exactly how he obtained this work he did not record; however, the out-of-town papers were delivered in bulk by rail, and subscribers collected their papers from the post office. It is not difficult to imagine the entrepreneurial young Daniels, who just happened to live at the post office, contacting the Raleigh papers and offering to serve as their local agent.

His remuneration for these activities came from a small percentage of the subscription and advertising monies he collected. Typically the newspapers themselves were sold at a discount to the distributor, in this case Daniels, and he in turn sold them to the subscribers. A paper that retailed for 2 cents—a typical price at the time—might be sold to Daniels for a penny. Thus, since North Carolina daily newspapers appeared six times a week (there was no Monday edition, as the staff had Sunday off in honor of the Sabbath), Daniels earned roughly a dollar a week for every seventeen subscriptions. If nothing else, the exercise taught Daniels about the newspaper distribution system beyond the city in which the paper was published. Years later, the stationery of his flagship paper would boast that the Raleigh *News and Observer* was "the only daily paper in the world having more subscribers than population in the city in which published."[5] In addition, Daniels seems to have always remembered the usefulness of diligently collecting payments from his customers whether they were distributors, subscribers, or advertisers. When three of his four sons began working at his Raleigh newspaper more than thirty years later, the first job he assigned each of them was collecting from customers.

Daniels's duties at the Wilson *Advance* expanded as he matured, and at the same time he approached the end of the curriculum at the Wilson Collegiate Institute. He did not return for the fall term in 1880. There appears to have been no formal commencement ceremony and no awarding of a degree. On his résumé, Daniels later claimed that he "completed a course at Wilson, N.C. Collegiate Institute."[6] At the same time, he gave up his regular job in Nadal's pharmacy as well as his less-regular job as Nadal's surveying assistant. He also surrendered his interests in the two free newspapers (though he kept his job as the local business agent for the Raleigh papers). He did all these things to become the full-time editor of the Wilson *Advance*. Except for three stints in public service, Daniels would be exclusively a newspaper editor and publisher for the next sixty-eight years.

This turn of events occurred shortly after Colonel Williams sold the paper to John Woodard. A member of the prominent local family that provided financial support for the Wilson Collegiate Institute, Woodard had studied at the bar of justice and then gone into politics. Prior to owning and editing the *Advance*, he had already established himself as a leader of the local branch of the Democratic Party, serving in the North Carolina House and Senate and as the state solicitor in eastern North Carolina. Woodard leveraged his social connections to obtain the local government printing contracts for Wilson and Wilson County, which helped make the *Advance* a profitable business from the time he acquired it. But the paper was never more than a part-time interest for him. Young Daniels felt that a little more aggressiveness in the paper's reporting, advertising, and circulation would make it an even more profitable enterprise. Apparently he did not do a good job of keeping these thoughts to himself.

NEWSPAPER ENTREPRENEUR

After Daniels served an apprenticeship of a few months as editor, during which he bombarded Woodard with ideas about improving the *Advance*'s management, Woodard decided to place the day-to-day operations in Daniels's hands. Although Woodard's management style at the paper might best be described as one of benign neglect, he was neither lazy nor stupid. Rather, he saw the paper, as many newspapermen of his day did, as an outlet for local Democratic opinion rather than as a capitalist undertaking. Thus he remained busy with what he considered more important, and perhaps more munificent, activities. Although his main interests were elsewhere, he was not about to surrender a profitable asset to the eighteen-year-old Daniels without some insurance. He persuaded, or perhaps he demanded, Daniels and Frank Connor, who as typographer oversaw the operation and maintenance of the paper's physical plant, to purchase shares in the company. (Daniels and Connor were the firm's only full-time white employees; there was also at least one African American worker, who did the actual printing.) It was a wise strategy on Woodard's part. He would receive an influx of cash from Daniels and Connor up front, and because Woodard continued to be the largest shareholder, he stood to realize any increase in the value of the firm. Daniels (and Connor) would benefit as well. They would share, beyond their weekly wages, in any gains in the value of the business. Daniels liked the idea of buying into the paper. The only problem was he did not have the money.

Of his financial condition at the time, Daniels merely said, "I hadn't a dollar in the world."[7] Like countless optimistic entrepreneurs before and since, Daniels got the money ($600, 30 percent of the firm) by borrowing it. To do so he turned to a local banker, Thomas Jefferson Hadley. In the South in those days it was uncommon for a town like Wilson, small and somewhat geographically isolated, to have a number of state or federally chartered commercial banks. In 1880, there were only sixteen chartered banks in the entire state (six state banks and ten nationally chartered ones) and only one in Wilson—the First National Bank. Its lending policies were decidedly conservative.[8] Eighteen-year-old newspaper entrepreneurs without collateral would have been wasting their time even asking for a loan.

Hadley on the other hand, with his partner Alpheus Branch, formed a "private" bank. The two colorful financiers complemented each other. Hadley represented the kind of old-fashioned southern gentleman that became increasingly scarce as the region industrialized and left its agrarian roots behind. Branch, on the other hand, was a man of the Gilded Age. An aggressive investor, Branch, according to Daniels, possessed "a sixth sense in buying and selling [cotton] futures, as well as in all business and banking lines. Others lost heavily. He almost always won."[9] Branch would eventually obtain a state charter and form the commercial Branch Banking Company, a forerunner of the large financial institution known as BB&T. At the time Daniels needed a loan, the firm of Hadley and Branch bought and sold cotton futures as well as a variety of other short-term credit instruments. They also directly loaned money, generally on collateral such as land or crops. The firm did not accept deposits, issue banknotes, or offer checking accounts as state or federally chartered commercial banks could. Also, unlike the town's chartered bank, Hadley and Branch were unregulated. Because there were no depositors to protect, no federal or state auditors questioned their loans. In the futures market, Hadley and Branch made money by buying low and selling high. Similarly, in the loan market, they borrowed at a low rate and loaned at a higher one. Their portfolio of loans could be as risky as they wanted it to be. Thus they operated more like a modern hedge fund than a commercial bank.

Although Daniels was and would remain on good personal terms with Hadley, the financier would not make a $600 loan to a teenager who possessed no tangible assets. Even financial players like Hadley and Branch, who took financial positions the more stolid commercial banks would never touch, placed a limit on the risks to which they would expose themselves. Thus, to obtain the loan, Daniels had to find someone with collateral who would "sign his note"—that is someone who would offer Hadley collateral in Daniels's name. For this Daniels turned to T. A. Wainwright, his former Sunday school teacher at the town's Methodist Church, which was conveniently located a block from Mary Cleaves's home.[10] Like Hadley, Wainwright was a man of some means, and with his guarantee Hadley lent Daniels the money. With the note secured, Daniels was in business, as was his colleague Connor, who also purchased 30 percent of the paper. At the time, long-term commercial loans were rare, particularly for a small business, so the note was probably a short-term loan of at most twelve to thirty-six months. Since Daniels's living expenses were minimal (he still lived in his mother's home), it is likely that he planned to pay off the loan in no more than a couple of years.

The arrangement at which Woodard, Daniels, and Connor arrived was such that Daniels would handle the news and the business ends of the paper, Connor would be in charge of the printing, and Woodard would write the editorials. This arrangement lasted no more than a couple of months. By the end of the year, Daniels approached Woodard and Connor with a proposition to buy them out. Exactly why Daniels decided to do this he did not record. However, the fact that his subsequent references to

Woodard were terse and detached, contrary to his tendency to be effusive in characterizing old friends and mentors, suggests that the two did not see eye-to-eye on politics, business, or both. In any case, the value of the paper, including physical plant, working stock (that is paper, ink, and so forth), and "goodwill" (an accounting entry for the difference between the market value of a firm and the value of its tangible assets), was $2,000. Although Daniels nominally owned 30 percent of the business, his share had been purchased on credit, and he had retired at best a very small portion of that debt between the time he incurred it and the time he bought out his partners a few months later. To purchase the paper, he would be forced to borrow the full price of the firm.

The original $600 loan was as far as old Wainwright would back the young, would-be capitalist. To issue a loan of $2,000 (more than ten times per capita income in North Carolina at the time, the equivalent of half a million dollars today), Hadley insisted on collateral in the form of government bonds or a mortgage on prime agricultural land or town real estate. Daniels had none of these, but he knew someone who did: his mother. She agreed to back the new loan from Hadley, in the process retiring her son's previous note, which Hadley still held. Whether Daniels turned to his mother for the money or whether the loan was her idea, he did not say. She had suggested that he approach Hadley about the original loan to purchase a stake in the paper, so it is probable that she also suggested the larger loan to buy out his partners.[11] In any case, Daniels's gratitude at his mother's generosity was deep and lifelong. Mary Cleaves did not have $2,000. In fact, she had no liquid assets. She had sold her home in Washington and her stake in her family's Hyde County property to purchase her house in Wilson. To raise the money for her son's loan, she mortgaged her house, which was worth roughly the value of the firm. "It was everything she had," Daniels said years later.[12] Hadley agreed to provide the loan, with the deed to Mary Cleaves's home as collateral.

When Daniels took over the *Advance* in the winter of 1880–81, it had a circulation of 1,000. By the time he sold the business in 1885, the circulation was 2,500, an average annual compounded growth rate of more than 20 percent, rapid by any standard. (Woodard might have been wise to listen to the suggestions of his young employee.) Within a year, Daniels could claim the *Advance* was "the largest weekly newspaper in the state."[13] In addition, to accommodate the growth in circulation, Daniels soon updated the paper's physical plant, replacing the old printing press, which like the one he used for the *Cornucopia* was a hand-operated Washington, with a new Cottrell. The Cottrell offered two advantages over the old Washington. The new machine printed two sides at once, and it had a mechanical feeder. (At that time, each issue of the *Advance* was four pages, printed on one sheet folded in the middle.) Together, these changes probably increased by a factor of four the speed of printing the weekly paper.[14] It was not an unsubstantial investment. Even the least expensive Cottrell sold for around $1,000. Daniels was increasing his investment in the firm by 50 percent, but his business was in the process of growing by 150 percent. Although the *Advance* was a weekly, the printing could not be done until the last minute; otherwise, late-breaking news would have been omitted. Thus, Daniels printed the paper the night before it was released, like a daily. Hand-printing 1,000 newspapers one side of one sheet at a time was trying; printing 2,500 in a night using the Washington was impossible. The Cottrell more than paid for itself.

Daniels also hired more workers, and he maintained an integrated workforce, not a common feature of southern capitalism at the time.[15] (Then and later, his African American workers were strictly segregated into manual jobs.) Among the key hires was H. B. "Ben" Hardy, who took over the circulation department. Hardy "whistled and cajoled many hundreds of people into subscribing," and with his help, Daniels made the *Advance* the must-read "paper for Wilson, Nash, and Greene counties."[16] Daniels's efforts confirmed his vision of the *Advance* as a profitable enterprise. From the beginning, Daniels oversaw every aspect of the paper's operation except one. Curiously, he initially farmed out the editorials, paying a prominent local judge $1.00 a week to handle the task. Perhaps eighteen-year-old Daniels lacked confidence in his writing skills, or perhaps he was simply overwhelmed with the other tasks associated with building the firm. In any case, the arrangement did not last long. Despite the fact that the judge was a loyal Democrat, Daniels quickly became disenchanted with the tone and quality of the editorials, and gaining confidence in his own opinions and his abilities with the pen, he fired the judge and took over the editorial page in the summer of 1881.

With all of these changes, the paper was soon, in Daniels's words, "on a paying basis," by which he meant it was yielding more profit than it had under Woodard's management.[17] About this time, Daniels began a business practice that he would follow well into middle age. From the paper's revenues he paid himself a salary, as if he were an employee. At first the figure was $75 a month, but in a couple of years he increased it to $100, where it stayed for many years. Any profits beyond that would then be plowed back into the firm in the form of improvements in or expansion of the physical plant. These profits, which modern accountants refer to as retained earnings, fueled the early growth in Daniels's businesses. Also, even after he bought the *Advance*, Daniels continued to work as the eastern North Carolina business agent and correspondent for the Raleigh papers. This work added to his cash flow, albeit modestly, but more importantly it allowed him to keep one foot in the bigger political and business world of the state capital. The connections he made in this way would pay off dramatically in just a few years.

Although the newspaper business was steady, in the sense that newspapers were published daily or weekly, the economy of Wilson County was highly seasonal. Much of the economic activity of the area revolved around the cotton crop. Newspaper subscribers often could not pay for their annual subscription until the cotton crop was harvested and sold. Similarly, advertisers could not pay for the ads they ran in the *Advance* until their customers paid them, which often was not until the cotton crop came in. Thus through the summer months Daniels faced a cash-flow crisis. Fortunately, his success as a newspaper entrepreneur soon opened new avenues of financing. After a couple of years of generating profits, Daniels managed to obtain credit from the town's sole commercial bank. The terms were onerous enough, 12 percent annual interest on short-term loans (usually no more than 90 days), but Daniels was now in a position to sign his own notes. His reputation and the equity he had in his business were enough to grant access to bank credit (which in turn allowed him to buy the Cottrell press). Modern readers should not underestimate the importance of this step to a budding nineteenth-century capitalist. Easy credit was a feature of later economies. Access to short-term credit was more than a validation of Daniels's business acumen; in a fluctuating economy, it could often mean the difference between success and failure. Credit could sustain a firm through the fluctuations of the business and crop cycles. By obtaining a line of credit at a commercial bank, Daniels had cleared a hurdle that many of his aspiring business colleagues, young and old, never would. It served as a milestone on his road to success.

The lack of credit access was not the only potential barrier to success in the newspaper business at the time. Given the relatively high cost of transportation, there was only so much Daniels could do to expand the *Advance*'s circulation. A small town such as Wilson was "quintessentially a retail place, and counted for its customers on rural residents who lived in its immediate vicinity."[18] In 1880, Wilson County contained only 16,000 people, many of whom were illiterate. The only way to reach much of the county was by wagon over roads that would grow impassable with even the smallest amount of rainfall. At the time, the post office did not offer free delivery to rural areas; thus the cost of circulating a newspaper beyond the town limit would quickly overwhelm any revenues derived from the effort.

Newspapers in large metropolitan areas did not face this problem. They had more potential subscribers than they could satisfy with their physical plants. Even the largest New York City papers supplied only a fraction of the city's total readership. (At its peak, Joseph Pulitzer's New York *World* reached a million subscribers when New York City's population was over 3.5 million.)[19] In addition, these big city papers could find customers in the hinterlands, as beyond municipal boundaries the papers were delivered in bulk, by rail. Even the Raleigh, Wilmington, and Charlotte newspapers were distributed to Wilson. However, the economics of the business did not run in reverse: Few of Raleigh's citizens were interested in reading the Wilson *Advance*. Obtaining a circulation of 2,500 for a newspaper in a town the size of Wilson was a considerable achievement, but further expansion would have to come at other margins. Although Wilson was growing, its growth was not extraordinary by the standards of nineteenth-century commerce. To expand further, Daniels would have to look beyond Wilson's boundaries. So, in the short run, he had his sights on establishing or acquiring newspapers in nearby towns. He closely monitored the region's other newspapers, and in 1882, upon learning that one of them, the Kinston *Journal*, was being moved to New Bern, Daniels decided to start a new paper in Kinston.

Located on the Neuse River thirty miles southeast of Wilson, Kinston mirrored Wilson in many ways. It was a natural place for Daniels to expand his business interests at the time, but he faced obstacles. He knew folks from Kinston, but he had no business contacts there. Both Wilson and Kinston were crossroads towns with a rail line, but there was no direct rail route between the two county seats. Going overland on a daily basis was too time-consuming; thus Daniels would need a partner in the venture. He turned to his younger brother, Charles. Seventeen at the time, Charles was a bright though occasionally indifferent student, and he was preparing to leave the Wilson Collegiate Institute at a younger age than either of his older brothers had. Charles proved to be a talented but erratic and difficult colleague from a young age. At this stage of their lives, Josephus looked after his younger brother, as he would continue to do off and on for the rest of his life. Although Josephus was not blind to Charles's shortcomings, he also recognized that Charles possessed intelligence and drive, and Josephus attempted to channel those talents by making Charles his partner. The brothers would call the new Kinston paper the *Free Press*. Josephus planned to finance the start-up through the profits he had retained from the *Advance*, and through advance advertising sales. To this end, he turned over to his employees the management of the *Advance*, temporarily moved to Kinston, and began going door-to-door soliciting advertising from merchants there—much as he had done in and around Wilson to build the advertising and subscription bases of the *Advance*. Once the paper was up and running, he returned to Wilson, leaving Charles in Kinston to oversee the day-to-day operations of the *Free Press*, though Josephus continued to edit the paper's final edition and write its editorials.

Interestingly, rather than pay off his mother's mortgage from the *Advance*'s profits, Daniels chose to expand his operations, upgrading the *Advance* with the new printing press and expanding into Kinston. It was a bold plan, and it worked. Daniels later claimed that within two days he had secured more advertising than the old Kinston *Journal* had run at its peak.[20] Charles proved to be a good newspaperman, and after a brief time working on both newspapers, Josephus withdrew from editing the *Free Press*. Henceforth, he only supplied its editorial content. He did not record the capitalized value of the *Free Press*, of which he and Charles were equal partners, but it would have been unlikely to exceed the $2,000 he had in the *Advance*, which was, after all, an established paper with a relatively large circulation. An estimate of $1,000 would not be unreasonable. Josephus fronted all of the initial capital, and Charles purchased his half on credit from his brother by forgoing his share of the profits.

Once the *Free Press* was up and running, Daniels added its profits to those coming from the *Advance*, and he purchased a half-interest in yet a third paper, the Rocky Mount *Reporter*, which was owned by another small-time newspaperman, W. J. Fitzgerald. In Nash County, fifteen miles north of Wilson, Rocky Mount was another coastal plain town that, like Wilson and Kinston, was growing as a result of the region's burgeoning cotton and tobacco markets. In addition to new financial capital, Daniels supplied the *Reporter* with editorial content. As with the *Free Press*, Daniels did not record the purchase price of his share of the *Reporter*, but as its circulation and market value would have been similar to those of the *Free Press*, half of the firm would have cost Daniels roughly $500. Thus, after consummating all of these transactions before his twenty-first birthday, Daniels owned two newspapers (though one had been purchased on credit and half of the other was pledged to his brother) and a half-interest in a third paper.

Daniels was a diligent businessman, always paying careful attention to the accounts even if he did not keep the books himself. However, he considered journalism more important than finance. If it came down to covering a hot story or sweating over the firm's accounts, Daniels chose journalism over accounting. It was always his view of the newspaper business that if he got the journalism right, the money would take care of itself. Of the many things that Daniels learned in the business during his Wilson days, one of the most important and lasting was that "the measure of a commercially successful newspaper is not simply how well it reports the big events, but what it does when there are no dying statesmen, bloodthirsty desperadoes, or heinous crimes to write about."[21] As the British newspaper magnate Lord Northcliffe put it, "The people relish a good hero and a good hate."[22] Like other successful newspapermen at the time and thereafter, Daniels realized that "news is not a phenomenon that exists in the real world. . . . An event becomes news only when journalists and editors decide to record it."[23] The prices of cotton and tobacco had fluctuated with the vagaries of the market for as long as people had been trading cotton and tobacco, but fluctuations that appeared on the front page of the Wilson *Advance* became news. The journalist's art was to give mere facts a context that made people discuss them over dinner or at the Wilson Post Office. Cotton was just a widely traded commodity; 5 cents a pound, just a number. But cotton at 5 cents a pound meant Wilson County farmers could not pay off their debts. People lost their farms. Short sellers got rich. That was news.

Similarly, gambling, legalized or not, was a well-entrenched human pastime. The Gospels tell us soldiers gambled at the foot of the True Cross. In the postbellum era, lotteries were big moneymakers for the state governments that oversaw them, the people who ran them, and the newspapers that advertised them. When Daniels took over the *Advance*, his biggest advertising client was the Louisiana Lottery, the nation's most prominent state-run lottery. Daniels soon refused to run the lottery's ads in his newspaper. That small act of conscience became local front-page news. On the day Daniels made the announcement in the *Advance*, people who had for years taken the lottery for granted buzzed in conversation all over town.

Whether it was taking a principled stand on the lottery or telling the human story of the cotton market's vicissitudes, Daniels understood that "if there were no discernible heroes or villains, no mysteries to uncover, no climaxes, denouements, triumphs or failures, if no one wins or loses in the end, then there is no story to tell," that is to say, there is no news.[24] It was the newspaper's job to provide that news. Thus in the pages of Daniels's newspapers, cotton became more than a commodity; it was the lifeline of the community. The Louisiana Lottery became more than a game of chance, more than a source of advertising; in the Wilson *Advance* it became a villain that defrauded otherwise God-fearing Wilson County folks out of their hard-earned cash. The lottery's managers, which included the revered Confederate generals P. G. T. Beauregard and Jubal Early, became villains, and in vilifying them Daniels created a storm of outrage. Like the waves generated by a tsunami that recede and then come crashing back onshore, the reaction to the denunciation itself became news. Everything needs context to have meaning. Journalists and editors supply that context to the news. They give it meaning, and in so doing they make a living. This was Daniels's chosen trade.

Another lesson Daniels took from those days was that politics, the news, and newspapers were never separate entities. With radio and television in the distant future, people received their news from the paper, which prior to rural delivery could only be obtained in town. Once the news was spread in town, it could make its way into the countryside—in edited form, perhaps—by word of mouth. But if one did not witness a news-making event or hear about it from someone who did, then the news came from the newspaper. Politics influenced and reflected public events, great and small, national or local, and so politics was news, and the newspaper, as the medium of the news, was simultaneously the medium of politics. But at the time Daniels entered the business, those who paid for the paper typically did not expect to be paying for the facts, whatever those might be. Rather, they bought opinion, editorial opinion, from the front page to the back page. As Benjamin Franklin, who spent time in the newspaper business, had written a century earlier, "The Business of Printing [newspapers] has chiefly to do with Men's Opinions." One of Franklin's contemporaries added that any claims of impartiality in a newspaper were "perfect nonsense."[25] The business had changed little in the intervening decades. Indeed, it would not change on a wide scale until Daniels's generation of newspapermen changed it.[26]

Of course, the opinions of editors often offended subscribers and advertisers, as well as potential subscribers and advertisers. This was the conundrum of the newspaper business at the time: A clearly defined political slant in reporting, coupled with a hard-hitting editorial page, was sure to offend and anger at least one side of any dispute. This would prove costly when it came to seeking advertisers and subscribers. However, an editorial approach that offended and angered no one also interested no one, and without a critical mass of subscribers, advertisers balked at purchasing advertising space. Daniels understood the basic economics of this situation from the time he spent hanging out at the Wilson Post Office, reading the newspapers from around the region. It was a lesson further impressed upon him at the Wilson *Advance* even before he became an owner of it. (Local government contracts had made the difference between profit and loss under Woodard's control.) Daniels determined that the solution to this problem was the separation of news and opinion. An opinion-free, or reasonably opinion-free, news section would accompany a nakedly opinionated editorial section. Following the model established by the big city papers, he aspired to separate the news from the editorials in the same paper, with the hope of selling newspapers even to subscribers who might object to the paper's editorial stand. They would pay for the news and accept the editorial position. This combination proved to be the future of the newspaper business across the United States and, indeed, the free world. In the management of his three papers, Daniels was creating what subsequent generations would come to know as the modern newspaper.

As a business enterprise, Daniels's vision would rise or fall on his firms' profits. In writing about his business success (or failure) Daniels seldom used the word "profit." He typically used more folksy expressions, such as "a paying basis" or "good money." It is difficult to say how much money Daniels made from his business ventures, because the accounting, never clearly reported, could be quite complex. Many of the necessary records have not survived, and those that have seldom follow anything like what modern readers would consider standard accounting practices. Still, it is possible to estimate how much he earned at the time. During the first few years he owned the *Advance*, Daniels paid himself $75 a month. In addition to his operating costs, he was amortizing his $2,000 loan from Hadley, and within three years of receiving Hadley's loan, Daniels had managed to generate the earnings to purchase one and a half other newspapers, which, if combined, were arguably equal in value to the *Advance*. Assuming he earned a few dollars a week from his activities as the local business agent for the Raleigh papers, and something comparable to that from his other local printing contracts, his newspaper would have had an annual accounting profit (that is, his personal income plus retained earnings) of about $1,500 a year. Since he had a total investment of $3,500 (including $2,000 in the *Advance*, $1,000 in the *Free Press*, and $500 in the *Reporter*), counting his income as part of the profit would have yielded annual returns on equity of around 40 to 45 percent. Subtracting his income from this calculation still left him with a respectable rate of return of between 15 and 20 percent.

With average annual rates of return in southern manufacturing around 20 percent at the time, and farmland and government bonds typically yielding less than 10 percent, it appears that when Daniels said he had the business on a "paying basis," he meant more than simply "profits were greater than zero."[27] He clearly meant that his operations were earning a superior rate of return. Even with such a high rate of return, however, Daniels was not getting rich, because the amount of capital he controlled was relatively small, and of course he still owed Hadley for the debt on the *Advance*, the interest and principal on which must be included as a cost in these calculations. A high rate of return on a small investment is still a small net income, but at roughly $1,000 a year (five times per capita income at the time), by age twenty-one, Daniels was well on his way to middle-class comfort and financial security.

Daniels quickly learned that while one had to take an editorial stand to sell papers, and hence to make money in the business, readers angered by one's stand would not always swallow their anger. They often struck back, sometimes by canceling their subscriptions. The threat of customer cancellations resulting from editorial opinions did not worry Daniels, because he expected the quality of his papers' news coverage to cushion such pressure, and he had the local government printing contracts to fall back on. But there were other ways angry readers could lash out, particularly politically powerful readers. Although later Daniels would have enough wealth and political capital to withstand almost any retaliation, during these early years, it took a great deal of moral courage to continue down a path when his livelihood was threatened. The first major crisis was in some ways the worst he would ever face.

The immediate cause was the election of 1882. At the time the underlying issue in Wilson County was prohibition. The election itself merely served as the manifestation of the prohibition debate. Daniels would prove to be a longtime, though not always an especially ardent, prohibitionist. He followed the spirit, though not the letter, of the Methodist doctrine against imbibing alcohol. Always better at disciplining his own behavior than he was at chastising others, Daniels would only partly follow his church's strict teaching on the subject. In this as in many things, he tended to follow his mother. In addition to belonging to the Methodist Church, Mary Cleaves was a member of the Good Templar Lodge, a prohibitionist organization.

Despite her prohibitionist beliefs, she was well known for basting her desserts in wine and brandy. When challenged about the practice by an ostensibly more devout Protestant, she said, "I defy you to point to anyone who became a drunkard by what he ate. It is the drinking that causes the trouble." Her son adopted her see-no-evil approach to cordial-infused desserts. Daniels stated, "I have followed her example—taking nothing alcoholic as a drink, but not looking too closely as to whether the cakes or ices contained wine or brandy."[28]

Daniels might have been personally ambivalent about prohibition, but at the time, drinking was associated with the saloon. The saloon was associated with machine politics, especially urban machine politics, and Daniels was no friend of any political machine of which he was not a part. Furthermore, following his own dictum that editorial indifference to sensitive public issues was a recipe for failure in the newspaper business, his papers took an unambiguous antialcohol position. As a result, following the election of 1882, his family's fortunes, modest though they were, were dashed upon the rock of prohibition.

Mary Cleaves's Good Templars antedated the Woman's Christian Temperance Union by more than twenty years. The convergence of small, local groups like the Wilson Lodge of the Good Templars and a broader national movement (which was overwhelmingly white and Protestant) focused the political spotlight on prohibition from the late 1870s. The temperance movement grew to prominence in North Carolina around the time Daniels entered the newspaper business. At its annual conference in 1879, which coincidentally was held in Wilson, the Methodist Church formally called upon the state legislature to adopt prohibition. (The Baptist Convention, in a slightly different form, did likewise soon thereafter.) It would be another thirty years before the state would formally go "dry," but the battle had begun. In the coastal plain the political split tended to mimic that of Reconstruction. Much of the Democratic Party, including Daniels's progressive wing, was unambiguously white, Protestant, and dry; the Republican Party, which was numerically dominated by its African American members, was "wet." Although Reconstruction in North Carolina had formally ended in 1868 and the Bourbons had retaken the state house following the election of 1870, blacks had not yet been systematically disenfranchised in the state, and antiprohibition proved to be a rallying point for Republicans of both races.

In the election of 1882, following an unsuccessful statewide prohibition referendum, which Daniels and his newspapers strongly promoted, the Republicans managed to elect James O'Hara, an African American carpetbagger, to the U.S. House seat representing Wilson County. O'Hara's victory was a triumph for African Americans and Republicans and a sound defeat for Daniels, who was a vocal opponent of the wets in general, Republicans in particular, and O'Hara specifically. In Daniels's opinion, O'Hara merely served as the black frontman for his white "Republican idols," who in turn controlled the "ignorant Negro vote," and Daniels openly opposed him.[29]

Daniels's strident support of a losing proposition, prohibition, and his opposition to a successful candidate, O'Hara, would prove costly. Daniels never would have guessed that the Republican leadership in Washington, including President Chester A. Arthur and Postmaster General Timothy O. Howe, read the Wilson *Advance*. They probably did not read it on their own accord, but someone, probably O'Hara, brought Daniels's scathing anti-Republican and antiblack language to their attention, and someone, again probably O'Hara, pointed out that the mother of the owner of the *Advance* was the Republican-appointed postmistress of Wilson. (It did not help that Mary Cleaves's oldest son, Frank, was also becoming an increasingly important voice in the area's Democratic Party, though Frank's voice was never as loud, rabid, or influential as his younger brother's.)

Daniels's anti-Republican and antiblack rhetoric was harsh by any standard. With respect to the election of local officials in Lenoir County, Daniels wrote in the Kinston *Free Press*, "The Democrats must show no quarter to any Republican, and the [Lenoir County] Court House must be cleaned from top to bottom, and this means the Clerk of the Court and his Negro allies." He went on to offer an inflammatory eyewitness account of a black political meeting:

> Wilson was in the center of the Second Congressional (Black) District, and therefore the Conventions to nominate a candidate for Congress were held there. The majority of the delegates were Negroes, with a mere handful of white delegates. As soon as the door of the courthouse was opened, the Negroes crowded in so that there was no room for white participants. A few seats were reserved for reporters, and I squeezed into one of these. . . . Think of five hundred perspiring Negroes packed into a courthouse, wrangling and near-fighting on a red-hot day! It was stifling and the odors were rank.[30]

One can forgive O'Hara if he took exception to such portrayals of the party, process, and people who sent him to Congress, and one might understand why he sought to oust Mary Cleaves from a patronage position that he would reasonably consider his to dispense. Still, in 1883 it was no easy task for a black man to get a popular white woman fired from the post office, even when his own party was in power. However, after much wrangling, O'Hara did obtain Mary Cleaves's discharge. The resulting decline in the family's income was costly but not catastrophic. With Charles and Frank gone, only Josephus and his mother remained in the house, and the two of them got along well enough financially. According to Josephus, his income from the newspapers was such that he "kept the interest on the mortgage paid, and later I paid the full amount of the mortgage. But it took close living and a long time."[31] In fact, thirteen years passed before he retired the mortgage on his mother's home, which Hadley conveniently continued to roll over.

Financially, Daniels was able to withstand the loss of his mother's respectable annual income because he secured an additional source of revenue. Since taking over the *Advance*, he had controlled the local government printing contracts, and he also had other printing jobs, including a decent business printing for various Baptist periodicals.[32] When it came to earning a profit in the nineteenth-century newspaper business, government contracts or the patronage of another powerful interest were often required to supplement subscriptions and advertising on the revenue side of the ledger. However, to get the government contract required a party-line editorial stance with which some subscribers and advertisers would disagree. On the cost side of the ledger, Daniels understood that money tied up in idle capital—in, for example, a printing press that was not printing—was money not drawing interest in a bank, paying down debt, or being used to purchase more printing presses or other newspapers. The government contracts helped keep the presses running. Thus, for his first fifteen years in the newspaper business, Daniels supplemented his cash flow by using his presses to print things other than his own newspapers. Government printing contracts proved to be the most lucrative of these non-newspaper publishing jobs. But the contracts did not go to just anyone. They went to printers who would circulate opinions that were consistent with and complimentary of the politicos issuing the contracts, which is to say they went to local newspaper publishers, but only politically *loyal* newspaper publishers.[33]

At the time, state and local governments did not normally maintain their own printing offices. Thus they contracted their printing to local party loyalists, and newspaper firms were the most likely to have a printing press and a ready audience. In this way, government printing contracts linked politics to a newspaper's revenues. Although Republicans and African Americans could occasionally get elected to state and federal offices, as O'Hara had done, the Democratic Party controlled local politics within the town of Wilson (and Kinston and Rocky Mount), just as it controlled most of North Carolina at the time. As a hard-core party loyalist, Daniels received the local printing patronage, which consisted of printing election and referendum ballots, court documents, laws, government announcements, and so forth. The fees for these contracts—which, as patronage payments, exceeded their costs—helped make the difference between profit and loss in the newspaper business at the time, just as they had done since Benjamin Franklin's day.

The economics of the newspaper business was different in large cities, where the market was large and dense enough that a paper could survive on subscriptions and advertising alone. Daniels aspired to copy that model, making a smaller-town newspaper work like those in larger cities. By way of comparison, when William Randolph Hearst entered the newspaper business, there were three newspapers in San Francisco with circulations between 15,000 and 37,500. At the same time, in New York City, a market into which Hearst would eventually move, there were no fewer than eight dailies, and two of those, Pulitzer's *World* and the *Herald*, had circulations above 200,000; they would eventually approach 1 million in Pulitzer's case.[34] Newspapers with circulation and advertising bases that large could eschew the quest for political patronage that kept afloat small-town papers all over the country, including the papers owned by Daniels.

The small towns in which Daniels tried to sell papers were potentially very competitive arenas. Just about anyone with access to a bit of capital could start a paper in a town like Wilson or even Raleigh. But the market could not support three or four competitors. The key to surviving was to have a source of income separate from subscriptions and advertising (as well as a line of bank credit), preferably a source to which one's competitors did not have access. Thus if one could not monopolize the local newspaper business outright, one could at least keep potential competitors out of the market by monopolizing the political printing contracts. In Wilson these contracts were small, but they could still make the difference between profit and loss. In Raleigh, the state capital, the contracts were large and were crucial to a newspaper's long-term survival. From Daniels's perspective during his Wilson days, the good news was that as long as he held the local government contracts, he had a competitive advantage over any potential rivals. The bad news was that his paper became, in essence, a wholly owned subsidiary of the local Democratic Party. If he ever strayed from the party line, then his livelihood was threatened. There were factions within the party, and to keep the local government printing business he had to maintain good terms with whichever faction held power.

Although Daniels was neither a Hearst nor a Pulitzer, he was already making a name for himself in North Carolina by creating a small coastal plain empire by the time he was in his early twenties. His achievements were recognized by his peers in the state's newspaper business when, in 1884, the members of the North Carolina Press Association elected him to be their president. It was a tremendous honor to bestow upon the twenty-two-year-old editor, and he recognized it as such. Claiming it was "wholly unexpected, and [an honor] which I highly appreciated," he served proudly. The highlight of every president's tenure was supposed to be the speech he gave as the outgoing president at the following year's convention. Unfortunately, revealing himself to be a poor public speaker, a trait he would take with him to his grave, Daniels delivered a forgettable speech warning against arrogance in the press.[35] Although Daniels was a good conversationalist, his voice was soft and tended to break as he raised it to make a point. Had Daniels sought a career in elected office, his failure as a public speaker would have been a handicap. With no microphones, radios, or televisions, let alone Internet access, a candidate for public office could rise or fall on the stump. Daniels's career as an elected politician never rose, and he was destined to forever be the man pulling the levers offstage, just behind the curtain.

Taken together then, by 1885, Daniels's ownership of the Wilson *Advance* and the Kinston *Free Press*, his partial ownership of the Rocky Mount *Reporter*, his correspondence and collection work for the Raleigh papers, and his local government printing contracts had propelled him well on his way to comfortable, middle-class respectability. A year earlier, he had borrowed an additional $600 from Hadley and purchased a house adjacent to his mother's on Tarboro Street. (He rented out the house until he sold it for a nice capital gain years later.)[36] His success in the newspaper business and the equity he built as he paid down his mother's mortgage served as collateral for the new loan. Although Daniels still owed on Hadley's initial loan to purchase the *Advance*, he had no trouble servicing the debt, and if he had liquidated his shares in his papers, he could have paid off the mortgage and had cash to spare.

His net worth was positive, and after increasing his monthly income to

$100, he had an annual net income over $1,200, which was several times, perhaps as much as four or five times, larger than the per capita income in North Carolina at the time. (A comparable multiple today would put Daniels's income at roughly $250,000). Still, with newspapers in three of the largest towns in the area, Daniels's opportunities for subsequent expansion were limited. At twenty-three, he confronted a crossroads that the young often face though perhaps recognize only in retrospect. He could settle down, cultivate his local business and political connections, and enjoy the small newspaper empire he had created in North Carolina's coastal plain. In so doing, he could become a respected member of Wilson's professional class, with all the local emoluments such a position entailed. Or he could look for a bigger challenge. Had his vision been limited, had he desired to settle in Wilson, had he sought nothing more than to spend the remainder of his days comfortably hobnobbing with the economic and social elite of the coastal plain, he could have done so with relative ease. But his eyes were on a larger prize. Daniels was intent on moving to the state's capital, Raleigh, and he had a plan for getting there. But the route would be a bit circuitous, and it would lead through Chapel Hill.

CAPTAINS AND GENERALS

As a boy growing up in Wilson, Daniels claimed to have no greater aspiration than to run a daily newspaper in Raleigh: "The farthest point West that I dreamed of or desired to reach was the capital of my state. . . . Early, everything about Raleigh intrigued me."[37] Despite that ambition, when he finally did leave his mother's home in the spring of 1885, he was going neither to Raleigh nor deeper into the newspaper business. Rather, he left to attend law school at the University of North Carolina in Chapel Hill. Why, after working so hard to master the newspaper business in the coastal plain, Daniels suddenly decided to pursue a career at the bar of justice he never explained in any detail. In the five volumes of his memoirs covering thousands of pages, of this monumental decision Daniels wrote exactly one sentence: "I conceived the idea, after the election of 1884, that I could practice law and also edit the Wilson *Advance* with the help of a young reporter and bill collector."[38] None of his surviving personal correspondence, which also runs to thousands of pages, elaborates on the decision. Though Daniels's failure to discuss the matter is odd, the decision itself was not. For an aspiring young Tar Heel, then and later, the law offered an opportunity to move from the lower to the higher rungs of the socioeconomic ladder.

The law had provided an avenue for social and economic advancement for Daniels's older brother, Frank, and his dear friend Charles Brantley Aycock. Daniels had taken a different path, choosing a business career. In doing so, he had learned that the newspaper business was potentially profitable, but he also might well have envisioned a career in politics beyond newspapers. Many of the local movers and shakers who passed through or otherwise hobnobbed at the Wilson Post Office had a foot in politics—men like his mentor at the *Advance*, John Woodard. Thus immediately following the election of 1884, Daniels began planning a move to Chapel Hill to study law—the surest avenue for a man without means to enter politics and a broader social circle in postbellum North Carolina. He went to the right place. At the time, the University of North Carolina was emerging as a place through which many of the state's connected, or hoped-to-be-connected, young men would pass on the way to bigger things.

When Daniels moved to Chapel Hill in the summer of 1885, Wilson, in the heart of the state's cotton and tobacco belts, was the city on the move. Chapel Hill, though a recognized place of learning, was still a sleepy piedmont village. Daniels quickly became all too aware of the disparity. Upon arriving at the university, he expressed shock at the relatively primitive living conditions there. "In those days," he wrote, "there was not a bathroom in Chapel Hill, no modern toilet facilities, no heating system, no comforts or conveniences deemed essential now."[39] In short, Chapel Hill was backward even by Wilson standards. Then as now, Chapel Hill's fate was inextricably tied to that of the university, and the university had suffered mightily in the immediate post–Civil War era. As one local historian put it, "The university and the village were so interdependent that they were bound to either sink or swim together."[40] During Reconstruction they sank. Only a little more than a decade before Daniels arrived there, the town was described as "a desolate, silent wilderness."[41] Of its Reconstruction days, a former governor, Zebulon Vance, lamented that "an air of melancholy, of ruin, pervades everything where once was so much active and intelligent life."[42] Neither the town nor the university stayed down for long, and Daniels arrived relatively early in the town's renaissance. By the time he matriculated in the spring of 1885, there were roughly 200 students enrolled in the university. The undergraduate curriculum was heavy in the classics, as was, albeit to a lesser extent, the law curriculum. Daniels's enthusiasm in continuing his study of the classics in Chapel Hill was matched only by his joy at no longer being forced to wrestle with mathematics.

As for the faculty, Daniels never understated the talents and reputations of his professors at Chapel Hill. Although with the perspective offered by the passage of time his praise seems a bit too floral, they were an impressive lot. According to Daniels, John Manning, professor of law, "had dignity and a certain Jove-like air" and "distinction"; John deBerniere Hooper, professor of Greek, "was the gentlest of gentlemen"; and Dr. Adolphus W. Mangum, head of the Department of Moral Philosophy, was eloquent and a "delightful conversationalist." (Mangum possessed a well-earned reputation for deflating the opinions his students held of their own work. "Nothing a schoolboy ever wrote had lived," he told them.)[43] More importantly from Daniels's perspective, Mangum had "charming daughters." Of all of these solons, Daniels reserved his greatest praise for his brother Frank's mentor, George Winston, professor of Latin, who was in Daniels's opinion "the most brilliant man with whom I came in contact and the most versatile."[44] Collectively, these men and their colleagues were for a generation the keepers of the curriculum at the university, and as such, they continued to run an institution that maintained its lofty status as an elite and erudite finishing school for the state's future leaders. Given his socioeconomic background, Daniels was fortunate to have access to such an education and the network of privilege that it granted him.

Despite enjoying the challenge of law school, Daniels finished nowhere near the top of his class. Indeed, in later years, he claimed his performance was barely adequate, and he finished well behind the distinguished scholars and future members of the bar who were at or near the top of the class of 1885.[45] (In Daniels's law class of ten, there were no fewer than four future state legislators, two superior court judges, and two members of Congress. Among the other important acquaintances Daniels met during his university days was future U.S. senator Lee Overman, the brother-in-law of Mangum.)[46] Still, despite the subsequent success of Daniels's more highly regarded classmates, none achieved anywhere near his renown. An intelligent striver who enjoyed study for its own sake, Daniels was not an intellectual, at least not by the standards of his faculty mentors. Throughout his life, those who knew him—friend and foe alike—described him as exceptionally bright, possessing a "high natural intelligence,"[47] but when it came to the application of that intelligence, Daniels preferred the empirical over the theoretical. He appreciated the intellectual challenge of law school; but it was a challenge, and Daniels later referred to his law school days as a "hard summer."[48] Daniels's subsequent financial and political success resulted from a mix of experience, insight, common sense, and sheer physical drive rather than abstract philosophical reasoning. He was proud of the university and his legal and humanist studies there, but he was not fundamentally changed by the university experience. Nor did his appreciation for his professors' erudition lead him to consider the pursuit of an academic career. Daniels remained a doer not a thinker.

Postbellum North Carolina maintained a keen sense of socioeconomic hierarchy, but the middle of that hierarchy was expanding rapidly. Many of the young men in Daniels's class were, like Daniels, ambitious members of a growing and aspiring middle class whose wealth was not tied to the old economic anchor of land and slaves but to a new one, knowledge. At the top of the hierarchy one still found the old planter elite, occasionally supported by, and through marriage or business diversification increasingly attached to, the mercantile and manufacturing families of the growing towns and villages of the piedmont and coastal plain—towns like Wilson. Through his entrepreneurial activities in the newspaper business, Daniels could now claim membership in this aspiring class. The old money was still around, and its scions still showed up at the university. Some of the old families had managed to maintain their wealth and social status, through the postwar booms in cotton and tobacco, but the New South was generating new wealth.

Rapidly joining the group at the top of the economic hierarchy, if not the social hierarchy, was the still relatively small number of families who derived their wealth from railroads or manufacturing, families like the Dukes of Durham. The two sets of wealth were not mutually exclusive, as some families from the old planter elite made the transition into industrial capital. Daniels was never a member of either group—the old landed elite or the new industrial plutocracy—which he collectively referred to as "that set."[49] Although Daniels always played up his impoverished boyhood, by the standards of his day, his upbringing, education, and family connections placed him well within what one might call the middle class today. Thus, Chapel Hill's "elevated social life," as Daniels described it, and learned climate suited the aspiring young publisher.[50] For him the town had just the right mix of privilege and meritocracy, and he never forgot the friendships he made there.

As for actually acquiring an education, in Daniels's day there was nothing like the organized curriculum that would greet subsequent generations of law students. Instead he and his classmates "read the law" for a term, which in practice meant much independent study of ancient legal treatises. The university assigned William Blackstone's *Commentaries on the Laws of England* as the standard reading. Sir William had been dead for more than a century by the time Daniels read his text, and no one in Daniels's class expected to practice law in England; however, recognizing that American common law came from English common law, the faculty had yet to find a better text than Blackstone. The other much-relied-upon volumes came from Joseph Chitty, another Englishman, whose series on the practice of various types of law, including especially his *Treatise on Commercial Law* and *The Practice of Law in All Its Principal Departments*, were almost as important as Blackstone.

It is difficult to imagine Daniels warming to Blackstone or Chitty, and his remarks on them were phlegmatic. For a man of action who had already been a successful entrepreneur, and one whose tastes in reading material leaned toward the exploits of antique heroes like Odysseus and Aeneas, Chitty's exposition on the game laws of England must have been a grind. The professors were of little help in the classroom. Student interactions with Manning, Winston, and the other solons of the faculty were as much social as they were academic. In Daniels's day, students regularly dined and socialized with the faculty and their families, an increasingly rare occurrence over subsequent generations. By Daniels's accounts, he spent more time chatting over dinner with his professors (and their daughters) than he did listening to them profess.

After a term of study, law students presented themselves before the justices of the North Carolina Supreme Court for examination and, hopefully, admission to the bar. After passing the exam, which was entirely oral, a novice lawyer had to pay the clerk of the supreme court a $20 fee, no small sum at the time, to obtain a license. At that point, the young counselor could "hang out a shingle" and practice law. The court's clerk at the time of Daniels's admission to the bar in 1885 was a former Confederate officer, Major W. H. Bagley.

Before the war, Bagley had been a Unionist and political moderate, as well as a newspaper publisher. He had nonetheless followed his state out of the Union and joined the Confederate army as a private. He subsequently earned a commission and attained the rank of major. After the war, the Major, as he would always be known to Josephus Daniels, had returned home as destitute as most of the men he had led in battle. The Major's fortunes appeared to turn when, as a result of his Unionist past, he was offered the sinecure of superintendent of the U.S. Mint at Charlotte. However, the war had changed the former Unionist's views on the Union, and the Major refused to take the oath of allegiance required of ranking Confederate officers seeking citizenship (and thus federal employment). All was not lost, however, as through his wartime political connections, the Major managed to become the private secretary, essentially chief of staff, to the postwar governor Jonathan Worth, who had been elected under President Andrew Johnson's relatively moderate Reconstruction plan.

The Major's fate took yet another turn when he was bounced from office, along with Worth, when the Radical Republicans in Congress wrested control of Reconstruction from the more accommodating Johnson. As part of the subsequent procedure for being readmitted to the Union, North Carolina was required to ratify a new state constitution. To that end, the Union general in charge of the state, E. R. S. Canby, oversaw elections in the spring of 1868. The election was a clear victory for the state's Republicans. The new constitution was ratified, and with the exception of a few offices, the Republicans dominated all branches of state government. (To what extent this outcome was the result of Republican chicanery and military coercion or the fact that in protest 30,000 voters boycotted the election remains an open question.) In either case, Governor Worth, his term unexpired, considered himself legally elected under Johnson's original Reconstruction plan, and thus he simply refused to leave office. Canby, a career officer and West Point graduate, had not achieved the august rank of general by flinching when it came to a fight, especially since he had an army at his disposal and Worth did not. Worth was removed metaphorically, if not literally, at the point of a bayonet. The Republican gubernatorial candidate, William Holden, was in; Worth and Major Bagley were out.

Although out of a job, the Major managed to create a happy family life, marrying Adelaide Ann Worth, the governor's youngest daughter. When, following the election of 1870, the conservative (now largely Democratic) regime in the state legislature impeached and exiled Holden, the Major was put back on the state's payroll as clerk of the supreme court. In this capacity he formally presented Josephus Daniels with a license to practice law in North Carolina. (Within three years of their meeting at the supreme court chambers, Daniels would be married to the Major's oldest daughter, Adelaide Worth (Addie) Bagley, though the Major died before Daniels met his bride-to-be.) Daniels expressed happiness and pride upon obtaining his license to practice law. But at the time he was already well along on his career as a newspaperman, and except for a few minor pro bono cases he handled for down-on-their-luck acquaintances, he never practiced law.[51]

After completing his term studying law at the University of North Carolina in the summer of 1885, Daniels remained in Chapel Hill, preparing for the bar exam. Even as he prepared for admission to the bar, he actively sought a way of entering the newspaper business in Raleigh and achieving his boyhood dream of editing, and possibly owning, a successful daily paper in the state's capital city. Fortune smiled on the young editor when a series of seemingly unrelated events converged to set Daniels on course to become the owner of the region's most politically powerful and economically successful newspaper.

———

At a number of key junctures in his life, Daniels relied on the support and patronage of important men. Never an ingrate, he freely gave these men credit for his subsequent success. One of his most famous and oft-repeated homilies was "There is no such thing as a self-made man."[52] Perhaps he pursued the favor of such men for narrow, even calculating, professional reasons, or perhaps he sought a relationship that he had missed as a result of the early death of his father. Regardless, at each stage of his personal and professional development, a father figure appeared to look after Daniels's interest. In his Wilson days it had been Colonel Henry Williams, and then more prominently Edward Morse Nadal, Daniels's longtime teacher, employer, and mentor. These were modest local figures who influenced Daniels through either the power of their personalities or the kindness they bestowed upon him and his family. It would take a more financially and politically powerful figure to launch Daniels's career beyond Wilson.

The man who first offered Daniels a chance to move into the Raleigh newspaper business was Walter Hines Page. Page was born into a prosperous family in 1855 near Cary, North Carolina. He graduated from Trinity College, which later became Duke University, and went on to become the successful editor of *Atlantic Monthly*, a founder of the publishing powerhouse Doubleday Page, and U.S. ambassador to the Court of St. James in London during World War I. Daniels had met Page and befriended one of Page's brothers at the 1884 wedding of Daniels's old school chum Edward Oldham. Page would cross Daniels's path on more than one occasion as the years wore on, and he would go on to become one of the state's more distinguished native sons. However, at the time he met Daniels, Page was a struggling journalist who had expanded into publishing, founding, in 1883, the weekly *State Chronicle* in Raleigh. A progressive, well-written, and reasonably well-researched paper, the *State Chronicle* proved to be a stepping stone to bigger things. Page's newspaper, which he was publishing daily by the end of its first year in existence, offered a New South alternative to the capital's leading paper, the reactionary Raleigh *News and Observer*, known locally as the *N&O*. At that time the *N&O* was owned and edited by the die-hard unreconstructed Confederate Samuel Ashe. Ashe's paper served as the mouthpiece of the capital's Bourbon faction of the Democratic Party. Although Daniels respected Ashe's skill as a businessman and envied his paper's success, he would eventually get to know Ashe personally and grow to dislike him immensely. It did not work to Ashe's credit that Daniels never favored the backward-looking Bourbons, and he found Ashe's paper in particular "too conservative" and thought it "belonged to the old order." In contrast, Daniels thought "Page had freshness and brightness; he believed in a New Day and in getting away from old hitching posts. His style was nervous and vigorous."[53]

What Daniels found "vigorous" in Page's approach others considered unnecessarily provocative. Among the provocations for which Page was known was his refusal to use military rank as a prefix when referring to former Confederate officers. Postbellum southern society revered the Glorious (albeit lost) Cause, and former Confederate officers, including those who had obtained their rank in veterans' organizations rather than on the field of battle, clung to their titles like European aristocrats. Page revered neither the cause nor the men who lost it, and so he refused to recognize such titles. It was a principled position, which Daniels admired but did not imitate.[54] Though personal opinions of Page varied, all factions of the Democratic Party could see that Page attempted to offer a "clear news beat" in contrast to the more opinion-oriented papers of the day, including Ashe's *N&O*.[55] As Daniels was trying to demonstrate in his coastal plain papers, this strategy was the beginning of a revolution in the newspaper business beyond the largest, most densely populated cities. In addition to sharing a view of the future of the newspaper industry with Page, Daniels aspired to move among the company he kept in Raleigh.

Daniels was quite familiar with the newspaper business in Raleigh long before he moved there. Even after he bought the Wilson *Advance*, he continued to serve as the correspondent and business agent for the old Raleigh *Observer* and *Hale's Weekly*. Peter M. Hale, with William L. Saunders, had founded the *Observer* in 1876, which was merged with the Raleigh *Sentinel* (founded 1865).[56] Hale was the son of Edward J. Hale, a leading figure in publishing and Whig politics before the Civil War. As an adolescent, Daniels read the *Observer* religiously and considered it an exceptional paper for the day. It was not exceptionally successful, however, at least not in a financial sense, and in 1879 Hale and Saunders sold out to Samuel Ashe. Two years later Ashe merged the *Observer* with the Raleigh *News* (founded 1872) to form the *News and Observer*.[57] Ashe had dabbled in publishing since the end of Reconstruction, and the *N&O* became his flagship property. Hale was neither a friend nor an admirer of Ashe, and after selling the *Observer*, Hale soon founded the weekly that bore his name, which itself failed a few years later.[58]

A significant economic step in the newspaper business at the time was the move from a weekly to a daily. However, moving to a daily increased the operating costs of the firm substantially, and those costs could only be off-set by some combination of increased circulation and advertising. It took more than a good wordsmith to make that happen. A tireless and savvy businessman was also required. Thinking he had what it took, only months after founding the weekly *State Chronicle*, the up-and-coming Page made the paper a daily. To further contrast his paper with the city's only success-ful daily, Ashe's morning *News and Observer*, Page put out the *State Chronicle* every afternoon. Thus Page's paper became a competitor of Ashe's *N&O*.

The publishing and social community in Raleigh was quite small at the time, so Page undoubtedly knew about Daniels's subscription and business work for Hale. Page had hired Daniels as his coastal plain business agent, and Daniels also supplied Page with news. Shortly after Page moved the *State Chronicle* to the daily format, much of the village of Wilson was dam-aged or destroyed by a fire. Wooden structures and open fires for cooking and heating created a literally combustible combination, and such destruc-tion was not an uncommon occurrence at the time. A fire in Wilson had destroyed the home into which the recently widowed Mary Cleaves Daniels had moved her boys in 1865, and Wilson had suffered even more extensive damage in the Great Fire of 1878.[59] After the fire of 1883 was brought under control, Daniels opportunistically wasted no time in sending the story, in-cluding details concerning the value and insurance coverage of the struc-tures that were damaged, to the *State Chronicle*, and Page published it the next day. There was no corresponding piece in the morning *News and Ob-server*, and thus Daniels helped Page scoop the more established paper. This was exactly the kind of day-to-day news that Page figured would make a daily paper profitable without political patronage. Page would not forget Daniels's scoop.

At the time of the Wilson fire, Page's *State Chronicle* faced two daunt-ing challenges. First, it competed with the formidable daily *News and Ob-server* in a town with fewer than 10,000 residents in 1880. This was a rela-tively small market for two daily papers. Second, Page, the *State Chronicle's* founder and manager, was determined to become a bigger fish in a bigger pond. To that end, in the winter of 1884–85 Page left Raleigh to investigate opportunities in New York City. Page was sufficiently impressed with the news and business savvy of his coastal plain agent, Josephus Daniels, to invite the younger man to move to Raleigh and run the *State Chronicle* while Page went to New York. In a letter posted shortly before Christmas 1884, Page wrote, "Dear Joe, I find that I must go to New York for two weeks and there is nobody here with whom I can leave the *Chronicle* while I am away. You could do the job better than anybody I know. Weekly papers [such as Daniels's Wilson *Advance*] suspend for the holidays. Will you not come to Raleigh and run the paper while I am gone? You will make me happy and you'll enjoy the chance to try your hand on a daily. You can sleep at my house and eat at Mosely's."[60] This letter would lead the reader to believe that the two men were lifelong chums. They were not. Page's usage of the diminutive "Joe" suggests a familiarity that they did not share. The letter struck a tone that Page must have suspected would flatter the younger and lesser-known Daniels.

The ploy worked. Daniels later admitted frankly that he was flattered by the offer and accepted it immediately. His management of Page's paper was relatively uneventful, though more than fifty years later Daniels still remembered the record-setting cold of that winter in Raleigh. "I slept in [Page's] house without heat or hot or even tepid water," he wrote. "I shiver yet to think how cold I was! It was too cold to take a real bath—if there had been a tub in the house."[61] This is a remarkable passage. In the thousands of pieces of Daniels's personal correspondence that survive, he rarely makes a point of discussing his own physical discomfort. He possessed incredible physical and mental stamina and enjoyed good health throughout his life. He scoffed at physical adversity and discomfort, working excruciatingly long days, week in and week out for more than sixty years. After his political career took off, he traveled extensively on overnight trains, by horse and buggy, and in automobiles over roads that could shake the dental work from a traveler's mouth. He slept in different beds night after night, ate indifferent food, and spoke to crowds at dusty country crossroads or in big-city auditoriums. Yet he never displayed more than a gentle contempt for the discomfort that accompanied such a lifestyle. Thus one can only conclude that he must have been truly miserable that first winter he spent alone in Raleigh. In any case, Page, unsuccessful on his trip to New York, soon returned, and Daniels moved back to Wilson. Years later, after Daniels and Page experienced an irreparable rupture in their relationship, Daniels concisely summarized their first business transaction: "Of course, [Page] paid me nothing except board."[62]

Shortly after these events, Page was back in Raleigh, and, struggling financially, he converted the *State Chronicle* back to a weekly. He announced the change, with what Daniels called "characteristic audacity," through an editorial titled "Change But Forward." Bravado does not hurt in the world of commerce, but it can only carry one so far. Ultimately the *State Chronicle*'s financial trouble outpaced Page's credit, and the business teetered on the brink of failure. Competition kept profit margins tight for most of the newspaper industry's participants, and newspapers came and went frequently. In Wilson, Daniels's public printing contracts were small, but they supplemented his profits. In Raleigh, the state printing contract was worth several thousand dollars a year, and the contracts could make the difference between a large loss and a large profit.[63]

Page tried to obtain the state contracts, but he consistently failed. Humorless, touchy, and prone to offend rather than humor those with whom he disagreed, Page did not fit in the Raleigh social scene. Notorious for keeping to himself and focusing on his journalism rather than his social or professional contacts, Page seldom went out socially. He was an awkward conversationalist, as his biographer notes, and even in his own home, "dinner-table talk was rare." Furthermore, "except for the Watauga Club and the Methodist church, neither Page nor his wife joined any organizations."[64] In Daniels's overly charitable assessment, "Page was no politician, not even a general mixer," and he never won the state contract.[65] During this period, Page's main competitor, the politically better-connected Captain Ashe at the *N&O*, usually procured the contract. Without the state contracts, the *State Chronicle*'s losses piled up. However, the status of Page's Raleigh business became moot, as he received a job offer from a daily paper in Brooklyn.

In the process of moving to New York, Page began closing the books on his North Carolina operation, and thus in the spring of 1885 he offered to sell the *State Chronicle* outright to Daniels.[66] Daniels, who was making plans to head for law school that summer, refused the offer. His mother's mortgage was still hanging over his Wilson paper, and there was no way he could put together the financing to take over the Raleigh business at that time. Page was disappointed, but the two men remained on good terms for many years afterward, though they would eventually have an acrimonious political and personal parting.

Although Daniels was never as impoverished as the lore surrounding him would one day claim—a lore much promoted by Daniels himself—at the time Page offered him the *State Chronicle*, he had neither the personal financial capital nor the access to credit that would have been required to purchase the physical plant and goodwill associated with Page's newspaper, valued at $2,000. Daniels had built a reputation in the coastal plain similar to Page's in Raleigh, and the other Raleigh publishers had gotten to know him, but he had no reputation with Raleigh readers or advertisers. More importantly, he had no reputation with Raleigh lenders. He had borrowed to the limit in Wilson, and he had neither the personal savings nor the cash flow to allow him to accept Page's offer.

The balance sheets of his newspapers were in reasonably good shape, but even if he had liquidated all three of his coastal plain papers (and the lot he had purchased adjacent to his mother's house) and paid off his mother's mortgage, Daniels still could not have scraped together enough cash to purchase Page's paper. Furthermore, with roughly $2,000 in debt still hanging over his operations, Daniels could not hope to borrow another $2,000 to purchase the *State Chronicle*. Even though he now had access to commercial bank credit, there were limits on the amounts he could borrow. The bank only granted Daniels short-term loans to cover the new Cottrell press and operating expenses during the summer months, before the cotton crop came in. So in 1885, Daniels passed on Page's offer and remained in Wilson. Although Daniels's personal monthly cash flow was by his own admission "a large income for that day," it was not enough to purchase Page's paper.[67] Despite this setback, Daniels had not given up on his boyhood dream of running a Raleigh paper. Once he arrived in Chapel Hill later that year, he began developing a long-run strategy for moving into the Raleigh newspaper market. Ironically, the *State Chronicle* would figure in that plan.

After Daniels rejected the offer to purchase the *State Chronicle*, he continued with his plans to attend law school that summer, while Page began casting about for another buyer. He soon found one closer to home in F. B. (Falc) Arendell, the *State Chronicle*'s business manager.[68] A Falstaff-like character with a barrel chest and a drooping walrus moustache, Arendell would one day prove to be a tireless political correspondent (and equally tireless political ward heeler) for Daniels. (More profitably, in old age, Daniels's friendship would secure for Arendell the job as superintendent of the state prison in Raleigh.) At the time Page sold out, however, given the *State Chronicle*'s financial past, it is not surprising that the paper did no better financially as a weekly under Arendell than it had done as a weekly or a daily under Page, and after only a few months as owner and publisher, Arendell had the paper on the market once again. Fortunately for Daniels it was purchased by a man who did not have long to live.

That man was Randolph Shotwell, or Captain Shotwell, as he was known in Raleigh circles. Shotwell owned yet another financially troubled Raleigh weekly, the *Farmer and Mechanic*. Upon learning of Arendell's financial distress at the *State Chronicle*, Shotwell proposed a merger between the two papers, and Arendell, a good field soldier but no captain of industry, accepted.[69] Shotwell was a Civil War veteran and another unreconstructed Confederate whose voice carried weight around the state capitol.[70] A Virginia native, at age nineteen Shotwell survived Pickett's Charge, earning a battlefield commission for his courage. Later he was captured and spent the remainder of the war as a Union prisoner. After the war, he moved to North Carolina, and he became a strong supporter, though reportedly never a member, of the Ku Klux Klan. During the Klan purges launched by Governor Holden's Reconstruction regime, Shotwell was arrested, tried, and convicted in federal court for violating anti-Klan ordinances. Offered a pardon in return for his testimony against other accused Klan leaders, Shotwell refused and was sentenced to six years in a federal penitentiary in Albany, New York. Although President Ulysses S. Grant pardoned Shotwell after he served a little more than a year, his treatment at the hands of the Reconstruction government earned him a place in the state's hall of martyrs. As such, he was an ideal candidate for state office after Reconstruction. Accordingly, Shotwell spent time in the state legislature, and at the time he proposed the merger of his *Farmer and Mechanic* with Arendell's *State Chronicle* he enjoyed the sinecure of state librarian.

Although diligent and scrupulous in his business dealings, Shotwell had not previously been successful in his management of the *Farmer and Mechanic*. Like most newspapers of the day, Shotwell's paper suffered from some combination of a lack of subscribers, advertisers, and political patronage. In the cutthroat world of Raleigh newspaper publishing, the long-run survivors had access to all three. Thus, like the *State Chronicle*, the *Farmer and Mechanic* was destined for failure. However, just before his paper went under, Shotwell found a financial patron in the form of Durham industrialist, financier, and fellow Confederate veteran Julian Shakespeare Carr. Through the serendipity wrought by Shotwell's failure as a businessman (and eventual death), the futures of Carr and Josephus Daniels would become inextricably linked. In Daniels's long life, only Woodrow Wilson would come to play a larger role than Carr.

Born in Chapel Hill in 1845 to Eliza and John Wesley Carr, Julian Shake-speare, or Jule, as he was known to close acquaintances, was seventeen years older than Daniels.[71] By the time they met in the early 1880s, Carr had a small fortune which he was on his way to turning into a large fortune. After serving in Robert E. Lee's Army of Northern Virginia, Carr mustered out at the exalted rank of private. (His generosity to indigent veterans eventually earned him the rank of lieutenant general in the United Confederate Veterans of America, and Daniels typically referred to him as General Carr.) Like countless veterans since time immemorial, Carr had a difficult time returning to a stable and successful life in the years immediately following his Civil War service. He remained at loose ends until October 12, 1870, his twenty-fifth birthday, when he and his father became partners in the firm of Blackwell and Day, a Durham flue-cured tobacco business. The names of Blackwell and Day have been superseded in the history of North Carolina by the trademark they made famous: the Genuine Durham Smoking To-bacco, known more commonly by its label as Bull Durham. Fortunes were guaranteed in North Carolina's flue-cured tobacco industry after occupying Union troops returned home and began to request shipments of the noxious, though uniquely mellow, product the troopers enjoyed smoking during the war and Reconstruction. The Bull Durham trademark had been established soon after the war when the Durham tobacco manufacturer John Ruffin Green sought to differentiate his product from that of other local manufacturers. While seeking a unique trademark, so the story goes, Green was dining on oysters with a friend from nearby Hillsborough. After listening to Green lament his inability to find an appropriate symbol, the friend pointed to the logo on a jar of mustard from Durham, England. The emblem was a Durham bull's head. The icon lasted.[72]

Strapped for cash, Green sought an influx of new operating capital. He found it in W. T. "Buck" Blackwell and J. R. Day, tobacco brokers from Kinston, in the heart of the "down east tobacco belt." Cotton, not tobacco, had been king when Daniels and his brothers toiled in the fields of the coastal plain. Around the time Blackwell and Day were considering expanding their tobacco operations, Daniels spent his late summer days picking cotton, but tobacco was about to take off. By the time Daniels reached adulthood, tobacco was in a position to challenge cotton for supremacy in the region, and as a young newspaper publisher a few years later, Daniels (who never smoked in his life) extolled the financial virtues of diversifying the coastal plain's agriculture by increasing the production of flue-cured tobacco at the expense of cotton. Initially, the tobacco belt bypassed Wilson, stopping in the coastal plain around Kinston. A few years later, with the continued growth in demand for smoking products, it pushed further inland to Wilson. "Up to that time the only tobacco raised in Wilson was that of some farmers who grew a few stalks in fence corners for their own use," wrote Daniels. Soon, however, the tobacco boom was on. When Daniels entered the newspaper business, he quickly became a promoter of tobacco, and "in the next decade Wilson would be the 'biggest bright tobacco market in the world.'"[73]

Blackwell and Day eventually joined Green's firm, purchasing one-half of the concern for $1,500 in 1869. They took over 100 percent of the firm when Green died shortly after the partnership was formed. With a physical plant in Durham and a purchasing network in the coastal plain, the tobacco entrepreneurs sought to expand the business in response to the growing demand for their Bull Durham brand. Like their former partner, however, they lacked operating capital, which they sought through a loan. Blackwell and Day discovered, as Daniels discovered a decade later, commercial bank loans to budding capitalists were often unobtainable in the postbellum South. Like Daniels, the tobacco men sought more credit for a longer period of time than the commercial banks of that day were willing to lend. The South's primitive financial markets had a hard time accommodating even a sure winner like cigarettes.

However, through mutual acquaintances, the Chapel Hill merchant John Wesley Carr received word that the Durham tobacconists were seeking a loan. So Carr went to Durham in the spring or early summer of 1870 and met with Blackwell and Day. Negotiations stretched over the next few months, and in the end, rather than making a loan, Carr senior purchased one-third of the firm for $4,000—a substantial amount of capital at the time. The fact that a year earlier Blackwell and Day had purchased 50 percent of the firm for only $1,500 suggests the business had quadrupled in value in a year or so, an indication of the flue-cured tobacco industry's growth during those years. To look after his considerable investment, Carr sent his son, Jule, into the tobacco business.

A physically small man with piercing eyes and an indomitable spirit, Jule Carr turned out to be an outstanding businessman. After working with Blackwell and Day for a short time, Jule saved his salary and bought into the firm on his own account. Soon thereafter, he bought out his partners, including his father. Carr eventually became one of the richest men in the South, selling, in 1898, Blackwell's Durham Tobacco Company to the Union Tobacco Company for $3 million. By that time, his tobacco holdings comprised only one of the jewels in the Carr industrial crown. Before the rolled cigarette became the rage, smoking tobacco was shipped in small cotton bags to facilitate hand-rolling. Recognizing the profit opportunities offered by vertical integration, Carr went into the textile business, ultimately creating an empire that numbered eight mills, including one on the edge of nearby Chapel Hill that spawned the neighboring town of Carrboro. Among Carr's other holdings were a nationally chartered bank, a Durham electric power company, a machine tool firm to manufacture textile equipment, and a hotel.[74] He was also a landlord to hundreds of his employees who lived in his mill villages.

Generous to the point of imprudence when it came to certain causes, Carr seldom turned down a fellow Confederate veteran in need, and he was often equally generous in his patronage of journalists and politicians of the right persuasion. The right persuasion was invariably Democratic. Though conservative when it came to social issues, Carr was no Bourbon when it came to economic matters. He was a solid member of the party's New South industrial wing. In the spring of 1885, soon-to-be-insolvent Raleigh publisher Captain Randolph Shotwell sought Carr's charity. As a scarred Confederate veteran, die-hard Democrat, and social conservative, Shotwell was a good candidate, and indeed Carr's munificence kept Shotwell's paper afloat in the months leading up to its merger with Falc Arendell's *State Chronicle* in the early summer of 1885. When the merger took place, Shotwell, unbeknownst to Carr, formally registered a majority of the stock in Carr's name. In essence, Shotwell converted Carr's debt to equity in the newly combined firm, a common business maneuver. It was a remarkable move because Shotwell did so without asking Carr's permission or even informing him in person. By the end of the summer of 1885 Shotwell was dead, and the executor of Shotwell's estate sought to place the firm on the market. (After the reincorporation of 1885, the joint newspaper was known simply as the *State Chronicle*. The name of Shotwell's paper was dropped from the masthead.) At this point, Josephus Daniels showed up in Raleigh.

At the time Shotwell joined the ranks of his Confederate colleagues in the next life, Daniels, who had just completed his term studying law at the University of North Carolina, remained in Chapel Hill studying for admission to the state bar. Daniels later candidly professed that he actively investigated the purchase of the *State Chronicle* from Shotwell's estate immediately following the captain's death. He hoped to purchase the paper, which now included the *Farmer and Mechanic*, at a discount from the $2,000 price

Page had demanded earlier in the year. If Daniels cashed in his interest in his three coastal plain newspapers and paid off his mother's mortgage, he could have mustered about $1,000, depending on exactly how much his mother still owed Hadley for the original mortgage loan for the Wilson *Advance*.

Recalling the events after the fact, Daniels wrote, "As soon as Captain Shotwell was buried, I hurried to Raleigh." There Daniels spoke with Shotwell's executor. In going through Shotwell's papers, the executor discovered that the estate did not have legal claim to the *State Chronicle*'s assets. Further investigation followed, and Daniels "learned [from the executor] that General Carr owned the majority stock and nobody in Raleigh knew his plans."[75] Shotwell, with more of Carr's money, had only recently bought out the cash-strapped Arendell, and in an effort to retire his debts to Carr, Shotwell had subsequently transferred all of the *State Chronicle*'s stock to the Durham industrialist. In short, Shotwell's estate did not own the paper; Carr did. After learning of this, Daniels took the next train to Durham, where he found the true owner of the *State Chronicle*. The intrepid young man approached the general at his considerable home and got straight to the point. Daniels wanted to know about Carr's plans for the paper. Carr replied, "What paper? I am not in the newspaper business."[76] After Daniels described his consultations with Shotwell's executor and explained why he thought Carr *was* in the newspaper business, Carr called his personal secretary from an adjacent room and explained the situation. After an investigation of various papers on their respective desks, an investigation that took place as Daniels waited in Carr's office, the secretary finally determined that Carr did, in fact, own the *State Chronicle*. It seems Shotwell had sent to Carr the stock certificates in a letter that, while among Carr's business papers, had never passed before Carr's eyes.

Daniels recognized his opportunity to take over the *State Chronicle*. Seizing the moment, he recited his résumé and frankly shared his ambition to publish a newspaper in Raleigh. Daniels explained how he planned to expand the subscription base and increase the advertising revenues—and perhaps even convert the paper back to a daily. The primary objective was to offer a New South competitor for Ashe's Bourbon-friendly *N&O*. Citing his successes in Wilson, Kinston, and Rocky Mount, Daniels tried to convince Carr that a Raleigh paper could be managed profitably. Carr reflected silently, no doubt sizing up the younger man. Although the two had met briefly the year before at a Methodist conference in Wilson, Carr being as devout a Methodist as Daniels, neither could have known at that time

that their futures were to be linked. Although Daniels had proven himself
as a newspaperman, and although he was clearly a young man with a bright
future, he was only twenty-three and could claim a net worth of no more
than $1,000. With the financial backing of one of the state's most important
business figures at such an early age, he would have a tremendous start in
the Raleigh newspaper business and whatever else he might pursue, including politics. It was the absence of such financial backing that had forced
Daniels to pass on Page's offer to buy the *State Chronicle* earlier in the year.
Having a man like Carr in his corner was an even bigger opportunity.

Carr listened as Daniels recited his résumé and plans for the *State
Chronicle*. Then Carr calmly reviewed the inauspicious financial history of
the newspaper business in Raleigh, going over one failed paper after another. Daniels knew this history all too well. Indeed, as the coastal plain
business agent for several of these firms, he understood the Raleigh market
better than Carr, though he wisely kept that to himself. After his mono-
logue on the risks of the venture, Carr explicitly confronted Daniels, asking the young man if he really thought he could run a profitable enterprise. Daniels tersely replied, "Of course I do, or I would not wish to try
it." To which Carr, impressed by such cheek, responded, "That is the stuff
that wins!"[77] On the spot Carr transferred to Daniels the ownership of the
stock, telling the young newspaperman that should the enterprise prove
financially successful, Daniels could pay Carr whatever Daniels thought the
stock was worth. This proved to be an even better deal than Daniels could
have reasonably hoped for, as he was not forced to immediately liquidate
his coastal plain papers to purchase the *State Chronicle*. Daniels's main goal
had been to acquire the paper for less than the $2,000 Page had demanded
earlier in the year. According to Carr's biographer, Daniels eventually returned $1,000 for the stock (the par value, which differed substantially from
the firm's higher market value), without interest. Upon receiving the payment for the stock, Carr supposedly said that, despite Daniels's brave show
of confidence, it was $1,000 more than he ever expected to receive from the
enterprise.[78]

In the long run the price proved to be a bargain for both Carr and
Daniels, though the fact that Daniels was able to make the paper profitable
can be better attributed to his success as a politician rather than as a businessman. Although Daniels was unable to make the *State Chronicle* succeed
strictly as a medium for the news and advertising, he made a profit the old-
fashioned way in the nineteenth-century newspaper business: by securing
the state printing contract through his political connections. This he did

through the largesse of the legislatures of 1887, 1889, 1891, and 1893. (The printing contracts ran for two years.) It was an impressive run and indicates Daniels's political savvy. Although the paper itself limped along from issue to issue, the public monies that went with being the state printer provided Daniels with a nice income, and those contracts substantially enhanced the goodwill value of his newspaper.

Never lacking in personal discipline, financial or otherwise, Daniels continued to pay himself a salary of $100 a month from the paper, and he received another $200 to $350 a month for being the state printer. Much of this latter amount he put back into the business, just as he had done in Wilson. However, there was a difference between the economics of the newspaper business in Raleigh and in Wilson. After taking over the *Advance*, Daniels had immediately expanded its circulation and advertising revenues, but beyond his initial efforts in those activities, he could do little more to make the paper more profitable. Wilson and its hinterland simply were not large enough to support expansion beyond what Daniels had been able to achieve. Thus, he had expanded his operations by starting the paper in Kinston and purchasing 50 percent of the paper in Rocky Mount. In Raleigh, however, Daniels could expand his operations by increasing circulation considerably both in and beyond the city, and he could always make the leap to a daily. These were, in fact, his goals.[79]

Thus Daniels began reorganizing his businesses and financial situation. First, he sold his interest in the Rocky Mount *Reporter*. The amount of the sale went unrecorded. While it was unlikely Daniels sold at a loss, any capital gains would have been small, given the nature of the market. Similarly, he and Charles sold the Kinston *Free Press*. The two brothers agreed that Charles would move to Wilson and purchase the Wilson *Advance* from Josephus. The way they arranged this was somewhat complicated.[80] Since Charles had been forgoing his claim on any profits from the *Free Press* in return for purchasing an ownership position in it, Daniels took Charles's share of the *Free Press* and applied it toward Charles's purchase of the *Advance*. No money changed hands between the two brothers. In short, Josephus received the cash from the sale of the *Free Press*, in the neighborhood of $1,000. Charles then borrowed from Josephus the money to purchase the *Advance*, and in return Charles would amortize this loan by paying Josephus from the subsequent profits of that newspaper.

Thus in order to begin operating the *State Chronicle* in Raleigh, Josephus had converted his ownership in the *Reporter* and the *Free Press* into a cash value of around $1,500, money he immediately put into upgrading the physical plant of the *State Chronicle*. As he had done with the *Advance*, he ordered a new printing press. He also was entitled to some of the cash flow from the profits of the Wilson *Advance*, which he was owed in return for surrendering its ownership to Charles. Interestingly, after these transactions, Daniels paid neither Carr the $1,000 for the *State Chronicle* nor Wilson financier Thomas Jefferson Hadley the remainder of the $2,000 he owed on his mother's mortgage (or his other nearby property). Rather, in typical Daniels fashion, he put the entire amount into a new press, type, and other improvements at the *State Chronicle*. Although Daniels fretted about the debt hanging over his mother's home, he nonetheless upped the ante, extending the business that her loan had leveraged.

Of course Daniels had every intention of making his Raleigh newspaper a journalistic and financial success. He had reason to be optimistic. The Raleigh market had room for growth that Wilson, Kinston, and Rocky Mount never would, and the eventual move to a daily would further expand the paper's reach—both financially and politically. The problem Daniels faced in Raleigh was that, unlike the coastal plain markets he had earlier penetrated, the Raleigh market already had a well-established major player, Samuel Ashe's *News and Observer*. To be successful in the newspaper business in Raleigh in the 1880s meant beating Ashe. A reasonable observer at the time would have concluded that the unknown younger man from Wilson had little chance of pulling off that feat. Ashe was an honored Confederate veteran; he had deep pockets financing his firm; and he had political connections in Raleigh, connections that had secured for him the state printing contract in the past. Ashe was Goliath to Daniels's David. It would take a long time, and it would be a hell of fight, but in the end Daniels would break Ashe.

3. Center Stage

In this country, everyone must pay for everything he gets.

—THE WIZARD, in *The Wonderful Wizard of Oz*

In becoming the owner of the *State Chronicle* in 1885, Josephus Daniels laid the foundation for a move up the economic ladder. His next objective was to move up the social ladder. A judicious marriage might help on that front. Those who knew Daniels well would have expected him to marry and settle down. Despite the fact that he remained at home with his mother until he was twenty-three, relatively late for that time and place, he was definitely the "marrying type." The product of a stable home headed by a strong woman whom he admired deeply, Daniels remained comfortable with and sincerely enjoyed the company of members of the opposite sex. He was a family man at heart, and it was just a matter of time before he settled down with a wife. He enjoyed the quest almost as much as he did his rise in the newspaper business.

At the time, courting was strictly proscribed. The Methodists in particular could be quite strict regarding social interactions between their young men and women. It was said, in jest one assumes, that Methodists objected to the act of making love while standing upright because they feared it might lead to dancing. Still, Daniels never let his religious convictions stand between him and female companionship, and just as he skirted his church's strictures on alcohol, he was known to dance now and then. His memoirs and correspondence contain frequent references to dalliances with Tar Heel daughters, especially those from prominent families. During his brief stay in Chapel Hill, this seems to have particularly been the case. In his description of John Manning, professor of law at the University of North Carolina, Daniels made a point of noting the good doctor's daughters, whom Daniels visited frequently. Similarly, of Adolphus Mangum, head of the Department of Moral Philosophy, Daniels observed that Mangum possessed "eloquence and [was] a delightful conversationalist. Sometimes he monopolized me when I would have preferred to talk to his daughter."[1] Daniels's ease of manner around women had been a prominent feature of his personality since his days studying at the Wilson Collegiate Institute and hanging out at the Wilson skating rink.

If Chapel Hill offered more and brighter prospects than Wilson, then Raleigh must have been a Babylon of female companionship. Of the Raleigh scene, Daniels said with humorous understatement, "I found in Raleigh a difference in the social life from that I had known in Wilson." In some cases he chose friends based on the possibilities of interacting with young women in their households. "I made friends, among them the Moores (there was a good-looking daughter)," and he befriended Colonel J. M. Heck, an influential Raleighite whose daughter was "an accomplished lady, Miss Susie Heck." Daniels even pursued the daughters of his professional competitors, including one in the Hale family, the Raleigh publishing family for whom Daniels had once worked and with whom he now competed in the city's newspaper market.[2]

Daniels clearly had an eye on a long-term relationship that he hoped would lead to marriage with a daughter of one of the area's more prominent families. Because he was from a lower socioeconomic class than the women he longed for, however, he could only maintain the most formal connections with them. Although he mixed well enough in polite company, in his search for a suitable mate, he found it difficult to cross the social chasm between petit bourgeois Wilson and haut bourgeois Raleigh.

Part of the problem for Daniels was that the social stratification of Raleigh was better defined and more intimidating than anything he knew in Wilson or even Chapel Hill. Years later Daniels would joke about the difference between Raleigh and Wilson, and one can still feel the sting in his social alienation: "My boyhood home was both Democratic and democratic, whereas Raleigh was politically not so Democratic and even less democratic in its social atmosphere."[3] Now in his early twenties, and showing every sign of being on his way to a reasonably successful newspaper publishing career, Daniels had bright economic prospects, but he lacked both a distinguished name and wealth. Thus if he found an eligible young woman from a higher rung of the social ladder, he could settle down and start a family while simultaneously gaining entrée into a more elevated social sphere. On the plus side, his business had a positive cash flow that put him at the higher end of the state's income distribution at the time. However, from a social perspective, his cash was all new money and thus tainted, at least from the perspective of Raleigh's old money. It would take just the right woman to help Daniels make the leap from the striving middle class to a loftier social position.

Having failed to find that woman by the spring of 1887, Daniels appeared to have abandoned the possibility of "marrying up" in Raleigh. Instead he turned to what he must have considered a safe, though disappointing, choice. He informed his mother that he was preparing to marry, probably sometime the following winter. The bride-to-be was Addie Marsh, a schoolteacher in Wilson. Exactly how the courtship transpired or the engagement came about is difficult to reconstruct. Although in his personal correspondence and memoirs, Daniels discussed many of the women he encountered at this stage of his life, Marsh was not one whose name he recorded with any regularity. He much more frequently and favorably wrote about the women in Raleigh he was *not* going to marry. This was not a good sign. Daniels seems to have never been particularly excited about the wedding or his bride. The best spin he put on life with his future wife was "We will be brave & poor," which was hardly a ringing endorsement of the union, particularly since Daniels's business success in Raleigh had moved him well beyond poverty.[4] In the event, for reasons unknown, though Daniels's foot-dragging must be suspected, the engagement fell apart in September 1887. It is probably no coincidence that at exactly that time Daniels began his formal courtship of another Addie. This one lived in Raleigh and possessed a much more blue-blooded background than the one he left behind in Wilson.

Among the friendships Daniels cultivated in those days was one with Herbert Worth Jackson. He and Daniels would remain friends and professional colleagues for the rest of their long lives. Jackson was a grandson of the state's post–Civil War governor Jonathan Worth. Young Jackson had parlayed the family name and a good head for financial figures into an appointment at the state treasurer's office, another state office once held by his Grandfather Worth. In Raleigh, Jackson boarded at the home of his aunt, Adelaide Worth Bagley, widow of the same Major Bagley who, as clerk of the North Carolina Supreme Court, had formally presented Daniels with his legal license in the summer of 1885 and who had passed away the following year.

The widow Bagley, a masculine-looking woman whose capacity for kindness was as great as her countenance was imposing, could count herself among Raleigh's social elite. As the daughter of a former governor and the wife of a distinguished Confederate officer, Adelaide Bagley could claim title to "old money," even if by the time Daniels entered her family's life there was not much money left, old or otherwise. But in the post-Reconstruction South, social rank and economic wealth did not always go hand in hand.

Besides a small Confederate pension (paid by the state), some land here and there in Wake and nearby Chatham Counties, and a comfortable home, the Major had not left his wife with much more than six surviving children, all of whom were still living at home when Daniels became acquainted with the family.

Not long after the Major's untimely death, young Jackson invited Daniels to dinner at the Bagley home, where Jackson resided. At the time, Daniels lived and dined at the Yarborough House hotel, Raleigh's finest and arguably the best hotel between Richmond and Atlanta. Although the hotel was known for its fine cuisine, Daniels probably welcomed the respite from another day of hotel dining. (When the legislature was in town, Daniels seldom dined alone, but between sessions, he often found himself unaccompanied at dinner, and he typically used mealtime to catch up on his correspondence.) Another incentive was the three young women in the Bagley household. Adelaide Bagley's oldest daughter, seventeen-year-old Addie, whose Christian name was the same as her mother's, might have caught the eye of the young publisher if she had made any effort to do so. But at dinner and on other social occasions over the next year or so, Addie showed no interest in this older man of no renown—at least no renown that mattered to a haughty teenaged product of Raleigh's social elite.[5]

Exactly what Daniels thought of Addie is unrecorded. Later he claimed that he "liked her fine and easy bearing, her manner and face," but he was initially uninterested, as the young girl could not hope to compete with his more mature "female friends [who] were well in their middle twenties."[6] Indeed, when he first dined at the Bagley home at Jackson's invitation, Daniels was already formally courting the older Addie Marsh from Wilson. Subsequently, however, Addie Bagley in Raleigh began to mature from a somewhat haughty girl into a somewhat haughty but attractive young woman. (Her grandfather, the former governor Worth, described her as "spoilt to death.")[7] Although not classically beautiful, Addie's face was outlined by a well-defined bone structure, and in her youth she could be described as handsome rather than pretty. She also possessed a rapidly developing buxom figure of the type much appreciated by men at the time. Ever a keen observer of the emergence of an attractive and socially prominent marriage prospect, Daniels began to take notice. Having gained entrée to the Bagley household via his friendship with Jackson, Daniels decided to get to know Addie Bagley better, and he began visiting Jackson regularly. When Adelaide Worth Bagley was out of town for a brief stint, Jackson wrote to her noting that "he (Mr. D.) has been a frequent visitor since you left. . . . Always stays until a few minutes before the clock strikes 12."[8]

Their first correspondence, which survives in Daniels's papers in the Library of Congress, is dated September 1887, sixteen months after they first met and the same month in which his engagement to Addie Marsh ended. (Marsh immediately passed from all subsequent family correspondence.) Daniels initiated formal contact with Addie Bagley through a note asking, "Do you receive? If so, at what hours? If so, do you want to see me?"[9] She did receive, and she accepted, without exactly welcoming, his overture. He followed up, but she continued to remain lukewarm to his advances. Daniels, however, was persistent in love as well as business. After several weeks of flirtatious cat-and-mouse, Addie yielded, and they soon became something of an item around town. The advent of Daniels's quick and timely courtship of Addie Bagley, coinciding as it did with his breakup with Addie Marsh, is certainly consistent with crass social climbing. From a strictly social point of view, Addie Bagley was obviously the more desirable catch. She was from one of Raleigh's most distinguished families, though with the early death of Major Bagley and six children in the house, it was a family on the verge of Dickensian hard times.

Adelaide Worth Bagley welcomed Daniels's courtship of her daughter, perhaps counting as a blessing the matching of her eldest daughter to an up-and-coming businessman. Daniels might have been from a family of no distinction, but in addition to the generous cash flow from his newspaper, he had some positive qualities. There were no hard edges to his personality, at least when it came to his family life. He was humorous, kind, and hard working; a mother, particularly a widowed mother with six children, could not have reasonably hoped for more from a prospective son-in-law. There was little chance that he would mistreat her Addie, and his economic and political prospects looked bright. All in all not a bad match, and Adelaide Bagley said so. Although she was a bit of social snob, according to family members, in summarizing her view of Daniels, she concluded, "I think he is an unusually good man."[10] In the ancient language of mothers-in-law, she meant "He is a good catch."

The correspondence between Josephus Daniels and Addie Bagley during courtship reflects the flowery rhetoric, absent of irony, which was common at the time. Daniels often began his day by writing to Miss Addie, as she would forever be known to him, while he ate breakfast at the Yarborough House. Beginning with "Good morning," he would continue in his nearly illegible handwriting, which would only worsen with age, to tell her about the prospects for his day or, if they had not been together, the happenings of the previous evening. On a bad day, or after some professional or personal difficulty, he might brighten the tone with "Disagreeable as the day is my heart is light and my sky is as bright as when the sun shines. For that I have you."[11]

Despite the florid tone of much of the surviving correspondence between the two lovers, their relationship was not without conflict. Addie was stubborn, as was Josephus, and she had a mind of her own from an early age, as did Josephus. That two such independent people could survive in a happy marriage for more than five decades suggests a deep mutual affection and respect. When they clashed, however, it was usually Josephus who gave ground. During their early years together, and indeed throughout the rest of their lives, Josephus generally let Addie do exactly as she pleased, as long as her wishes did not conflict with his newspaper businesses or his religion. For her part, Addie never stood between Josephus and the business that fed her family. He would on occasion seek, and she would provide, counsel concerning the family business, but theirs was not a business partnership. The arrangement worked fine for both parties.

Religion was a bit trickier. Although Major Bagley had been raised as a Methodist, Adelaide Worth Bagley and her children were Presbyterians, and Josephus would never accept the Presbyterians' embrace of predestination. Similarly, Addie refused to convert to Methodism. To a devout Presbyterian of that day, a Methodist was nothing more than a poor man's Episcopalian, and an Episcopalian was little better than a Catholic who owned a nice suit and spoke English rather than Gaelic. The couple quickly agreed to disagree on religion, a pact they kept unto death.

Josephus undoubtedly learned during their early courtship that trying to constrain Addie resulted in conflict, and he was more likely to shy from their battles than she was. When he did not let her have her way or when he challenged her, she could be quite difficult. After one minor dispute, which apparently involved one of her many trips without him, Josephus tried to make up. "My heart yearns over my own little girl," he wrote in her absence; "I cannot go to work without sending her a line. Please forgive me for being a bad boy. God knows that I did not mean a word I said and that I have been punished terribly by my own feelings. Please forgive me." Addie's reply (postmarked "Wilmington") included her forgiveness and began affectionately with "My precious, precious, precious boy." Even after receiving her absolution, Josephus could not stop doing penance. "When I think about all the sunshine you have put into my life," he replied the following day, "it makes me feel very mean to have given you a moments pain or trouble. . . . God help me, I will make the next year fuller of happiness."[12] Such exchanges would be repeated more than a few times over the years.

Josephus proposed in October, and although Addie accepted quickly, a dispute arose over when the wedding would occur. He wanted it sooner rather than later; she wanted it later. On this rare occasion, she came around to his point of view, and they settled on the following spring: May 2, 1888. Addie turned nineteen on May 1, and Josephus would be twenty-six on May 18. Just as Josephus thought he finally had everything in hand, shortly before the wedding day, his bank, the State National Bank, failed, taking his life savings and the cash balances of the *State Chronicle* down with it. The intercession of two friends, D. E. Everett and Joseph G. Brown, saved the young couple's immediate future. Everett helped with the wedding bills, while Brown, the president of a competing bank, Citizens National, extended a generous personal loan. Brown subsequently became Daniels's banker.

The marriage came off as planned, "on the most beautiful May morning in all history," according to Daniels.[13] As a compromise, the wedding took place in Raleigh's Presbyterian Church, adjacent to the state capitol, but the minister employed the Methodist rite. It was a large wedding with more than thirty groomsmen, bridesmaids, and other attendants. Josephus's best man was his younger brother and erstwhile business partner, Charles. Among his groomsmen was the man most responsible for bringing the couple together, Herbert Jackson. The social prominence of the bride's family made the wedding *the* social event of the season. The day after the affair, even Captain Ashe's *News and Observer* reflected the tone by describing its guests as the "crème de la crème of Raleigh society." From Josephus Daniels's perspective no greater compliment could have been offered. As for the newlyweds, they "were said to be among the most popular and well-known of Raleigh society. . . . Altogether it was one of the most beautiful marriages ever witnessed in Raleigh."[14] Given the competition between Ashe and Daniels, the wedding must have been an event of great social distinction to merit such generous coverage in the *N&O*. With the loan from Brown, the newlyweds were able to enjoy a grand honeymoon. They left Raleigh on the afternoon of their wedding day, taking the train to Washington, D.C. There, through the good offices of Matthew Whitaker Ransom, North Carolina's senior senator, first lady Frances Cleveland formally received the young couple at the White House the following week. Ransom made sure that Josephus Daniels, an up-and-coming Democrat from back home, and Addie got the royal treatment around town. It had the desired effect on Addie, who was visibly impressed.

After returning to Raleigh, the young couple rented a room from one of Addie's aunts, but they soon sought accommodations elsewhere, as the quality of the dining in their new residence proved less than acceptable to them. The Bagley home was blessed with an excellent cook, a former slave known as Aunt Zilphia, and Addie, whose physique, like her mother's, would soon reach a robust proportion, missed Aunt Zilphia's cooking.[15] Josephus could eat anything. Digesting it was another matter. There appears to have run in the family a digestive disorder that at the time went by the name dyspepsia. The rich menu Josephus had enjoyed at the Yarborough House probably did not help. At the time, the hotel's menu included "Oysters, Lobsters, Consomme Imperial, Sheepshead Hollandaise, Potatoes a la Maitre, Quail au Champignons, Chicken Liver Patties, Orange Fritters, Glace au Rhum, Roast Sirloin, Lamb with Mint, Stuffed Turkey, Roast Canvasback Duck, Plum Pudding with Brandy Sauce, Vegetables, Pies, Fruits, Raisins, Cheese, Spanish Olives, and Jelly a la Russes."[16] Josephus avoided most of this, claiming "hotel food—or something—had impaired my digestion. . . . [I] lived on baked apples and rare steak."[17]

For the rest of his life, when given a choice, Josephus Daniels usually stuck to simple meat and potatoes dishes. A typical meal included a rare steak or lamb chops (with mint jelly), baked fruit, potatoes variously prepared or a vegetable garnish, and toast, accompanied by tea (hot or cold, depending on the season). Josephus's brother Frank suffered even more severely from intestinal problems. While it is possible that the boys inherited a food allergy, it is just as likely they suffered from an unnamed digestive disorder that "merely caused chronic diarrhea and other discomforts that people in preindustrial countries—then and later—simply learned to live with."[18]

Because of their unhappiness with the dining situation, and perhaps for other, more personal reasons, Josephus and Addie spent most of their free time at Adelaide Bagley's. Since the death of her husband, Adelaide Bagley had taken boarders from time to time, and in the late summer of 1888, a room opened when one of the boarders moved on. Upon hearing this, Josephus's mother persuaded Addie and her mother that the young couple should move into the Bagley home. There Josephus could serve as the male head of the household; he could help support the family financially; Addie could be close to her mother, with whom she got along so well; and they could all enjoy Aunt Zilphia's cooking. That is exactly what the young couple did, and the arrangement worked famously—so famously that Josephus and Addie lived in the Bagley home for the next twenty-five years. Indeed, Josephus Daniels never owned a home of his own until he returned to Raleigh from Washington in 1921 after serving as secretary of the navy. He was fifty-eight years old at the time.

PRINTER TO THE STATE

As Josephus Daniels climbed Raleigh's social ladder through his marriage to Addie Bagley, he was simultaneously climbing the economic ladder through the growth of the *State Chronicle*. Raleigh's newspaper world continued to include a varying number of small-circulation, weekly newspapers that came and went just as they had done since the end of the Civil War. But within a year after Daniels moved to Raleigh, two newspapers dominated the market, his *State Chronicle* and Ashe's *News and Observer*. There were two main differences between the newspapers. First, the *Chronicle* was a weekly, while the *N&O* was a daily. In the newspaper world, dailies were the big leagues; weeklies, no matter how successful, were the minors. Daniels stewed about the *Chronicle*'s status relative to that of the *N&O*, and he planned to make the *Chronicle* a daily as soon as he could secure the financing. The other difference was in the editorial tone of the papers. Although both men were die-hard Democrats, Ashe served as the spokesman for the party's older, conservative Bourbon faction. Daniels spoke for the party's younger, progressive wing.

A New South progressivism always dominated the editorial views of Daniels's newspapers. In the 1880s, in places like Wilson and Raleigh, progressive meant anti-Bourbon. The Bourbons included unreconstructed planters, tight-fisted legislators, railroad magnates, and more generally, conservatives of any stripe. To Daniels, progress meant agricultural reform, which in turn meant diversifying the region's cotton culture, increasing the use of chemical fertilizers, and capping the rates railroads charged for hauling crops. Progress also meant public support for education, promotion of industrialization (which included recruiting northern capital), and regulation of railroads and trusts. At the national level, progressivism would come to mean some of these things, and later, when Daniels emerged on the national stage, he would play a role in their incorporation into the Democratic Party's national platform. At the time Daniels moved to Raleigh, however, a good bit of local idiosyncrasy marked his version of progressivism. Racial issues in particular were especially difficult to get over or around in North Carolina. "Progress" would come to mean eliminating racial conflict from southern politics.

In Raleigh the intellectual leadership of this progressive movement revolved around the membership of a recently founded social group called the Watauga Club, which might just as well have been named the Anti-Bourbon Club. To an extent, the Raleigh social scene was also split along generational lines, with the younger Wataugans on one side and the aging Bourbons on the other. The Wataugans met at the Yarborough House, and shortly after he moved to Raleigh in the early fall of 1885, Daniels was invited to join the club, which had been founded in 1883.[19] The Wataugans recognized that in social, political, and economic terms the South in general and North Carolina in particular lagged behind the rest of the country. To address that matter, they met regularly, presented scholarly papers on various topics, and generally complained, as the young are wont to do, about the older men who more or less ran the city of Raleigh and the state of North Carolina.

At the time Daniels joined it, the group was led by the triumvirate of W. J. Peele, a Raleigh lawyer and an outspoken proponent of higher education for women; Charles Dabney, a chemist and fertilizer expert employed by the woefully backward state department of agriculture; and Arthur Winslow, an engineer. Joseph G. Brown, Daniels's banker, as well as several other energetic young professionals rounded out the membership. Walter Hines Page had been a key player in setting the club's political agenda. Page was a poor mixer but a bright fellow and a possessor of considerable vision when it came to the South's modernization, and his departure to New York was a double-edged sword. The loss of a publisher, especially a gifted one like Page, who could distribute broadly the club's views was a blow to the Wataugans' political objectives; but there was also a social side to the club, and Page contributed little at that margin. As Daniels now held the reins of the *Chronicle*, and as he was a better social fit than Page, the other Wataugans welcomed Daniels as Page's replacement.

The number one issue on the club's agenda at the time Daniels joined was agricultural reform. North Carolina's primary economic problem from the Wataugans' view was that the state was overwhelmingly rural and its workforce heavily agricultural. At the time, only about 5 percent of the state's population lived in an urban area, and over 80 percent of the labor force was directly employed in farming. Although the Wataugans possessed a New South affection for the economic miracles promised by a rising manufacturing sector, the simple arithmetic of the state's economy worked against manufacturing's role as an economic savior. The manufacturing sector was so small relative to the agricultural sector that to effect an improvement in the material status of the state's population would, at least in the short run, require improvements in agriculture.[20] That meant increasing the productivity of labor, increasing crop yields, diversifying crop portfolios (including growing more tobacco), and modernizing more generally (including mechanization and the use of chemical fertilizers). The state possessed a department of agriculture, of which Dabney was a leading light, but the department's revenues and expenditures were controlled by the Board of Agriculture, and the board was dominated by old planter interests, which were in turn supported in print by Daniels's main competitor, Samuel Ashe at the *News and Observer*.

Ashe and his *N&O* remained at the top of the Raleigh market by maintaining Bourbon-friendly editorial positions and staying on the good side of men like Montford McGehee, the Bourbon who headed the state's Board of Agriculture. Daniels had long detested Ashe's pro-Bourbon editorial stance, and after moving to Raleigh and taking control of the *Chronicle*, Daniels found that he did not much like Captain Ashe himself. Although they belonged to the same party, they represented decidedly different branches of it. In Daniels's own words, "Captain Ashe stood for the status quo and viewed with alarm the organizing farmers. I didn't like the status quo and viewed with joy any movement inside the Democratic Party that would give it new life and bring to it some new leaders."[21] Daniels left little doubt concerning which newcomer he had in mind for a leadership position. From the time he arrived in Raleigh in 1885, he openly challenged Ashe for the unofficial position of Democratic Party publisher. A distinguished Civil War veteran, a devoted Democrat, an able journalist, and something of a man of letters, Ashe possessed characteristics that should have made him sympathetic to Daniels, but personal animosity and economic competition prevented them from recognizing their common interests and overcoming their differences.

Though Daniels and Ashe had philosophical differences, the most acute dispute between them was the state printing contract. The economics of the contract were simple. The Raleigh printer who possessed the contract secured the cash flow that tended to make the difference between profit and loss, which is to say success or failure, in the newspaper business. Ashe, who had served in the legislature after Reconstruction, had secured the contract through three consecutive legislative terms (1879, 1881, and 1883). His most recent competitor, Page, was not much competition, as Page was better at alienating than at cultivating potential allies. But after control-ling the contract for six years, in 1885, a few months before Daniels pur-chased the *Chronicle*, Ashe lost the contract to another competitor, Major Edward J. Hale, publisher of *Hale's Weekly*. The conflict between Hale and Ashe went back years. Hale was another Confederate veteran, but in the prewar era, he had been a Whig. Like Daniels, Hale took a more modern view of the South's social and economic development than did Ashe. Hale's earlier paper, the *Observer*, had been taken over by Ashe in 1879 and later (in 1881) combined with the *News* to form the *N&O*, and there was no affection between the Hale family and Ashe. By the time the state printing contract came up for renewal in 1887, *Hale's Weekly* had folded, and Hale himself was out of the running for the contract. Daniels immediately decided to seek the contract. Ashe sought to reclaim it.

It was a bitter fight. In addition to the fact that Ashe's views on most local matters reflected his Bourbon bias, while Daniels's were progres-sive, they had already clashed in print over a number of issues, including the management of the agriculture department and prohibition. Daniels got little leverage from his attacks on the agriculture department, but he quickly learned that prohibition was a hotter topic. That a man of means might take a drink now and then did not trouble Daniels; that such a man might occasionally drink a lot was not even all that bothersome; but that poor men drank a lot in saloons where their political allegiance could be bought and where political deals were done—deals to which Daniels might not be a party—did trouble him. In those days, votes were purchased with alcohol. Daniels's prohibitionist tendencies were driven more by his anti-saloon proclivities than by his feelings toward alcohol. In his view, taking alcohol out of the saloon took the saloon out of politics. There had been prohibition referenda at both the state and local level before. In Raleigh, the saloon keepers kept their thumbs on the political pulse and always man-aged to defeat efforts to proscribe their trade. The prohibition referendum of 1882, which had cost Mary Cleaves Daniels her position as Wilson post-mistress, had gone down statewide by a margin of 3 to 1, but in Raleigh the vote had been much closer (1,180 to 780).

Daniels blamed the black vote for the statewide debacle. However, with much of the black vote effectively gerrymandered out of Raleigh city poli-tics, Daniels was optimistic about a prohibition referendum in Raleigh itself. In 1886, the issue came up again following the successful prosecu-tion of a local publican named James Miller, whose drinking and gambling den was the most upscale of Raleigh's downtown establishments. This time

Daniels beat the tocsin hard, while Ashe was, in Daniels's words, a "passive opponent."[22] Daniels had found a wedge issue. The Democrats were increasingly becoming a dry party, while the Republicans and their African American supporters were overwhelmingly wet. Thus Daniels's vocal advocacy for prohibition put Ashe in a difficult spot. If Ashe followed his personal inclinations, which were wet, then he would be going against his party, and so the *N&O* remained largely on the sidelines while the *Chronicle* led the prohibitionist charge. Daniels won; by a vote of 1,237 to 1,177 Raleigh went dry.[23] Prohibition had made a name for Daniels. He decided to leverage that name into bigger things, the most important of which was the state printing contract.

For various reasons having to do with political power and the logistics of printing state documents, it was clear that the contract would go to a Democratic newspaper in Raleigh. Republicans and out-of-town printers need not apply. The contract was designed to offer patronage to a local printer, who could in turn circulate the party line in his newspaper. By 1887, only two such printers possessed the physical plant, circulation, and political connections to compete: Ashe and Daniels. Of the two, the older man was the low-risk choice for the party. Solid and conservative, Ashe was a loyal Bourbon who had handled the contract efficiently in the past. Daniels was the newcomer, the unknown entity. He was clearly less conservative than Ashe, and some Democratic legislators could have been forgiven for thinking Daniels was a loose cannon, a progressive who leaned toward Populism before the term became a rallying cry of the political left. On the issues Daniels had openly addressed and supported, such as prohibition, agricultural reform, and railroad regulation, he took the more controversial and, from the perspective of many legislators, the more politically risky positions. Daniels had demonstrated his independence and, in the view of some, his reckless side in rejecting advertisements from the Louisiana Lottery when he took control of the Wilson *Advance*. A man who would throw away profit on principle was a man politicians mistrusted.

For both Ashe and Daniels, the contract could make the difference between profit and loss for the next two years. (The contract was issued anew by each legislature, which stood for election every other year.) Recognizing the financial stakes, Ashe used all of his political muscle in his attempt to keep the contract away from Daniels. He argued that Daniels was too young and inexperienced and that as a prohibitionist Daniels would alienate the party's wet wing; most damagingly, Ashe claimed that Daniels's agrarian Populism had split the party and cost it a majority in the state house in the most recent election. There was something to be said for each of Ashe's anti-Daniels arguments. Daniels was young; he could be reckless in print; and to a certain extent he had split the party on prohibition and agrarian reform. However, the tectonic plates of North Carolina's social and political strata were shifting under Ashe's feet. A number of younger Democrats without Confederate titles had been elected to state office in recent terms. They included Daniels's friend from Wilson Henry Groves Connor in the state senate and future ally Robert Glenn in the house. Denigrating Daniels was not a winning strategy with these younger men, who along with Daniels were sowing the seeds of their eventual takeover of the party.

The 1886 election had been more tightly contested than recent ones, and a faction of Democrats (called Independent Democrats at the time) led by John Webster of Rockingham County had split from the mainstream of the party in a dispute that revolved around the personality of Webster himself as much as any political or ideological issue. The Republicans sided with the Independents, making Webster speaker of the house. Mainstream Democrats harbored concerns that Webster and his rebels might formally cross the aisle and become Republicans, giving them control of the house. In addition to prohibition, a key issue at the time was the state's local-government law, which called for the state legislature to appoint local officials, such as magistrates and justices of the peace, in unincorporated areas. The objective of the law was to place white Democrats in office in black-majority areas. Daniels wrote that the Republicans' primary objective of the 1887 legislative session was "to repeal the County Government legislation."[24]

Ashe, through the pages of the *N&O*, overreacted to Webster's defection and, in print, waged a war against the new speaker, urging all Democratic members of the house to reject committee chairs offered by Webster. Governor Alfred Scales, a friend of Ashe's, tried to remain above the fray, but he was certain that Ashe's strategy would give control of the house to the Republicans by driving Webster further into their camp. To avert a disaster, Scales called on Daniels to arbitrate the dispute. This Daniels did, going door-to-door among the legislators' residences and office to office in the state capitol trying to avoid a schism. In the end, Daniels smoothed enough feathers to keep the Democrats in control of the house and ultimately defeat Republican efforts to repeal the county government legislation. It was Daniels's first big success in the political back rooms of Raleigh. Perhaps not coincidentally, Daniels won his first state printing contract soon thereafter. It was both a financial and a political coup.

Even before Daniels won the state contract, his name was becoming prominent beyond Raleigh. During the fall of 1886, in the run-up to the prohibition vote, Daniels was approached by a group of Durham industrialists, including the Dukes, and invited to move his newspaper to Durham. A local lawyer, William W. Fuller, represented the group, and he intimated that if Daniels were to move, then the physical plant and working capital of his paper might be substantially enhanced through local financial support. By this he meant, or at least Daniels took him to mean, Duke money. These upgrades would in time be expected to lead to a larger circulation, which would lead to more advertising, with larger profits to follow. The offer tempted Daniels. "I gave the matter for consideration," he wrote; but with the return of the legislature in the spring, he hoped to secure the state printing contract, and despite its industrial success, Durham was still viewed as a provincial backwater compared with Raleigh. Daniels rejected the deal and placed his bet with his Democratic colleagues in the legislature in Raleigh rather than with the Dukes of Durham.

After winning the state contract, Daniels immediately attempted to leverage it into control of the *News and Observer*. Although in a letter to Ashe Daniels tried to sell his proposal as a merger, he was in fact trying to buy out his competitor. Daniels offered $8,000 in cash (money he did not have but which he no doubt could borrow from Julian Shakespeare Carr) and later offered to assume Ashe's debts, which Daniels estimated at $12,000.[25] But Ashe had no intention of folding just because he had again failed to obtain the state printing contract. The *N&O* faced hard times, but Ashe was not yet on the verge of insolvency. Not only was his paper a daily, whereas Daniels's was only a weekly, but the *N&O*'s circulation exceeded the *Chronicle*'s. Daniels added insult to his offer by telling Ashe that he could stay on as an employee. The offer did not endear the younger man to the old Confederate soldier.

As Daniels's political connections expanded, and marrying into the Worth-Bagley family in 1888 did not hurt him in this regard, he became the front-runner to get the contract again when it came up for renewal in 1889. His earlier leadership of the successful prohibition campaign had raised his profile among the growing number of the state's militant Protestants. Increasingly desperate for the contract, the usually capable Ashe made an uncharacteristic blunder during the 1889 campaign. He offered to do the job for 15 percent less than the legislated rate. While a lower price for a government contract might in retrospect appear to have been good public policy, in fact, many legislators viewed the offer as bad form. It cost Ashe any number of votes. The idea of the contract in the first place was to provide political patronage, with profit built in at the expense of the taxpayers of course, in return for favorable press. The party that controlled the legislature was in essence renting a local newspaper. The contract was designed to be a transfer from the taxpaying public to a favored local publisher who would be a rabid partisan through his newspaper. Low cost and efficiency, beyond minimum competence, were never intended to be part of the bargain. That Ashe signaled his willingness to be a cut-rate political hack did not endear him to the political hacks in the legislature, and Daniels, who never released the pressure on his allies, received the contract by an even larger margin than he had in 1887. Upon hearing of her son-in-law's success in securing the contract again, Adelaide Worth Bagley enthused, "I have never seen a man have such magnetic influence among men. He is honest & that is the reason, & he is fearless to do right."[26] The irony of his mother-in-law's praise for his "honesty" concerning such crass political patronage as the state printing contract would not have been lost on Daniels.

The two publishers repeated their battle for a third time in 1891. At the time the state printer received $4,000 a year, a considerable sum.[27] Although the job was not without its costs, it was a certain net money-maker for the winner. The $2,000 or so in expected net profit was more than Daniels could earn from the *Chronicle*'s circulation and advertising bases alone. Ashe wanted the contract back, and having lost the last three contests (one to Hale and two to Daniels), he figured that continuing to go directly to the legislators was the wrong strategy. So he decided to influence the members of the legislature indirectly by persuading their constituents that a vote for Daniels was the wrong vote. Accordingly, Ashe attacked Daniels directly in the pages of the *N&O*. Ashe had spent the last thirty years in the Confederate army, the state house, and the Raleigh newspaper business. He had not survived that long in those cutthroat environments without learning a thing or two about bare-knuckled, in-the-dirt brawling, and he put his learning to use against Daniels.

At the time, one of the more emotional issues across the South was the pensions of Confederate veterans. Union veterans approaching old age in large numbers were relatively well provided for by the federal government.[28] But Confederate veterans were at the mercy of their state governments. In North Carolina, surviving veterans received roughly $50 a year, a fraction of per capita personal income at the time. Ashe openly called upon Daniels to forgo remuneration as state printer and challenged him to place the money in the state's Confederate veterans' fund. "The wounded old veterans who have rendered service to the State and their condition appeals for aid," Ashe wrote. "Mr. Daniels was too young to have rendered similar service. The two are on the scales! Will the donation be to the one or the other?"[29] Daniels could handle an attack in print. He knew how to handle challenges concerning policy positions, and since he himself was only three years old when the war ended, no one could have taken seriously any suggestion that he had shirked in avoiding military service. But Daniels remained sensitive about his father's contribution to the Confederate cause. Rumors circulated about the suspicious nature of his father's death, coming as it did at the hand of Confederate forces on a Union-commandeered vessel. One need not stretch one's imagination too much to guess that Ashe promoted the spread of those rumors. In any case, Daniels chose to take Ashe's remarks about Confederate service as a thinly veiled attack on his dead father and thus as a personal slur. Daniels called it the "last straw."[30]

It was not the last straw, however. Early one afternoon, while members of the state assembly still debated the contract behind closed doors, Daniels and S. J. Payne, a member of the legislature, were walking north to the state capitol after leaving the Bagley house, where they had just had lunch. The Bagley house, on the corner of Blount and South Streets, was two blocks east of Fayetteville Street, which ran from the site of Raleigh's future Memorial Auditorium (near the site of the old governor's mansion) to the capitol, four blocks north. Fayetteville was Raleigh's main street, with shops lining either side. When going between home and the capitol, Daniels typically strolled up Fayetteville, window-shopping and chatting with the merchants and assorted acquaintances along the way. In the block just north of where the auditorium would one day stand were the offices of the *News and Observer*. As Daniels and Payne crossed the entryway to the firm, Ashe and two of his nephews stepped out and confronted Daniels. After a verbal exchange, Ashe swung at Daniels and missed. The two men then grappled and traded swings, but according to Daniels, neither landed a solid blow. Ashe's nephews, though a menacing presence, did not come to their uncle's assistance, and Payne quickly stepped in and separated the two combatants before much physical damage was done.

Following their encounter, Ashe made the mistake of issuing a press release claiming that he had "cowhided" Daniels, an expression which readers of that day would have interpreted to mean that Ashe had either literally or metaphorically whipped Daniels.[31] On learning that this statement was circulating as news, to be picked up in newspapers around the area, Daniels became livid. Daniels possessed a bad temper, though he was usually good at controlling it or at least letting it out in print rather than through physical violence. However, on this occasion he failed to keep it in check, and early the next day both men showed up at the state capitol to cover the day's legislative events. As soon as Daniels saw Ashe, he went directly toward him, and even before words could be exchanged the fight was on. This time it was an old-fashioned donnybrook. Daniels was younger by many years. At nearly six feet, he stood above average height for his day, and he possessed a stout build, making him a formidable physical presence. But Ashe was a tough old codger whose physical courage had been tested in war. Following the initial clash of bodies, the two combatants fell to the floor and rolled among the legislators' desks as they wrestled and exchanged blows. After the initial shock wore off, a group of legislative bystanders intervened and separated the two pugilists. Other than scrapes and bruises, neither man was badly hurt. The battle was the talk of the town for days, and while the physical tension between the two men appears to have climaxed with the fight, they kept at each other in print in the weeks that followed.

While their fisticuffs might have come to a draw, their business battles were increasingly no contest. Daniels's professional and political star rose; Ashe's descended. Although they had some further journalistic conflicts over the next three years, those disputes never approached the bitter tone of those surrounding the state printing contract in 1891, which in the end Daniels won handily. Daniels would go on to win the contract again in 1893 by a comfortable margin. Many years later, with some understatement, Daniels summarized the campaigns against Ashe, noting that "though the result was never in doubt, there was always a contest that involved bitter personalities and sometimes personal altercations."[32] Daniels had gotten the best of Ashe. Without the cash flow from the state contract, Ashe had been forced to raise money from outside investors, including his father-in-law, W. H. Willard, who was president of the successful Durham tobacco manufacturing firm R. F. Morris and Son. Willard put together a consortium that infused cash into Ashe's firm, and in return, Ashe issued stock to his new partners, diluting the firm's ownership. The *N&O* limped along, for now.

POWER BROKER

When Daniels first entered the Raleigh newspaper market in 1885, and especially after he went for his first state contract in 1887, he recognized that given his current financial situation and prospects, the best way to reach the next rung on the political and economic ladders was to use the *Chronicle* as leverage. The best way to do that was to make the *Chronicle* a daily again. In Daniels's own words, the only way "to become a powerful influence in the State" was to control a daily.[33] After six years of building up the paper's circulation and advertising, and after winning the state contract for the third time in the spring of 1891, Daniels was finally ready to set the wheels in motion to compete with Ashe on a daily basis. Page had tried this and failed in the year before Daniels took over the paper. But Page did not have the cash flow from the state contracts to fall back on, and in the ensuing years, Daniels had turned the *Chronicle* into Raleigh's top weekly. Indeed, it was probably the most-read weekly in the state. As the leading Democratic publisher in a Democratic town, with the state contract, the retained earnings from the *Chronicle*, and the revenues he received from his brother Charles, who was still paying off his loan for the purchase of the Wilson *Advance*, Daniels was in good financial shape. He had every expectation of increasing his profits from a daily newspaper and finally driving Ashe out of business to boot.

Still, Ashe's *N&O* remained the capital city's only morning daily. Since he first purchased the Raleigh *Observer*, Ashe had successfully fought off all comers for the morning market. By 1891, there were two afternoon papers, the *Visitor* and the *Evening Call*. Both hovered on the edge of failure. Of these, Daniels considered the *Call* to be the more financially viable and the one more amenable to his editorial positions. Never a proponent of afternoon papers—Daniels liked his news first thing in the morning, and the market seemed to indicate most of his potential customers did too—Daniels decided to approach the ownership of the *Call*, propose a merger, and if successful, convert the combined paper into a morning daily. Daniels had been planning the move for some time. In fact, he had begun putting the deal together in 1890, even before the battle with Ashe for the 1891 state printing contract. With a bank loan (probably from Joseph Brown) Daniels closed the deal with the *Call* later in the year.[34] Daniels now owned a daily.

In the months immediately following the conversion of the *Chronicle* to a daily, Daniels worked as hard as at any time during his life, which is a strong statement, given his physical and mental capacities for work. Other than the time he took for rest, meals, and worship, he basically worked all the time. He had no real hobbies to speak of, other than following baseball. He was not much of a hunter or fisherman; he did not collect coins, stamps, or butterflies; his primary pastimes were the news and politics, which also happened to be his trade. Initially, it looked as if his efforts in converting the merged *Chronicle-Call* into a viable daily newspaper would pay off. Although circulation figures for this period are often unreliable, as publishers would sometimes report optimistic figures to persuade advertisers of a newspaper's reach, by the accounts that have survived it is safe to say that Daniels quickly made up the ground between the *Call*'s daily circulation (before Daniels purchased it) and that of Ashe's *N&O*. Indeed, the *Chronicle* passed the *N&O* in circulation early the following year. Not only did Daniels best Ashe, but by the spring of 1892, with a circulation of roughly 5,000, the *Chronicle* could lay claim to having "the largest circulation of any daily paper in North Carolina."[35] At age thirty, Daniels had achieved his boyhood dream.

Circulation figures did not tell the whole story, however. Despite Daniels's efforts, the *N&O* remained a popular paper and a tough competitor. Also, Ashe could fall back on the new capital he had received from his father-in-law just a year earlier, and name recognition meant something in the newspaper business. Still, Daniels *had* passed Ashe in circulation, and Daniels still possessed a competitive advantage over Ashe in the form of the state printing contract. The younger man clearly had gotten the best of the older one. Furthermore, unlike Ashe, Daniels did not answer to stockholders. He continued to pay himself a monthly salary of $100, a good living at the time to be sure, but everything else he plowed back into the *Chronicle*'s physical plant. The paper now had new Cottrell presses and was overall in pretty good shape financially. In contrast, the physical plant of the *N&O* was shot, and the primary asset of the venerable old firm was the accounting "goodwill" associated with its name. Recognizing the contrasting trends in the fortunes of Raleigh's two leading newspapermen, *N&O* creditors and stockholders began to pressure Ashe to make changes.

The first creditor to lose confidence in Ashe was his former law partner, Augustus Merrimon, a former U.S. senator and, at the time, chief justice of the North Carolina Supreme Court. Merrimon had loaned Ashe a total of $10,000 to purchase the Raleigh *Observer* in 1879 and then to merge it with the Raleigh *News* in 1881. Now sixty-one years old and in declining health, Merrimon had little tangible wealth and wanted to provide for his family in the event of his death. Ashe had never repaid the initial loan. He had, in fact, explicitly refused to do so when Merrimon demanded repayment. Ashe had apparently even stopped paying interest on the loan. Extrapolating recent trends in Ashe's fortunes, Merrimon guessed that he would go to his grave without ever seeing the return of his original $10,000. Hoping to avoid a potentially messy and time-consuming court proceeding, Merrimon went to Daniels with a proposition. Merrimon would, in the language of the day, sell Ashe's note to Daniels. Daniels could then demand payment from Ashe, who could not pay. Then Daniels, rather than Merrimon, could execute the legal process that would help him take control of the *N&O* as its chief creditor. Merrimon would get what he wanted: his $10,000. Daniels would get what he wanted: control of the *N&O*.

Daniels's comfort at the thought of having Ashe's fate in his hands must have equaled his satisfaction at consummating a good business deal, and he accepted on the spot. However, in his own words, Daniels confessed that he "had no such sum of money."[36] His commercial banker, Brown, would not lend that kind of money, but Daniels was confident that his old financier, Julian Shakespeare Carr, would. There was only one possible hitch. Either for old-time's sake or out of some gentlemanly notion of honor, before selling the note to Daniels, Merrimon insisted on giving Ashe's other stockholders, which included Ashe's wealthy father-in-law, Willard, a chance to settle the account by Monday of the following week. To Daniels's chagrin, Willard came through, persuading the other stockholders to pay up. Merrimon accepted the cash, and Ashe kept control of the *N&O*.

However, the settlement of Merrimon's account did not sit well with the other stockholders at the *N&O*. A group of them soon approached Daniels and quietly inquired about a merger. It is doubtful Ashe knew of this potential coup. Daniels wisely refused for two reasons: First, the *N&O* stockholders proposed to absorb the *Chronicle* at considerably less than the value of the *N&O*, which would make Daniels a minority owner in the combined firm. That was bad enough, but the other stockholders were not of Daniels's choosing. In short, Ashe would be out, but Daniels would come in as the junior partner. On paper, this was a fair deal. The *N&O* was capitalized at $10,000; the *Chronicle*, at $2,000.[37] Of course at some point Daniels could offer to buy out his new partners, but that was the second problem. According to Daniels, "The *News and Observer*'s press outfit was old, its type was old, and it had nothing of real value."[38] The firm's goodwill, specifically the name *News and Observer*, was all that remained of Ashe's years of management. Still, that was worth something. A few weeks earlier, Daniels had been willing to pay Merrimon $10,000 for the *N&O* name. Although the amount he was being offered for the *Chronicle* went unrecorded, it was considerably less than that figure and was probably in the neighborhood of its $2,000 capitalized value. Daniels's foot-dragging with the stockholders was most likely an attempt to get them to increase their offer for the *Chronicle*, giving Daniels more cash to leverage a future buyout of his new partners.

Sensing he had Ashe and his fellow owners on the ropes, Daniels nibbled at the deal, but he did not bite. The negotiations dragged on, and eventually the deal collapsed.

Although in the long run, Daniels's rejection of the merger with the *N&O* proved to be a wise decision, at the time he underestimated Ashe's staying power. Ashe had powerful friends in addition to his wife's family, and some of them had deep pockets. Among these was Major Rufus S. Tucker, a director of the Seaboard Air Line railroad. Ashe was a supporter of the state's railroad barons. Daniels was their enemy. Tucker and Daniels had been combatants since the day Daniels took over the *Chronicle*. Daniels, as part of his progressivism, consistently called for the creation of a railroad commission to regulate the state's railroads, including the rates they charged. As a spokesman and the chief lobbyist for the railroad industry in North Carolina, Tucker had spent the past six years fighting a rearguard action in the state legislature against Daniels's calls for a regulatory commission. (Daniels thought the rate of return on railroad capital should be capped at 6 percent. When asked if he would settle for the same rate of return on his business, he answered that the state did not subsidize him the way that it had the railroads, a disingenuous argument, given his possession of the state printing contract for eight years.)

Tucker now led the group of *N&O* stockholders who wanted to merge the *N&O* and the *Chronicle* and thus silence Daniels by making him a minority stockholder. Tempting as it was to be part of the famed *N&O*, Daniels saw through Tucker's scheme, which explains why he held out for a better offer that never came. Rather than join Ashe, Daniels wanted to bury him, and if that meant driving the *N&O* under with him then so be it. But in Tucker's calculus, if Daniels would not join the *N&O*, he could not be allowed to put it out of business. Raleigh needed a conservative Democratic voice. It would be costly, but Ashe and his paper had to be kept afloat. With yet another shot of new money, this one from the railroads, Ashe's paper limped on.

This was not the first time the railroad interests had tried to silence Daniels by writing him a check. After Daniels had won the state printing contract in 1889, he had been approached by Colonel A. B. Andrews, vice president of Southern Railway. "How would you like to edit the daily *News and Observer?*" the colonel asked straight out. Daniels, suspicious, hesitated. Andrews was known for drawing up pro-railroad legislation and sending it to the state legislature with the expectation it would be passed verbatim.[39] Daniels, on the other hand, had been a foe of the railroads in print and on the floor of the state house. "I knew that Colonel Andrews had no reason to advance my ambitions," he wrote of the offer, and after much give-and-take, it became clear that Daniels was being asked to sell out to the railroad. He turned down the offer.[40]

Having failed to take over the *N&O*, Daniels went to work destroying it. Converting the *Chronicle* to a daily initially looked to be a financially successful move. But there was a downside, perhaps more than one, to this success. Despite what appeared to be prosperity, Daniels was not clearing any more money than he had when the *Chronicle* was a weekly, yet he was working much harder. Furthermore, to buy out the *Call* and expand operations to a daily, he had taken on new debt.[41] As Daniels had discovered earlier, chartered commercial banks of this period maintained relatively conservative loan policies, and the loans were short term. To obtain long-term financing, a borrower had to roll over the short-term loans. This exposed Daniels to the vagaries of interest rate movements, since he often had to roll over debt at a higher interest rate. Daniels had taken on the new debt with the expectation that he would drive Ashe out of business, collect most of Ashe's subscribers and advertisers, and see the *Chronicle*'s profits boom. The paper's revenues did grow, but the debts grew faster, and thus profit stagnated.

Another downside was that balancing work and family became an increasingly difficult chore. The work was especially taxing. Having a morning paper out the door six days a week (there was still no Monday edition) required late nights six evenings a week. Running a weekly had required hard work as well, but the pace for much of the week was more leisurely. The increasing demands of the daily paper coincided with increasing demands at home. The Danielses' first child, a daughter named Adelaide after her mother and maternal grandmother, had been born in January 1892. Josephus Daniels was by all accounts a dedicated father by the standards of his day, but tied up as he was with the *Chronicle*, that dedication did not extend much to the day-to-day care of his daughter. This was left almost entirely to Addie and the female members of her family, a common domestic arrangement at the time.

At work Daniels drove himself and his staff hard. He worked fourteen- to sixteen-hour days (except on Sundays, of course), and although initially he was successful in expanding the paper's circulation, for the first time in his life, he questioned whether the success was worth the effort. Despite earning a decent income, he remained in debt, and the strain of running a daily started to show. It got worse quickly. With the additional physical plant and employees that came with running a daily paper, Daniels was forced to expand his subscription and advertising revenues dramatically. This took time. In the short run, to cover operating expenses, he borrowed more from a local bank (again, probably Brown's Citizens National), and the cost of servicing this debt expanded faster than his revenues. Daniels understood that he had to spend money to make money, but he was spending borrowed money. For the first time in his life, Daniels saw one of his businesses fall into the red. "The *State Chronicle* was losing money," he recalled. "It [began] losing more than I was receiving as State Printer. I was in debt several thousand dollars and the paper was going into the hole more and more all the time."[42] Moving to a daily had been a success at one margin: Circulation, advertising, and revenues rose dramatically, as did the paper's goodwill and overall capital value. But the up-front costs had been high, and Daniels was having a difficult time amortizing the short-term loans that had financed the expansion.

Ironically, the *Chronicle* had quickly become the most widely read daily in the state. The paper's circulation, its brand name, and Daniels's growing reputation as a publisher made the *Chronicle* a valuable property, especially as a progressive voice within the Democratic Party. However, the recent increase in value had been generated with borrowed money and Daniels's sheer physical energy, inputs that could not continue to grow at their current rates. The competition between Ashe and Daniels was destroying both of them. Daniels began to look for a way off the fast track he had worked so hard to get on. Events surrounding the gubernatorial campaign of 1892 gave him the opportunity to take a well-earned break and enjoy a financial windfall.

The agrarian discontent sweeping the country at the time hit North Carolina. The increasingly vocal Populists—a party composed largely of small farmers—threatened to split the Democratic Party. Daniels took it upon himself to keep together the state's Democrats. The party maintained a clear majority in the state, and whoever won the Democratic primary, whether they were progressive or conservative, would most likely win the governorship. A year earlier, the governor, Daniel Fowle, had died in office, and his term was completed by Lieutenant Governor Thomas Holt. As the incumbent, Holt began the race with the upper hand, but he could not hold it.

The Fowle family was close to the Bagleys, and Addie counted Fowle's daughter, Helen, among her closest friends. Accordingly, Daniels and Fowle maintained a warm personal friendship. Daniels did not have the same regard for Holt, who was the product of a prosperous textile dynasty. Holt sought to retain the governor's office. Daniels, who saw Holt as a tool of the state's railroad owners, Colonel Andrews in particular, opposed his candidacy.[43] The Holt forces expected Daniels to attack the governor through the pages of the *Chronicle*, and they feared that the absence of Daniels's support would be the difference between winning and losing the party's nomination. Recognizing that Daniels would not support Holt under any conceivable terms, in the spring of 1892 Holt decided to buy Daniels out. According to Daniels, "Colonel Holt thought that if the *State Chronicle* could be bought and made a Holt organ he would certainly be nominated" and thus remain governor.[44] Holt, probably with Andrews's support, financially backed a local journalist, Thomas Jernigan, who approached Daniels with an offer for the *Chronicle*. This was the fourth time in the past few years Daniels had received an offer for his paper or an offer to merge it with the *N&O*. Daniels had seriously considered selling to Tucker in the most recent negotiations, but that deal had fallen through.

Daniels bargained hard with Jernigan, but not too hard this time. After some negotiating, a deal was struck. The deal had three primary components: First, Daniels would keep the state printing contract, but he would subcontract the actual printing. This would cut into Daniels's net income from the contract but still leave him with a little less than $1,000 in (annual net) profit.[45] Second, the new debt Daniels incurred while expanding the *Chronicle* from a weekly to a daily would be paid off, as would his $1,000 debt to Carr for the original stock. Finally, Daniels would hold the mortgage on the *Chronicle*'s physical plant, now valued at $2,600, which Jernigan, with Holt's money (or, possibly, the railroad's money), would retire under unspecified future terms. (In seven years, Daniels had increased the value of the *Chronicle* 160 percent, an average annual rate of growth of 15 percent.) Daniels summarized the deal: "For the first time since I had gone into the newspaper business [in 1880] I was out of debt and had a few hundred dollars [annually, from the residual of the state contract] and the $2,600 coming to me [for the *Chronicle*'s physical plant and equipment]."[46] (Ironically, the *Chronicle* was soon swallowed by Daniels's old enemy, Captain Ashe, and the two papers were jointly published as the *News and Observer-Chronicle*.) At the time, observers could be forgiven for concluding that Ashe had bested Daniels. However, with the mortgage debt hanging over it and without the state printing contracts, Ashe's combined operation remained in the red, and Daniels was now in effect an *N&O* creditor. His immediate business debts in Raleigh were paid. He was earning a decent upper-middle-class income. Though he still owed roughly $1,000 on his mother's mortgage in Wilson as well as $600 on his own Wilson property, balancing these against the mortgage he held on the *Chronicle*, he had a substantial positive net worth. But for the first time in thirteen years he was out of the newspaper business.

After Daniels, by now the state's leading progressive voice, sold the *Chronicle*, the conservative Holt thought he had the nomination in the bag. But Holt was by no means a beloved figure in the party. As an industrialist, he lacked support from the state's still-dominant agrarian interests, and in a year of Populist unrest, many party insiders thought Holt was all too beatable. Some of them went in search of a better candidate. Thus Daniels's old patron, General Jule Carr, had been persuaded to join the race. Although, like Holt, Carr was an industrialist, he was untainted by previous office, and thus his political reputation was clean. Furthermore, while Carr was capable of driving a hard bargain in the mart of commerce, party insiders considered him honest and charitable to a fault, and he was widely respected in ways Holt was not. It followed that the choice of Carr over Holt was an easy one for Daniels. Unfortunately, Daniels now had no newspaper to throw behind Carr's nomination. Proving that a weak campaign could undo an otherwise strong candidate, Carr, who was a poor stump speaker with no political machine to fall back on, saw his candidacy go nowhere. Once again, it appeared Holt would continue as governor. But the race soon became even more confused.

Agrarian unrest, which Daniels had helped cultivate since his attacks on the state's Bourbon-controlled Department of Agriculture years earlier, had finally boiled over. Low farm prices contributed to the strengthening of the Populist movement across the country. In North Carolina the Farmers' Alliance, led by Colonel Leonidas Polk (not to be confused with the Confederate general of the same name), voiced the farmers' complaints. For the time being, the alliance remained part of the Democratic Party. But Holt was a conservative businessman with no ties to the state's small farmers, and a strong faction within the alliance opposed Holt's nomination as governor. At the Democratic State Convention, with the threat of schism in the air, a group of anti-Holt alliance men managed to win the nomination for yet another candidate, Elias Carr.

An unlikely populist, Elias Carr was the scion of an old coastal plain family, and as the owner of several plantations and a solid member of the state's planter elite, he had the classic résumé of a Bourbon. However, his sympathies for the alliance members, while paternalistic, were nonetheless real. There remained those within the alliance who questioned Carr's devotion to their cause, arguing that a landed Bourbon was little better than the industrialist Holt, but a deal was hammered out. The party leaders agreed to support one of the alliance's main causes, Free Silver, at the national level (about which more will be said below), and in return, the more radical elements of the alliance would remain in the party and support Carr. The deal fell apart when the Democratic National Convention, meeting in Chicago, nominated Grover Cleveland, who favored the gold standard. From the day Cleveland was nominated, his affection for gold over silver would cause Daniels and the Democratic Party no small amount of trouble at both the state and national levels.

In North Carolina that trouble began immediately. As one historian of the period observed, Carr's nomination did not "unify the Alliance or vanquish anti-Alliance Democrats."[47] Alliance members, feeling betrayed by the national party's support for gold, organized their own convention to meet in early August. In the meantime, realizing how much he missed the rough and tumble of politics and journalism, and hoping to keep his party from splintering, Daniels quickly decided to leap back into the world of papers and politics. Accordingly, he spent July putting together yet another newspaper. He would go back to the weekly format he knew well, and the paper would be titled the *North Carolinian*. Its primary objective was to elect Grover Cleveland and Elias Carr.

Because Daniels still possessed the state printing contract and the cash flow from the sale of the *Chronicle*, he could afford to break even on the *North Carolinian* and perhaps even run a bit in the red, at least for a while. The competition with Ashe was put aside temporarily. Daniels understood that his new firm might or might not be a long-run operation. (Daniels did not explain how he obtained the funds to jump-start the *North Carolinian*. Most likely, using the mortgage on the *Chronicle* as collateral, he borrowed the money from Joseph Brown's Citizens National Bank.) With a new press and a new location in the Holloman Building on Fayetteville Street, he published the first edition of the paper on Friday, August 12. He was too late. On the following Wednesday the radical alliance men met in Raleigh and nominated W. P. Exum for governor. The alliance's choice of Exum was only slightly less curious than the Democrats' choice of Elias Carr. Exum's sole qualification appeared to be that he was unobjectionable to the leadership of all of the key factions within the radical wing of the alliance.

Daniels feared that the mainstream of the Democratic Party would go for Carr, while the radical wing led by the alliance would go for Exum.

The split in the party's vote would lead to the election of the Republican candidate, David Furches. To prevent this from happening, Daniels put together a team of younger Democrats to rally the vote. It included his old schoolmate Charles Brantley Aycock; Robert Glenn, a former member of the state house from the piedmont and currently a state solicitor; and the senior member of the group, Furnifold Simmons, an experienced politico from the coastal plain. Daniels could not have foreseen it at the time, but with the subsequent addition of Locke Craig, this group would eventually run the state for a generation. Aycock, Glenn, and Craig were future governors, and Simmons would be a long-serving U.S. senator. Their immediate roles would be repeated later in the decade. (Craig, the junior member of the group, had not yet reached the prominence of the other three.)

Aycock and Glenn, as physically tireless as Daniels, took to the stump speaking at every crossroads they could reach. Daniels turned the *North Carolinian* into a subsidiary of the Cleveland and Carr campaigns. Swallowing Cleveland's support for the gold standard, Daniels claimed, "The readers of this paper [i.e., the *North Carolinian*] know our estimate of Grover Cleveland. He is the uncrowned king of the world." In a few years Daniels would regret those words, but for now Cleveland, the only Democrat to make it to the White House between James Buchanan (in 1857) and Woodrow Wilson (in 1913), carried the party's hopes at the national level. As for Carr's candidacy, the hyperbole was more local in color. Raising the fear of a return to the bad old days of Republican (and, hence, African American) control during Reconstruction, Daniels wrote, "We appeal to every man who loves reform and loves his State, now that it is apparent that all divisions [within the Democratic Party] mean a return to Negro supremacy, to come together and elect Elias Carr."[48]

In Daniels's view, the key to the election was Simmons, "a talented and ruthless organizer and tactician," as one Tar Heel political correspondent subsequently and accurately described him.[49] Accordingly, Daniels sought Simmons's elevation to chair of the state Democratic Party, arguing that Simmons, more than Carr, was the key to the election. But Daniels faced a problem. By tradition the gubernatorial candidate chose the party chair, and that choice was then simply ratified by the state committee. Daniels recognized these were dangerous times for his party. At the national level, the Republicans held the White House, and they had controlled both houses of the 51st Congress (elected in 1888). Although the Democrats had taken the House of Representatives in the midterm elections of 1890, the Senate remained solidly Republican, and the split between the mainstream and radical elements of the Democratic Party increased the probability of Republican gains at the national level in 1892. More threateningly to Daniels, the national scene foreshadowed a resurrection of Republican power in North Carolina. The Democratic Party had to be held together, and the better man, Elias Carr, had to be elected, even if that man was not very good in Daniels's opinion. As Daniels summarized the campaign, a split vote "would give the Republican Party control of North Carolina and put the Negro back into office."[50]

Carr, whom Daniels considered to be "a baby in politics," was not much help and, indeed, hindered the campaign from the start.[51] He had chosen as his state chairman Richard Battle, a former chair who was, in Daniels's view, past his prime and not up to the fight the party was about to undertake. Simmons, on the other hand, was younger and a two-time U.S. representative from the "black" second congressional district that included Daniels's hometown, Wilson. Daniels considered the fact that Simmons had managed to outmaneuver the African Americans and white Republicans, who had previously dominated the second district, sufficient evidence of his political capabilities. In fact those capabilities, which were indeed considerable, were only beginning to reveal themselves. Daniels was absolutely correct in his appraisal of the relative talents of Battle and Simmons. Accordingly, he began maneuvering to obtain the chairman's position for Simmons. This involved much behind-closed-doors persuading, but Daniels had carefully built up his local political capital during his seven years in Raleigh, and with some deft back-scratching and deal-making, he secured the state chairmanship for Simmons, a landmark achievement in Daniels's rise to power. During his time in Raleigh, Daniels had gone from being nobody from Wilson to a backroom power broker. Still only thirty years old, he was already powerful enough to override the wishes of the party's gubernatorial candidate concerning who would be party chairman. Daniels wanted Simmons, and he got what he wanted. Other powerful and aspiring men saw this outcome, and it strengthened Daniels's hand in subsequent battles. He had graduated from a voice of the party's progressive wing to mainstream insider.

With Simmons orchestrating the campaign, Daniels promoting it in the pages of the *North Carolinian*, and Aycock and Glenn seeming to be everywhere on the stump, Elias Carr won the election. But it was hardly a landslide. Together, the other two candidates, Exum and Furches, outpolled Carr by nearly 10,000 votes.[52] The underlying problems the Democrats faced in North Carolina were hidden by their success at the national level.

Cleveland reversed the outcome of the 1888 election, beating the incumbent Benjamin Harrison, and the Democrats took the U.S. Senate. For the first time since before the Civil War, they controlled both houses of Congress and the White House.

Daniels's finances were not doing as well as his party. With an initial circulation of 3,500, the *North Carolinian* looked to be a winner. It had taken several years to get the *Chronicle*'s circulation in that range. With the value Daniels's name brought to the paper, it reached that figure in a few months, and the excitement of the election kept circulation up. However, after the fall elections, circulation began to drop off. The economic crisis continued to plague the state's rural areas. The decline in crop prices had driven the alliance supporters to their recent rebellion. The price of cotton (the state's leading economic indicator) soon hit a post–Civil War low of 6 cents a pound, and it continued to trend downward.[53] This in turn affected the cities, as the state's economy remained tied to its agricultural sector. Merchants, lawyers, and financiers lived in town, but their professions were inextricably tied to what happened on the farms surrounding the town. The economic fate of a newspaper was also tied to the farm. A newspaper subscription was often one of the first things to be cut from a family's budget when hard times hit.

At the national level, although the Democrats had lost seats in the U.S. House, they maintained a majority, and with Cleveland heading for the White House and the Democratic Party now in control of the Senate, the party's fortunes were on the rise. But Daniels's personal fortune continued to fall. Interest in the *North Carolinian* declined; its circulation hit 2,000 by early 1893. The financial losses piled up more quickly than Daniels had anticipated when he returned to the business. However, Cleveland's victory brought Hoke Smith, a lawyer and newspaperman from Atlanta with whom Daniels was acquainted, into the new administration, and in Smith's appointment Daniels saw a new opportunity for a job in Washington, D.C. Smith had once offered Daniels a job at Smith's Atlanta newspaper. Daniels had turned down that offer, but he now maneuvered for another one.

Smith's mother was the sister of General Robert F. Hoke. A fighting general who saw action up and down the eastern theater during the Civil War, Hoke had been the youngest major general in the Confederate army. After the war, he embarked on a successful career as a New South industrialist, and he maintained a home in Raleigh. A prominent Democrat, Hoke was familiar with Daniels's rise in the political world and his role in the victory of 1892. Hoke's word carried weight in Democratic circles well beyond

Raleigh. Despite his previous interactions with Smith, Daniels hesitated to approach him directly and instead went to Smith's uncle, the general, for a recommendation. General Hoke told Daniels that he would gladly offer a good word, but he added that "Hoke [Smith] thinks so much of you that you need no recommendation. All you have to do is tell him you would like to go and he will hold a place for you if he can." The general did support Daniels, who was forever grateful. Years later, he eulogized Hoke, noting that "he was wise in counsel, and his advice was sought by governors and other able state leaders." In a subsequent Confederate Memorial Day speech, Daniels admonished North Carolina's youth to "get you a hero," and he cited Hoke's life as a heroic model to be followed.[54]

Daniels's strategy to go through Hoke worked. By telegram Smith directed Daniels to be in Washington for Cleveland's forthcoming inauguration. Leaving the operation of the newspaper in the capable hands of his managing editor, Fred L. Merritt, Daniels boarded the next day's train for Washington, D.C. There he attended Cleveland's inauguration on March 4, 1893. As directed, Daniels contacted Smith and reiterated his interest in a position. Smith conferred with Cleveland, who had tapped Smith to head the Interior Department. Smith then got back to Daniels with the news that Cleveland was pleased to welcome Daniels into the administration. Excited, Daniels wrote to Addie: "While at Dinner [in the Arlington Hotel] Hoke Smith came in. He spoke cordially and invited me to call at his room after dinner. . . . He said that the President had determined to make the appointments himself to the places one of which he has hoped to save for me."[55] The official job offer came later that week.

At the time, there were only eight cabinet positions, and head of the Interior Department was among the most important. The department's mandate included the administration of federal pensions, including military pensions, which with the aging of the Civil War veterans proved to be an enormous administrative undertaking. Indeed, veterans' pensions represented one of the federal government's largest programs. When Cleveland took office, the U.S. Army, Navy, and Marine Corps combined had fewer than 40,000 men in uniform, whereas the Interior Department administered pensions for more than five times as many veterans.[56] The department also served as the human resources office for the other federal departments, as nonpatronage civil servants were hired through the department.

The relative importance of Daniels's responsibilities can be seen in his salary, which was $1,600 a year, seven or eight times per capita income in North Carolina, which would be comparable to more than $300,000 today.

It is easy to see why Daniels so quickly changed from struggling newspaper entrepreneur to political appointee. Smith soon recognized Daniels's superior characteristics and almost immediately elevated him to the head of what was then called the Appointment Division, which served as the human resources office of the federal government, at an annual salary of $2,000. In this position, Daniels personally oversaw the hiring of all nonmilitary and non-cabinet-level government employees; he essentially served as the federal government's chief civil servant.

As soon as Daniels began receiving his federal salary in March, he stopped paying himself a salary from the *North Carolinian* or the state printing contract, putting those monies back into the firm. For the first few months after taking the position in the Interior Department, he lived in the Metropolitan Hotel on Pennsylvania Avenue, while Addie and young Adelaide stayed in Raleigh. After his promotion to the head of appointments, he arranged for his wife and daughter to join him in Washington. Ever a good social mixer, Daniels fit in well in Washington's salons, and he could be one of the boys in a smoked-filled room. However, he never enjoyed late-night drinking and carousing more generally, and the arrival of Addie and Adelaide provided a great deal of emotional comfort.

Throughout the spring and summer of 1893, Daniels demonstrated his capabilities, professionally and politically, in managing the Appointment Division. In an age in which senior bureaucratic positions were largely patronage appointments, Daniels brought an unusual amount of business savvy, intelligence, and vigor. Secretary Smith recognized as much, and when the department's most senior position (unimaginatively titled chief clerk) opened up in September, Smith gave the job to Daniels at a salary of $2,750, a figure almost unheard of back in Wilson, or Raleigh for that matter. Daniels had more than doubled his annual income from his newspaper days in only a few months in Washington. The promotion also yielded a large political return to Daniels, for he was now second in command in the Interior Department, serving as Smith's right hand for the department's day-to-day business and as the secretary's chief advisor on political matters. He was essentially what would later be called Smith's chief of staff. Daniels was near the top of the Cleveland administration's hierarchy. Indeed, counting only the president and vice president, the eight cabinet heads (and in some cases their assistant secretaries), and the heads of the army and the navy as senior to him, Daniels was now among the top thirty or so individuals running the executive branch of the federal government.

At the time, the great political questions faced by the Cleveland administration were primarily domestic and economic. In *The Wonderful Wizard of Oz*, L. Frank Baum's allegorical tale of late nineteenth-century America, the inhabitants of the Emerald City, Baum's version of Washington, D.C., viewed the world through money-colored glasses. Indeed money, finance, and economics were at the heart of American politics at the time.[57] When Daniels took up his post in 1893, four great economic issues faced the administration: the tariff, the rise of big business in the form of trusts, civil service reform, and monetary policy, which was largely debated in the context of the gold standard versus Free Silver. Daniels arrived in Washington at the height of the Pax Britannica, that century-long period of general peace among the Great Powers. The great issues of the day were all domestic, and to the extent they had international implications (as the tariff and the gold standard did), domestic considerations dominated international ones.

Of these issues, the first Daniels hoped to see addressed was the tariff. Regarding international trade issues, Daniels was an ardent free trader, remaining for nearly fifty years one of the country's leading advocates of tariff reform, which to Daniels meant simply a reduction in tariff rates. Daniels viewed many public policy questions in terms of the rich versus the poor, and unless race was involved, Daniels unambiguously sided with the poor. In Daniels's view, the conflict over the tariff fell into this category. But in his opposition to the tariff, he also saw the tariff question in terms of the North versus the South. In Daniels's calculus, the tariff could be reduced to this: It protected and further enriched already wealthy northern industrialists while further impoverishing already poor southern farmers. To Daniels the tariff fight represented an economic version of Reconstruction all over again. Daniels saw the tariff as the single most important domestic policy issue. "When I went to Washington I expected to see tariff reduction made the first and paramount reform undertaken," he wrote.[58] He constantly harped about the tariff to his boss, Smith, who served as Daniels's conduit to Cleveland.

Disputes over the tariff had a long history. Until the twentieth century, the tariff served as the single largest source of federal government revenue. As late as 1900, nearly 50 percent of total federal revenues came from the tariff.[59] The root of the tariff mischief could be found in the advantage it offered to domestic producers who faced international competition. Because the tariff raised the price of imported goods, it put foreign producers at a competitive disadvantage. Since domestic producers played a role in electing the politicians who set the tariff rates, and foreign producers did not, domestic capitalists used the political process to eliminate foreign competition. As Chief Justice of the U.S. Supreme Court John Marshall famously wrote in the case of *McCulloch v. Maryland*, "the power to tax involves the power to destroy," and destroying foreign competition was exactly the objective of the tariff's proponents.[60]

The tariff tended to be disproportionately placed on manufactured goods, and manufacturing activity was disproportionately located in the Northeast and the Midwest. Conversely, the southern economy was overwhelmingly agricultural. For the South, then, the tariff proved to be burdensome in two related ways. First, as net purchasers of manufactured goods, southern farmers and southern consumers paid a higher price for the goods they purchased. Second, as a large exporter of agricultural products, the South witnessed a decrease in the foreign demand for southern output as a result of the fact that foreign incomes were reduced because foreign producers could not sell their wares in the American market. As Daniels summarized the issue, "Congress [which had been dominated by the Republicans since the Civil War] levied high tariff taxes, compelling cotton farmers to buy everything at high prices in a highly protected market, whereas cotton—their only money crop—was sold in the free trade market of the world."[61] Accordingly, southern Democrats referred to the protectionist Republicans in Congress as the "tariff gang."[62]

It followed naturally that the Democrats, the South's dominant political party, would be the party of free trade; the Republicans, the dominant party in the North and the party of northern capital, remained the protectionist party throughout the late nineteenth and early twentieth centuries. As long as the Democratic Party expressed the voice of free traders, such as Daniels, the party offered southerners and farmers more generally a clear alternative to the Republicans' high-tariff, pro-capitalist policies. Daniels would argue for the rest of his life that free trade was an important component of any winning strategy for the Democrats.

Unfortunately for Daniels's efforts in support of tariff reduction, the deepening recession of 1893 almost immediately derailed Cleveland's domestic policy agenda, which had initially included lower tariffs. The tariff, always a double-edged sword politically, proved even more so during an economic downturn, and Cleveland, a New Yorker, turned out to be less than the ardent free trader that Daniels had hoped. Domestic producers, who were cutting back production and laying off workers, sought even more protection during the recession, and politicians were susceptible, just as they are today (especially when unemployment is high and increasing), to the charge that free trade costs domestic jobs. Hailing from New York, Cleveland was more sensitive to these cries than he was to those of small farmers across the South.

In the summer of 1893, Smith treated Daniels as a sounding board for the administration's domestic agenda. After meeting with the president, the interior secretary asked Daniels for his views of the falling economy and what the administration should do about it. Daniels explicitly placed tariff reduction and the silver issue (which is addressed in Chapter 4) at the top of his list. To Daniels the matter was simple: Cut tariff rates across the board and coin more silver into money to inflate the money supply. Lower tariffs would cut farm costs, and Free Silver would put upward pressure on farm prices. Smith responded that the recession had led Cleveland to waver on both issues. This was a bad sign from Daniels's perspective.

More susceptible to the lamentations of Wall Street than Daniels had suspected, Cleveland quickly lost the will for the trade fight, and he had never favored silver. In a subsequent meeting, Daniels told Smith that if the president retreated from free trade and if he did not loosen his commitment to the gold standard, then the economic crisis would worsen, and a political crisis for the Democrats would ensue. "I could not refrain from telling my superior that I feared the wreckage of the Democratic Party in the next election," Daniels wrote.[63] Daniels had faith in Cleveland's moral courage. Cleveland did not flinch when it came to a fight, but Daniels now feared that Cleveland's tenacity was aimed at free trade and Free Silver rather than at the capitalists and goldbugs on Wall Street, most of whom were Republicans. In the end, Cleveland sided with the northern industrialists and financiers, and while average tariff rates did come down during his administration, the decrease was small compared with Daniels's expectations. In the year before Cleveland took office, the average tariff rate was 49 percent. The year he left, it was 42 percent, still high by almost any standard.[64] Daniels always felt Cleveland's failure to press tariff reform represented a broken promise, as well as a missed opportunity, and it was one that would hurt the party in the next two elections. As for the silver issue, Cleveland remained hostile even to the entreaties from within his own party.

———

The fight over Free Silver would eventually bring down Cleveland and the Democratic Party with him, but before that happened, Daniels found a new enemy to attack: the trusts. He landed in Washington on the eve of the period economists and historians would later come to call the era of "the Great Merger Movement."[65] More generally, the era marked the rise of big business in America. While it is easy to toss around a term like "big business," a quick glance at the data suggests the term fits the era. In the decade following Daniels's arrival in Washington, "over 1,800 manufacturing firms relinquished their separate identities and combined with former rivals. One-third of these combinations resulted in a market share in excess of 70 percent."[66] Any way one slices the economic data, the mergers of the era created an unprecedented number of very large firms, and many of these firms dominated the industries in which they operated.[67]

The key to the merger movement was the relatively high fixed costs of the technologies of many of the leading industries of the late nineteenth century. The advantage of these technologies was that they offered economies of scale—that is, low average total costs of production, but *only at high levels of output*. Thus during a downturn in the economy, as the demand for products fell, so too did their prices and quantities sold. The capitalists who controlled the large firms, including Andrew Carnegie (in steel), John D. Rockefeller (petroleum), and North Carolina's James B. Duke (tobacco), therefore struggled to amortize the high fixed costs associated with the initial investment in their capital-intensive industries. Furthermore, competitors might attempt to capture market share by cutting the price of their product, thereby starting a price war. Hence the owners of these large businesses sought to protect themselves by merger or collusion. The trust was born.

For a progressive like Daniels, if the trust was successful in controlling an industry, then it might exert its monopoly power through higher prices to consumers. Of course, many trusts could produce at lower costs, in many cases much lower costs, than the smaller firms they were replacing. Thus the large firms could price *below* the small firms and still earn enormous profits. (It should be remembered in this regard that the ultimate "smoking gun" in the antitrust case against Duke's American Tobacco Company would be "predatory" pricing, through which Duke employed *low* prices to drive his smaller competitors under.)[68]

In Daniels's view, when the trusts successfully monopolized an industry and raised prices, that was bad, because consumers were harmed by higher prices. However, when the trusts successfully monopolized an industry by having lower costs and driving smaller businesses under with low prices, that too was bad, because the country's small business owners were harmed by lower prices. So when the trusts charged either higher prices or lower prices, that was bad for someone. In short, the trusts were bad! In print Daniels usually focused his attacks on James B. Duke's American Tobacco Company. In Daniels's words, "The organization of the American Tobacco Company with Mr. Duke at the head presaged the world of monopoly of tobacco manufacture." He continued: "The tobacco trust would swallow all competitors or drive them out of business. It was a buccaneering process . . . carried on with the genius of totalitarian rulers."[69] Daniels used Duke's firm as a metaphor for big business, but he had a specific complaint against Duke, namely his perceived mistreatment of tobacco farmers. Daniels argued that the hardships faced by North Carolina's tobacco farmers were not the result of the impersonal forces of supply and demand; rather, they were the collateral damage from the control exerted on the industry by Duke, who had enough power to drive down the price he paid for tobacco. In this Daniels was almost certainly wrong. The factors determining tobacco prices were more complex than the machinations of James B. Duke. As one historian of the tobacco market observes, "It thus appears that the chief critic of the trust [i.e., Daniels] did not understand what caused low prices of cotton and tobacco."[70] The logic of economic theory did not keep Daniels from blaming Duke for the blight of North Carolina's tobacco farmers.

Although James B. "Buck" Duke was only one among equal partners with his father, Washington Duke, and older brother Benjamin, more than either of them Buck deserves the credit for creating the Duke family fortune, a fortune generated from the machine-rolled cigarette business. It was Buck who leveraged that fortune into an even bigger fortune via the electrical power industry. In both of these pursuits, Daniels used all of his journalistic and political influence to frustrate Duke's objectives. Against Duke, Daniels enjoyed little success.

At first glance it would appear that Daniels and Duke had much in common, and one might suppose that they would be allies and perhaps even friends.[71] Both lost a parent at an early age—Daniels his father, Duke his mother. Both experienced a hardscrabble childhood amidst the turmoil wrought by the Civil War and its immediate aftermath—Daniels in the coastal plain, Duke farther upcountry in the Orange (now Durham) County piedmont. At the end of the war, Daniels's mother owned little more than the clothes on her back; Duke's father possessed only a small Orange County farm, which had been abandoned and fallen into disrepair while he served in the Confederate army. Both were self-made men in the most basic sense of the expression. Duke created one of the world's great industrial fortunes in tobacco processing and electrical power; Daniels created a considerably smaller fortune in the newspaper business. Both were devout Methodists and financial supporters of the church and its works—Daniels modestly, Duke much more prominently. Both displayed traits the other admired—personal integrity, hard work, and courage in the prosecution of their convictions. Why were they the bitterest of enemies?

Daniels was a Duke family acquaintance of long standing. Surviving documents suggest that, through the Methodist Church, Daniels knew Benjamin Duke from early adulthood. Daniels was occasionally a guest in Benjamin's home, and he described Benjamin as "a quiet unassuming gentleman of few words." Further Daniels claimed, "I never heard Benjamin talk politics and do not think he took much interest in it."[72] Unlike Benjamin Duke, his brother and father did take an interest in politics, and both men were "Republicans of the deepest dye." This fact and their growing wealth would bring them into Daniels's editorial sights. Daniels did not record when he first met Buck Duke, but in the years immediately following Daniels's move to Raleigh in the fall of 1885, he saw Benjamin Duke regularly. During one stay in Benjamin's modest Durham home, Daniels met for the first time the clan's patriarch, Washington Duke. By his own admission, Daniels liked the elder Duke from the beginning, and despite their political differences the two men hit it off. Although a biographer described Washington as "taciturn," Daniels considered the old man to be somewhat loquacious.[73] According to Daniels, unlike Benjamin, or Buck for that matter, the elder Duke "had more conversational qualities. In fact the old man loved to talk and to tell his experiences."

Washington Duke had formally created the partnership of W. Duke, Sons, and Company in 1878. By the time Washington later stepped aside, the firm's brains, energy, and vision were centered in his youngest son, Buck, who turned the modest family business into an industrial empire. Hand-rolled cigarettes were the fastest-growing component of the tobacco business at that time. After being convinced of the efficacy of the Bonsack cigarette-rolling machine, Buck gradually moved the firm out of the labor-intensive, hand-rolled cigarette and into the more capital-intensive, machine-rolled type. Between 1885 and 1888, he entered a series of complex negotiations with the Bonsack Machine Company, first securing favorable terms and later getting the manufacturer to limit production of Duke's competitors' cigarettes. With a competitive advantage built into his close and mutually beneficial relationship with Bonsack, Duke persuaded four of his competitors to merge, and in 1890 they formed the American Tobacco

Company, which in Duke's own words could claim "90 to 95% of the entire paper cigarette business in the United States."[74]

Duke would not be satisfied with *just* 95 percent of the cigarette business. Indeed, he was not the kind of man to settle for 95 of anything when there was 96 or 100 to be had. In the same year that the American Tobacco Company was organized, Congress passed the Sherman Antitrust Act, but it would take more than two decades before the U.S. Supreme Court would pass judgment on Duke's masterpiece. Daniels battled Duke every step of the way. However, little progress was made on the antitrust front during the Cleveland administration. Although the president supported a progressive antitrust policy, like his tariff policy, his antitrust efforts were quickly swamped by the economic crisis that was dragging his administration down with the economy. A number of firms were prosecuted during Cleveland's tenure, but the federal courts' rulings in all of the cases turned out to be disappointments for Daniels.[75] Thus the trust issue would still be simmering when Daniels returned to Washington twenty years later. Using Duke as the archetype of the piratical trust builder, Daniels's newspapers would help keep the issue on the front burner of national politics.

Through his position as Smith's chief of staff, Daniels played only an advisory role in the Cleveland administration's tariff and trust policies. He more directly affected the other two major issues of the day: civil service reform and Free Silver. As the head of the Interior Department's personnel branch, Daniels oversaw appointments to the federal civil service, which was undergoing dramatic reform. Civil service reform may not seem like the kind of issue upon which political careers are made or ruined, but in fact in the late nineteenth century it was a major political battleground. Theodore Roosevelt first made a name for himself in Washington over the issue, and so did Daniels. On the front page of the first issue of the *State Chronicle*, after Daniels took control in 1885, he published a piece advocating civil service reform.[76] To understand the importance of a civil service in the political firmament, one need only understand its alternative—patronage. In the absence of a civil service, government jobs were largely handed out as part of the spoils system. In nineteenth-century American politics, the admonition "To the victors go the spoils" became a way of life.

However, with the expansion of the federal government in the late nineteenth century, patronage became difficult to manage. Between 1871 and 1901, federal civilian employment grew from 51,000 to 240,000.[77] The value of the time and energy elected officials spent allocating patronage appointments rapidly dominated the value of controlling the appointments. Thus,

Congress sought relief from the patronage beast. The relief would come via the creation of a professional, bureaucratized civil service. The Pendleton Act of 1883 did this by authorizing "the establishment of a Civil Service Commission of three persons, appointed by the president, to draw up rules for the administration and enforcement of a merit system" for federal civil servants.[78] Thus the conversion from patronage to merit would in theory be overseen by the commission, and importantly, only two members of the commission could be from the same political party. While the problem appeared to be solved, or at least passed off to the bipartisan commission, in practice, Congress and the president meddled with the process.

Benjamin Harrison, the outgoing Republican president, had appointed up-and-coming New York politician Theodore Roosevelt (TR) to the commission. Although a Republican, TR was a progressive and by all accounts an honest and energetic commissioner. Rich, flamboyant, and caustic, he represented Cleveland's home state. Cleveland was no novice politico. He knew that keeping a loose cannon like TR bound to the commission in Washington was better than having him rolling around on the political decks back in New York. So TR remained on the Civil Service Commission. There was much about TR that Daniels admired. (Later Daniels wrote that TR's "patriotism and courage were a national asset.")[79] As progressives, both men were dedicated to increasing the role of merit and reducing that of patronage in the federal civil service—at least nominally. Daniels was anti-saloon politics in Raleigh, just as TR was anti–Tammany Hall in New York, but Daniels was not opposed to all political machines, only the ones he did not control. In the pages of his *State Chronicle*, Daniels had been a vocal supporter of a merit-based civil service, both in Washington and in Raleigh, but in practice he was a machine politician.

Powerful elements in Congress and back home, wherever back home might be, were not always supportive of civil service reform, so the Civil Service Commission was perpetually underfunded. Thus the conversion from patronage to a system of merit in filling federal government positions took years. Indeed, nearly a decade after passage of the Pendleton Act, only a small percentage of the eligible federal jobs had been formally converted to merit positions. Because of the chronic underfunding, the commission had to seek staff from the various cabinet departments, and at the time, TR's commission was staffed with men from Daniels's department. Since Daniels was at least nominally a supporter of the commission's objectives, the staffers served with Daniels's blessing. As evidenced by his continued service on the commission during a Democratic administration, TR was never the hard-core partisan that Daniels was, and TR thanked Daniels for providing support for the commission. The two men became friends, and all things considered, they should have continued to get along well. Sometimes they did; other times they did not.

Despite Daniels's generosity in providing civil servants to help run the commission, he almost immediately ran afoul of TR while hiring in his own department. When a position came open, Daniels surveyed the names of the three candidates forwarded by the commission, as directed by the law. He identified one of them as a Mississippian—and thus not only a southerner but also a Democrat—and sent an envoy on an information-collecting mission to the Democratic congressman from the candidate's home district. This action violated the civil service statutes, which required that the politically appointed administrator, Daniels in this case, simply review the resumes of the candidates and choose one without investigating the candidates' political connections.

When TR got wind of Daniels's violation, he heatedly stormed into Hoke Smith's office—"with his teeth showing," in Daniels's evocative words. Threatening to seek indictments against Daniels, the aide, and the congressman, TR demanded an explanation.[80] Smith, who knew Daniels was a party loyalist but also honest by the standards of the day (*Time* magazine would later call him "unpurchasable"), simply summoned Daniels with TR still in the room.[81] Once Daniels appeared, Smith presented him with TR's charges and asked Daniels to explicate. Quickly sizing up the situation and realizing he had been caught committing a grave error, Daniels pleaded guilty to ignorance of the law (and, by inference, a degree of incompetence) but innocent to influence-peddling. By Daniels's own admission, he supported the civil service laws in theory but claimed to have never actually read the acts themselves. This has a ring of truth to it. Daniels was exactly the kind of man who was confident enough of his own abilities and efforts to admit such a lapse. A lifelong journalist with a knack for clear communication in the written word, Daniels had little patience with legalese. Thus he claimed to have skipped the details of the hiring regulations. Of course, Daniels was also capable of sweating the details of any matter in which he took an interest, and it is possible he knew the law well. Daniels frequently wielded patronage strategically, and he had been testing the limits of the act through a series of political hires. TR, perhaps decently or perhaps naively, chose to take Daniels at his word and dropped the matter. However, getting in the last word, TR concluded the session by admonishing Daniels with "Don't let it happen again." When the two next met under less heated circumstances, TR chided Daniels with "All three of you ought to have been in jail."[82]

The relationship between Daniels and TR remained unstable over the years. During Daniels's remaining time in Washington, they worked reasonably well together on the conversion of federal jobs from patronage to merit, but Daniels never fully forgave TR for the dressing-down he received in Smith's office, and they would eventually become the bitterest of enemies. As for Cleveland, the man Daniels had referred to the year before as the uncrowned king of the world, his failure to deliver on the tariff caused Daniels to question his earlier support for the president. But Cleveland's mishandling of that issue was nothing compared with the disaster that the silver issue was rapidly becoming. The Free Silver movement would cause Daniels to abandon Cleveland, adopt a new hero, and leave Washington. In so doing he would open a new chapter in his life.

4. Fusion

You may talk tariff, revenue, corruption, fraud, pension
and every other evil . . . till doomsday and not one man in ten will
remember what you said three minutes after you stop. . . . But when you
talk negro equality, negro supremacy, negro domination to our
people, every man's blood rises to boiling heat at once.

—W. W. KITCHIN, North Carolina governor and *N&O* stockholder

The Democratic Party's success in the election of 1892 did not usher in an era of Democratic dominance in Washington or Raleigh. The party soon faced a disastrous schism over the gold standard (backed by the so-called goldbugs) and the silver standard (backed by the Silverites). In North Carolina, Democratic governor Elias Carr proved to be an ineffectual leader, and the split between the radical Farmers' Alliance, whose members increasingly drifted to the broader left-wing group known as the Populists, and the rest of the Democratic Party only widened. The Populists' fanatical commitment to silver contrasted with the conservatives' commitment to gold. Some radicals even called for a fiat currency backed by nothing. More troubling, the Populists and the Republicans had closely studied the results of North Carolina's 1892 campaign, and leaders from both groups recognized that a marriage of convenience would give them a majority of the state's voters. Together they could break the hold on the state government that the mainstream Democrats, whose leadership now included Josephus Daniels, had maintained for more than two decades.

However, because the Republican Party was numerically dominated by African Americans, formation of this majority coalition would bring to the fore the "Negro question": What role would African Americans play in the state's political alignment?[1] By raising this question, the Populist-Republican coalition opened the Pandora's box of racial politics in North Carolina. The coalition was made possible by the dispute between the goldbugs and the Silverites, which almost fatally weakened the Democratic Party. The silver movement reflected the fate of the Democratic Party in the 1890s. What at first appeared to be a sure winner, leading to certain

Democratic gains, turned into a fiasco. Daniels was not only an eyewitness to the disaster; he had a front-row seat.

Daniels stood, as one writer put it, "at one" with the Free Silver movement, which advocated the unlimited coinage of silver at the pre–Civil War gold-to-silver price ratio of 16 to 1. However, he lamented the split that resulted over the battle between gold and silver.[2] After only a short period of time in Washington, Daniels came to understand that Free Silver was the most important grassroots economic issue in the country, even dominating the tariff. Writing to Addie, who remained in Raleigh until Josephus was settled in Washington, he observed, "There are more free silver men in this country than I had ever imagined. The crowds [to hear Free Silver speakers] have been immense and the enthusiasm cannot be told."[3] The issue would only grow in importance over the next few years.

As silver was more plentiful than gold, a silver-based coinage promised a more rapidly expanding money supply, higher prices, and lower real interest rates to the farmers, who, according to Daniels, "had felt the grind of low-priced cotton and hard times [e.g., high interest rates]." Thus the farmers' commitment to a silver-based coinage was "such as might characterize a religious gathering."[4] From the Silverites' perspective the problem was the Coinage Act of 1873, passed by a pro–gold standard Republican majority in Congress. Because of this act, the U.S. Mint coined large-denomination gold coins but only a limited number of small-denomination silver coins. Thus the act, in effect, put the United States on the gold standard almost exactly when the world price of silver was falling dramatically relative to gold.

Farmers, who borrowed annually to put the crop in the ground and harvest it, tended to be net debtors. Since deflation caused the money farmers paid back to be more valuable than the money they borrowed, the Coinage Act of 1873 (subsequently referred to as the Crime of '73) effectively kept upward pressure on the real interest rate (the nominal interest rate plus the rate of deflation), while putting downward pressure on the prices farmers received for their crops. Thus at the 1896 Democratic National Convention in Chicago, which Daniels attended, soon-to-be Democratic presidential candidate Williams Jennings Bryan could cry out, "You shall not press down upon the brow of labor this crown of thorns, you shall not crucify mankind upon a cross of gold."[5] Because silver was no longer being coined in significant quantities, Bryan, Daniels, and the other Silverites used the expression "demonetized" to describe the metal's status. Thus during the recession of 1893, Daniels wrote that he and his Silverite colleagues "traced the [economic] trouble to the demonetization of silver."[6] The Silverites' solution to the crisis was simple: Remonetize silver, which in practice meant the unlimited coinage of silver at the (fixed 16-to-1) mint price, which would increase the money supply and inflate crop prices.

In the give-and-take world of Washington politics, silver, the tariff, trusts, and civil service reform were frequently shackled to one another, and so it was in the early 1890s with silver and the tariff. In response to agitation from various farmers' groups and western mining interests, Congress had since 1878 directed the mint to purchase limited amounts of silver and to begin once again coining silver dollars, which had been omitted from the 1873 act. Despite the limited silver purchases, with the Republicans in control of the White House and the Senate for much of the period, there was little chance of currency reform along Silverite lines, and just as northern financial interests pushed for the gold standard and sound money, northern industrial interests pressed hard for tariff increases. They got them. The result was the McKinley Tariff of 1890, named for future president William McKinley, at the time a leading Republican in the House of Representatives. The act raised tariff rates more or less across the board, driving the average rate above 50 percent. With stiff opposition from free-trade Democrats, including Daniels and most politicians across the export-based South, the northern Republicans needed to throw a bone to their sometime western allies in order to ensure passage of the tariff act. The bone they threw was the Sherman Silver Purchase Act, which increased the amount of silver the mint was directed to purchase. While the payment for western silver was an economic boon to western mining interests, the amounts purchased ultimately had little impact on the deflation gripping the country. The limited quantities of silver purchased were not large enough to substantially increase the price level.

Following the midterm elections of 1890, in which the Democrats gained control of the U.S. House, the outgoing (lame-duck) Republican majority attempted to advance their party's standing in the South. The leader of the movement, Representative Henry Cabot Lodge, sponsored the so-called Fair Election Bill, which called for the federal government's management of local congressional elections. It quickly became known as the Force Bill, a term that had a turbulent history in the South. In the tariff disputes of the early 1830s, South Carolina had "nullified" federal tariffs and refused to collect customs duties on imported goods. President Andrew Jackson then attempted to obtain a Force Bill from Congress, which would allow Jackson, as commander in chief, to force South Carolina to collect the federal duties. The conflict between states' rights southerners and hard-core unionists (including Old Hickory, who despite his southern roots was a staunch nationalist) was perceived to have been a milestone on the road to disunion and the Civil War. By labeling Lodge's bill the Force Bill, Democrats tried to stir up regional resentment against it.

Thanks to Daniels and other southern editors, the bill, which passed the House, was greeted with only slightly less loathing in the South than Jackson's bill had been nearly sixty years earlier. The act was a naked attempt by the Republicans to increase their numbers in the South, largely by using federal troops to assist black voters, who, while not yet formally disenfranchised, often faced intimidation at the polls. North Carolina's Leonidas Polk, head of the Farmers' Alliance, summarized southern opinions on the bill: "Its passage," he declared, "will be fatal to the autonomy of the states."[7] The Republicans held a slim seven-vote majority in the House; but they led by an even slimmer two-vote margin in the Senate, and it was there that the Democrats chose to wage battle over the bill. Daniels, no friend of black voters, came out strongly against Lodge's bill. "This bill infuriated the South more than anything that had happened since Reconstruction," he wrote. "It had only been a few years since the Southern white people had come into control of their affairs, and up to that time no measure had been passed which legally disqualified the mass of ignorant Negro voters in the South."[8] That Daniels added the word "legally" indicates that whites had begun intimidating African American voters even before blacks were formally disenfranchised later in the decade, which was, of course, the reason for Lodge's bill. If blacks had enjoyed the same voting rights in practice as whites did, the number of Republicans elected in the South would have been much greater than it was. The Republican majority in the Senate meant that the Democrats would have to induce some Republicans to defect to defeat the bill. They needed a wedge to drive into the Republican block. They found it in Free Silver.

Daniels claimed to have mobilized the (white) citizens of North Carolina "against that measure as they had not been against any measure since the end of the Civil War."[9] With the public aroused, Daniels helped devise a strategy for killing the Force Bill. The key player in the Senate was North Carolina's senior senator, Matt Ransom. Over the years, Daniels had carefully cultivated his relationship with Ransom, especially during the older man's campaigns across the piedmont and coastal plain. During one such stop in 1884, the year before Daniels moved to Raleigh, Ransom was scheduled to speak on the lawn of the Wilson County courthouse. In the hours leading up to the speech, Daniels let it be known around town that Ransom would be working on some correspondence at a spare desk in the back room at the Wilson *Advance*, and that the former major general in the Confederate army would not object to visiting with his old comrades-in-arms and other supporters.

Although he had once been a Whig and had advised against secession, Ransom eventually came to venerate "the great cause of the 'Rights of the States,'" and as a commander he saw much action with Lee's Army of Northern Virginia.[10] However, nearly twenty years had passed since Ransom had worn a uniform, and he could not realistically have been expected to remember the name and face of every rank-and-file soldier who served under him. In fact he knew practically none of them. But Daniels worked out a plan in which Ransom would sit in the back room of the shop and Daniels, who knew everyone worth knowing in the county, would greet any visitor seeking the senator's presence loudly and by name in the outer room. Daniels might even follow up with a question or two on some other matter that would reveal a bit of information about the visitor. That person would then be admitted to the inner sanctum, where Ransom sat at a desk appearing to be seriously engaged in paperwork. Having heard Daniels's greeting, the senator, giving every appearance of being deep in thought or hard at work, would leave his correspondence, rise, and warmly greet the person by the name. With their plan in place, the two conspirators waited for the traffic to begin flowing.

When the first visitor, a local Confederate veteran named Tom Eatman, appeared at the front door, he was greeted loudly by Daniels and then shown to the senator's room. The old general, hearing Daniels call Eatman's name, greeted his former comrade warmly: "How are you, my old friend Tom Eatman, God bless you. It is good to see you again, and I recall the courage you displayed on the battlefield in the terrible days when we followed [General Lee]." After a brief chat, Eatman proudly went around town telling anyone he could find about how after all these years the general still remembered him and his exploits on fields of battle long ago and far away. On that one day in 1884 Daniels claimed to have ushered into Ransom's presence more than 100 people.[11] Men like Ransom did not forget efforts like that.

Daniels's exertions on Ransom's behalf were about to pay off. Ransom was a good choice to drive the silver wedge between northern and western Republicans. A courtly gentleman and an old-time political operative (in Daniels's words, "a sort of glorified feudal lord"), Ransom proved equally capable in the smoke-filled rooms of Washington and the ice cream socials of small-town North Carolina. Daniels understood Ransom's strengths and weaknesses, writing, "All in all, in native gifts I never knew his superior, but he was as eloquent and learned at forty as he was at sixty. After he reached forty he never gave himself to hard study and in the Senate was regarded more as a conciliator than as a statesman."[12] For this particular job, a conciliator was exactly what Daniels needed.

Ransom's friends among the Republicans included two westerners.[13] One was a tough former sheriff named John Percival Jones of Nevada. The Coinage Act of 1873 had been detrimental to his and his state's financial health. The free and unlimited coinage of silver at the fixed mint price, which was above the world price, would have been a tremendous windfall to Nevada mine owners, of which Jones was one. Along with his colleague Senator Henry Teller of Colorado (another silver-mining state), Jones was ripe to be recruited into the anti–Force Bill movement. Through Ransom, Jones and Teller were persuaded that the (largely southern) Democrats might adopt a more strident pro-silver position in return for support against the Force Bill. Jones and Teller brought their western colleagues onboard, and when the vote finally came in, nearly the entire western wing of the Republican Party joined the southern Democrats in defeating the bill. Daniels considered the southern and western alliance a triumph for both the South and Free Silver. It was ultimately a triumph for white supremacy. It did nothing for the silver movement.

Always chary of the silver wing of his party, Cleveland had openly declared for gold, and after taking office, he threw down the gauntlet before his party's Silverites. Daniels—lamenting the president's pro-gold strategy in conversations with Hoke Smith, who also leaned toward gold—was among the first to predict that Cleveland had chosen a disastrous course.[14] The problem was that in the spring and summer of 1893, the country was stuck in a severe economic recession. At the time there was neither the theory nor the precedent for direct government intervention on the demand side of the economy. Great public works projects, federal agricultural subsidies, and public welfare programs were decades in the future. (As for intervening in financial markets, the United State did not even have a central bank at the time.) Accordingly, the economic orthodoxy, as Cleveland received it from Wall Street, was sound money, and at the time that meant gold, not silver. In a letter to a colleague, Cleveland summarized his view of the silver movement, calling it a "dangerous and delusive notion."[15] By the time Cleveland took office, the treasury's gold reserves had fallen to $100 million, and there were rumors that the government might start meeting its liabilities with silver, which was rapidly depreciating in value, rather than gold. This led to a minor panic on Wall Street. Following the advice of Treasury Secretary John Carlisle, Cleveland planned to instill confidence in financial markets by repealing the Silver Purchase Act of 1890.

Although the silver purchases authorized in 1878 and 1890 had done little to combat the deflation sweeping the country, they had undermined the confidence international financiers had in the country's commitment to gold—or at least that is what Wall Street told Cleveland. Daniels lobbied Smith hard to oppose the president's move against silver. Daniels, ever the good newspaperman, had his ear to the ground, and the sounds he heard were those of left-leaning Democrats stampeding out of the party and into the arms of the Populists because of Cleveland's firm commitment to gold. Daniels bluntly told Smith that repeal of the Silver Purchase Act "will bring no [economic] relief and it will split a victorious party."[16]

Daniels knew what he was talking about. The Populists attracted many of the country's radical agrarian groups, including the Farmers' Alliance. The Populists would cost the Democrats more votes than they would the Republicans. Smith was no fool, but he was not committed to silver, and he did not think Cleveland would change his position. After subsequent consultation with the cabinet, Smith told Daniels that when it came to repeal, "I doubt if [Cleveland] will budge an inch. . . . [He] is adamant."[17] In this Smith was correct. Cleveland called a special session of Congress in August, and after a filibuster was defeated in the Senate, the purchase act was repealed in November. Daniels summarized the result: "Cleveland won, but it was a Pyrrhic victory."[18]

The period leading up to Cleveland's repeal of the Silver Purchase Act was one of great personal trauma as well for Daniels. Tragedy struck in July 1893, when his daughter, Adelaide, only eighteen months old, died from an unknown ailment, most likely dysentery, a common early childhood killer at the time.[19] Although Josephus frequently referred to his daughter in his correspondence with his wife, he was more obsessed with Addie than with their daughter, and his feelings for his wife only deepened with the death of their first child. Josephus, usually closely attuned to his wife's emotional needs, recognized that Adelaide's death hit Addie harder than it did him. After she left Washington and returned to Raleigh following their daughter's death, he wrote to her, "I seem to feel the blow harder than ever though I know my own loss is less than yours." As difficult as the tragedy was, Josephus put his faith in God and hoped Addie could do so as well, adding a classical metaphor in his letter to her: "We must drink the cup and be as resigned as possible."[20] Even during this greatest of all challenges, Josephus's faith remained steady, as, ultimately, did Addie's. Although she spent nearly two months in seclusion after Adelaide's death, she rallied thereafter and was soon pregnant with their second child.

As for the economic crisis, the administration's renewed commitment to gold did not stop the recession, which continued into 1894. Just as Daniels predicted, the midterm elections that year proved to be a disaster for Democratic hopes. Using a biblical metaphor, first-term Democratic congressman Champ Clark described the election of 1894 as "the greatest slaughter of Innocents since the time of Herod."[21] It was one of the greatest changes of fortune in American political history. On the eve of the election, the Democrats enjoyed an 84-seat majority in the House; in the next Congress, the Republicans would have a 140-seat majority, a swing that covered well over half of the 348 seats in the House at that time.[22]

In assigning blame for his party's rupture, Daniels unequivocally pointed at Cleveland. In Daniels's view, had Cleveland and his conservative supporters not been so adamant for gold over silver, both the political and economic crises could have been averted, and the election of 1894 would not have been such a disaster. Still, despite what Daniels considered to be a gross error in judgment, Cleveland, as president, remained at the head of the party, and Daniels conceded that Cleveland knew a thing or two about politics. The president had earned a certain amount of loyalty, an attribute Daniels possessed, and so despite misgivings about the administration's direction, he stayed on in Washington after the election.

At the national level, the leader of the schismatic Democrats was William Jennings Bryan, who was among the individual losers in the 1894 elections. Attempting to move from the U.S. House to the Senate, Bryan got caught in the landslide. However, the loss invigorated Bryan, freeing him from the constraints of being a party insider. Henceforth, unshackled from the party's mainstream, he sought the leadership of an alliance between progressive Democrats and the various radical groups that now collectively formed the Populist Party. Daniels liked Bryan personally, agreed with most of his positions, and deeply admired his passion for the issues he embraced. He would eventually become an ardent follower, but at the same time he remained wary of splinter groups within the party.

Born on the eve of the Civil War in Salem, Illinois, Bryan studied for the bar and became a small-town lawyer in Jacksonville.[23] In 1887, to satisfy an ill-defined restlessness, he moved to Lincoln, Nebraska. Earning enough money at the bar of justice to enter politics, Bryan leveraged his speaking skills (which earned him the sobriquet "Boy Orator of the Platte") into a seat in the U.S. House in 1890. He was thirty years old at the time. By the force of his personality, he soon took over the Free Silver movement, and as much through his power as a public speaker as through the ideas he promoted, he quickly became a national figure. Every bit as stubborn as Cleveland on the currency issue, Bryan was generally even less disposed toward political expediency than the president. Never a man to be led astray from a righteous path he had taken, Bryan welcomed political martyrdom, remaining, in the words of his biographer, "a godly hero."[24] Losing as a result of mulish stubbornness was not a Daniels trait, but the Cleveland-Bryan rift forced him to choose between two losing propositions: gold and Cleveland or silver and Bryan. Daniels ultimately chose silver and Bryan.

Uniting race and silver as campaign issues, Daniels started referring to the Democrats as the party of those "who believed in white men and white metal."[25] He quickly became one of the country's most vocal pro-silver publishers. But given Bryan's devotion to the topic, neither Daniels nor anyone other than "the Great Commoner" (another Bryan nickname) could claim to lead the movement. It was Bryan's crusade, and on crusade Bryan proved to be a dynamic (and tireless) stump speaker in an age when the skill could carry one far in politics. Silver was not the only thing Bryan stood for. He spoke on the tariff, trusts, and liquor, all of which he was against. On almost every great issue of the day, Daniels's views aligned with Bryan's. From their first meeting in 1893, Bryan impressed Daniels. Although only two years in age separated them, Bryan was clearly the more senior of the two, and Daniels became something of a protégé. From Bryan, Daniels learned how the politics of class resentment could be used to foment a movement that could then be used to control the party. It was a lesson Daniels would apply to racial disputes back in North Carolina later in the decade. But from that experience Daniels would learn another lesson: Drumming up a movement based on anger and resentment and leading it responsibly were two different tasks, and the former was easier than the latter.

The sympathy Bryan and Daniels had for the poor—a group both men too often defined as small-scale white farmers—was sincere enough, yet they leveraged that sympathy into an "us-against-them" politics that too frequently led to scapegoating. Bryan practiced it on the economic front; Daniels did so with race. More importantly for the political careers of both men, the approach gave rise to a politics of anger. For Bryan, who had national aspirations, the resentment proved difficult to sustain in a dynamic culture of economic opportunity like that of late nineteenth-century America. In the long run, economic growth lifted millions of downtrodden Americans and their families to a level of comfort largely unknown in the rest of the world, and Bryan was left with the angriest and most intransigent of the country's agrarian malcontents.

Bryan also demonstrated a staying power that any politico might envy, especially given that he lost more often than he won. A truly great orator in the style of the times, Bryan was, like Daniels, incorruptible by the standards of his day, took unequivocal well-defined positions, and sincerely believed that the powers of the state could and should be better employed to aid his downtrodden constituents. Bryan was also an inflexible demagogue who proved poor at critically evaluating his own positions. As a recent biographer put it, "His fame and influence depended on his adherence to a worldly faith shared by millions of citizens, one that resisted the compromises endemic in policy making."[26] Although smart and tough, he was also stubborn, a weak political organizer, and a poor horse trader in the smoky back rooms of Gilded Age politics. His gifts would allow him to approach the pinnacle of American political success; his shortcomings would keep him from ever reaching it.

Torn between Cleveland, on one hand, and Bryan, on the other, and with no compromise forthcoming between them, Daniels finally had to choose. At the national level, silver beat out gold, and he chose Bryan over the conservative Cleveland. The choice meant he would have to leave the administration and return to Raleigh. There, he chose the exact opposite course, supporting the more conservative mainstream of the Democratic Party *against* the Populists. Over the next six years, he would put a great deal into that effort. This split decision—national Populist, local conservative—makes sense only when one understands that the dispute between the two groups played out differently at the national level than it did in North Carolina.[27] At the national level, the Populists remained in the Democratic Party, more or less, for the time being. In North Carolina, however, the Populists broke away completely from the mainstream Democrats. They had, in fact, defected to the Republican ranks, and after the magnitude of that disaster became apparent, Daniels prepared to leave Washington to save what he could of his beloved party in his home state.

Daniels's decision to back Bryan over Cleveland proved painful in more ways than one. Financially, it cost him. Daniel's $2,750 salary was more than he could hope to make in the near term back in Raleigh. Furthermore, at age thirty-two, he held a position of great responsibility. But Daniels could not openly break with Cleveland and remain in the administration. In the end, the advantages of staying in Washington were outweighed by his urge to return home, because by the time the full magnitude of the Democratic defeat in the election of 1894 became apparent, Daniels was already planning to leave Washington and return to Raleigh. There he once again had the opportunity to take over Samuel Ashe's *News and Observer*. This time he accepted the challenge.

OLD RELIABLE

Members of the Daniels family recall Addie frequently telling acquaintances, "Mr. Daniels loves only four things: the *News and Observer*, the Democratic Party, the Methodist Church, and his family."[28] While she occasionally tinkered with the ordering, no matter where she placed the other three loves, the *N&O* always came first. Daniels claimed he had been driven since adolescence to become the editor of the top daily newspaper in the state capital. In the summer of 1894, he realized that ambition. Henceforth, no matter what roles he would play on the national or world stage, to North Carolinians, Josephus Daniels would always be most closely associated with the Raleigh *News and Observer*. And that was the way he wanted it. He and the *N&O* became so closely associated in the minds of Tar Heels that to this day he is commonly, and erroneously, thought of as the paper's founder.[29] For better and sometimes worse, under his management the paper would inform, entertain, instruct, cajole, and rebuke the people of the state and their leaders for more than fifty years.

While in Washington, Daniels had remained active in the Raleigh newspaper and political spheres through his ownership of the weekly *North Carolinian*, and although the paper was hardly a financial success, it served as an outlet for Daniels's editorial positions. (The paper's increasingly pro-silver voice left Daniels in an awkward position in Cleveland's administration.) He also remained in possession of the state printing contract, and so the paper broke even, roughly. The same could not be said of the *N&O*. In the spring of 1894, the paper's cash flow fell below the critical level. In the depth of the worst recession in decades, the capital markets dried up, and this time no new money was forthcoming. The venerable old paper finally succumbed to the inherent logic of profit and loss. The business (formally known as the News and Observer Company, chartered in 1881 when Ashe had merged the *News* with his *Observer*, and rechartered in 1885), failed in the summer of 1894. Ashe was bankrupt.

Bankruptcy was handled in state court in those days, and the court ordered the Wake County sheriff to auction the company's assets on the steps of the county courthouse on July 16, 1894. The buyer, who paid cash, was J. N. Holding, a local lawyer, who bought the *N&O* at the direction of Daniels and Julian Shakespeare Carr. For Daniels, it proved to be the triumph of his professional life. In just over a decade he had risen from hustling subscriptions and advertising for his weekly papers in the coastal plain to become an owner of the state's best-known newspaper. The paper would remain in the Daniels family for the next 100 years. Of the *N&O* at the time Daniels wrote, "I was very anxious to get the paper and would do anything to secure it."[30] Among the things he would do was go deeply into debt to Jule Carr. But with Carr's capital, Daniels finally secured the newspaper.

The means by which Daniels became the owner of the Raleigh *News and Observer* seems to have become obscured by the number of times the story has been retold. A quick perusal of the secondary literature gives no less than five versions, not all mutually exclusive, but not all accurate or consistent. For example, the *North Carolina Biographical Dictionary* claims that after his service in the Cleveland administration, Daniels returned "to Raleigh, North Carolina where he founded the *News and Observer*."[31] This is blatantly incorrect, as Ashe had founded the *N&O* in 1881. Furthermore, Daniels did not leave the Cleveland administration until a year after he bought the *N&O*. Another version from an earlier biography of Daniels states that Julian Shakespeare Carr "bought the Raleigh *News and Observer* as a distressed property in 1894 and turned it over to the energetic Daniels to operate as the organ of the North Carolina Democrats."[32] However, elsewhere in the same volume Carr is referred to as merely a "majority stockholder" of the firm.[33] Another version, from the *Dictionary of North Carolina Biography*, avoids the financial component of the deal, simply stating that "an agent of Julian Carr in collaboration with Daniels purchased [the *N&O*] with the understanding that Daniels would be its editor."[34] Carr's biographer offered yet another version: "Knowing that Daniels was eager to buy [the *N&O*], Carr offered to back him 'up to the limit with needed finances.'"[35] This last version, which is repeated from a commemorative volume celebrating the centennial of Carr's birth, reflects closely Daniels's own version in his memoirs, which appeared in a chapter titled "I Purchase the *News and Observer*."[36]

In fact, the weight of the primary sources—some of which are in Daniels's own hand and are housed in the Library of Congress—indicates that Daniels purchased *part* of the *N&O*, albeit with a loan from Carr, while Carr also purchased part of the paper. Later Daniels purchased Carr's share of the business, and Daniels eventually paid off the loan from Carr for Daniels's initial stake. In defense of the earlier authors, we should note that the exact details of Daniels's financial dealings would have been inaccessible to anyone not familiar with his private correspondence. The title of the chapter in Daniels's memoirs that covers the event only adds to the confusion. It would seem to be self-explanatory. "I Purchase the *News and Observer*" is as unambiguous as it is untrue. Indeed, in the very chapter in which Daniels claimed to have purchased the paper, he noted that "with the lawyer's fees and the money General Carr *had put into the purchase of* [the N&O] and the paying of its [old] debts, it had cost him [i.e., Carr]" the $10,000 purchase price.[37] According to this passage, Carr bought the paper, turning its management over to Daniels. To confuse matters further, the new firm included the formal merging of Daniels's *North Carolinian*, which itself was nominally capitalized at $2,000. Even if, as the earlier biographies suggest, Carr had purchased the paper rather than loaning Daniels the money to purchase it, the inclusion of the *North Carolinian* would have given Daniels at least 20 percent of the reorganized *N&O*—though as Daniels himself noted, this "capital" included no cash, only the physical plant of his paper and its goodwill. In this case, goodwill meant literally a market valuation of Daniels's reputation as a publisher.

These confusing stories can only be untangled by a close look at Daniels's personal correspondence, which reveals that, in fact, Carr never owned *all* or even a majority of the *News and Observer*, though he was a stockholder *and* a major creditor of the firm from the day Holding purchased it. After the transactions were consummated, Daniels, who was in Raleigh, explained the details in a letter to Addie, who remained in Washington caring for the recently born Josephus Jr. (The new baby arrived in July just as Daniels and Carr closed the deal for the *N&O*.) From Carr's offices in Durham, and on Carr's stationery, Daniels wrote to his wife: "Our plan is to put the N&O in at $10,000 . . . put the North Carolinian in at $3,500 & to issue stock . . . [at] $100 a share. . . . If [an additional] $6,500 is subscribed the capital stock will be $20,000. Mr. Carr will take $1,000 of the [original] ten thousand in his name [i.e., 5 percent of the total recapitalized value of the paper] and the other $9,000 [i.e., 45 percent] will be in my name, to be held to his credit & transferred to him when he wants it."[38]

To understand this otherwise confusing correspondence, one must recognize that Daniels was conflating the financing of two separate transactions. The first involved purchasing the newspaper, and the second involved the recapitalization of the firm. With respect to the purchase, Carr paid $12,000 in cash—$10,000 for the firm and an additional $2,000 for legal fees and the retirement of old debt hanging over Ashe's enterprise.[39] In return for this outlay, Carr would receive a 10 percent equity position in the paper (the $1,000 Daniels refers to in the letter), and, in the commercial language of the day, Carr would hold Daniels's "note" for the remaining $9,000. Daniels would receive 90 percent of the stock, but he would in turn owe Carr $9,000 for it.

The second transaction brings in new capital: The $6,500 in new stock to be sold to outside stockholders would bring the recapitalized value of the firm to the $20,000 figure quoted in Daniels's letter. In return for merging the *North Carolinian* (nominally valued at $2,000 in his memoirs and $3,500 in his letter to his wife) with the *N&O*, Carr would credit Daniels for $3,500, making Daniels the majority stockholder of the newly combined newspapers. He would own 62.5 percent of the firm ($12,500 out of the soon-to-be-recapitalized $20,000). Carr would own 5 percent ($1,000 in stock), and new stockholders would own 32.5 percent (the remaining $6,500) of the corporation. In addition, Daniels would still owe Carr $9,000. This was the plan at the time Holding purchased the *N&O*. Though altered slightly by events, as explained below, this was essentially how Daniels obtained his initial stake in the *N&O*. It was a complicated transaction, involving private capital, of a type not uncommon at the time.

Ultimately, the financial accounting mattered, because ownership meant control of the paper's editorial positions, and here the deal got even more complex. If nothing else, Daniels's explanation showed that there were no practicing lawyers present when the two southern gentlemen made their agreement. Daniels explained more details in his letter to Addie. He noted his $9,000 loan was "to be held to [Carr's] credit & transferred to him when he wants it." That is to say, Carr could call the loan, which Daniels would be forced to pay in cash or more likely stock, at any time. However, "we [i.e., Daniels and Carr] will make a contract by which he [Carr] will give me the chance to buy when I want to do so, and will execute a paper to that effect in the event of his death."[40] So in Daniels's own words, the two men had agreed that Carr could buy out Daniels whenever Carr wanted, and Daniels could buy out Carr whenever Daniels wanted. The possibility that each party might want to exercise his mutually exclusive option must have occurred to the two principals, given their combined business acumen, but it was a true gentlemen's agreement. Although in retrospect, this transaction seems as odd as it does amateurish, similar deals were not uncommon at the time.

The North Carolina business world was small. Credit markets were thin. Carr could offer credit, and Daniels needed it. Carr was a veteran business-man, and Daniels, while no longer a novice, was clearly the junior partner in the venture. While their manner of doing business seems unprofessional today, it was in fact the standard in small communities across the country at the time. If either man subsequently behaved in a manner detrimental to the other, there would be a cost to pay in lost reputation, because the party that acted in bad faith would be excluded from such transactions in the future. As one observer put it, "The middle class [business]man was meticulous in fulfilling his contractual obligations, even though these were supported only by his pledged word; there were few papers that changed hands. . . . The only enforcement agency was public opinion. In the circum-stances, personal integrity in the middle class community was taken for granted; anyone who did not live up to his obligations was well advertised and lost his credit standing."[41]

Daniels had only been able to secure his first loan in Wilson because his Sunday school teacher trusted his word and capacity for work. He received his initial loan from Carr to purchase the *State Chronicle* on his pledge that he would repay Carr if the venture proved successful. Victorian notions of honor may well have driven such men, but so did cold calculation. There was no local capital market to which an aspiring capitalist like Daniels could turn for financing. Daniels's banker Joseph Brown might offer a few thou-sand dollars in short-term credit, but not $10,000 indefinitely. Carr was the surest means through which Daniels could obtain the *N&O*. If Daniels vio-lated Carr's trust, he would forfeit control of the paper, and future credit would be tougher to come by.

Despite the gentlemanly goodwill, the deal was not yet finished. Arrang-ing the financing for the purchase of the paper was only the first step in Daniels's grander business and political strategy. Another key was to sepa-rate the financial side of the paper from political patronage. In order to achieve this objective, Daniels knew the *N&O* had to do two things. First, the revenue side of the paper's books had to be dominated by subscriptions and advertising. In the future Daniels would forgo the state printing con-tract. Daniels had learned from watching and contributing to Ashe's profes-sional demise that papers that lived and died by government printing con-tracts would sooner or later end up dead. However, in order to maintain a critical mass of subscriptions and thus potential customers for advertisers, the paper had to maintain a solid "news beat," as Daniels frequently put it. Here Ashe had failed. Regardless of the editorial positions the paper took,

some were bound to offend many if not most readers at some time. To offset that fact, the paper had to provide readers angered by the editorials with
enough news of sufficient quality to maintain them as subscribers and as
potential customers to advertisers. Just as when, as an adolescent, Daniels
had gone door-to-door in Wilson, Kinston, and Rocky Mount signing up
subscribers and commercial advertisers for his first papers, at the *N&O* he
perpetually sought more subscribers and advertisers.

Second, Daniels recognized that a financially successful paper that was
the party organ—but an organ that maintained its independence from any
particular party faction, person, or legislative agenda—could be used as an
instrument of power itself. Rather than going to politicians hat-in-hand for
printing contracts or outright subsidies for the publication of opinions, as
he had been doing for the past fifteen years, Daniels envisioned a paper that
stood the previous economic relationship between politics and newspapers
on its head. If he could establish in the state capital a daily newspaper that
was profitable via subscriptions and advertising, which in turn were based
largely on its news content—that is to say, profitable without political patronage—then politicians would henceforth come to Daniels seeking his
support for their careers, rather than Daniels seeking the politicians' support for *his* career. A financially successful *N&O* would then be a platform
for Daniels's political aspirations.[42]

In order to set this plan in motion via the newly acquired *N&O*, Daniels
immediately needed one more thing: additional financial capital. The problem earlier local newspaper entrepreneurs—such as the Hales, Page, Shotwell, Arendell, Ashe, and Daniels himself—had faced was that they did not
possess either the cash flow or the necessary physical plant to see the business through the initial losses that they would inevitably face while establishing large subscription and advertising bases. This was how Daniels had
ended up in debt expanding the *State Chronicle* and the *North Carolinian*.
Daniels aimed to solve this problem by leveraging his vision into new financial capital—via equity rather than debt. As he noted in his letter to Addie,
from the day he and Carr hatched their plan to buy the *N&O*, Daniels anticipated bringing in at a minimum an additional $6,500 of new capital to be
plowed into the paper's physical plant and marketing and news-gathering
infrastructures. Although this would be troublesome, in the sense that he
would be taking on additional partners who would have a voice in the company, Daniels decided that potential headache was worth the risk.

Before raising the new capital, for reasons not altogether clear, Daniels
and Carr altered slightly their original financial plan for the *N&O*, as Daniels

had spelled it out in writing to Addie. After further negotiations, in the end, the deal was as follows: Carr put up $10,000 in cash, which included $2,000 in legal expenses, the retirement of old debt, and start-up costs; he took $1,000 in stock; and he made a $7,000 loan to Daniels, who put up $2,000 in the form of the *North Carolinian*, giving him 20 percent of the firm. Thus before they formally recapitalized the firm as the News and Observer Publishing Company, Daniels owed Carr $7,000 for the loan to purchase 70 percent of the company; Daniels owned 90 percent (20 percent purchased with the *North Carolinian* in addition to the 70 percent purchased with Carr's loan); Carr owned the other 10 percent of the firm; and he held Daniels's note for the $7,000 loan. (In addition, they had spent $2,000 on the acquisition, all of which was Carr's cash.) Now that they owned the firm, Daniels and Carr set about raising new capital to upgrade the physical plant and keep the newspaper running until its subscription and advertising bases had been expanded.

To this end, on July 30, 1894, just two weeks after Holding had purchased the *N&O*, Daniels wrote a letter from the Interior Department to 100 men in North Carolina offering them (new) shares of *N&O* stock to be issued after the firm was formally reorganized as the News and Observer Publishing Company. The handwritten version of this letter, which survives in the Library of Congress, states in the clearest language Daniels's financial needs and political objectives.[43] The key passages state frankly that the paper will serve as "an aggressive exponent of Democracy"—that is, the Democratic Party—but to do so it must be "thoroughly independent," and to achieve that independence required "sufficient" capital. All of the recipients were prominent Democrats. Daniels offered each of them one share of stock at $100 par value, and in lieu of dividends the stockholder would receive a free annual subscription to the *N&O*. Since the current annual subscription rate was $7.00, each share would earn a minimum 7 percent rate of return, and Daniels guaranteed the subscription even if no other dividends were paid. He requested that interested individuals notify him "this week, enclosing a check or authorizing me to draw on you for $100; or if you prefer, send $50. cash and your note for $50. payable Jan. 1, 1895." Since Daniels handpicked the names on the list, he was fairly confident of a good response, and it was overwhelming—"better than I expected," he confessed. More than 70 of the 100 potential subscribers accepted the offer, and "some offered to take additional stock."[44]

The list of new stockholders in the reorganized company reads like a who's who of North Carolina power brokers in the 1890s. It includes future

U.S. senators Furnifold Simmons and Lee S. Overman; future governors Charles Brantley Aycock and W. W. Kitchin; Raleigh businessman Needham Broughton, who was the uncle of future governor J. Melville Broughton; and Raleigh banker Joseph Brown. It also includes Addie's cousin and future *N&O* financier, Herbert Jackson; Daniels's brother Frank but, curiously, not Charles; and several prominent longtime Daniels associates, such as F. A. Woodard of Wilson. Daniels himself purchased 5 of the new shares and 9 of Carr's original 10 shares ($1,400 worth in all).[45] With those shares, Daniels owned 104 of the company's 200 outstanding shares, giving him 52.5 percent of the firm. Carr owned just 1 share.[46] The remaining 95 shares were distributed among the 70 or so individuals who had favorably responded to Daniels's letter of invitation.[47] After all of the financial dealing, Daniels still owed Carr $7,000 for the loan for 70 of Daniels's original 90 shares, though Carr charged no interest on this loan.

With the new capital, Daniels's ownership had been diluted, but he was still the majority stockholder and president of the corporation, as no other stockholder owned more than two shares. Almost immediately he began pouring the new financial capital into the physical plant and equipment, including new printing presses, type, and building repairs, all of which Ashe had neglected during the last years of his management. He also immediately began buying out his new partners. Daniels had no intention of indefinitely sharing the company with other stockholders. Even though his son Joe Jr. was merely an infant, Daniels intended to buy out his new partners and someday leave the firm to his heir.

There was more to the strategy than paternal altruism. Because of his strong views about the editorial side of the business, Daniels was personally disinclined to have anyone looking over his shoulder. "Early I resolved to work on my own," he wrote. "In my career as a publisher I have never wished to have a partner. . . . A newspaper to be influential should be guided by a single hand. . . . The best way to run a newspaper is for one mind to direct the policy. Division often works for such compromises as prevent effective influence on public opinion. Boards of directors can govern where only business is to be considered. A journal to be useful must never be controlled by financial considerations. Counting house direction is not compatible with the best journalism."[48] So even before Daniels took on new partners, he had resolved to buy them out. It took a long time. More than thirty years passed before Daniels once again reorganized the newspaper in 1926; by then he was the sole stockholder.

Decades later, as Daniels tried to consolidate the stock and take sole possession of the firm, a few holdouts refused to allow him to buy back their stock. For one thing, the return on the initial capital proved to be above 7 percent. Before the last of the initial stockholders was bought out, the price of an annual subscription had increased to $10; thus the free subscription given to stockholders yielded a 10 percent annual return on the original investment of $100. Daniels was undeterred; he wanted to own the paper outright with no debt and no stockholders to which he or his sons had to answer. By 1906, Daniels had retired the original $7,000 note he had sold to Carr when the two of them finalized the *N&O* deal—allegedly, as he had done with Carr's earlier loan, without paying any interest.[49] His acquisition of the remaining stock would take considerably longer. In fact, his youngest son, Frank, who eventually became the paper's business manager, was charged with buying out the remaining original stockholders when he joined the firm in the 1920s.[50]

Daniels's takeover of the *N&O* inspired the creation of several competing newspapers. Conservatives, mainly Republican business interests but some Democrats as well, saw the need for a local voice to counter Daniels's. Railroad magnate Colonel A. B. Andrews, who only a few years earlier had offered to purchase the *N&O* for Daniels in return for a more pro-railroad position, financed two morning papers, the *Daily Tribune* and the *Morning Post*. Neither was successful. A new afternoon paper, the *Times*, achieved a modicum of success. Although the *Times* was not owned by the railroads or their big investors, Daniels exposed the fact that its editor was being paid by the Southern Railway. Unlike the other Raleigh papers that challenged Daniels, the *Times* survived, limping on for decades only to be taken over by the *N&O* after Daniels's death.

As for the day-to-day operations of the *N&O*, Daniels reorganized the firm, focusing on four areas: the physical plant, editing, subscriptions, and advertising. Although the new capital would not be fully paid in for some months, the initial cash flow was enough for Daniels to purchase new type for the presses. The benefits of this purchase would be short lived, because the infusion of new capital also allowed Daniels to make a technological leap, employing a new printing system. Like many such economic changes, it involved upfront costs that were subsequently amortized in the long run through increased efficiency.

From the time Johannes Gutenberg first created the printing press in the fifteenth century, commercial printing had been accomplished by "setting" type—that is, by creating words, one letter at a time, with small pieces of metal similar to those at the end of each key on a typewriter. The process was labor intensive and expensive. As printing presses developed in size and speed, typesetting became a technological bottleneck, and typesetters' unions were among the most powerful of the early labor organizations in the United States. German immigrant Ottmar Mergenthaler solved the problem posed by the typesetting bottleneck in 1886 with his so-called linotype machine. By converting a keystroke into a piece of metal type, the machine basically allowed an operator to cast an entire line of type through a process that combined typing with metal casting. It greatly reduced the time and labor involved in publishing in general and in printing a daily newspaper in particular.

Daniels had been interested in the linotype process since he had first heard of it in the late 1880s. He began exploring the purchase of one or more of the machines even before the ink dried on his contract with Carr to buy the *N&O*. But he faced two obstacles. First, there was not a single Mergenthaler machine in use in North Carolina at the time.[51] Daniels solved this problem by consulting L. F. Alford, an old colleague from his Wilson *Advance* days. Alford had worked for Daniels and his brother Charles in the early 1880s and had eventually become the manager of their physical plant in Wilson. Later, after Josephus and Charles sold out of their coastal plain newspapers, Alford moved to Washington, D.C., and worked for the U.S. Government Printing Office. There he became familiar with the linotype technology, and when Daniels consulted him, Alford convinced Daniels that the linotype would meet the needs of the *N&O*.

The second problem Daniels faced in purchasing a Mergenthaler was the typesetters themselves. Although Daniels expected to expand the *N&O*'s circulation, increasing the demand for labor within the firm, the increased productivity that would result from introducing the linotype technology would more than offset the expected increase in the demand for labor as the firm expanded. The question arose: What to do with the superfluous typesetters? Daniels maintained conflicting views on organized labor. As a progressive who generally advocated public policies that redistributed wealth, he was sympathetic to the labor movement, at least on some theoretical level. However, Daniels was also a successful capitalist, and like any capitalist, he understood that every dime he shared with his workers was a dime that did not go into the profits of the News and Observer Publishing Company, which is to say into Daniels's pockets.

Daniels drove a hard bargain with his workers, but he convinced himself that he offered a fair bargain. To the extent that the *N&O* never experienced serious labor troubles, he might have been justified in believing that. But

Daniels dealt only with the elite typesetters. He never faced the ire of the United Mineworkers; he never required twelve hours a day from children in a textile mill; and he never laid off dozens of unskilled workers with no ready alternative employment opportunities. He might have been personally sympathetic to workers on the other side of industrial disputes, and as such he could praise the labor movement at some level of abstraction; but he never openly or stridently sided with the industrial unions against his fellow southern capitalists. He never pushed a strong labor agenda in his newspapers the way he pushed other components of his progressive agenda—Free Silver, antitrust, railroad regulation, and free trade. When it came to economics, at heart he would always be a bourgeois from Wilson. He was no Duke or Rockefeller, but neither was he a Eugene Debs or even a Samuel Gompers. He sympathized with labor in theory, but he sided with capital in practice.

Thus with the infusion of new capital, he ordered three of Mergenthaler's linotype machines. (In his memoirs Daniels claims that before purchasing the machines, he put the proposal to the firm's typesetters. Somewhat predictably, the older ones were against adoption, and the younger ones were for it.)[52] After placing his order, Daniels asked Alford to leave his government printing job to return to Raleigh and oversee the installation of the Mergenthalers and, after they were installed, to become the manager of the *N&O*'s printing operations. Alford accepted, and he held the position for more than twenty-five years. In making this move, Daniels rendered technologically obsolete many of the firm's typesetters, who were subsequently laid off, but in so doing he increased the productivity of the remaining typesetters and hence the firm's long-run profitability.

Once the plan to modernize the physical plant was in place, Daniels turned to the content of the newspaper. He installed Fred L. Merritt, his managing editor from the *North Carolinian*, in that capacity at the *N&O*. Merritt, like Alford, was a steady, somewhat colorless character, and he proved the perfect manager for the more lively journalistic staff Daniels put together. It included eccentrics like William Christian and John Wilbur Jenkins, both excellent writers in the florid style of the day. Daniels consciously put together this team, noting that the senior man, Merritt, was "methodical, careful, and accurate," while the more erratic Christian "had done some brilliant writing on New York papers. . . . He had an original style . . . the type of journalist who worked brilliantly when the spirit moved him but was not suited for the regular work day by day."[53]

Another colorful contributor was the paper's traveling political correspondent, Falc Arendell, the former owner of the old *State Chronicle* before Daniels acquired it. Arendell was a jovial, swashbuckling Falstaff, the type of hail fellow who proved to be as adept at slapping backs as he was at lifting a pint. He worked the saloons at night and followed the state's politicians from stump to stump by day. A peripatetic correspondent, he provided lively copy from all over North Carolina. Although a teetotaler and prohibitionist himself, Daniels was not above employing hard-living and hard-drinking types like Christian and Arendell as long as they produced good journalism. The sober Merritt rode herd over this unruly bunch, and through his calm day-to-day management turned the *N&O*'s news coverage into a model for regional papers across the country.

After reorganizing his journalistic staff, Daniels turned to the business side of the firm. From the day Daniels formally entered the business at the Wilson *Advance*, he understood that without political patronage a newspaper must rise or fall through its subscriptions and advertising revenues. Advertising depended on subscriptions, and subscriptions depended on the quality of the paper's news coverage. He recognized from his own experience knocking on doors in the crossroads towns of the coastal plain that there was no magic formula for increasing subscription and advertising revenues. It was all about making personal contact with potential subscribers and advertisers and then knocking on the same doors to collect the monies they owed. For this he chose three men. One was Arendell, who doubled as political correspondent and roving business agent. Daniels called Arendell the paper's "travelling representative."[54] The other two, H. B. Hardy and Wiley Rogers, Daniels called his field marshals. Like Arendell, they served as roving reporters, ad and subscription salesmen, and collection agents. Whereas Arendell was most likely to pick up customers (and a good scoop) in a saloon, Hardy specialized in covering the state's more genteel set. An accomplished musician, he would work the upper-end salons, where—in an age before radio or television—a musician could hold an audience with an evening of playing for the hosts and their guests. Rogers was the only major holdover at the *N&O* from the Ashe regime. From his days with Ashe, Rogers had staked out local politics and the business trends of the state's central piedmont region—from Raleigh to Greensboro and down to Charlotte—and Daniels always looked forward to Saturday evenings at the paper, when Rogers would return from his weekly rounds with the new subscriptions and ads and the political report from surrounding towns and counties. Daniels knew a good man when he saw one, and he never let his judgment of Rogers be colored by Rogers's ties to Ashe. It was Rogers who coined the term "Old Reliable" for the paper, a name that can still be found on the editorial page. According to Daniels, Rogers never called it anything else.[55]

Formally, at the top of the *N&O* hierarchy rested the eight-man board of directors of the News and Observer Publishing Company, but Daniels ran the company with the counsel of three men. Initially, the most important of these was W. N. Jones. A former typesetter turned lawyer, Jones sat on the board of the reorganized corporation and soon became vice president of the firm. He was a close personal friend of Daniels and often served as a sounding board for Daniels's ideas. As important as that role was, Jones made no important decisions in the firm. He offered advice, but it was Daniels who decided whether to heed that advice. Another friend who served on the board was R. T. Gray, the firm's legal counsel. He also handled Daniels's personal legal affairs.

The third member of this de facto executive committee was the man who introduced Josephus to Addie, her cousin Herbert Jackson. Formally his title was secretary-treasurer, but he was also the firm's business manager and, later, its financier. In addition he handled Josephus and Addie Daniels's personal financial matters, serving as their investment advisor and broker as they accumulated wealth. Despite the fact that Jones held the title of vice president, Jackson was in fact the number two man at the *N&O*. He was the only senior employee who could issue orders to the staff without having them first approved by Daniels, but he appears to have rarely exercised this authority. It is likely that had he done so more regularly, he might have lost the power to do so. Daniels delegated authority; everyone at the firm understood that any authority they had was delegated by Daniels, and he did not lightly share power at the *N&O*. Although Jackson would eventually leave the *N&O* and Raleigh for Richmond, Virginia, to become head of the Virginia Trust Company, he remained the family's and the firm's chief financial consultant until Daniels's youngest son, Frank, took over in the 1920s.

Although reliable figures would not be available for another decade, the paper's circulation when Daniels took over was probably between 1,000 and 2,000, with the higher figure the more likely one.[56] A copy of the *N&O* sold retail for 5 cents, up from the 2 cents Ashe had charged. (In fact, in a last desperate attempt to expand circulation, Ashe had cut the price to a penny per issue.) The paper was published six days a week; there was still no Monday edition. An annual subscription (312 papers) cost $7.00, or a little over 2 cents per issue. The paper contained eight pages (two sheets, four pages to a sheet). There was as yet no "funny page" containing cartoons or a separate sports section—though Daniels regularly published baseball scores and included the occasional sports feature. Even though the sports coverage was light by subsequent standards, it was dominated by baseball, and some readers complained that the paper printed too much about such a frivolous activity that, in their view, crowded out real news.[57] Daniels, a big baseball fan, ignored their complaints. The physical plant was where it had been since Ashe had combined the *Observer* with the older Raleigh *News*, on South Fayetteville Street in the block just north of the old governor's mansion and the future home of the Raleigh Memorial Auditorium. (Daniels eventually moved the firm around the corner to West Martin Street, where it remains to this day.) Daniels was now ready to realize the vision he had first experienced as a youth in Wilson. Henceforth, rather than working for the politicians, they would work for him, or so he hoped.

STRANGE BEDFELLOWS

The election of 1892 had propelled Daniels to the top of North Carolina's Democratic Party. His ascendancy, along with that of Furnifold Simmons and Charles Brantley Aycock, was part of a transition within the party through which the progressives replaced the Bourbons as the mainstream core. As the leaders of the dominant faction of the majority party, Daniels and company could look forward to taking over the state's government. However, the Populist revolt and the rise of a new political movement, the Fusionists, disrupted that process. The Fusionist movement represented the formal cooperation ("merger" might be too strong a word) between the Republicans and the Populists in North Carolina. The combination was a serious electoral threat to the Democrats.

Although Democrats outnumbered Republicans in the state, Cleveland's antisilver policies and the lingering recession, which hit the agricultural sector especially hard, had split the Democratic Party. Following the rise of the Populists as a clearly defined political party, and one that was largely populated with angry former Democrats, the Democrats no longer possessed an outright majority on their own. To maintain control of the state would require careful parliamentary maneuvering of the type Daniels had employed to secure victory in 1892. Unfortunately, from Daniels's perspective, no deft leadership had emerged in Raleigh during his time in Washington. Elias Carr, as much a cipher in office as he had been before he was elected, eventually sold out to the railroads. Simmons, now a customs official, and

Aycock, the U.S. attorney for eastern North Carolina, were both tied up with their federal appointments. This vacuum in political leadership created the opportunity for the Fusionists to become the new majority party. In short, following their victory in 1892, the young Turks had not leveraged their success into power in Raleigh. Their complacency cost them.

Prior to the mid-1890s, except in a few eastern congressional districts, defeating the Republicans (black or white) had been relatively easy for Daniels and the Democrats. More difficult was keeping united the various factions within the Democratic Party. The tension between conservative and progressive elements of the party created an opening for the Republicans, their first real opportunity to obtain power in more than twenty years. And they took it. In the election of 1894, the Republicans reached across the political void and grasped the hands of the disgruntled, overwhelmingly poor and white elements among the state's radical Populists. Together these groups—black and white Republicans, on one hand, and white Populists, on the other—formed the Fusionist Party.[58]

Politics makes for strange bedfellows, sometimes too strange, and the inherent contradictions among the Fusionists would ultimately doom their political control of the state. In the mid-1890s, however, they had the votes to control the state legislature. The problem was the underlying groups that generated those votes wanted, indeed demanded, mutually exclusive policies. Because African Americans composed the largest voting block within the coalition, particularly in the coastal plain, Fusion rule would mean black rule in those regions. It remained to be seen whether the white Populists in the Fusionist coalition would permit that to occur.

White Fusionists were nakedly cynical when it came to the "Negro question." A contemporary observer compared their treatment of blacks with the way the Irish were treated in northern cities, noting that Fusionists "accept [blacks] precisely as Northern men in cities accept the ignorant Irish vote—not cheerfully, but with acquiescence in the inevitable. . . . Any powerful body of voters may be cajoled today and intimidated tomorrow and hated always, but it can never be left out of sight." In short, "as a voter, the Negro was both hated and cajoled, both intimidated and courted, but he could never be ignored so long as he voted."[59] The Fusionist Party was not created out of racial harmony; it was created in spite of racial animosity among its members.

With the Fusionist victory of 1894 Daniels realized that his party's progressive agenda—which at the state level included railroad regulation, agricultural reform, and prohibition—could not go forward as long as it was blocked by the integrated Fusionist coalition. Progress, as Daniels and his fellow progressives came to define it, demanded that the coalition be broken, and that could only be achieved by driving a wedge between the coalition's poor white members and their new African American colleagues. This was part of the so-called Negro question. As long as blacks had political power, it would most likely be exercised in support of the Republican Party, and it would be a source of contention and social turmoil throughout the region. That was not the kind of progress Democrats had in mind. Henceforth, from Daniels's perspective, progress would require taking African Americans out of politics.

While the broader issues in the "Negro question" were the social standing and economic status of African Americans, the specific issue was narrowly political. In particular it involved voting rights. It would be difficult to overemphasize the animosity among white Democrats resulting from an active African American presence in the state's political life. Men like Daniels grew up amalgamating defeat in the Civil War, the Union army's occupation that followed, and subsequent economic hardship with the political empowerment of the state's African Americans. The animosity resulted from a sense of social chaos, relative economic decline, and the raw power that came from controlling political office. During Reconstruction, southern Republicans and carpetbaggers relied on the force of the occupying Union army to ensure Republican control at the ballot box, and this control extended to African American voters. Sixteen African American representatives were elected to the North Carolina legislature in 1870, and as late as 1874, after the state had been "redeemed" by white Democrats, the figure still stood at fourteen. However, on the eve of the election of 1892, the number was down to three.[60]

The withdrawal of Union bayonets after Reconstruction made the ballot box more contested. Perhaps because he had come of age during a period of violent political conflict, for the remainder of his life, Daniels would view politics as a Darwinian process in which there was only victory or defeat. As a Tennessee state senator put it immediately following Reconstruction, "The Radicals [i.e., Republicans] disfranchised us, and now we intend to disfranchise them."[61] This was a policy Daniels pursued with vigor. The squabbles between North Carolina's Bourbon and progressive Democrats for control of the state's politics had been minor family spats compared with the battles during Reconstruction and now those with the Fusionists. A "war to the knife" was a commonly employed Daniels metaphor. The struggle between the Democrats and the Fusionists was about to become such a war.

That the struggle existed at all resulted from the radical politics that had engulfed the South during Daniels's time in Washington. The region had not experienced such political turmoil since Reconstruction. The thirty years immediately following the Civil War represented a high-water mark of black political power in the region, certainly relative to the decades immediately before or after that period.[62] According to a detailed history of the era, "The impression often left by cursory histories of the subject is that Negro disenfranchisement followed quickly if not immediately upon the overthrow of Reconstruction. It is perfectly true that Negroes were often coerced, defrauded, or intimidated, but they continued to vote in large numbers in most parts of the South for more than two decades after Reconstruction."[63]

The relatively benign, even paternalistic, view of African Americans as held by the Bourbons, who dominated southern politics after Reconstruction, meant that the coercive powers of the state had not yet been fully unleashed through a de jure white supremacy regime. Following Reconstruction, whites reestablished their de facto supremacy across the region, and for the most part their conservative leaders were confident enough of that status that they seldom needed state-sanctioned pogroms to enforce or alter the status quo. As evil as that status quo appears in retrospect, it was in many ways better, or at least less openly destructive, than the changes wrought by the political upheavals of the 1890s.

At the national level, Free Silver, rather than racial politics, formed the initial unifying theme of the Populist movement, but the silver issue merely reflected a more general discontent, in the face of which the national Democrats seemed to offer only warmed-over Republicanism. Cleveland stood by gold, and the mainstream of the party stood by Cleveland. With cotton headed to 5 cents per pound, how much worse could the rural economy get? As William Jennings Bryan asked rhetorically of the conservatives, "Can you cure hunger by a famine?"[64] How much worse could poor white farmers do by forming their own political party? Not much, they answered by the time the 1894 election rolled around.

In North Carolina, Marion Butler emerged as the Populist leader. Head of the state's Farmers' Alliance, which by 1894 could best be described as a trade group with strong lobbying activities, Butler ("the shrewdest and most capable of the Alliance men," according to Daniels) proved to be as smart at political maneuvering as he was good at political organization.[65] The Populists offered the alliance members a stand-alone political party, which meant they were no longer the neglected country cousins of the Bourbon and progressive elites who made up the power base of the state's Democratic Party. Through the power of his personality and sheer physical and mental energy, Butler seized control of the movement. Under Butler the North Carolina Populists formed what was essentially a parliamentary faction that determined which way the state legislature would swing. In 1894, the Republicans offered the best deal.

Daniels identified the leaders of the Fusionist regime as Hiram L. Grant, Daniel Lindsay Russell, and Butler—a formidable triumvirate. Of the three, Daniels credited Grant with being the "father of the fusion" in North Carolina.[66] According to Daniels, Russell and Butler, successful politicians in their own ways, were elevated to the state's highest political rungs by Grant's machinations. Daniels considered Grant the true power behind the throne, the head of the Fusionist state; Butler was its prime minister.[67] A carpetbagger from Rhode Island, Grant secured the postmaster's position in Goldsboro, the Wayne County seat, shortly after being mustered out of the Union army. He prospered there as a merchant, land developer, brick manufacturer, and politician. According to Daniels, Grant was generally recognized as the "Republican leader in Eastern North Carolina." Daniels granted that Grant's personal honor was above reproach. "Although an intense Republican," Daniels wrote, Grant "was a successful business man . . . and had the confidence, in his business affairs, of the solid people of Goldsboro." In Daniels's lexicon, "solid people" meant white Democrats like himself and his brother Frank, who practiced law in Goldsboro, and the kind of people Daniels regularly dealt with personally and professionally. But according to Daniels, Grant's failings included his tendency to regard "a Negro as a black white man. In all political relations he was cheek and jowl with [African Americans] and was much hated and feared by the Democrats of his section."[68] In short, Grant was the kind of man with whom Daniels could disagree and still respect. The other two leading Fusionists, Marion Butler and Daniel L. Russell, did not fit that description.

At first glance, Butler had the most to recommend him to Daniels. Reared on a hardscrabble farm "down east" in Sampson County, Butler had nonetheless attended the University of North Carolina, which, as it had done for many upwardly mobile Tar Heels of the day, including Josephus Daniels, gave him a boost up the socioeconomic ladder.[69] After returning to Sampson County following the death of his father, Butler became a teacher and administrator at the local academy and soon turned to politics, becoming president of the local Farmers' Alliance. He then branched out, publishing a local weekly newspaper, the Clinton *Caucasian*. After the death of Leonidas Polk in 1893, Butler took control of the National Farmers' Alliance. He soon led the various farmers' groups in North Carolina out of the Democratic Party and into the Populist Party. Butler was only thirty years old when he ascended to the top of the Farmers' Alliance, but his youthful countenance masked a tough backroom political dealmaker who possessed few scruples. Known as "the sly fox of Sampson County," Butler was an intelligent, hardworking young politician with a bright future, one that would include many clashes with Josephus Daniels.

Unfortunately for his political future, like more than one sly fox before and since, Butler would raid one henhouse too many. Although Butler and Daniels agreed at some philosophical level about many of the great political questions of the day, they differed in the details. For example, Daniels favored silver over gold; Butler also supported an unlimited silver coinage, but he wanted it accompanied by a fiat currency issued by the treasury. Daniels favored rigorous government regulation of the railroads; Butler favored government ownership.[70] But their greatest dispute was over the politics of race. Butler compromised with the state's African American political leadership, to whom Daniels offered only the back of his hand. The combination of Butler's brand of racial politics and his tendency to wheel and deal too freely always led Daniels to view Butler as a slippery opportunist, and thus Daniels suspected Butler's motives even when the two opponents agreed on an issue. As a result, Butler lost any support he might have otherwise expected among the state's progressive Democrats. Butler's tendency to discard old political alliances and make new ones for what proved to be short-term gains, and his failure to build through trust a broader coalition that included some critical mass of progressives, would eventually lead to his downfall.

Daniels perceived his own progressive wing of the Democratic Party to be the Populists' natural allies. Even though his party still carried some conservative baggage—Cleveland's stand on the gold standard being the most obvious—Daniels understood that time was on the side of the party's progressive wing. As the inevitable arithmetic of the mortality table claimed the lives of the old Bourbons and as American society shifted, Daniels calculated, correctly as it turned out, that the Democratic Party would be well positioned at both the national and state levels to pursue a more progressive domestic program. It would take another two decades, the election of a Democratic Congress, and the elevation of Woodrow Wilson to the White House, but it *would* happen. All the progressives had to do was keep their message out among the populace and not burn too many key bridges to the older power structures that still controlled money and votes within the party—two steps forward, one step back, and over time the party would belong to the progressives, and the progressives would win elections. This was Daniels's view, and it drove his political and editorial actions.

Butler did not share Daniels's confidence in the long-run trends of American political life. Headstrong and ambitious, he did not possess Daniels's calculating patience. In the early 1890s, Butler saw in the disaffection of the Democratic Party's radical agrarian wing an opportunity to boost his own career, which he valued more than the party itself. Like Daniels, Butler thought the party was a means to an end, but unlike Daniels, Butler would discard the party when he thought it stood in the way of his personal objectives. Daniels was not above using the party for his own aggrandizement, but he felt that internal squabbles would come and go; in the long run the greater Democratic good, and thus the greater good for Daniels, would be achieved through, rather than without, the party. Daniels saw strength in unity, even if internal dissent sometimes had to be squashed, and even if it meant sometimes supporting a candidate with whom he disagreed. Conversely, Butler saw strength in schism. Butler went one way, Daniels another; Daniels would rise and Butler would fall, eventually. Before Daniels won the war against Butler's Fusionists, however, he lost some major battles.

After gaining control of the Farmers' Alliance, Butler set his sights on the North Carolina legislature. Having recently expanded his newspaper into Goldsboro, Butler got to know Grant, and according to Daniels, Grant convinced Butler of the logic of Fusion.[71] The various Republican and African American coalitions of the late 1880s and early 1890s had controlled roughly 45 percent of the overall vote in the state's gubernatorial elections.[72] If Butler could persuade enough of his Populists to fuse with Grant's Republicans, then the two men could divide the state's political spoils. This they did in the midterm election of 1894. Daniels was still in Washington as the election approached, and he was tied up reorganizing the *N&O*. Still, he found time to make a speaking tour of the piedmont on the eve of the election. The leaders of the Fusionist movement maintained an explicit policy of secrecy while they were assembling their coalition; as a result Daniels was not well informed about their efforts.[73] When he learned of the talks, Daniels dismissed the news and thus badly underestimated Butler's sway among the Populists, as well as the number of rank-and-file Populists who would follow Butler and vote with the Republicans. Butler had fused the Farmers' Alliance to the Populists, and now he was fusing the Populists with the Republicans.

Thus Daniels did not immediately recognize the election of 1894 for what it was: a disaster for North Carolina's Democratic Party. The day after the election, the *News and Observer*'s front page headline read, "Big Democratic Losses: The whole country turns against the party of the people." But the streamer read, "The State Safe. North Carolina Democratic By A Large Majority. Nine [the state's total at the time] Democratic Congressmen. The [state] Legislature Will be Organized By The Democrats."[74] Seldom would Daniels be more wrong. In an age when each ballot was tallied by hand, the results came in slowly. As they did, the magnitude of the defeat began to sink in, and the tone of the *N&O*'s headlines changed. Two days after the election it read, "The Legislature is Close. Republicans and Populists Confident"; two days later, "The Democrats Have Lost Everything."[75] After the votes were counted and certified, six of nine congressmen were Fusionists; all four Fusionist candidates were elected to the state's supreme court; the Fusionists controlled the state senate, thirty-seven to twelve, and the house, seventy-nine to forty-one.

Butler quickly moved to consolidate Fusionist control of the state and prepare for the upcoming gubernatorial election in 1896. The mechanism through which he hoped to secure his control was an arcane though common political issue in postbellum America called Home Rule for local governments. Home Rule in this context meant the state's counties and municipalities would largely be free to govern themselves. Home Rule would be the first major battle Daniels would fight with the Fusionists. Each state government created within its boundaries various "minor" or "subordinate" political units, such as counties and municipalities, and because voting took place at the local level and much political patronage could be dispensed there, the party controlling the state legislature had an incentive to control local governments through special legislation or the outright appointment of public officials. This control was intended to serve as a self-perpetuating cycle: By one means or another, the legislature appointed local officials; out of gratitude and party loyalty, these officials did what they could, legally and otherwise, to ensure their party remained in power. In much of the old Confederacy, the post-Reconstruction period contained an additional complicating factor: black versus white rule.

Before the Union army withdrew, former slaves, at least the adult males among them, could vote without fear across the South. As Reconstruction came to an end, however, the fate of African Americans varied. In some regions white terrorist groups, often aided by local officials, prevented black voters from exercising their rights. In other regions blacks fared better if not well. The diversity of experience across the region has been well documented by subsequent generations of historians of the era.[76] In the absence of the Union army, the experiences of blacks were largely determined by local whites, among whom a clear socioeconomic divide emerged. Upper-class planters and New South industrialists sought peace, though not equality, among the races, while working-class whites, who often competed with black labor, took a much more reactionary view of black freedom. The peace sought by white elites was reflected in economic paternalism that appeared in retrospect like exploitation. Bourbon planters wanted cheap black labor in the fields, and New South capitalists wanted cheap black labor in the factories and mines. For blacks, in most instances the paternalism of the planters, Bourbon or Republican, despite its downside, was preferable to direct competition, and thus conflict, with working-class whites, Democratic or Populist. A black legislator in Virginia claimed "that he and his race relied for the protection of their rights & liberties, not on the 'poor white trash' but on the 'well-raised' gentlemen."[77] The paternalism of the "well-raised" whites may have been the lesser of two evils, but it was a clear choice. The alternative was violent confrontation with "the developing phobias of the hillbillies of the white counties . . . as the two races were brought into rivalry for subsistence wages in the cotton fields, mines and wharves."[78]

As a result of this mixture of forces, the period between Reconstruction and the end of the nineteenth century "was a complex time for black North Carolinians. It was a time of growth and progress in many ways . . . a time of vitality and change. . . . Yet, these were also years of retrogression and ultimate disappointment."[79] This combination of promise and disappointment is reflected in the racial composition of the state legislature. Between North Carolina's readmission to the union in 1868 and the election of 1900, more than 100 African Americans served in the state legislature.[80] However, the long-run trend was clearly downward. In the legislative sessions of 1868 and 1870, at least fifteen state representatives and three state senators were African American. In the 1895 session, which directly followed the Fusionist victory of 1894, African Americans received only three seats in the state house and none in the senate. However, the postelection figure does not fully capture the revolution in the political status of the state's African Americans following the Fusionist victory in 1894. While the African American presence in elected offices was down, Butler delivered what were even more-sought-after political prizes, namely, hundreds of patronage positions accompanied by Home Rule in African American communities.

In addition to the occasional act of terror designed to cow black voters, the ruling Democrats had maintained control of state and local government across the South in two primary ways without explicitly disenfranchising blacks: through gerrymandering African American residential districts in the cities and then prohibiting Home Rule in the unincorporated areas of the counties, where blacks were most likely to live. Because the state's cities had their own charters, their citizens elected local municipal officials. To prevent African Americans from controlling the cities in the eastern parts of the state, where they often possessed a numerical advantage over white voters, those municipalities were, in Daniels's approving words, "governed by special acts" of the state legislature.[81] These acts essentially concentrated black voters into one or a few voting districts or gerrymandered their neighborhoods outside a city's or town's boundaries, formally making the town's African Americans residents of the county's unincorporated areas, which, by state law, were denied Home Rule. In those unincorporated areas the white-dominated state legislature appointed government officials. Thus in North Carolina, the white-controlled cities received Home Rule from the legislature, which their white residents, in conjunction with the legislature, used to exclude blacks from urban politics. Simultaneously, these gerrymandered blacks were denied Home Rule, as the legislature appointed county-level officials. In short, despite holding the franchise and being able to elect representatives to Congress and the state house, blacks found it almost impossible to hold local offices in North Carolina after Reconstruction.

Residents of gerrymandered black neighborhoods, whether they were inside or, as was often the case, just beyond municipal limits, could expect no public services to speak of. Eyewitness accounts of black residential areas contradict the notion that a move to town represented a rise in socioeconomic status. Such accounts described "long rows of crazy shacks of shambling rookeries, packed as close as might be along fetid brooks and creeks, railroad tracks, alleys, or unpaved red gullies which answered for roads, or abutting directly on swarming sidewalks, with from three to a dozen Negroes per room, all but universally letting in the wind and rain, lighted by oil lamps or a smoking fire (when there was a fire), often without sanitary facilities, almost never with more than a stingy privy here and there. And the whole area generally without street lights."[82] Effectively without participation or representation in local government, the residents of these areas had no means of overcoming the negative externalities associated with poverty, the most obvious of which were crime and disease.

The North Carolina Constitution of 1876 "abandoned the simple and uniform court system created in 1868, and gave the legislature authority to determine the jurisdiction of courts . . . [and it] authorized the legislature to revise or abolish the form and power of county and township government."[83] In other words, the white Democrats who controlled the state legislature also ran the county and township governments. With the addition of the authority to create and amend municipal charters, this was the means by which subsequent Democratic legislatures would control the state's politics at the local level. Whites would get Home Rule in the cities, while blacks would be denied Home Rule in unincorporated areas. Primarily through what was left of the post-Reconstruction Republican Party, African Americans sought to circumvent if not overturn the enabling legislation authorized by the state constitution. They were largely unsuccessful until the rise of the Fusionist movement.

Given the antiblack intent of the state's byzantine Home Rule laws, it followed that prior to the Fusionist triumph of 1894, blacks held virtually no local offices around the state. After the new Fusionist legislature met in 1895, however, African Americans fared well under Butler's regime, securing more than 300 magistracies alone, mostly in the eastern counties.[84] At the time, this was a great political victory for the state's African American population, arguably the most important since Reconstruction. Even as Butler was handing out these patronage appointments to African Americans, their leaders sought more from the coalition. Raleigh's James Young emerged as a spokesman for the coalition's African American contingent, and he demanded changes in the state's Home Rule laws. Hoping to solidify African American gains, Young wanted the state's municipal charters amended to allow blacks to have a voice in local politics, and he demanded repeal of the state's county government laws. In short, he sought Home Rule for the black-majority areas.

A gifted politician, Young was also a renowned newspaperman, publisher of the Raleigh *Gazette*, arguably the state's most influential black newspaper. He was also a resident of Raleigh's East Lenoir Street, making him a neighbor of Daniels, who lived one block away, literally just a few hundred feet south and west, in the Bagley home on South Street.[85] Daniels grudgingly recognized Young's competence: "[Young] was as smart as he could be, and generally managed to secure what he wished." However, in giving full credit, race could be an insurmountable barrier for Daniels. He qualified his praise by noting that Young "was a very bright mulatto and was reputed to be a son of a prominent white man in Vance County. I guess that was true. His political astuteness was attributed by Democrats to his white blood."[86]

Young recognized that the Fusionist coalition might not hold together. If it should collapse, Young wanted to ensure that his constituents got as much as they could for the long haul. If the city charters were not amended, or if the county government legislation was not repealed, then African Americans would be right back where they were prior to the Fusionist victory. However, if the state's idiosyncratic form of local rule could be killed, then the black majority in many eastern counties could control municipal elections and the county courthouse, which included the sheriff's office. This would be a big political step for the state's African American population, which found local government to be at best benign and at worst murderous during the Democratic reign that had followed Reconstruction. Even if the coalition held, Young saw no reason not to demand a larger share of the state's political lucre. Blacks represented the largest identifiable voting block within the coalition. Without black votes, there was no Fusion.

Butler, no fool, recognized that tampering with Home Rule was playing with fire. It was one thing for poor whites in his Populist Party to join African Americans in a common cause to capture the state assembly and reward blacks with a share of the patronage that came with that accomplishment. Black magistrates in black townships were acceptable, but to end the state's racist Home Rule statutes meant the de facto sanctioning of black rule in the parts of eastern North Carolina where African Americans formed a majority. Many of the poor whites on the left of the Fusionist coalition would balk at this step, or as Daniels bluntly put it, the "country Populists gagged" at the thought of black rule. Butler understood this, and he faced his own Rubicon. Driven by personal ambition, he crossed it. Doing what was necessary to round up the votes, Butler handed Young the Home Rule legislation he wanted. White control of local politics died in eastern North Carolina.

Butler made this deal because he wanted to be a U.S. senator. He planned to be the Fusionist replacement for Daniels's old colleague Matt Ransom, whose term expired in 1895. Prior to the passage of the Seventeenth Amendment to the U.S. Constitution in 1913, senators were elected by the legislatures of their state; thus Butler had to deliver on local Home Rule in order to obtain Republican support for his bid for Ransom's seat. The legislation was complicated because, although the counties could be granted Home Rule easily enough through blanket legislation, the eastern cities, including the key political strongholds of Raleigh, New Bern, and Wilmington, were governed by the special legislative acts that had to be amended or over-turned one by one. In the absence of such an effort, blacks did not control enough seats in the legislature to hold up Butler's agenda, but black votes in subsequent elections would be needed to keep the coalition in power. Butler was determined, however, and he managed to ram through part of Young's agenda, which handed county control to popularly elected three-man commissions, and which meant black rule in much of the eastern part of the state.[87] As for the cities, that issue was much more problematic.

Daniels thought Butler was foolish in turning local government in the coastal plain over to African Americans. However, Butler's position within the Fusionist coalition was more precarious than Daniels imagined. Be-cause Daniels wrote off the black vote, he simply assumed the state's Afri-can Americans would vote in lockstep with Butler. Although blacks did vote overwhelmingly Republican, their turnout on Election Day depended on their enthusiasm for the slate, and they maintained a well-placed skepti-cism about the Fusionist movement. (In addition, many votes, white as well as black, were up for bid on Election Day). As one history of the period noted, initially "Fusion did not prove popular with the Negroes of North Carolina."[88] Butler had to deliver the tangible reward of Home Rule in re-turn for black support. If he failed to deliver, subsequently putting together the votes to perpetuate Fusion control would be difficult, especially in the crucial upcoming gubernatorial election.[89]

However, in shattering the monopoly whites held on local government, Butler altered the racial equilibrium in post-Reconstruction North Caro-lina. The state's arcane laws regulating local government were not the result of political serendipity; rather, they were the well-thought-out legal mani-festation of de facto white supremacy. Whites could not maintain their su-perior social status if they surrendered the coercive powers of the govern-ment to blacks. A black magistrate, justice of the peace, or deputy sheriff represented an extension of state power. In the exercise of that power a black man dominated a white man. No one understood this better than Daniels, who quickly became the spokesperson for the state's white power establishment. Under the state's pre-Fusionist system of local government, Daniels wrote, "the control of the finances of the county was in the hands of magistrates appointed by the Legislature and not elected by the people. This prevented Negro magistrates in the East and Negro power in county finances. The Democrats believed that a change in the system would bring the State back to the bad conditions that existed in the days of reconstruction. They would have sacrificed almost anything to keep the county government system."[90] These were ominous words, foreshadowing what was to come, and they demonstrate that Daniels understood the sociology of his state better than Butler did. Daniels predicted that Butler's Home Rule strategy "would be the undoing of the Fusion."[91]

When Butler began bringing the Home Rule acts to the floor of the legislature during its 1895 session, Daniels and the Democrats fought a ferocious rearguard action. In the end, from all perspectives, the legislative session proved to be decidedly mixed. On one hand, there were some notable Fusionist successes. Jeter Pritchard, a Republican Fusionist, had been elected to replace Senator Zebulon Vance, who had died in office the previous year. (Vance's seat had been temporarily occupied by former Democratic governor Thomas Jarvis.) Also, as planned, Butler replaced Ransom. Thus the state's two U.S. senators were Fusionists. The state's supreme court was solidly Fusionist. The constraints on Home Rule in the unincorporated areas of the state's counties were removed, ensuring African American and Fusionist gains in the next election. The state's patronage had been carved up among Fusionist groups, and as noted, the legislature had already appointed hundreds of African Americans to local offices before the Home Rule laws were reformed. Of these gains, the writer W. J. Cash observed, "In Craven County [in the coastal plain], North Carolina, as the peak and crown of it all, sixty-two Negroes got back into office. In more than fifty of the Tar Heel counties black magistrates sat again in judgment of white men—and, as the [white] orators did not fail to note, white women. Black inspectors passed into white schools and gave orders to white teachers, most of them women."[92] Such scenes did not play well with the white Populists in Butler's coalition. Still, despite disputes over the spoils of victory, the Fusionist coalition held, and with gubernatorial elections approaching, its leaders had every expectation of further advancing their cause.

These were clearly gains for Butler's forces. Yet when compared with Fusionist expectations, the 1895 legislative session must be qualified as a disappointment. Other than their exploitation of the spoils system and the demise of white rule at the county level, the Fusionists achieved little of significance. In particular, the Fusionists failed to overturn the legislation that maintained white rule in Raleigh. Young was the strongest proponent of this particular effort both behind the scenes with Butler and in the legislature. Daniels excoriated Young and Butler in the *N&O*, claiming they were trying to "Negroize Raleigh."[93] Daniels and the supporters of white rule won the day, keeping Raleigh in the Democratic camp. The battle was a harbinger of things to come and should have been a warning to the Fusionists, because the Democrats won through the defection of a faction of local Fusionists led by Wake County Populist A. C. Green.

Daniels guessed correctly that by carefully manipulating the issue of race he could leverage white Populists back into the Democratic fold. (The vilification of J. B. Duke's American Tobacco trust, which Daniels presented as the enemy of small-scale tobacco growers, was part of this strategy. That Butler was backed by Duke money only helped Daniels's cause.)[94] Thus Raleigh was safe for now. As for the other major cities, according to Daniels, "The Republicans in the Legislature set out to gerrymander the towns and cities so as to put them under the rule of Negroes and their cohorts."[95] In other words, the Fusionists attempted to pass legislation that would overturn the city-by-city Home Rule acts the Democrats had passed and enforced since Reconstruction. In Raleigh the Fusionists had failed. Daniels had won. Importantly, however, Democratic efforts to keep Wilmington in the exclusively white camp failed.

In his efforts to keep Young from taking over Raleigh's municipal government, Daniels learned that in regard to race, demagoguery worked, a strategy William Jennings Bryan had been using successfully with respect to class. The threat of African Americans holding local offices, and thus having some control over whites, was enough to drive some white Populists back into the arms of the Democrats. But Daniels needed more. Miscegenation—the mixing of races—was an especially volatile aspect of black-white relations, and Daniels exploited it during the Fusion wars. It was one thing to rail about race mixing in general, but like the threat of black rule in Raleigh, what Daniels needed was a specific example of Fusionist support for miscegenation. In the battle for control of the municipalities, Butler, generally a deft politician, handed Daniels such a case.

African American abolitionist Frederick Douglass died on February 20, 1895. Innocently enough, in honor of Douglass, a Fusionist in the North Carolina house introduced a resolution calling for the house to adjourn for a day. The resolution was adopted. Daniels pounced. Douglass's first wife, an African American, had died many years earlier, and Douglass subsequently married a white woman twenty years his junior. This was high scandal in social circles, in the North as well as in the South. The day after the Douglass resolution passed, the *N&O* claimed that the act was a thinly disguised Fusionist endorsement of miscegenation, and the paper made the case that promotion of miscegenation would follow endorsement of it. Indeed, Daniels went so far as to turn Fusionism itself into a metaphor for miscegenation. "Fusion is a marriage of two parties having no principle in common. The endorsement of a miscegenationism leader is the legitimate heir of that union. . . . The essence of Fusion is to break down all barriers and solve the Negro question by marriage between the races." It was, in short, "the climax of infamy."[96] One need not be a high school English teacher to appreciate the careful use of the words "marriage," "union," and "climax."

Daniels also noted that the same legislature that had elevated Douglass's death to a holiday refused to adjourn in honor of the birthdays of George Washington or Robert E. Lee. White Populists now openly denounced their leader, Butler, and many claimed the Douglass resolution was rushed through without their knowledge. Butler was steamrolled by the episode. To salvage some goodwill among the racist elements of his own coalition, Butler quickly arranged to have passed an appropriation of $10,000 to complete a Confederate monument on the west side of the state capitol (where it remains to this day, mutely glorifying "Our Confederate Dead").

With the 1895 session of the legislature behind them, the various players prepared for the gubernatorial battle of 1896. Despite the Frederick Douglass fiasco and the failure of the Raleigh Home Rule act, the Fusionists held the upper hand, and the Democrats clearly remained on the defensive. With Fusionists in control of the legislature, the courts, and the state's patronage, the election of 1896 would possibly usher in the beginning of a long Fusionist reign, or so hoped Butler and, behind the scenes, Hiram Grant. Unfortunately for the visions (and careers) of Butler and Grant, the man to whom they turned to wear the crown of their polyglot empire, Daniel Lindsay Russell, proved to be a poor choice.

With the puffy eyes of a turtle, a double chin, and a protruding midsection, and sporting his ever-present hat, dapper waistcoat, and cigar, Russell looked like the very embodiment of the self-satisfied Gilded Age plutocrat. In fact, his complaisant countenance and deportment hid the soul of a swashbuckling politico. The product of the union of two old and rich Brunswick County slave-owning families, Russell might have been the quintessential Bourbon were it not for the fact that he was an ardent Republican. Even more odd was that Russell's Republicanism did not reflect a venal Reconstruction opportunism. Although Russell was more than capable of such opportunism, his Republicanism came honestly. Russell's father had been a leading Whig and antisecessionist before and during the Civil War. It was a principled and unpopular position among the social elite of the lower Cape Fear River valley, and after the war, like many old Whigs, the Russells joined the Republican Party.

The postbellum economy was not kind to the Russell estate. Whereas North Carolina's coastal plain was well suited for tobacco, cotton, and "the hog and hominy," the swamps and sandy wastes of the lower Cape Fear were best suited for rice. Although the crop had been grown there successfully since early colonial days, the end of slave labor and the subsequent shift of rice production to the Gulf eventually ended North Carolina's contributions to the world rice market. Although Russell still owned much land, it was no longer very valuable, and so he turned to politics. More successful in politics than agriculture, Russell and a few of his white Republican colleagues formed what became known as the "Wilmington Ring."[97] Russell's white colleagues were indeed few in number, as whites were a minority within a minority party; roughly 90 percent of southeastern North Carolina's Republicans were African Americans.[98] Still, the Wilmington Ring did well enough in local politics in the years after Reconstruction, and Russell spent time as a judge, a state legislator, and a U.S. congressman. But none of these offices fully satisfied Russell's piratical nature. Fusion offered him a chance to seize a bigger prize, control of the state's government. Grant and Butler would hand it to him. These three men—Grant, the Yankee war hero turned carpetbagger; Butler, the up-and-coming Populist publisher; and Russell, the Republican planter—formed the trinity of North Carolina's Fusionist movement.

Daniels did not consider these men his moral equals. He always preferred an honest opponent, like Hiram Grant or Buck Duke or Theodore Roosevelt, men he respected, to a wily former ally and apostate like Butler. After Butler's first speech in the U.S. Senate, in which he made negative remarks about the Democratic Party in North Carolina, Daniels showed no mercy in the pages of the *N&O*, calling Butler a "turn-coat and blatherskite" and threatening "to peel the hide off this young boastful slanderer of his betters."[99] The reference to peeling the hide off Butler would not be lost on the African American members of Butler's coalition.

Recognizing that the election of 1896 would probably not go well for Democrats in North Carolina, for the first time in his career, during a political campaign Daniels focused more of his energies at the national than the state level. Daniels gambled that the national candidate, his new political hero William Jennings Bryan, who was in the process of fusing Populists with the Democrats at the national level, largely through the silver question, would help offset Fusionist momentum in North Carolina. In this Daniels's hopes were dashed. The election of 1896 was a disaster for the Democrats at both the state and national levels. Bryan took the Democrats down to defeat. But in North Carolina, the election of 1896 would be the low point for the Democratic Party. After that, the party's fortunes would ebb and flow at the national level, but in North Carolina, it would be the last electoral debacle in Daniels's lifetime. More than any other person, Daniels would be responsible for the subsequent long string of Democratic victories.

5. A Nuisance and Disturber

The big question that now loomed was the best plan of
withdrawing from the ignorant Negroes, who had been used as tools
for the bad government that cursed the State, the right of suffrage.

—JOSEPHUS DANIELS

Daniels resigned from the Cleveland administration in the summer of 1895, and he was soon back in Raleigh full time, running the *News and Observer.* The infusion of new capital and Daniels's vigorous management revived the *N&O.* The paper had no serious daily competitor, and its circulation quickly reached 10,000 at a time when Raleigh's population was only a bit more than that. Although a complete reconstruction of the firm's accounts is not possible for these years, it is clear from Daniels's correspondence that the business was a financial success. A conservative estimate would yield annual profits of $6,000 to $7,000.[1] As the firm paid no regular dividend to its outside stockholders (they received only their annual subscriptions), Daniels was essentially the residual claimant of the company's profit. Within a year of taking over the paper, Daniels was clearing between $3,000 and $4,000 (more than ten times North Carolina's per capita income at the time), more than he had made as Hoke Smith's chief of staff in the Interior Department. Only thirty-three years old at the time, Daniels had moved well beyond middle-class comfort.

During the first eighteen months Daniels owned the *N&O,* on a day-to-day basis, combating the Fusionists was the primary editorial objective of the newspaper. However, in the spring of 1896 Daniels turned back to national politics and the upcoming presidential campaign. In those days, the national conventions were the means by which the parties actually nominated their presidential candidates. The state parties typically conducted an election for delegates to the national convention. These delegates, usually local politicos of varying degrees of prominence, would on occasion formally announce their support for a presidential candidate, or they might quietly signal their support for a particular candidate. But frequently they were elected to exercise their judgment based on what transpired at the convention itself. Thus to be a state delegate was to be recognized as a key player in party affairs and offered the possibility of being a kingmaker at the convention.

By the spring of 1896, Daniels was clearly a leader of North Carolina's Democratic Party, but he was among the youngest members of the shifting inner circle in Raleigh. Accordingly, he thought that if he were elected as a delegate to the upcoming Democratic National Convention, to be held in the Chicago Coliseum between July 7 and 11, his new, lofty standing would be recognized. Unfortunately for Daniels, the number of convention delegates was much smaller in those days than it is today.[2] Under national party rules, North Carolina would only send twenty-four delegates to the 1896 convention. Thus the seats became valuable political property.

Daniels had attended the 1892 Republican National Convention in Minneapolis on his way back from a vacation in California (taken after he sold the *Chronicle*), but he had never attended a Democratic convention. He understood that any number of older party loyalists, men who had shed more blood over more years than he had, sought the position. Still, he had ambition alloyed with hope, frankly confessing that he "was anxious to be elected to that convention."[3] To that end, he quietly began sending out feelers to see who else might be in the running and who among the local sachems might be willing to back his candidacy. His heart fell when he learned that Wake County sheriff Mack Page was in the running to be the local delegate.[4] Despite his yearning for the position, Daniels could not hope to beat Page, a former Confederate officer, and Daniels settled on accompanying the delegation as a journalist.

Feeling, in his own words, "quite miserable about" not being a delegate, Daniels soon achieved a more important position in the party. Page and Daniels traveled on the same train to Chicago, and during the trip Page initiated a campaign to have Daniels elected as the delegation's representative to the Democratic National Committee. The position was open because its longtime occupant, former senator Matt Ransom, was stepping down. Having lost his Senate seat to the Fusionist Marion Butler the previous year, Ransom was now U.S. ambassador to Mexico. Daniels professed surprise at Page's proposal. "I had not the remotest idea at being elected national committeeman," he wrote.[5] This claim is disingenuous at best. Daniels knew Ransom was out of the running, and Daniels must have suspected that if the delegation sought a younger man to fill the slot, then as the foremost member of the party's younger generation, he had a better than 50-50 shot at the position.

Among the North Carolina delegates, the leading senior candidate for the national post was Thomas Jarvis, a former governor and former senator against whom Ransom held a long-standing grudge. Before accepting the U.S. Senate seat of Zebulon Vance, who died in office, Jarvis had challenged Ransom for his long-held seat, and the two had been competitors for party leadership while both served in the Senate.[6] The Fusionist victory in 1894 rendered moot the dispute, sending both old Democrats into retirement. While filling his new diplomatic sinecure, however, Ransom cultivated his bitterness toward Jarvis. When he received word that Jarvis sought to replace him on the Democratic National Committee, Ransom served his revenge by promoting a younger alternative candidate—Josephus Daniels. At first, this was done behind the scenes, but within the delegation, the pro-Jarvis forces suspected Ransom of boosting the younger candidate's chances.

Soon the issue came out into the open, and Daniels was forced to declare his interest in the position or renounce any claim to it. Having passed on the opportunity to challenge Sheriff Page for a delegate's seat, Daniels decided to contest Jarvis's claim to the national position, and so Daniels declared his interest in the job. Not surprisingly, Jarvis, more than twenty-five years Daniels's senior and yet another ex-Confederate officer, expressed outrage at the upstart's challenge. Daniels, as usual, downplayed the internecine strife his candidacy initiated, noting only that Jarvis became "aloof" once he understood that his seat on the committee would be challenged.[7] Jarvis also should have been worried. The vote-counters figured Daniels to be the winner. The Baltimore *Sun*'s correspondent at the convention observed that Daniels's "candidacy has reached a point where he will be hard to defeat."[8] And so it was, as both youth and Matthew Whitaker Ransom's revenge were served. Daniels won by a vote of 13 to 9 (with 2 abstentions). He was now on the Democratic National Committee and would remain there for the next twenty years.[9]

CROSSES OF GOLD AND SILVER

After being elevated to the national committee, Daniels pursued two mutually supportive objectives. One was to see that the party's platform was built of silver rather than gold, and the other was to see that Bryan received the nomination for president. The former proved easier than the latter. Many in the party blamed Cleveland and his goldbug supporters for the recession of 1894 and the party's disastrous defeat in the election of that year. Daniels claimed that Cleveland wanted to be renominated, but there was little hope of that. Cleveland's supporters and his detractors battled over a resolution to endorse his administration. It went down by a vote of 564 to 357. Cleveland's long political career was over.

The vote on Cleveland was really a referendum on gold. However, supporters of silver demanded a formal vote on the inclusion of a Free Silver plank in the party platform. They got it, and silver beat gold by a vote of 624 to 301. With that vote, the return to the pre–Civil War bimetallic standard, under which the U.S. Mint would coin unlimited amounts of silver at a fixed gold-to-silver price ratio of 16 to 1, became the official position of the Democratic Party. Summarizing the matter, Daniels wrote, "In the atmosphere of the hour a man had to be militant for 16 to 1."[10] Cleveland was not such a man. Bryan was, and his hour approached.

The party's broad sentiment for silver soon became difficult to disentangle from its sentiment for Bryan. However, the Great Commoner's nomination was no sure thing. As Bryan's biographer notes, "The old guard [of the Democratic Party] was not going to yield without a struggle."[11] Bryan's own seat in the Nebraska delegation had been challenged by his state's conservatives. Bryan was an underdog to win the nomination, but it would be incorrect to say that he came from nowhere. In fact, six weeks earlier, on May 26, Daniels had declared for Bryan in the *N&O*, calling him "the most eloquent public speaker in America." To rally Tar Heel Democrats around Bryan, Daniels employed a comparison sure to resonate with party loyalists, writing that Bryan "is a sensible, honorable, and brave man and would create an enthusiasm that would be as surprising to the whole country as Vance's [gubernatorial] campaign of 1876 was in North Carolina."[12] Evoking the name of the recently departed Vance tied Bryan to the state's hallowed past, especially its salvation from Reconstruction. This, Daniels knew, would give Bryan's candidacy a popular boost in North Carolina.

Once the convention opened, Bryan's name quickly moved near the top of the list of potential nominees. The convention schedule placed the five key speeches on the third day, Thursday, July 9. Although nominally the party platform was the topic to be addressed, all those present recognized that the nomination itself hung in the balance. In addition to Bryan, the speakers included the agrarian radical "Pitchfork Ben" Tillman and three conservatives who would make the case for perpetuating Cleveland's policies if not his reign. Confidant he could upstage this crew, Bryan arranged to speak last. This was fortuitous for the Silverites, as Tillman nearly sank their cause with a needlessly inflammatory speech that, incredibly, threatened secession if the radicals' Free Silver demands were not included in the platform. Daniels admired Tillman, a South Carolinian, and the two became close friends over the next few years, as increasing racial tensions in North Carolina brought out the worst in each man. Tillman's speech created a storm of protest within the party, but Daniels hardly mentioned it at the time or later. His tendency to keep intraparty disputes from public scrutiny, or to downplay them after they became public, overcame his sense of journalistic responsibility. As luck would have it, all three of the conservatives who spoke between Tillman and Bryan gave speeches as dull as Tillman's had been fiery. As the last of the three wound down, a reporter passed Bryan a note that read, "You have now the opportunity of your life." Bryan replied, "You will not be disappointed."[13] Bryan's hour had arrived.

With virtually no fanfare, Bryan delivered one of history's most memorable speeches. Daniels wrote, "Bryan had not been speaking five minutes before he held the convention rapt. I had never dreamed that a mortal man could so grip and fill with enthusiasm thousands of men."[14] Daniels often succumbed to the temptation to be too effusive in his praise of certain men, and Bryan was one of those men, but on this occasion Daniels recorded it as it occurred. Bryan began by wrapping the progressive program in a holy shroud. "The humblest citizen in all the land, when clad in the armor of a righteous cause, is stronger than all the hosts of error. I come to speak to you in defense of a cause as holy as the cause of liberty—the cause of humanity."[15] He made the case that the country's conservative forces, whether they were Republican or Democrat, had sold out "the cause of humanity." The tariff and the trusts were the instruments of exploitation by "the few financial magnates who, in a back room, corner the money of the world."[16]

In Bryan's worldview, however, one transgression transcended all others: the gold standard. As Daniels summarized Bryan's position, "Free silver was the expression of the hope for legislation of a people who had been through the panic and hard times and were seeking to strike at a government of privilege," whereas gold was the policy of the money men.[17] Thus the great political question of the day became silver or gold? That was the fault line Bryan clarified for the audience, the grievance to which he had distilled the differences between the conservatives and the progressives in his own party. And on that point, he brought his speech to a rapid climax and triumphant conclusion: "We will answer their demand for a gold standard by saying to them: You shall not crucify mankind upon a cross of gold."[18] Mimicking Christ on the cross, Bryan stood onstage motionless for several seconds. As his words echoed through the coliseum and he posed with his arms stretched wide, the crowd made not a sound. And then, all at once, the room exploded. Daniels's eyewitness account read, "It was spontaneous. Attempts to shorten or quell it were as impossible as the attempt of Canute to drive back the waves of the ocean."[19]

Bryan won over the convention with his Cross of Gold speech. His candidacy rose with each subsequent round of voting, and he was nominated on the fifth ballot, becoming at age thirty-six the youngest presidential candidate before or since. The power brokers now considered a running mate. Daniels joined the handful of other solons who gathered backstage to choose a vice president. The group settled on national committeeman Arthur Sewall, a Maine shipbuilder who had never held elective office, as the least offensive of the potential candidates, and so the names Bryan and Sewall headed the ticket. At the time, Daniels acquiesced in the nomination of Sewall. The choice seemed logical enough. It appeared that Sewall satisfied the Hippocratic oath of vice presidential candidates. He did no harm to the ticket, so Daniels went along with the group.

Following the convention, Daniels returned to Raleigh. After checking in at the *N&O* and collecting a clean set of clothes, he left for the Populist Party convention, which was held in St. Louis on July 21. Daniels traveled to St. Louis as a journalist, accompanying the North Carolina Populist delegation led by Marion Butler. According to Daniels, Butler wanted to control the national Populist apparatus and fuse it with the national Republicans. As Daniels put it, Butler "wanted to trade, in the nation, as he had traded in North Carolina."[20] This became unlikely after the Republicans nominated William McKinley, a gold standard advocate, at their convention in June. According to Butler's biographer, prior to the Democratic convention, Butler expected the Democrats to also nominate a pro-gold candidate, which would allow the Populists to offer a pro-silver alternative to the two main parties.[21] However, by choosing the radical Bryan, the Democrats outflanked Butler on the left. Although many Populists supported a fiat currency—that is, money backed by neither gold nor silver—Butler could not hope to nominate a candidate to the left of Bryan with a reasonable chance of success; thus the Democrats had forced Butler to support Bryan, or at least to feign support.

The only other potential Populist candidate of any note was Thomas Watson, a one-term congressman from Georgia. A radical, Watson had abandoned the Democratic Party, as Butler had, but Watson's virulent racism kept him from joining any Fusionist coalition. So in his challenge to

Bryan, Watson found himself between the pro-Democratic faction and the pro-Republican Fusionist forces at the convention. Watson's vitriol resonated with a substantial proportion of the disaffected whites who formed the foundation of the Populist Party. Once turned loose in St. Louis, he threatened to either splinter the coalition or take control of it. Butler, perhaps recognizing the threat posed by Watson, became the staunchest of Bryan supporters if for no other reason than to offer a counter to Watson. According to Daniels, who knew both men well, "Butler did not want Watson. He disliked him. He knew Watson would take the scepter from him if he could. [Butler] wanted to hold the reins but he feared Watson."[22]

Butler was wily, and his cunning allowed him to see a deal in the making. Although many Populists preferred leaders whose positions were as radical as their rhetoric was inflammatory—men like Watson—they were nonetheless prepared to accept Bryan's candidacy, but not Sewall's. Yankee capitalists were near the top of their list of enemies to be punished should they obtain power. They were not going to accept one on the ballot. Recognizing as much, Butler threw his weight behind Watson for the vice presidency. Butler hoped to stick the Georgia firebrand in a do-nothing job while simultaneously weakening the national ticket. Butler's objective, according to Daniels, was to sacrifice the 1896 race, and in so doing he would convince the Populists that the Republicans offered a brighter future than the Democrats. Daniels, lamenting the negative impact of two vice presidential candidates running simultaneously with Bryan, saw through Butler's game but could do nothing to stop it.[23]

Thus the selection of Sewall, a relatively conservative northeasterner to the right of Bryan on most issues, opened the door for the Populists to nominate someone more radical than Bryan as their vice presidential candidate. Daniels realized a catastrophe was in the making and thought it was the single biggest issue in the campaign. He noted that the Populists "drove a nail into the coffin of the Democratic victory when [they] refused to endorse the nomination of Bryan and Sewall and threw a discordant and demoralizing element into the campaign by the nomination of Watson."[24] Still, Daniels had to pay homage to Butler's clever outmaneuvering of both Watson and the pro-Democratic wing of the Populist Party. Watson was "more audacious than Butler but neither so cunning nor so shrewd," wrote Daniels with disgusting admiration. Butler, he added, "made the leaders of the Democratic Party think [he supported Bryan], although those who knew him best never fully trusted him."[25]

For the Democrats, what had started in the spring as a hopeful, unified

movement away from Cleveland's brand of conservatism to a more progressive candidate and platform had by late summer turned into a messy
battle between the party's progressives and the Populists. To add to the
confusion, the so-called Gold Democrats, what was left of Cleveland's conservative wing of the party (the "Yellow Bellies," in Daniels's lexicon), held
a convention in Indianapolis in September and nominated two Civil War
generals, John Palmer and Simon Bolivar Buckner, to run for president and
vice president, respectively. Palmer was seventy-nine and Buckner was
seventy-three. Both had reached the rank of general before Daniels had
even been born. The old warriors did not put up much of a fight as candidates, but they did threaten to split further the already fractured Democratic vote. As the hard campaigning got under way, the three most identifiable Democratic factions had between them two presidential and three
vice presidential candidates. Inauspicious was perhaps the most generous
way to describe the party's chances of keeping the White House.

Despite the awkwardness of having two running mates, Bryan was a
tireless campaigner, and Daniels accompanied him on his campaign tour
through the East. They parted shortly before the election with great hope,
but that hope was thwarted, as the 1896 election proved to be an even greater
disaster for North Carolina's Democrats than that of 1894. The Democratic
gubernatorial nominee, Cyrus Watson, was a decent enough legislator
from the state's central piedmont region. He might well have won, replacing the ineffectual Carr; but unlike the national Populists who nominated
the same presidential candidate as the Democrats, the state party—which
is to say the rump that remained after the Populist leaders fused their party
with the Republicans—had nominated their own candidate, W. A. Guthrie,
who split the anti-Fusionist vote. To make matters worse, Watson became
ill during the height of the campaign season and was forced to leave the
stump. Although the Fusionist camp was not of one mind—after a bitter
fight between the old-guard Republicans and their new Fusionist allies, the
party nominated Dan Russell from the Lower Cape Fear region—the party
possessed enough votes to put their man in the governor's mansion.

At the national level, gold crushed silver, as McKinley and his running
mate, Garret A. Hobart, defeated Bryan and his duo of running mates by
an electoral count of 271 to 176. Bryan carried North Carolina handily, but
he carried Republican-Populist Fusionists with him rather than either the
mainstream Democrats or Guthrie and the rump Populists. The diver-
gence between the national and state political alignment of parties confused efforts to interpret the state's election results along national lines.[26]

By any accounting, however, the fortunes of the state's Democratic Party were lower than they had been at any time since Reconstruction. Russell won the governorship in a landslide. The Democratic seats in the North Carolina senate sank to 9 (out of 50), while in the house the figure was 35 (out of 120).[27] In addition to the general rout, Daniels suffered a personal affront in the election. His close friend and publishing colleague Needham Broughton stood for Raleigh's North Carolina house seat against the Fusionist James Young. Daniels campaigned hard for Broughton with the expectation that the white Baptist Broughton would defeat the upstart African American Young no matter what happened elsewhere in the state. Daniels was wrong again. Young won by ten votes, a difference that before Fusionist rule would have easily been within the Democrats' margin of ballot-box prestidigitation.

After the elections of 1894 and 1896, the Fusionists decisively controlled North Carolina's political machinery. In response, Daniels vowed to "wag[e] war on those Populists and Republicans who were responsible for the disgrace that came to the State under the Fusion administration."[28] During the 1895 legislative session, the Democrats' power had still been robust enough to allow Daniels to frustrate much of Butler's political agenda. In particular, the movement toward "black rule" in much of the eastern part of the state had caused many white Populists to question their allegiance to Fusionism. However, as the 1897 session approached, Butler appeared to have solidified the Fusionists' hold on state politics. With Russell in the governor's mansion, overwhelming majorities in both houses of the legislature, and control of the judiciary, Butler could look forward to running the state as if he were its prime minister. What he wanted, he expected to get.

Fortunately for Daniels and the Democrats, the battles in Raleigh were temporarily abated, as the campaigns of 1896 and 1898 bracketed the escalation of the U.S. conflict with Spain that ultimately resulted in the Spanish-American War. As the decrepit Spanish monarchy tried to hold on to the remnants of a once glorious empire, Cuba became the center of a dispute between Washington and Madrid. Native Cubans rebelled at the high-handedness of their Spanish rulers, who found no middle ground between subjugating the locals and granting them complete independence. The Spanish chose subjugation. Cuba soon became a cause célèbre among certain circles in the United States, including the rising group of American imperialists, many of whom were businessmen who wanted Spanish influence replaced with U.S. capital. Assistant Secretary of the Navy Theodore Roosevelt served as their leading voice in the McKinley administration.[29] Another circle included a bellicose branch of the press led by William Randolph Hearst. Generally a progressive in domestic politics, internationally Hearst was an imperialist. Together these forces exploited a minor diplomatic dispute and blew it up into a war between the United States and Spain, a war that, although brief, would generate decades-long repercussions.

Aggravating tensions between the two countries, on February 15, 1898, the USS *Maine* experienced an explosion and sank to the bottom of Havana harbor, taking 266 U.S. seamen, marines, and officers down with it. Blaming the Spanish and invoking the Monroe Doctrine, pro-imperialist Americans led by Roosevelt and Hearst demanded retribution. Although the exact cause of the Maine's sinking was never determined, Roosevelt pointed his finger at Spain: "The Maine was sunk by an act of dirty treachery on the part of the Spaniards I believe."[30] McKinley, a more savvy politico than generally thought, was not about to let jingoes like Hearst and Roosevelt prod him into an unpopular war. McKinley had experienced firsthand the horrors of combat during the Civil War and had spent the intervening years in a different kind of warfare. He knew well enough that the jingoes who excoriated him for not immediately declaring war on Spain could just as fiercely attack him when U.S. soldiers started dying in Cuba.

To play for time, McKinley ordered an investigation into the sinking of the *Maine*. When the investigative commission concluded that the explosion had come from outside the ship's hull, the finding implied sabotage. (Subsequent investigations disputed that conclusion.) Quickly, the public fell in with the march to war. Adopting a more bellicose tone, McKinley stayed ahead of the martial pace, but just barely, as angry pro-war crowds began to burn him in effigy. McKinley eventually delivered an ultimatum to the Spanish government, the essence of which was Cuban independence. Madrid temporized, and on April 11 McKinley asked Congress for authority to send troops to Cuba. After Congress granted that authority, Spain declared war on the United States, and on April 25 Congress in turn declared war on Spain. Despite the grumbling of TR and Hearst, in retrospect McKinley's handling of the march to war was a political masterpiece. By dragging his feet, he appeared statesmanlike, and by judiciously moving toward the use of force, he let Spain declare war first; thus he could go to the world, and history, with "clean hands."

Unlike Hearst, Daniels had little interest in Cuba, and he certainly disagreed with Hearst's and TR's calls for a more imperialist foreign policy. Though Daniels grudgingly admired McKinley's handling of the diplomatic crisis with Spain, he was well on his way to becoming a staunch anti-imperialist, a position that dated from his days in the Cleveland administration when Hawaii had been the object of U.S. imperialist designs. U.S. sugar interests had organized coups against Hawaii's ruling house in 1887 and again in 1893, the second time with the assistance of U.S. marines. Benjamin Harrison, the outgoing Republican president, proposed Hawaii's annexation, but Cleveland withdrew the proposal after becoming president in March. Thus Hawaii's fate was delayed. Daniels thought Hawaii's eventual subjugation offered an ugly object lesson in the evils of the Great Power imperial game, and he linked the fates of Hawaii and Cuba: "Whenever a greedy strong nation wishes to annex or exploit a weak nation, it calls its avidity 'Manifest Destiny.'"[31] Daniels understood the game. In 1898, McKinley, flush with the imperialist fever surrounding the war with Spain, eagerly accepted the entreaties of U.S. sugar producers (led by Sanford Dole), and Hawaii was finally annexed.

Daniels remained angry about the Hawaiian episode for years, and the U.S.-engineered coup and subsequent annexation colored his view of the war with Spain, which he saw as just a bigger version of Hawaii. The *N&O* ran Associated Press reports on the events leading up to the *Maine* crisis, but it did not emphasize Spanish wrongs or expend its own journalistic capital on the matter. Daniels had no interest in promoting conflict with Spain. Although never a McKinley backer, Daniels supported the president's cautious approach to the conflict, and McKinley's avoidance of war earned him rare, if lukewarm, praise from Daniels and the *N&O*. "With the blowing up of the *Maine*," Daniels wrote, "the feeling in Raleigh and all over the country ran high. McKinley's serious attempts to secure adjustment of the difference between this country and Spain were both denounced and approved." The *N&O*, which supported McKinley's cautious stance, noted disapprovingly that "there were many jingoes in Raleigh."[32]

Once war came, Daniels never doubted the outcome, and the *N&O* put little effort into laying out the grand international implications of a U.S. victory. Rather, the newspaper's coverage focused on the day-to-day life of North Carolina troops engaged in the war. More importantly, Daniels's perspective on the war also revolved around its implications for the political career of William Jennings Bryan. Since the Civil War, six men had been elected to the presidency: Grant, Hayes, Garfield, Cleveland, Harrison, and McKinley. Of these, Grant, Hayes, Garfield, and Harrison had all achieved the rank of general during the war, and the youngest, McKinley, had been promoted to major by the war's end. Only Cleveland (the sole Democrat on the list) had not served. It would be difficult to understate the importance of honorable military service to Daniels's generation, the generation that had been too young to reap military glory from the war. Daniels was thirty-six when Congress declared war on Spain; Bryan was thirty-eight. While Daniels might have been the more physically robust of the two, Bryan still possessed great physical energy. At the time, local politicos of a certain standing and (minimum) physical fitness were liberally given commissions. Thus both Bryan and Daniels were excellent candidates for command of their state's volunteer troops. But Daniels saw no net gain in a commission. He did not seek elected office; he had no quarrel with Spain; his Methodist conscience counseled against war; and he continued to build a family business in Raleigh.

For Bryan the calculus was different. He planned to run for president again in less than two years. He had little interest in business beyond his political career. Although he too had no quarrel with Spain and a pacifistic conscience, his political interests dominated these. So Bryan enlisted in the Nebraska National Guard and quickly became a colonel of the Third Nebraska Regiment. He was shipped to Florida, supposedly for staging and training, but it became clear that the War Department had no intention of sending him close to any action that might make him a hero. Mosquitoes were the only thing he would fight. "I had five months of peace in the army" was how Bryan later described his service.[33]

Bryan took his treatment better than Daniels, who saw in the administration's handling of the Third Nebraska a calculated move to bury Bryan. The *N&O* emphasized the contrast between the War Department's handling of Bryan's volunteers and those of Theodore Roosevelt, who had resigned as assistant secretary of the navy to lead a cavalry regiment—the famed Rough Riders. As was frequently, though not always, the case when it came to detecting the rumblings of future political earthquakes, Daniels guessed correctly that TR was being marked for a higher office than he had held in the Navy Department. In the pages of the *N&O*, Daniels protested "the opportunity the McKinley administration gave to Roosevelt [relative to] that given to Bryan." He "denounced the administration for favoritism, pointing out that Bryan had been marooned in Florida and his regiment, which was trained by experienced officers, had been denied any place where they might render real service, while the Roosevelt Rough Riders had been immediately taken to Cuba and given the opportunity, which Roosevelt embraced" to make the conflict "a Republican war."[34] Having slowly gotten in front of the war party, McKinley now wanted to be the commander in chief of a successful campaign, and he defined success in partisan political terms as well as military terms, with Roosevelt serving as the administration's martial surrogate in Cuba. At least that was how Daniels saw it.

Daniels's perspective on the war was also acutely personal. While Daniels fumed about the failure of the war to make a military hero of Bryan, his brother-in-law, Worth Bagley, was serving as an ensign aboard the torpedo boat USS *Winslow* in Cuba's Cárdenas harbor. On May 11 the *Winslow* came under fire from Spanish gunboats and shore batteries. The little boat was shattered but remained afloat and was eventually towed to safety, but Bagley and four crewmen were killed. According to correspondence between the ship's commanding officer and the Navy Department, Bagley was killed with the first shell and was listed in department correspondence as the first U.S. casualty of the war.[35] Adelaide Worth Bagley and Addie Daniels were shaken, but neither woman was devastated, nor did either retreat from society. (Addie was soon pregnant with the couple's second son, named Worth Bagley Daniels in honor of the fallen hero.) An enormous public funeral in Raleigh followed, and thanks to Daniels's support, a statute of Worth Bagley was erected on the lawn of the state capitol, where it remains to this day.

While Roosevelt's Rough Riders obtained the favorable press coverage that Daniels feared they would, the sinking of Spanish fleets at Santiago de Cuba and Manila Bay settled the war's outcome. A cease-fire was arranged in August, and the Treaty of Paris formally ended the war in December. The annexation of Hawaii and the aftermath of the Spanish-American War ignited in Daniels an interest in international events that he had not previously shown. The peace treaty granted to the United States the territories of Puerto Rico, Guam, and the Philippines, and it made Cuba a U.S. protectorate. The treaty explicitly allowed the United States to join the ranks of the imperial powers. During the ratification debate, Daniels denounced the treaty in the *N&O*, derisively referring to it as the product of "McKinley's 'benevolent assimilation' program." Daniels expected the treaty's ratification to fail. But then something curious happened: Bryan undermined his anti-imperialist colleagues by coming out in favor of the treaty. Stunned, Daniels called it Bryan's "great mistake." Bryan was being either naive or disingenuous when he justified his position by arguing that after the war formally ended via the treaty, "the American people could be mobilized to compel the withdrawing of the troops and to give the Filipinos their independence."[36] Daniels more clearly understood that once key U.S. business interests staked a claim in the Philippines, withdrawal of the troops that protected U.S. investments would be difficult. It would not be the last time that Daniels and Bryan differed over U.S. foreign policy.

WHITE SUPREMACY AND WILMINGTON

The war with Spain wound down just as the 1898 election season heated up. After fighting in the party's rear guard following the election debacles in 1894 and 1896, Daniels set his sights on the 1898 campaign. Writing almost half a century later, after the social costs of that campaign had been fully revealed, Daniels still unrepentantly referred to it as the "White Supremacy Campaign," and he typically used military metaphors to describe it.[37] The earlier Fusionist victories had changed dramatically the political status of North Carolina's blacks. Home Rule was restored to the counties, and African Americans began to hold office on a large scale at the local level for the first time since Reconstruction. Daniels grudgingly granted his enemies their due. "Shrewd manipulators," he called them.[38] Unfortunately for the supporters of the Fusionist movement, its gains were short lived, and no one was more responsible for that short life than Daniels.

If the Democrats were to return to power, Daniels would need to neutralize at least one element of the numerically superior Fusionist coalition. In fact, he planned to turn one faction of the coalition against the other two. The Populists, most of whom had originally been Democrats, were the logical choice for defection. Daniels learned in the legislative fights following the elections of 1894 and 1896 that race served as an effective lever among the radical white Fusionists. He guessed that the white Populists in the Fusionist coalition had not foreseen the extent to which the coalition's success would advance black political power. By appealing to what W. J. Cash called the "dear treasure of [the Populist's] superiority as a white man," Daniels would offer a devil's bargain to the largely poor, rural whites who made up the majority of the state's Populists: Come back to the Democratic Party and together white Populists and white Democrats could disenfranchise the state's black voters and thus end "black rule" before it got too far out of hand.[39]

Even before the 1898 election campaigns formally got under way, Daniels had orchestrated the appointment of Furnifold Simmons, the field marshal who would formally lead the Democrats. Daniels had been instrumental in getting Simmons appointed as chairman of the state Democratic Party earlier in the decade, and Simmons had rewarded Daniels's confidence by organizing the victorious 1892 campaign. Before that, Simmons had served in the U.S. House of Representatives, and until being recently ousted in favor of a McKinley supporter, he had enjoyed the sinecure of federal internal revenue collector. Out of a job and hoping to return to Washington, D.C., rather than his law practice in New Bern, Simmons had every incentive to put the Democrats back in power in Raleigh.

Simmons was a man of many contradictions, and portraits of him do not do justice to his formidable character. With protruding ears and a pie-shaped head crossed by a bristle-brush mustache, he was homely of countenance and a poor stump speaker in a day when the skill carried much weight. But Simmons's métier was backroom, political horse-trading. Before the Civil War, Simmons's family had owned a successful plantation in Jones County, a little south and east of Wilson. But like other upwardly mobile young Tar Heels, Simmons made his own way in the world at the bar of justice, and he eventually went into politics. Daniels and Simmons would have their disagreements, but the two men got along well enough personally and worked closely together off and on for nearly forty years. For the approaching 1898 campaign, Daniels needed a hard-nosed politico and a proven winner who would fight to the last man in the last ditch. Simmons was such a man.

Recognizing that "[l]eaders routinely molded support against a villain, and for most politicians a skillfully cultivated foe could become a source of advantage, energy, idealism, even comfort,"[40] Daniels and Simmons vilified blacks whose political power had grown under Fusionist rule. In doing so, Daniels aimed to shame the Populists who had abandoned the Democratic Party while simultaneously motivating party members who had remained faithful. Daniels kicked off the campaign even as war with Spain continued, delivering an indictment of Fusionist rule in speeches on the state's political circuit. At this he was a failure. Public speaking was one of the few things in Daniels's life at which he failed completely. Possessing a rare ability to cut to the quick in print, Daniels never created a similarly successful style on the stump. Furthermore, he had a soft voice that rumbled quietly like the surf but tended to break as he raised it to make a point. Accompanied by his coastal plain accent that still possessed a touch of the Outer Banks "hoi toid" of his ancestors, his tone and speaking style worked splendidly in the salons and dining rooms of Raleigh and Washington but did not serve him well on the stump.

In addition to a weak voice, Daniels had a tendency to read from a script that sounded better on the page than it did to the ear. Those who heard him speak did not consider him among the great, or even good, orators of the age. "His style was flowery, excessively so," one eyewitness recalled.[41] An organized thinker and a concise writer when constrained by the time and space demands of a daily newspaper, Daniels struggled to find those qualities on the stump, and he could not forcefully capture a crowd in the way other great speakers of his day could. Always more diffident in person than he was in print, without microphone or other means of amplification, he never mastered the physical elements of the stump, a forum in which the speaker had to impose his or her will on the crowd. By his own admission he "wasn't much on speaking."[42] Recognizing that he could carry more weight publishing newspapers in Raleigh, Daniels quickly gave up speaking around the state and returned to the *N&O* to carry on the fight from there.

As Daniels hammered his readers daily with attacks on the Russell regime—"Vile and Villainous" being among the more sanitary headlines the paper ran above articles describing Fusionist rule—he and Simmons recruited three of the state's most promising young Democrats to promulgate the party's case: Locke Craig, Robert B. Glenn, and Charles Brantley Aycock.[43] Daniels marked each for high leadership positions within what had become, with the continued demise of the Bourbons and the defection of the radicals, the progressive mainstream of the state's Democratic Party. Each would leverage his success in the white supremacy campaign into a term as governor.

A native of Bertie County in the state's northeastern corner, Craig (no relation to the author) had moved to Asheville after attending law school at the University of North Carolina. Almost immediately he became a force in local politics and thereafter served as the leading voice of the Democratic Party in the western part of the state. With a patrician's sharply defined countenance, piercing eyes, and a thick head of hair showing a distinguishing touch of early gray at the temples, Craig exuded a scholarly air that matched perfectly his speaking style, which Daniels described in glowing terms. "[Craig's] sentences were beautiful, his speeches ornate, and he had fire and oratory," Daniels wrote.[44] A handsome though physically small man, Craig became known as the "Little Giant of the West."[45] In contrast, Glenn, who represented the piedmont region in the state's geographical center, was a less subtle, more direct speaker. With a bullet-shaped head and oaklike trunk, Glenn targeted his speeches further down the socioeconomic ladder. He was pugnacious where Craig was erudite. As Daniels succinctly put it, on the stump, "Glenn used the meat axe."[46]

Despite the estimable qualities of Craig and Glenn, of the campaign's three star speakers, Aycock proved to be the most impressive. A fellow alumnus of the Wilson Collegiate Institute, Aycock had graduated from the University of North Carolina (where Craig had been a contemporary), married into the distinguished Woodard family, and established, with Daniels's older brother, Frank, a successful law practice in Goldsboro. With his high, prematurely bald pate and beaked nose, Aycock possessed the countenance of a fierce bird of prey. Honest, reserved in private, and as intellectually daunting as he looked, Aycock would have probably succeeded at anything he pursued. Somewhat unusual for a man of such self-effacement and intellectual capacity, Aycock was an outstanding stump speaker with the ability to cut to the point of an issue while simultaneously eviscerating an opponent's positions. In Daniels's concise summary, when it came to public speaking, "Aycock used a rapier."[47] Craig, Glenn, and Aycock proved to be an imposing trio. Unlike Daniels or Simmons, these men could force their will on an audience through speaking styles that, while differing from one another, allowed each man to dominate a crowd.

The background material for their speeches, and the campaign more generally, came from Daniels's indictment of the Fusionists, which was published in the pages of the *N&O*. Years later, Daniels would proudly recall that the "*News and Observer* was the printed voice of the campaign."[48] The self-effacing Aycock, deflecting well-earned praise for his stump speeches, agreed. "Any man can make speeches if he would read the *News and Observer*," he said.[49] The outrages documented by Daniels's newspaper focused on the exercise of local political power by African American officeholders under Fusionism. These charges, as reported in the *N&O*, included

- "young white women in Wilmington [were] pushed off the sidewalks by Negro policemen on their beats";
- "a Negro man struck a young white girl in the face";
- in Greene County there was a report of a "burglary and attempted rape by a Negro";
- an African American member of the state legislature was convicted of forgery;
- in Craven County a white woman was tried by an African American justice of the peace;
- "a Negro deputy sheriff in Wake County served subpoenas on leading white men";
- in Fusion-controlled counties, African American prisoners were chained to white prisoners;

- African American congressman George White, from Daniels's old second congressional district, attempted to sit in a whites-only section of a circus in nearby Tarboro;
- Daniels's Raleigh neighbor Jim Young was appointed director of the state's Blind Institution, "where white girls were being taught";
- in some Fusionist districts, "Negroes and whites [served] on the same school committee";
- "white ladies in Vanceboro were compelled to go to a Negro to list their taxes."[50]

The primary journalistic source of most of these complaints was Daniels's paladin Falc Arendell. The events reported above represented just a few examples of "the horrors of Negro domination" that Arendell reported and Daniels published.[51] Seemingly indefatigable, Arendell worked the state's small towns, digging up racist dirt for publication in the *N&O*. He would set up shop at a local tavern, where he could hear, swap, and embellish news and gossip about the operation of the Fusionist machine in the area. The *N&O* told its white audience that going to jail was bad enough, but to go to jail on the order of or chained to a black man was intolerable, as was an African American justice of the peace sitting in judgment of whites.

In addition to these legal interactions, which were often petty, the threatened virtue of white women was a recurring theme; the threat came from the politically liberated, and thus socially emboldened, black man. As one southern writer later explained, "The sex and race taboo that grew from [the] roots in slavery remained a mighty oak."[52] In his standard stump speech, Aycock declaimed, "The goddess of North Carolina Democracy is the white womanhood of the state."[53] The worshipful concern for white women was such that W. J. Cash could famously refer to it as "gyneolatry."[54]

Bryan had used class as the wedge political issue with which he leveraged his movement. Daniels now applied Bryan's techniques to race-baiting. Many of the rural and working-class white Populists who had helped propel the Fusionists to power were overt racists. As generations of social commentators and historians have observed, whites at the bottom of the socioeconomic ladder were most likely to resent black progress. The Populists could be as violently antiblack as the progressives who remained in the Democratic Party. This was the inherent contradiction in the Fusionist movement: "A special difficulty of the Populist-Negro combination lay in the historical position of the upland whites toward the blacks, an antagonism with roots in slavery days. The regions where Populism made its strongest appeal were the very regions that found it most difficult to over-come racial feeling."[55] Thus, the Fusionists were swimming against the cul-tural tide.

Still, the Fusionists did not yield in the face of the Democrats' attacks. At every stage of the campaign, they challenged the white supremacists on the stump and in the press. Governor Russell, a backroom politico like his Democratic opposite Simmons, was no help on the stump, and Hiram Grant, a carpetbagger with no credibility among the majority of the state's white voters, remained behind the throne. But Butler was an energetic and effective public speaker, a "bullying" force arguing with "sledgeham-mer logic and facts."[56] He traveled up and down the state, matching Craig, Glenn, and Aycock speech for speech. The state's African American leaders understood the implications of a Democratic victory. It would bring back white rule in the cities and end Home Rule in the counties, which meant effectively the end, or at least the sharp curtailment, of hard-earned and only recently enjoyed black political power. Thus, the state's black leaders did not back down from the Democratic challenge.

Within the Fusionist coalition, disputes continued over the spoils of power, and the efforts of white Fusionists to appease the African American members of the coalition continued with mixed success into the 1898 cam-paign season. On one hand, African Americans had managed to obtain a form of Home Rule, as locally elected, three-person commissions now gov-erned the unincorporated areas of the counties. This was no small achieve-ment because it meant that in the black-majority counties, primarily those between Raleigh and the coast, African Americans could control the county government. However, the cities were another matter. Raleigh and Char-lotte were safe from Fusionist domination for now, but Wilmington had been taken over by the Fusionists and became the key city, the pivot around which white supremacy would revolve. The state's major port, Wilmington was in the heart of Russell country, and it offered a relatively prosperous home to a large African American population. Furthermore, there was no local Democrat as powerful as Daniels was in Raleigh; thus with no one of equal stature to broker a deal with disaffected Populists to keep Wilming-ton's municipal government white (and Democratic), Wilmington became a Fusionist city. Young managed to obtain for Wilmington what he had failed to get for Raleigh: a legislative act amending the city's charter.[57] An integrated "Police Board" now ran the city and began appointing African Americans to municipal jobs, including on the police force. This was an especially controversial move, as sooner or later black police officers would be in a position to exercise their authority in dealing with whites, which in turn would shake the foundation of the post-Reconstruction racial status quo. Thus, Wilmington was a political flashpoint in the campaign of 1898.

As the campaign wound down and Craig, Glenn, and Aycock talked themselves hoarse on the stump, Daniels beat the tocsin daily in the *N&O*, with the evils of black men in power as the main theme. In the North Carolina campaign of 1898, Daniels had to reverse much of the work he had done with William Jennings Bryan in the most recent presidential campaign. Then, Daniels had helped send to oblivion the Democratic Party's gold standard wing and Grover Cleveland's career along with it. The Democratic Party became a Free Silver party, but Bryan's and Daniels's efforts in vilifying the party's more conservative elements had been all too successful. They had delivered many radical Democrats into the Populist Party, and in North Carolina that meant into the Fusionist ranks. Daniels now tried to lure Populists back into the Democratic Party with race-baiting and Free Silver, or as he regularly put it in print, into the party of "white men and white metal."[58]

Daniels was a pugnacious man who looked for a fight in every newspaper he published, and there was no chance he would turn away from challenging Fusionist control in Wilmington. He assigned Arendell to cover the city, and he published the details of every crime, as if it were the inevitable product of black corruption or Fusionist incompetence. Whatever the facts on the ground, Wilmington came to represent the worst of Fusionism in the eyes of the white supremacists.[59] For Daniels, however, the temerity of an African American newspaper publisher exceeded all other outrages associated with Wilmington. Alexander Manly, publisher of the Wilmington *Record*—"the Negro organ and chief advocate of Fusion," in Daniels's words—boldly upheld black prerogatives under the Fusionists.[60] Among other things, Manly's writings broached the ultimate taboo in black-white relations: sex. While much of the white supremacists' case against Fusionism revolved around the elevated political status blacks had come to enjoy, the *N&O* specialized in the added allure of sexual innuendo, especially when the accused was a black male and the victim a white female. Nowhere was Cash's gyneolatry more openly displayed than in the pages of the *N&O*. For example, under the headline "A Nameless Crime" (which anyone over the age of twelve could name), the paper reported that

> Charles Lassiter, a fifteen-year-old negro, assaulted a highly respectable white girl on the public road near [Rich Square, a coastal plain

crossroads] yesterday afternoon, but was frightened off before he could accomplish his purpose. Today and tonight a posse has been scouring the country but up to this hour has not arrested the brute. The assault was made in open daylight and in one of the most densely settled sections of the county. The community is aflame with indignation and the probabilities are that if the negro is caught he will be lynched in short order. The young girl . . . [against] whom the foul crime was attempted is a member of a family highly esteemed in this section.[61]

Noting other outrages against the virtues of white womanhood, Daniels's journalists made the case that white women were not safe from the animalistic impulses of the state's now unrestrained black men.

As the campaign wore on, the African American publisher Manly, as combative as Daniels, began to challenge the implications of such pieces, openly taunting the white supremacists. Manly focused his attack on lower-class whites, comparing them unfavorably to the African American miscreants Daniels highlighted in the *N&O*. "The morals of the poor white people are on a par with their colored neighbors," Manly wrote. "Our experience among poor white people in the country teaches us that the women of that race are not any more particular in the matter of clandestine meetings with colored men than the white men with colored women."[62] By openly addressing such a touchy subject as miscegenation and indicting a whole class of the state's whites in doing so, Manly was playing with fire. Furthermore, by equating poor whites with blacks he played into Daniels's strategy of separating the Populists from the Fusionists. Lower-class whites did not welcome Manly's comparison of the races. In the *N&O* Daniels wrote that Manly's boldness was the "legitimate result of the political situation, and that" he had "inflamed the white people of the State. They blazed their indignation." Indeed, Wilmington was about to become a metaphor for the white supremacy campaign. Daniels predicted as much: "People reaped what they sowed, and . . . the slanderous article of the Wilmington Negro [that is, Manly] had so aroused the people that a race riot was imminent in Wilmington."[63] That was true enough, and Daniels would help make it so.

In the closing weeks of the campaign, parts of the state approached anarchy.[64] Among the demagogues who got in on the campaigning was South Carolina's Ben Tillman, the same "Pitchfork Ben" who, two years earlier, had nearly sunk Bryan's nomination chances by threatening secession at the Democratic National Convention. He made a whirlwind speaking tour in North Carolina near the end of the 1898 campaign, openly exhorting whites to once again "redeem" the state. As Daniels wrote, Tillman "had spoken violently . . . saying that the white folks of South Carolina would chunk enough Negroes in the river before they would permit their domination."[65] Tillman aroused large crowds of angry whites wherever he spoke, and he was determined to raise North Carolinians to a higher level of racial animosity. Regarding Manly, Tillman asked, "Why didn't you kill that damn nigger editor who wrote that?"[66]

Keen to capitalize on the success of Tillman's tour, Daniels and Simmons immediately followed it with a last great push before Election Day. They called a meeting, which they named the White Supremacy Convention, in Aycock's home base of Goldsboro. It would be held only two weeks before the election. While the convention contained much speechifying, the primary purpose was to organize a get-out-the-vote campaign across the state, especially in the white-dominated western regions. Afraid that complacency would prevent a complete Democratic victory, Daniels resolved to "ask the people of all Eastern North Carolina to come together at Goldsboro to declare the conditions that existed in the East and to make an appeal to the whole State."[67] In other words, the west, largely white and heavily Populist, must be convinced of the dreadfulness of black rule in the east.

Daniels identified two speeches delivered by former Confederate officers W. A. Guthrie and Alfred Moore Waddell as "the high-water marks of the convention." Likely to trouble the consciences of modern readers, excerpts of these speeches are nonetheless illuminating. Following up on Tillman's threat to commit mass murder against African Americans should they attempt fusion in South Carolina, Waddell said that whites must overthrow the North Carolina Fusionists even "if they have to throw enough dead Negro bodies in the Cape Fear to choke up its passage to the sea." Only slightly less bellicose, Guthrie, who began his speech by reading from the Bible, openly declared, "The Anglo-Saxon . . . has carried the Bible in one hand and the sword in the other and with these emblems of religion, we say to the nations of the world 'Resist our march of progress and civilization and we will wipe you off the face of the earth.'"[68] Daniels objected strenuously when imperialist Republicans trampled on the rights of indigenous peoples in Cuba, the Philippines, and Hawaii, but it was the great paradox of Daniels's personality that his concern for the non-Anglo races did not extend to North Carolina's African Americans.

Daniels recognized all too well that "the world tested causes by com-

bat."[69] And so it would be with white supremacy. In promoting the explicitly violent views of men like Tillman, Guthrie, and Waddell, Daniels sowed
the whirlwind. Immediately following the election the reaping began. Election Day that year fell on Tuesday, November 8. As the results rolled in the
following day, it became clear that the Democrats had achieved a complete
victory, one of the most resounding in American political history. Going
into the election, the Democrats held less than 20 percent of the seats in
the state senate and less the 30 percent in the house. When the next session
of the legislature met, the party would control more than two-thirds of the
seats in the legislature.[70]

A coalition built on hate had been cobbled together, and the hatred became difficult to control once victory was secured. On November 10 a group
of armed whites led by Waddell marched on Manly's Wilmington office.
Estimates of the group's size vary; Daniels, who probably got his version
from Arendell, put the figure at 400.[71] A riot ensued, and what followed
in its wake was essentially a coup. The city's Fusionist government was
ousted by armed force. Manly escaped, but the mob destroyed his printing
facilities. The mayor, Silas Wright, and most city government officials were
simply removed from office. Many of the most prominent blacks, along
with leading Fusionists, were later banished from the city. Another 2,000
African Americans soon left the city, some as the result of overt intimidation. At least 22 African Americans died and 9 were wounded, though some
estimates put the number of dead as high as 60. The *N&O* reported 11 African American deaths and 3 whites wounded.[72]

Initially, the *N&O*'s coverage followed the white supremacist line. The
day immediately after the coup, the *N&O* headline read, "A DAY OF BLOOD-
SHED," with the sub-headline, "Negroes Precipitate Conflict by Firing on
Whites." The newspaper's position was that Wilmington was out of control
and the city government had to be "changed legally."[73] However, Daniels
wanted to see blacks ousted from power at the ballot box, not at the point
of a gun, and as more information came in, he changed his view of what
had happened. Eventually he concluded that Waddell had incited the riot.
Daniels explicitly discounted Waddell's claim that whites only responded
to being fired upon by African Americans. "If that is the true statement,"
Daniels wrote, then the blacks "did not fire until four hundred armed white
men led by Colonel Waddell marched to [Manly's] office to destroy it." As
for the burning of Manly's property, Daniels noted cynically that "some
papers said it caught fire in an unaccountable way, evidently meaning that
nobody knew who applied the torch."[74]

Although Daniels questioned Waddell's version of events, he remained unapologetically bellicose about what happened in Wilmington. He was, according to his third son, Jonathan, in person "a very gentle man, and he was also a very violent man . . . editorially."[75] Living up to that reputation, Daniels wrote, "If any reader is inclined to condemn the people of Wilmington for resolving to expel Manley [sic] from the city, let him reread the libel upon the white women of the state that appeared in the *Daily Record*."[76] In the end, despite his questions about Waddell's methods, Daniels felt the Wilmington rioters had merely taken his war metaphors to their logical conclusion. Although for Daniels the 1898 campaign was, as one of his grandsons put it, "a political activity and not a racial activity," that was not how it played out for his white supremacist allies in Wilmington.[77] The violence there was not about politics or the virtue of white womanhood. It was about the open display of the dominance of one race over another. It was the violence of victory. *Vae victis.* Woe to the vanquished. Daniels, a dedicated student of the classics, understood this better than anyone.

In his old age Daniels came to see that, whatever the merits of his positions during the heat of the debates in the late 1890s, the policies he pursued had produced considerable hardship for North Carolina's African Americans. He described his own tactics as "cruel, . . . too cruel."[78] Some in Daniels's circle recognized as much at the time. Daniels's former colleague Matt Ransom complained about the white supremacists' tactics before and after the election. In a letter to Julian Shakespeare Carr, Ransom protested the movement's illegal tactics: "The law is as necessary to the preservation of government and society as the 'attraction of gravity' is to the solidity and permanence of the mighty systems of nature of which the earth is a part."[79] However, Ransom's censure carried little weight, as the Fusionists' earlier victories had sent him into retirement. As one commentator put it, in politics "doing the right rather than the expedient thing is often excruciating, and virtue is seldom rewarded."[80] In the white supremacy campaign Daniels chose expediency over virtue.

Daniels thought the problems facing the state's African American community were "due more to the men who led the Negroes than to the Negroes themselves,"[81] by which he meant Butler and the Republicans. The implication was that only enlightened Democrats, such as Daniels, could help the blacks. But help, in this context, did not include the granting of equal social, political, or economic status. Indeed, when it came to race, late nineteenth-century progressives were not all that progressive. As one historian described the situation, the progressives "spoke of racism as the linchpin of the progressive movement, meaning that progress could be made only when white supremacy mooted the race question in politics."[82] Thus the Democratic Party's leaders viewed blacks as a political problem to be solved, rather than as a political asset to be accommodated. To the progressives, racial progress meant taking the "Negro question" out of politics. There was a New South dimension to this as well, because northern capital would not flow freely into a region marred by racial strife; yet every social, economic, and political issue had a contentious racial dimension. Taking that dimension out of play would bring social order; order would bring investment; and investment would bring economic and social progress to the New South.

To the Fusionists, African Americans might have been many things, including farmhands, sharecroppers, and, potentially, industrial laborers. They might be patronized or accommodated. But most of all they represented votes. Since Reconstruction, "the [Republican] party still appealed for the votes of a propertyless electorate of manumitted slaves."[83] As the party of northern capital, the Republicans could not hope to be very successful among North Carolina's white farmers. Thus the Republicans became the party of black farmers. Thus African Americans were not the white man's burden but a chief asset in the Republican Party's battles against post-Reconstruction Democratic rule.

To modern readers it may seem paradoxical that progressives, such as Daniels and Aycock, should be among the nation's leading white supremacists. However, from the perspective of their New South ideology, removing African Americans from the political equation was the shortest avenue to economic and social progress. Indeed, "racism was conceived of by some as the very foundation of Southern progressivism."[84] The rise of the Fusionists taught Daniels that every major political issue—educational funding, agricultural reform, prohibition—could be held hostage to the demands of black voters. Under the Fusionists, African Americans formed the largest voting bloc in the majority coalition. As a result, Butler's parliamentary coalition could only move forward by appeasing James Young's demands for political spoils. Henceforth any ruling coalition would have to do likewise. This was unacceptable to white Democrats. The combination of ideology and circumstances prevented them from dealing with blacks as political equals. In the antebellum era, slavery's staunchest defender, John C. Calhoun, had predicted exactly the situation Daniels found himself in during the 1890s. "The next step [after emancipation] would be to raise the negroes to a social and political equality with the whites . . . [but slavery] exempts us from the disorders and dangers resulting from this conflict."[85] Slavery was no longer an option to end the "disorders," but disenfranchisement was.

As a later observer noted, "Violence had opened the way to political action, [the Democratic] party became the institutionalized incarnation of the will to White Supremacy."[86] In fact, the Democratic Party had served as the "will [of] White Supremacy" since Reconstruction, but now that will was about to be formalized in the state's constitution. Even while the embers of Manly's office smoldered in Wilmington, Daniels and Simmons began planning for the 1900 elections. They concluded that the best way to ensure that there would be no Fusionist resurgence was to deny the coalition access to the necessary votes. In Daniels's estimation, this insurance could be had through the disenfranchisement of the state's African American citizens. As Daniels had equated Fusionism with corruption, moral and political, it was not a great intellectual leap for a progressive to associate disenfranchisement with good government. Thus, "in part disenfranchisement was also presented as progressive reform, the sure means of purging Southern elections of the corruption that disgraced them." "Cheating at elections is demoralizing our whole people," said one Democrat.[87] Daniels counted on the "disgrace and public shame of this corruption [being] more widely and keenly appreciated than the circuitous and paradoxical nature of" disenfranchising African Americans.[88] In short, as odd as this might seem to subsequent generations of readers, Daniels could sell disenfranchisement as part of a progressive movement. Progress—which in Daniels's view included state funding for public education, agricultural reform, railroad regulation, and prohibition—could only be obtained when race was no longer an element of southern politics.

Daniels and Simmons decided that the optimal strategy would be to offer voters a disenfranchisement amendment to the existing constitution. At the time, three other southern states had disenfranchised their black citizens. Broadly speaking there were two avenues for doing this. One was informal, in that the "law put it into the hands of the poll [workers] in each precinct to determine the eligibility of a voter."[89] This was the so-called Mississippi plan. It revolved around enforcement of the state's requirement that voters be "literate." Since literacy was verified by white Democrats, who controlled voter registration and the actual voting process at the poll, blacks were, in effect, prohibited from voting in the majority of precincts. The poll tax offered another, arguably more formal option. To be safe, in North Carolina the joint legislative committee charged with drawing up the amendment included both a literacy requirement and the poll tax.[90] To prevent the amendment from effectively disenfranchising a large number of the state's white voters, many of whom were as poor and illiterate as their black neighbors, an additional section "grandfathered" the voter registration of whites. The amendment passed by a 54,000-vote majority of 310,000 ballots cast, or 59 to 41 percent. Given that blacks participated in this election, the last one in which they would play an important role for more than sixty years, the final tally suggests overwhelming white support. In the *N&O*, Daniels called the passage of the amendment "a history-making day."[91]

The gubernatorial race that same year was never in doubt. Aycock beat the Republican candidate, Superior Court Judge Spencer Adams, by 60,000 votes. Race continued to be the key issue. The *N&O* quoted Adams as having said that "nine times out of ten, if you will chase down the fellows who are trying to stir up race prejudice, you will find that the most vigorous one is sleeping with a negro woman."[92] Two years earlier, Manly, an African American, had nearly been killed for less inflammatory remarks. The white politician Adams was simply kept from the governor's mansion. Simmons defeated Daniels's old financier, Julian Carr, in the Democratic primary for Butler's senate seat and was then elected easily by the new legislature. The white supremacy campaign effectively ended the careers of Marion Butler and Dan Russell, and it buried the state's Republican Party. It would be seventy-two years before another Republican would be elected senator or governor in the state, and more than a century would pass before the Republicans would again control both houses of the state legislature.

———

Daniels's other accomplishments during these years included the continuing financial success of the *N&O*. The publicity attending the white supremacy campaigns provided the paper with a dramatic increase in circulation and helped make Daniels a wealthy man. Circulation grew from roughly 1,800 in the last year of Samuel Ashe's ownership to nearly 10,000 by 1903, an average annual compounded rate of growth greater than 20 percent, at a time when the U.S. economy was growing around 4 percent a year on average. Thus revenues from subscriptions alone were in the neighborhood of $70,000 annually, and by the end of the next year the paper was completely free of debt, as Daniels retired the note originally held by Carr.[93] Furthermore, with advertising revenues roughly 75 percent of those from subscriptions, the newspaper's gross income exceeded $100,000.

During this period, the paper contained eight pages during the week and sixteen on Sundays. There was as yet no separate sports section or comics and still no Monday edition. Although Daniels continued to take a monthly draw, the majority of his income now came from his share of the profits. During this period he increased his efforts to buy back the stock that he had issued during the corporate reorganization of 1895. Daniels listed his annual salary as $3,000.[94] Assuming he was earning a return on equity comparable to what he had earned in the 1890s, a conservative estimate given the paper's growth, and recognizing that he owned substantially more than 50 percent of the paper, then it follows that he was probably clearing $4,000 to $5,000 a year, which would have been roughly fifteen to twenty times per capita income, or the equivalent of more than $700,000 today. Such a figure would be consistent with the size and number of the investments he was beginning to make with his financial advisor Herbert Jackson.[95] Although still not rich by the standards of Carr or the Dukes, in his first decade at the helm of the *N&O* Daniels was by Raleigh standards a wealthy man.

Among the changes to the newspaper business that facilitated this growth were the spread of literacy, public investment in rural roads, and the post office's expansion of rural free delivery. The combination of these forces was a windfall for Daniels. Rural delivery was especially valuable. In the decade following rural delivery's expansion into eastern North Carolina in 1905, *N&O* subscriptions doubled, for an average annual compounded growth rate of 7 percent, slower than the first decade of Daniels's ownership but still roughly twice the growth of the economy overall during this period.

———

In addition to his six-year war against the Fusionists, Daniels waged many fierce political battles in those days, earning the *News and Observer* the sobriquet "Nuisance and Disturber."[96] None was more hard-fought than the so-called Bassett affair. In October 1903, John Spencer Bassett, a Trinity College (as Duke University was then known) history professor, had published in the *South Atlantic Quarterly* a piece on racial antipathy in the South. It included the following passage: "There is today more hatred of whites for blacks and blacks for whites than ever before."[97] Bassett went on to express relatively liberal ideas on race, adding that the African American educator Booker T. Washington was "the greatest man, save General Lee, born in the South in a hundred years."[98] These words generated a storm of protest. By implication, Bassett accused Daniels, Aycock, and the other white supremacy leaders of "stirring up the fires of race." In Daniels's view, rather than stirring the fire, the white supremacy campaign had extinguished the fires of race, the embers of which Bassett was now stoking. The primary idea behind the white supremacist movement was to remove race from public debate, thus promoting social "harmony" and economic growth. Bassett's arguments posed a threat to the hard-earned stability that the return of white Democratic rule had brought to the state. The *News and Observer* served as a primary outlet for the resulting rage. Among the more temperate headlines Daniels ran were "SOUTHERN LEADER SLANDERED," and "THE PEOPLE FEEL THAT PROFESSOR BASSETT'S UTTERANCES ARE AN OUTRAGE."[99]

The storm raged for the next three months. (Henceforth, the *N&O* referred to Bassett as bASSett.) Daniels would often cleverly adopt a news topic because it allowed him to achieve other objectives. Daniels now used Bassett's unfortunate juxtaposition of Booker T. Washington with the South's white heroes as a means of settling old scores with Bassett's boss, the Reverend John C. Kilgo, president of Trinity. The longest-standing conflict between Daniels and Kilgo was over state funding for public education. As the leader of one of the state's prominent private institutions, Kilgo, along with Baptist leader Columbus Durham, was an outspoken opponent of state support for higher education. Daniels was on the other side of that fight. Among Kilgo's other offenses was, in Daniels's mind, his close relationship with the Dukes. It should be remembered that at that time Trinity served as the state's leading Methodist seminary, and its president played a much more public and important role in the state than do presidents of today's secular private universities. (Later, as bishop, Kilgo would hold another position that carried much more weight at the time than it does now.) As a Methodist with considerable public standing, Daniels felt free to offer advice on the college's management, and because of the political power wielded by Trinity's president, Daniels had a stake in placing an ally in the seat. Kilgo was no ally. In Daniels's view, the Republican Dukes bought Trinity with tobacco money, and their lapdog Kilgo had turned the Methodist institution into a Republican institution, one that did not support white supremacy. (It did not help Kilgo's reputation among white supremacists that the Dukes had financed Marion Butler and the Fusionists in the 1890s.)[100] As one of Daniels's sons later summarized the dispute, when Daniels "fought Kilgo over the Bassett case . . . also involved was the fact that at the same time he was fighting the Dukes as the tobacco trust."[101]

Thus, Daniels saw in Bassett's anti-white-rule article an opportunity to attack Kilgo. By attaching Bassett's views to the university, Daniels forced Kilgo to take a formal stand on his professor's views.

To his credit, Kilgo, who never shied from a fight, stuck by Bassett. He refused to accept the professor's letter of resignation and vocally defended him in public. Rallying support from the Trinity community, Kilgo made the case one of academic freedom. He attended a special meeting of the Trinity trustees on December 1. He brought letters of resignation from every member of the faculty, though he did not threaten the trustees with a mass defection. Instead he hoped they would listen to his case and support on its merits his recommendation to retain Bassett. Daniels's main contact on the board of trustees was none other than Furnifold Simmons. The Bassett affair occurred at the peak of the Simmons-Daniels relationship. The two giants grew apart later; but they were still allies in 1903, and Simmons had as much at stake in ousting Kilgo as Daniels did. The meeting lasted for seven hours, running into the early morning of December 2. The outcome was not reported in the early editions of that morning's *N&O*, but the next day the headline told the story: "Eighteen [for keeping Bassett]—Seven [against]—Thus They Voted. Senator F. M. Simmons . . . Led the Fight against the Retention of Professor Bassett."[102] Daniels had lost. After another month of carping in the *N&O*, he let the matter drop. But he was not through hounding Kilgo. It took seven more years and a promotion of sorts—Kilgo left Trinity to don a bishop's robes, a position Daniels considered less politically harmful—but eventually Kilgo left. He was replaced by William Preston Few, a scholar who meddled in politics less than Kilgo. Daniels considered it a good trade.[103]

———

Daniels's triumphs in business and state politics were not matched at the national level. In the election of 1896, McKinley had soundly beaten Bryan in the electoral college, but the popular vote had been much closer, with McKinley securing only 51 percent. Furthermore, Daniels blamed Bryan's defeat on the disastrous split ticket offered by the Populists. (In this he was almost certainly wrong. It is difficult to imagine that running Sewall for vice president on the Populist ticket would have propelled Bryan over McKinley in the electoral college.) From the center to the left wing of the Democratic Party, the thinking was that Bryan could beat McKinley the second time around. With the increase in the world's gold supplies, the price of silver relative to gold had leveled off, ameliorating the downward price spiral of the 1890s, and thus Free Silver no longer served as the party's rallying cry. Instead, with the successful U.S. war against Spain, anti-imperialism became the new mantra. Even the old Silverite "Pitchfork Ben" Tillman, who had threatened secession over the issue only four years earlier, saw that silver no longer possessed the same magic. He declared at the party's 1900 convention in Kansas City, "The paramount issue of this campaign is imperialism." Bryan, who had earlier turned his back when McKinley had taken the Philippines from Spain, now stuck with the party's anti-imperialist rhetoric and won the nomination easily. Bryan, Daniels wrote, "still completely dominated the party. So we all left the convention and went home, feeling that the time for Mr. Bryan to win had come."[104]

Daniels was wrong. The more conservative elements of the party rebelled at Bryan's nomination. Among the defectors was Joseph P. Caldwell, editor of the Charlotte *Observer*. The leading paper in the south-central part of the state, the *Observer* challenged the *N&O* as North Carolina's most influential newspaper. With the demise of Samuel Ashe's career, Caldwell, a gold standard advocate, became the loudest voice of the state's conservative Democrats. Caldwell argued that anti-imperialism was not a winner at the polls at a time when America was becoming one of the Great Powers. Caldwell was correct. With a general return to prosperity, McKinley, at the peak of his popularity following the victory over Spain, defeated Bryan by even wider margins in both the electoral and popular votes than he had in 1896. For Daniels, the pain of the loss was compounded for the Democrats when McKinley died at the hands of an assassin shortly thereafter and Theodore Roosevelt moved into the White House.

Roosevelt was immensely popular, and his personality transcended his office in a way that, among his predecessors, only Andrew Jackson could match. He mixed just the right amounts of jingoist imperialism and anti-business populism with enormous physical and mental energy. No thinking Democrat questioned TR's general attractiveness as a politician, and when he announced that he would seek a term on his own in 1904, no leading Democrat wanted to run against him. Bryan, a recent two-time loser, sat this one out, and although Daniels made a token effort to rally his fellow Democratic editors, his heart was not in it. TR defeated conservative New York jurist Alton Parker in an electoral landslide of 336 to 140. At the national level, the Republicans continued to control both houses of Congress, as they had done since the disastrous 1894 election.

Daniels's personal relationship with TR, forged during their time in Cleveland's administration, ended during these years. It had run hot and cold over the years, but Daniels's increasingly outspoken opposition to the president's bellicose foreign policy served as the proximate cause of their permanent split. TR's time in office increased Daniels's awareness of international affairs, which had been ignited by Hawaii's annexation and the events leading up to and following the Spanish-American War. Thus Daniels perpetually clashed with the president, who called for America to join the European powers in imperial pursuits. When TR visited the North Carolina State Fair in Raleigh in 1905, Daniels managed to see the president briefly, but TR snubbed Daniels by not inviting him to the formal reception and luncheon held later on the president's behalf. This was a calculated jab at the city's top Democrat. Although the slight was clearly a political power play, Daniels uncharacteristically took it as a social affront. It also signaled to Daniels that TR had consciously chosen to end what was left of their friendship. Of the event Daniels wrote, "There was a struggle among the socially prominent as to who should be invited [to lunch with the president]. The number was limited and I don't know whether it was because I was not socially prominent or that I was politically undesirable, but my wife and I were about the only people who were accustomed to go to such places who were left [off of the invitation list]."[105] Addie was probably more angered and embarrassed than her husband was, but he was stung by the rebuff all the same. To have become a regular in the Raleigh social scene, and thus "accustomed to go[ing] to such places," had required a long, hard effort the socially conscious Daniels never forgot. He resented that TR could not put their political squabbles aside for what Daniels considered to be a social affair.

———

In North Carolina, despite the total victory of the white supremacists in the campaigns of 1898 and 1900, in the years that immediately followed, there remained the issue of exactly how those victories would be manifested on a day-to-day basis in the state's politics. At the time Daniels observed that although the whites "had disenfranchised the illiterate Negroes . . . the question of whether this disenfranchisement would stand made anything that touched upon it a matter of great importance politically."[106] Daniels expected the Fusionists to test the limits of white rule. As Charles Brantley Aycock waited to take office early in 1901, he laid down the new racial ground rules. In an effort to discourage African Americans from considering any kind of challenge to the new regime, he said, "Let the Negro learn once and for all that there is unending separation of the races; that the two peoples may develop side by side to the fullest, but they cannot intermingle." The threat was clear enough: Blacks should not think about crossing racial lines or challenging the new order. Calling upon whites to enforce that order, he added, "Let the white man determine that no man shall by act or thought or speech cross this line."[107]

Other state leaders backed the white supremacy program. During the recent campaign, another future governor, Locke Craig, had divided whites into two groups: those who supported African American advancement and those who supported white supremacy. "If you wish to find the lowest type of public man," he would declaim, "it is the man who associates on the terms of political equality with the negroes. . . . [In contrast] consider the poor [white] man. . . . He may not know anything about books. He maybe careless, indifferent as to his condition, but that man has flowing in his veins the blood of fifty generations of slave governing ancestors."[108]

Despite the admonitions of the state's white leadership, the new order was tested all the same. The first major political challenge came over an old topic, prohibition. Daniels's earlier prohibition battles had taught him that, like race, prohibition could serve as a political wedge issue. In general, the most ardent prohibitionists tended to be white, low-church Protestants, ranging from the middle of the Democratic Party to its radical Populist fringe. On the "wet" side were the white Republicans and their largely black supporters. Two traditionally Democratic groups split from the party when it came to prohibition: Catholics, largely Irish and located in the state's ports and few cities of any size, and some high-church Episcopalians who appreciated a fine aperitif before dinner and a cordial or glass of port afterward. But in North Carolina their numbers were small relative to those on either side of the black-white, Democrat-Republican divide on prohibition.

Prohibition remained a hot topic, primarily because Daniels's victory in the Raleigh prohibition campaigns of the mid-1880s had not been as decisive as he might have hoped. The earlier ban on alcohol applied only to Raleigh Township, which included the heart of city; however, the saloon keepers merely moved their operations to the far edges of town, just beyond the township limits, and soon after the referendum one or more saloons stood beside every road leading into Raleigh. Furthermore, during the period of Fusionist rule, enforcement had taken more than a few steps backward, and by the time the 1900 campaign came around, the city was as wet as it had ever been. The Democratic machine that had taken over Wake County and Raleigh, the county seat as well as the state capitol, following the victories of 1898 kept Daniels at arm's length. Its leader,

Raleigh lawyer Armistead Jones, maintained an outwardly courteous relationship with Daniels, but there were few progressive crusaders among the machine's minions. As Daniels observed, "The Democratic organization in Raleigh [was] composed of those who made politics a business and [it] had most of the county and city offices."[109] Jones himself served as the county's attorney and, after 1900, the state solicitor.[110] The machine conducted its behind-the-scenes business in the city's saloons. Thus while the state party—led by Simmons, Daniels, and Aycock—went dry, the Raleigh Democrats remained wet. Daniels recognized that a victory in Raleigh and Wake County would give the state prohibition campaign a boost. He had made Raleigh dry once. He would try to do so again.

The prohibition movement had been picking up steam around the country in the closing decades of the nineteenth century. Daniels, suspecting that the tides of public opinion were with prohibition, backed the Raleigh machine into a corner. At the Wake County Democratic Convention in 1900, the local machine planned to nominate for state senator a pro-wet lawyer named William Snow. Daniels had nothing against Snow, and in fact, beyond their split on prohibition, the two got on well and saw eye-to-eye on most issues. From Daniels's perspective, the local machine could have done a lot worse than Snow. However, Daniels, expecting whomever the Democrats nominated to win the state senate seat in the upcoming election, saw an opportunity to get his close friend Needham Broughton elected. Broughton was a staunch Baptist as well as the publisher and a co-owner of the *Biblical Recorder,* a leading Baptist journal. Daniels persuaded Broughton, who was more puritanical in his prohibitionist beliefs than Daniels (though generally less vituperative in print), to allow his name to go forward as a candidate. Knowing Broughton's hallowed place in the hearts of Raleigh's low-church white community, the wets within the machine expressed their outrage at what they saw as a schismatic act. How, they asked, after they had spent four years in the wilderness and had just patched together a winning political coalition, could Daniels threaten that coalition by forcing a referendum on prohibition in the form of Broughton's candidacy?

This was exactly the question Daniels expected the wets to ask. He had used Broughton's candidacy like a stiletto, passing it into the abdomen of the pro-wet local machine. Now he would twist it just enough to get what he wanted. Daniels offered the machine leaders the following deal: If the machine withdrew its support from Snow and threw everything behind Broughton, then Daniels would see to it that the General Assembly passed no legislation regulating Raleigh's liquor trade without including a local referendum. Since the local prohibitionist forces (led by Daniels himself) were demanding some kind of action in Raleigh and Wake County, Daniels offered the machine the lesser of two evils. In exchange for Broughton's nomination and almost certain election, Daniels could guarantee a local referendum on alcohol rather than an act from the legislature without a local vote. Of the threat to go to the legislature, Daniels wrote, "I knew that would put the fear of God into their hearts."[111] Recognizing Daniels's clout in the state assembly, the machine took the deal. Broughton was elected (though, never a happy politician, he served only one term), and Raleigh got its referendum on alcohol the following year.

The formal proposal on the referendum ballot represented yet another compromise worked out by Daniels. Rather than outlaw alcohol outright, he proposed that the city offer a referendum on a publicly run "dispensary," a forerunner of the state and local alcohol control boards that would dot America following the repeal of national prohibition in 1933. Daniels argued that the dispensary would be a better deal than a winner-take-all war over prohibition. It was a tough sell all the way around. The saloon keepers in particular objected to the deal. They did not care that alcohol would still be legal if they could not sell it directly. Broughton and his fellow Baptists did not like it either. As Daniels noted, "It was not easy to induce strong prohibitionists to accept the service [of the dispensary]."[112]

Despite their reservations, in the end the prohibitionists went along, albeit reluctantly, with Daniels's plan. The wets did not. A bitter referendum fight ensued. And it was during that fight that prohibition became inextricably linked with disenfranchisement. The Republicans were all too happy to aid the saloon keepers in using the dispensary referendum to challenge the disenfranchisement amendment. The wet forces had a reputation for using alcohol to induce blacks to go to the polls, and in general African Americans were perceived to be in the wet camp. As with so much of state politics during the period, one could never separate race from an issue. As a contemporary observed, white Democrats and Populists "believed that to forbid the sale of legal liquor, and so presumably force up the price of the bootleg product, would be to deprive [African Americans] of alcohol altogether and so make it easier to keep [them] in their place. Certainly the argument was much used in winning over the hard-drinking poor whites."[113] Republicans as well as Democrats understood this too well, and they prepared to use the referendum as a challenge to the recent disenfranchisement amendment.

Daniels witnessed firsthand the challenge to the law. He and Addie still lived in Adelaide Worth Bagley's home on east South Street, in a neighborhood that had become almost entirely African American in recent decades, as whites had fled to the more fashionable north side. The local voter registrar, "a saloon advocate," in Daniels's words, had registered the neighborhood's blacks without deference to the literacy clause in the disenfranchisement amendment. In response Daniels formally challenged every registered African American in his ward, "except the school teachers and preachers and those known to have education."[114] Daniels described in detail what happened on Election Day:

> The news got out that all were to be challenged, and on the day of election hundreds of people were surrounding the polls in that ward near [historically black] Shaw University [across the street from the Bagley home]. . . . Every Negro who came up to vote, having been challenged [by Daniels himself] was compelled to stand in the middle of a ring with scores of people looking on and read parts of the constitution. None on trial knew what *ex-post facto* law was and none could correctly pronounce "Lieutenant Governor." . . . I justified my act by reflecting that these Negroes were being used by the liquor forces to their own undoing in the debauchery of their race. I fortified myself by the fact that they and the white registrar were violating the law. But it was cruel. . . . After a dozen had made the attempt and failed, the other uneducated Negroes did not seek to vote.[115]

With the black vote all but eliminated, the dispensary won, 677 to 483. On the same ballot was a referendum to prohibit the production of alcohol within Raleigh's corporate limits. Again, the drys won, 751 to 187.[116] It also signaled an end to the black franchise. Although there were subsequent attempts to put together a legal challenge, no state court would hear the case.

To get Broughton elected, Daniels had promised the Raleigh wets that he would keep the legislature from doing anything to damage them without a referendum, but he had promised nothing to the unincorporated parts of the county. Accordingly, early in 1903, the legislature passed a set of acts that limited the manufacture and sale of alcohol in the state of North Carolina to incorporated cities. In one swipe, prohibition had been imposed on the state's rural areas. This aided the liquor trade in cities like Raleigh, as rural dwellers in the surrounding area, as well as those in nearby towns that had gone dry by referendum, came to Raleigh for their pint or dram. Raleigh's liquor business boomed.

The epilogue to the prohibition battles in Raleigh contained no small amount of irony. The dispensary proved to be a great financial success. As Daniels explained, "Instead of injuring [the liquor] trade the dispensary rather increased it, for people came from the dry surrounding territory to get their wet supplies."[117] During its first three years in operation, the dispensary generated a profit of nearly $1 million, an astronomical sum at the time.[118] The success of the dispensary caused its advocates to reevaluate its usefulness. The idea had been to regulate alcohol out of business, but instead the regulators had become the region's most profitable distributors. They decided to kill the monster they had created. In the winter of 1907–8, they put a new prohibition referendum to the city's voters. As Daniels described it, "It was a rather peculiar situation. The men who four years before, were fighting to keep the saloons open, were now fighting to keep the dispensary and, in the main, the men who had fought to drive out the saloons by means of the dispensary, were now fighting to destroy their own creature and put an end to the sale of liquor in any legal way in Raleigh."[119] Despite the liquor monies flowing into the city's budget, the drys won a resounding victory. In the end it mattered not a bit, because a few months later the entire state went dry when a statewide prohibition referendum passed overwhelmingly. Alcohol would not be sold legally again in North Carolina for twenty-seven years.

———

Another long-running fight in which Daniels remained a combatant involved the state's dreadful public education system. Many self-made men who received a good bit of their education at the school of hard knocks belittle formal education. In Daniels's day the list of such men included Thomas Edison, one of Daniels's heroes, who "considered conventional education to be perfectly useless."[120] Unlike Edison, Daniels never underestimated the boost in life he received from his formal schooling. More than that, Daniels considered education an ennobling act, and his commitment to the school movement was consistent with his theology. Protestantism contained a strong element of spiritual self-improvement, a quest for "the means of elevating universally the intellectual and moral character" of its adherents.[121] Since firsthand knowledge of the Bible required, at a minimum, literacy, the public school movement and the Protestant component of the progressive movement were strongly aligned in nineteenth-century America, and thus Daniels became one of the South's most vocal and persistent advocates of public spending for education at all levels. However, the state's Protestant leaders, who supported public funding for primary education, fought appropriations for public universities.

Since Reconstruction, North Carolina's public school system, such as it was, had been mired in low spending, low returns, low expectations, and racial disharmony, but the state's universities formed the occasional oasis of learning in an otherwise arid landscape. Their very success threatened their future, however, as public financial support for the universities soon came under attack from the state's leading private institutions. As Daniels put it, "Representatives of the Baptist, Methodist, and Presbyterian colleges had gone to the Legislature and protested against appropriating money, particularly to the University [of North Carolina], unless it would agree to change its course so as to admit only post-graduates."[122] At its core the conflict can be understood as a simple one of ideology and, more acutely, competition. The organized churches in America had long maintained their own institutions of higher learning separate from those supported by the public. In North Carolina the early leaders were Wake Forest (Baptist), founded in 1834; Trinity, later Duke (Methodist), founded in 1838; and Davidson (Presbyterian), founded in 1836. Over time, the schools came to see themselves as *the* providers of undergraduate education in the state. By the 1890s, the leaders of the private schools, supported more broadly by influential personages within each denomination, sought to limit state funding for the growing university system. They saw their opening in the turmoil surrounding the rise of the Fusionists.

Prior to solidifying their control of the state, the Fusionists sought support where they could. Since much of their power came from the Populists, almost all of whom were low-church Protestants, the Fusionists cultivated a relationship with church leaders, with the hope that those leaders would use the pulpit to promote Fusion. This strategy yielded some success. The president of Trinity, future Methodist bishop John C. Kilgo, fervently supported the efforts to impoverish the state universities. Among the Baptists, the most outspoken antiuniversity leader was Columbus Durham, who served as the secretary of the Baptist State Convention, a position Daniels described as having "more power than a Bishop." Daniels gave a grim assessment of Durham, describing him as "an intense man without the least shadow of humor. He asked no quarter and gave none. He convinced himself that the prosperity of the University [of North Carolina] would work to the injury of Wake Forest College. He believed the success of Wake Forest College was essential to the Baptist Church. With this premise, he set out to destroy anything that stood in his way."[123] What stood in Durham's way was the legislature's financial support for the state universities.

Despite the vocal support of Kilgo and Durham and the victories of the Fusionists at the polls, the antiuniversity forces still had to kill the state funding of the various institutions. Daniels and Aycock were the universities' most vocal defenders, Aycock on the stump and Daniels in the pages of the *N&O*. The debate quickly turned personal. Durham, as combative as he was self-righteous, was accustomed to the internal battles of his denomination, but he proved less adept at the public persuasion necessary to swing votes in the legislature. In an effort to salvage victory, he began waging an ad hominem attack on Daniels. Among the more curious stones he hurled was "Josephus Daniels is not fit to run a newspaper."[124] Daniels's co-religionist Kilgo displayed more decorum but was no less antagonistic.

Meanwhile, the wily leader of the Fusionists, Marion Butler, realized that the university system was more popular than the demagogues Kilgo and Durham. Butler recognized that the universities, and public schools more generally, were also mechanisms for funneling jobs and construction contracts in key towns around the state, as well as a means of raising working-class boys, such as Butler himself, to the middle class. Thus Butler reneged on any deals, implicit or otherwise, that had been made during the campaign. Of Butler's support, Daniels wrote, "In all the political bitterness of the day—and no words can describe it—University men always felt that they were under obligation to Butler in that crisis."[125] It was one of the few positive comments Daniels ever offered about his political enemy. Thus the "war on the university," as Daniels called it, ended with a whimper as Butler sold out his religious supporters.

No sooner had university funding been saved than the debate over funding for the state's primary and secondary schools began to heat up. During Daniels's school days, North Carolina's public school system was, by any reasonable measure, nonexistent. At the time, state law permitted local individuals of initiative to promote public education, and it permitted local taxpayers to tax themselves to support such initiatives. But across vast swaths of the state, no such local initiative had been taken. In the early 1880s, that began to change with the graded-school movement. The state legislature passed legislation in 1881 and 1883 that facilitated the referendum process by which local taxpayers could approve the establishment of a segregated graded-school system. Following the passage of the 1883 act, while Daniels still owned the *Advance* and held the local government print-ing contracts in Wilson and Wilson County, public school advocate Alex-ander Graham (the "father of the North Carolina graded school system" as well as the father of future University of North Carolina president Frank Porter Graham) came through town and, with Daniels's support, persuaded the locals to submit the graded schools to a referendum.

The school referendum law called for ballots to be printed as FOR and AGAINST, and voters cast one or the other depending on their preference. As the local public printer, Daniels received the ballot contract from the local school committee. However, Daniels printed only ballots that said FOR. On Election Day, when one voter demanded an AGAINST ballot, the polling officer had to confess that none had been delivered. Daniels was called for, and the voter ("a wealthy time merchant," in Daniels's words, which meant he loaned money to farmers while holding a lien on their crop as collateral) demanded to know why Daniels had not printed any AGAINST ballots. Daniels replied that he had not been paid to print any. When asked who paid him to print the FOR ballots, he said the school com-mittee, chaired by his old benefactor Thomas Jefferson Hadley, who was as pro-school as Daniels. The voter demanded an AGAINST ballot, but Daniels refused to print one. By the time the AGAINST forces could supply bal-lots, the polls were closing. The Wilson graded-schools referendum passed that day.[126]

Despite his early success in getting a school in Wilson, Daniels recog-nized that it would take decades of bitter town-to-town fighting to create graded schools across the state. What the pro-school forces needed was blanket legislation from the state assembly. With the rise of the Fusion-ists, such support would not be forthcoming. The African Americans in the Fusionist coalition rightfully demanded that any comprehensive edu-cational legislation address the needs of both black and white students. (Although the expenditures on North Carolina's black schools were not as low, relative to white schools, as they were elsewhere in the South, they were low by absolute standards. Furthermore, the state's overall per pupil spending was roughly 20 percent of the national average.)[127] Conversely, whites in either party would object to any "pro-Negro" school legislation. Further harming the chances of statewide legislation, the Populists rejected any system that concentrated power at the state level and thus threatened their "democratic localism," which in practice meant low tax rates and thus meager funds for local schools.[128] Thus the school issue, one of the pillars of Daniels's progressivism, languished during the Fusionist reign. It was exactly the type of "progressive" issue that Daniels thought could be settled by disenfranchisement.

In 1899 the legislature appropriated $100,000 to support the state's schools. It was "the first state appropriation for schools in thirty years," which is to say since Reconstruction.[129] Aycock's election in 1900 accelerated the change. Per pupil expenditures nearly doubled for white students, as the state went on an educational spending spree. During Aycock's term as governor, the number of school districts voting for the local options tax increased from 30 to 229. The state helped finance the construction of nearly 700 new school buildings.

The momentum continued into the next administration. Robert Glenn, another leader of the white supremacy campaign, followed Aycock in the governor's mansion and continued the school building program. In 1907 the legislature passed a bill promoting the construction of high schools in rural areas, and within a year 160 new schools opened. Over the period, the state's contribution to secondary and primary education grew by more than 1,200 percent. Ironically, despite the openly racist component of the state's pro-school movement and the fact that the school system was rigorously segregated, Aycock managed to increase the aggregate support for black schools, though relative to spending on white schools, spending on black schools lagged following disenfranchisement. Although nearly 100 new black schools were built, and although North Carolina's ratio of black-to-white funding was the highest in the South, that ratio fell over time.[130] As one historian put it, "Discrimination in schooling closely followed the extreme new discrimination in voting, a correlation unlikely to have been coincidental."[131]

Through Aycock's and Glenn's years in office, the state remained solidly in Democratic hands. As Glenn's term drew to a close, at the national level the Democrats were more optimistic than they had been for some time. For one thing, upon being elected in 1904, Theodore Roosevelt had pledged not to seek reelection in 1908. His political heir was the competent but not especially colorful Secretary of War William Howard Taft. Although a two-time loser, Bryan still held top billing on the Democratic Party marquee. Thinking this might be his year, Bryan declared his candidacy, and at the party convention in Denver he was, in Daniels's words, "nominated by acclamation," which in practice meant he received 90 percent of the votes on the first ballot.[132] Bryan could still electrify a crowd on the campaign trail. With the world's gold supplies continuing to expand and deflation (and thus Free Silver) no longer an issue, Bryan had turned to the tariff, the trusts, and imperialism as the planks in his platform.

If all of the stars in the heavens had aligned, Bryan might have pulled off an upset. But few stars aligned for the Democrats that year, and in the end, Bryan did only marginally better against the stolid Taft than Parker had done against TR four years earlier. Carrying only the South, Colorado, Nevada, and his home state, Nebraska, Bryan went down by an electoral vote of 321 to 162. The Democrats only gained three seats in the House, and the balance in the Senate remained unchanged. For Democrats, as much as Daniels would have hated to say or hear it, perhaps the best thing that came out of 1908 was that it ended William Jennings Bryan's quest for the White House. Perhaps the second-best thing that followed the election was that the longtime president of Princeton University lost a series of minor, and otherwise meaningless, internal squabbles of the type that perpetually plague the academy. That discouraged university president was Woodrow Wilson, and his defeats caused him to consider a move into politics.

Josephus Daniels standing in his office at the News and Observer. *At the height of his power, he was the most politically influential person in the state. (Courtesy of Frank Daniels Jr.)*

(top) *The Wilson County Courthouse. Daniels grew up around the corner to the left, and his first newspaper, the Wilson* Advance, *was across the street.* (Courtesy of the North Carolina Office of Archives and History, Raleigh, North Carolina)

(bottom) *The Yarborough House Hotel, one of the South's finest hotels. Daniels lived here his first three years in Raleigh.* (Courtesy of the North Carolina Office of Archives and History, Raleigh, North Carolina)

Josephus and Addie Daniels at the time of their golden wedding anniversary, taken while Daniels was U.S. ambassador to Mexico. (North Carolina Collection, University of North Carolina Library at Chapel Hill)

Addie Daniels with her mother, Adelaide Worth Bagley, and infant daughter, also named Adelaide. The child died shortly after this photograph was taken. (North Carolina Collection, University of North Carolina Library at Chapel Hill)

(top) The Bagley home, located in what became an African American neighborhood. Josephus and Addie Daniels lived here from 1888 to 1921. (Courtesy of John Lapp)

(bottom) Furnifold Simmons, leader with Daniels of the white supremacy campaign. Daniels called him a political "genius." (North Carolina Collection, University of North Carolina Library at Chapel Hill)

Charles Brantley Aycock, Daniels's boyhood friend and future governor. (North Carolina Collection, University of North Carolina Library at Chapel Hill)

Locke Craig, future governor, known as the "Little Giant of the West." (North Carolina Collection, University of North Carolina Library at Chapel Hill)

Daniels at his desk at the N&O during the white supremacy campaign. (Courtesy of the North Carolina Office of Archives and History, Raleigh, North Carolina)

John C. Kilgo, president of Trinity College (later Duke University) and bishop of the Methodist Church. He and Daniels had many battles. (Duke University Archives)

Marion Butler, the "Sly Fox of Sampson County," leader of the N.C. Fusionist Movement. (Southern Historical Collection, Wilson Library, University of North Carolina Library at Chapel Hill)

Daniel Lindsay Russell, Fusionist governor. Daniels eventually destroyed him. (North Carolina Collection, University of North Carolina Library at Chapel Hill)

James Young, African American leader and publisher and, ironically, Daniels's Raleigh neighbor. (North Carolina Collection, University of North Carolina Library at Chapel Hill)

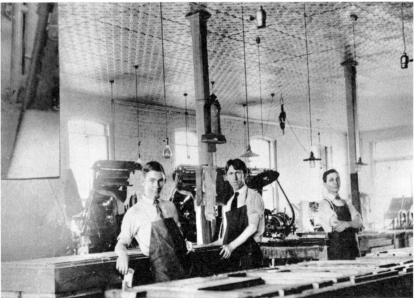

(top) The News and Observer *building, the first building from the right, on West Martin Street. Today the newspaper occupies most of this block. (Courtesy of the North Carolina Office of Archives and History, Raleigh, North Carolina)*

(bottom) The typographers at the N&O, around the time Daniels took over the company. He replaced these men with the new linotype technology. (Courtesy of the North Carolina Office of Archives and History, Raleigh, North Carolina)

*Julian Shakespeare Carr,
Confederate veteran, successful
industrialist, and Daniels's
financier. (North Carolina
Collection, University of North
Carolina Library at Chapel Hill)*

*Woodrow Wilson. Daniels and
Wilson maintained a complex
relationship, but Daniels stuck by
Wilson because he was a political
winner. (Prints and Photographs
Division, Library of Congress,
LC-USZ62-88979)*

(top) Wilson's first cabinet. Daniels is seated third from Wilson's left. William Jennings Bryan sits immediately to the president's right. (Courtesy of Frank Daniels Jr.)

(bottom) Franklin Delano Roosevelt and Josephus Daniels at the Navy Department. The future president learned a great deal about politics and life while serving under Daniels. (Courtesy of Frank Daniels Jr.)

(top) *Franklin Delano Roosevelt and Josephus Daniels during the 1932 presidential campaign. After winning, FDR tapped Daniels to be ambassador to Mexico. (Courtesy of Frank Daniels Jr.)*

(bottom) *Daniels and his youngest son, Frank, and Frank's son, Frank Jr., the year before Daniels died. (North Carolina Collection, University of North Carolina Library at Chapel Hill)*

(top) Wakestone, the facade. Daniels claimed to have built the house with all the stones that had been hurled at him by his enemies. (Courtesy of John Lapp)

(bottom) Daniels shortly before his death. Taken late in 1947, this is the last known photograph of Daniels before his death in January 1948. (North Carolina Collection, University of North Carolina Library at Chapel Hill)

(top) Statue of Josephus Daniels in Nash Square near downtown Raleigh. The statue faces the front door of the News and Observer building. (Courtesy of John Lapp)

(bottom) Stone facade of the current N&O. Although the newspaper was not created until 1881, Daniels traced its lineage to an earlier paper founded in 1865. (Courtesy of John Lapp)

6. Cup-a-Joe

A small-town Southern newspaper editor with radical agrarian and pacifist views, [Josephus Daniels] was a hopeless landlubber.

—NATHAN MILLER, *The U.S. Navy: A History*

If the pen is mightier than the sword, then Josephus Daniels was arguably the mightiest man in North Carolina following the white supremacy campaigns of 1898 and 1900. Of the state's other leaders during those years, only Furnifold Simmons could rival Daniels in political clout, and beginning in 1901, Simmons spent much of his time serving in the U.S. Senate. In the decades that followed the victories of 1898 and 1900, no one else spent as much time at the apex of the Democratic Party's hierarchy as Daniels did. Those who would dispute this claim might point to the fact that Daniels never held elected office, but the two most powerful offices, governor and U.S. senator, placed constraints on the power of the men who held them. At the time, under the state's constitution, governors were limited to one four-year term. Thus the only place to go from the governor's mansion was the U.S. Senate, but except for the one-term Fusionists, senators tended to hold their seats for a very long time. (Simmons spent thirty years in the Senate; his colleague Lee Overman, who replaced the Fusionist Jeter Pritchard in 1903, served for twenty-seven years. Before them, Matt Ransom served for twenty-four years.) Furthermore, as Daniels had learned during his days in Cleveland's administration, it was difficult to control local politics back in Raleigh from Washington, D.C. Each of the great triumvirate of stump speakers during the white supremacy campaigns—Charles Brantley Aycock, Robert Glenn, and Locke Craig—made it to the governor's mansion for a term. None made it to the Senate. The Democratic machine that ran the state during these years was called the Simmons Machine, but there would have been no Simmons Machine were it not for Daniels. Twice Daniels had put Simmons in control of the state party apparatus, leading to the creation of Simmons's political organization. Similarly, Aycock, Glenn, and Craig were formidable men, destined to be movers and shakers among the Tar

Heels of their generation, but it was Daniels's support that proved crucial in making each governor.

Daniels was a friendly man, but he never feared making an enemy. He once attributed the failed political career of his financial mentor Julian Shakespeare Carr to the fact that Carr "was no politician. . . . He was so agreeable he didn't like to run against anybody."[1] The observation tells as much about Daniels as it does Carr. Daniels loved the rough and tumble of a political campaign. The *News and Observer* endorsed a large number of political candidates over the years, and it often went to lengths to vilify those it did not endorse. But of all the state-level campaigns Daniels would wade into, perhaps none proved as personally treacherous as the 1912 campaign for the state's U.S. Senate seat. It was a monumental struggle dominated by Tar Heel legends. (That campaign also serves as a landmark of another sort, as it was the last Senate seat appointed by the state legislature rather than elected by direct popular vote. The Seventeenth Amendment to the U.S. Constitution would be ratified before the next seat was contested.)

Since the Democrats controlled the state apparatus following the white supremacy campaigns, whoever they chose would get the seat, which was currently held by the redoubtable Simmons, who had been handed Marion Butler's Senate seat following the election of 1900. Simmons had faced little opposition for reelection in 1906, but 1912 was shaping up to be a different campaign. Simmons's brand of backroom horse-trading went over well in Washington, but in the intervening years the luster on his reputation back home had begun to tarnish. In old age Daniels dedicated an entire chapter of his memoirs to Simmons's transgressions, the most offensive of which was his support for the tariff. Simmons, never an idealist, abandoned, to the extent he had ever signed on in the first place, much of the progressive agenda, which had dominated the party since the downfall of Grover Cleveland. Daniels thought Simmons had sold out to the Yankee "tariff gang," and Aycock joined Daniels in his disenchantment with their erstwhile colleague.

The two old schoolmates remained in close contact, personally and professionally, as Aycock and Daniels's older brother, Frank, resumed their legal partnership in Goldsboro after Aycock left the governor's office in 1905. By the fall of 1911, Aycock had decided to challenge Simmons's reelection. Aycock let Daniels in on his plan well before formally announcing his candidacy. In preparation for backing Aycock, Daniels openly broke with Simmons, and the *N&O* began a campaign against the incumbent senator months before Aycock's plans were widely known.[2] Simmons and Daniels had worked closely for twenty years. The *N&O* would not have begun campaigning against the powerful senator without a popular alternative candidate to tout. Aycock was *the* most popular man the paper could support. However, he was not the only Tar Heel titan seeking Simmons's seat. The soon-to-be-former governor, W. W. Kitchin, was looking for a job, and he too wanted to replace Simmons. To cloud the picture further, state supreme court chief justice Walter Clark also announced his candidacy.

Daniels had close ties to each of these powerful men. He and Simmons, an *N&O* stockholder, had led the party to its resurgence in the late 1890s. Kitchin, another *N&O* stockholder, had become governor with Daniels's aid, and Kitchin's brother, Claude, a U.S. congressman, was a longtime Daniels confidant. Clark, too, owed his position as chief justice to Daniels's support. (Daniels, as part of the white supremacist movement, had helped orchestrate the impeachment of Fusionist David Furches, Clark's predecessor as chief justice.) Despite these ties, none could transcend those that connected Daniels to Aycock. Other than the members of his and his wife's immediate families, Daniels would never be closer to anyone than he was to Aycock. They were "like kin," as Daniels put it, and Daniels prepared to put the full force of his own considerable political clout and the voice of the *N&O* behind Aycock's Senate campaign. Unfortunately, on April 4, 1912, just as Aycock prepared to launch his challenge to Simmons, Daniels's boyhood friend died of heart failure while speaking in Birmingham, Alabama. He was fifty-two.

Daniels faced a difficult decision. Of the remaining candidates, he preferred Clark, going so far as to call him the "better qualified man" and a "truly national progressive."[3] A man of moral strength, Clark possessed a haughtiness of a kind not uncommon among Victorian gentlemen, perhaps too much so. "Judge Clark was a martinet," as Daniels succinctly described the jurist, and more importantly, although Clark "wrote with force and power . . . on the stump [he] had neither eloquence nor driving power."[4] Furthermore, at age sixty-six Clark's best years were clearly behind him. But perhaps his biggest handicap was that, unlike his opponents, during his long years on the bench, he had built up no political machinery. Backing a loser for the sake of principle never appealed to Daniels. He preferred winning, and Clark could not win.

Daniels had worked closely with both Kitchin and Simmons, but he had also crossed each of them in recent years. Simmons had been vilified recently in the *N&O*, and Daniels's feud with Kitchin went back to the 1908 gubernatorial campaign. Glenn had followed Aycock in the governor's mansion with little controversy. As Glenn's term approached its end, Daniels backed Craig as Glenn's successor. However, Kitchin challenged Craig for the governorship. As an *N&O* stockholder and the product of a prominent eastern political clan, Kitchin felt he had as much right to Daniels's support, and their party's nomination, as Craig. Daniels did not agree, and he stuck by Craig, who battled Kitchin for the nomination. To further complicate the governor's race that year, there was a third candidate, Ashley Horne, yet another *N&O* stockholder. The battle went to the state convention, where it continued for four days encompassing sixty ballots.[5] The fratricidal affair made for great political show, but it was exhausting and distracting.

Although the *N&O*'s coverage of the governor's race was clearly pro-Craig, its editorial section remained officially neutral. It was well known that Daniels supported Craig, but he recognized a hopeless political deadlock when he saw one. To move the process forward, he cloistered himself with Horne in a proverbial back room to work out a compromise. Daniels persuaded Horne that he could not win. Horne then renounced his candidacy and released the delegates committed to him. Since it was understood that enough of these would go to Kitchin to give him a majority, Daniels was in effect handing the election to Kitchin. Daniels then persuaded Craig's followers to accept Craig's defeat, but only after Daniels reached a separate backroom understanding with the Kitchin forces "that Craig would be next in line for the governorship."[6] Thus while Daniels had helped make Kitchin governor, he had only done so after failing to secure the post for Craig, a point Kitchin had not forgotten four years later when he sought to replace Simmons.

In attacking Simmons in preparation for Aycock's run, Daniels had taken a holier-than-thou attitude, emphasizing Simmons's ties to the state's railroad, lumber, and tobacco interests. Unlike Simmons, Daniels never held or even ran for elected office; thus he never had to answer to political constituents to remain in office. Like former senator Matt Ransom, Simmons understood that to convert his elected office into a feudal duchy, he had to collect and distribute political booty and patronage. Simmons's vision of the Democratic Party was limited to that of obtaining power. Neither especially sinister nor cynical for a politician of his day—which is to say he was both sinister and cynical by most other standards—Simmons differed from Daniels when it came to their views of the Democratic Party. Daniels viewed the party as the means toward achieving both broad and specific social objectives—lower tariffs, Free Silver, and antitrust at the national level, and white supremacy, railroad regulation, and increased educational funding at the state level—which for him represented a progressive agenda. For Simmons, however, the party's success was the end in and of itself. Thus he had a very simple view of divisive issues like the tariff. If powerful constituents, such as North Carolina's lumbermen, could benefit from tariffs on goods shipped by their foreign competitors, and if Simmons could only obtain such tariffs by supporting similar requests from other congressional colleagues, then he would support tariffs.

Thus backed into a difficult choice between Kitchen and Simmons, Daniels did something unusual. He did nothing. Claiming illness, an unlikely situation given his strong physical constitution (Daniels was ill no more than a handful of days in his adult life), he turned the management of the paper over to his subordinates during the primary campaign, and he formally refused to endorse any candidate. The *N&O* sat out the senatorial race. The newspaper openly backed Craig for the governorship, which he won, and in the end, the party returned Simmons to the U.S. Senate.[7]

BACK TO WASHINGTON

Daniels's physical absence from the state during the Senate race was at least partly due to the fact that he was helping put Woodrow Wilson in the White House. Daniels was well acquainted with Wilson long before the professor-turned-politician became the Democratic candidate for president that summer. Indeed, Daniels claimed that as early as 1886 Walter Hines Page had told him, following dinner at the Yarborough House, where Daniels then lived, that Wilson, with whom Page had been acquainted for several years, might someday be president.[8] In the intervening years, Page touted Wilson as the antidote to the bland Civil War generals that the Republicans had been successfully running for president since U. S. Grant's victory in 1868. Page was eventually proved correct, though it would be a few decades before the Republicans finally ran out of Civil War heroes.

The third child and eldest son of a distinguished Presbyterian minister, Thomas Woodrow Wilson was born in 1856 in Staunton, in western Virginia.[9] After a boyhood in Georgia and South Carolina, he studied at what was then known as the College of New Jersey—the future Princeton University—and graduated in 1879. Graduate study at Johns Hopkins followed a brief stint studying law at the University of Virginia and practicing it in Atlanta. Like Daniels, Wilson would come to find influencing the law more interesting than practicing it. The two men differed, however, regarding the philosophical side of the law and, by extension, politics. Daniels viewed both law and politics through the lens of expediency, as means to an end, and his political strategies evolved as a result of his experiences rather than from abstract reasoning. He had little interest in theories of law or government. His days in Chapel Hill studying Blackstone and Chitty had done nothing to whet his appetite for legal or political theory. Although, like Daniels, Wilson would prove to be an opportunistic political practitioner, unlike Daniels, Wilson found political theory fascinating, and indeed, he spent much of his young manhood studying it. An average student as an undergraduate and an uninspired legal practitioner, Wilson prospered intellectually and personally at Hopkins. He received a Ph.D. in 1886 after completing his well-regarded treatise, *Congressional Government*.[10] After leaving Hopkins, Wilson began a happy and successful career as an academician. Elevated to the position of president of Princeton in 1902, he spent the next eight years leading it into the ranks of the truly great modern universities.

Somewhat austere by nature, in public Wilson often seemed distant and unapproachable. He confounded political friends and enemies alike by addressing them as if they were students in his class. In fact, this harsh public persona hid sensitivity and a considerable reserve of personal warmth and humor, which he usually revealed only in small, private settings. Before he left Hopkins, Wilson had married Ellen Louise Axson, who like her husband was the offspring of a well-known and well-regarded southern Presbyterian minister. Despite evidence of an extramarital liaison on Woodrow's part, the marriage proved to be happy enough. Ellen subordinated her artistic aspirations to her husband's academic and, later, political ambitions. In the privacy of his home, among family and close friends, Wilson could be caring and gracious, and he was a loving and devoted father to his three daughters.

During his Princeton years, Wilson honed the personal characteristics that would mark his political career, namely, an enormous intelligence and capacity for work coupled with a supercilious attitude that would eventually cost him as many friends (and votes) as his positive qualities earned him. Wilson's personal flaws tended to be particularly costly when he became involved in the horse-trading element of politics. French premier Georges Clemenceau said talking to Wilson was "something like talking to Jesus Christ."[11] To British prime minister David Lloyd George, Wilson appeared to believe "in mankind but distrusted all men."[12] Senator Henry Cabot Lodge described Wilson as a master of "low cunning."[13] Although each of these men was at one time a political foe, and thus their views should be weighed accordingly, the man they describe can be recognized clearly enough in Wilson.

Since he was never the product of a political machine and never had to stand for reelection until he ran for a second term as president, Wilson underappreciated the efficacy of compromise. Indeed, Wilson's biggest flaw as a politician—or at least the flaw that would ultimately destroy his presidency and, in essence, Wilson himself—was his habit of wrapping his opinions in a self-righteousness that he confused with noble idealism; thus, in his own mind, he insulated them from dissent. And so Wilson often backed himself into uncompromising corners from which the only outlets were victory or defeat. On more than one occasion, Daniels compared Wilson to Martin Luther, another of history's great figures not known for compromise. Daniels put Wilson's creed as "God defend me against compromise."[14] It made a better campaign slogan than a strategy for governing a republic.

Although Daniels had known of Wilson since his after-dinner conversation with Page in 1886, he first met the future president in January 1909. Wilson, having recently been engaged in a battle with Princeton's trustees over reforms he proposed for student social life at the institution, stopped by Raleigh on his way to deliver a speech in Chapel Hill commemorating the centennial of Robert E. Lee's birth. An unswerving Democrat, Wilson followed party politics closely enough to know that Daniels was the man to see in Raleigh, so he dropped by unannounced at the *News and Observer*'s office. There he found Daniels bent over copy for the next day's paper. The two chatted for a while, and Daniels invited Wilson to stay with him and Addie at the Bagley house in Raleigh. Wilson politely declined, preferring the quietude of a hotel room. (The choice was a wise one, as the Bagley house was getting crowded. The Danielses had added two more sons to their growing family: Jonathan Worth, born in 1902, and Frank Arthur, born in 1904.)

Wilson did visit the Bagley home later that evening. Before dinner, Addie informed Wilson of the long association, through the Presbyterian Church, of members of her family and Wilson's late father. Wilson showed little interest in much beyond what was on his own mind, however, and he spent the evening lecturing his hosts on his battles at Princeton. Even Daniels, who quickly acquired the habit of fawning before Wilson, noted the professor's "absorption" of the topic that evening. Only after he discharged his speaking obligation in Chapel Hill the following day did Wilson reveal his better social qualities. He became "the soul of the company at the dinner in his honor [and] . . . charmed the entire company" later that evening.[15]

In that first visit, Daniels witnessed Wilson's bad and good sides, the self-absorption but also the fire that Page had noted more than twenty years earlier. Although not a physically dominating public speaker in the mode of Bryan or even Aycock, Wilson had honed his oratorical skills from years in the classroom. An organized thinker and coherent writer, Wilson was good at clearly conveying his thoughts to his audience. Although Wilson was personally conservative, his politics and the points he emphasized in his public speeches increasingly came from the progressive wing of the Democratic Party. By the time Wilson visited Daniels in Raleigh, his policy prescriptions included a low tariff and antitrust. Later he would add currency reform by supporting the creation of a central bank (the Federal Reserve System). Daniels and other leading Democrats approved. Many especially liked that Wilson's progressivism lacked the backwoods Populism that Bryan had pushed to defeat in three of the last four presidential elections. Although Wilson had not backed Bryan in 1896, and he was sometimes referred to as an anti-Bryanite, by the time Daniels came to know Wilson, the core of the professor's political views coincided with Bryan's. Leading Democrats could see Wilson as Bryan wrapped in a more socially acceptable veneer. In addition, Wilson had resided long enough in New Jersey to be a northerner, while still claiming southern roots. Thus Wilson appeared to be the thinking man's Bryan from the Northeast. In 1909, this combination of traits put him on the short list of contenders for the 1912 Democratic presidential nomination.

The problem was Wilson had no political experience. But that was about to change. George Harvey, president of Harper and Brothers publishing house, sought a means of leveraging his own power within the national Democratic Party. In the days when candidates were put forward out of smoke-filled rooms, one way to rise in the party was to tout a candidate who emerged from the back rooms and won an election. Before a candidate could emerge, however, he had to become a serious contender. To this end, in *Harper's Weekly*, Harvey had been running the slogan "For President—Woodrow Wilson."[16] In an age devoid of electronic media, such publicity in a reputable, nationally distributed magazine helped make Wilson a household name. However, Wilson was then in his mid-fifties, too old (and probably too egotistical) to begin his political career at the bottom or even a middle rung of the ladder. If he were to leap from the top of academia to politics, it would only be to an important executive position. The looming 1910 New Jersey gubernatorial race offered both Wilson and Harvey the opportunity they sought.

Despite Wilson's growing popularity, it would have been very difficult for a political novice, and an outsider, to obtain the Democratic Party's nomination for governor without the support of the New Jersey political machine. Harvey managed to persuade the leaders of the machine that Wilson was a "safe" choice, progressive but not radical. Daniels would argue later that Wilson remained aloof from any backroom negotiations and thus entered the race with his hands clean. But in fact Wilson was in on Harvey's deal with the machine. He explicitly told a Princeton colleague that the bosses understood that his gubernatorial nomination was "the mere preliminary of a plan to nominate me in 1912 for the presidency."[17] As evidence of Wilson's supposed virtue in the matter, Daniels offered the fact that once he was in the governor's mansion, Wilson refused to support the reelection of New Jersey machine boss U.S. Senator Jim Smith. (Interestingly, the first record of Daniels's correspondence with Wilson involved Wilson's renunciation of Smith. Daniels sent the governor a clip from the *N&O* in which the paper denounced Smith.)[18] Wilson needed no encouragement. He used Smith's support to obtain the governorship and then, aiming at the White House, he betrayed Smith while appearing to be a selfless reformer. Wilson had cleverly traded Smith's local machine support for the national appeal that came with being viewed as an antimachine progressive.[19] The episode serves as an example of Wilson's ruthless cunning. As a Wilson biographer put it, the Smith case "presented Wilson with a nearly foolproof opportunity to reap political advantage."[20] It would not be the last time Wilson was charged with ingratitude toward Democratic colleagues.

In fact, Daniels's handling of two subsequent cases concerning Wilson's less-than-generous treatment of party elites elevated Daniels into Wilson's inner circle and ultimately into the office of secretary of the navy. Daniels sincerely liked and admired Wilson, and later, to an extent, Wilson would return the feeling; however, at this stage of their association, Wilson's affection for Daniels was primarily utilitarian. The first incident in which Daniels displayed his value to Wilson concerned Harvey. Daniels later claimed to have jumped on the Wilson-for-president bandwagon "shortly after his visit to North Carolina" in 1909, and the *N&O* did speak favorably about Wilson for at least two years prior to his run for the presidency. However, only after Wilson's renunciation of Smith and the New Jersey machine did Daniels, always against the machine, except the one he and Simmons ran in Raleigh, got fully behind Wilson for president. Wilson justified that support when he subsequently turned on Harvey and Harvey's Wall Street colleagues.

In the winter of 1911, after Wilson became governor of New Jersey but before he turned on Smith, Harvey had invited Daniels to a meeting at a hunting lodge near High Point, North Carolina. There Harvey recounted how he had been instrumental in placing Wilson on the New Jersey throne, and he declared that he was planning a similar role for himself in Wilson's elevation to the presidency. A key component of Harvey's plan was that Wilson's journey to the White House would have to go through Wall Street, where, Harvey argued, one could find moneymen who would support a Democrat, but not one named Bryan. Harvey did not think a Democrat could obtain the presidency without such support. Daniels, recalling Cleveland's efforts to appease Wall Street during the 1894 crisis, did not embrace Harvey's plan and extricated himself from the meeting with a folksy admonition about not skinning rabbits before they had been shot. Soon thereafter Wilson betrayed the New Jersey machine and was off and running for president. Clinging to Wilson's coattails, Harvey accepted the career assassination of his erstwhile colleague Smith and quietly organized a Wall Street pool to fund Wilson's upcoming presidential campaign.

In addition to editorial support in the *N&O*, Daniels contributed to Wilson's campaign by seconding his former Washington correspondent, Tom Pence, to serve as Wilson's press secretary. Daniels, his ear always to the political ground, discovered that Harvey was proceeding with his Wall Street funding scheme. Through Pence, Daniels got Wilson to renounce the deal publicly. Daniels argued that the publicity value of renouncing Wall Street money would far exceed anything Wall Street would put into Wilson's campaign. Wilson listened to Pence, followed Daniels's advice, and broke with Harvey, who quickly became a vocal enemy. The subsequent fallout was messy, but as Daniels had predicted, it was to Wilson's political advantage. Taking no public credit for his own role in the affair, Daniels disingenuously wrote in the *N&O*, "Woodrow Wilson has been born to good luck. George Harvey has come out against his nomination. Harvey and his [J. P.] Morgan connections had become a dead weight around the candidacy. Now that Wilson, from no act of his, has lost that deadly support, the prospect of his nomination has brightened."[21] At this stage of the campaign Daniels might or might not have been considering a position in a future Wilson cabinet, but helping to eliminate Harvey increased the odds of such a position. (Harvey would obtain his revenge by attacking Daniels in print during his time in Wilson's cabinet.) Daniels's next service to Wilson almost certainly assured him a cabinet position.

Like many intellectuals on the left of American politics in those years, Wilson despaired at his party's continued support for Bryan. In 1907, during the run-up to the 1908 presidential campaign, Wilson, in written correspondence with a Princeton alumnus, disparaged Bryan. The letter contained innocuous criticism of no particular importance, but it included the following passage: "Would that we could do something, at once, dignified and effective, to knock Mr. Bryan, once and for all, into a cocked hat."[22] Bryan won the nomination that year but lost the election. Wilson's private correspondence remained private. However, Wilson subsequently fell out with some of his Princeton supporters, and in January 1912, as the presidential race was about to get under way, Wilson's letter was leaked to the New York *Sun*. On the very day the letter was released, Bryan was visiting Daniels in Raleigh. The Commoner had stopped by to spend some time at the Bagley home before he and Daniels left together to attend the Democrats' annual Jackson Day Dinner in Washington.

In an act of journalistic courtesy, an insider at the *Sun* forewarned Daniels of what was about to happen. In Daniels's words, his "heart sank" upon reading the letter. He shared it with Bryan and then persuaded Bryan to make no remarks of any substance until they had a chance to hear Wilson's explanation of his letter. (Daniels knew how damaging communicating through the press could be.) Later, the *Sun* reporter caught the two at the Raleigh train station. When asked about the matter, Bryan simply made an offhand remark about how the affair seemed all too appropriate, as the *Sun* had been trying to knock him into a cocked hat for years. Meanwhile, Wilson, already in Washington, decided to consult Daniels before saying anything else about the conflict with Bryan. Upon reaching Washington, Daniels and Bryan parted company, and Pence took Daniels to meet privately with Wilson, who wanted to know Bryan's state of mind. Daniels explained that he had persuaded Bryan to keep an open mind and to say nothing of consequence in public until Wilson addressed the matter. Wilson then ran through several versions of formal remarks, some in the form of a press release, others in his speech to be delivered that evening, January 8. After some back-and-forth, both men agreed that a press release should be avoided but that a warm tribute to Bryan should be included in Wilson's speech. In that tribute, Wilson called Bryan the Democratic Party's "fixed point," and he closed the speech with an appeal to party unity, making no reference to his earlier anti-Bryan letter. When Wilson sat down, Bryan patted him on the shoulder and said, "Splendid . . . splendid." Daniels claimed that "Bryan was moved as I never saw him before or afterwards."[23] Bryan would speak the following evening.

It appeared that with Daniels's aid a crisis had been avoided, but most narrative accounts of the period overlook the most important event of those crucial days. Daniels offered an even greater service to Wilson the night before Daniels and Bryan went to Washington. While cloistered in the Bagley home after dinner, Bryan freely discussed his chances for the party's nomination in the upcoming presidential campaign, and he asked Daniels for his opinion. It was difficult to share the bad news with his long-time friend and hero, but Daniels was not optimistic about Bryan's chances and he said so. Daniels's critical assessment of another run for the White House caused Bryan to conjecture, perhaps rhetorically, that he could not win without the support of the northeastern machines. This was exactly the kind of support Wilson could obtain. Taking Bryan's question as if it were not rhetorical, Daniels concurred that Bryan could not win without the Northeast and added that he was unlikely to get it. Summarizing their conversation, Daniels wrote, "The conversation ended. I did not doubt that Bryan, having reached the conclusion he had unfolded to me in the sacred precinct of friendly communion, had given up ambition for the presidency."[24] Daniels helped Bryan reach that conclusion. It is not known if Daniels shared this conversation with Wilson when they met privately in Washington the next day, but two days later, in his speech before the Jackson Day crowd, Bryan completely avoided any mention of Wilson's disparaging letter. Bryan noted, perhaps with a nod toward Wilson, "No friend of mine need to be told that I am much more interested in the things for which we are struggling than I am in office."[25]

And so Bryan offered an open hand to Wilson. More importantly, by deciding not to seek the nomination, he had increased Wilson's chances of obtaining it, a state of events brought about by Daniels's careful maneuvering over the previous forty-eight hours. Daniels had helped keep Bryan from standing in Wilson's path to the nomination, but, coyly, the Commoner did not immediately come out in support of the professor. As the Democratic National Convention opened in Baltimore in late June, Bryan, following the Nebraska delegation, committed to House Speaker Champ Clark of Missouri. Clark, who had only become speaker with the Democratic takeover the year before, was a gifted political operator who entered the convention with a majority of the delegates on his side. No Democrat holding a majority of the delegates before the convention had failed to win the nomination since Martin Van Buren had been defeated by James K. Polk, coincidentally in Baltimore, in 1844. But the Clark forces, which included the party's conservative Wall Street wing as well as Tammany Hall, poorly played their hand at the convention. Instead of cultivating Bryan, they alienated him, and he began to think he would have no influence in a Clark administration. Thus out of righteous conviction or cynical self-interest, Bryan dramatically switched his support from Clark to Wilson.

No one could deny the impact of Bryan's backing, but it did not automatically give the nod to Wilson. Clark still had the upper hand, but it was a weaker hand than it had been before Bryan's defection. Three other men played crucial roles, and without their efforts, Wilson would not have benefitted from the votes Bryan swung his way. Two of those men—Albert Burleson, a seven-term congressman from Texas, and A. Mitchell Palmer, a Pennsylvania lawyer and businessman turned politician—had steered their large state delegations into the Wilson camp before the convention. Without the grassroots efforts of these two, Wilson would have entered the convention with even fewer than the 248 delegates (of 1,088 total) pledged to him. The third key player was Daniels, who managed to keep Wilson's nomination alive at the convention even when his cause seemed hopeless. Wilson knew he faced an uphill battle against the Clark forces, which had history on their side. Some in Wilson's camp thought he should cut the best deal he could with Clark. Among these was Wilson's campaign chair, William F. McCombs, who had, in Daniels's words, "given up." Wilson, following the custom of the time, remained away from the convention. He hesitated to take McCombs's advice and release his delegates. He called Daniels.

As Daniels recalled, Wilson asked, "How does this situation look to you, Daniels? Some of my friends [meaning McCombs] think that as Clark has a majority I should release my delegates. What do you advise?" Daniels understood the power of Bryan's support, and after canvassing the convention floor, he discovered the support for Wilson was broad. Later, recalling his thoughts at the time, Daniels wrote that those who expected an easy Clark victory "figured without appreciating Bryan's resourcefulness." Daniels frankly told Wilson, "It may take several days but you are sure to be nominated." Wilson, taken aback by Daniels's blunt confidence, asked how that could be. Daniels then gave a lengthy tally of which key Dems were in Wilson's camp but had yet to declare officially their position. He closed with "My experience in politics is that men find a way to do what at heart they desire to do. It will be so with enough delegates [currently] in other camps to nominate you."[26] Wilson, though skeptical, followed Daniels's advice and held on to his pledged delegates. He would soon realize the value of Daniels's political opinions. It took forty-six ballots, but Wilson won the nomination.

The 1912 presidential campaign quickly became Wilson's to lose. As an incumbent Republican in a Republican-dominated era, William Howard Taft should have had an edge; however, after supplying the winner in eleven of the last thirteen presidential races, the Grand Old Party was not so grand. Earlier that summer, Taft had won the Republican nomination over Theodore Roosevelt, who had not happily adjusted to the role of former president. While competent enough, Taft brought to the presidency none of the fire the country had experienced with TR in the White House (TR called his successor, among other things, a "puzzlewit" and a "fathead").[27] The Democrats had taken control of the House in the most recent midterm elections (the first time they had done so since the debacle of 1894), and they had cut substantially the Republican majority in the Senate. TR sought to bring back the fire, but the hard-nosed men who ran the Republican machines around the country handed Taft the nomination. TR, never a man to back down from a fight, ran on a third-party "Progressive" ticket.

McCombs had run Wilson's campaign before the convention, but his recommendation that Wilson yield to Clark had cost him some of the nominee's respect. To make McCombs's position worse, several party leaders, including Daniels, placed little confidence in his ability to run a presidential campaign against an incumbent *and* TR, the best-known name in American politics since U. S. Grant. Wilson wanted a new chairman for the campaign, and in principle Daniels agreed he should have one. However, Daniels, in concert with Burleson and Palmer, counseled against tossing McCombs overboard. Correctly sensing that, after the Smith and Harvey affairs, Wilson had already earned a reputation within the party for "ingratitude," they persuaded Wilson to keep McCombs. But they all agreed that he should be saddled with a strong vice chair. That person would be New York financier and engineer (and Wilson's future treasury secretary and son-in-law) William Gibbs McAdoo. In Daniels's words, McAdoo was "a man of initiative, independent, courageous, and able to lead."[28]

Before, during, and after his time serving Wilson, McAdoo proved himself in many different spheres, including law and engineering. In addition to his unqualified success at financing America's eventual participation in World War I, he earned a national reputation by overseeing the construction of the tunnels linking New York and New Jersey under the Hudson River. A native Georgian, McAdoo always got on well with Daniels. In particular, the two men agreed completely on two of the more prominent social issues of the day: women's suffrage and prohibition, both of which they supported.

McCombs bristled at the appointment of such an important figure to a position he considered to be that of his assistant. But the other insiders had turned against him, and he had no choice. McCombs's churlishness eventually led to his omission from Wilson's cabinet. Subsequently offered the ambassadorship to France, McCombs refused in a huff, though Daniels urged him to accept.[29] Daniels was happy to see McCombs shipped anywhere outside Wilson's inner circle, as his absence was to Daniels's advantage. Although Daniels considered McCombs an energetic and competent drummer for the party, he had no faith in McCombs's counsel on matters of state. Apparently neither did Wilson, and McCombs was never again a part of Wilson's inner circle. As McCombs's star fell, Daniels's rose, and Wilson named Daniels chair of the publicity campaign. Wilson's press secretary, *N&O* reporter Tom Pence, would now report to Daniels.[30]

Daniels's disenchantment with McCombs reflected the growing rivalry among those competing for a position in Wilson's inner circle. Another individual who eventually joined that inner circle and with whom Daniels would compete for favor was "Colonel" Edward House. A rich Texan with ties to the New York financial community, House's political dabbling was not unlike that of George Harvey. House latched onto Wilson and ultimately became his intimate personal confidant. Daniels clearly resented House's role in the party, the presidential campaign, and eventually Wilson's administration and personal life. In his memoirs, Daniels made a point of noting that when he received the crucial phone call during which Wilson inquired about conceding the nomination to Clark, House was not even in the United States. Furthermore, while some narratives give House credit for leading the Texas delegation into Wilson's camp, Daniels gave the credit to Burleson.[31] Later, in personal correspondence with Newton Baker, a leading Democrat who would become secretary of war, Daniels referred to House as nothing more than a "yes man."[32]

As head of publicity, in July and August Daniels spent much time at Wilson's summer home in Sea Girt, New Jersey, developing what Daniels called their "campaign textbook." Over the past few years, Wilson had been drifting leftward, and by the time he won the nomination, he could be classified as a full-blown progressive. Daniels's only fear was that Roosevelt would maneuver to Wilson's left, making the Democrats "look like a sort of conservative party standing between" Taft and Roosevelt. Thus, Wilson and Daniels organized a "militantly progressive" campaign focusing on what came to be called the New Freedom. An exclusively domestic program, the New Freedom emphasized lower tariffs, antitrust, support for labor, and a central bank. In short, the New Freedom was the 1910s version of the 1890s progressivism.

Despite concerns about TR's popularity, overall Daniels found Wilson "confident he would be elected."[33] Daniels, too, was confident, but since the Fusionist victories of the mid-1890s, he worried over every election until the votes were counted. As students of national politics, both men understood the basic arithmetic of the electoral college and expected TR to cost Taft a second term. Their confidence was well placed. Although Taft and Roosevelt together collected 1.3 million more votes than Wilson, the professor won in an electoral landslide—435 to Roosevelt's 88 and Taft's 8. In addition, the party increased its control over the House by an additional 63 seats, and it even took control of the Senate. Wilson recognized Daniels's contribution to his nomination and eventual election, and he had become personally closer to Daniels during the campaign. Shortly after his victory, in a letter to Homer Cummings of the Democratic National Committee, Wilson wrote, "Anybody who speaks in behalf of Josephus Daniels speaks to my heart as well as my head. I have a real affection for him as well as a very high opinion of him."[34] Wilson's biographer notes that of "the men who had worked for his nomination, Wilson most liked and respected Josephus Daniels."[35] As a reward for Daniels's efforts—and, it should be added, for helping Wilson dispose of Harvey, Bryan, and McCombs—Wilson invited Daniels into the administration as secretary of the navy. Daniels accepted.

There was initially some talk of Daniels taking the postmaster's slot, but that post eventually went to Burleson, who had better connections in Congress. Although Wilson appears to have been set on bringing Daniels into his cabinet, there were objections. Among those who reviewed Wilson's list of potential appointees were House and Wilson's old acquaintance Walter Hines Page.[36] Both House and Page strongly recommended David Franklin Houston, president of Washington University in St. Louis and a native Tar Heel. This was an ominous sign for Daniels's chances of being in the cabinet. Political expediency dictated that cabinet positions be distributed geographically. There were only ten seats in the cabinet in those days, and thus room for only so many Tar Heels. Daniels had already marked House as a rival, and House reciprocated the sentiment. As for Page, he also strongly supported Houston as a strategy for keeping Daniels out. The two Tar Heel editors were no longer on friendly terms.

Nearly thirty years had passed since Page and a young Josephus Daniels had collaborated on Page's *State Chronicle* in Raleigh. The warmth of their relationship had chilled considerably. Exactly why is difficult to determine.

The gradual disappearance of references to Page is noticeable in Daniels's memoirs and correspondence, but from Daniels's side, there was no big break. Years later, Daniels ascribed their split to Page's rejection of Bryan during the silver wars of the 1890s, and it was true that Page thought Bryan a bumpkin who would destroy the Democratic Party.[37] To Daniels, however, this was merely a political dispute of the type he dealt with daily at the *News and Observer* and in the party's backroom deal-brokering sessions. It was not the kind of thing that should rupture an old friendship. Daniels continued to be friends with men with whom he shared much larger disputes. Page's biographer noted that his "onetime friendship with Daniels had curdled into enmity, at least on Page's side. He [Page] had come to despise his successor on the *State Chronicle* because of his racist demagoguery and his championship of Bryanite agrarian radicalism and, perhaps, for having succeeded where he, Page had failed."[38] Daniels had certainly engaged in racist demagoguery and had supported Bryan, and the suggestion of Page's resentment at Daniels's success in Raleigh is consistent with Page's personality.

Whatever the cause of the Page-Daniels split, according to Page, Wilson asked him for cabinet recommendations. Page touted Houston while explicitly denigrating Daniels. House, who was in communication with Page, reported that "Page was very earnest in his belief that Daniels should not go into the Cabinet. He thought he was not big enough."[39] The irony is, of course, that Daniels was bigger than Houston by any standard other than academic achievement, though it should be noted that academic credentials mattered to Wilson, a point with which Page was surely familiar. So it is easy to interpret Page's outspoken support of Houston as a means of sabotaging Daniels, since Page himself held cabinet aspirations, and he knew that there was a limit on the number of native Tar Heels Wilson would appoint.[40] Page reasoned that if he and Houston were in, then Daniels would be out. In the event, Page's plan backfired. Wilson, proving to be a better judge of Page than Page was of Wilson, happily accepted Page's recommendation of Houston and rejected his blackball of Daniels. Page eventually became Wilson's ambassador to the Court of St. James in London. And so Daniels became head of the U.S. Navy.

The most prominent member of Wilson's cabinet was William Jennings Bryan, with whom Wilson entrusted the portfolio of state. Bryan was without question the most imposing character in the cabinet. Wilson and Bryan made an odd couple. Austere by any standard, the president often seemed the very embodiment of the reserved, haughty academic. His rigorous mind and self-righteousness often combined to form a mulelike stubbornness. Bryan, although as stubborn as Wilson, in contrast possessed the moral courage of an Old Testament prophet. Whereas Wilson's stubbornness resulted from rigorous, self-justifying intellectual exercises, Bryan's stubbornness came from Bryan simply being Bryan. It was his greatest personal trait. It also kept him out of the White House and would eventually ruin him.

That a split would eventually come between the president and his secretary of state did not surprise many observers at the time. There were those in Wilson's camp who, expecting the dynamic Bryan to upstage the sometimes grim professor, urged Wilson to leave the Great Commoner out of the cabinet. McCombs had advised Wilson, even before he secured the party's presidential nomination, to renounce Bryan as a candidate for the cabinet. This Wilson honorably refused to do.[41] Given Bryan's role in eventually making Wilson the nominee, Wilson's refusal to cast Bryan adrift proved wise. And not just Wilson's friends were suspicious of any Wilson-Bryan pact. Not a few of Bryan's friends were distrustful of the northeastern wing of their party. Many remembered the apostasy of Grover Cleveland all too well. Despite Wilson's southern roots, Bryan's people viewed the professor as a New Jersey man, which was little better than a Tammany man. According to Daniels, who at this stage maintained ties to both camps, Bryan's ever-loyal friends expected Wilson to honor the party's "four-year" plank, which, if Bryan were free from the shackles of a cabinet post, would allow him to campaign to become the first in line for the White House in 1916. Bryan, all too aware of the controversy surrounding his appointment and uncharacteristically in doubt, sought Daniels's advice on the matter. Daniels urged his old hero to join his new hero and accept the post.[42] This advice, which Bryan followed, seemed sounder at the time than it proved in retrospect.

DREADNOUGHTS AND U-BOATS

From the time Daniels took over the navy, he envisioned it as an instrument for promoting the broader social objectives of the Wilson administration. Daniels viewed the navy's enlisted men as he viewed Wilson County cotton farmers: as the downtrodden to be lifted through public policy. He intended to use the navy as a school to educate seamen and advance their moral and social development. To achieve this objective, Daniels quickly realized that he would need to change the navy's organizational structure. This and other actions, such as competitive bidding for navy contracts, ruffled the feathers of more than a few senior officers who viewed the navy's institutions as inviolable. Of equal importance, the officer corps viewed those institutions as a trust that they alone controlled. As the navy changed under Daniels's leadership, the officers who opposed him blamed Daniels for the subsequent shortcomings of the service. As one officer wrote shortly after Daniels took charge, "The fleet is deteriorating like an eagle in a cage."[43]

The navy that Daniels took over in the spring of 1913 represented one of the republic's great paradoxes. Its socially hidebound officer corps, byzantine organizational structure, and arcane customs resembled something from a Gilbert and Sullivan opera. Officers still wore swords, braided epaulettes, and bicorns—a fore-and-aft pointed headdress that was as antiquated as it was impractical. By any reasonable standard, the social barrier between officers and men was insurmountable. In Daniels's view it was also intolerable. According to the new navy secretary, naval officers regarded themselves "as belonging to a superior caste, while the enlisted personnel live in a different compartment." Shortly after taking office, Daniels offended a senior naval aide by addressing newly enlisted men as "young gentlemen," an expression that had been reserved strictly for officers-to-be. In the aide's view, enlisted personnel were unworthy of the title "gentlemen." He advised Daniels to "use some other term, as it might be misunderstood. It has never been done in the Navy."[44] Daniels ignored such advice.

The navy also maintained a dangerously antiquated command structure. In 1913, the navy still possessed no central staff organization, such as the U.S. Army had adopted in 1903 (and, ominously, as the Prussians had adopted nearly a century earlier). In the navy, form appeared to drive function. Only half-jokingly, John Holland, the father of the modern submarine, observed that the navy initially rejected his submarines because the officers had "no deck to strut on."[45] Holland's complaint about the service rang true enough with the egalitarian Daniels, who could do little, at least in the short run, about the haughtiness of the officer corps and the treatment of the enlisted personnel. But almost immediately he began addressing the navy's organizational structure. He would encounter resistance, and as a result, some heads would have to roll.

The naval command structure that Daniels inherited had worked reasonably well in the age of sail. In the absence of information technologies that would allow a centralized command to control geographically dispersed ports and operations at sea, seven largely autonomous bureaus formed the pillars of the navy's organizational structure. These bureaus, each commanded by a rear (i.e., two-star) admiral, included navigation (which despite its name was essentially the navy's personnel bureau); supplies and accounts; engineering; construction and repair; ordnance; yards and docks; and medicine and surgery. With the U.S. Marine Corps, headed by a commandant who held the rank of major general, and the judge advocate general's office, headed by a navy captain, these nine units and the men who led them formed the organizational backbone of the navy. Over time the bureaus, which operated separately from the fleet command, had become not unlike medieval fiefdoms with their commanders enjoying semi-autonomous and essentially perpetual sinecures.

Nominally, the bureau chiefs reported directly to the secretary of the navy, who had a civilian assistant secretary and four uniformed naval aides. Each aide covered a specific piece of naval turf: operations, personnel, matériel (supplies), and inspection. In practice the naval aides formed what Daniels's predecessor in the Taft administration, George Meyer, called the "Council of Aides."[46] According to Daniels, in theory these aides were to serve as the "eyes and ears" through which the secretary administered the navy. In practice they were often neither. By the dawn of the twentieth century, this system—created in 1842—had been rendered obsolete by technological change and a new strategic vision that had captured the imaginations of leading naval theorists.[47] The antiquated system would not survive Daniels's tenure as navy secretary.[48]

Despite its arcane structure, the navy, which on the surface remained among America's most culturally insular institutions, was in the process of undergoing a transformation—a revolution in which Daniels would play a key role. Here was the great paradox of the early twentieth-century U.S. Navy: dramatic upheaval amidst stifling tradition. Many naval historians attribute this upheaval to one man: Alfred Thayer Mahan. The son of Dennis Hart Mahan, a renowned West Point professor of strategy, the younger Mahan graduated from the U.S. Naval Academy in 1859.[49] He embarked on what began as a mediocre career, notable only for the publication of a minor tract on naval operations during the Civil War. However, this publication marked Mahan as something of an intellectual among his fellow officers, and in 1884 he was offered a post at the newly formed U.S. Naval War College in Newport, Rhode Island—an advanced graduate school for naval officers. He accepted, and in 1886 he became president of the college. It proved to be an ideal posting for a man with intellectual aspirations who liked to socialize almost as much as he hated sea duty.[50] Just prior to this appointment, Mahan had, by his own account, experienced a near-religious epiphany from which emerged a vision of modern naval strategy.

In Mahan's vision, offensive striking power, in the form of a great concentrated naval fleet, served as a key, perhaps even *the* key, instrument of national policy. The fleet would be designed for the decisive battle in which it would destroy an opponent's fleet, thus exposing the enemy's coast and ports to the will of the victors. This vision, based on historical experience, was not particularly new. Indeed, Mahan was in essence extending an ancient metaphor of land warfare to the sea. The quest for the decisive battle had captured the imagination of generals since Hannibal defeated the Romans at Cannae more than two millennia earlier.[51] However, it represented a different vision, certainly a different vision of and for the navy, than that held by U.S. leaders up to that time. The older, pre-Mahan navy was seen as a necessity in case of war, but the navy was not viewed as an important day-to-day instrument of national policy.

The British had perfected the use of their navy to protect and promote trade throughout their far-flung empire. With an economic base anchored to trade between their geographically dispersed imperial holdings, the British clearly saw trade and national security as inextricably linked. Without open sea lanes, there was no British Empire. As Joseph Chamberlain, one of the empire's leading promoters, put it, "It is not too much to say that commerce is the greatest of all political interest and that Government deserves most the popular approval which does the most to increase our trade."[52] The United States, in contrast, had a huge and rapidly growing domestic population, a continentlike landmass, a large diverse economic base, and no empire (yet), so Congress had not funded a navy to compete with the British. Indeed, since Waterloo, the economically developed nations of Western civilization had relied largely on the British navy to serve as, in effect, the navy of the West, and it could be counted on to keep the seas open and safe for everyone. Thus, prior to Mahan, the primary objective of the U.S. Navy was not national security, at least not in any context in which that term was subsequently employed.[53] A small, decentralized navy, in conjunction with army coastal batteries to protect key ports and waterways against invasion, would serve well enough. In 1889, the United States was, by almost any meaningful economic measure, already the world's richest country, yet it possessed the world's twelfth-largest navy.[54] That was about to change. Mahan supplied the philosophy for that change.

Despite his singular devotion to a singular vision—an increase in naval power—Mahan thought broadly, and his great thesis, which is often reduced to "sea power equals national power," was in fact based on a well-informed understanding of history, politics, geography, and economics. Surprisingly, given that it was the militarists who most fondly adopted Mahan's thesis, his book can be understood as a treatise in economic history. Though Mahan was a militarist by upbringing, training, and profession, the implications of his key insights rested upon economic pillars: Trade generated wealth; only a strong navy could guarantee trade; and the circle was completed by the fact that the resulting wealth could be taxed to generate an even more powerful navy, which would help ensure more wealth, and so forth, creating a virtuous cycle of naval strength and economic prosperity.

The war college post also offered Mahan the opportunity to put his thoughts on paper. *The Influence of Sea Power on History, 1660–1783,* published in 1890, was his principal treatise. Among Mahan's readers was Theodore Roosevelt, who became Mahan's most ardent and important supporter. Upon reading the volume, TR wrote to Mahan, congratulating him on the achievement: "I can say with perfect sincerity that I think it very much the clearest and most instructive general work of the kind with which I am acquainted. It is a very good book—admirable: and I am greatly in error if it does not become a naval classic."[55] In a related piece, also written in 1890, Mahan further endeared himself to TR by emphasizing the importance of gunboat diplomacy in the Caribbean, tying it to a big navy and a canal through Panama, which at the time was part of Colombia. "Militarily speaking," Mahan wrote, "and having reference to European complication only, the piercing of the Isthmus [of Panama] is nothing but a disaster to the United States, in the present state of her military and naval preparation."[56] This was a manifesto for TR's future foreign and naval policies: Dominate the weaker Caribbean states, build and control the canal, and construct a big navy to enforce the Monroe Doctrine; in short, dominate the Western Hemisphere and frighten off the other Great Powers.

Accordingly, TR and other Mahanians became known as the "Big Navy" faction. For Daniels, Mahan's legacy was decidedly mixed. The two men would eventually have a nasty clash, but, never one to begrudge another man's fame, Daniels, even after they parted ways, referred to Mahan as "the great Naval statesman."[57] The success of the U.S. Navy in the war with Spain demonstrated all too clearly the efficacy of Mahan's theories and boosted the Big Navy advocates. In the two main naval engagements of the war, U.S. forces completely destroyed beyond salvage their antiquated Spanish counterparts. In 1898, at opposite ends of the world, Commodore George

Dewey and Rear Admiral William T. Sampson commanded naval forces that faced off against the Spanish. In the Philippines, Dewey commanded a squadron of cruisers displacing several thousand tons each and sporting eight-inch guns. Off the coast of Cuba, Sampson commanded a larger force, including battleships of 10,000 tons and a combination of twelve- and eight-inch guns. As one naval observer summarized those engagements: "An hour or two at Manila, an hour or two at Santiago, and the maps of the world were changed." So, too, was naval warfare.[58] The other Great Powers watched and learned from what happened to Spain's forces at Manila and Santiago. The battleship was the key.

The battleship's main role in the history of naval warfare would be relatively brief, as the aircraft carrier would soon replace the battleship as the primary instrument of a Great Power navy. But the age of the battleship would coincide exactly with Josephus Daniels's control of the U.S. Navy, and Mahan's system approached its zenith during Daniels's tenure. The event that made real Mahan's vision was the construction of the HMS *Dreadnought* in 1906.[59]

Only rarely does a single event fundamentally alter everything that comes after it. The launching of the *Dreadnought* was such an event. By raising the killing effectiveness of naval vessels (and their cost), and thus precipitating the naval arms race that contributed no small amount to the onset of the Great War, as much as any other single technological innovation in history, the *Dreadnought* changed the world. Upon taking over as secretary of the navy, Daniels wrote that he "had decided to include in my estimates [of naval expenditures] money for the construction of two dreadnaughts" per year.[60] As Daniels's correspondence indicates, the very word "dreadnought" became synonymous with the modern battleship, and these ships formed the core of modern navies. Daniels represented the first generation of political leaders who had to deal with the full ramifications of this upheaval in naval warfare.

British ingenuity and industry, guided by First Sea Lord Admiral of the Fleet Baron Fisher, built the *Dreadnought*, though the Americans, Italians, and Japanese all had plans for large battleships when the *Dreadnought* was launched.[61] In the previous half-century, naval technology had evolved slowly, with each new vessel or class of vessels slightly different from the last. The *Dreadnought*, however, differed in every way from its forerunners. At 17,900 tons and capable of reaching speeds of twenty-one knots, it was larger and faster.[62] In addition, it was more heavily coated in protective armor, and perhaps most crucially, the *Dreadnought* had more firepower than any ship in history to that point. With five turrets, each containing two twelve-inch guns, it became the first "all big gun" ship. No pre-dreadnought carried more than four twelve-inch guns.

Because of its size and the size of its guns, the *Dreadnought* could fire accurately at 10,000 yards—nearly six miles—depending on weather conditions. (Dewey had opened fire with his eight-inch guns at Manila at 5,000 yards.) Thus, the *Dreadnought* could kill anything afloat at a distance that would eliminate the need for smaller guns. In the words of a contemporary report, "It is hardly too much to say that, given her speed, gun power, range and the smashing effect of the concentrated force of heavy projectiles, the *Dreadnought* should easily be equal in battle-worthiness to any two, probably to three, of most of the ships now afloat." Upon being informed about the *Dreadnought*, Germany's Kaiser Wilhelm II supposedly said, "In my opinion, this is the armament of the future."[63]

After learning of British plans to build the *Dreadnought*, the United States followed almost immediately with its own all–big gun ships.[64] Launched in 1909 and displacing 16,000 tons each, the first two American dreadnoughts, the *Michigan* and the *South Carolina*, were a bit smaller than the *Dreadnought*, and they only had eight twelve-inch guns. But because the guns were on the center line of the ship, whereas two of the *Dreadnought*'s turrets were offset in the middle of the ship, the American battleships could fire an eight-gun broadside equal to that of any ship afloat. These were soon followed by the 20,000 ton, ten-gun *Delaware* and *North Dakota*. Any one of these ships would have decimated Dewey's victorious fleet at Manila before the older vessels could even get their guns in range.

British ingenuity did not stop with the *Dreadnought*. Since the all-big-gun ship could outshoot anything afloat, the next frontier was speed. At the time, the large German cruisers, the so-called armored cruisers that were smaller than battleships, could reach speeds of twenty-four knots; thus they could outrun the new dreadnoughts. To bring the firepower of the *Dreadnought* to bear on the armored cruisers, Fisher came up with a hybrid: the battle cruiser, an all-big-gun ship with the speed of a cruiser. To obtain the necessary speed, the battle cruisers were given even larger engines and slightly narrowed hulls. In addition, they sacrificed armor. The first of these swift monsters was put into British service in 1909. (Unfortunately, in battle the light armor proved to be a fatal flaw, and on a single day in May 1916, at the Battle of Jutland, four battle cruisers and 5,000 men would go to the bottom of the North Sea.)

Thanks to the initial efforts of TR, the United States had moved toward the upper tier of the world's navies by the time Daniels took over in the spring of 1913. Determining the size of a navy is an inherently risky exercise, but as measured by gross displaced tonnage (arguably the crudest of empirical indicators), the changes wrought by Mahan's theories and TR's obsession with a big navy helped propel the United States from the world's twelfth-largest navy in the late nineteenth century to the third-largest by 1914.[65] On the eve of the Great War, the United Kingdom possessed, by any accounting, the world's most powerful navy, with more than 20 modern dreadnoughts and 10 modern battle cruisers, as well as more than 80 other capital ships, which included older, pre-dreadnought battleships and the older armored cruisers. In addition, the United Kingdom had built more than 50 newer or "light" cruisers. The United Kingdom's gross size of nearly 3 million tons more than doubled that of its closest rival, Imperial Germany, which in 1914 could send to sea 13 modern dreadnoughts, 6 modern battle cruisers, more than 40 other capital ships, and roughly 25 light cruisers.[66] The United States came next, followed by France, with just under a million tons each. No other navy in the world could compete at the time with the big four, though Japan was building rapidly.

Upon taking office, Daniels found himself in the middle of this international naval arms race. The Roosevelt administration's naval building program—the first in the United States to include dreadnoughts—which was continued with a few updates during Taft's administration, yielded, by the spring of 1913, eight dreadnoughts sporting twelve-inch guns. The last two of these, the *Wyoming* and the *Arkansas*, were enormous (over 27,000 tons each), even by the standards established by the HMS *Dreadnought* only a few years earlier. They were followed by two *New York*–class ships, which were under construction when Daniels took office. Similar in size to the *Wyoming*-class ships, the *New Yorks* sported ten fourteen-inch guns. As noted, once in office, Daniels proposed to continue this "two-a-year" building program.

The dreadnought was not the era's only major technological innovation in naval warfare. While the British were perfecting the battleship, they were also experimenting with the submarine. Whereas the efficacy of a battleship was immediately obvious, few military strategists could claim to have fully grasped the possibilities of the submarine, which, unlike the battleship, was as yet untried in war. Still, by 1913, each of the Great Powers had constructed a submarine fleet, and each was in the process of expanding their fleet. As with most things naval, the United Kingdom led the race, with nearly 80 subs. It was followed by France with 67, the United States with 39, and Germany with 30. Although slow to see the sub's value, the Germans were about to discover that the *Unterseeboot* (or U-boat), was, as one British politician put it, the ideal "weapon of the weaker nation."[67]

Although smaller than the surface vessels it hunted, the submarine possessed all the firepower it needed, since the killing force of a torpedo was vastly multiplied by the energy unleashed when it struck at or below the waterline. The submarine merely punched a hole in a vessel and let physics do the rest. Stealth and low price were the sub's main advantages. Even after the development of sonar toward the end of the Great War, finding and catching a submarine was much more difficult than locating a surface vessel. Thus the submarine made an ideal commerce raider. Indeed, in practice it proved far superior to the surface raiders it replaced. The submarine era would last longer than that of the dreadnought.

Daniels may or may not have read Mahan before taking over the U.S. Navy, but he was certainly familiar with Mahan's treatise and its primary theses. Initially, the hubbub over Mahan's theories and the revolution in naval technology embodied in the *Dreadnought* had little impact on Daniels's day-to-day management of the navy. Because he did not expect to fight a major war at sea, he wisely left matters of strategy and tactics to his admirals. However, Daniels's plans to change the navy's organizational structure and to turn the navy into an educational institution were not universally embraced by the navy brass, and he soon became dissatisfied with several officers in key positions. Despite the officers' protests, Daniels was determined to reform the navy, and eventually the recalcitrant officers would go the way of their bicorn caps.

Daniels's primary uniformed assistant, the so-called operations aide, was Admiral Bradley A. Fiske. Daniels made a point of noting that he had "inherited" the admiral, whose "consuming passion was to confer all power in the head of Operations," that is, in his own hands. Physically small and verbally combative, Fiske proved to be a formidable opponent. Initially, the two got on well enough. Fiske even described Daniels as "a delightful gentleman, companionable, sympathetic, and apparently open-minded."[68] However, once Fiske realized Daniels's plans for the service, their relationship deteriorated, and one of Fiske's most vocal supporters among the navy's officers described Daniels as "a small minded despot, bigoted and narrow in his views."[69]

Despite their differences, like Daniels, Fiske recognized the inefficiency of the navy's current organizational structure. Even before Daniels took over, Fiske was working hard to turn his own office into that of an overall commander of naval operations. He hoped to centralize the command structure such that the ranking uniformed officer would report to the secretary and would issue orders directly to the fleet commanders and the bureau chiefs.[70] According to Daniels, Fiske imagined himself occupying the new position, and he might have if he had been more politically savvy. Even Daniels acknowledged that Fiske possessed a great deal of energy and a keen naval mind. Indeed, from Daniels's perspective, Fiske was all too lively, and he and Daniels eventually differed on so many issues that both parties recognized their days together were numbered. The only question was who would break first.

Fiske came to see Daniels as little more than a meddling political hack. Daniels may well have been some of the things Fiske suspected him of being, but Daniels was also a tenacious political infighter. Nearly thirty years of state and local battles in Raleigh had taught Daniels that victory often went to the man who played the best hand behind the scenes. Fiske's unhappiness with Daniels's appointment mattered little to Daniels, who expected a good officer to follow orders regardless of whether he liked them. Despite their disagreements about who was in charge, their relationship might have survived had their battles not been accompanied by major policy disputes as well. The main issues over which they conflicted included the size of the navy, with the Mahanian Fiske being a hard-core Big Navy man, and the role of Fiske's office, wherein Fiske wanted authority for operations consolidated. Once the Great War began in the summer of 1914, Fiske wanted the U.S. fleet consolidated to begin joint exercises in the Atlantic. In addition, Fiske saw no reason for Daniels to meddle with the navy's customs or its treatment of its enlisted personnel.

Daniels disagreed with Fiske on each of these issues. He saw no reason to expand the navy faster than what he and Wilson called the administration's "second to none plan," even if, despite its name, it would leave the U.S. navy second to that of the British and the Germans for the foreseeable future. At this stage of his tenure, Daniels was happy with the "two-dreadnoughts-a-year" plan. Fiske wanted more. In addition, Daniels fully supported organizational reform, but he wanted the chief of operations to serve more as an advisor and as a conduit of orders from the navy secretary, rather than as an independent naval commander in chief, as envisioned by Fiske. When war came, Daniels objected to consolidating the fleet and organizing joint maneuvers in the Atlantic because at the time the navy was engaged in ongoing campaigns in the Caribbean (see Chapter 7) and because he thought such a move on the part of a neutral power would appear too belligerent to the Europeans already at war. Fiske hoped that he could hold on long enough for the political winds to change and blow Daniels out of office. Daniels, who read political winds better than Fiske, developed a successful strategy for getting rid of the recalcitrant admiral.

Soon after he took office, Daniels recognized that he would have to scrap the Council of Aides and reduce the power of the bureau chiefs. The activities of the bureaus themselves would remain, but Daniels would break the feudal status of the bureau chiefs by simply commuting to four-year terms what had previously been open-ended billets. Under Daniels's policy, at the end of their terms, the chiefs could go to sea or into retirement. This became known as the "Single Oak" policy. (Admiral Samuel McGowan, Daniels's loyal chief of supplies and accounts, coined the term as a double entendre after the Danielses' Washington home, Single Oak, which was located in the northwest part of the city, adjacent to what is today Woodley Park.)[71] Henceforth, younger men could compete for Daniels's favor to obtain a bureau posting, which would now open more frequently than in the past. Some officers resented the change, and the service became divided into those who supported Daniels's policy and those who did not. One of Daniels's enemies wrote that he was "unrelenting in the misuse of [his] official power to punish officers of the Navy who incurred his official disapproval."[72]

Daniels decided to dispose of the Council of Aides. He did so by ignoring the officers in place until they were assigned to sea duty and then simply refusing to replace them. Thus, of the four aides Daniels inherited from his predecessor, all but Fiske were quickly eliminated, which certainly streamlined the command structure. Orders now flowed directly from the secretary to the bureau chiefs and fleet commands, and information flowed unabridged from them to the secretary. The problem was that Daniels instituted this system when naval strategy, following Mahan, called for a centralized command structure *within* the uniformed hierarchy. The new strategy called for a chief of naval operations (CNO), in a structure similar to what modern armies had developed in the form of the general staff. Fiske saw this development as inevitable. In a memo to Daniels, Fiske noted, "Our Navy Department has no machinery for doing what a general staff does."[73] Initially, although Daniels wanted to change the bureau structure, he was not sure the naval equivalent of a general staff was a good idea, and he resisted Fiske's urge to "Prussianize" the U.S. Navy; however, after war came to Europe, Daniels recognized the efficacy of such a centralized system. Perhaps of more immediate importance to Daniels was the fact that he saw in the creation of a CNO a chance to rid himself of Fiske.

After more than a year of being hounded by Fiske on the topic—that is, during the period in which Daniels was purging the bureau chiefs and his aides—Daniels permitted Fiske to make a formal presentation on his proposal to reorganize the navy's command structure. According to Fiske's proposal, all command and bureau functions would pass through the CNO's office, making the CNO essentially the navy's commander in chief.[74] Daniels formally rejected the plan. But Fiske managed to have his CNO plan circulated among sympathetic congressmen. Exactly when Daniels first got wind of Fiske's back-door machinations is not known, but he had received a lengthy written warning on the matter from his normally demure private secretary, Howard Banks. A Tar Heel newspaperman, Banks had published the Hickory *Democrat* before joining Daniels's staff in the spring of 1913. In the fall of 1914 he wrote to Daniels with concerns about "intrigue [that he had uncovered] within the Department."[75] Daniels was aware of the general direction of Fiske's plans. When he had taken over the Navy Department, Daniels had been warned by Senator "Pitchfork Ben" Tillman, a member of the Committee on Naval Affairs, that there were "spies" in the department.[76] Still, he might have been caught off guard by the breadth and depth of the "conspiracy" within the naval command structure. Daniels left no written reply to Banks's letter, but the correspondence left no doubt that Fiske would have to go.

After learning that Fiske had taken his general staff plan to the halls of Congress, Daniels struck. He called Fiske in and gave every appearance of having had a change of heart. Daniels averred that while he objected to some minor details of Fiske's plan in its original form—that is, the form Daniels had formally rejected earlier—he had decided to support the creation of a CNO office in principle. Recognizing that the devil would be in the details of the legislation creating a CNO, Daniels gambled that he could beat Fiske at that game. More cunningly, Daniels recognized that by taking ownership of the reform of the command structure, he could simultaneously rid himself of the Council of Aides as an administrative structure and, eventually, Fiske as the uniformed head of the new apparatus. Daniels gambled that he had more, and more powerful, friends in Congress than Fiske. Daniels guessed correctly. Once the matter formally and openly entered the halls of the Capitol, Fiske's plan was replaced by Daniels's plan, which was ultimately passed by Congress in 1915. (One of the key differences in the two plans was that in Daniels's plan the bureau chiefs still reported to the secretary rather than to the CNO.)[77] Thus, with Fiske's help, Daniels replaced the old system with the new Office of the Chief of Naval Operations, which, like the army's chief of staff, would coordinate planning, training, and supply functions but would only issue orders to bureau chiefs and fleet commanders with the approval of or in the name of the secretary of the navy. And just as Daniels planned, he got to choose a new uniformed chief to be the first CNO. Fiske had achieved his objective to Prussianize the navy and, with Daniels's smooth support, maneuvered himself out of a job. There was no way Daniels would appoint Fiske as the first CNO, and Fiske retired soon thereafter. The man Daniels chose was William Shepherd Benson, a solid uninspiring chief and a sound organizational type who almost always deferred to the civilian leadership, exactly what Daniels wanted in a CNO.

———

In addition to changing the organizational structure of the navy and replacing ineffectual or difficult personages in the key billets, Daniels had to deal with a number of diverse groups that affected his control of the navy. Among the most important of these associations, from the perspective of the Big Navy faction, spurred on by TR, was the Navy League. Among the least important of these, from Daniels's perspective, was the Navy League. Founded by TR in 1902, the Navy League serves, in its own words, as "a civilian organization dedicated to the education of our citizens, including our elected officials, and the support of the men and women of the sea services and their families."[78] During Daniels's tenure, it was headed by former naval officers and served as an unabashed advocacy group for an expanded navy. Initially, Daniels and the league's leadership got along well. However, once war broke out in Europe, the league adopted an explicitly belligerent stance, demanding ever-greater naval expenditures. Daniels (and Wilson) did not support these for several reasons, not the least of which was the provocative nature of such a position if taken by a neutral power. Daniels called the subsequent clash with the league a "war to the knife," a metaphor he reserved for the bitterest political battles.

After the sinking of the *Lusitania* by a German submarine in May 1915, the league moved closer and more publicly to an outright pro-war position, including public attacks on Wilson and Daniels. Despite any merits of the league's position, it was a gross miscalculation by the league's leadership, which was directed by Robert M. Thompson, an Annapolis graduate. The league had no independent political power base of its own and could only affect naval affairs through its contacts in Congress and the administration; thus, taking a hard antiadministration line when the Democrats controlled both houses of Congress and the White House threatened the league's access to power. The break came in August when Daniels, labeling the league "unpatriotic if not traitorous," issued an order banning league representatives from naval vessels and bases.[79] With the administration at the height of its popularity and power (Wilson was about to embark on a successful reelection campaign under the slogan "He kept us out of war"), the league's political influence dwindled to insignificance. (Wilson's unwavering support of Daniels was helpful in these turf battles. The president, no militarist, was all too happy to see Daniels break recalcitrant officers like Fiske and bellicose meddlers like Thompson.)

Another organization with which Daniels clashed almost from the outset of his tenure was the Joint Army-Navy Board. The Joint Board, also created by TR, had the sensible charge of more closely coordinating army and navy planning and operations in the event of another war. As such, the Joint Board served as a primitive form of the Joint Chiefs of Staff, which would be adopted by Franklin Roosevelt during World War II. However, some of the more bellicose members of the Joint Board adopted a strong aversion to the unmartial leanings of the administration; in turn, Daniels charged them with politicizing their task. In Daniels's view, civilian control of the military meant that officers should not try to influence policy. The administration would make policy, and the generals and admirals would see that it was carried out. Some members of the Joint Board sought to influence policy as well as carry it out.

The Joint Board had been chaired since its inception by the navy's highest-ranking officer, the Conqueror of Manila, Admiral George Dewey. Dewey was long past his active command days; he was seventy-six when Daniels took office. In May 1913, at the peak of a dispute with Japan over immigration issues (see Chapter 7), political officers, possibly at the instigation of Fiske or Army Chief of Staff Leonard Wood, leaked to the press the board's opposition to Wilson's relatively passive response to Japan's belligerency. Wilson and Daniels decided they had had enough of the board, since its members were serving officers who were now openly disputing their secretary's and their commander in chief's policies. The president and Daniels considered Wood and Fiske impertinent at best, insubordinate at worse. On Wilson's formal order, Daniels (and Secretary of War Lindley Garrison, who was more sympathetic to the board's position) disbanded the board. (It would be reconstituted, on Daniels's recommendation, only after the Great War began in Europe.) As with the banishment of the Navy League, the (albeit temporary) end of the Joint Board can be seen as an unambiguous political victory for Daniels.

Because of Dewey's reputation, and because he apparently played no role in the Joint Board's insubordination, Daniels went to great lengths to make sure Dewey was neither offended by nor tarred with the board's termination. Daniels sincerely revered the old admiral and showed him much respect. Daniels always insisted on calling on Dewey, rather than the other way around, and Daniels sat at Dewey's right hand during meetings. Both actions violated protocol, for which Daniels cared little, and as Daniels suspected, the violations nourished Dewey's petty vanity. The two struck up a warm personal friendship, and Dewey (who called Daniels "a great, if not *the* greatest Secretary of the Navy") was generally, though not uncritically, a Daniels supporter.[80] Whenever Daniels was attacked by other officers or the Navy League, Dewey's public support often did much to undermine the attacks.

One final group that could not be as peremptorily handled as the Navy League or the Joint Board was the General Board of the Navy, which Daniels referred to variously as "The Board of Naval Statesmen" or "The Supreme Court of Naval Policy." Dewey had been president of the General Board since shortly after its creation in 1900. The board's overarching charge was to "prepare for war in times of peace"—that is, it was created to make sure that the long-run strategic factors in naval warfare did not get overlooked in the short-run political machinations in the White House and on Capitol Hill. Like the Navy League, it served as an advocacy group, but one focused narrowly on issues pertaining to naval strategy and preparation for future conflicts.

Despite Daniels's fondness for Dewey personally and respect for his military accomplishments, the board was more supportive of naval expansion and naval traditions than Daniels would have liked. Although Daniels always professed reverence for the board and advertised its views whenever they supported his own, he ignored its recommendations and admonitions whenever they conflicted with his objectives. As one naval historian characterized the relationship between the board and the secretary, "While deferring to the General Board on many aspects of the strategic and operational overview, [Daniels] would not concede political decisions," and political calculations usually dominated military ones.[81]

———

In addition to dealing with personnel and organizational concerns, Daniels had to manage the massive naval construction program. On this issue, Daniels was wedged between the Big Navy advocates and the more frugal fiscal policies of the administration, as well as, more tryingly, its neutrality after war came to Europe. The fundamental problem Daniels faced was the administration's position on U.S. expansion as an imperial power. With Western colonialism approaching its zenith, imperialists viewed a strong navy as an empire's guarantor. Great Britain had proved the efficacy of this view over the past two centuries; through its navy, that windswept collection of rock in the North Atlantic had controlled a quarter of the world's landmass and population. In the United States, the bellicose Big Navy faction envied Britain's imperial success, and for the Big Navy types there could never be enough naval power. This faction included Mahanian naval theorists, rapacious imperial traders and financiers, and social Darwinists, who supplied the intellectual justification for the military and economic actions of the first two groups. This latter group was led most conspicuously, if somewhat erratically, by Daniels's old nemesis Theodore Roosevelt, who summarized the Big Navy faction's view: "The American people must either build and maintain an adequate navy or else make up their minds definitely to accept a secondary position in international affairs, not merely in political, but in commercial, matters."[82] The onset of the Great War would only exacerbate his and his supporters' stridency.

At a more prosaic level, the imperialists were strongly supported by the manufacturers and shipbuilders (and their congressional representatives) who expected to benefit directly from the government spending associated with a large navy and by many military officers who saw in the country's imperial activities the opportunity for promotion. Concerning the latter group, Daniels wrote, "The military as whole believed in colonial expansion and wished Uncle Sam to emulate the example of Great Britain by 'taking up the white man's burden'—a polite way of describing the exploitation of the weaker races." Daniels referred to the civilians who supported a big navy as "Dollar Diplomats," who he said "were virtually the agents of Big Business."[83]

In response, a coalition of progressive anti-imperialists and fiscally conservative politicians formed to counter the Big Navy faction. A big navy was not cheap. Indeed, with the technical advances of the early twentieth century, a small navy was not cheap. The cost of admission to the rarefied realm of the Great Powers had gone up dramatically with the advent of the *Dreadnought*, and there were few players in the Great Powers games by the time Daniels took control of the navy. By 1914, construction of a single state-of-the-art battleship could cost $14 million, excluding any subsequent operating costs. The 1914 fiscal-year budget of the U.S. Navy was $139 million, nearly 20 percent of the entire federal budget, up from less than 7 percent only a generation earlier.[84] If one rejected imperialism, as Daniels did, then there was no reason to support such an expenditure on instruments of war that were likely never to be unsheathed in the name of any morally defensible cause. Let the British taxpayers keep the world's sea lanes open, argued U.S. critics of the Big Navy group. On the other hand, outright pacifism was a political loser at the national level; there were simply too many votes to the right of such a position, as both Daniels and Wilson recognized. Thus, the politically correct slogan adopted by the Wilson administration was "the most adequate navy in the world." Of course, interpretation of the adjective "adequate" left much room for political maneuvering.

War in Europe distilled the differences between the Big Navy and the adequate navy factions. To a certain extent, the war played into the hands of both groups, at least initially. Because neutrality was overwhelmingly the most popular political position at the outset, both sides argued that their view was most consistent with remaining out of the war. According to the Big Navy supporters, the war at sea, fought primarily between the British and the Germans, demonstrated the efficacy of naval power. In the absence of a great navy, the other Great Powers would be able to dictate U.S. foreign policy. To hypernationalists, such as TR, this was intolerable. On the other hand, Wilson and Daniels could argue that an aggressive building program following the onset of war would only demonstrate a lack of good faith with respect to neutrality and thus only embolden potential foes to strike preemptively before the United States could bring its new battleships online. This, Daniels argued, would lead the country into exactly the situation the administration most hoped to avoid, specifically, being drawn into the Great War on the terms of a belligerent power. As Wilson famously put it, if the United States were, in fact, to end up in the war, it must "come into the court of history with clean hands."[85] In Daniels's view, a large navy, especially one employed aggressively, was inconsistent with this position. The Big Navy types were not worried about clean hands. Indeed, in their view a little blood on the hands might not be such a bad thing.

As for the naval building program itself, by Daniels's accounting, at the time he took office the United States had eight dreadnoughts operational, two soon to be operational (the *New York*–class ships), two under construction (the *Nevada* class), and two already approved by Congress (the *Pennsylvania* class).[86] Daniels had approved of this program before he took office, and not foreseeing war in Europe, he professed support for the "two-battleship ratio," as he called it. Thus he advocated continuing the current dreadnought-building program. In practice, as a fiscal measure, Daniels was forced to "stretch out" the plan; only one dreadnought was laid down in 1913 and one in 1914, after four consecutive years of two dreadnoughts a year. Daniels claimed his building plan would yield a "Navy second to none." Given the size of the building programs in Britain and Germany, as well as those in Japan and France, such a claim was difficult to justify. Indeed his initial dreadnought program—the "two-battleship ratio"—was half the size of that proposed by the General Board of the Navy.[87] Thus, calling the plan "second to none" while not advocating for the physical resources to match such a phrase made Daniels appear hypocritical at best. In the eyes of the Big Navy faction, it made him incompetent. At the same time, a navy second to none did not have much to recommend it to more pacifistic voters, who wanted the administration to focus on its progressive New Freedom program. Daniels took heat from the Big Navy group for his lack of aggressiveness in building capital ships, and he took heat from the progressives because his program was too aggressive.

The war in Europe, which came in the late summer of 1914, especially the war at sea and Germany's subsequent aggressive U-boat campaign, changed Daniels's view of the navy and its role in national security. He decisively moved toward the Big Navy position, and in 1915 he developed a new building program, which would be approved by Congress the following year. The administration's new construction program, which greatly exceeded the second-to-none plan, included 10 battleships, 6 of the faster battle cruisers, 10 smaller scout cruisers, 50 destroyers, 100 submarines, and various support ships. If completed in a timely fashion, this armada would have proved formidable, yielding a navy on par with that of the British on the eve of the Great War. However, since the plan was only adopted three years into Daniels's administration of the navy, and since Daniels had earlier resisted calls to increase and accelerate the building program he inherited, he came under much fire at the time and subsequently for what was perceived as a fundamental lack of naval preparedness. Unfortunately, Wilson began describing Daniels's new plan as one that would lead to "incomparably the greatest Navy in the world." This phrase soon caused problems for both men, because the program would still not surpass that of the British and it was still not bold enough for the Big Navy supporters. Thus, the administration fell back on the "most adequate navy" slogan, which reflected the maxim that politics was the art of the possible. All things considered, a most adequate navy was the Wilson administration's compromise between the Big Navy and progressive political factions. No one who had strong views on the matter was happy with the compromise.

———

As the naval building program expanded, Daniels insisted on competitive bidding on navy contracts.[88] The navy placed large orders for many goods, including cigarettes, uniforms, and coal. However, the two primary big-ticket items were armor plate and fuel oil, which newer naval vessels used rather than coal. Even before he took office, Daniels had convinced himself that the big U.S. suppliers of these products had cartelized the navy's contracts and thus rigged the bidding. Daniels's solution was simple. He argued that the federal government should manufacture its own steel and expand its ownership of petroleum reserves. He got half of what he wanted. There would be no government steel plant, but in 1915, the navy purchased a petroleum reserve at Teapot Dome, Wyoming, a name and place that would, after Daniels left Washington, live in infamy among the great public scandals of history.

During Wilson's first term, federal government expenditures hovered around $700 million annually.[89] With a single dreadnought costing $14 million, the post-1915 naval building program would need hundreds of millions of dollars, a huge share of the overall federal budget. Since Congress annually appropriated a certain dollar figure for the navy, every dollar Daniels let go in excess profit was a dollar he could not spend on other ships or programs. He became especially incensed at the country's big steel producers for submitting what he considered to be collusive bids. (He called them "steal prices.") On one occasion, he tore up the bids submitted by the heads of the three largest firms and demanded new ones by noon the next day. He then let it be known that he was in touch with a senior manager of a British manufacturer who was visiting New York on the same day. If the U.S. producers could not come in with lower bids, Daniels hinted, perhaps a foreign manufacturer could. Not surprisingly, the U.S. manufacturers offered lower, less similar bids.

On another occasion, after the United States entered the war, Daniels called in an executive of a navy contractor and demanded the man's firm submit a lower bid, which Daniels had conveniently drawn up for him. The executive refused, at which point Daniels reached into his desk drawer, pulled out a piece of paper, and claimed it was the man's draft notice. If the executive still refused to submit the bid Daniels wanted, then Daniels would draft him into the naval reserve and order him to sign the bid. The man signed.[90] Congress soon gave Daniels the authority to force contractors to accept a standard markup on the goods they supplied. If they refused, Daniels did not have to coerce their executives; he could simply seize their goods at 75 percent of their assessed value. (While Daniels strong-armed some of the navy's suppliers, he treated others more gently. In 1914 he awarded a contract for 400,000 pairs of socks to his former financier, textile magnate Julian Shakespeare Carr. There was no bidding.)[91]

In addition to reorganizing the navy and changing its bidding process (and eventually its building program), Daniels planned to improve the quality of the lives of the enlisted men. These improvements took two forms: educational and moral. With respect to the men's education, Daniels saw the navy as an enormous community college. Many of the enlisted billets involved a skilled trade, and petty officers and warrant officers handled much of the day-to-day administrative work that kept the navy running. These jobs required skills that transferred well into civilian life, but many of the navy's 65,000 men performed routine chores of mind-numbing monotony that required neither literacy nor numeracy. Daniels envisioned the navy as both a trade school and a general secondary school ("a great university," as he called it) so that young men could leave the service and enter civilian life on a higher rung of the socioeconomic ladder than that at which they had entered the service.

Accordingly, in Daniels's first annual report to Congress, submitted in December 1913, he emphasized the educational role of the service, and he rebuked his predecessors and the officer corps for spending more effort and thought on "the guns than to the men behind the guns." He offered a plan for correcting that oversight. "Every ship should be a school," he wrote, "and every enlisted man and petty and warrant officer should receive the opportunity to improve his mind, better his position and fit himself for promotion."[92] While well received among the progressive Democrats on Capitol Hill, this strategy was not equally appreciated by the officers who would be charged with carrying it out. They preferred training and leading warriors rather than scholars. As Lieutenant Collins, the stern naval commander in Richard McKenna's *Sand Pebbles*, lamented, "The naval uniform marked men whose primary purpose in life was to deal in violent death. People would rather not have to know that, even some who wore the uniform. . . . The current recruiting slogans were pure Josephus Daniels: *Join the navy and learn a trade. Every battleship a school.* It was no wonder the men tended to forget the primary purpose of their lives."[93]

The objection to turning ships into schools was comparable to that which came in response to Daniels's next directive. He decided to democratize the officer corps by admitting enlisted men into the naval academy. A few admirals, "influenced by a sort of spirit of caste," as Daniels put it, fought to hold up the proposal in Congress.[94] The effort failed. Emboldened, Daniels began pushing members of Congress, who controlled the seats in the academy's freshman class, to choose their midshipmen by competitive examination rather than through personal contacts.

After addressing the educational needs of his men, Daniels turned to their moral and spiritual needs. He focused on three things: religion, alcohol, and prostitutes, with the objective of increasing the importance of the first and decreasing the prevalence of the other two. Giving religion a higher profile in the service was easy enough. After settling into the secretary's post, Daniels visited naval bases and ships, and he was angered by the absence of religious ceremony in the service. Subsequent investigation revealed that the navy had as many chaplains in 1913 as it had in 1841, though the service had grown considerably during the interval. Daniels persuaded Congress to increase substantially the number of chaplains. He had at least one chaplain billeted to every dreadnought, and he ordered chaplains to wear the same uniform as other officers (another outrage in the eyes of McKenna's fictional Lieutenant Collins). Finally, Daniels insisted that religious services be conducted every Sunday on every ship.[95]

Reducing the number of prostitutes around naval bases proved much more difficult than increasing the number of chaplains. Daniels exerted political pressure on local politicians to clean up the red-light districts beyond the gates of navy posts. (He also prohibited the navy from issuing condoms to its men.) At the peak of wartime expenditures, Daniels controlled hundreds of millions of dollars in government contracts. While he did not have complete discretion over any of it, he had some discretion over much of it. Port cities that refused to make an effort to clean up their seediest districts could see a reduction in their military-related funding and thus local employment. Daniels successfully threatened city leaders in Chicago, New Orleans, and Charleston, South Carolina. (Daniels has been blamed, or credited, for the jazz diaspora—the spread of jazz up the Mississippi and beyond—as a result of his efforts to clean up New Orleans's legendary Storyville area.)

He had the most trouble with Newport, Rhode Island, where certain government officials had ties to the illicit activities of the town. Never one to back down from a challenge, Daniels determined that if the Newport police would not do their jobs, the navy would, and he stationed Shore Patrol officers outside every house of prostitution in the city. When that did not work, he threatened to move the naval war college and to remove the funding for one of the navy's main torpedo manufacturing plants. The effort was successful but was not universally embraced, as Daniels himself noted. "I was not as popular as I deserved to be," he lamented, with tongue in cheek, at the ingratitude of the young men and fallen women his actions saved.[96]

Daniels tied prostitution to his perception that the service also suffered from an alcohol problem. He obtained even less support for his war on alcohol than he did for his war on prostitution. It would take national prohibition to win the war beyond naval bases, but Daniels waged the war within the navy. Accordingly, on June 1, 1914, he issued General Order Number 99: "The use or introduction for drinking purposes of alcoholic liquors on board naval vessel, or within any navy yard or station, is strictly prohibited, and commanding officers will be held directly responsible for the enforcement of this order."[97]

With that, the navy's long affinity with alcohol came to an end.[98] Most of the men, from the lowliest tar to Admiral Fiske were livid: "white with resentment" was how Daniels characterized Fiske's response.[99] Fiske spent an entire day trying to persuade Daniels to revoke or amend the order. Daniels refused. The navy went dry. As a substitute, stewards increased their purchases of coffee, among other beverages, and Daniels's name became linked to the daily drink of millions around the world. A cup of coffee became disparagingly known as "a cup of Josephus Daniels," and as legend has it, this was soon shortened to a "cup of Joe."

7. Splendid Little Wars

I am going to teach the
South American republics to elect good men.

—WOODROW WILSON

At daylight we marched right through Vera Cruz.

—MAJOR SMEDLEY BUTLER, U.S.M.C.

American diplomat John Hay will forever have a place in the history books if for no other reason than for his characterization of the Spanish-American conflict as that "splendid little war."[1] The phrase has come to be associated with wars that might or might not have been little but were by no means splendid. Among these were several Latin American campaigns overseen by Josephus Daniels during his tenure as secretary of the navy. They included Nicaragua, the occupation of which Daniels inherited from the Taft administration in 1913; Mexico (1914); Haiti (1915); the Dominican Republic (1916); and Cuba (1917).[2] In addition, from its first days, the Wilson administration faced crises in China and disputes with Japan that involved the navy.

The imperialistic policies of the three Republican presidents who immediately preceded Wilson—McKinley, Roosevelt, and Taft—foreshadowed subsequent complications. Initially, however, Daniels expected the administration to concentrate on its domestic agenda, and he was optimistic that Wilson would not perpetuate the gunboat diplomacy of his predecessors. In this he would be disappointed. Wilson was to the right of his party's mainstream when it came to imperialism. Indeed, he had "publicly argued that America should take Hawaii, Guam, and the Philippines as colonies."[3] Thus Daniels's day-to-day business would be overwhelmingly dominated by foreign affairs, including overseeing Wilson's own version of gunboat diplomacy.

One of Daniels's first major acts after taking office in March 1913 was to choose an assistant secretary. In those days of leaner bureaucracy, the navy secretary had only one civilian assistant, so the choice was crucial. Franklin Delano Roosevelt, the rich Harvard alumnus Daniels chose, possessed a famous name, a well-stocked family treasury, and a forceful personality, all of which destined him to fill a position of leadership in American public life. There is little doubt, however, that Daniels greatly facilitated FDR's route to the pinnacle of American politics. When Daniels offered the assistant secretary post to the thirty-one-year-old FDR, the two had only known each other for a few months. At the time, FDR was in the process of modeling his own career on that of his cousin Theodore, the former president and recent presidential candidate. TR offered a good, though ambitious, model for a young, patrician politician.

There is no shortage of biographical information on FDR.[4] His leadership during the Great Depression and World War II, while he coped with the ravages of polio, elevated him to the pantheon of history's greatest statesmen. FDR himself, never much given to sharing the limelight, rightfully credited Daniels for a good portion of his subsequent success.[5] The only child of an aged but kindly patrician father and a loving but authoritarian mother, FDR inherited a large fortune that originated in international trade.[6] On his father's side, a great-grandfather descended from Dutch traders made the Roosevelt fortune in the New World in the eighteenth-century sugar trade. On his mother's side, the de la Noyes were French Protestants. His mother's father, Warren Delano, who took the anglicized version of the family name, made his fortune in, among other things, the opium trade.

FDR himself was the product of the Hudson Valley (Whig and, later, Democratic) branch of the Roosevelt family, as opposed to the Oyster Bay (and Republican) branch that yielded TR. (The respective branches of the family had split in the eighteenth century.) Educated at Groton and Harvard, FDR was a mediocre student who tried perhaps a bit too hard to fit in among America's social elite. Raised in the insular world of his parents' estate, the boy developed a glib and ingratiating manner that made him more popular with adults than with his adolescent peers. Physically active though not a great athlete in competitive sports, FDR fit in well enough but did not excel at either of the elite schools he attended. Living off his family's wealth and at loose ends as a young man, he entered New York state politics. When he first met Josephus Daniels at the 1912 Democratic National Convention in Baltimore, FDR held the office of state senator.

Contrary to Daniels's subsequent protestations in his memoirs, written at the height of FDR's power and popularity, their first meeting, brief and hectic, could not be described as portentous.[7] One of FDR's frequent illnesses prevented an extension of their initial contact, and they met only briefly during the subsequent presidential campaign and not at any length again until the inauguration in March of the following year. Although well built and handsome, FDR suffered from poor health throughout his life and would be dead at age sixty-three. Even before he was struck by polio in the 1920s, he was "plagued by sinus infections and vulnerable to bacterial infections and severe illnesses, including typhus [and] pneumonia." The contrast with Daniels could not be starker. Uncharitably, though not in-accurately, characterized as "obese and dumpy," Daniels was overweight—though never excessively so—and he never exercised a day in his adult life. As one of his sons observed, the only exercise Daniels ever took was "walk-ing to lunch."[8] Still he rose early and worked late almost every day for nearly seventy years, especially during his years in the Wilson administration. Yet, in those eight years in the high-pressure post of secretary of the navy, he never took a day of sick leave. Indeed, other than common childhood ail-ments, he was sick for no more than a few days during his entire life, which lasted a considerable eighty-six years.[9] His physical energy, capacity for ex-tended periods of mental work, and overall constitution were truly remark-able. FDR had physical and mental energy too, but he lacked the ability (or perhaps the good luck) to ward off disease, and he suffered physically throughout his life.

Daniels was usually a shrewd judge of character. As one observer put it, "Daniels undoubtedly could pick men."[10] He may not have foreseen all that FDR would become, but he liked what he saw and knew. Daniels also recognized how valuable a bright, energetic young assistant with northern political connections could be. Furthermore, Daniels envisioned a public relations coup in bringing a Roosevelt into Wilson's Democratic adminis-tration, and he offered him the job at Wilson's inauguration. An early biog-raphy of Daniels and a recent one of FDR both mention FDR's Yankee patri-cian background as appealing to Daniels in contrast to his own upbringing. According to one, "They made an oddly assorted pair, this provincial editor and the patrician from Groton and Harvard."[11]

Later, Daniels would claim to have followed FDR's career in the New York legislature, and upon receiving Wilson's letter requesting his service as navy secretary, he claimed he told Addie, "I will ask the President to appoint Franklin Roosevelt as Assistant Secretary."[12] Neither claim is preposterous, but both are questionable. FDR had a famous name and was considered a reformer in the New York legislature. Daniels followed New York politics, and he maintained a strong antisaloon political line in general and an anti–Tammany Hall line in particular, attacking both in the editorial pages of the *News and Observer*. Roosevelt was never antisaloon, but he openly broke with Tammany, which took courage and endeared him to Daniels, who like his contemporary Winston Churchill thought "that courage is the most important political virtue."[13] Of the young Roosevelt, Daniels said simply he had "that stuff—there is no other word for it."[14]

Despite Daniels's claims of prescience, the primary accounts of the individuals involved in the creation of Wilson's cabinet suggest that several members of Wilson's inner circle who knew FDR better and for longer than Daniels did had already tapped the young patrician for a place in the administration. More tellingly, on the day FDR was to officially begin his duties in Washington, Daniels's diary refers to "Mr. Frederick D. Roosevelt, who had been appointed Assistant Secretary of the Navy."[15] It is curious that Daniels, who at the time was clearly keeping his diary in good order for posterity, should record the wrong name for his assistant, a man he supposedly knew so well. In any case, Daniels offered the job to FDR in the lobby of Washington's Willard Hotel on inauguration day, March 4, 1913. Daniels was sworn in the next day, and on March 6 he sought Wilson's approval of FDR's appointment. Wilson, having just fought a nasty presidential campaign against a Roosevelt, displayed justifiable skepticism. With the exception of the State Department after the Great War began, however, Wilson did not micromanage his cabinet. When Daniels remained firm on FDR's appointment, Wilson acquiesced.[16]

Although FDR remained in the right party and possessed the right ideological leanings, Wilson was shrewd enough to be wary of letting Daniels invite a Roosevelt into the administration. Furthermore, there was no shortage of FDR detractors. As Republican senator Elihu Root, a former secretary of war and secretary of state, famously put it, "Whenever a Roosevelt rides, he wishes to be in front."[17] Daniels possessed enough self-confidence that he was not intimidated by FDR's name or ambition. To these concerns, Daniels replied, "A chief who fears that an assistant will outrank him is not fit to be chief."[18] Wilson's and Root's skepticism would prove to be prophetic. FDR would cause no small amount of trouble for and within the administration as he fed his bellicose cousin Theodore inside information. In the end, however, FDR's positive traits would compensate for his negative ones, though perhaps just barely.

Whereas Daniels boasted that his assistant secretary had "that stuff," FDR's early assessment of Daniels could not have been less charitable. "When I first knew him," FDR said of Daniels, "he was the funniest looking hillbilly I had ever seen."[19] In retrospect, FDR's appraisal tells us more about the arrogant young assistant secretary than it does his boss. That even an educated, well-traveled northeasterner like FDR could not tell the difference between a self-made entrepreneur (and southern gentleman) like Daniels and an Appalachian cracker exposed his Yankee prejudice. If FDR thought Daniels was a hillbilly, then it was only because FDR had never seen or spoken with the real thing.

Initially their relationship, while cordial on the surface, was poisoned by FDR's bitter exemplar, TR. Until war came, FDR largely limited his attacks on Daniels to matters of personality and taste, and these were launched behind his chief's back, typically at social functions or in writing to TR. FDR aimed his criticism at Daniels's personal attire and demeanor, his teetotaling, and his religion. As FDR's initial observation about Daniels being a "hillbilly" suggests, Daniels's clothes and coastal North Carolina drawl marked him as someone from well beyond the pale of FDR's patrician Yankeedom. Daniels's "aw shucks, good ol' boy" act and antiquated clothing were designed to disarm northeastern sophisticates like FDR. Young FDR got the impression Daniels wanted to give.

As for the teetotaling, despite his public support for prohibition, Daniels never preached abstinence to individuals. He even went so far as to excoriate fellow Protestants who took a holier-than-thou attitude toward alcohol. "If all laymen who occasionally transgressed [by drinking alcohol] had been turned out of the church," he wrote, "the membership would have been considerably decreased."[20] However, his willingness to forgive the weakness of individuals did not prevent him from pursuing public policies that made drink more costly and difficult to abuse, and if it could be outlawed altogether, so much the better. For his part, FDR drank consistently, if not heavily, throughout his life, and he belittled Daniels (and Secretary of State Bryan) for serving grape juice rather than wine at formal Washington events. (Not surprisingly, very early in FDR's first administration, the country approved the Twenty-first Amendment to the Constitution, repealing national prohibition.)

As for Daniels's religion, FDR and his wife, Eleanor, were high-church Episcopalians, and they "must have been culturally and theologically horrified," according to a biographer, at Daniels's backwoods Methodism.[21] Although Methodist founder John Wesley was an ordained member of the Anglican clergy, after the American Revolution the point became moot, as Wesley's New World followers left the discredited Church of England and founded their own church. Subsequent generations of American Methodists tended to align culturally, if not theologically, with their low-church separatist colleagues, who at the time could be found among the country's

Baptists and Presbyterians, and the cultural ties between Methodists and the non-Episcopal Protestant sects tended to dominate their theological differences. It was a common saying at the time that a Methodist was nothing more than a Baptist who could read.

As he displayed in his relationship with Daniels, FDR could be vain, mendacious, ruthless, and ambitious and appear shallow. But he was also hardworking, intelligent, courageous, earnestly patriotic, and, in fact, inscrutable rather than shallow. FDR's candid view of his new boss also starkly demonstrates one side of his complex relationship with Daniels, which was initially one of condescension. Later—much later in fact—FDR would recognize Daniels's virtues and, more poignantly, recognize that their relationship was one of master and apprentice. Indeed, Daniels contributed considerably more to FDR's professional development and subsequent career than FDR's more famous cousin TR ever would. Daniels groomed FDR, even as FDR ridiculed and undermined Daniels. Only the passage of time would cause FDR, the least introspective of men, to appreciate fully what Daniels had put up with and done for him. Years later, referring to Daniels, FDR told Rexford G. Tugwell, "Rex, this is a man who taught me a lot that I needed to know."[22] For the rest of his life FDR referred to Daniels as "Chief." When other, more powerful men deferentially referred to FDR as "Mr. President," Daniels called him "Franklin." Except for the short time they would spend in the political wilderness of the Republican-dominated Roaring Twenties, their careers would be inextricably linked for the rest of their lives. Daniels relied heavily on FDR, and he needed a good assistant, because for the next eight years the navy would be putting out fires all over the world.

GOD, GOLD, AND GUNBOATS

God, gold, and glory, the so-called three Gs of imperialism, were all present in the first foreign policy crisis the new administration faced in the spring of 1913. It occurred in China, where a year earlier the empress dowager had formally surrendered control of the government to revolutionary leader Sun Yat-sen. To placate the military, Sun offered the presidency of the Republic of China to General Yuan Shikai, who had established important contacts with Western financiers when he held key commands during the declining years of the Qing Dynasty. Yuan hoped to leverage those contacts into financial support for his new regime. The immediate problem facing Wilson was Yuan's request for loan guarantees from a U.S. banking syndicate organized by the House of Morgan. Morgan's people wanted the administration formally to request that the syndicate join banks from the other Great Powers—including the United Kingdom, France, Germany, Russia, and Japan—in offering loans to the new Chinese government. A formal request from the administration carried with it, in Morgan's view, a guarantee of the loan in case China defaulted. Loan guarantees of this type often resulted in U.S. navy gunboats enforcing the terms of the loans. One way or the other, the gold would be paid; U.S. taxpayers would see to that. The navy would get what little glory there was to be had in the bargain.

Wilson, Secretary of State William Jennings Bryan, and Daniels had been informally discussing the China loan since the inauguration.[23] Taft's foreign policy with respect to weak, economically undeveloped states was to support U.S. investments in those countries and to back those investments with military force. Thus he had approved the U.S. banking syndicate's participation in the international loans to China. (Combining money, via loans and direct investment, with diplomacy earned Taft's policy the sobriquet "dollar diplomacy," which in practice differed little from the gunboat version. During each of the recent Republican administrations, interest on U.S. loans was collected via the threat or use of military intervention.) Despite Taft's approval, the final terms of the big China deal had not gone through before Taft left office; now that Wilson was in the White House, the bankers wanted the new administration's formal blessing on Taft's China policy. Wilson, supported by Bryan and Daniels, balked at backing the loan, and the president formally rejected the plan only a few weeks into his administration.

In rejecting the loan, Wilson offered a new foreign policy toward developing countries. Repudiating Taft's dollar diplomacy, the president rejected any government backing of private U.S. investments abroad. Unfortunately, the logic surrounding Wilson's rejection of the loan plan was not consistent with events on the ground either in China or in Central and South America, the other hot spots of U.S. investment in economically undeveloped and politically unstable countries. The alternative Wilson offered was not much more than lofty rhetoric, which subsequently proved to be politically untenable. Under Wilson the only policy the United States would formally support in China was the so-called Open Door, which in theory meant trade with no strings attached and no formal annexation of Chinese territory by other Great Powers. The no-annexation component was important, because without it, one or more of the other powers might close the door to China or, more likely, charge a fee to go through it.

Wilson foreshadowed his response to the China crisis when, only a week into his term, he outlined his new foreign policy as it related to Central and South America. The essence of the policy was that the United States proposed to be good friends on equal terms with like-minded democratic regimes. Wilson wrote:

> We can have no sympathy with those who seek to seize the power of government to advance their own personal interests or ambitions. . . . As friends, therefore, we shall prefer those who act in the interests of peace and honor, who protect private rights, and respect the restraints of constitutional provision. Mutual respect seems to us the indispensable foundation of friendship between states as between individuals. The United States has nothing to seek in Central and South America except the lasting interests of the people of the two continents, the security of governments, intended for the people, and for no special group or interest, and the development of personal and trade relationships between the two continents, which shall redound to the profit and advantage of both and interfere with the rights and liberties of neither.[24]

The problem was that many, perhaps even most, of the regimes to which this message was addressed were run by people who did, in fact, seek power to "advance their own personal interests," who had no intention of protecting "private rights," and who did not respect "the restraints of constitutional provision." Furthermore, the references to trade and profit were disingenuous, since the administration was adopting an explicit policy of refusing to support this rhetoric with force, which was ultimately the only thing that worked with the strongmen and warlords to whom the message was addressed. Viewed in the context of what subsequently happened, this message can be seen as foreshadowing a muddled U.S. involvement throughout East Asia, Central America, and the Caribbean. Daniels would be the person most responsible for carrying out the administration's interventionist policies.

As for the immediate problem in China, it was too early to tell what course the Chinese revolution would take, but Daniels and Bryan thought the Morgan loan would put the Chinese under Wall Street's heel and force the administration to use gunboats to collect the loan payments. They persuaded Wilson, who did not need much persuading, that he was giving Yuan and Sun a vote of confidence by vetoing the loan plan, while simultaneously recognizing China's new republican regime without consulting the other Great Powers. In other words, they argued that Wilson was doing the Chinese a favor by slapping Morgan in the face. According to Daniels, Bryan crowed that he loved Wilson's "audacity and his courage."[25]

In essence, Wilson's foreign policy with respect to China and Central America was to be good friends with good friends and good neighbors with good neighbors. What the president intended to do with bad friends and bad neighbors went unanswered. For all of the exploitation and jingoism associated with gunboat diplomacy, at least it offered well-defined carrots and sticks. Friends who supported the expansion of U.S. economic and military interests would receive loans and direct investment; those who inhibited U.S. economic and military interests or failed to honor their debts faced gunboats. The policy might not have been moral; but it possessed an inherent logic and consistency, and it is difficult to argue that the world's poorest regions would have been economically better off without U.S. investment.[26] In contrast, Wilson's policy was incomplete, offering only the carrots of goodwill and no sticks. Though Daniels initially supported Wilson's rejection of gunboat diplomacy for reasons both practical and philosophical, Daniels soon recognized better than either Wilson or Bryan the problems associated with the replacement of gunboats with rhetoric.

Daniels began to move away from Wilson's Good Neighbor policy as soon as he realized it placed him between several "fires," as he put it.[27] On one hand, powerful domestic financial and political forces lobbying for access to developing economies argued that if U.S. money did not flow to these countries, other Great Power money would. On another hand, progressives argued that U.S. tax dollars were being used to prop up ruling kleptocrats (or replace them with other kleptocrats) who did nothing for their largely poor, uneducated, and disenfranchised subjects. Instead of paying for gunboats, those dollars could be used to support struggling American farmers, through, for example, a new rural finance program that allowed farmers to obtain federally backed loans using their crops as collateral.[28]

On yet a third hand, during this period an increasingly strident missionary lobby emerged. Described as that "curious blend of gunboat diplomacy and gunboat Christianity," the missionary lobby rejected the hands-off foreign policy of the progressives, but it was not interested in profits for the House of Morgan.[29] Rather, it sought to convert heathens into Christians as fervently as Morgan sought to convert heathen land into profitable territory. The missionary lobby felt comfortable demanding that the U.S. government support efforts to proselytize to the natives. China, which had hundreds of millions of potentially convertible souls, proved especially dear to the missionary diplomatists. As one keen observer of U.S. policy in East Asia wrote, "China had long fascinated Americans, many of whom felt a deep, if curious paternalism toward the poor, struggling Chinese."[30] There was more than a slightly racist undertone to the U.S. version of gunboat Christianity. Senator Albert Beveridge well captured this sentiment when he spoke of "the divine law of human society which makes of us our brother's keeper. God has been preparing the English-speaking and Teutonic peoples to bring order out of chaos. . . . He has made us adept in government so that we may administer government among savage and senile peoples."[31] Increasingly, Wilson listened to these demands, which only complicated U.S. foreign policy.

Although from the administration's perspective the immediate problem was the China loan syndicate, the policy adopted toward the syndicate would establish a precedent for other interventionist groups. If Wilson supported the loan, then he attached to it the implicit protection of U.S. capital. This he would not do. For now, Daniels agreed with the president (and Bryan) when it came to China. Sun and Yuan would have to make do without U.S. financial support. Open doors, good neighbors, and Wilson's professorial admonitions were in; dollar diplomacy and gunboats were out. It was not a policy destined for a long life.

The administration's policy toward China, such as it was, quickly became more complicated as it became inextricably linked with its policy toward Japan. China and Japan, uncomfortable neighbors, were headed in different directions on the Great Powers ladder. China was moving down; Japan was moving up. Japan's transition from the feudal shogunate to a modern polity nominally headed by the emperor (a process referred to in the West as the Meiji Restoration) fifty years earlier initiated the country's leap into the modern era. Wrapped in the ideology of nationalism, the process included the modernization of Japan's military forces, and since the end of the nineteenth century, Japan had prosecuted successful wars against China and Russia, securing a foothold on the Asian mainland through its control of the Korean Peninsula. Despite Japanese protestations, the other Great Powers, as well as weaker East Asian states that might stand in Japan's way, naturally anticipated further Japanese expansion into the heart of China. This possibility had been openly discussed at the highest levels of the U.S. military since Japan's victory over Russia in 1905. Theodore Roosevelt, who was at the time still president, openly shared his concerns about the newly powerful Japan.

The nominal causes of the impending conflict between the United States and Japan went back decades. With a booming economy and a vast landmass to fill, the United States had maintained an open-door immigration policy until 1880. In that year, in response to racial animosity that had been building primarily on the West Coast, the United States and China agreed to the terms of a treaty in which the Chinese formally recognized the U.S. right to exclude Chinese immigrants from the open-door policy, which Congress did in 1882. While the Japanese and the Chinese maintained highly refined and distinct racist views of their own, along much of the western coast of the United States, whites made little distinction between the two groups of East Asians and informally discriminated against both with impunity. By the early twentieth century, political forces in California were driving toward formal, state-sanctioned discrimination. In 1906 the local board of education in San Francisco designated segregated schools for East Asian children. China, politically weak and facing the threat of dismemberment by the Great Powers, was in no position to resist, but the Japanese government, fresh from its recent martial victories over larger, supposedly more powerful neighbors (China and Russia), strongly protested. Japan's ruling elites refused to accept the insult when their compatriots were treated in the same manner as blacks in the American South.

Just as Japan was joining the Great Powers following its recent military victories—and as it was negotiating with the United States as an equal with respect to China—Japanese were being openly reviled along the West Coast of the United States. Seething with resentment, the Japanese government nonetheless subsequently signed off on the so-called Gentlemen's Agreement to limit the outflow of Japanese migrants to the United States. But anti-Asian riots in San Francisco and Japan's lukewarm adherence to the immigration agreement kept the problems between the two countries just below the boiling point. The conflict with Japan reemerged as a full-blown crisis when, at the end of Taft's term, the California state legislature passed a law that prohibited Japanese (and other Asians) from obtaining a deed to or even a lease on land. In rural areas, the blatantly racist act, a form of economic Jim Crow, was clearly designed to keep Japanese immigrants (and their immediate descendants) as agricultural laborers rather than farm owners. Similarly, in urban areas they would remain tenants rather than landlords or homeowners. Taft passed the problem to Wilson.

As Daniels took the oath of office in the first week of March, "public meetings were held in Japan denouncing [the law] and the Japanese in California were in an ugly mood," he noted, adding, "Undoubtedly the Japanese were so aroused that their government officials could have carried them into war over what they regarded as a studied insult."[32] Though neither Daniels nor Wilson wanted to admit it, the new administration, Secretary of State Bryan in particular, was completely caught off guard by the explosive reaction in Japan. The unexpected nature of the situation made it all the more disconcerting. According to Daniels, the Japanese, who lived in a country in which the national government could dictate to local leaders, did not understand how the U.S. federal government could claim amity between the two countries while letting the Californians openly discriminate against Japanese residents.

As word of Japan's anger reached the United States, a war party emerged in Washington led by the army's General Leonard Wood and Daniels's chief aide, Admiral Fiske. Secretary of War Garrison represented this group within the cabinet. Bryan and Daniels led the peace party. Wilson, too, wanted peace, but he knew that he could not take an openly weak stance against Japan in the first big international confrontation of his administration. Thus he chose a two-pronged approach. Publicly, he would remain friendly with Japan but firm on principle. The U.S. government would not run roughshod over the federalism embedded in the Constitution. However, more quietly, in April he sent Bryan to California to see if the state's political leaders could be persuaded to adopt a more benign policy toward California's Japanese population.

While Bryan went to California and relations between the United States and Japan teetered on the brink of conflict, Daniels dashed home to Raleigh to survey the results of a fire that had nearly destroyed the *News and Observer* building and equipment. (The plant was not totally lost, but the damage was greater than the fire insurance coverage. Fortunately, the *N&O* yielded large profits during these years—as evidenced by Josephus and Addie's tens of thousands of dollars in investments with Herbert Jackson at the Virginia Trust Company—and through Jackson's intermediation Daniels borrowed the money to rebuild the plant.)[33] Both Daniels and Bryan returned to Washington for a cabinet meeting on May 13. Bryan reported that he received no concessions from the Californians. He then immediately left Washington to represent the administration in an address to the Pennsylvania state legislature. Other than serving as a conduit of information, he would play no further role in resolving the East Asia crisis, and this might well have been by Wilson's design. If so, it did not go unnoticed by either Daniels or Bryan. At the next cabinet meeting, Daniels recorded that Bryan told the cabinet that "if the President sent him [Bryan] on many other missions . . . he would not have time to attend the duties of his office." Daniels observed that Bryan made this comment "laughingly," and Wilson might have smiled at the jibe; if so, one can imagine clenched teeth behind the smile.[34]

At the same meeting, Wilson read aloud the formal protest from Japan's ambassador to the United States, Viscount Sutemi Chinda. As Daniels recorded it, "The words of protest were very strong—stronger than the circumstances seemed to warrant. The language, while diplomatic, was such as to cause" some members of the cabinet to fret that if the Japanese demands for redress were not met, then war would follow.[35] At this point Chief of Staff Wood and Admiral Fiske weighed in and attempted to carry the country into war through the ill-timed and ill-considered bellicose positions of the Joint Army-Navy Board. When Daniels returned from Raleigh early on the morning of May 13, he was met by Fiske, who supplied him with a ten-point memorandum on naval preparations for war with Japan. In addition, Fiske recommended the movement of U.S. ships, then in Chinese waters, to the Philippines, where they could transport and support army troops and then commence offensive actions against Japan. Daniels did not support the move, which bore Wood's imprimatur, thinking it premature and too provocative. (Daniels called Wood the "instigator" of the plan.)[36] However, Daniels saw in Fiske's plan a single solution to two thorny problems: the Japan crisis and the overreaching Joint Army-Navy Board. Fiske saw the board as a forerunner to the Joint Chiefs of Staff, and more importantly, he saw it as a means to gain a degree of independence from the secretaries of the army and the navy. Daniels encouraged Fiske to give him all of the information pertaining to the Joint Board's plans, with the understanding that Daniels would share it with the cabinet.

Thus Fiske, in a typically clumsy fashion, naively revealed the war party's plans to Daniels. Rather than quietly securing support among powerful forces in the administration and Congress before springing his proposal, he divulged everything to Daniels, who, in a seemingly conscientious fashion, agreed to put Fiske's proposal before the cabinet. Daniels might even have given Fiske the impression that he would serve as an honest broker and present Fiske's plan without actively attacking it.[37] If so, he misled the admiral. In the subsequent cabinet discussion surrounding the military's plans, Wilson and the others in attendance sought Daniels's view on military conflict with Japan. In reply, Daniels offered a homily: "I have observed that if a man puts a gun to his shoulder and walks down the street, particularly down a street in which he knows there is a man with whom he has some misunderstanding, it is pretty likely to cause the other man to get a gun himself and that death or something else serious results, whereas if the man had not started out with a gun on his shoulder the difficulty would have ended peaceably."[38] The metaphor won the day, and the cabinet supported Daniels's rejection of the Joint Board's plan, though War Secretary Garrison disagreed with the decision.

Daniels knew that while the cabinet was rejecting the Joint Board's plan, the board itself was meeting. Later that evening the board resolved that the army and the navy should consolidate their Far Eastern forces in the Philippines, exactly the action the cabinet had rejected earlier in the day on Daniels's recommendation. The difference of views between the Joint Board and the cabinet hit the newspapers the next day, May 14.[39] Daniels suspected Wood and Fiske of leaking the details to the press. In doing so, however, they only played into his hands. On both the 14th and the 15th, Daniels had heated discussions with Garrison behind closed doors, and at cabinet meetings on the 15th and 16th, their dispute, probably with Daniels's encouragement, spilled into the open.

The lines were now clearly drawn. Garrison and the uniformed leaders of the army and the navy sought actions likely to lead to war; the cabinet wanted to avoid those actions but had not yet come up with an alternative strategy. Wilson did not want war, but the author of *Congressional Government* had no intention of trampling the rights of the state of California, nor did he want to appear timid before Viscount Chinda's hectoring. The government was at an impasse, but it did not last long. Daniels never claimed to be the source of the solution to the standoff, but following the cabinet meeting on May 16, he met privately with Wilson at the White House. They discussed the crisis and the actions of the Joint Board, the members of which both the president and the navy secretary considered insubordinate in intent if not in deed. The offending generals and admirals would have to be dealt with severely. At the end of their talk, without elaboration, Wilson claimed that the course advocated by Daniels "cheered my heart." The next day he announced that the Joint Board would be "abolished."[40]

The insubordination and subsequent dissolution of the Joint Board offered the administration a face-saving way out of the crisis. Wilson and Daniels were happy to rid themselves of the Joint Board, because in its actions it revealed itself to be an obstacle to their objectives; however, Wilson decided to frame the action diplomatically, offering the Joint Board as a sacrifice to the Japanese, who Wilson correctly surmised would appreciate such a gesture. Bryan was dispatched to Chinda with two messages, one formal and the other informal. The formal message explained, in the mind-numbing language of diplomacy, that while the administration offered the "utmost friendliness" to the people of Japan and deplored the actions of the state of California, under the U.S. system of government, it could not unilaterally abrogate those actions. The informal message stated that the president had disbanded the Joint Board, which had acted in a hostile manner without the approval of either the secretary of the navy or the commander in chief, and that the "administration had no thought of war and no intention of moving any of its ships in the Far East while negotiations for peace were pending." "This assurance was given so promptly," Daniels recorded, "that the Japanese government was able to quiet superheated demonstrations in their country."[41] It is possible Wilson, on his own, recognized the opportunity presented by the Joint Board's actions. However, given Daniels's central role in the handling of the board's proposal (encouraging Fiske to share it and then shooting it down in the cabinet), his wishes concerning the outcome of both the crisis and the board's ultimate fate, and his private conversation with Wilson just before the denouement, one cannot dismiss the notion that the resolution was his idea all along. For his part, Daniels took no credit, instead yielding the stage to Wilson.

————

Following the crises in the Far East, the administration turned to problems in Central America and the Caribbean. Of these regions, Wilson said, "We must prove ourselves their friends and champions upon terms of equality and honor. You cannot be friends at all except upon terms of equality. We must show ourselves friends by comprehending their interest whether it squares with our own interest or not."[42] This was a lofty goal, one that Daniels supported, but it would not be realized in practice. Even as Wilson trumpeted a policy of "equality," he was backing away from it, and in fact, his subsequent policies differed little from those of his predecessors.

The U.S. Marine Corps served as the sharp end of those policies, and as secretary of the navy, Daniels maintained responsibility for the marines. Although the Marine Corps had been created by the Continental Congress in the fall of 1775, only months after the battles of Lexington and Concord, the mission of the corps was about to be expanded. Under Mahan's theories, the navy became the embodiment of national power on and across the seas. In extending that power beyond the ship itself, naval officers often had to deploy shipborne infantry. The marines handled the bulk of the navy's fighting on terra firma, and imperialism proved to be a task for which the Marine Corps was particularly well suited.

In February 1914, corps commandant William Phillips Biddle retired. The scion of an old and well-known conservative family, Biddle did not endear himself to Daniels. Although Daniels was clearly relieved to see Biddle go, he faced a difficult decision in choosing Biddle's successor. There were three main candidates. The first was an irrepressible officer with the imposing name of Littleton Waller Tazewell Waller. Born in 1856 in Virginia, Waller joined the corps in 1880 and had seen nearly as much controversy as he had action in his long career, which had taken him from one end of the earth to the other. Daniels never questioned Waller's courage or his leadership under the most trying of combat conditions. But on two occasions, once in China and once in the Philippines, Waller had nearly gotten his command wiped out, and he had faced a court-martial following the debacle in the Philippines.[43] Daniels decided Waller was a warrior, not an administrator.

After rejecting Waller, Daniels turned to the second candidate: John A. Lejeune. Another southerner, Lejeune was born in Pointe Coupee, Louisiana, and graduated from Annapolis in 1888. With a striking visage and stiff-backed gait, Lejeune looked like the marine officer in a recruiting poster. More importantly, unlike Waller, who struck first and worried about the details later, Lejeune exuded a calming demeanor that comforted rather than rattled political nerves. Although ten years Waller's junior, Lejeune had already earned a reputation as a solid leader in the field and, more importantly, as a man who could be trusted to negotiate the political land mines of Washington—a trait not apparent in Waller. Lejeune was clearly Daniels's first choice, but he was much too junior for the position. Even a revolutionary like Daniels recognized the limits on his powers of appointment, and he hesitated to challenge the extreme seniority-consciousness of the armed forces. To promote Lejeune to commandant of the corps, Daniels would have to advance Lejeune three grades, from lieutenant colonel to major general—the rank held by the commandant. The grades did not matter as much as the attitudes of the scores of other officers who would have to go from being Lejeune's senior—in some cases by many years—to his subordinate over night. So Daniels passed on Lejeune for the time being.

The final candidate, the colorless Colonel George Barnett, was in many ways the anti-Waller. Like Lejeune, Barnett was an Annapolis graduate, class of 1881. A midwesterner with a small frame, sad eyes, and a milquetoast mustache, Barnett did not at first glance inspire confidence in the way that either Waller or Lejeune did. But Barnett was every bit as tough as his competition. Furthermore, he had commanded troops in roughly as many theaters as Waller, a considerable achievement for any soldier in any age, and by all accounts Barnett was an outstanding marine officer. Unlike Waller, however, Barnett was a safe candidate without a questionable past or a political following, and unlike Lejeune, Barnett had enough seniority to be an uncontroversial candidate among his uniformed colleagues. Daniels settled on Barnett. Succinctly summarizing his three candidates, Daniels wrote, "[Barnett] was not as vigorous or able a man as General Waller. He was not as able and learned a soldier as General Lejeune, but he had a good record, and he was appointed. I found him capable and agreeable. . . . [He] had his department well organized. It made a fine record."[44] Daniels kept Barnett on for the next six and a half years. At a personal level, neither man ever fully embraced the other, and in the end they would have an ugly split. But for the years they served together, they maintained a good working re-lationship.

The Marine Corps that Daniels took over in 1913 was small but had many responsibilities, and it would be stretched thinly throughout Daniels's tenure. Despite the number of "splendid little wars" in which the corps would find itself before being called to serve in the Great War, there were fewer than 10,000 U.S. marines in 1913, including only 331 officers on active duty. Often starved for resources in a naval hierarchy that increasingly valued the dreadnought, the marines would be repeatedly called to pro-vide thankless and dangerous service. They were undermanned and often poorly supplied, and their can-do spirit and successful record as the iron fist in the velvet glove of Wilson's version of gunboat diplomacy has gener-ally gone unappreciated by subsequent generations.[45]

Daniels always maintained a somewhat ambivalent attitude toward the Marine Corps. On one hand, the corps was never as hidebound as the navy, in Daniels's opinion. In the field, the social distance between officers and enlisted men was never as great as that between the wardroom and other ranks in the navy, and so in the marines Daniels never saw the class distinc-tions that so appalled him when he reviewed the navy. On the other hand, the Marine Corps was the most strictly martial of the military services. The technical demands placed on a modern navy—mechanical, electrical, and metallurgical demands that required numeracy and literacy—meant that the navy could serve as a federally funded vocational training school. This was Daniels's view of the service, and thus he saw in the navy the opportunity to better the economic status of the enlisted personnel. No such opportunities existed in the Marine Corps. The marines served solely as the violent extension of U.S. foreign policy. Although under Daniels the corps engaged in small-scale public works projects in a number of countries, overall the corps was not a good place to learn much beyond discipline, personal hygiene, and how to administer violent death. The resulting hard-charging ethos on the battlefield was matched only by the corps' reputation for hard drinking and riotous living off it. A near-pacifist like Daniels could never fully embrace the corps' violent battlefield credo, but political expediency would lead him to exploit it. Wilson would give him a number of opportunities to do so, because the president's Good Neighbor policy had a short life.

It was easy to be good neighbors, even with bad men, when thousands of miles lay between you. With respect to problems in the Far East, it helped when the Pacific Ocean made up most of those miles. No matter how bad things got in China and Japan, neither was an immediate threat to the United States or its strategic interests, and the amount of U.S. capital invested there was relatively small. However, when bad neighbors lived much closer, when they threatened U.S. interests, and when large amounts of U.S. capital were invested there, *then* it became difficult to be good neighbors with bad men. Many of the Western Hemisphere countries carved out of the Spanish Empire failed to enjoy political stability following their independence. When it was achieved, stability was often maintained by strongmen who cared little about being good neighbors with the United States. Indeed, anti-U.S. sentiment served as a common rallying point for many of the warlords who reigned between the Rio Grande and Tierra del Fuego. Such men laughed at Wilsonian rhetoric, which was tested almost immediately after the inauguration.

Of the major Latin American expeditions that would be undertaken or extended during Daniels's time at the helm of the navy, Cuba produced the longest-standing problems. As the producer of a high-demand European luxury—sugar—Cuba had been a valuable part of the Spanish Empire since 1511. With a class structure that was the product of four centuries of Spanish rule, Cuba had a small number of very rich and a larger number of very poor citizens. The U.S. war with Spain, while nominally about Cuban independence, was really about removing a decrepit European power from a nearby island. Through the Treaty of Paris signed at the end of 1898 and ratified the following year, Cuba gained nominal independence but became a de facto U.S. possession. Initially, the U.S. occupation of Cuba was uneventful, especially in contrast with the end of Spain's reign. The Cuban insurgents, recent U.S. allies, were paid a bounty and disbanded. A mosquito eradication campaign, motivated by the work of U.S. Army doctor Walter Reed, contributed to dramatic reductions in the incidence of yellow fever and malaria, and sugar production rebounded. Honoring the slogan "Cuba for the Cubans," in 1902 the army prepared to leave. "Cuba for the Cubans" made for good propaganda, but the reality of it made the sugar interests and their creditors nervous. Congress eased their concerns.

Determined to "safeguard" U.S. economic and military interests in Cuba, Congress passed an army funding bill that had attached to it the so-call Platt Amendment. "Under its terms," one writer observed, "Cuba would be obligated to obtain Uncle Sam's approval before signing any foreign treaty; maintain low foreign debt; ratify all acts of the U.S. military government; and give the American armed forces the right to intervene at any time to protect life, liberty, and property. In addition, Cuba would have to provide the U.S. long-term leases on naval bases; it was this provision that would lead to the creation of a naval station at Guantánamo Bay in 1903."[46] The army left the following year only after the new Cuban regime pledged to honor the Platt Amendment; the navy and the marines remained, always ready to enforce the terms of the amendment.

Within three years of the troops' departure, rival factions within Cuba sent the island to the brink of open civil war. President Theodore Roosevelt called out the marines, and under the command of the tenacious Littleton Waller, they restored order and kept a moderate political faction nominally in control of the island. The marines served as the de facto Cuban constabulary for three years. With order restored and a U.S.-trained Cuban army in place, President Taft pulled the marines out. Three years later the island's black population—the poorest of the poor—revolted. Once again U.S. property, largely in the form of sugar mills, was threatened, and once again Taft called on the marines to bring order.

The revolt and the subsequent marine landings took place in May 1912, and the timing could not have been worse for Taft. Caught between's TR's Bull Moose campaign and Wilson's scholarly brand of progressivism, Taft recognized that he was vulnerable to charges of fiscal profligacy for spending tax dollars to secure the profits of a small number of sugar magnates, as well as to charges of imperialism from those who thought Cuba for the Cubans sounded just fine. Accordingly, with the so-called Negro revolt quickly put down, Taft recalled the marines in July. The essence of Taft's Cuba policy had been to keep in power a friendly regime that would enforce the Platt Amendment, which itself was merely a means by which U.S. sugar producers and Wall Street bondholders received the profits from and interest on their Cuban investments. Judged by this narrow financial objective, one must conclude that Taft's policy was successful, but it was not a policy that offered long-run stability absent U.S. force, as Daniels would soon discover. When Daniels took over the navy, Cuba again teetered on the brink of insurrection.

In contrast to the strategy of keeping a friendly regime in power in Cuba, Taft's policy in Nicaragua focused on removing a recalcitrant regime and replacing it with a friendly one similar to Cuba's. The troublesome regime, run by José Santos Zelaya, derived revenue from selling or exercising monopoly rights to exploit the country's natural resources, primarily rubber and bananas. When U.S. companies decided they wanted a slice of the pie, Zelaya could not be induced to offer favorable terms. The American capitalists, supported (as was so often the case in these situations) by the U.S. consul, calculated that it would be cheaper to replace Zelaya than bargain with him, and so they funded a revolt in the Nicaraguan outback.

Initially, U.S. involvement included only encouragement, funds, and a few mercenaries. But when Zelaya succumbed to U.S. pressure and resigned, his replacement, José Madriz, pressed the campaign against the U.S.-supported rebels and all but shattered the revolt. With the remnants of a rebel force encircled in the remote town of Bluefields, late in 1909 the consul persuaded Taft to back U.S. policy with military force, and a company of marines was dispatched from Panama to resolve the situation. The U.S. force in Nicaragua never exceeded a few hundred marines, but they were capably led by Major Smedley Butler, a bantam rooster of a man who had been raised in a prominent Pennsylvania Quaker family. A resourceful field officer, Butler reorganized the rebels, and by midsummer his outnumbered and outgunned force had routed the Nicaraguan army and established a friendly regime in the capital, Managua. Butler's coup, a tremendous military feat, proved to be a political failure, as forces that had previously been loyal to the Madriz regime were turned into rebels, and they proved better at guerilla warfare than conventional combat. To compound the new, pro-American regime's problems, the rebels were soon joined by various splinter groups, and by September the country again faced a full-blown civil war. Butler returned, now joined by a larger force led by Colonel Joseph Pendleton. Two months of sometimes hard fighting followed, but U.S. victory was never in doubt. The U.S. puppet remained president, and a force of U.S. marines remained in Managua as his imperial guard. More importantly, they ensured U.S. access to Nicaraguan rubber, banana plantations, and mining concessions. The marines were still there when Daniels took over as their chief five months after the victory, and they stayed until 1925, long after he had left office.

U.S. involvement in Cuba and Nicaragua antedated the Wilson administration, and Daniels inherited fragile Cuban and Nicaraguan governments propped up by U.S. marines. Problems in both countries would blow up soon enough; but an even larger and more important crisis erupted in Mexico just as Daniels took office, and it would continue to plague him for years to come. The problems in Mexico provided the most troublesome example of the muddle that was Wilsonian foreign policy in the hands of William Jennings Bryan. Not forceful enough to be effectively imperial, the policy was just strong enough to be offensive to those with anti-imperial leanings. Mexico would represent the beginning of Daniels's transformation from pacifist and isolationist to imperialist.

In 1910, longtime Mexican dictator Porfirio Díaz announced he would step down following a presidential election; instead, he changed his mind and ran for reelection. His primary opponent was reformist aristocrat Francisco Madero. On the eve of the election, which given the extent of the regime's control was never in doubt, Díaz had Madero arrested. After securing victory, Díaz released Madero, who, instead of returning to a quiet private life, initiated an open revolt and declared himself president. Disparate rebel elements, including forces under Pancho Villa in the north and Emiliano Zapata in the south, supported Madero, and the Díaz regime quickly collapsed. Another round of elections was subsequently held, and they confirmed support for Madero's insurgency with his elevation to the presidency.

The poverty of the vast majority of the Mexican people, the country's weak economy, and the decay surrounding the late Díaz regime contributed to Mexico's political instability. Although Madero had been a successful revolutionary, and he was arguably a less corrupt leader than Díaz, he had little success as the head of state. One of his generals, Victoriano Huerta, with the support of U.S. Ambassador Henry Lane Wilson, staged a coup, and Huerta had Madero executed on February 22, 1913, just two weeks before Daniels took office. Huerta had achieved the rank of general under Díaz, and Madero had kept him on—just one of the well-meaning Madero's many mistakes. In the struggle for power under Madero, Huerta had run roughshod over the men who had led the military struggle against Díaz. Among these was Villa. Arrested by Huerta, Villa managed to escape and once again took his army of the north into the field. Villa's old comrade in arms, Zapata, joined the fight against Huerta, and the two rebels were in turn supported by a group of middle-class economic interests, the members of which correctly surmised that a banana republic would not provide the political road to wealth. The leader of this group was a northern politician named Venustiano Carranza.[47] Very quickly Mexico descended into chaos.

Despite the role of Taft's ambassador in putting Huerta on the throne, the general quickly resorted to demagoguery concerning U.S. investment in Mexico. U.S. investors, especially those in the oil industry, interpreted this as a threat to their financial interests and to the well-being of their workers in the country. Accordingly, they turned to the new Wilson administration for support. Thus the affair offered an early test of Wilson's Good Neighbor policy. Huerta was not a good neighbor.

According to Daniels, the administration's leading advocates of U.S. military intervention in Mexico included Interior Secretary Franklin Lane and Bryan's counselor, Robert Lansing, both of whom, again according to Daniels, represented U.S. oil interests. In addition, Postmaster Albert Burleson, a Texan, wanted to restore order south of the border. Outside the administration, among the loudest voices calling for a U.S. invasion was that of Daniels's publishing colleague William Randolph Hearst, who had extensive landholdings in Mexico. "There is only one course," Hearst wrote. "That course is to occupy Mexico and restore it to a state of civilization by means of American MEN and American METHODS."[48] Daniels strongly objected, and to lessen the chance that the United States would become involved, Daniels lobbied for support for his plan to recall to U.S. ports naval vessels stationed off the coast of Mexico. Removing the vessels, he argued, lessened the chance that a random incident between U.S. and Mexican forces might get blown out of proportion and lead to armed conflict between the two countries. This was the majority view in the cabinet, where the interventionist party had not yet gotten the upper hand. Daniels noted that among the cabinet members "there was a general feeling that no steps ought to be taken looking toward intervention and nothing done which might cause the Americans at this juncture to make it necessary to interfere."[49] As a result, in April the ships came home.

However, Mexico descended into civil war, and Daniels realized that withdrawing any threat of U.S. involvement solved nothing. "What to do with Mexico is the great problem," he wrote in his diary just a few weeks after the navy had been withdrawn at his insistence.[50] As the situation in

Mexico continued to deteriorate, Daniels began to see the hollowness at the core of Wilson's Good Neighbor rhetoric, which had no impact on men like Díaz or Huerta, or Villa and Zapata. According to Daniels, after the China and Japan crises had passed, the major question, the "most pressing foreign problem," in his words, was whether to extend formal recognition to the Huerta regime. If the administration recognized the regime, that would send a strong signal to interested parties that the United States disapproved of Carranza's revolution, and those on the fence might swing toward Huerta.

The Taft administration had complicated Wilson's Mexican policy by supporting Huerta's coup. As a result of that intervention, some observers in Washington and Mexico saw Huerta as Washington's man. Although one could make a cynical case for supporting Huerta on the grounds that his regime might have been more "stable" than Madero's, Daniels thought that H. L. Wilson had simply been a stooge for American business interests, oil in particular, that viewed Huerta as more welcoming of dollar diplomacy than Madero was.[51] The timing of events was important, as Huerta acted before Taft left office with the promise, either explicit or implicit, that his regime would be recognized. Huerta was wrong. Taft dithered, and the Wilson administration was not yet ready to grant Huerta recognition. Huerta had Mexico, but he was not Washington's man.

The administration considered three options. One was outright recognition. War Secretary Garrison, who wavered between intervention and recognition, was skeptical that the Mexicans would ever obtain a truly democratic government; thus he thought recognition the easiest path, arguing that it would be cheaper to persuade Huerta to be reasonable than it would be to do nothing or replace him. The problem with such a strategy was that it exposed the Wilson administration to the risk that Huerta would turn out to be an even worse neighbor than he already was. Viewing Huerta as nothing more than a warlord, Daniels did not support recognition.

A second option was to invade and put a U.S.-backed strongman on the throne in Mexico City. Interior Secretary Lane argued that if Wilson refused to recognize Huerta, then he should go ahead and use force to put a friendly ruler in Huerta's place. While this morally questionable strategy was logically consistent, it did not appeal to Bryan, Daniels, or Wilson, all of whom were more inclined to tread lightly on their neighbors' sovereignty than the recent Republican administrations had been.

A third option would be to play for time. Under this strategy, although the administration would not formally recognize Huerta, it might treat with him and his envoys, while at the same time (quietly) offering support to Carranza, with the hope that his forces would drive Huerta from power.[52] Bryan recommended this option, and initially Daniels, who called Huerta a "brute," agreed with it.[53] Wilson, by nature a scholar rather than a man of action, went along with Bryan and Daniels, calling his administration's strategy "watchful waiting."

This strategy satisfied neither Huerta nor the U.S. business interests, which included Wall Street bondholders and U.S. oil firms. The latter were willing to deal with a dictator, but they preferred the explicit backing of the U.S. government in doing so. That support, they assumed, included military force should Huerta decide to do something really rash, such as nationalize U.S. property in Mexico. The result would be the replacement of Huerta, possibly with Carranza (but certainly with neither Villa nor Zapata). Complicating the administration's strategy of doing nothing was that it allowed the European powers to secure what should have been American markets in Mexico. It also gave the Europeans greater access to Mexican resources, the most important of which was oil. Thus the administration remained under pressure at home to pacify Mexico.

Subsequent events caused Daniels to sour on the president's watchful waiting strategy. The British, soon followed by the other European powers, recognized Huerta, and word came back from Mexico that the Europeans, especially the Germans, planned to supply Huerta with arms. With German arms and advisors, Huerta could afford to be indifferent to U.S. concerns, whether those concerns emanated from Wall Street or the White House. More troubling was what the Germans might seek in return for their support. Among the worst-case scenarios was a naval base in Mexico. Although Daniels initially supported Wilson's watchful waiting strategy, should push come to shove, as head of the navy Daniels would have to deal with a German naval contingent in the Gulf of Mexico. A violation of the Good Neighbor policy would be, in Daniels's view, less costly than a German naval base in Mexico. Wilson's watchful waiting threatened to turn into a renunciation of the Monroe Doctrine.

Viewed through the lens of time, the interventionists' position on Mexico seems cynical and anachronistic, but at least it was realistic. With the involvement of the European powers in Mexico, Daniels realized that intervention might be necessary. The European powers recognized an opportunity in Mexico, while the Wilson administration vacillated. The interventionists, led by Lane, saw that if the administration was not going to recognize Huerta, then it should publicly declare as much and develop an aggressive strategy to replace him, challenging the Europeans before any of them got a toehold in Mexico. Even if Daniels disagreed with Lane's recommendation of putting a U.S. puppet in power in Mexico City, he recognized that Lane saw more clearly than Wilson and Bryan what would happen in Mexico in the absence of U.S. force. Lane's view disturbed Daniels, but with the threat of Germany running guns to Mexico, Daniels now understood and appreciated it. Though Daniels continued to keep his increasing skepticism from Wilson, his actions spoke louder than words. Without fanfare, he sent a U.S. Navy flotilla back to Mexican waters.

It is possible that Daniels took this martial step anticipating that it might force Huerta's hand. He certainly was not going to let Germany make Mexico a protectorate, and so he must have understood that if the navy attempted to stop Germany from running guns to Huerta, there would be shooting. In any case, the situation blew up on April 9, 1914, when nine seamen aboard a U.S. Navy whaleboat sent to collect supplies in Tampico were taken into custody by forces loyal to Huerta.[54] The supply boat had been sent under the command of Admiral Henry Mayo, whom Daniels had ordered to Mexico's coastal waters "for the protection of Americans." When Mexico's regional military governor heard of the arrest, he immediately ordered the men released and issued an apology to Mayo. Without consulting Daniels or anyone else in Washington, Mayo rejected the apology and demanded that the governor "hoist the American flag in a prominent position on shore and salute it with twenty-one guns."[55] In addition, Mayo demanded a formal written apology, which was to include a disavowal of the act, all within twenty-four hours. A minor incident between the armed forces of otherwise peaceful neighbors was about to become a war.

Huerta quickly recognized that Mayo had handed him an opportunity to play a clever double game. In Mexico, for domestic political purposes, his allies denounced the "Tampico incident" as an example of America's arrogant imperialism, claiming it was a prelude to another U.S. invasion of Mexico (the first having occurred during the Mexican-American War in 1848). In Washington, however, Huerta quietly signaled that he could be reasonable. Although he would not accede to Mayo's demands, Huerta claimed to regret the incident, and he tried to use the communications between the two countries as a means of obtaining de facto U.S. recognition of his regime. By now Huerta had exhausted Daniels's patience. The threat of military intervention in Mexico by Germany was the last straw. The naval arms race was bad enough, but the thought of European encroachment in Mexico was too much for Daniels. He would not be the navy secretary who repudiated the Monroe Doctrine. Huerta would have to be slapped down.

At that moment the president was out of Washington tending to his wife, who was battling a kidney disease that would ultimately prove fatal. He left Bryan in charge of the communications with Mexico. Bryan was not a great secretary of state. Indeed, he was the most parochial of men, and America's standing as a Great Power meant little to him. He hoped to continue to play for time and sought Daniels's support, thinking the navy secretary agreed with him on international matters in general and on Mexico in particular, and he hoped the navy would back down. Daniels offered Bryan a sympathetic ear but backed Mayo's play in Mexico, and when Wilson returned to Washington, the president agreed with Daniels's strategy. To hedge his political bets, however, Wilson went to Congress seeking support in case things should go wrong in Mexico. There he received approval for the use of armed force.

Wilson made up his mind that he would not be further bullied by Huerta, but when Secretary of War Garrison proposed a formal declaration of war, the president demurred. It is not clear exactly what Wilson was prepared to do in confronting the Mexican strongman. However, events took a dramatic turn less than forty-eight hours later when Bryan received a message from the U.S. consul in Veracruz that included reliable information that the German steamship *Ypiranga* would arrive early on April 21 to unload a large arms shipment. Bryan informed Wilson, who called Daniels. "What do you think should be done, Daniels?" the president asked. Daniels, crossing the martial Rubicon, said the administration could not allow the Germans to arm Huerta. To do so would be a repudiation of the Monroe Doctrine and would create a potential military crisis and certainly a political one. Thus Daniels advised a military invasion of Mexico. Wilson concurred. Before dawn on the 21st, Daniels wired Admiral Frank Fletcher, commander of the force off Veracruz: "Seize custom house. Do not permit war supplies to be delivered to Huerta government or to any other party."[56]

What followed was two days of nasty urban warfare. Fighting house-to-house from street to street, U.S. naval and marine forces led by Smedley Butler drove the Mexican army from the town. Both sides suffered a combined 500 casualties, and Fletcher and Butler, along with 53 other seamen and marines, received the Congressional Medal of Honor for their roles in the engagement, "the most for any battle before or since."[57] Butler became the de facto ruler of Veracruz, and he prepared to march to Mexico City.

Mayo and Fletcher would have ordered him to do so if they had not received orders from Daniels to halt their forces in Veracruz. Daniels, aghast at the thought of expanding the beachhead, figured that if U.S. troops marched on Mexico City, Huerta's regime would collapse, and the United States would be forced into running Mexico. Wilson agreed with Daniels's analysis. Huerta remained in power, but not for long. Carranza's forces proved victorious in the field, and with Veracruz closed and Mayo and Fletcher blockading the coast, Huerta could not be resupplied from outside the country. In addition, the threat of further U.S. involvement remained. With his regime on the verge of collapse, Huerta retired later that summer, just as the world's attention turned to the war in Europe. As Mexico faded from the front page of the newspaper, U.S. forces left Veracruz in November, and the Wilson administration formally recognized Carranza the following year.

While Carranza's victory over Huerta and the marines' evacuation of Veracruz appeared to signal the stabilization of the political situation in Mexico, the Caribbean nation of Haiti collapsed. To observers at that time it would have been difficult to imagine that things in Haiti could get worse than they had been in recent years. As Daniels put it, "Haiti was killing its presidents rapidly—seven from 1911 to 1915—most of them removed by violence."[58] Although there was little direct U.S. investment in the impoverished country, which had once been a part of the French Empire (the island of Hispaniola had been divided between the French and the Spanish by the Treaty of Ryswick in 1697), during the Taft administration a Wall Street consortium had taken over the Haitian national bank, the Banque Nationale de la Republique d'Haiti. Following a coup in 1914, the investors, concerned that the bank's gold reserves would be plundered, convinced Bryan to persuade Wilson to order Daniels to send marines to protect the bank's vaults. Without comment, Daniels followed the State Department's "request" and ordered a gunboat to land a squadron of marines, who then seized the bank's reserves, which were subsequently transferred to Wall Street. It was a transparent reminder that in practice there was no difference between dollar and gunboat diplomacy, and that by 1914, other than the rhetoric, there was little difference between Wilson's brand of gunboat diplomacy and that of his Republican predecessors.[59]

Taking control of the Haitian national bank on behalf of Wall Street investors was exactly the type of imperialist bullying that Daniels deplored, but Daniels was not a rigid ideologue. If Wilson ordered it, he would follow orders, though it is probably not a coincidence that he did not mention the event in his memoirs. However, he soon became more interested in

Haiti for strategic reasons. The war in Europe made the Caribbean islands tempting bases for the belligerent countries. In particular, recent German investments in Haiti created a strong Teutonic presence there—too strong, in Daniels's view. Indeed, it was rumored that the Germans decided who would and would not reign in Port-au-Prince, the country's ramshackle capital. Accordingly, Daniels worried about the Imperial German Navy "obtaining bases in these near-by islands" and thus threatening "the approaches to the Panama Canal."[60] This concern had turned Daniels into an advocate of using force in Mexico. Daniels wanted no part of the war in Europe, but he also had no intention of letting it spread to the Western Hemisphere in the form of naval bases in his own backyard.

Thus Daniels followed closely a coup attempt on July 27, 1915. The deposed Haitian president, V. G. Sam, took refuge in the French legation, while his police chief did the same in the Dominican legation. However, both men were subsequently dragged from their respective sanctuaries and hacked to death in the streets. On the flimsy pretext that the new regime had violated the territorial integrity of France and the Dominican Republic, the Wilson administration—at the urging of the new secretary of state, Robert Lansing, who had replaced Bryan only a month earlier—decided it was time to stop the merry-go-round in Port-au-Prince and bring political stability to the island. As Lansing wrote, the objective "was to forestall any attempt by a foreign power to obtain a foothold on the territory of an American nation."[61] In short, the administration chose to uphold the Monroe Doctrine to keep the Germans out of Haiti. Daniels ordered the navy to land marines with the objective of seizing the Haitian capital. This they did on July 28. The marine in charge of the operation was none other than Littleton Waller Tazewell Waller, one of whose chief subordinates was the peripatetic gunboat diplomatist Smedley Butler.

Although the marines encountered courageous resistance from various Haitian factions opposing U.S. intervention, they soon seized control of the country's few coastal towns. To prevent a continuation of the string of coups and countercoups that had plagued the country for decades, Lansing arranged for a U.S.-backed strongman, Phillipe Durtiguanave, to be placed in the presidential "palace." Daniels supported intervention in Haiti, but he thought little of Durtiguanave. In his memoirs, Daniels noted that Durtiguanave had been "hand-picked" by the State Department.[62] The new Haitian president did not impress Butler either. With classic military understatement, in his formal report to Daniels, Butler wrote, "I won't say we put [Durtiguanave] in. . . . Anyway he was put in."[63] Rumor had it that when

Durtiguanave balked at signing the country's new constitution as drawn up by the State Department, rather than argue the point Butler simply held a pistol to the president's head until he signed. Daniels, who never refuted the story, phlegmatically summarized the Haitian expedition with "My job in Haiti was to furnish the ships and the marines. They acted as policemen. The State Department directed the policy."[64] As distasteful as Daniels found this business, the Germans were kept out. Daniels agreed to keep the marines on to train a new Haitian constabulary, a process that proved more challenging than Daniels might have hoped. The U.S. Marines stayed in Haiti for nineteen years, even longer than in Nicaragua.

To Daniels, there seemed to be no end to the turmoil in the region. About the same time his marines were securing the reserves of the Haitian national bank in 1914, he ordered them into the neighboring Dominican Republic. To force the repayment of interest and principal on U.S. loans, President Theodore Roosevelt had ordered marines to seize the Dominican customhouses in 1905, and the country's debts to U.S. lenders were subsequently serviced by force of arms. Even with marines running the Dominican customs service and serving by default as a constabulary in the port cities (and as Wall Street's bill collectors), the country had only a bit more political stability than Haiti. Following the assassination of its president in 1911, the country descended into the type of chaos all too common in the region at the time. In 1914, Wilson, in consultation with the State Department (which increasingly meant consulting with Lansing rather than Bryan), decided to make the Dominican Republic a model for his supposedly benevolent form of gunboat diplomacy. Wilson concluded that he had been forced to intervene in Mexico and Haiti because the respective heads of state had not been elected by popular vote. Thus he charged Daniels with ensuring that the Dominican Republic held fair elections in the fall of 1914. This effectively made Daniels the receiver of the politically and economically bankrupt nation. Accordingly, Daniels increased the number of marines in the country and ordered them to oversee the elections held in October. The result was that Juan Isidro Jiménes became president. Despite being popularly elected, Jiménes had no credible military force at his disposal, and the marines were obliged to run the country for him. To make sure U.S. investors were paid interest on their loans, the marines forced the president to surrender control of his country's treasury and police force.

With the marines in control of the Dominican police, customs, and treasury, some order was finally brought to the country, but resentment at U.S. power led to a revolt against Jiménes two years later. In the interim, the war in Europe had spread to the shipping lanes of the Atlantic, and as Daniels had done in Haiti in 1915, he used the threat of the Germans seizing a base in the Dominican Republic as an excuse to invade the country. Daniels ordered the marines to increase their forces and to seize the capital. They did so, but that did not quell the revolt, which spread across the country. After several weeks and the deployment of an additional marine contingent, they took control of the major towns and ports. After the marines finally drove the last insurgents into the hinterlands, the Dominican Republic became another wholly owned subsidiary of the U.S. Navy Department, which ran the country until 1924.

U.S. invasions of its neighbors did not end there. The following year, 1917, yet another revolt broke out in Cuba. The nominal cause was an election supposedly stolen by U.S. sugar interests. Wilsonian rhetoric declared that the United States would support fair elections. In Cuba, the most likely outcome of such an election was victory for the Cuban rebels. However, as a historian of U.S. military efforts during the era put it, "the U.S. had just entered World War 1 and needed assured access to the Cuban Sugar crop. So the Wilson administration backed [the Cuban regime's] suppression of the revolt and, at the Cuban president's request, [Daniels] landed 2,600 marines."[65] The marines stayed to ensure five more sugar crops before leaving in 1922.

All told, the United States "intervened 33 times in Latin-American countries, during the era."[66] But in the end, Wilson's Good Neighbor imperialism, as administered by Daniels, amounted to little. As tactical military operations, the invasions must be judged unequivocal successes. The navy and the marines achieved every objective Daniels assigned to them with no significant setbacks, and they did prevent Germany from obtaining a foothold in the Western Hemisphere during the Great War, which was a legitimate threat in Haiti and Mexico and possibly the Dominican Republic.[67] However, as strategic political operations, they must be considered failures. Despite the creation of some economic infrastructure, largely in the form of local public sanitation and road building, the efforts brought no long-term stability to the region, while they arguably worsened relations between the United States and its Latin neighbors. Daniels and Wilson may or may not have had better intentions than Roosevelt and Taft, but they were gunboat diplomatists all the same. No matter how hard Daniels tried to dress up his role in these affairs, by 1917 he was effectively running Nicaragua, Haiti, the Dominican Republic, and Cuba. He became derisively known in the region as "Josephus the First—King of Haiti."[68] The moniker was not unearned. As the end of the Great War approached, the empire Daniels oversaw was larger than those of the German kaiser, Russia's czar, or the Ottoman sultan.

THE DOMESTIC FRONT

During his time at the helm of the navy, Daniels kept the same schedule as he had as publisher of the *News and Observer*. He rose early, returned home for dinner in the early evening, and then frequently worked until late at night and often into the early hours of the next day. His mental and physical stamina were remarkable by any human standard. His diet remained bland—meat and potatoes unimaginatively prepared—for the most part. He and Addie tried to transfer their daily life in Raleigh to Washington, and Josephus was never entirely free from the management of the *N&O*; nor could he escape the quotidian chores of family life, though it must be noted that at home Addie was in charge. When asked about the allocation of family responsibilities, one of Josephus and Addie's sons recalled, "I would say this: my mother was always in charge of the home."[69] Josephus gladly turned over the management of the household to his wife, and with respect to his immediate family, his early years in Washington were happy.

By upbringing and personality, Addie was a society maven, and she competently discharged her social duties as the wife of a cabinet minister who was also one of the president's closest confidants. She recalled her most pressing duties as a cabinet minister's wife: "What to reply when a queen says that her clothes closets are dusty. How to feed fifteen hundred women at a reception when eight hundred have been expected. Where to find the time to make from two hundred and fifty to four hundred calls every week. What to do when a lady blurts out a government secret at a tea."[70] Of course the family's teetotaling constrained their socializing to a certain extent. For Washington's many regular drinkers, a dry dinner at the Danielses could be trying, no matter how insightful or pleasant the conversation.

The Danielses' three younger boys were all old enough to view the move from Raleigh as something of an adventure. (Addie had given birth to the couple's sixth and last child, a girl, in 1911, but she died shortly after birth.) Josephus looked forward to moving his oldest son, Josephus Jr., soon to be nineteen, into a management position at the *N&O*. Content in his personal life, the elder Daniels could eagerly look forward to his time near the top of the American political hierarchy. Unfortunately, some family issues beyond his own household were not progressing smoothly, and several problems emerged at the *N&O* almost immediately after the family departed from Raleigh.

Initially, the most trying of these problems involved two family members left behind: Josephus's younger brother, Charles, and Addie's younger brother, Henry Bagley. During the first few years Josephus Daniels spent in Washington, he perpetually dealt with problems surrounding these two people, neither of whom seemed capable of bringing the kind of order to their own lives that he and Addie had brought to theirs.[71] As a teen, Charles had been a steady partner for Josephus in two of the three newspapers he owned in Carolina's coastal plain, but Charles eventually gave up the newspaper business and followed his brothers in studying the law. After obtaining a license, he had a hard time settling down to a successful practice. Quarrelsome, he made a difficult junior partner for anyone other than Josephus.

While serving in the Cleveland administration, Josephus helped secure an appointment for Charles in the Bureau of Indian Affairs. Moving west, Charles handled legal matters related to Indian property rights on reservations. After the Republicans recaptured the White House following the election of 1896, Charles returned to a desultory legal practice in Wilson. In 1901, Governor Charles Brantley Aycock rescued Charles's career by securing his appointment as state solicitor for the judicial district surrounding his home. There can be no doubt that this was done out of friendship for and gratitude to Charles's older brothers, as Frank was Aycock's law partner and Josephus had helped make Aycock governor. For reasons not altogether clear, Charles left that position after a few years, and at the time Josephus joined Wilson's administration in 1913, Charles was maintaining a marginal legal practice back where he had begun in Wilson.

From the time Charles learned that Josephus would hold high office in Washington, he beseeched his brother to secure a patronage position for him, hopefully something in the Justice Department. After considerable back-and-forth on the topic, Josephus finally persuaded Attorney General James McReynolds to appoint Charles to a position as U.S. attorney in Minnesota. Charles's experience in Indian affairs from his days in the Cleveland administration helped him secure the position, as tribal disputes involving timber and mineral resources took up much of the time of the U.S. attorneys in the region. While Josephus knew that in the right circumstances Charles, who was intelligent and worked hard when he wanted to, was a good subordinate, this particular appointment would later prove troublesome.

While working out the details of Charles's position in the Justice Department, Josephus had asked Charles to look after a few legal issues related to the *News and Observer* in Raleigh. Among the most important of these was the prosecution of a lawsuit against the Wake Water Company concerning the April 1913 fire at the *N&O* building. Much of the physical plant was destroyed. The plaintiff in the original suit was technically the News and Observer Corporation, but by that time the corporation was almost entirely Josephus Daniels, since he owned the vast majority of the stock. Charles argued that the Wake Water Company had failed to supply the fire department adequately with water so that the fire could be extinguished before extensive damage was done. Unfortunately, the water company had failed prior to the suit, and by the time Charles pursued damages, the company was already in receivership. Ever the cautious businessman, Josephus had earlier purchased fire insurance; however, the loss was valued at more than the $40,000 covered by the policy.[72] Despite the failure of the water company, Charles pursued whatever he could get from the rump of the now defunct company, which turned out to be little.[73] (The *N&O* building would burn again two years later under essentially the same conditions.)

Shortly before he left for Washington in March 1913, Josephus, in a letter, had asked Charles to "keep in touch with the News and Observer."[74] Innocent as Josephus might have thought these words were, Charles almost immediately exceeded his charge and began meddling in the operation of the paper. In preparation for his departure, Josephus had divided the firm's management into three departments. Day-to-day editorial matters were to be overseen by Edward E. Britton, a longtime Daniels confidant, who would later join Daniels's personal staff in the Navy Department in Washington. Britton was a competent though colorless editor, exactly the type of manager Daniels valued, and Daniels never surrendered overall editorial control. He determined the *N&O*'s position on any policy issue of importance and regularly supplied Britton with news and opinion pieces from Washington. Lee Alford, Daniels's longtime collaborator, continued to manage the "mechanical department," which included the actual printing and distribution of the paper. Alford had been a printer thirty years earlier on Daniels's first paper, the Wilson *Advance*, and he had been instrumental in upgrading the *News and Observer*'s physical plant after Daniels took over in 1895. Ever a steady hand, Alford kept the operations side of the business humming in Daniels's absence and took the lead in rebuilding the physical plant following the fire.

The third member of the triumvirate was Josephus's brother-in-law,

Henry Bagley, who was to be the business manager. Because his short-comings manifested themselves more directly in the management of the *N&O*, Henry would prove to be an even more troublesome family member than Charles. Among Henry's problems, though from Josephus's view not necessarily the most important one, was that Henry had a reputation for liking more than one woman, while he was married to a woman he apparently did not like. In addition to his constant womanizing, which was scandalous for an individual from such a prominent family in turn-of-the-century Raleigh, Henry, though not without talent, could be a somewhat erratic colleague. Unlike Charles, who worked well under Josephus but no one else, Henry did not work well under Josephus, but he would later prove to be a good employee working for other newspapers. Opinionated and chafing under his brother-in-law's command, Henry took obstinate positions on rather minor managerial issues that merely alienated others at the firm. Overall, he turned out to be considerably less than the team player Josephus needed in Raleigh. Although a capable newspaperman, Henry's inability to order his personal life would eventually rupture his relationship with Josephus (and more importantly, Addie).

Of more immediate concern, however, was Charles's meddling at the *N&O*. While conversing with Britton, Alford, and Henry Bagley during a visit to the paper, Charles learned that Josephus continued to provide direction concerning the paper's editorial content. Why this fact should have surprised Charles is an open question. Josephus had too much capital invested, financial and personal, to abandon the *N&O*, and his position in Washington only increased the weight of his editorial opinions. In any case, Charles strongly urged his older brother to let go of the management of the paper and turn it completely over to the triumvirate. In particular he admonished Josephus to give complete editorial control to Britton: "You advised [Britton] to write editorials on good roads, good health and some other dust like subjects, which I have forgotten. . . . I cann [sic] conceive of nothing that will destroy the power of the News & Observer so completely and effectively as for him to follow your suggestion and I hope he has too much sense to do so. . . . You have no business being editor of the News & Observer while you are in the cabinet."[75] Given Josephus's love of the *N&O* and his obvious skill at managing it, in retrospect Charles's letter appears somewhat ridiculous. Charles should have known his brother well enough to understand that Josephus would not consider surrendering the paper's editorial position to Britton or anyone else. The *N&O* was more than Josephus's love; it was his family's wealth and, he hoped, his sons' future. And

Josephus knew the newspaper business as well as anyone in the United States at that time.

Charles did not stop there, though. Displaying his customary lack of awareness in interpersonal relationships, he referred specifically to Britton's status, claiming, "I know there were two reasons why you did not take Britton to Washington as your private secretary. The first and foremost was that Addie did not want Mrs. Britton there, and the second was you had nobody to put on the News & Observer. You told [Britton] you were going to make him editor and give a free hand. Instead of that you put a straight jacket on him."[76] It is almost certain that Britton, whom Daniels did eventually bring to Washington as his personal secretary, did not initiate this correspondence, and in fact his relationship with Josephus was such that he probably would have been horrified to learn that Charles was so clumsily promoting his cause. Bringing Addie into the dispute was a mistake, as any perceptive person would have recognized. Josephus dearly loved his wife, but beyond that he had a reverential Victorian view of women in general and his wife in particular. Even if he understood and agreed with Charles's characterization of the situation, he would not approve of Charles mentioning Addie in a managerial dispute at the *N&O*. If Josephus suspected Britton in any of this, he would have never brought Britton to Washington. Exactly what Mrs. Britton's transgressions were is not recorded—though it was not unheard of for Addie to dislike, hold a grudge against, or otherwise banish a member of the Raleigh social circle. (One suspects that the Brittons' social standing did not meet Addie's standards.) In any case, Josephus wisely ignored Charles's advice and ranting.

In addition to seeking a job at the Justice Department and meddling at the *N&O*, Charles badgered his older brother constantly about patronage or other special treatment for friends, colleagues, and even friends of friends. This grew worse as war approached and people pursued Josephus's largesse through his younger brother. Officer commissions, draft exemptions, and early discharges were among the favors for which acquaintances sought a conduit to the secretary of the navy. Charles proved all too willing to be such a conduit. Charles's poor judgment also extended to his financial affairs, and later in life money became a problem. In this matter, too, Josephus would aid his younger brother, making loans that eventually summed to tens of thousands of dollars.

Although victimized throughout his adult life by his own poor choices, Charles was not without virtues. Like his older brothers, he possessed the same terrierlike determination when pursuing a matter that was dear to him, and Charles enjoyed a good fight. Unfortunately, unlike Josephus, Charles was not always wise in identifying a good fight, nor did he know when he was beaten. He was never as steady as either of his older brothers, and although he had more than a touch of Josephus's ambition, Charles could never match Josephus's intuition or ability to learn from his mistakes in either business or politics.

In the summer of 1913 Josephus finally secured, through Attorney General McReynolds, a position for Charles. Brotherly love aside, Josephus was eager to get Charles away from the *N&O*, where he was driving to distraction the officially deputized management team. Charles's practice in Wilson was stagnating, but he undoubtedly hoped for something better than the position in Minnesota. He expected something closer to the seat of power in Washington. Still he accepted reluctantly and almost immediately found trouble by becoming mixed up in an old Indian land dispute. Charles nobly defended the communal property rights of the Chippewa against the encroachment of white capitalists seeking to obtain timber and mineral rights. Admirable as Charles's stand might have been, politically his position was a loser, as the whites had powerful connections in Washington. The Chippewa did not.

Although Josephus Daniels could generally be counted on to take the side of the downtrodden (excluding southern blacks, of course), some causes were too far gone even for him. Thus it was with the Indians. He had no intention of expending political capital on their behalf. Charles received more than a few warnings from the Justice Department that his pursuit of the case was too diligent and that the invective he hurled at those on the other side, all of whom were wealthy white voters, was too antagonizing. Rather than cutting a deal or acquiescing, Charles, to his personal credit but professional detriment, continued to pursue the case. Unfortunately, lacking his older brothers' wisdom and perhaps relying too much on the cover offered by his highly placed brother, Charles never understood that he could not win. By early 1916, Attorney General Thomas Gregory, who by that time had replaced McReynolds, sent a new man to handle the case. Charles was to be reassigned. In bad temper he resigned.[77]

Reluctantly, he returned to Wilson. Once again, through Josephus's goodwill and connections, opportunity knocked for Charles. An old Daniels friend, Judge Francis D. Winston, offered to set up a legal practice with Charles in the nearby town of Tarboro. The kindly judge even offered to let Charles continue to reside in Wilson and do as much or as little work as he wanted in Tarboro. Charles declined. Ungraciously, he wrote to Josephus and requested assistance in setting up an office in either New York or Chicago.[78] He did eventually set up his own practice in New York and then requested his brother's help in finding gilt-edged clients such as Henry Ford, Thomas Edison, and popular author Thomas Dixon.[79] Although Josephus did not deliver either Ford or Edison, he did pull some strings with Bernard Baruch and Henry Morgenthau, two wealthy and powerful New Yorkers and leading members of the Democratic Party. (The choice of clients is curious, because Charles was a notorious anti-Semite.)[80] That Josephus would direct such serious men to his brother says as much about his considerable confidence in Charles as a lawyer as it does about brotherly love. For the time being, Charles's situation stabilized.

By the time Charles was settling down in New York, the storm over Henry Bagley had come and gone. And Henry had gone with it. Henry's womanizing had been a sharp, though relatively small, thorn in Daniels's side even before Daniels joined Wilson's administration. Although strictly a one-woman man himself and censorious in matters of marital infidelity, Daniels was not self-righteous. If Henry could organize his life in such a way that it did not interfere with Daniels's professional or political goals, then Daniels could turn a blind eye to the indiscretions. Unfortunately, Henry's lifestyle did begin to interfere with Daniels's professional and political goals. Henry's adultery first became public during the 1912 race for the U.S. Senate.

Following Charles Brantley Aycock's death, Daniels remained aloof from that campaign. The Kitchin and Clark forces argued correctly that Daniels's neutrality in fact favored the incumbent Simmons. Hoping to turn the tide, the anti-Simmons forces threatened to reveal some rather sordid details about Henry's philandering if Daniels did not disavow Simmons.[81] This type of pressure never worked on Daniels. His own conscience and record were clean, and there were no skeletons in his closet—at least none that would scandalize Raleigh's white society. If his opponents wanted to tar him by targeting Henry, Daniels considered them free to do so. Daniels calculated that weathering that storm would be easier than further crossing Simmons. In the event, he simply called his blackmailers' bluff and ignored the threat, accurately surmising that anyone of any importance in Raleigh already knew that Henry was a skirt-chaser. The storm passed, and Henry remained at the *N&O*. But Henry's troubles were only beginning.

Addie, who played no small role in her brother's eventual banishment from Raleigh, seemed more scandalized by Henry's behavior than Josephus did. Perhaps it was because, in terms of social status, the Bagleys had more of a reputation to lose than the nouveau Danielses did. Or perhaps, as Henry was her brother, she felt his moral failing more acutely than Josephus did. Although a reasonably liberal woman for her time—she supported women's suffrage, spoke her mind whenever she liked, and expected other women to do so as well—unlike her husband, Addie was not tolerant of drinking, smoking, vulgarism, or any type of "carrying on." One of Franklin Roosevelt's biographers erroneously described Josephus Daniels as "puritanical." Although he himself lived a puritan life, Daniels was never much of a proselytizer, and he let his personal behavior speak for itself. Addie was the more puritanical of the two. An ardent Presbyterian, and thus a predestinarian, she took a more judgmental view of human nature in the belief that it revealed something more (or less) divine than just human nature.

For a while Henry's career appeared to have not only survived the storm of 1912 but to have actually taken a positive turn. With Wilson's election, Josephus moved to Washington, and Henry, as business manager, became the boss in residence in Raleigh. He ran a tight ship at the paper. Almost immediately after taking over in March 1913, he fired a sales representative, Garwood, for "getting drunk at Salisbury and at Shelby." Paying him $187.00 to bring in $200.60 in subscriptions did not seem to be a good return on funds. Henry watched every dime that passed through the newspaper's accounts, and his record keeping offers the first detailed look into the firm's finances. On one occasion he even encouraged Josephus to chastise a Washington stenographer who sent Henry a 5:20 P.M. telegram at one cent per word. Henry noted that if the individual had waited until 6:00 P.M., the rate would have dropped to one-half of a cent per word. Henry also handled a few personal financial matters for Josephus and Addie. Although Herbert Jackson took care of the couple's investments beyond Raleigh, Henry looked after their growing real estate portfolio.[82]

Despite these credits, Henry sabotaged himself by quarreling with Alford and Charles, and once Josephus Jr. joined the *N&O*, Henry made the professionally fatal error of mistreating Josephus Daniels's eldest son. Henry might have been out the door sooner were it not for the crisis created by the fire of April 1913. Henry and Alford diligently oversaw the reconstruction of the firm's physical plant and finances following the fire. Still, there were warning signs of Henry's professional demise. Reports of Henry's continuing mischief between the bedsheets made their way to Washington, and in August, Josephus, no doubt at Addie's prompting, had a pointed written exchange with Henry. Although not all of the relevant correspondence has survived, the essence of their dispute emerges from a letter Henry sent to

Josephus in response to an earlier exchange: "Your undated note asking me to give you by Monday at Washington answers to a number of questions about a purely personal and private matter of mine is received. . . . Without admitting or denying any of your expressions, I may say that . . . I have done my duty by all connected with me in both personal and business matters to the best of my ability. Of course, I am answerable to myself alone for the personal and to you alone for the business. . . . My personal devotion and respect for you requires that I ask that there be no reopening of the private matter referred to."[83] Henry's careful tone suggests he suspected Addie's hand in this. Requesting a Monday deadline for a reply to an undated letter was not Josephus's style, and Henry's reply that he conscientiously answered to Josephus on business matters, but on business matters only, was a calculated risk. If the complaint had originated with Josephus, then the demand that he stay out of Henry's personal affairs would have forced Josephus's hand in the matter. Henry guessed correctly that if he turned stubborn on the personal issues while remaining a loyal professional underling, then Josephus might let the matter drop, and in fact he did—for the time being.

Daniels had good reason to ignore Henry's personal behavior: Business was booming. In the first full (fiscal) year during which Henry ran the *N&O*, the firm earned a profit of $26,500, of which more than $20,000 went directly to Daniels (on top of the $3,000 annual salary he now paid himself).[84] The paid-in capital for the firm, from its 1895 charter, was only $20,000, yielding a return on equity of greater than 100 percent. This calculation overstates the market rate of return, because by 1914, had Daniels chosen to sell the newspaper, of which at that time he owned more than 75 percent, it would have sold for considerably more than $20,000. But for how much more? Since the company's stock was not publicly traded—in fact, other than the shares of the original outside investors, which Daniels continued to buy back, it was not traded at all—determining the true market value is not possible. However, the fact that after buying out the original outside investors Daniels rechartered the firm in 1926 with a capitalization of $100,000 suggests that it was probably worth around $60,000 in 1914, assuming the appreciation in the firm's value between 1895 and 1926 was reasonably steady. Such a figure is not inconsistent with (roughly) the cost of rebuilding the whole operation after the 1913 fire and suggests an annual market rate of return of 44 percent, which was comparable to what Daniels earned on his earlier papers in the 1880s, but now that return was on a much larger capital investment. More importantly from Daniels's perspective was the fact that he and his family could live on half of his $12,000 salary as navy secretary, and thus he could plow nearly $5,000 in retained earnings back into the *N&O* and still invest roughly $30,000 ($6,000 from the navy, $3,000 from his *N&O* salary, and $21,500 from *N&O* profits) with Herbert Jackson at the Virginia Trust Company. The following year, 1915, was not quite as profitable (as the *N&O* had suffered the second fire), but even after reinvesting roughly $10,000 in the firm, Daniels personally received another $11,000 to invest at the Virginia Trust Company. With another $6,000 from his unspent government salary, Daniels had $17,000 in new investments with Jackson. In short, Josephus was growing rich with Henry's help, and thus he could tolerate Addie's carping about Henry's behavior as a cost of doing business.

Despite Henry's skill at putting money into his brother-in-law's pockets, he remained on a collision course with Josephus and Addie. Throughout 1914 and 1915 Henry quarreled with Alford about the printing and distribution end of the business. Alford ran a tight shop, too; but he had to confront the powerful local typographer's union, and he was liberal with wages and benefits. In this Daniels generally supported him. A paternalistic and altruistic capitalist of the type rarely seen today, Daniels sincerely tried to look after his employees. Among other things, he paid for their funerals and those of their immediate families out of his own pocket.[85] Henry, ever the bean counter, simply saw wages and benefits as a cost to be kept down. Daniels intervened on Alford's behalf, and in so doing he took a conciliatory but firm tone with Henry, explicitly demanding that Henry give Alford "entire charge of the mechanical department."[86] Daniels did not like arbitrating the disputes back in Raleigh, but he continued to do so.

The straw that eventually broke the back of Henry's career at the *N&O* was his dispute with Daniels's eldest son. After joining the firm, Joe Jr. struggled to earn respect, especially among the triumvirate his father had left to run the paper. Of this group, Uncle Henry proved to be particularly difficult. For some reason, Henry resented Joe Jr. and treated the boy badly. In one of Daniels's many trips back to Raleigh to check on the business, late in 1915 he had to settle a severe disagreement between the two. Addie, who had a stake in this fight, must have demanded to be kept informed, because Daniels wrote a mollifying letter to her. "Now on to Josephus [Jr.]! . . . Certain people did not want him in the office. . . . Had a heart to heart with [him] and Henry. Henry talked very lovingly of Josephus and [says] he will do anything for you [that is, Addie]. I know you will work it out in the best way but I hate to always let you bear [Joe Jr.'s] burdens."[87] The letter suggests Henry tried to persuade Daniels that everything was fine in Raleigh. It also indicates a father who wanted his son to takes his lumps while learning to work things out on his own, as well as a mother who was not prepared to let her own brother issue those lumps to her son.

Despite his comforting words to Addie, Josephus must have been convinced on this trip that Henry would have to go, profits or no profits. With Charles shipped off to Minnesota, Henry appeared to be the cause of most of the turmoil that remained at the *N&O*. Earlier in the year, Daniels had written to Herbert Jackson (who, it should be recalled, was also Henry's first cousin) inquiring about getting rid of Henry.[88] Henry's continuing disputes with and perceived bullying of Joe Jr. sealed his fate, and in 1916, Daniels finally got rid of his brother-in-law. When Henry started openly cavorting with a married woman, Addie had had enough. Probably at her instigation, Josephus wrote to Henry: "If you are resolved in this course, no action should be taken and no lawyer consulted until you have made your home in some other place than Raleigh, North Carolina."[89] Instead of firing his family member, Daniels "bought out" Henry, giving him a $10,000 personal loan and setting him up with a position at the Fort Worth (Texas) *Record*. Over the next two years, Josephus and Addie would loan Henry another $17,000. Unlike Charles, however, Henry appears to have done well in business beyond Raleigh, and he eventually paid off the loans (though there is no record of him paying any interest).[90]

Thus during Daniels's first years in Washington there was much turmoil at the newspaper back in Raleigh. Twice the physical plant had burned to the ground, and Daniels had been forced to run his brother and his brother-in-law out of town. However, overall, business was booming, as the industry grew and underwent important changes. By 1913, a regular sports section (still emphasizing baseball) had been added. The following year, the *N&O* began publishing seven days a week (an innovation introduced by Henry Bagley, a less pious businessman than Daniels). In 1916, the funny page became a regular feature, and in 1917, the company began offering suburban delivery by carrier. At the time, an annual subscription was $7.00, the same figure Daniels had set in 1894 (though it had been $6.00 between 1903 and 1913). The daily price had gone up to 5 cents in 1895 and remained there. Circulation had expanded dramatically. Though exact figures are difficult to verify, by 1917, daily circulation was between 20,000 and 25,000. Assuming revenues were split 50-50 between subscriptions and advertising, the firm's annual revenues would have exceeded $500,000. At an annual rate of return on capital of 40 percent (a conservative estimate), Daniels cleared around $20,000 a year during these years, or roughly 40 to 50 times per capita income at the time. This would be about $2 million a year in today's money. Daniels was getting rich, slowly by the standards of a Duke or a Rockefeller, but rich all the same. That was good, because Daniels's attention to his beloved *N&O* would decline during the next few years. The United States was about to go to war.

8. The Great War

Any little German lieutenant can put us
into the war at any time by some calculated outrage.

—WOODROW WILSON to JOSEPHUS DANIELS

On June 28, 1914, the presumed heir to the Austro-Hungarian throne, Archduke Franz Ferdinand, and his morganatic wife, Sophia, toured the imperial outpost of Sarajevo. As they were driven through the streets, Gavrilo Princip, a young Bosnian nationalist, emerged from the sparse crowd and shot the archduke and his wife. Both soon died from their wounds. Under the headline "HEIR OF AUSTRIA AND WIFE KILLED," the *News and Observer* offered readers a front-page story covering the details of the assassination but gave no indication that it would lead to an international crisis. (Ironically, only the day before, the paper had run an article about Germany's military prowess.)[1] However, despite the general unpopularity of the Habsburg heir, his reactionary views had a strong following in the highest reaches of the imperial government, particularly in the army and the foreign ministry, and the assassination of such an eminent figure demanded some response from Vienna. The authorities quickly rounded up the conspirators, and under intense interrogation, they revealed their link to Serbian military intelligence. This complicated matters considerably. Russia backed the Serbs; thus, Serbia's involvement opened a Pandora's box that would only be closed more than four years and 20 million deaths later.

What had seemed like an internal Austrian affair was about to become Europe's worst crisis since Napoleon. Daniels got wind of the heightened risk of war from the State Department, and the *N&O*'s tone grew more worried even before the world knew what Austria's response would be. "ANXIETY IN THE BALKANS," screamed the *N&O* headline. The related article, probably much influenced by information supplied by Daniels, tied the impending crises to the Habsburg succession: "This anxiety is considered likely to increase during the short period before the aged emperor . . . finally disappears."[2] During the first week of July the anxiety indeed heightened, as both the Germans and the Austrians called high-level councils to

289

discuss Austria's response to the assassination and Serbian involvement in it. The Germans subsequently granted their famous "blank check" to the Austrians, who in turn prepared to invade Serbia. However, before the Austrian war machine could formally launch a cross-border attack, Hungarian prime minister István Tisza persuaded the government in Vienna to present the Serbs with a stern ultimatum demanding satisfaction.

The document, submitted to the Serbs through official diplomatic channels on July 24, contained ten points that can be put, roughly, into three categories: those demanding that Serbian authorities actively suppress terrorist activities aimed at Austria and organized within Serbia, those demanding an investigation of the assassination and the roles of Serbian authorities in it, and those demanding Austrian participation in the investigation *within* Serbia. Austria demanded a reply within forty-eight hours. In its response, Serbia met the deadline and agreed to the first set, temporized while seeming to agree with the second set, and rejected the third set.

Bismarck had famously claimed that "some damned foolish thing in the Balkans" would set off the next great European war, and it looked as if the archduke's assassination might be that foolish thing.[3] But Serbia's response seemed reasonable to most observers, including Daniels. The Serbs conceded a few points while maintaining their territorial integrity. Certainly, there was nothing in their reply that could be interpreted as bellicose or welcoming war with Austria. Daniels interpreted the Serbian reply favorably, and the information he received from the White House, which followed reports from Colonel Edward House, Wilson's confidant and roving representative, who at the time was in Europe, suggested war would be averted. According to House, Germany's Kaiser Wilhelm II asserted that there would be no war.[4] Unfortunately, nobody who discounted the possibility of war had authority in Vienna. Despite the fact that Wilhelm considered Serbia's reply "a brilliant performance . . . a moral triumph for Vienna [and] . . . with it every reason for war ends," the Austrians rejected it outright. On July 28 they declared war on Serbia and bombarded Belgrade the next day.[5]

During the crisis, rather than go through formal diplomatic channels, Wilson, perhaps as a rebuke and certainly as a gesture of no-confidence, had circumvented Bryan and deputized House as his personal, though unofficial, commissioner to treat with key European heads of state. The assignment was emblematic of Wilson's sloppy handling of U.S. foreign policy. Wilson, though generally gifted in interpreting shifts in domestic culture and politics, did not possess the same facility on the international front. In a rare moment of sincerely critical (and accurate) self-evaluation, Wilson confided to a friend, "It would be an irony of fate if my administration had to deal with foreign problems, for all my preparation has been in domestic matters."[6]

A war had begun between Austria and Serbia, but that war had not yet spread beyond the Balkans to become *the* war. In Daniels's view, Germany was now the key. So long as Germany remained on the sidelines, the war would remain localized. Earlier in the week, however, the French ambassador to Moscow, Maurice Paléologue, assured Russia's Czar Nicholas II of France's support in a general war. With that guarantee, and despite personal entreaties from his cousin the kaiser, the czar succumbed to the wishes of his generals and partially mobilized the Russian army on July 29. Telegrams flew between the capitals of all the Great Powers. All eyes turned to Berlin. German chancellor Theobald von Bethmann-Hollweg, realizing that Europe stood on the edge of the abyss, hesitated to push the continent over. Meeting with the British ambassador, Sir Edward Goschen, he offered the English a treaty of amity if they would remain out of the war while Germany dealt with Russia and, most likely, France. The British cabinet rejected the proposal the next day. On July 30 the czar signed the order for full mobilization. The next day Austria ordered full mobilization of its forces in preparation for war against Russia.

At the White House, during those last days of peace, the flow of information through official State Department channels, which pointed toward war, began to override House's unofficial forecast of peace. Wilson, who had perhaps lost some confidence in House, whose predictions about the impending continentwide war could not have been more wrong, now turned to Bryan and Daniels for counsel. According to Daniels, Bryan proposed to mediate under "Article 3" of the Hague Convention of 1907. (Either Daniels or Bryan got this wrong, as Article 3 covers belligerents; however, Chapter III of the convention covers negotiations under "Flags of Truce.") Bryan's main contribution was to insist that all of the belligerents place their demands on the table. Ignored or ridiculed at the time, this was exactly the position Wilson would take later in the war, after Bryan had left the administration and a few million people had already been killed. Both House and Ambassador Walter Hines Page, who had little respect for the secretary of state, rejected Bryan's recommendation and discouraged Wilson from offering to mediate, because, in their view, there was "not the slightest chance" of the offer being accepted.[7] Wilson took this advice, at least partly. He did not turn Bryan loose on Europe, but the president did issue a blanket offer to tender "the good offices [of the United States] to the belligerent countries."[8]

Those good offices might have been valuable if any of the belligerents would have taken advantage of them, but when Russia ignored a German demand to halt mobilization, on August 1, Germany declared war and mobilized its army, with the expectation of fighting a two-front war against Russia and France. Portentously, to reach Paris, German war plans required the violation of Belgian neutrality, which had been guaranteed by the Great Powers, including Prussia, in the 1839 Treaty of London. Beginning the race to Paris, on August 2, Germany demanded passage through Belgium and gave the Belgian government only twelve hours to accept or face a de facto declaration of war. Belgium refused. The German army prepared to march. The next day, August 3, Germany declared war on France and formally breached Belgium's neutrality on the 4th. In response to Germany's violation of the Treaty of London, the United Kingdom declared war. The Great War had begun. The British foreign minister, Sir Edward Grey, summarized the view of a generation: "The lamps are going out all over Europe; we shall not see them lit again in our life-time."[9]

NEUTRALITY

Daniels followed the events in Europe in his official capacity as secretary of the navy, and through the *N&O*'s editorial position he speculated on the subsequent course of the war. The newspaper reported the broadening of the conflict on August 2. "GERMANY DECLARES WAR ON RUSSIA; FRANCE ANSWERS ULTIMATUM WITH SWORD; Greatest War In All Time," the paper announced. Highlighting Daniels's role in the conflict, the lead article focused on the U.S. Navy's responsibilities once the shooting started. Foreshadowing future crises, the piece emphasized the potential problems the war at sea would present for the United States, noting that the navy was "preparing to protect trade."[10]

Highlighting the trade angle was prescient, because at the time the article was written, Germany was the only sea power in the war. But once Germany entered, Daniels anticipated the conflict would spread to Britain and thus become a world war. In the past three centuries the British had swept, in order, the Spanish, the Dutch, and the French from the seas, and they had kept the Russians bottled up on land. The German leadership had read Mahan and adopted his vision of the navy as the guarantor of Great Power status. Thus Germany became the latest in this string of continental threats to British sea power. The British could not let Germany win the war on the continent and then use whatever spoils it took to strengthen its growing navy and rapidly expanding overseas empire. Daniels understood that a war at sea would soon follow Britain's entry into the conflict and that U.S. shipping would be caught in the crossfire. Wilson was out of action during those crucial days in August, as his wife, Ellen, was in the final stages of a battle with terminal kidney disease. Inauspiciously, on the day she died, August 6, a German U-boat pack attacked Royal Navy ships in the North Sea. The war at sea had begun.

With the onset of the war at sea, Daniels began a battle of wits with his German counterpart, the head of the Imperial German Navy, Grand Admiral Alfred von Tirpitz. By challenging British mastery of the seas, Germany had all but guaranteed Britain would be on the other side of any major war in which the Germans fought. In his diary, Daniels listed Tirpitz immediately after the kaiser as the leaders to be hanged at the end of the war.[11] Although Germany's invasion of Belgium was the immediate event that led from a war in the Balkans to a world war, Daniels attached that smaller war to a broader one through the naval arms race between Germany and Great Britain. Belgium was only a hand to be played in a larger game. Germany was the first of the Great Powers since Napoleon to challenge the British at sea. Tirpitz fathered the strategy.

In 1892, as chief of staff of the Baltic squadron, with the rank of captain, Tirpitz attended a dinner at Kiel Castle over which the kaiser presided. Here Tirpitz entered history. After being prodded for an opinion on the overall state of military affairs, Tirpitz presented to Wilhelm a vision of imperial glory. Wilhelm wanted a colonial empire, "a place in the sun." Tirpitz told the kaiser that in order to achieve that objective, one had to emulate and be prepared to compete with the British, who would not lightly yield their dominance in overseas markets or control of the sea lanes. Tirpitz persuaded the kaiser that he could succeed where the Spanish, the Dutch, and Napoleon had failed. He told Wilhelm that with Germany's new industrial might, a big navy would yield "such a measure of maritime influence which will make it possible for Your Majesty to conduct a great overseas policy."[12]

For all his faults, no one ever criticized Wilhelm for thinking small. In Tirpitz, the kaiser recognized a man with a vision that matched his own. Rising in rank over the next few years, in June 1897, Tirpitz became state secretary of the Naval Office, a post he would hold for nearly twenty years. During his years as naval secretary, Tirpitz would achieve two of Imperial Germany's supreme distinctions. In 1900 Wilhelm elevated Tirpitz into the hereditary Prussian nobility, and in 1911 Tirpitz achieved the empire's highest naval rank, grand admiral. Unlike the British or the Americans, the Prussians had no use for sentimental parliamentary affectations, such as civilian control over the military. Thus, on the eve of the Great War, Tirpitz was not only the ranking uniformed naval officer in Imperial Germany; he was also, like Daniels, secretary of the navy.[13] Although Tirpitz began life with the advantages offered by an upper-middle-class upbringing, his climb to the top of a more caste-driven society was arguably even more remarkable than Daniels's own ascent in the United States.

As for Daniels's view of the war, from the editorial position of the *N&O*, his diary, and his memoirs, three things are clear. First, familiar as he was with the latest military technology, Daniels expected the war to be long and painful; this was a minority view at the time. (Expressing popular opinion, the Dallas *News* claimed that the war would be over "long before cotton season is"—that was supposed to be the cotton season of 1914, not 1919. Maintaining a more informed and ultimately more accurate view, Daniels's position was that "the war might last for years.")[14] Second, he did not desire U.S. participation in the war, and he had every expectation that his country could remain on the sidelines, even though that might be difficult once the war at sea began. This, too, was the majority position at the time. Third, he blamed Tirpitz and the "three Kaisers" for the war (adding Austria's Franz Joseph and Russia's Nicholas II to the list that already included Germany's Wilhelm II). Their quick leap to arms "would be laughably ridiculous, were it not so ghastly," claimed an unsigned *N&O* editorial that was most likely penned by Daniels.[15] Some variation of this view was also probably held by the majority of Americans, since Austria had invaded Serbia, Germany had invaded Belgium and France, and Russia had invaded Germany. Britain and France had invaded no one. As for Wilson's view of the war, the administration's formal response would be neutrality, which seemed natural enough. But what exactly did that mean in practice?

Daniels publicly and privately supported Wilson's neutrality proclamation, which called upon Americans to be "impartial in thought as well as action."[16] When the war broke out, Daniels took Wilson at his word, which was "Every man who really loves America will act and speak in the spirit of true neutrality."[17] In practice, true neutrality would be difficult to define, and though Wilson's rhetoric never wavered, once the naval war between Britain and Germany escalated, neutrality became impossible to maintain. For many Americans—particularly East Coast social elites who had close economic and cultural ties to the British and the French; financiers and trade unionists who, through war, enjoyed an increase in the demand for their capital and labor; many high-ranking military officers; and eventually Wilson himself—neutrality in thought and action would prove too difficult. But that was not true for Daniels and William Jennings Bryan.

To show support for that policy, Daniels was determined to formally enforce neutrality within the uniformed ranks of the navy. On August 6, 1914, two days after the Germans crossed into Belgium, he issued a general order "directing all officers of the Navy, whether active or retired, to refrain from public comment of any kind about the war in Europe, and to observe in spirit and in letter the neutrality proclamation of the Commander in Chief."[18] In this position, Daniels thought he was perfectly in tune with his heroes, Bryan and Wilson; however, a rift within the team appeared almost immediately. Although Bryan was not the pacifist his more bellicose enemies, including Franklin and Theodore Roosevelt, made him out to be (Bryan had, after all, accepted an officer's commission in the war with Spain, and he had subsequently supported annexation of the Philippines), the Commoner wanted no part of the European war.

Wilson, too, hoped to keep the country out of the war, but quickly his primary concern turned to keeping Britain from losing; after that, his major concern was his role as a potential peacemaker. As for Daniels, despite his expanding role as a perpetrator of the administration's ad hoc version of gunboat diplomacy, the Great War only reinforced his pacifistic leanings. Unleashing a few companies of marines in Haiti to keep out German U-boats was one thing, but clashing with the Germans or the British on the high seas was another level of conflict, which Daniels would do almost anything to avoid. To define U.S. neutrality in practice, however, as commander in chief and the head of the Democratic Party, Wilson sensed the need for more subtle leadership than did Bryan or Daniels. Wilson's neutrality proclamation stated that the American people were "true friends of all the nations of the world, because we threaten none, covet the possessions of none, desire the overthrow of none. Our friendship can be accepted . . . without reservation because it is offered in a spirit and for a purpose which no one can even question or suspect. Therein lies our greatness. We are the champions of peace and concord."[19] Nothing in the record suggests Wilson wanted anything other than peace; but despite his neutrality proclamation, he maintained broader objectives than merely the absence of war, and as the war encroached on those objectives, his commitment to strict neutrality faltered.

Daniels agreed that the United States should remain out of the war, but

that was not the same as championing peace. He supported a strict interpretation of neutrality for philosophical as well as practical reasons. The
philosophical reasons were simple: Daniels's religious convictions and personal temperament were such that, on moral grounds, he could never align
with the more bellicose elements in American politics. As for the practical
reason, 1914 was a midterm election year. By Daniels's accounting, as the
election approached, the Democrats maintained an "unprecedented" 153-
seat majority in the House and a 10-seat majority in the Senate.[20] Midterm
elections typically resulted in losses for the party in power, and 1914 would
prove no different. Daniels, like other leading Democrats, fervently hoped
to minimize the losses, and he expected peace to be a more likely winner
at the polls than war. It was a majority view. Few U.S. politicians wanted
to stand for election on a plank of sending America's youth to die in Flan-
ders's fields merely to avenge Serbia or to protect the British Empire from
the German navy.

Even Daniels's old nemesis Theodore Roosevelt, the most bellicose and
jingoist figure in American politics, supported neutrality, at least nominally and at least for the time being. In August, during the crucial battles
in France, TR wrote publicly, "It is certainly eminently desirable that we
should remain entirely neutral."[21] He would soon repudiate this position.
But in the fall of 1914, even an imperialist like TR did not want to campaign
against the Democratic slogan "War in the East! Peace in the West! Thank
God for Wilson!" TR never thanked God for Wilson, but he knew the country was not yet ready for war.

As Daniels predicted, peace proved to be a winner at the polls. Both sides
could claim victory of a sort in the off-year elections. Although the Democrats lost sixty-three seats in the House, they maintained a strong majority
there, and they kept their ten-seat lead in the Senate. Overall, both within
and beyond the party, the election was considered a plebiscite on Wilson's
policies. Those included the tariff—rates had been reduced; the trusts—
they continued to be pursued by the attorney general under the recently
passed Clayton Act, which also offered new protections for organized labor;
the currency issue—the Federal Reserve System had been created; and of
course peace—through neutrality. Daniels was completely justified in pro-
claiming the election "a vote of confidence in the administration and approval of the New Freedom legislation. It was also a test of Wilson's popularity."[22]

As 1914 drew to a close, stalemate gripped the war on the Western Front,
where massive armies dug in for what would be four years of bloody trench

warfare. That stalemate threatened to lengthen the war, a development that could only increase the probability that the United States would get involved. The deadlock in the land war on the Western Front moved both the Entente (as the British- and French-led allies were called) and the Central Powers to seek some way of outflanking their opponents—in Russia, in the Balkans, in the Dardanelles, in the Middle East, and at sea. Of these efforts, only the war at sea would ultimately have a major impact on the outcome of the Great War.[23] Despite Germany's Herculean attempt to outbuild the British navy during the years leading up to the war, on the day Germany invaded Belgium, the German navy faced an arguably small, but nonetheless decisive, disadvantage in the war at sea. The resulting struggle would fundamentally alter the course of history. It is ironic, given the emphasis on the dreadnought in prewar strategies, which revolved around Mahan's theory of the decisive battle of the great ships, that the United States ultimately entered the Great War because of Germany's use of a different weapon altogether—the U-boat.

More than any other country, in the prewar years, Germany, led by Tirpitz, had attempted to follow Mahan's vision, and the logic of that vision, embodied in the dreadnought, called for the decisive battle between those great "castles of steel" on the high seas.[24] Yet when war came, the German admiralty confronted situations that would end the quest for the decisive battle; thus the Germans would seek victory not in one great naval battle, but in a thousand small ones involving U-boats rather than dreadnoughts. From a strictly military point of view, during Daniels's eight years at the helm of the navy, the U-boat war in the Atlantic proved to be the most important challenge he faced. Even before his country entered the war, Daniels recognized the importance of protecting allied shipping from the U-boats. Every U.S. ship that went to the bottom supplied the pro-war party with ammunition for its cause. Daily, Daniels filled his diary with entries related to these problems: "Everything possible done . . . to protect American shipping"; "No cost & no effort spared to protect shipping"; "Stop or lessen sub-marine warfare"; "Consider every method to protect our shipping."[25] The threat was constant that the United States might be dragged into the war. As Germany attacked U.S. shipping, from the navy's view, nothing would be more important than combating the U-boats initially while trying to avoid war and, later, while waging it.

The U-boat campaign below the waves resulted directly from Germany's failure to win Mahan's decisive battle on the surface. Despite all the treasure the Reichstag had poured into Tirpitz's naval building program since the end of the nineteenth century, the British still maintained an advantage over the Germans. It was a small advantage, but an advantage all the same, and in war, as in more prosaic matters, small advantages can be decisive. Time began running out on Germany from the day the United Kingdom declared war, because while the British continued to trade with the rest of the world, they simultaneously blockaded the continent. Nearly two millennia had passed since Cicero observed that economics was the essence of war (*Nervo belli, pecuniam infinitam*).[26] But the principle was as sound in 1914 as it had been in antiquity. The German high command and admiralty could not let the Royal Navy blockade starve Germany into defeat while keeping the Entente fed and armed.

Since the German high seas fleet was incapable of inflicting a decisive victory on the British, the German admiralty turned to an older naval strategy—commerce raiding on the high seas. Here too, the Germans found themselves at a disadvantage. When war broke out in August 1914, besides the high seas fleet, which faced the British navy in the North Sea, the German navy maintained ten cruisers of various ages and sizes stationed around the world. Within six months, the Royal Navy would sink seven of these ships, and two others would be chased from the sea. Early in 1915, it was clear that Germany was losing the war at sea.

Daniels studied closely the experience of the German navy in these first months of the war and how it was driven to the U-boat campaign. That study eventually led him to believe that the United States needed a two-ocean navy equal to that of any other power on earth. Before the war, and even through its early months, Daniels had thought a strong navy unnecessary and, indeed, antagonistic. Germany's difficulties in the war at sea caused him to change his position 180 degrees. "Peace through neutrality" became "peace through strength." After watching the failure of the German navy, he wanted to increase substantially his naval building program. Germany's failure turned Daniels into a Big Navy supporter. Because Daniels came to this view later than the Big Navy faction, he was subjected to much criticism at the time and after the war. The specific charge was that the navy was unprepared for the U.S. entry into the war.[27]

Just as Daniels was proposing to increase the naval building plan, a budget shortfall that started in the late fall of 1914 and ran into 1915 forced Wilson to cut federal expenditures. The resulting fiscal tightening cost Daniels one new battleship per annum from the old building program, which Daniels now viewed as inadequate. Wilson broke the news at a cabinet meeting on January 22. The cuts came primarily from the army and the navy budgets. Daniels went along and became the public face of the now-even-more-stretched-out naval building plan. Later that evening, however, he confessed his frustrations in his diary. Angrily he noted that the reductions had come from the military and "No others," meaning no other cabinet departments.[28]

While Wilson was trimming Daniels's budget, Germany's situation worsened. As its capital ships were sunk or chased from the high seas, the German admiralty turned to the next option—the U-boat. While planning for the decisive battle in the prewar years, the Germans had neglected their U-boat fleet. When war broke out, Germany had only thirty U-boats in operation. Both the British and the French had more than twice as many submarines; ironically, even Daniels controlled more submarines than Tirpitz.[29] However, with the British blockade now firmly in place, Germany's commerce-raiding cruiser force wiped out, and no chance for the decisive fleet-sized victory envisioned by Mahan, the Germans saw no alternative to the U-boats. Their mission would be to put pressure on the British economy by sinking its merchant vessels faster than they could be replaced. Economic pressure via the U-boats, they hoped, would result in political pressure in Parliament to seek peace on terms favorable to Germany.

The naval hopes of the Entente focused on keeping the high seas fleet in port (or destroying it, should it venture out) and blockading Germany. The British proved largely successful at both. With the exception of a few minor North Sea skirmishes and one great fleet battle off Jutland in 1916, the naval war distilled into one of British blockade versus the German U-boat campaign. Daniels quickly recognized the danger to the United States resulting from the path the naval war was taking. The U-boat campaign against the British was bound to affect neutral shipping, as was Britain's blockade of Germany. By early 1915, both Britain and Germany were in clear violation of international law, and Daniels foresaw that the courses taken by both countries would lead to conflict with the United States. He privately questioned how the United States could maintain strict neutrality when the main belligerents violated international law in ways that were bound to infringe upon the rights of the world's largest neutral power. But Daniels confined his frustration to his diary. There, following a cabinet meeting of February 5, he noted in particular the hypocrisy of the British, who, as they nakedly broke international law, demanded the Germans follow it to the letter. Daniels wrote that the British were "insisting upon" terms they themselves ignored.[30]

The relevant rules of naval warfare under which the belligerents were expected to operate and which neutrals were expected to respect were not laws but, rather, generally recognized practices, as laid out in four doctrines: The so-called Cruiser Rules, two Hague Conventions (1899 and 1907), and the Declaration of London (1909).[31] The first of these was quite old. The Cruiser Rules dated from the sixteenth-century reign of England's Henry VIII. In principle the Cruiser Rules were quite simple. Belligerent ships of war could be attacked on sight and without warning, but "an unarmed merchant ship could not simply be attacked on sight. She must be stopped and searched to establish her identity and the nature of her cargo. If neutral, she must be allowed to continue on her way after any contraband had been impounded. If hostile, the ship and her cargo could be seized as prizes or, if far from land, destroyed. Whatever the case, proper provision had to be made for the safety of the passengers and crew."[32] These rules, which Daniels called "old-time rules of the sea," served Western civilization for better or worse for nearly 400 years.[33] The Great Powers formally codified them in the Declaration of Paris in 1856; however, the Cruiser Rules contained many loopholes. For example, what exactly was contraband? What was the status of ships other than naval vessels and merchant ships—for example, a hospital ship or a passenger ship capable of transporting troops? How were disputes to be adjudicated? In response to these and other questions, the Great Powers had attempted to further codify the rules of war more generally in the various Hague Conventions of the late nineteenth and early twentieth centuries. Of these, the conventions of 1899 and 1907 had attempted to address specific issues related to war at sea, including details related to the Cruiser Rules. The subsequent London Naval Conference produced a more comprehensive pact in what became known as the Declaration of London.

The declaration determined that with respect to blockading and commerce raiding, all ships were to adhere strictly to the Cruiser Rules as they had evolved over time (that is, as laid out above). Goods shipped by sea fell into three categories: absolute contraband, conditional contraband, and noncontraband. Neutrals could trade freely with belligerents, but contraband was subject to confiscation. Absolute contraband included goods with an indisputable military use, including weapons and munitions. Conditional contraband included key goods that could be used for either civilian or military purposes, including coal and petroleum as well as gold and silver bullion. Noncontraband goods were those that could be used for military purposes, but only indirectly or after processing. These included foodstuffs, nonprecious metal ores, and raw cotton and wool. Absolute contraband could be seized. Conditional contraband could be seized only if a belligerent destination could be determined. Noncontraband could not be seized.[34]

The Cruiser Rules also covered blockading. A blockade was recognized as legitimate only if it directly blocked *all* belligerent ports and attempted to intercept *all* shipping in and out of those ports. In other words, the British could not declare a blockade of Germany and then randomly search ships coming out of New York to see if they were destined for a German port. A British blockade of Germany required a British blockade of *German* ports. This became known as the "close" blockade, and it was the only legal blockade. The close blockade was unacceptable to the British admiralty because of the losses the navy would take as a result of maintaining ships so close to German ports. Given the geography of the North Sea, the close blockade was unnecessary in the admiralty's opinion. The navy could simply retreat to the English Channel and the North Sea outlet between Scotland and Norway and prevent anything from going in or out of Germany. This "distant" blockade would be just as effective as the close blockade required by the Cruiser Rules, with the advantage of a much lower risk to men and ships. However, it violated both the letter and the spirit of international law.

Tirpitz had predicted that when war came, the British would simply ignore the Cruiser Rules and close the channel and the North Sea, which they did. The grand admiral understood the economic risk Germany faced from such a blockade, but Tirpitz did not fret; he expected the decrease in trade with the rest of world to be made up through increased trade with Germany's European neighbors, and the diplomacy was put in place to bring about that outcome. Initially, this strategy appeared to work. The decline in the value of trade with the United States from 1913 to 1914 was almost exactly offset by increases in trade with neutral Scandinavia and the Netherlands.[35] It is difficult to say how long this situation might have continued had the British not taken steps to counteract it.

The British responded by unilaterally redefining the Cruiser Rules, effectively declaring every conceivable item destined for Germany, including cotton and foodstuffs, as contraband. Furthermore, the Royal Navy adopted what was known as the doctrine of "continuous voyage." "This meant that the ultimate destination of seaborne cargoes, not their initial stopping point, would become the determining factor" in seizure.[36] Thus, for example, U.S. goods on U.S. ships destined for trade with the Netherlands or Sweden were subject to seizure by the Royal Navy if the officer in command of the search determined that the ultimate destination of the goods was Germany. This effectively extended Britain's distant blockade to neutrals trading with other neutrals that in turn *might* trade with Germany. In short, British policy could be reduced to this: Nothing could go in or come out of Germany by sea, and nothing could go into the continent if its ultimate destination was determined to be Germany.

This unilateral amending of the Cruiser Rules outraged Daniels; he complained that in response to "voluminous" diplomatic correspondence the British would only agree to "generally [follow] the rules of the Declaration [of London] subject to certain modifications," which included the "steadily increasing definitions of lists of contrabands and . . . other radical modifications."[37] In short, the British blockade was a bald violation of international law, and unless the United States severely constrained its seaborne trade with much of Europe, these actions set a course to bring the United States into the conflict. Daniels's concern was well founded. During the first few months of the war, forty-five neutral ships leaving U.S. ports for neutral destinations were seized by the Royal Navy. Although only a fraction of these were eventually liquidated as prizes, Secretary of State Bryan was quick to cast the British as the real threat to Wilson's neutrality policy. Here was the beginning of the rift between Wilson and Bryan, with Daniels in the middle.

Wilson, who "thought it immoral to stifle commerce on the seas," objected to British treatment of U.S. ships. But his protests were slow and tepid, a response that can be attributed somewhat to the advice he received from the pro-British Colonel House and Ambassador Page in London.[38] But Wilson was no dupe. He listened to House and Page because their counsel reinforced his own inclinations. The war at sea forced Wilson to choose between the British and the Germans. He chose the British. In retrospect, one can see the emergence of a clear asymmetry in the administration's expressions of concern for the legality of the actions of the British versus those of the Germans. The resulting unequal treatment of the two countries caused U.S. neutrality to crumble. The difference between the U.S. response to British and German violations of international law was not lost on German leaders in Berlin, where the heads of the admiralty and the high command expressed outrage at the lack of outrage coming from the United States over British violations of the Cruiser Rules. Of the blockade, observers in the United States quipped, "Britannia not only ruled the waves but waived the rules."[39] Tirpitz was not laughing. He told an interviewer, "America has raised no protest and has done little or nothing to stop the closing of the North Sea against all neutral shipping."[40] Daniels and Bryan would have been hard pressed to disagree with the grand admiral. However, before Daniels and Bryan could construct an effective front against British naval policy, the German admiralty rescued the British from what would most likely have been, at a minimum, a major public relations problem with the United States.

The Hague Convention of 1907 also addressed the use of mines in naval warfare, in effect subsuming the issue under blockading and, hence, the Cruiser Rules. Under the convention, mining was limited to a three-mile zone along belligerent coasts. The Germans violated the three-mile rule immediately, and in response the British followed. The North Sea soon became a vast minefield. In response to German mining, the British declared the entire North Sea a war zone, another clear violation of international law. Since there was no international body to which Germany could legitimately protest, and since the Germans' own mine-laying activities were not above reproach, the German admiralty responded in the only way it could: by unleashing its U-boat fleet on merchant shipping. Daniels wrote, "On February 14, 1915, Germany declared the waters surrounding the British Isles and the whole English Channel a war-zone. It also announced that in retaliation for Britain's violations of the [Cruiser Rules], all enemy merchant vessels found in the zone would be destroyed after February 18."[41] Unrestricted submarine warfare had begun.[42]

The U-boat posed problems for all sides because its activities were not well defined under any relevant international conventions. Because of their small crews and vulnerability on the surface, submarines could not effectively follow the stop-and-search procedures dictated by the Cruiser Rules. If a U-boat surfaced and attempted to stop a commerce vessel to determine its nationality and the contents of its holds, one of three scenarios could unfold, all of them bad from the U-boat captain's perspective. First, the stopped vessel could have hidden guns onboard and decide to shoot it out with the surfaced submarine. Since submarines usually only had one small deck gun and little armor plating, surfacing put the sub at great risk. Second, the merchant vessel could be neutral, would be searched, and no contraband would be found. This might appear to be a harmless situation, but depending on the merchantman's sentiments, the captain could reveal via wireless the submarine's presence to other ships in the area, including belligerent sub-hunters, thus placing the submarine at risk. Third, the vessel could be either a belligerent merchantman or a neutral carrying contraband. In this case the submarine's captain was charged with getting the crew safely off the ship before sending the vessel to the bottom (since confiscation was out of the question for a submarine). Even this violated the Cruiser Rules, because the crew's safety could not be ensured, and in many circumstance being abandoned in a lifeboat on the high seas was a de facto death sentence. Furthermore, sinking a neutral merchantman containing contraband would also send other, perhaps legal cargo down with the contraband, opening the issue of liability for the loss. Thus the submarine was most effective if it attacked without announcing its presence, but under any reasonable interpretation of international law, that was illegal.

German policy exacerbated pro-British feeling in the United States, and it allowed Wilson to move away from his position of strict neutrality, even if he would not admit it publicly. As Bryan's biographer put it, "Wilson did not consistently take his own advice" when it came to being "impartial."[43] The asymmetry between the British and the German naval positions and strategies defeated Wilson's call that Americans "be impartial in thought as well as action." As Bryan, Daniels, and the German admiralty recognized, once the British closed the North Sea to outside shipping, the United States basically became the breadbasket and arms supplier of the Entente. For the Germans, that situation was untenable, and so they fought back with the U-boat, the only naval weapon at their disposal.

Trying to maintain the role of honest broker, on February 20, 1915—two days after the Germans launched unlimited submarine warfare—Wilson called on the belligerents to "find a basis for agreement which will relieve neutral ships engaged in peaceful commerce from the great dangers which they will incur in the high seas adjacent to the coast of the belligerents."[44] Unfortunately for U.S. neutrality, the status quo favored the British. Wilson understood this, and more than one historian claims that favoring the British was exactly Wilson's objective.[45] Bryan's supporters were particularly keen to note the implicit pro-British result of American neutrality. Bryan's biographer accurately summarized the situation: "Wilson regarded the German tactic of submarine warfare as a devious, dishonorable mode of combat. With the aid of his U-boats, the kaiser might also win the war. For Wilson, a great admirer of England's laws and institutions, that would be a great calamity." In contrast, neither Bryan nor Daniels admired the British to any great extent. Daniels largely confined his complaints to his diary, private correspondence, and to a lesser extent, cabinet discussion. Bryan shared Daniels's outrage at British interference with legal U.S. trade, but Bryan did not share Daniels's ability to hold his tongue. Once Germany commenced unrestricted submarine warfare and the administration began to tilt clearly toward the British, Bryan challenged Wilson openly. Plainly juxtaposing the German and British modes of naval warfare, he asked, "Why be shocked at the drowning of a few people if there is no objection to starving a nation?" He recommended that Wilson simply embargo U.S. shipping to the continent and prohibit U.S. passengers from traveling in the proscribed areas. Wilson responded by rejecting his secretary of state's recommendations as well as the way he framed the issue. Privately, Wilson shared his hope that Bryan would resign.[46]

The first U.S. death caused by a U-boat occurred on March 24, when the British passenger ship *Falaba* was torpedoed in the Irish Sea. Wilson bypassed Bryan and had State Department counselor Robert Lansing compose a formal protest. The press swung unambiguously against the Germans. U.S. firms were profitably engaged in supplying the belligerents with all kinds of goods, contraband and otherwise, and it was generally recognized that the wheels of commerce were less constrained by the British blockade than by the German submarine campaign. After all, Britain's violations of the Cruiser Rules still permitted the United States to trade with the Entente. It was also the case that death from a U-boat torpedo resonated more viscerally than death from Britain's blockade. In the end, public opinion was determined (and Bryan's fate was sealed) a few weeks later by the doom of the British passenger liner *Lusitania*.

On the morning of May 7, Captain Walther Schweiger of the *U-20* sighted a large ship in St. George's Channel between Ireland and Wales. Schweiger submerged and fixed a course to intercept the ship off a promontory called Old Head of Kinsale near Queenstown. A German merchant marine officer, assigned to the *U-20* to identify the nonnaval vessels that were potential military targets, clearly identified the ship as either the *Lusitania* or the *Mauretania*. From the intelligence available to him at that time, the officer informed Schweiger that these ships were "Royal Navy Reserved Merchant Cruisers" fitted with guns and potentially serving as troop transports. (The *Lusitania* carried neither deck guns nor troops, but at that moment, less than 150 miles away, the *Mauretania* was boarding 5,000 British soldiers on their way to the Dardanelles.) At 14:10 GMT, Schweiger, assuming the *Lusitania* was a legitimate target, ordered the firing of one torpedo from half a mile away. It struck the forward starboard portion of the ship and was followed by a secondary explosion. The damage was catastrophic, and the ship went down in less than twenty minutes. Of the 1,965 people onboard, only 764 survived. Of the 1,201 dead, 94 were children and 128 were Americans.

The international outrage was pronounced and nearly universal. As Daniels put it, "Indignation was stirred to white heat."[47] Daniels managed to swallow his own rage and, with Bryan, counseled Wilson to take a moderate tone in addressing the Germans. On this issue, Wilson's administration split. It would not be stitched together again until the United States entered the war, nearly two years later. On one side were the hawks, including Secretary of War Garrison, Assistant Secretary of the Navy Franklin Roosevelt, and to a slightly lesser degree, the State Department's Lansing and Treasury Secretary McAdoo. Of this group, Daniels later wrote, "There was demand in some quarters that war be declared at once on Germany, but the preponderating American sentiment was with President Wilson, and of the course he pursued. There was no suggestion of war coming from Congress."[48] On the other side were those hoping and praying, literally, for peace. In the cabinet Bryan and Daniels led this group, which stood steadfastly against war and against the use of diplomatic language that might induce the Germans to an even stronger reaction, which would then increase the probability of the United States entering the war. Daniels's diary entries for the days surrounding the issuing of Wilson's message are missing, and he was careful in his personal correspondence to avoid the appearance of disagreement with the president. However, before the administration formally responded to the sinking, on May 9, the *N&O* called for calm: "There should be no hysteria." Writing years after the event, Daniels gives the impression that he felt Wilson subsequently adopted exactly the right tone. "Wilson used the period of neutrality diligently to find a way to end the war and to insure a warless world," Daniels wrote. "It called for the skill of an experienced navigator."[49]

Daniels wrote that after events revealed that Wilson possessed no such skills. The president's pro-British version of neutrality left the Germans with few options, and Daniels sided with Bryan in recognizing as much. Bryan's biographer notes that Daniels "sympathized with his good friend's views," but Daniels did not openly break with Wilson, because Daniels "had worked too hard and long to elect a Democratic president to risk a break with Wilson."[50] Bryan, Daniels's old hero, the man of iron principle, was not going to join the Great War just so American capitalists could profit from the resulting trading opportunities with the Entente. Wilson, Daniels's new hero, a man of more supple principle, found in his own interpretations of international law a more important goal than peace. He did want peace, but he did not want the British to lose the war; so he would risk a break with Germany over his interpretation of the laws of the sea, a risk he never seriously considered in response to British violations of those laws. Daniels agreed with Bryan in private, but publicly he supported the president. Wilson was an electoral winner; Bryan was not. In Daniels's calculus the Democratic Party needed Wilson more that it needed Bryan, and Daniels would risk war to avoid a schism in the party.

Daniels suspected that keeping the Bryan-Wilson marriage together was going to take a good bit of counseling, but he nonetheless tried to supply it and keep Bryan in the cabinet. Daniels's calendar for Saturday, May 8, 1915, only twenty-four hours after the full horror of the *Lusitania*'s sinking was known in Washington, shows that he arrived at the office at 9:10 A.M. Almost immediately he "went to call upon the Secretary of State," in whose office he spent the rest of the day, consulting with Bryan until 5:45 P.M. Discovering that his two most antiwar cabinet members had been cloistered together all day, Wilson sent his personal secretary and advisor, Joe Tumulty, on a reconnaissance mission to Daniels's home later that evening. Exactly what Daniels told Tumulty concerning the meeting with Bryan is unknown, but Tumulty informed Daniels that Wilson had called a cabinet meeting at the White House for the following morning. After attending an early church service, Daniels arrived at his office at 9:40 A.M. and went to the White House at 11:00 A.M. It was the first of a series of long and occasionally stormy sessions in which Wilson constructed his formal response to the sinking of the *Lusitania*.

Declaring that a man could be "too proud to fight," he composed his reply accordingly.[51] Wilson had mastered the art of using the English language to split hairs, and he displayed that skill in his first note to the Imperial German government. Wilson appears to have relied heavily on Lansing, a lawyer by training, in formulating the reply. This was consistent with the recent trend in Lansing's standing in the administration. It proved to be an ill omen for Bryan's tenure. However, Bryan reluctantly but diligently signed and circulated the note on behalf of the State Department, though he played no important role in its construction.

The essence of Wilson's message to the German government was that submarine warfare, as waged by the German navy, was incompatible with the Cruiser Rules and thus a violation of international law. "The government of the United States," Wilson wrote, "desires to call the attention of the Imperial German Government . . . to . . . the practical impossibility of employing submarines in the destruction of commerce without disregarding those rules of fairness, reason, justice and humanity [i.e., the Cruiser Rules] which all modern opinion regards as imperative."[52]

While correct in its logic, Wilson's note did nothing to settle the dispute between the hawks and the doves in the United States. It was variously referred to as "careful," "pedagogic," and "doctrinaire." However, Wilson knew what he was doing. Along with Bryan and Daniels, he did not want war with Germany. His message flung no gauntlet at the kaiser's feet. However, domestic outrage demanded a stern response, and accordingly Wilson's tone was uncompromising. Still, a careful reading indicates that the president did not object to submarine warfare per se, merely its indiscriminate use against merchantmen and passenger liners. While denouncing the course of the German admiralty, Wilson left the German government plenty of room to maneuver short of war. He hoped that the kaiser would leash Tirpitz and his admirals, and thus avoid war between Germany and the United States, while the British maintained the upper hand in the war at sea. Wilson achieved these objectives for the time being.

Wilson's response aggravated the split in his cabinet between those, like Garrison, who thought it too tepid and those, like Bryan, who thought it too provocative. In disgust, Franklin Roosevelt placed Daniels in the pacifist camp with Bryan. While Daniels did publicly support Wilson, he privately feared the note would lead to a German declaration of war; indeed "nothing could" prevent it, he wrote.[53] Bryan agreed. Here Bryan and Daniels were wrong; they overestimated Berlin's resolve. The Germans were not ready to declare war on the United States over a piece of stern diplomatic correspondence. The immediate German response was to blame the British, claiming that the *Lusitania* carried guns on its deck and munitions in its hold and that it had at times (illegally) flown the American flag. Although the British and the Americans denied the charges at the time, subsequent scholarly research indicates that the Germans got two of three correct. The *Lusitania* had gun mounts but no guns; however, it was carrying munitions to the British, and it may well have flown the American flag at times.[54]

As relevant as this may have been in a court of law, what mattered at the moment was the court of public opinion, and here the more visionary among the German leadership, especially Chancellor Bethmann-Hollweg, recognized that this legalistic approach to the dispute would fail to alleviate the rising tensions with the United States. In a second, more conciliatory note, the German government recognized, albeit disingenuously, "the principle of the freedom of all parts of the open sea to neutral ships."[55] It went on to obliquely recognize that violations of this principle could be rectified with compensation. In short, the Germans proposed to continue their campaign, perhaps a bit less aggressively, and should neutral merchantmen be sent to the bottom, Germany was prepared to pay, literally, for the error. This message would seem to have dispelled Daniels's and Bryan's worst fear for the time being. The Germans were backing away, ever so slightly, rather than escalating the dispute. Wilson had stood for freedom of the seas for nonbelligerents, and the German government had formally conceded the point. However, Wilson was unsatisfied by this reply. Recognizing the all-too-subtle nature of the German response, he rejected it and issued another message to the Germans.

Wilson's second note, submitted on June 5, was in some ways even more strident than the first one. Perhaps Wilson interpreted Germany's somewhat conciliatory response to his first message as a sign of weakness and he was determined to exploit that weakness. That was not Wilson's style, however. He was much more comfortable with the give-and-take of the academic world than with the take-no-prisoners approach. It is more likely that he decided, in his stubborn professorial way, that he was not going to let the Germans wiggle through loopholes of their own making. The heart of Wilson's second note stated that the United States did not recognize or accept the breaching of the rights of its citizens to trade and travel on the high seas. Germany could not simply declare those seas to be a war zone for the purposes of military expediency and then offer to write a check for damages that resulted from such a policy. That Wilson took such an official and unequivocal position with the Germans but not the British, who had been seizing rather than sinking U.S. ships, was the last straw for Bryan, who argued that Wilson's second note increased the tension just as the Germans were backing down. He brusquely declared that neither his cabinet colleagues nor the president were truly neutral. Wilson rebuked Bryan before the cabinet, and Daniels, who held his tongue but agreed with Bryan, was finally caught between his old hero and his new hero. It was painful, but the choice was never in doubt; he chose Wilson and a policy with which he disagreed, renouncing Bryan and a position with which he agreed. Bryan went and Daniels stayed. Daniels saw that America's recognition of and tepid protests concerning Britain's blockade would bring the United States into conflict with the Germans. The German high command could not simply continue to wage a land war that had descended into a murderous stalemate and wait until the Royal Navy starved Germany into submission. Disingenuously splitting hairs, Daniels defended his pro-Wilson position by claiming that although he thought war inevitable, he "did not believe *the note* [i.e., Wilson's second message] would inevitably lead to war."[56]

As the final collision between Bryan and Wilson approached, Wilson held the whip hand, as Bryan served at the president's pleasure, but Wilson was not inclined to ask for Bryan's resignation. With the next presidential election season only a year away, Wilson had to be careful how he handled Bryan's exit. The Commoner was too powerful within the party to be discarded with impunity. Rather than firing Bryan, Wilson simply ignored him and used Lansing as his de facto secretary of state. Recognizing he had already pushed the envelope of what was acceptable dissent, Bryan was too loyal to his party to sound off any more than he already had while remaining in the cabinet, but his constitution prohibited him from serving as a figurehead.

The end came two days later. On the afternoon of June 7, Bryan and his wife called on Josephus and Addie Daniels at Single Oak. The two couples took tea and had a pleasant, inconsequential conversation. To Daniels, Bryan looked old and worn. He spoke little, which was not his custom in either professional or social settings. As he got up to leave, Bryan asked Daniels if they could meet early the following morning "upon a most important matter." When the two men met over breakfast the next day, Bryan gave Daniels a set of letters that had passed between Bryan and Wilson during the recent crisis. The last of these included Bryan's resignation and Wilson's acceptance. Daniels said "it was like a bolt out of the blue. It struck me between the eyes."[57] Losing himself for just a moment, Daniels excoriated Bryan for not consulting him before resigning, arguing that both their long personal association and their leadership of the antiwar front in the cabinet demanded such a consultation.

The harsh tone Daniels directed at Bryan might have called forth a reply tinged with righteous indignation. Bryan would have even been justified in asking why Daniels did not resign as well, given how he felt about the threat of the country entering the war. But on this occasion Bryan was neither righteous nor demanding. For the first time in Daniels's memory, the fire seemed to have gone out of the Commoner. He calmly told Daniels that he did not consult him because he did not want Daniels to be compromised by association. It is possible Daniels gave Bryan the impression that he might resign as well, because Bryan told him, "You must stay in the Cabinet. The President will need you."[58] Daniels accepted his old friend's argument, and in any case, there was nothing else he could do. Despite what he might have let Bryan believe at the time, Daniels left no evidence that he considered resigning. As they parted that day, Daniels was reminded of something Bryan had told a crowd in Raleigh just before the two men left on the train for Wilson's inauguration: "There will be no war while I am Secretary of State." According to Daniels, Bryan had made the same pledge on "a hundred platforms."[59] Certain that Wilson's asymmetric treatment of the Germans' submarine warfare and the British blockade would now lead to war with Germany, the Great Commoner would rather leave the ship of state than see his promise broken.

Thus the first major U.S. casualty in the Great War was the political career of William Jennings Bryan. That career had survived three presidential defeats and the guns of August 1914, but it could not survive the sinking of the *Lusitania*. Writing in the immediate postwar period, Daniels glossed over the personal differences and disputes between Bryan and Wilson. He wrote, "The separation did not affect their mutual esteem," but the closest interaction the two men ever had again was when Bryan and his wife lunched at the White House after the successful conclusion of the 1916 presidential campaign. In fact, despite Wilson's semipublic protestations of "personal sorrow" at Bryan's resignation, the president was happy to see Bryan go.[60] Lansing, a distinguished-looking man who had the bearing of a foreign minister, replaced Bryan at the State Department, but Wilson wanted no more Bryans. Henceforth, "Wilson was his own secretary of state."[61]

Daniels agreed with Bryan on the wrongheadedness of Wilson's policy, but he did not want to leave the administration on this particular point of conscience. Bryan recognized that Daniels was the most antiwar member of the cabinet. In a letter written shortly after he left the administration, Bryan contended that Wilson's arguments for supporting the British were irrelevant for ending the war and, more importantly, keeping America out of it. He noted that history would answer "'Who began the war?' or 'Which side has been most cruel in its conduct of the war?'"[62] But the real question was How could the United States avoid war? Agreeing with Bryan's analysis, Daniels had to be the insider who pointed out that the administration's policy was increasing the probability of war with Germany, and as the country drifted toward war, Daniels replaced Bryan as the administration's most pacifistic voice. In this capacity he would prove even less effective than Bryan.

Lansing's first task as secretary of state was to sign and forward Wilson's second message to the Germans. Wilson recognized that the Germans had nominally conceded the rights of neutral ships on the high seas, but that Germany had maintained the right to sink indiscriminately all vessels of belligerents and neutral vessels deemed to be engaged in "hostile acts," as determined by Germany. Were the president to unambiguously accept that position, he would be forfeiting the lives of Americans (as well as surrendering American goods) on British passenger liners and merchant ships.

Furthermore, he would be subjecting American merchant shipping to the endless legal morass of defining "hostile acts." This he refused to do. The key point of Wilson's second note was in its conclusion: "The United States cannot admit that the proclamation of a war zone . . . may be made to operate as in any degree an abbreviation of the rights . . . of American citizens bound on lawful errands as passengers on ships of belligerent nationality."[63] Of course, Wilson had allowed the British to declare the North Sea a war zone, but in any case, the note firmly rejected unlimited submarine warfare, or even submarine warfare subject to the ambiguous limitations offered by the Germans in their reply to Wilson's previous note.

Upon receiving this message, the Germans blinked. The kaiser, who had been oscillating between his bellicose admirals, led by Tirpitz, and the more cautious civilians, led by Chancellor Bethmann-Hollweg, swung toward minimizing the chance that the United States would be drawn into the war. He subsequently declared neutral merchantmen and all passenger liners off limits to the U-boats—unless they followed the stop-and-search procedures. Wilson announced that this placed the German navy "in substantial accord with the accepted practices of regulated warfare."[64] In short, submarines would have to follow the Cruiser Rules just as if they were surface raiders. The kaiser's decision to capitulate was made easier by a split among his military advisors. Some, such as the chief of the (army) general staff, General Erich von Falkenhayn, thought the best chance of victory lay in keeping America out of the war. Others, such as Tirpitz, were incensed that Germany was "kowtowing" (Tirpitz's term) to the United States. The grand admiral complained to the kaiser that "America is so shamelessly, so barefacedly pro-English" that it was dishonorable to behave as if the United States was in fact neutral.[65] More to the point, Tirpitz argued that even if unrestricted submarine warfare brought the Americans into the war, the U-boats would bring the British to their knees before the United States could materially affect the outcome. For seventeen years, the kaiser had taken his chief admiral's advice, but now Germany's supreme ruler grew faint at heart. He took the advice of the parliamentarian Bethmann-Hollweg and the soldier Falkenhayn over the sea dog Tirpitz, who, in a huff, offered his resignation. Wilhelm refused to accept it.

The U-boat campaign continued, but the kaiser's concession to Wilson meant that German submarine commanders would not sink passenger ships or neutral merchant vessels without stopping and searching them first. Since stopping and searching was impractical, U-boat commanders simply sank without warning those vessels that they thought were fair game. The list of legitimate targets was reduced to British naval vessels, merchantmen, and troop transports. Given the crude technology employed in identifying vessels, mistakes were bound to be made. The first major errors occurred on August 14 when a U-boat sank the British steamer *Durnsley*, which might have been fair game, and the passenger liner *Arabic*, which certainly was not. Four Americans died. The war party in America expressed outrage. Again, Daniels counseled caution, and Wilson, accepting his advice, simply asked Berlin, through diplomatic channels, if there had been some miscommunication between the two governments. The Germans replied, in effect, No, there had been no miscommunication, but mistakes happen. That answer was unacceptable to Wilson, and after much subsequent back-and-forth, on September 18, the Germans backed down and broke off the Atlantic campaign altogether, pulling their U-boats back from the western approaches to the British Isles. It was a major diplomatic victory for Wilson.

Before departing, Bryan had noted that international law, as recognized by previous U.S. administrations, did not recognize the right of citizens of neutral states to travel unmolested on belligerent ships. The Cruiser Rules offered no such protection. Wilson's deviation from the accepted rules of the sea and past U.S. policy did not go unnoticed. Wilson's demand for freedom of the seas appeared to be absolute. Thus, "taken to the extreme, Wilson's position was that American lives were sacrosanct," meaning "Americans traveling on Allied ships were indeed human shields, just as the Germans claimed."[66] There was an easy way to avoid conflict with Germany over the matter. The administration could have issued a formal alert to travelers on belligerent ships and let them go at their own risk. On strictly legal grounds, on this particular point Tirpitz (and Bryan and Daniels) possessed a stronger case than Wilson; but there was no court to which the grand admiral could appeal, and the kaiser was not yet willing to risk war with the United States over arcane points of the ancient and unenforceable laws of the sea.

Despite the U.S. administration's nakedly pro-British policy, the United States and Germany had avoided armed conflict. Daniels summarized the months of dispute in 1915 by noting that "after vigorous and unmistakable assertion of the position of the United States, Germany made the promises Wilson had demanded."[67] Though Daniels had not been a strong supporter of what had become Wilson's pro-British version of neutrality, he felt vindicated in sticking with Wilson after Bryan left. In a matter of weeks, the tide had completely turned on the fortunes of his two heroes. Bryan left under a cloud. Some of Bryan's critics claimed he abandoned Wilson with the thought of running for president in 1916. In any case, with the Germans backing down, Bryan appeared to desert in the face of a successful policy. Wilson's supporters could put the president up for reelection simultaneously claiming that "he kept us out of war" and that he defended American honor and the rights of the sea (and the profits that went with them, Bryan might have sarcastically added). Bryan's position and his subsequent career never had a chance once the kaiser's resolve wobbled before the force of Wilson's rhetoric. Despite his reservations, Daniels backed the winning horse. Soon enough, however, events would reveal it to be a warhorse.

WAR

As Mahan clearly explained, naval war is economic war. Daniels got the point. From the outset of the U-boat campaign, he followed the data on shipping and tonnages lost to the U-boats. He would have been correct to conclude that in the months prior to withdrawing their U-boats from the approaches to the British Isles, the Germans were winning the battle of the Atlantic. Basic arithmetic showed that the growth of British shipping tonnage fell below the tonnage sunk by the Germans. For a trading nation that relied on the sea lanes for food, among other key products, that trend could not continue indefinitely. Wilson's demand that the Germans adhere strictly to the Cruiser Rules while refusing to make such a demand of the British was a de facto pro-British policy. On this point, Tirpitz, Bryan, and Daniels all agreed. However, following the withdrawal of the U-boats, in the fall of 1915, the chances of the United States entering the war were lower than they had been since the previous winter. But the new status quo left Britain to starve Germany by blockade, while the Germans no longer tried to starve the British with U-boats. That, too, was a state of affairs that could not continue indefinitely. Germany would be forced to either alter the new arrangement or eventually it would lose the war.

Thus with the war at sea going badly by the end of 1915, the German high command decided to change the equation in 1916 by refocusing their attention on the continent, where Falkenhayn strove to knock the French out of the war by "bleeding them white." The place he chose, and failed, to do this was the fortified city of Verdun. More than a half a million men would die, but Verdun remained in French hands. Meanwhile, the British blockade permitted a constant flow of shells, some of which came from the United States, to French guns at Verdun while starving the German home front.

So "with each successive month, the British grip on German economic life tightened; by January 1916, the German people were showing signs of hardship."[68] Following Falkenhayn's failure to win the war in the trenches, the German admiralty demanded that the kaiser renew submarine warfare in the Atlantic.

With the German infantry being slaughtered at Verdun and no breakthrough on land in sight, Wilhelm yielded to the pressure from his admirals. On March 13, 1916, Germany resumed its submarine campaign in the Atlantic. The new campaign, while technically not "unrestricted," allowed its commanders more freedom than they had enjoyed under Wilhelm's order of June 1, 1915. The new orders contained no explicit mention of how neutrals were to be treated. Even if the Cruiser Rules were implied in the case of neutrals, all parties understood that, as had happened in the summer of 1915, aggressive U-boat commanders would make mistakes and the Cruiser Rules would be violated. Chancellor Bethmann-Hollweg warned anyone who would listen that the civilized world would treat Germany like a "mad dog," but no one in the German admiralty had renounced the U-boats following the diplomatic crisis of 1915. On the contrary, Germany's submarine fleet had been upgraded and enlarged during the timeout. In promoting the return to the submarine, the admirals again argued that despite the threat of angering the Americans, the British would be out of the war before the United States could enter it. Chief of the naval staff Admiral Henning von Holtzendorff reported that the improved submarine fleet was ready. At its peak, it could sink more than 500,000 tons of British shipping per month, whereas at peak production British shipyards could only add about 3 million tons a year; thus unleashing the subs would end the war "in at most six months."[69] For his part, Tirpitz was outraged that the kaiser denied the admiralty the freedom to return to unrestricted submarine warfare, and he again offered his resignation. This time Wilhelm accepted. They never spoke again.

The conflict between the United States and Germany entered its next phase when, on March 24, a German submarine mistook the passenger ship *Sussex* for a troop transport and sank it, causing several deaths, including those of four Americans. Wilson consulted his cabinet concerning the construction of a response. The pro-war party, now led by Lansing, called for language that would almost certainly lead to conflict. (War Secretary Lindley Garrison, often the most bellicose cabinet member, had recently been replaced by the more cautious Newton Baker, former mayor of Cleveland. Daniels got on better with Baker than he had with Garrison, and they worked well together throughout the war.) In contrast to Lansing's belligerence, Daniels argued that the country was not yet behind war, and the death of four Americans on a British ship was not enough to tip the scales. With the presidential election forthcoming, Daniels recalled William McKinley's strategy in the prelude to the Spanish-American War. Daniels, who did not want war at all, argued that it was bad politics for Wilson to get out in front of the pro-war crowd. With Bryan gone, Daniels remained the cabinet's most antiwar voice, and in his own words, he "took the ground that, aside from other questions, if Wilson brought on war with Germany except after exhausting every possible means to avert it, the country would rise up against him in the 1916 election."[70] Daniels's strategy of "peace for political reasons" might not have gone down well with either his hawkish colleagues or the high-minded followers of Bryan, who agreed with peace but turned up their noses at the political calculating, but it was sound political advice all the same. Wilson listened to Daniels. There would be no war, for now.

After considerable discussion within the cabinet, Wilson issued a to-the-point message to the vacillators among Germany's leadership, mainly the kaiser and Bethmann-Hollweg. Unless the Germans were prepared to return explicitly to the Cruiser Rules, Wilson wrote, the United States would be forced to sever diplomatic ties—an act to be interpreted as belligerent and likely to lead to war. At first glance, it appears that Wilson took a hard line, but it is easy to misinterpret his message, which he delivered to Congress on April 19. The message seems more belligerent in retrospect than it was at the time, and it reflects Daniels's view on the matter. Whereas some members of the cabinet (with Lansing being the most bellicose) interpreted the new submarine war as an escalation of the conflict, Daniels counseled that it was merely a return to the same impasse at which the United States and Germany had been the previous summer. He attributed no ill will to the actions of the German *government* but, rather, accused the German *military* of exacerbating tensions between the two countries. This approach, which Wilson followed to the letter, offered both the president and the kaiser a way out short of war. In his congressional address, as Daniels had advised, Wilson juxtaposed the behavior of the government and the military: "Again and again the Imperial German Government has given [the United States] its solemn assurances," yet Germany appeared to permit "its undersea commanders to disregard these assurances with entire impunity." Playing the role of the professor who merely followed logic to its necessary conclusion, the president concluded that "unless the Imperial German Government should now immediately declare its intention to abandon its present practice of submarine warfare and return to a scrupulous observance of the practice clearly prescribed by the law of nations, the Government of the United States can have no choice but to sever diplomatic relations."[71] In short, Wilson demanded nothing more than a return to the constraints agreed upon the previous summer. Again Wilhelm flinched at Wilson's resolve. On April 24, the kaiser ordered Holtzendorff to return to the state of affairs as they stood in the summer of 1915. In effect, Wilson's determined resistance to Germany's U-boat campaign and the kaiser's fears of forcing America into the war once again gave the British the upper hand in the war at sea.

With the U-boats defanged, the new commander in chief of the German fleet, Vice Admiral Reinhard Scheer (who, as a surface commander, "did not view the submarine war against commerce as a substitute for some other plan"), decided to initiate battle with the British navy.[72] On May 31, at the Skagerrak, where the North Sea narrows off Jutland, the two sides fought the greatest sea battle in history. More than 250 surface ships, including massive dreadnoughts on both sides, flung shell after shell at one another throughout the day. When the battle was over, the British had lost three battle cruisers, three smaller cruisers, and eight other ships. German losses were one battle cruiser and ten other ships. Ten thousand men went to the bottom in a matter of hours. Because their losses were smaller, the Germans could claim to have won the battle, but on the same day they lost the war at sea. The kaiser's fear of losing his beloved fleet caused the admiralty to keep the high seas fleet in dock for the rest of the war, and Scheer began to reconsider the usefulness of the U-boats.

On the other side of the Atlantic, Daniels closely monitored the results of the Battle of Jutland and eventually concluded that the sacrifice of armor for speed in the battle cruisers was a losing trade-off. The size and accuracy of the shells from the largest guns proved to be simply too much for the lightly armored behemoths. Although his top admirals split on what to do with the battle cruisers, Daniels delayed their construction, and two were eventually converted into aircraft carriers, the next technological marvel of sea warfare.[73]

Despite Daniels's fears that Wilson's pro-British policy would lead to war, the president had successfully walked the razor's edge between war and peace through the *Lusitania*, *Arabic*, and *Sussex* crises, and peace was the more popular alternative at the polls, if barely. In the election of 1916, the Democrats did reasonably well for the party in power, losing another fourteen seats in the House and two in the Senate while keeping control of both chambers. However, Wilson was reelected by the narrowest of margins. Although he earned nearly 3 million more votes than he had in 1912, he squeaked by in the electoral college, defeating jurist Charles Evans Hughes by only twenty-two votes, the closest race since Rutherford B. Hayes defeated Samuel Tilden in 1876. If only one state, Ohio, had gone the other way, Hughes would have been president. Daniels worried about Wilson's popularity in the North, and he had advised the president to reach out to northern Catholics by appointing one to the cabinet or to some other key position, a point with which Wilson's confidant House agreed.[74] Daniels thought Wilson did not try hard enough to leverage Democratic power among the northern and midwestern urban machines, many of which were maintained through the Catholic vote, and he persisted along this line as the cabinet began to turn over and as Wilson made appointments to the Supreme Court. Wilson replaced three cabinet members before the election, and he made three court appointments. None went to a Catholic. While Wilson had appointed Louis Brandeis, the first Jew on the Supreme Court, the Jewish vote was minuscule compared with the Catholic vote, which was concentrated in the weakest Democratic regions.[75]

Still, Daniels, who among Wilson's cabinet members remained the most consistent supporter of neutrality (even though he had misgivings about the manner in which that policy had been applied), considered the 1916 election a "mandate from the people," and so did Wilson.[76] However, whereas Daniels interpreted the victory as a mandate to remain neutral, Wilson increasingly interpreted it as a mandate for peace, which as the violent course of the naval war indicated, was not the same as neutrality. Despite Daniels's later protestations, as found, for example, in his memoirs, he and Wilson never saw eye-to-eye on how U.S. policy was actually practiced during these years. Like Bryan, Daniels thought Wilson's policy was more pro-British than truly neutral; however, unlike Bryan, Daniels never publicly revealed his misgivings. He only shared them with Bryan privately, in carefully phrased cabinet discussions, and in his diary. As the war dragged on through 1916, however, the president and his navy secretary began to have even more divergent views on the conflict. Wilson grew increasingly horrified by the carnage and began to see himself as an honest broker in the peace process, perhaps the one person in the world with the inclination and power to bring peace. In this he was seriously mistaken. It would be the first of several key diplomatic blunders over the next four years. Daniels, similarly horrified, concluded that the extent of the carnage was all the more reason for the United States to remain aloof from the slaughter. True neutrality, treating the British and the Germans the same, was, in Daniels's view, the surest way to avoid being dragged into the war. Again, Daniels did not jump ship but, rather, maintained a muted counsel while publicly following where Wilson led.

During the election campaign, the State Department officially gave notice that after he was reelected, Wilson would begin the peace process. Thus immediately after the election, Wilson worked on his formal peace proposal; however, more than a month went by before he presented it. Though he was skeptical of its usefulness, Daniels thought Wilson should have had the proposal ready immediately following the election, and he blamed the delay on the pro-British Colonel House and Ambassador Page. (In Daniels's view House and Page thought the British were winning the war and did not want Wilson to do anything that might be favorable to Germany.) Before Wilson could present his proposal, the Germans offered their own peace plan, which included no assignment of war guilt, no German retreat from Belgium or France, no surrender of Germany's eastern conquests, and no reparations—a proposal the Entente dismissed without seriously considering it.[77] With the hope of identifying a middle ground, Wilson's proposal asked that the belligerents formally present their war aims, and thus essentially list their conditions for peace. Ironically, this is exactly what Bryan had been calling for since the war began. Although the Commoner was not known for his sense of irony, he must have had a laugh when Wilson posed as Europe's potential savior using Bryan's plan for peace.

In response to Wilson's entreaty, the Germans offered nothing of substance and thus revealed the great diplomatic flaw in their war effort.[78] Initially, Germany's only specific war aim in 1914 was to defeat France and Russia and then dictate terms to both. When that did not happen, Germany had no other formal goals—other than not losing, of course. With the exception of what the Germans had proposed in their earlier peace offer, which was simply no retreat from their current positions, they gave no objectives for the war or conditions for ending it. They simply fought on.

Wilson's proposal, which in retrospect seems innocent enough, in fact angered both sides. The kaiser and his key generals and admirals saw no reason to surrender an inch of ground that the British and French could not force them to give up. The Entente, offended that Wilson's proposal treated the combatants as moral equals, saw no reason to give Germany any breathing room. The Germans might hold large patches of Europe, but the British controlled the seas, and their leaders guessed Germany would crack before it could extract enough resources from its conquered territories to produce victory. The logic behind Britain's blockade was that Germany would crack first economically, then politically, then militarily. The British, who had been listening to the Anglophiles House and Page, had been interpreting Wilson's asymmetric neutrality as an implicit show of support for their strategy, and thus they were deeply disappointed that the president's initial peace proposal did not reflect a more sympathetic view of the Entente's position. Daniels wrote, "News from London was that 'the King wept' when he read Wilson's suggestion."[79]

In August 1916, while the U-boat campaign remained in hiatus, Wilhelm dismissed Falkenhayn, whose disastrous Verdun campaign had bled the Fatherland as white as it had the French. Falkenhayn's replacement was sixty-eight-year-old Field Marshal Paul Ludwig Hans Anton von Beneckendorff und von Hindenburg, who would henceforth be known to the world as Hindenburg. With Hindenburg came his chief subordinate, General Erich Ludendorff. With peace off the table following the rejection of Wilson's plea for terms, Hindenburg and Ludendorff argued that the U-boats should resume their unrestricted quest for prey in the Atlantic. A showdown was in the making.

The economic strain of the blockade tested German resolve in the so-called turnip winter of 1916–17. (The German harvest had failed in 1916.) However, despite the economic hardships endured on the home front, the *N&O*'s headlines did not indicate that the Germans were losing the war. In the East, the kaiser's most consistently successful general, Field Marshal August von Mackensen, had in consecutive campaigns pushed the Russians out of Eastern Europe, knocked Serbia out of the war, and conquered Romania. Russia was on the verge of collapse, both militarily and politically. The Austrians held their own against the Italians, who had entered the war on the Entente's side in 1915. In the Middle East, in the past two years the Turks had defeated British armies at Gallipoli and in Mesopotamia. On the Western Front, the Germans still held Belgium and much of northern France. Success on the Eastern Front allowed the German high command to shift divisions to the West, and Hindenburg and Ludendorff planned a series of campaigns that, if successful, would lead to breakthroughs that, in turn, would end the war.

There existed only one dark cloud on the German horizon. It was apparent to all that as the war dragged on into its third year, it had become an economic fight to the finish. Hindenburg and Ludendorff, both old infantrymen, realized they could not defeat the British and the French in the field so long as those powers were supplied by sea from the nearly unlimited economic font of the United States. Thus they argued that the U-boat war would have to be restarted. Although the German high command did not fear the United States militarily, at least not in the short run, they did respect its economic prowess. They understood that confronting the United States on the high seas might ultimately lead to a formal declaration of war, but they were gambling that before the full force of the U.S. Army could be felt in France, the war would be over. So, as it had early in 1915, after stalemate had first set in on the Western Front, Germany turned to its navy, and after Jutland, the navy had only the U-boats to offer.

The final showdown on the U-boat war took place in a series of meetings on January 8 and 9, 1917, first in Berlin and then at German military headquarters at Pless. The high command and the admiralty demanded a return to unrestricted submarine warfare. Chancellor Bethmann-Hollweg went against the military one last time. The U-boats would bring America into the war on the Entente's side, he argued; at the same time, the economic damage the submarines wrought would not cause Britain to abandon France before the vast potential of the United States could be felt on the Western Front. Rather than winning the war in a year, unrestricted submarine warfare would lose the war sooner or later, probably sooner. After listening to the debate, the kaiser turned to naval chief of staff Holtzendorff. With a bearing and countenance only slightly less intimidating than those of Tirpitz, Holtzendorff supposedly replied, "I pledge on my word as a naval officer that no American will set foot on continental soil."[80] The kaiser made up his mind. On February 1, 1917, the Germans announced the return to all-out submarine warfare. No more Cruiser Rules. No more stop and search. Everything was fair game.

On the evening Holtzendorff gave his solemn pledge to his emperor, 4,000 miles away, Josephus Daniels was attending a revival meeting held by the legendary evangelist Billy Sunday. In Daniels's diary that day, he entered nothing about the conflict. Over the next two years, however, Daniels would oversee the landing of more than 2 million U.S. troops on French soil, 2 million more than Holtzendorff claimed Daniels could land, and "not one soldier aboard a troop transport manned by the United States Navy lost his life through enemy [naval] action."[81] By underestimating U.S. power, Germany's leaders lost the Great War on February 1, 1917, though the slaughter would continue for almost two more years.

Meanwhile, in Washington, on the evening of January 31, the German ambassador visited Secretary of State Lansing and informed him that as of midnight, the U-boat war in the Atlantic would be restarted. Upon being informed of this fact, Wilson told his personal secretary, Joe Tumulty, "This means war."[82] Although the president hesitated to ask Congress for a formal declaration of war, he followed up on his earlier threat and had Lansing break diplomatic ties with Germany.

Following the announcement of Germany's return to unrestricted submarine warfare, events moved very quickly toward war. The move was aided by the bungling of the German Foreign Ministry, which perversely followed a policy that increased tensions with the United States. Within a week of the kaiser's decision to unleash once again the U-boats, German foreign minister Arthur Zimmerman sent a message to his ambassador in Mexico. In the "Zimmerman telegram," as it became known, Germany announced that submarine warfare was about to recommence in the Atlantic. The message also noted that Germany preferred that the United States remain neutral. However, if unrestricted submarine warfare brought the United States into the war, then Germany invited Mexico to form an alliance "on the following basis: Make war together, make peace together, generous financial support, and an understanding on our [i.e., Germany's] part that Mexico is to reconquer the lost territory in Texas, new Mexico and Arizona."[83] The message, which vindicated Daniels's decision to interdict Germany's military shipment to Mexico in 1914, was intercepted by the Royal Navy and transmitted to Washington through official channels.

When Wilson shared the news with his cabinet, ferocious debate followed. Typically, Daniels, who was at the center of the storm as the most antiwar member, downplayed the acrimony among his colleagues. While Interior Secretary Lane wrote that "we had one of the most animated sessions of the Cabinet that I suppose has ever been held under this or any other President," Daniels does not mention the fight in his diary.[84] This was Daniels's strategy since his teen years running the Wilson *Advance*. He always understated conflict within the inner circles of the Democratic Party, whether the dispute concerned voting for public school appropriations in Wilson, North Carolina, or entering the Great War. He seemed to fear magnifying the dispute by openly recognizing it. As a newspaperman, Daniels was famous for magnifying and exploiting disputes among his opponents, and so he understood the risk of being too public with squabbles within his own political family.

The squabbles within the cabinet were noisy. War was now unambiguously the majority position. Among the most outspoken war hawks were

Lansing, McAdoo, Lane, and Houston. Following Daniels's counsel while ignoring the majority, Wilson would not declare war without a specific precipitating incident. Despite his hopes that the country could still avoid war, Daniels now had to prepare for the worst. His immediate concern was arming U.S. merchant ships. They would be the U-boats' primary targets. Wilson had the executive authority to do so, but still seeking political cover, he asked Congress for authorization. After the *New York Times* publicized the Zimmerman telegram, the U.S. House passed the bill overwhelmingly, but antiwar sentiment and everyday politicking held it up in the Senate. On Inauguration Day, March 4, Wilson authorized Daniels to arm the vessels under executive order. The guns were little help against U-boats that did not surface, and of course ships already at sea were at great risk. Accordingly, Daniels noted, "Within a few days of the inauguration, eight American vessels were sunk by U-boats."[85] There was no longer even a razor's edge upon which Wilson could walk.

Wilson called a cabinet meeting for Tuesday, March 20. Daniels called it "the Day of Decision." The war hawks spoke first. They made their case and displayed a united front. Daniels referred to what happened next as his "Gethsemane." After listening to the war party, the president turned to Daniels and explicitly asked for his view. Daniels, deep in thought, said nothing. As the cabinet waited for Daniels, two other holdouts, Secretary of Labor William Wilson and Postmaster Burleson, spoke up. Both said that although they regretted the matter, war was the only alternative. All eyes turned back to Daniels, the final holdout, who still had not spoken. He hesitated, and then arguing that the law of the sea was among the "cherished principles of the American people," voted for war, making the tally unanimous for the first time. Finally, with Daniels onboard, Wilson would ask Congress for a declaration of war.[86]

It is difficult to imagine that the president would have hesitated to go to Congress for a declaration if Daniels and the other doves had held out for peace. The political momentum for war was now simply too great to resist. But given that it was the war at sea that was bringing the United States into the Great War, riding roughshod over his navy secretary would have been a public embarrassment for Wilson. The president guessed correctly that Daniels was too much of a party man to cause an ugly public rift over the move to war. Over the past twenty years, with the exception of Bryan, Daniels had shed as much blood as anyone for the national Democratic Party. He would not be the one to tear it apart. Gethsemane was a poor metaphor, however, because unlike Christ, Daniels succumbed to worldly temptation. He did the politically expedient thing and made Wilson's call for war much easier.

On April 2, Wilson went to Congress, called into an extra session, and delivered a startling address. For all his personal faults, Wilson was a bold leader. (As one of his biographers accurately put it, "In situations where he had a choice, he would nearly always pick the grander riskier course.")[87] In his address, the president did more than ask for a declaration of war; he offered an entirely new vision of the war and of U.S. foreign policy. Wilson opened with a restatement of the events leading to the diplomatic breach with Germany, but he did not request a declaration of war based on the events that brought about the breach. Rather, he offered a revolutionary vision of America's entry into the war as an event to make the world "safe for democracy . . . [and] for the rights and liberties of small nations." Thus war was not a specific act to redress a specific wrong; it was a great crusade for peace. Calling for a declaration, he concluded by paraphrasing Martin Luther; of America's entry into the war, Wilson said, "God helping her, she can do no other."[88]

It was an incredible speech, one that broke with all precedent in U.S. foreign policy. When his mind was focused on the subject, Wilson could be a truly effective public speaker. But on this occasion his eloquence and his listeners' focus on the initial indictment of Germany and the call for war caused many of those who heard the speech to miss completely its broader import. In his summary of the speech—overlooking, or perhaps expediently ignoring, Wilson's grand commitment to world peace, a calling Daniels did not share—Daniels emphasized Wilson's mastery of the language, writing that the president spoke "in sentences so vascular they would have bled if cut."[89] More to the point, Wilson was proposing to take America down a path of international engagement so new that its very name, Wilsonian Idealism, revealed its recent paternity. More basely, like McKinley in his justification for conquering the Philippines, Wilson wrapped the venture in the sanctimony of a religious crusade. Wilson had once claimed God ordained his presidency, and on the day he invoked God's name in going to war, 12 million people had already died as a result of the conflict. Another 8 million would die following America's entry.[90] Congress followed Wilson's lead, passing the War Resolution Act by overwhelming majorities.

Even before Wilson signed the declaration on April 6, Daniels launched the navy on a crash course in preparing for war. In a volume titled *Our Navy at War*, published the year after he left office, Daniels went to some length to persuade readers that he had the navy on a sound footing before war came.[91] In a sense, he did. Daniels had been a diligent executive of the Navy Department. The officers, men, and ships were world class. However, the size and composition of the navy were not immediately up to the task of fighting a naval war on the scale that was expected by Mahan's doctrines. Fortunately, the war Mahan laid out was not the war the navy would be called upon to fight. At the outset of Daniels's tenure, the naval building program had been anchored by the "two-battleship ratio," which in theory meant two new battleships a year for the foreseeable future, but which for fiscal reasons meant one new battleship a year in the short run. The war had changed that plan. The fate of the German cruisers, hunted down one by one across the world's oceans, had taught Daniels that the United States needed a two-ocean navy equal to that of any other Great Power. As Daniels watched the war at sea unfold, he became a Big Navy advocate. Accordingly, late in 1915, Daniels created a new building program. This plan, which Congress approved in 1916, called for the construction of 157 new vessels, including 10 dreadnoughts, 6 battle cruisers, 10 smaller cruisers, 50 destroyers, 70 submarines, and other auxiliary ships. Most prominently, the dreadnought building program was immediately stepped up to three a year.[92] Mahan's doctrine still captured the imagination of Daniels, his admirals, and the navy's congressional supporters, but the war that was about to be fought would not require *any* of the new dreadnoughts.

Indeed, Jutland was the first and last great naval battle of dreadnoughts. The airplane and the aircraft carrier, which was being conceived during these years, rendered the great battleships obsolete. Daniels quickly realized that the kaiser's high seas fleet offered no danger to the United States, and his review of the battle cruisers' performance at Jutland ultimately caused him to exclude them from his new building plan. In the event, the dreadnoughts were not the keys to victory or defeat; commerce was. The flow of food and matériel would decide the war, and keeping the British and French in the war became Daniels's main objective. He would do this by feeding their people and supplying their troops and by delivering American troops to the front. Ironically, the primary contribution of the great battleships was their service as troop carriers.

Over the next few years there would be allegations that Daniels could have and should have done more to prepare the navy for war before it was declared.[93] These charges would come from several different directions, and not all of them would stand close scrutiny; but two are worth reviewing. One was that Daniels had not focused on preparing the navy for entry into the Great War. His initial foot-dragging on creating a chief of naval operations was the primary evidence on this charge. As one critic wrote, "The Navy until 1915 had no provision in its organization for the handling of military activities or for the conduct of war operations."[94] The second charge was that he was a latecomer to the Big Navy view. The evidence was that Daniels's recommendation for the construction of dreadnoughts had been half that recommended by the General Board.

But Daniels had embraced a version of the chief of naval operations as a means of addressing the organizational issues, and the Royal Navy's complete mastery of the Imperial Navy taught Daniels that the U.S. Navy must be the equal of the Royal Navy. By the time war came to the United States, he was a Big Navy man. In retrospect, his antiwar sentiments probably left him vulnerable to charges that he could have better prepared the navy for the war that eventually came. It was argued that because of Daniels's lack of enthusiasm for the fight, his leadership lacked vigor. (A related charge was that, given the nature of the war, Daniels actually had the navy doing the wrong things. To a certain extent, on this point Daniels was guilty. The navy did not need dreadnoughts to defeat the U-boats; it needed destroyers, the smaller, faster sub hunters.)

The settling of political accounts related to naval preparedness would have to wait until after the war; for now, Daniels focused on waging it. Daniels had no formal training in either economics or military science, but he had been observing the Great War carefully for two and a half years. He understood that the only way to end the war in the short run was to starve the German economy while breaking the German army in the field. Here he proved more prescient than either his fellow cabinet members, who claimed U.S. troops would not be needed in France, or the German high command, who claimed U.S. troops would not arrive in time to affect the war's outcome. One of the arguments the cabinet's war hawks employed to support U.S. entry was that no U.S. soldier would need to go to Europe to fight. (The argument was made explicitly in cabinet meetings by Interior Secretary Lane and Agricultural Secretary Houston.)[95] Daniels firmly disagreed, claiming that the war could not be won without employing U.S. ground troops in Europe. Even as the Germans and the war hawks dismissed the notion, Daniels wrote that the navy's "most important task [would be] to land American soldiers on French soil."[96] Hindenburg and Ludendorff knew more about war than the members of Wilson's cabinet did. The German warlords agreed with Daniels's strategic vision. The war would be won or lost in the trenches on the Western Front. Their mistake was to assume the war would end before Daniels started landing American regiments in France. They overestimated Holtzendorff and his U-boats and underestimated Daniels.

Daniels argued that defeating the U-boats and ratcheting up the blockade without forcing the issue in the trenches in France would allow the war to plod on, certainly through 1918 and most likely 1919. Simply focusing on naval issues—feeding Britain by defeating the U-boats and blockading Germany into starvation on the home front—would not end the war quickly. Germany could not be starved in a matter of months. Mackensen's victories in the East had freed manpower and made other material resources available for the effort in the West; thus as long as the Germans maintained control of vast stretches of Belgium and France on the Western Front, they could fight on, not indefinitely but certainly for another two years. Since the German war machine had first claims on economic resources at home and in the conquered territories, the blockade could only weaken the effort on the Western Front. It could not win the war outright. The hope was that the blockade could ultimately break morale on the German home front, which would in turn further erode support for the war, perhaps even fomenting revolution. Daniels did not doubt such a strategy would work; he just doubted it would work quickly, and Entente politicians were running out of time. The Entente's elected leaders were subject to more public pressure than Hindenburg and Ludendorff were. Hard men were needed to see the thing through quickly, and those men would soon be in place.

At the end of 1916, the government had fallen in Britain, and liberal Welshman David Lloyd George replaced H. H. Asquith. In Italy, before the end of the 1917, after a series of military disasters culminating in the German and Austrian victory at Caporetto (marked by the performance of young German infantry officer Erwin Rommel), the government would fall, and Vittorio Orlando would take over the helm of the new government. In France, one government after another had fallen. Shortly after Orlando took power in Italy, the president of the Third Republic, Raymond Poincaré, called on the "Old Tiger," seventy-six-year-old radical Georges Clemenceau, to form yet another government. In this impressive triumvirate—Lloyd George, Clemenceau, and Orlando—the Entente had the determined leadership to see the effort through to the bitter end; but when America entered the war, Lloyd George was the only one onboard, and his position looked precarious. All of the Entente's leaders—those in power and those soon to be—understood that if the end did not come sooner rather than later, then there was no predicting what course political events at home might take. Indeed, one would have been justified in guessing that the Entente, whose governments were more subject to popular will than Germany's, would break before the Central Powers. To prevent that from happening, Daniels would have to tighten the noose around Germany's neck.

From the outset of the war, Daniels had questioned both the legality of the British blockade and the preferential treatment afforded the British by the Wilson administration. He continually chafed at what he considered a less-than-wholehearted commitment to neutrality among many Americans, including his colleagues in Wilson's cabinet. More infuriating were British efforts to entice American entry into the war or, what to Daniels amounted to the same thing, British policies that led Germany toward a direct conflict with the United States. Of the latter group of transgressions, the blockade was item number one. Daniels was never an Anglophile. He blamed the British for rejecting Wilson's earlier offer to mediate between the warring parties based on their war aims, and he thought the British should be held accountable, as the Germans had been held accountable, for violations of the Cruiser Rules. After the war, and after Wilson was dead, Daniels disingenuously claimed that Wilson maintained an identical view. But Wilson never held the British to the same standards he did the Germans, and by continuing to allow U.S. trade with the British and the French while protesting German interference with that trade, the president's actions clearly favored the Entente.[97]

Once Congress declared war, however, debate about the asymmetric treatment of the Entente and the Central Powers was dismissed. The U.S. Navy now actively supported Britain's blockade. Daniels became a party to violations of international law he had spent two years chafing about. Written after the war, his justification for his subsequent actions amounted to the type of legalistic hairsplitting to which he seldom stooped. According to Daniels, under international law, specifically the still-unratified Declaration of London, "any country was at liberty to buy munitions in the United States. Britain could do so freely because of its strong Navy while Germany could not because of Britain's sea power. That was Germany's chief grievance [against the United States], and [Germany] continued to argue that this gave aid to Britain. If so, it was outside the control of [the United States]."[98] This was sophistry; Daniels ignored the British blockade and its closing of the North Sea, which Daniels himself noted time and again as a violation of international law.

Perhaps recognizing the disingenuous nature of his interpretation of British actions after the United States entered the war, Daniels later more honestly observed that both the British and the Germans were equally culpable in their respective violations, but that the impact on the United States from the conflict was not the same. "The difference between the wrongs inflicted by Germany and by Britain on the United States," he wrote, "was that Germany's policy resulted in the death of Americans, while the British wrongs affected merchandise. Germany would kill human beings while Britain killed commerce. In the final wind-up, human life was regarded as more sacred than trade."[99] Here Daniels laid bare the public relations and crass political facts that formed the essence of Wilson's asymmetric policy that ultimately led the United States into the war. The public relations issue was that death came more slowly to German children who starved as a result of the blockade than it did to the victims of U-boats who drowned quickly in the icy North Atlantic. The political issue was that U.S. arms and food suppliers and their employees voted in U.S. elections, while hungry Germans did not. To Daniels's credit, he never wrapped U.S. policy in religious sanctimony as Wilson did. Although Wilson was no evangelist, he increasingly invoked God's name in the support of his policies. As one of his biographers put it, "He did think of himself as an instrument of God's will."[100] Even Daniels grew tired of this side of Wilson's personality. At one point, after listening to Wilson justify a policy by invoking God's will, Daniels confided to his diary, "Personal religion & national [policy] have no relation."[101] As Daniels had said of McKinley's military conquest of the Philippines, Wilson laid the war on God.

Daniels might have put a more partisan, pro-British slant on his postwar summary of the dispute with Britain over its continental blockade. He did not do so, even though after the United States entered the war he proved to be a good ally, because he always saw the dispute between the British and the Germans as one of moral equals. His explanation of the public's juxtaposition of human life lost to the U-boats versus commerce lost to the British blockade was almost verbatim the administration's party line on the justification for treating the combatants differently during the war. (U.S. Ambassador James Gerard said as much to the kaiser.) Of course the sanctity of human life to which Daniels referred applied, in fact, only to *American* lives. The British blockade might have killed tens of thousands of Germans, and those deaths were concentrated among citizens on the home front—women, children, and the elderly—while the U-boat war killed a few hundred U.S. citizens, most of whom were merchant seamen. Daniels saw the truth clearly and had from the beginning of the U-boat war.

As a neutral, Daniels supported the Cruiser Rules, but as a combatant he found them inexpedient. Upon being briefed on economic conditions in Great Britain, Daniels began to fear for his new allies. The Cruiser Rules would have to go. Daniels recognized that to the British, after nearly three years of the most horrific slaughter in history, the war had become a double-edged sword. On one hand, their losses in lives and treasure had hardened the British against Germany, and this hardening placed a compromise peace out of reach. On the other hand, early in 1917, to many observers, Germany's war strategy appeared to be working. British losses at sea from the resumed U-boat campaign could not be borne indefinitely. Daniels understood that the crisis faced by America's key ally resulted from two arithmetic relationships: Ships sank faster than they could be built, and the finite human capacity for endurance was a function of nutritional consumption.

But the Germans had to eat, too. Although the U-boats sent ships to the bottom faster than new ones could be launched, the Royal Navy had virtually shut Germany off from the rest of the world. Despite the growing misery on the home front, the German leadership refused to lay out defensible and specific war aims, and by the spring of 1917, the strategy of Germany had been distilled to four main objectives: keeping its allies, Austria-Hungary, Bulgaria, and Turkey, in the war; bleeding the Entente in the trenches; executing a series of campaigns against Russia in the East, with the hope of knocking it from the war and thus freeing troops and securing grain lands; and, the key to the plan, starving the British via the U-boat campaign in the Atlantic. On the other side, Britain also had four objectives: keeping its allies, France and Italy, in the war; spreading the Central Powers by diversionary envelopment movements through the Middle East and the Balkans; protecting its empire; and, the key, starving the Germans via the continental blockade. Thus starvation of the home front became a shared strategy aggressively pursued by both sides. That fateful spring Josephus Daniels offered the best concise summary of the equation to which the Great War had been reduced. In his diary he wrote, "The stomach is the test."[102]

9. To the Bitter End

For all its agony of carnage and destruction,
the Great War of 1914–1918 settled little.

—DAVID KENNEDY, *Freedom from Fear*

As the Great War ground on, it disrupted Josephus Daniels's usually quiet domestic life. Following America's entry, his most acute personal concern was the appropriate role in the war effort for his two eldest sons, both of whom were old enough to perform military service. When the United States entered the war, Joe Jr. was twenty-two years old and serving his apprenticeship at the *News and Observer*. The second son, Worth, had just turned eighteen and was completing his first year at the University of North Carolina. The Old Man, as Daniels was often called to avoid confusion with his oldest son, was quietly agonizing over what to do about his sons when the Greensboro (N.C.) *News* settled the matter for him. Having taken an antiwar position during the diplomatic crisis with Germany, the paper, in an article Daniels labeled a "vicious, dirty" piece, published only two weeks after the United States entered the war, noted correctly that none of Daniels's four sons had yet enlisted. As Jonathan was only fifteen and the youngest, Frank, was thirteen at the time, the challenge was clearly meant for Joe Jr. and Worth. The oldest boy, physically frail and possessing poor eyesight, took the adverse publicity very hard. The Old Man noted in his diary that after the article was published, he and his eldest son "had a heart to heart talk and a cry." Joe Jr.'s "heart [was] in the paper," his father wrote, meaning the boy wanted to stay at the *N&O*, but yielding to pressure, much of which was self-generated, Joe Jr. joined the U.S. Marine Corps within the week.[1]

In his capacity as secretary of the navy, Daniels had to exempt Joe Jr. from the rigorous physical and eye exams, and concerns about his son's health caused the Old Man to suffer more than a little anxiety. In his diary the father confided that the boy "loves to be with me & all the time I am yearning to take his place & help him. The saddest thing about being a father is that striving to help a boy grow to age and not be able to do it." He added that the boy "isn't very strong. I had to waive defect in eyes for him to

331

enter & feared he would not be able to stand it; & that sleeping in room with 30-40 other men (etc.) would go hard with him." Despite these concerns, Daniels noted that Joe Jr. "takes it all bravely and cheerfully."[2] By February of the following year, Joe Jr. had earned a commission as a second lieutenant, and eventually he was sent to France. There he was subsequently promoted to first lieutenant while serving in a regiment commanded by his father's gunboat paladin, Colonel Smedley Butler. Although having a father who, as navy secretary, was nominally his superior probably did not hurt Joe's chances for a commission, the son made his own way in the corps, and though never a frontline solder, he became a solid marine. In the fall of 1918, Colonel Butler, never one to dissemble, wrote to Addie from France, noting that "Josephus is doing splendidly [as a marine]."[3] As the oldest son, and thus least protected from combat, Joe Jr. was his father's biggest concern, and the Old Man must have sighed in relief as his son managed to serve his country well without getting killed.

Daniels had hoped that Joe Jr. would be the only sacrificial lamb to come from his family. His hopes were dashed through the impetuosity of Worth. Of Daniels's four sons, unquestionably the one with whom he had the most conflict was Worth. Hardheaded and independent, Worth would be the only son who never worked at the *News and Observer* for any length of time, the only one who would not make the newspaper business his trade, and the only one who would not spend his adult life in Raleigh. From a young age, Worth sought his own way in the world, and with the country's entry into the Great War, he grew restless at the University of North Carolina in Chapel Hill. Sometime late in 1917 or early 1918, he approached his father about an appointment to the U.S. Naval Academy at Annapolis. The Old Man in turn approached Lee Overman, at the time the junior Democratic senator from North Carolina, about an Annapolis appointment for Worth. (Daniels had a better personal relationship with Overman than the state's senior senator, Furnifold Simmons. Daniels's relationship with Simmons never fully recovered from the 1912 senatorial campaign.) Overman promised that Worth would be the first alternate for an appointment in the entering class of 1918.[4]

In the meantime, seeking military service while hoping to avoid sacrificing his education, Worth had joined the naval reserves. On June 12, 1918, shortly after completing his sophomore year in Chapel Hill, he received a telegram calling him to active duty. Before Worth had to report for duty, however, his appointment to the naval academy came through (apparently Overman's first nominee withdrew), and he became a midshipman in July.

Not surprisingly, Worth's status as the son of the secretary of the navy did not sit well with some of his fellow midshipmen. He ended up in at least one knock-down fight over the charge that his father had secured him an appointment merely to help him avoid regular military service.[5] The charge stung. More critically, he left the academy after only one semester—during which the Great War ended—to return to the University of North Carolina. Daniels resented that his son quit the academy, and they argued violently. The Old Man tried to persuade Worth that, having entered the academy, he should have at least stuck it out, even though the war was over. But the headstrong Worth dropped out and returned to his studies in Chapel Hill.[6] It would not be the last time father and son clashed.

TRIUMPH

Daniels had more luck dealing with the Germans than with his second son. Combating the U-boat menace consumed most of his efforts, which largely revolved around three issues. One was the navy construction program. The expanded plan would include dramatic increases in the number of destroyers and sub-chasers, as well as an overall increase in the size of the navy. A second issue involved the use of mines to reduce the number of U-boats that escaped the North Sea to prowl the Atlantic. The third was the arrangement of convoys to protect U.S. shipping and troop transports.

With respect to the building program, Daniels, convinced that the United States must have a navy at least as large as the Royal Navy, presented Congress with a new, massive building program.[7] The result was the 2,000-ship navy. Daniels kept the dreadnoughts in the revised plan but dropped the battle cruisers. He added to his already expansive building plan 275 destroyers, 447 sub-chasers, 99 submarines, and more than 200 additional smaller ships and auxiliary vessels. When war was declared, the U.S. Navy had just over 300 vessels afloat; by the time the conflict ended, the figure was more than 2,000. Such an industrial and organizational accomplishment was tremendous by any historical standard. In the prewar period, a destroyer could be constructed in 20 to 24 months. By the end of the war, one was being constructed in less than 50 days.

As for mining the North Sea, the Hague Convention (1907) recognized mining as a legitimate act of war, so long as mining conformed to the rules associated with the close blockade. The convention declared that mines could only be deployed as "offensive" weapons in "hostile territorial waters."[8] Thus, they were viewed as an instrument in support of the (legal) close blockade. Both the British and the Germans had ignored the convention on this point, and they sowed wide expanses of the North Sea with mines. When first approached about an expanded mining campaign between Scotland and Norway—designed to keep U-boats from passing into the Atlantic via the northern route—Daniels agreed with his chief of naval operations, Admiral Benson, that it was not advisable. (The idea was pushed originally by Franklin Roosevelt and supported by Wilson; the fleet commander, Admiral Mayo; and the navy's representative in London, Admiral William Snowden Sims.) Daniels knew such an act would violate international law and Norwegian sovereignty, which troubled his conscience, especially after he had criticized the Germans and the British for two and a half years for similar transgressions. Less loftily, he questioned the technical feasibility of the barrage, and moreover, he thought the strategy too passive and too time consuming. In his diary, he expressed reservations, asking rhetorically if it would work: "North Sea too rough & will necessitate withdrawing all our ships from other work and then can we destroy the hornets nest or keep the hornets in?"[9] From the war's outset, the British had hesitated to move toward the mine barrage, though they had more reservations about the state of mining technology than any qualms about further violations of the laws of war.

FDR and the navy's technicians ultimately persuaded Daniels to push for the mining barrages despite Benson's and British objections. Daniels put aside his qualms about Norwegian sovereignty, and after much back-and-forth with the British concerning the technology and cost, which was ultimately borne by the Americans, the North Sea mine barrage was set up. In the event, the combined operations of the U.S. and British navies would lay nearly 80,000 mines. Daniels summarized mining as a "drab and perilous task . . . attended with disaster and deaths."[10]

Convoying was another point of dispute between Daniels and the British. Daniels became convinced that the surest way to get men and material across the Atlantic was through a convoy system. The senior admirals were not of one mind on this. Mayo, who had supported the mine barrage, was for convoying, as was Sims; Benson, who had been against the mine barrage, sided with the British against convoying.[11] Since the war began, the British had followed a strategy of sending single merchant ships out on the high seas. Their argument, which had merit and was supported by Benson in his correspondence with Daniels, was that convoys simply offered the U-boats a more visible target, and since a convoy could only travel as fast as its slowest member, the convoy system increased the collective exposure time of the ships in it. The British argued that the chances of a U-boat finding a single ship traveling as fast as it could were smaller than those of finding a group of ships traveling as slow as the slowest member.

What the Americans brought to the equation was the capacity to produce a large number of destroyers and sub-chasers to accompany and screen the convoys. The destroyers were small escort vessels that were fast enough to attack a U-boat. If a destroyer caught a U-boat on the surface, the sub could be sunk by the destroyer's superior firepower or by ramming; if the U-boat submerged, the destroyer could sink it or force it to the surface with underwater explosives called "depth charges." The sub-chasers were even smaller, faster craft that also carried depth charges. The speed and shallow draft of these vessels made them difficult targets for the U-boats; they were terriers to the U-boat's rats. The United States quickly geared up its industrial base for the construction of these small convoying vessels.

Once Daniels became convinced that convoying was the surest way to protect American goods and troops, he had to convince the British to go along, and then he had to get Congress to pay for the escort vessels. Neither was easy, but the British came around more quickly to convoying than to the mine barrage. Still, only after Congress agreed to supply the vast majority of the goods, ships, and men did the British agree with Daniels's plan. This outcome was, in part, the result of Admiral Sims's advocacy. On convoying he and Daniels saw eye-to-eye, and by July the system was in place.

When the United States entered the war, the majority of the cabinet held the view that defeating the U-boats and supplying the Entente with war matériel was all the United States would need to do to ensure victory. Daniels, earlier and more consistently than any of the other cabinet members, argued that the war would be won when the navy broke the U-boats at sea *and* when U.S. ground forces broke the German army in France. Only gradually did the rest of the cabinet come around to Daniels's view that ground troops would be needed for the war. Simply put, the entire cabinet finally agreed that the navy could not strangle Germany quickly enough to avoid political crises in London, Paris, and Rome. In the spring of 1917, the British admiralty was predicting that the British economy would collapse before the German economy did. Britain's senior uniformed admiral, First Sea Lord John Jellicoe, "calculated that Britain would run out of food and other needed raw materials before July [1917]."[12] When Sims reached London, his first communication with Daniels confirmed Jellicoe's pessimistic assessment. "The submarine issue is very much more serious than the people realize in America," he wrote, adding that the U-boats "constitute the real crisis of the war."[13] Sims went over the tonnage figures with Daniels, who concluded that the situation did indeed look grim for the Entente. America would immediately have to supply the British at home and the French in the field, but that would only forestall the next crisis. The war-ravaged Entente economies could not live off American credit indefinitely. For the war to end sooner rather than later, U.S. troops would be needed on the ground in France, just as Daniels had predicted.[14]

John J. "Black Jack" Pershing, who had led a punitive expedition into Mexico against Pancho Villa the previous year, had been tapped to be the commander of the American Expeditionary Force (AEF), and he was calling for 1 million men as soon as possible and 3 million in uniform over the next two years. Although Daniels objected to conscription ("Why introduce Prussianism to fight Prussianism?" he asked rhetorically in his diary),[15] he agreed that Pershing's figures would not be reached without conscription. Accordingly, Congress passed the conscription act on May 19, and the draft began the following month.[16] Daniels would have to haul these men across the Atlantic.

After the war, Daniels would frequently be asked for his opinion on the war effort and, in particular, on what was America's greatest achievement in the war. His standard answer consisted of two parts: first, raising an army of 4 million men and a navy of 600,000 men and, second, safely transporting 2 million soldiers and marines to France, all in a span of eighteen months. Daniels called it "the biggest transportation job in history."[17] Pershing agreed. After the war, the general wrote a personal note to Daniels congratulating him on the navy's success in transporting the army to France. Pershing arrived in England in June, only a month after his formal appointment as head of the AEF, and from there he went to France, where a small contingent of American troops, some supposedly shouting "Lafayette we are here," paraded through Paris on July 4. They were almost too late. The French army had mutinied in April, and Ambassador Walter Hines Page wrote from London that the British, too, were in "bad straits."[18] German leaders Hindenburg and Ludendorff shared Daniels's assessment of the war. They understood that the United States had to act quickly, but they erroneously thought that U.S. forces would not be in the field in Europe before 1919. Accordingly, they planned to end the war with a major thrust in 1918.[19] That winter, Ludendorff had told his field commanders that Germany had to strike the decisive blow "before the Americans can throw strong forces into the scales."[20]

The race was on. Would Daniels's navy be able to get the U.S. Army into the field before Germany's offensive broke the French and British on the Western Front? As the calendar turned to 1918, it looked as if the answer would be no. The problem from the administration's perspective was two-fold: creating an army and shipping it to France. On the eve of war, the U.S. Army had just over 100,000 men and a poorly trained and equipped National Guard composed of roughly the same number of troops. In eighteen months that force would grow to 4 million. But before the first three divisions could be brought into the line for an offensive in 1918, the Germans attacked. Ludendorff's offensives came in waves beginning in March 1918. In places the line buckled, and the Germans pushed the British and French back nearly fifty miles, bringing Paris within the range of German guns. In anticipation of the arrival of U.S. troops on a large scale, debate had been raging for months among the allied commanders concerning the best use of the Yanks as they arrived. British and French generals wanted the Americans fed piecemeal into already organized units, bringing the units up to full strength. Wilson and AEF commander Pershing opposed this strategy.

Wilson wanted the AEF to remain independent of the Entente, because he thought that would help the United States serve as an honest broker after the war. From the time he called for a declaration of war, Wilson had cultivated his conception of America's entry into the war as a crusade for world peace rather than victory over the Germans. In a speech to Congress on January 8, Wilson issued what became known as his Fourteen Points. In Wilson's mind, they would serve both as terms for peace and as the foundation for a new, postwar order.[21] The Fourteen Points were classic Wilson, lofty yet focused, ranging as they did from sweeping international issues of ancient origin, such as freedom of the seas, to specific acts, such as the evacuation of Montenegro. In his memoirs and in his biography of Wilson, written years later, Daniels was typically praiseworthy, calling them "Wilson's Magna Charta of World Peace" and adding that "they heartened despairing peoples."[22] At the time Wilson proposed his points before Congress, Daniels, fighting a life-and-death struggle with the U-boats while convoying supplies and troops to Europe, took a less generous view. At the cabinet meeting in which Wilson previewed the speech containing his points, Daniels conceded that Wilson's goals were exalted enough, but he argued that they should be tailored more closely toward ending the war rather than winning the postwar peace. Wilson's response to this suggestion went unrecorded, but it could not have been affirmative. Later that night, Daniels wrote in his diary that he did not think Wilson placed enough on the table to induce the Germans to end the war. "What bait is there for Germany to go into [the peace] Conference," he asked rhetorically.[23] Without that bait, the war ground on.

The situation in France in the spring of 1918 forced Pershing to compromise. In the face of Ludendorff's onslaught, some U.S. troops would have to be integrated with British and French forces. In addition to providing transport for the army, Daniels had committed a brigade of 8,000 marines to join U.S. ground forces. Pershing assigned these troops to the U.S. Army's Second Division, in which they were under the operational command of General James Harbord. As part of Ludenorff's surge toward Paris, the Germans had to clear a stretch of ground between Soissons on the Aisne and Château-Thierry. The maps called this area Belleau Wood, and beyond it lay the road to Paris, which was only thirty miles away. In a battle lasting nearly three weeks in June, the marines fought, often hand to hand, one German unit after another for control of the ground. Eventually, in a final assault that a navy report described as "tree to tree, stronghold to stronghold," the marines got the upper hand and cleared the area of Germans. The Entente line held. For their ferocity in taking Belleau Wood, the U.S. Marines supposedly earned from their battle-hardened opponents the nickname that would stick with them from that day forward, *Teufelshunden*, devil dogs. In Daniels's summary of the magnificent performance of his men, he simply said, "They saved Paris."[24]

As for the war against the U-boats, here, too, the tide turned. Earlier Daniels had written presciently that the "stomach was the test." The German economy failed the test as 1919 and the fifth winter of the war approached. It failed simply because the U.S. Navy supplied the Entente with more men and material than the German navy could sink. The war at sea and the war in the trenches were two sides of the same coin. Daniels had seen this since U.S. entry became a possibility. Mahan had synthesized how crucial the sea lanes were to a great nation, and if one interprets the ordering of Wilson's Fourteen Points as a ranking of their importance, then the naval war trumped all other military issues. In Wilson's view, freedom of the seas had been the point that led the United States into the war. Somewhat awkwardly, the notion of "freedom of the seas" was now being violated by his own navy. But in truth, when Wilson said "freedom of the seas," he meant an end to unrestricted submarine warfare rather than an end to British and American violations of international law. Subtleties of the Cruiser Rules and blockading could be worked out in the future, but in Wilson's mind even the most liberal interpretation of "free seas" would prohibit the U-boat war the Germans continued to wage. Daniels understood the hypocrisy of Wilson's position, as did the German high command, for whom Wilson's call for freedom of the seas canceled what little impetus existed to grasp his earlier peace terms. Ludendorff summarized the connection between the war at sea and the war in France: "To allow ourselves to be deprived of our submarine weapon would amount to capitulation."[25]

As Daniels predicted in his diary after first reading the Fourteen Points, Wilson had offered nothing to induce the Germans to end the war, and so they fought on; but later that summer, cracks appeared among the Central Powers. Ludendorff's offensives faltered, and the Entente and the AEF counterattacked. In the second week of September, shortly before Pershing launched his offensive, Austro-Hungarian Emperor Karl, who had been elevated to the throne following the death of the ancient Franz Joseph late in 1916, sent Wilson a peace offer. The president rejected it with little comment. Daniels, focused on Germany, did not even record a cabinet discussion of the matter in his diary. Ending the war was no longer Wilson's primary objective; the president now sought to change the world, and ending the war on Germany's or Austria's terms was not part of that equation.

Karl's offer had no impact in Washington, but it did in Berlin. The kaiser, who had been through three chancellors in the past year, now turned to his cousin, Prince Max von Baden. On October 4, the same day Prince Max took office, Bulgaria, another ally, which had left the war the last week of September, witnessed the abdication of King Ferdinand. As the dominoes began to fall, Prince Max moved toward peace. His first key act was to reject Scheer's call for more submarines, and then, hoping to secure the best terms possible in whatever form peace ultimately took, he demanded an end to unrestricted submarine warfare. When Scheer and Ludendorff refused, Prince Max obtained the kaiser's unequivocal backing, and the U-boat war ended on October 20. Daniels had won the war at sea.

After that victory, the end came quickly. Although the German army had taken a beating on the Western Front in recent months, the peace treaty with the new Bolshevik regime in Russia (signed earlier in the year) had freed manpower from the Eastern Front. Thus overall, the army remained in good enough shape to protect Germany from invasion, even though it could not muster the resources for another offensive of any size. However, Germany's economic outlook was grim at best. With winter approaching, despite the improved access to food supplies in the east, mass hunger remained a legitimate concern. With economic collapse came the specter of Bolshevism. Lenin's Russian regime threatened to spread communism throughout the disaffected areas of Europe. Although Germany had defeated Russia militarily and the Bolsheviks had agreed to a humiliating peace, communism's allure grew with the economic chaos the war had brought to Central and Eastern Europe.

Concern for the spread of communism soon became as pressing in Washington and London as it was in Berlin. Upon taking office, Prince Max had immediately addressed a note to Wilson appealing for an armistice and peace along the lines of Wilson's Fourteen Points. Prince Max's deference to the Fourteen Points was wise; Wilson did not immediately reject the German offer, as he had Austria's a month earlier. Shrewdly though, Wilson hesitated, seeking assurance that Germany sincerely sought peace rather than respite. Daniels feared that Wilson would lose the Germans if he waited too long or asked too much of them. He did not share Wilson's inclination to push the Germans a bit harder. Daniels wanted peace at almost any price the Germans were willing to pay at this stage. "I urged [Wilson] to express [his] views but not to close the door to peace," Daniels wrote of his counsel to president.[26] But Wilson was gambling that he held the winning hand, and it seemed to be working. In response to the president's hesitancy, Prince Max had sought and received an end to unrestricted submarine warfare. Wilson took this as a positive sign, and once he was convinced the Germans were serious about ending the war, he formally consulted the cabinet.

According to Daniels, the Bolshevik threat dominated other issues in that discussion. However, Wilson stubbornly refused to negotiate with either the kaiser or the military junta led by Hindenburg and Ludendorff. Despite Prince Max's efforts in the Reichstag, Hindenburg and Ludendorff essentially ran the country in the kaiser's name. Getting rid of the Hohenzollern Dynasty fit nicely in Wilson's postwar scheme, even if bringing it about would delay the end of the war. In his diary Daniels posed the question as Wilson had presented it to the cabinet: "How could he [i.e., Wilson] have correspondence with Germany under autocracy?" Daniels did not offer an answer, because he did not think the question was important. He considered just about anything to end the war as acceptable—even keeping the kaiser. In a cabinet meeting following the exchange of correspondence between Wilson and Prince Max, someone—Daniels's diary implies it was Wilson himself—suggested that if the United States could only find autocrats to speak for the Germans, "then we must go into G[ermany] and set up a government ourselves." In other words, Pershing would invade the German homeland. Daniels was aghast at this thought. In his diary, he recorded Wilson's suggestion to march to Berlin and overthrow the kaiser as "something unthinkable."[27]

Unfortunately at the time, if the Americans were not going to Berlin to set up a regime more to their liking, then the most likely postwar alternative was a Bolshevik regime seizing power as it had done in Russia. This, too, was anathema to Daniels. Although Daniels was a populist who never hesitated to use the coercive powers of the state to achieve objectives he valued, many of which were socialist in all but name, the overt atheism of the Bolsheviks led Daniels to reject their political program outright. A bit of socialism here and there to redistribute the wealth was one thing; Godless communism was, in Daniels's view, entirely different. Hoping for a bloodless coup in Berlin, Daniels confided to his diary, "Unless some sort of Gov. offers medium of communication, we might witness bolshevikism [*sic*] worse than in Russia."[28] He followed this with the rhetorical question, "Had you rather have the Kaiser or the Bolsheviks[?]"[29] Daniels thought the kaiser was the better of the two alternatives. In fact, the political leadership in Germany grew so desperate for peace while Wilson let them twist in the wind that a third option increasingly looked like a possibility.

Hindenburg and Ludendorff recognized that once peace was openly on the table, the army, which had been retreating since Pershing's late summer counteroffensives, might disintegrate quickly. If that happened, then the way to Berlin would be open. In discussing military priorities, Ludendorff supposedly said, "I want to save my army."[30] Daniels, unaware of the extent of the crisis within Germany and despairing that Wilson refused to close the deal on ending the war, prepared to fight to the bitter end. Just as the German government arranged to capitulate, he met in Washington with his British counterpart, First Lord of the Admiralty Sir Eric Geddes. Responding to intelligence reports of Scheer's plan for a new U-boat campaign, the two naval leaders prepared the strategy for combating what they expected to be an all-out submarine battle early in 1919. Following their meetings, Daniels accompanied Geddes to Washington's Union Station and then hopped a train back to Raleigh to rally the state's war bond effort. Noting in his diary that "NC had so far raised only ½ quota for bond [sales]. NC had failed & must not now," Daniels offered his *N&O* employees a sweet deal. For every $100 bond they purchased, Daniels would personally pay the first $10. He then told his department managers that he wanted 100 percent of his employees to subscribe, but if they did not, then from his own funds he would purchase whatever remained of the company's allotment.[31]

Those monies would not be necessary. After consulting with Daniels,

Secretary of State Lansing, and Army Chief of Staff Peyton March, on October 23 Wilson demanded that the kaiser abdicate before formal peace negotiations began.[32] Daniels disagreed with this strategy. He argued that the president should pursue an end to the war with whatever party controlled German forces, whether it was Wilhelm, Prince Max, or Hindenburg, but he could not convince Wilson to accept an immediate peace. In a calculated gamble, Wilson was forcing Germany to become a republic as the price of peace. Wilhelm was outraged, but he no longer had any leverage with either the Reichstag or the high command. In the *N&O* and his diary, Daniels had explicitly expressed the sentiment for hanging the kaiser and Tirpitz, and he now told Wilson that "public sentiment here wants blood or to put the Kaiser on St. Helena [the island in the South Atlantic where Napoleon had been exiled a century earlier]."[33] But that issue was separate from ending the war. The kaiser could be hanged in due time after peace was secured. Wilson dismissed Daniels's strategy. He now saw the kaiser as unimportant; peace was only part of his larger plan for a grand postwar settlement, and Germany's move to a republic would help.

While Wilson made demands for peace, the Central Powers collapsed. Talk of calling German leaders to account for the war unnerved Ludendorff, who abandoned his post and in disguise fled to neutral Sweden. On October 29, the Imperial German Navy began to mutiny; a full-scale revolt soon followed. Turkey left the war the next day. Austria's Emperor Karl sued for peace on November 3, and within forty-eight hours Prince Max accepted Wilson's terms. The kaiser had to go. On November 9, Prince Max simply proclaimed to the world Wilhelm's abdication as a fait accompli. Germany was now a republic.

The next day, Wilhelm left his homeland for exile in the Netherlands. On the same day, a Sunday, after receiving the Eucharist at an early service, Daniels met with Herbert Hoover, who had been appointed domestic food administrator. Without even taking time off to enjoy the impending armistice, they went to work on alleviating the economic situation in Europe, a situation Daniels had done much to create. In his diary, Daniels summarized his meeting with Hoover: "Allies would co-operate to secure food for people of conquered country. . . . Food must go to prevent bolshevikism & anarchy & help preserve the people. Danger of no government is call for our help."[34] On the next day, Monday, November 11, Armistice Day, Daniels rose at 2:45 A.M., and after breakfast, he again worked with Hoover, only taking time out to attend Wilson's address to Congress at 1:00 P.M. Late that evening, he attended a banquet for the Council of National Defense;

he finished a twenty-four-hour day with a late reception at the Italian Embassy that ran well past midnight.

Thus ended the War to End All Wars. "I felt the first thrill of joy in years—in fact, I had not been without distress and anxiety and strain since the beginning of the fighting in 1914," Daniels wrote.[35] By the time the armistice went into effect, the Great War had sent nearly 20 million people to their graves.[36] The influenza pandemic that began in 1918, the spread and severity of which is often attributed to the war, killed another 30 million.[37] Daniels closed this chapter of his life with a letter to his boyhood friend Henry Groves Connor: "I feel something good must come out of all this suffering and travail."[38] Daniels would live long enough to be bitterly disappointed in what came out of the Great War.

Less than a month after the armistice ended the fighting, Woodrow Wilson sailed for Europe to preside over the peace settlement and celebrate victory. Sadly, it proved to be merely "the illusion of victory."[39] That the war settled little was easy enough to see with the perspective gained from Stalingrad, Dachau, and Hiroshima—names from the abyss that was the next great war—but there were more than a few notables who predicted as much at the time. Among them was economist John Maynard Keynes, who wrote a treatise on how the Entente lost the peace. However, to many at the time, including Josephus Daniels, the war appeared to have ended with a great victory that laid the foundation for a settlement that would establish a new, more peaceful world order. He was wrong, but as one historian observes, "It is always easy, with the benefit of hindsight, to find fault with historical figures who fail to foresee revolutions."[40]

The most obvious transformation took place among the ruling houses of Europe. The Hohenzollern, Romanov, and Habsburg Dynasties—whose combined reigns of Prussia, Russia, and Austria-Hungary, respectively, had lasted more than a thousand years—became just so much ink in the history books. In Daniels's view, the world was better off. By the time the war ended, he had blamed it on the "three kaisers," who led those countries at the war's outset. From the remains of their ancient empires emerged the nation-states of Finland, Poland, Latvia, Lithuania, Estonia, Czechoslovakia, and Yugoslavia. Similarly, the Ottomans, heirs of the various Islamic empires that had threatened Christendom since the seventh century, saw their vast dominions dismembered. The resulting map of the Middle East was little more than the late-night work of cartographers in the British Foreign and Colonial Offices. They drew boundaries for the countries of Iraq, Iran, Syria, Lebanon, Saudi Arabia, and Trans-Jordan. Within five years of the war's end, Mustafa Kemal, henceforth known to the world as Atatürk, had deposed the sultan and created the Turkish republic from what was left of the Ottoman Empire.

Wilson worked on his upcoming report to Congress, and he intended his subsequent European tour before the peace conference got under way to be a victory lap. If, as Napoleon had supposedly said, victory goes to the last battalion, then Wilson, as the commander in chief of the last battalions thrown into the war, deserved the laurels. More than that, Wilson the idealist and Wilson the calculating politician recognized that winning the peace would be as important as winning the war. Daniels, whose view of monarchy was at best condescendingly dismissive, considered the abolition of the royal houses of the Central Powers an unambiguous plus for Western civilization. In this opinion he was probably joined by most Americans, but had that gain been worth the cost of the war? Both Wilson and Daniels understood that this was now the question before them. They had not always seen eye-to-eye maintaining neutrality and then fighting the war. But regarding Wilson's grand view of the peace, which was a treaty along the lines of his Fourteen Points, Daniels was onboard, at least initially.

VERSAILLES

The victors decided they would gather in Paris to discuss the foundation for a peace treaty. By the time the armistice went into effect, the Entente had grown to twenty-eight countries.[41] (Ironically, one of the last countries to join the alliance was Haiti. Its de facto ruler, Josephus Daniels, brought the country into the war on July 15, 1918.) Each country was invited to send a delegation, the size of which depended on the country's perceived contribution to the war effort. Bolivia was given one seat, for example, whereas each of the so-called Big Five—Britain, France, Italy, Japan, and the United States—would have five seats. Each delegation was, in turn, accompanied by any number of "experts"—soldiers, diplomats, and economists—with whom the delegates could consult. The experts attending the delegations of some countries numbered into the hundreds; thus the participants at the conference numbered into the thousands. As the size of the affair grew, the leaders of the Big Five decided to create a more manageable Supreme Council. This council would write the peace treaty.

Wilson told Daniels as early as October 17, more than three weeks before the armistice, that he intended to attend the peace conference.[42] Wilson's political enemies, and some of his friends, objected to his attendance. No president had ever visited Europe while in office. There was talk of a Constitutional crisis. In addition, Secretary of State Lansing thought Wilson's presence would only complicate the intense diplomatic negotiations that were certain to be a part of drawing up the treaty. However, the cabinet, with the exception of Lansing, agreed that Wilson should go. According to Daniels's diary, the matter was settled on November 12. The president was eager to accept the accolades of the civilization he imagined he had rescued, and with confidence in his powers to win the peace, he told Daniels, "I must go."[43] On December 4, Wilson left the country on the passenger liner *George Washington*. The battle of the peace was about to begin.

Wilson had listed the creation of a "League of Nations" among his Fourteen Points, and according to Daniels, from the conception of the list, the president "put the League first of all."[44] Everything else served simply as prologue to the league. "Wilson went to Paris," Daniels wrote "to secure the League as an integral part of the peace treaty. . . . To Wilson the League of Nations was as sacred as the Holy Grail."[45] In the pages of the *News and Observer*, Daniels "hailed the League as the long sought deliverance from the pestilence of war."[46] But as the head of one of the world's most powerful navies, he also recognized that the league's peacekeeping capacity would be directly proportional to the guns it had at its disposal, and in practice that would mean U.S. leadership in concert with the British and the French.

Daniels had grown personally close to Wilson during their years of service together; thus Daniels might have persuaded Wilson to temper his vision of a new world order and then helped him to develop a successful strategy for achieving a set of less ambitious goals. As it turned out, the administration's peace plan could not have been a bigger failure. Wilson deserves a good bit of the blame. In the months leading to the midterm elections of 1918, the president faced a cabinet crisis because he refused to dismiss Daniels and War Secretary Baker when they came under heavy opposition fire—for a perceived lack of preparedness, for a perceived mismanagement of the war effort, and for being, after Wilson, the most visible of the administration's members. The administration's critics demanded a more bipartisan war effort.

The length and cost of the war had led the British to adopt a coalition cabinet, which included liberals and conservatives. By the time the United States entered the war, the coalition was led by the liberal David Lloyd George, but Lloyd George's war council (confusingly also referred to as his "cabinet") was dominated by conservatives. Republicans in Washington, led from behind the scenes by Theodore Roosevelt, called for a "super cabinet," which following the British model would include some Republicans.[47] Specifically, they wanted to control the War and Navy Departments. One proposal placed former secretary of war and state Elihu Root at the head of the War Department, and none other than former president and assistant secretary of the navy Theodore Roosevelt at the head of the Navy Department.[48] The proposal made good political sense, if for no other reason than it would dampen Republican criticism of the conduct of the war, and it would give life to the administration's claims that "politics is adjourned" during the war.[49] Fortunately for Daniels's career, Wilson did not see the move as good politics; rather, he saw the proposal as "an attack upon his leadership," according to Daniels.[50]

Exactly why an arrangement that was working reasonably well for Lloyd George should be perceived as an attack on Wilson, Daniels did not address. It would have been to Wilson's credit if one could attribute his rejection of the plan to his loyalty to Daniels and Baker, but even Wilson's most ardent supporters, including Daniels, seldom emphasized loyalty as one of the president's great personal characteristics. Indeed, as Theodore Roosevelt noted, Wilson was "as insincere and cold-blooded an opportunist as we have ever had in the Presidency."[51] Wilson's rejection of the super cabinet proposal might have resulted from loyalty to Daniels and Baker, but it might just as well have resulted from his own tendency to turn "controversial questions into matters of principle, with himself occupying a moral high ground from which there could be no retreat."[52] Furthermore, his personal views of Root and, especially, TR prevented him from giving the matter the serious consideration it deserved.

The absence of any active Republican participation in the management of the war, other than that of the minority party in Congress, unleashed the more partisan elements of the party to attack the administration's own conduct of the war. The Republicans could get away with the most bitter denunciations of the war's management without taking any responsibility for it. The midterm elections cost the Democrats twenty-six seats in the House and six in the Senate; both figures were large enough to swing each house to the Republicans. Equally damaging in the long run was the bitterness sown by Wilson's partisanship at the peak of the campaign, after months of saying "politics is adjourned" during war. With the Republicans now in control of Congress, the administration would have to pay for its errors. Any treaty Wilson brought back from Europe would have to pass muster with a Republican-controlled Senate. Of this prospect, Wilson told Daniels, "We are all sick at heart."[53]

The jubilation surrounding the armistice, which went into effect the week after the election, helped pick up the morale of the cabinet. Furthermore, wrapping up the war, feeding Europe, and planning for the peace conference kept the key players, including Daniels, busy. But Wilson almost immediately compounded his errors in the recent campaign by making a series of disastrous choices for the U.S. commission to the peace conference. Wilson appointed himself to head the delegation, and counting Lansing, who had to go, that left three openings. A case could be made for any number of strategies. One would be to name a bipartisan commission. Another would be to name a commission of elder statesmen whose reputations were above reproach. What was needed was a group of men whose counsel might be rejected but whose motives would never be challenged. Such a group could bring home a peace that the people and the Congress would embrace.

Daniels saw this clearly enough. Tied up with the navy and deemed ultrapartisan, he was never seriously considered for one of the posts. (He would join Wilson later, when the postwar naval issues were being negotiated.) Still, the president sought his counsel on the matter, and in a letter dated November 14, Daniels proposed that the president blend the bipartisan and the "great man" approaches by appointing a sitting senator (either a Democrat or a sympathetic Republican), Bryan, and former president Taft. A senator would represent consultation with the legislative branch, a wise bridge-building exercise in light of the recent election returns. As for Bryan and Taft, no one would question the integrity of either man. Both had recently been giants of domestic politics; neither was a political threat in the future; and they represented both sides of the political spectrum. It was a good recommendation, but Wilson rejected it. Using the sophistry of the political theorist that he was, Wilson argued that appointing a senator would violate the separation of powers, as the man would be called upon to vote twice on the resulting treaty, once as a representative of the executive branch and once as a senator when the document was submitted for ratification. (Daniels might have pointed out that this was exactly the idea!) Concerning Bryan, Wilson argued that his detractors would think him "too easy," and as for poor Taft, Wilson did not offer a reply.[54]

In fact, Wilson did not appoint a member of the cabinet, a senator, a leading Republican, or an elder statesman. Wilson had lost faith in Lansing, a man with "little real ability of any kind," according to the president, and so Wilson had decided to be his own foreign minister.[55] That was a mistake. As a leading diplomatic historian put it, Wilson "lacked experience in diplomacy and hence an appreciation of its limits."[56] John Maynard Keynes, who attended the conference as a member of the British delegation, was even harsher in his judgment of the president's subsequent performance, noting that Wilson possessed the troubling "intellectual apparatus of self deception."[57] The peace conference was to be Wilson's great performance, and it was to be a one-man show. Thus he filled in the other three slots on the commission with men who would either support his efforts or, at least, stay out of his way. One of these was his confidant and roving ambassador, Colonel House. The military representative would be General Tasker Bliss, who played no role of any substance in Paris. The final member of the team was the diplomatist Henry White, whose primary role was to educate the other members of the party about diplomatic protocol and etiquette.

As Wilson and his team left for Europe to ensure world peace, Daniels remained in Washington focusing on four tasks: shipping food to Europe, bringing the troops home from Europe, planning for the postwar navy, and planning for a renewal of the blockade should Germany refuse whatever peace terms the victors offered. Food supplies were delivered in conjunction with Herbert Hoover's Food Administration. Daniels respected Hoover and was in awe of the future president's efforts at feeding, first, Belgium and, later, much of continental Europe. In print Daniels referred to Hoover as "the Almoner" and described his efforts as "holy work." But even before Hoover revealed himself to be a partisan Republican, the two men did not hit it off personally. After getting to know Hoover and working with him closely, Daniels described him as a technocrat, an "able administrator" but a cold man with no sense of humanity.[58] Despite the lack of personal warmth between the two, they worked well together, and in the winter of 1918–19, along with shipping board head Edward Hurley, they prevented much of Europe from starving.[59]

Daniels conducted his planning of the navy's future on two fronts, one in Congress and one in Paris. Daniels and his enemies in Congress had rotated their respective positions 180 degrees since the war began. At the outset of the war, as a means of maintaining neutrality, Daniels had hesitated to expand the navy too rapidly, thinking that this would be seen by the British and the Germans as needlessly provocative, perhaps leading them to aggressive actions that would bring America into the war. Now he realized a large navy was the key to peace. If the British had feared Germany's navy, they might have negotiated a bit harder in 1914. Similarly, if the Germans had feared U.S. naval power, they would not have been as aggressive in their pursuit of the U-boat war. Daniels proposed to extend his earlier massive naval building program for at least three more years. Confusingly, Daniels's original major building plan—drawn up in 1915, passed by Congress in 1916, and expanded and accelerated in 1917 and 1918—was sometimes referred to as the "three-year program." Since all of the ships in the plan had not been constructed by the time the armistice went into effect, in his "new" three-year program, Daniels was arguing for the completion of the original plan with some subsequent revisions, such as the removal of the battle cruisers and the addition of aircraft carriers, but which would now take six years to complete. By 1919, the program had been extended in time and reduced in size, but even with the changes, Daniels observed that after the completion of the plan, the U.S. Navy would be at least "equal to the most powerful [navy] maintained by any other nation in the world."[60]

Among the advances Daniels proposed was an expansion of the navy's aviation activities. Daniels has been criticized as an opponent of naval aviation. This criticism, which was largely the result of a dispute with army aviator and strategic bombing proponent General Billy Mitchell, is unjust. Daniels's dispute with Mitchell came over claims that land-based bombers made the battleship obsolete. As the story has it, when told of Mitchell's claim, Daniels supposedly said, "That idea is so damned nonsensical and impossible that I'm willing to stand bareheaded on the bridge of a battleship while that nitwit [i.e., Mitchell] tries to hit it from the air."[61] This version of events, which given the language and syntax ascribed to Daniels is almost certainly not accurate, nonetheless does reflect Daniels's skepticism about some of the claims of the early advocates of air power. In fact, Daniels was a proponent of naval aviation.[62] He was the first navy secretary to fly, and he commissioned the first transatlantic flight by a group of U.S. naval aviators. (Charles Lindbergh's later flight earned fame as the first *solo* crossing.) Furthermore, it was Daniels who scrapped the battle cruisers that ultimately became the navy's first aircraft carriers. Indeed, in Daniels's 1919 annual report to Congress, he wrote of "the necessity of developing aviation as an integral part of our military and naval forces. When an airship can fly from America to Europe in a few hours, the ocean is no longer a dependable protection against possible attack."[63] Those were not the words of a man who was skeptical about naval-based air power.

Hoping to see his revised building program approved, Daniels would be sorely disappointed by the final session of the 65th, and now lame-duck, Congress. Testifying throughout the winter before the House and Senate Naval Affairs Committees and the joint Military Affairs Committee, Daniels argued for the funds to create his two-ocean navy, the largest in the world.

As the sessions dragged on, he began to think that war weariness and fiscal concerns would prevent the Democrats from acting before the Republicans took over in 1919. He confided to his diary, "Are they [i.e., his Democratic colleagues] resolved not to let the bill pass at this session?"[64] He even persuaded Wilson to send a cable from Paris in which the president said, "It would be fatal not to build the [new] three year programme."[65] In fact, the session would expire without Congress passing a new naval appropriations bill. The next time Congress convened, the Republicans would be in charge.

With little to show for his efforts on the home front, Daniels left for Paris. There he would negotiate the status of the navy in the postwar settlement. Although Wilson's initial objective when he left the country in December had been to lay the foundation for *a* peace conference that would produce a treaty, by the time Daniels got to France, the conference in Paris had turned into *the* peace conference. As one historian of the treaty put it, "By the end of January 1919, the main outlines of the peace settlements were emerging."[66] Negotiations progressed rapidly because the leaders of the Great Powers had decided that their fellow countrymen as well as the lesser powers would have no voice in the peace. On January 12, the Big Five—Clemenceau, Lloyd George, Orlando, Prince Saionji of Japan, and Wilson—decided that, along with their respective foreign ministers, they would form the Supreme Council, or the Council of Ten, as it was sometimes called. During January and February, the Supreme Council laid out the key issues its members would address: territorial settlements, the fate of minority populations, reparations, and the creation of a League of Nations, which was expected to establish, in turn, the postwar naval balance.

With the decision-makers and the issues identified, the leaders took a midwinter break to return to their homelands to shore up support for what was to come in the spring. Wilson arrived in the United States on February 24. He remained for two weeks, and politically things went very badly. For a man who had spent only two years in elected office before becoming president, Wilson proved to be a deft politician on many fronts, successfully maneuvering through any number of political minefields. His domestic New Freedom program was an unequivocal success. He had remained behind the march to war while it was a political loser, leaping to the front just as the momentum inexorably shifted.

Despite this record of success, Wilson's inability to compromise when convinced of his own righteousness was about to cost him what he saw as his greatest victory. In his two years as governor of New Jersey and six as president, he had never been forced to deal with an opposition that controlled both houses of the legislature. Wilson's experience as chief executive had been more like that of a prime minister, who could obtain the legislation he wanted, than the head of state forced to defer to the legislative branch. Despite his rhetoric concerning the other issues at the peace conference, Wilson had distilled his contribution to the new world order down to creating the League of Nations. Getting it approved in Paris and ratified in Washington became an ordeal.

In February, the league's prospects remained bright. The Democrats still followed the president, and although Lansing and Wilson were undergoing a nasty split, the rest of the cabinet, led most vocally by Daniels, supported the league. In contrast, though they now controlled both houses of Congress, the Republicans were split on foreign policy. Since its formation, the Republican Party had been the party of northern capital; more recently it had become the party of international engagement, the party of amity with the Entente in general and the British in particular. In short, northern capital decided there was more money to be made in trade than in isolationism, and the northeastern wing of the Republican Party wanted to profit from that trade. However, the midwestern branch of the party contained a hardcore isolationist faction.

The leader of the international faction was Henry Cabot Lodge of Massachusetts. Cultured and haughty, a product of Harvard when it was the finest Protestant finishing school in the country, Lodge could not have found a single social equal among Wilson's cabinet or inner circle. The fact was that Lodge could not stand Wilson. But that did not prevent the politician in Lodge from doing business with the president. The idea of creating a new world order that would ensure the future peace appealed to Lodge. Daniels even wrote that Lodge "had been one of the earliest advocates of a league to secure peace."[67] Like Wilson, he saw the war as a costly and avoidable mistake. (He was also a vocal critic of Daniels's management of the navy). But one fundamental disagreement kept Lodge and Wilson from hammering out a deal on the postwar order. They disagreed on the terms of the best policy to ensure the peace. The path to the Great War convinced Wilson and Daniels that the balance-of-power approach—the collection of treaties and military alliances—that the Great Powers had used to maintain the prewar peace had, in fact, only led to war. They placed their faith in what came to be referred to as collective security. All members of the league would support all other members of the league.

In contrast, Lodge saw this as folly. It would only drag the United States into an endless number of disputes among the small nations with which

America shared little or no strategic interest. Why should the United States enter *any* agreement that involved it in a dispute between Lithuania and Latvia? And what if those disputes spilled over into the Soviet Union or the newly independent Poland? Wasn't this how the Great War got started in the first place? The nation-state of Serbia, where the war had begun, no longer even existed. Lodge argued that the failure of the prewar order had been a failure of will on the part of the democratic powers, Britain and France, to project enough military might to intimidate the militarist Germans and keep them from starting a general conflagration. Fear, not amity, prevented war. The solution was to keep the Germans down, ignore the smaller states, and align with the British and French, while maintaining enough military strength to trounce either if it became in the country's interest to do so. Although this position became known as the balance-of-power argument, it was really about maintaining an unambiguous surplus of power in the hands of the world's major democracies. While perhaps a minority position in Washington at the time, Lodge's thinking was not without logic.

The line between collective-security and balance-of-power arguments was drawn during Wilson's visit in late February. Through speeches and meetings with members of Congress, Wilson revealed his strategy. Lodge went to work combating it, as Wilson prepared to return to the conference to finalize the peace treaty's details. The president returned to France during the first week of March. Josephus and Addie Daniels followed on the 15th. They sailed on the USS *Leviathan*, which, prior to being interned at the outset of the war, had been the German passenger liner *Vaterland*. The party arrived at Brest on March 23. There, Josephus and Addie had an emotional reunion with their oldest son, Joe Jr., who was now a captain on Smedley Butler's staff. Butler generously assigned young Daniels to accompany his father during the navy chief's time in Europe.

From Brest Daniels visited various Marine posts on his way to Paris. He reached the City of Lights late on March 25, and early the next day he began consultations on the naval terms in the peace treaty. So began what Daniels would come to call the Sea Battle of Paris. The fight over the size of the world's postwar navies was really just an extension of the fundamental dispute of the terms of the League of Nations, a battle between collective security and a balance of power. Proponents of the league argued that, under the terms of collective security, the league's navy would be the world's navy, and thus league members could cut the size of their navies and thus their naval expenditures. This would leave the British with the world's largest

navy, and in the aggregate, there would be a much smaller number of war-
ships on the earth. The British advocated this view. They currently had
the world's largest navy (though if the new Republican Congress approved
Daniels's plan, the United States would soon catch up); they still had a vast
global empire to protect; and they were broke. Thus another naval arms
race like the one they had just gone through with the Germans was out of
the question. In short, the British saw the league as a way to maintain their
supremacy of the seas without having to pay for the privilege.

The primary advocates of British policy in Paris were First Lord of the
Admiralty Walter Long, Daniels's civilian counterpart who had only recently replaced Geddes, and First Sea Lord Admiral Sir Rosslyn Wemyss,
who had replaced Jellicoe at the end of 1917. Lloyd George charged Long
and Wemyss with persuading Daniels and Admiral Benson, who joined his
chief in Paris, to go along with Britain's plans for the postwar naval settlement. Daniels, whose distrust of the British quickly led him to reject collective security when it came to naval power, summarized the British position:
"Admiral Wemyss made the direct proposal that . . . [the parties] agree to
a fixed ratio of Naval strength, conceding to Great Britain continued pri-
macy. . . . Wemyss felt strongly that the far-flung British Empire was entitled
to be mistress of the seas."[68] Long supported his admiral. "It was a fundamental of British policy," a historian observed, "that its navy must be larger
than any other, ideally larger than any two other navies. But the British
knew they could not keep up financially in a naval race [with the United
States]."[69] Thus they hoped to persuade the Americans to avoid such a race
and surrender naval supremacy to Britain, as the world had done in the
century following Napoleon's defeat. This position was supported by the
isolationists back in the United States, who asked, Why should U.S. taxpayers pay for a big navy, when the British were willing to patrol the world's
sea lanes at no cost to Americans?

Recognizing that Wilson put the league above all other considerations,
the wily Lloyd George had Long use the league as both carrot and stick in
his negotiations with Daniels. According to Daniels's notes, in their first
meeting Long told Daniels that Lloyd George and the British people "would
not support the League of Nations if the United States accompanied it with
a big Naval building program, for Great Britain could not consent for any
other nation to have supremacy of the seas."[70] Although Daniels supported
the league, he rejected British naval superiority. The British strategy was to
drive a wedge between Wilson, on one hand, and Daniels and his admirals,
on the other, and to an extent it worked. Before leaving for France, Wilson

had said of the postwar naval settlement that he wanted "as many weapons as my pockets will hold as to compel justice."[71] But now, focusing on obtaining the league, Wilson did not get directly involved in the naval issue, and he hoped Daniels could work out a compromise with the British on his own. Whereas Long had the explicit support of Lloyd George, Daniels felt as if he were being abandoned by Wilson. Disappointed, he confided to his diary, "President hoped we [i.e., Daniels and the British] would talk it over and reach some right understanding."[72]

The negotiations with the British caused Daniels to alter his view on a postwar collective security agreement. Demands by the British that they remain the world's maritime power simplified his position in Paris. He stuck to his naval building program, which would put the U.S. Navy ahead of the Royal Navy in a few years. In Daniels's view, league or no league, the United States must have a two-ocean navy, and that navy must be equal to or better than any other navy in the world. Other than naval policy, Daniels stuck with Wilson's collective security objectives, but if collective security failed, then he wanted to be able to fall back on the world's most powerful navy. Since the British had no effective postwar building plan (the money simply wasn't there), Daniels's plan would soon, certainly by the early 1920s, achieve his objective.[73] If the British were to support the league, and if the members of the league, including the British, were to agree to an across-the-board reduction in their navies, then Daniels would be willing to trim his current program to keep it on par with Britain's end-of-war strength. This would give him enough dreadnoughts and cruisers to fill out Atlantic and Pacific fleets and still, over time, put the United States ahead of the Royal Navy. If all of those conditions were met, then he was prepared to go before the new Republican Congress and lower the spending profile of his plan. However, on one point Daniels remained firm. British mastery of the seas was over. If Daniels had his way, the United States would have the world's strongest navy. If the British wanted an arms race, he would give them one. Daniels shared these thoughts directly with Lloyd George at a breakfast meeting on April 1. In turn, Lloyd George directly threatened Daniels with the league. As Daniels put it in his diary, "L.G. said L[eague] of N[ations] would be worth nothing if we continued to build."[74] Despite Wilson's quest for the league, in negotiating with the British, Daniels was choosing a large navy over collective security. Nothing was resolved. The two sides remained at an impasse.

After a brief tour of the continent with Addie, which he temporarily interrupted to meet with Pershing in a ceremony honoring the Marquis de

Lafayette, Daniels went to England and stayed at Windsor Castle as a guest of George V and Queen Mary.[75] Daniels went back to Paris to confer with Wilson but returned to London on May 1. After another visit with the king, at Buckingham Palace—during which George V chided Daniels, the press lord, that freedom of the press had created a press "autocracy" in the United States—Daniels met with Long and Wemyss and was prepared to resume the battle where they had left it in early April. On this occasion, however, the British leaders did not immediately renew the dispute with their American cousin; rather, displaying a uniquely British grace, Long honored Daniels with a dinner at Parliament attended by nearly 100 members of the House of Commons. After dinner, Daniels met privately with a prominent guest: Winston Churchill.

The Churchill whom Daniels met that evening over brandy and cigars, all of which were consumed by Churchill, was not the great man he was to become twenty years later, but even then he was impressive. The grandson of the Duke of Marlborough, Churchill had become a household name in England when, as a young cavalry officer, he wrote a series of newspaper dispatches from three legendary colonial expeditions. Incredibly, between 1897 and 1899 Churchill managed to see action with the Malakand Field Force against Pashtuns on India's northwest frontier; with General H. H. Kitchener's expedition up the Nile to Omdurman, where Churchill witnessed the last great cavalry charge of the British Empire; and in the Boer War. These experiences later became the basis for best-selling books on Britain's colonial wars in India, the Sudan, and South Africa. He subsequently leveraged his famous name and literary success into a political career and served as secretary of state for war when Daniels met him.

The two men did not get along well. Daniels made the case for continuing the planned U.S. building program. His experience in Europe had not diminished his enthusiasm for building the world's largest navy. The machinations of the Europeans, the British in particular, only reinforced his conviction that the United States must be prepared to be self-sufficient militarily. That meant a two-ocean navy, and that meant building the world's largest navy in competition with the British, if necessary. He had arrived at this point entirely through experience. Unlike Mahan or Tirpitz, Daniels was no naval theorist, just as he was no political or economic theorist. His convictions as the head of the navy, in politics, and in economics were all based on empirical observation. As one of his sons put it, "He didn't philosophize about things."[76] As was said of his hero Carlyle, Daniels "was interested not in axioms and systems but in characters and situations."[77]

Daniels's arguments on his navy's behalf did not impress Churchill, himself a former first lord of the admiralty. The future prime minister was as blunt as Long and Wemyss had been, perhaps more so. No matter the cost, he told Daniels, the British simply would not become a second-class naval power. If Daniels wanted to up the ante, then he could do as he pleased with the U.S. naval building program, but as Daniels stated in his diary, Churchill added that Great Britain "would build as big ships & guns as any" other country.[78] Daniels doubted the British had the money to match his naval building plan, but it would be up to Parliament to decide whether the effort was worth it. With that, the two men parted civilly if not amicably.

Back in Paris, the situation had not improved for the Americans. Since returning in March, Wilson had decided that Lloyd George and the British were doing everything they could to protect and promote the British Empire, while Clemenceau and the French were doing everything they could to keep Germany down. All other considerations were secondary to his partners in peace, or so Wilson had convinced himself. In any case, by the time Daniels returned to Paris later in May, Wilson's view of the conference had evolved. Wilson was convinced that if the British and French could focus single-mindedly on what they wanted, then so could he, and he wanted the League of Nations. In return for focusing on the league, Wilson was prepared to surrender on many other issues that he now persuaded himself were unimportant. Wilson had also come to the view that the British would never compromise on the naval issue, and more importantly, that British naval supremacy would threaten the league. Thus he now backed Daniels and his admirals completely on the three-year building program. (In a private note to Daniels, marked "Confidential," Wilson noted that the British had misused their mastery of the seas: "As you and I agreed the other day, the British Admiralty had done nothing constructive in the use of their navy." It was now the Americans' turn to rule the seas.)[79] If the British objected and wanted to match the United States dollar-for-dollar, then that would be up to Parliament and the British taxpayers. Daniels had already created the organizational apparatus for a much larger Pacific fleet (in the prewar navy, the size of the Atlantic fleet dominated U.S. forces in the Pacific), and soon the navy was moving ships to the West Coast. In his memoirs, Daniels proudly proclaimed that by refusing to compromise at Paris, "I gave the country a Two-Ocean Navy."[80] By the time he left office, ten dreadnoughts would be stationed in the Pacific.[81]

Daniels was relieved that his chief had agreed to disagree with the British and would not sign any peace agreement or other treaty that surrendered

U.S. supremacy of the seas. Wilson asserted to Daniels that the three-year program remained the administration's formal policy. Uncharacteristically, Daniels requested this in writing. This was not his normal way of dealing with Wilson, and the request probably reflected House's influence on the negotiations. For reasons known only to himself, House had been playing a double game between Wilson, Daniels, Benson, and the British.[82] To Daniels, House preached flexibility with the British. To Benson, House hinted that Daniels was going soft during the negotiations, so Benson asked Wilson to keep Daniels away from Paris during the negotiations. (This Wilson wisely refused to do.) To Wilson, House recommended taking an inflexible position on naval matters, while to the British he hinted that a compromise might be possible. Daniels was known to refer to House as a "yes man." After discovering House's double dealing, Daniels referred to him as the "yes-yes man."[83]

Before he left the president, to ensure no meddling by or misunderstanding with House, Daniels wrote a note in Wilson's voice and showed it to the president for his explicit approval, "to be sure," in Daniels's words, "of no error." It read, "Please say that you [i.e., Daniels] have seen the President and have found him deeply concerned about the whole method with which the entire peace program is being handled and that you have been instructed by the President to say that he cannot make any sort of agreement until he sees what the outcome is going to be." In other words, the Sea Battle of Paris was over. Regardless of what happened with the league, the peace treaties would contain no grand naval arms settlement. Although the battle was a draw, Daniels won the larger war. The U.S. naval program would go forward to Congress just as Daniels had planned, regardless of the outcome of the conference. Of course, getting his plan approved by the new Republican Congress would be a different war altogether.

———

Upon Wilson's return to Paris in March, the leaders of the four Western powers decided that the Supreme Council included too many members. The key players agreed that a smaller group would more efficiently cut through the knots of postwar diplomacy than the larger group would. Accordingly, the Council of Ten became the Council of Five, with only the heads of the Big Five delegations admitted. This quickly became the Council of Four, as the Japanese representative was excluded from the final round of bargaining.[84] Japan's delegation had been charged with two objectives: obtaining territorial concessions in East Asia and the Pacific and getting a "racial equality clause" inserted into the treaty through the League of Nations covenant.[85] They got half of what they came for. The conference granted to Japan China's Shantung Peninsula, which had been controlled by Germany before the war, and the Council of Four confirmed Japanese control of Port Arthur and the Korean Peninsula. These three holdings gave Japan a firm foothold on the Asian mainland that represented "a dagger pointed at the heart of China."[86] There was to be no self-determination or political independence for the Koreans and no territorial integrity for the Chinese. The deal cut with the Japanese violated as clearly as any other at the conference calls for "self-determination" and "political independence and territorial integrity." The compromise cost the president much credibility.

The British had brought the Japanese into the war and onto the Supreme Council as their new partners in the Far East, a buffer against Germany's imperial aspirations. Lloyd George supported their claims. Clemenceau saw no threat from Japan to France's holdings in Indochina, so he went along with Lloyd George. It was clear that the Japanese were going to get something for siding against the Germans. However, Wilson was inclined to be stubborn with the Japanese. The administration had averted exchanging shots with Japan during the first foreign policy crisis of his administration, and Daniels advised Wilson that Japan posed an immediate threat to America's interests in the Pacific, specifically, the navy's base at Pearl Harbor in Hawaii.[87] Furthermore, American Christian groups were actively engaged in evangelism in China, and they opposed Japan's encroachment there. Finally, Japanese demands for the explicit recognition of racial equality in the treaty rubbed Wilson and Daniels the wrong way. Despite his years at Princeton, Wilson never abandoned the sense of racial superiority he acquired growing up in the South. The president had supported the segregation of employment in the federal government, and his strongest political support came from the region in which African Americans had been disenfranchised. Racial equality was not a concept from which he took any comfort, and he did not want it embedded in his treaty. Japan could keep Korea and have a slice of China, but that was it. There would be no equality clause, and with that the Japanese were excluded from all subsequent discussions of any significance.

Thus the Council of Ten was reduced to the Council of Four. It soon became the Council of Three. On May 5, while Daniels was still in London lunching at the Ritz, the Italian delegation left Paris in protest of the territorial settlements in Eastern Europe. While Western Europe had stabilized and been fed through the efforts of Hoover and Daniels (and the army, which had assisted with food distribution on the ground), the East descended into chaos. Within six months of the armistice, still months from the signing of the major peace treaties, there were no fewer than fourteen "small" wars being pursued actively in Europe.[88] The subsequent battles for Danzig and Fiume would cause much hardship. Daniels was involved in both.

In an age and region in which land transportation was primitive and costly, ports offered crucial economic access to the rest of the world. As such, the Baltic port of Danzig and the Adriatic port of Fiume became key sticking points in the forthcoming treaties. Daniels only advised Wilson on Danzig, warning against taking it from Germany (sound advice, as it turned out, which was ignored), but he found himself in the middle of the fight over Fiume. When the war ended, the Italians demanded territory from Austria: the South Tyrol; a slice of Slovenia, including Fiume; and various holdings up and down the Adriatic. These claims dated from the Treaty of London in 1915, which had helped bring Italy into the war on the Entente's side. Wilson, again ignoring the principle of self-determination, handed the German-dominated Tyrol to the Italians. Orlando was not satisfied. He demanded the Adriatic holdings promised under the London agreement. However, the subsequent creation of Yugoslavia complicated that arrangement. The British wanted a friend in the Balkans. Lloyd George pressured the Italians, who were willing to surrender other claims in the Adriatic, but Italy would not surrender the Istrian Peninsula, southeast of Venice, and the naval base at Fiume.

Wilson told Daniels that "Italy had no just claim to Fiume," and the president, agreeing with Lloyd George, argued that a pro-Western Yugoslavia would reduce the risk of another crisis in the region like the one that had started the Great War in 1914.[89] More importantly to Wilson, the creation of the viable state of Yugoslavia was a corollary of one of his Fourteen Points, which called for autonomy from Austria for the South Slavs; giving Fiume to the Italians was not. Still, Wilson appeared willing to listen to arguments on the matter, and he charged Daniels with looking into the issue when he visited Rome. The Italian ambassador to the United States, Count Macchi di Cellere, who was in Paris at the time, visited Daniels before he left for Rome. Cellere was one of Daniels's best friends in the diplomatic corps (Daniels had celebrated the armistice at the Italian Embassy in Washington), and the two men spoke frankly on the subject. Cellere confided that if the Big Three denied Fiume to the Italians, then Orlando would walk out on the peace talks. Daniels made no promises. In Rome, King Victor Emmanuel was a gracious host, but he, too, pushed Italian claims in the Adriatic. In meetings with Daniels, the king emphasized the historic animosities between the Italian and Slavic peoples that occupied either side of the Adriatic. Since the armistice, much violence had accompanied the pressing of Italian claims to territories up and down the Yugoslav coast. Daniels concluded that there was no easy solution to the territorial disputes in the region. He considered Italy a more stable polity than Yugoslavia, and the Italians a more civilized people than the Yugoslavs. After speaking with Cellere and the king, Daniels began to question Wilson's intransigence with respect to Fiume. Daniels agreed with Italian foreign minister Sydney Sonnino, who questioned Wilson's strategy for the region by offering a challenge: "Go to the Balkans and try an experiment with the Fourteen Points."[90] Daniels had been there, and as a result he sided with the Italians.

However, before Daniels could speak to Wilson again about the subject, his admirals in the region advised against giving Fiume to the Italians, arguing that Yugoslav friendship was more valuable than satisfying Italy. Called back to Paris to report, Daniels was again met by Cellere. This time, the ambassador held nothing back in pleading Italy's case to his friend. Daniels recorded the details in his diary. According to Cellere, the communists and the nationalists were tearing Italy apart. If Orlando could not secure Fiume, his government would fall, the country would descend into chaos, and "Bolshevism would be enthroned." Daniels claimed that the ambassador "spoke almost with tears in his eyes so deep was his feeling."[91]

Daniels met with Wilson the next day, April 10. Going against the wishes of his admirals, he clearly went into the meeting determined to soften Wilson's position on Fiume, having failed to move the president on Danzig. In his memoirs and diary, for any given subject of import, Daniels had developed a way of communicating his position relative to that of Wilson's. If the two men agreed, Daniels said so. When they did not agree, Daniels rarely stated as much; rather, he would carefully juxtapose their positions in a distant or philosophical way. His summary of the debate over Fiume offers an example. "I asked myself," he wrote, "whether Wilson was right in the rigid attitude he had taken."[92] This was Daniels's way of saying he disagreed with the president. Furthermore, with respect to Fiume, Daniels offered no support for the Yugoslavs; all of his recorded sympathies were with the Italians. Accordingly, Daniels advised Wilson to reconsider the harsh line he had drawn through the Adriatic.

As he had concerning their disputes over the administration's pro-British neutrality, Wilson rejected Daniels's position on Italy. The Italians did not get Fiume. Orlando walked out of the conference the first week of May, and his government fell in June. In September, a group of Italian nationalists led by Gabrielle D'Annunzio seized Fiume and established an independent state. A year later they declared war on Italy, which had descended into the chaos Cellere had predicted. Italy was not extricated from that chaos until two years later, when former newspaper editor Benito Mussolini, who had studied D'Annunzio's coup in Fiume, staged a coup of his own in Rome and established Europe's first fascist dictatorship.

With Orlando's departure, only Clemenceau, Lloyd George, and Wilson—the Big Three—would be left to determine the terms of the peace. The peace agreement they created, thus officially ending the Great War, is typically referred to as the Versailles Treaty. But in fact, the peace conference ultimately generated five separate treaties, one for each of the former members of the Central Powers—Germany, Austria, Hungary, Bulgaria, and Ottoman Turkey. Each treaty was subsequently referred to by the location at which it was signed. The first and most important of these was the treaty dealing with Germany, and as it was signed at Versailles (symbolically, the site of the creation of the German Empire forty-eight years earlier), it became known as the Versailles Treaty. It was the most controversial of the five treaties. The Fiume crisis had not occurred in a vacuum. At the same time that the Big Three were drawing lines between Italy and its neighbors, they were carving the German Reich into the new German Republic. As Orlando stewed over Fiume, the German government was sending a delegation to receive what it expected to be a proposal of terms for peace.

By the time the Germans arrived in Paris, the Big Three agreed that the German treaty would contain the following: Germany would lose roughly 13 percent of its prewar territory and 10 percent of its population; plebiscites would be held in parts of East Prussia and Silesia, two German-dominated regions that were no longer part of Germany; Germany would be excluded from the League of Nations; and it would be prohibited from maintaining a credible army or navy. The main sticking point was reparations. After much abstruse calculating, the matter was turned over to a commission, which after even more abstruse calculating, came up with a figure of 34 billion gold dollars. The figure was astronomical for the time. On a per capita basis, in today's money, the figure would have been roughly $40,000 for every man, woman, and child in Germany. It dwarfed the sum of the reparations attached to the other four treaties ending the war—though in the end Germany would pay relatively little of this amount.[93] The Big Three were about to sow the seeds of the next world war.

To his credit, Daniels maintained reservations about the settlement. He had been ignored on Danzig, and presciently he wrote in his diary that without a strong international peacekeeping force, to be maintained by the future League of Nations, which he suspected would never be created, there would be war with Germany over the settlement: "Without League [of Nations] there will be trouble with Germany."[94] On this he agreed with embittered German veteran Adolf Hitler, whose political career would soon rise on, among other things, his speeches denouncing the treaty.

As the German delegation arrived in Paris, Daniels prepared to return to the United States. On the positive side of the ledger, he had maintained a good working relationship with the civilian and military leaders of the Entente, despite their disagreements. Simultaneously, he, more than any other person, had prevented the peace talks from moving toward a naval arms treaty that would have been, in his view, detrimental to the United States. He had become the country's most prominent advocate of a big navy. On the other side of the ledger, he had disagreed with Wilson over the settlements in the Adriatic and the Baltic, and on both counts the president had ignored Daniels's position. Given that those settlements eventually contributed to the rise of Mussolini and Hitler and thus to World War II, one must entertain the thought that Wilson would have done better to take Daniels's advice on the territorial settlements.

When the Germans arrived at Versailles, contrary to their expectations, the treaty was presented to them as a take-it-or-leave-it offer, with the alternative to signing being the renewal of hostilities. The nonnegotiable nature of the settlement meant Germany had no recourse to the unfavorable territorial revisions, and an article establishing German guilt for the war led logically to the demand for reparations. The German foreign minister and head of its delegation, Count Ulrich von Brockdorf-Rantzau, said of the Big Three, "They could have expressed the whole thing more simply in one clause—'*L'Allemagne renounce à son existence*' (Germany surrenders all claims to its existence)." The German chancellor, Philipp Scheidemann, supported his colleague's view of the treaty. "What hand would not whither," he said, "which placed this chain upon itself and upon us?"[95] Refusing to offer that hand, Brockdorf-Rantzau resigned. However, with no alternative (the German navy had been scuttled by its own men while the ships were interned at the British naval base at Scapa Flow, and the army was in no position to resist the Entente), Scheidemann's government ultimately agreed to the terms and directed the new foreign minister, Hermann Müller, accompanied by Johannes Bell, minister of transportation, to sign, which they did on June 28. Over the next year, treaties would be signed with the other four members of the Central Powers, but in everyone's mind the Great War was officially over. The following day, Sunday, June 29, Daniels honored the event with his mother by receiving Holy Communion in the little church at Mount Vernon.

The treaty never had a chance in the United States. Partisan wrangling, Wilson's unwillingness to compromise on the treaty's terms, and concerns about the efficacy of collective security doomed it. The change of power in Congress following the recent midterm elections gave the Republicans, led by Henry Cabot Lodge, leverage to demand concessions, the most important of which revolved around the League of Nations. Isolationists, as well as many internationalists, were troubled by the league's role as the guarantor of collective security. Critics saw the league as a sure means of involving the largest number of nations in the smallest disputes. Despite publicly supporting the treaty and the league, Daniels was not unsympathetic to these concerns. Regardless of any collective commitment, the experience of the German navy in the late war had taught him that the United States must have a navy equal to that of any other country, and the Sea Battle of Paris taught him that the British saw the league's collective security arrangement as a means of ensuring their superiority at sea. Daniels wanted the league *and* a navy large enough to make the league irrelevant to U.S. national security. A compromise might have been worked out, but Wilson was having none of that. As one senator put it, in Wilson's refusal to compromise with the Senate, "the President strangled his own child."[96]

To get the Senate to ratify the treaty, the president went directly to the people for support. Despite Daniels's confidence in Wilson's oratory skills, he advised the president against this strategy, arguing instead that Wilson should speak individually or in small groups with every senator, Republicans as well as Democrats, "except for the handful who are impossible." If Wilson insisted on speaking publicly about the treaty, then, Daniels suggested, he should do so in a formal address delivered in the Senate chambers.[97] Wilson ignored this advice and embarked on a speaking tour in early September. According to Daniels, who accompanied Wilson for part of the trip, the president was not in good health. (Indeed, this might have been why Daniels discouraged the strategy.) In Seattle Wilson complained of a "splitting head-ache," and a few days later in Colorado he collapsed. Daniels's diary noted that "the President was sick, returned to Washington."[98] Upon returning to the capital, Wilson had a stroke. He had delivered his last public words on the treaty. Daniels summarized the result: "The League of Nations was dead."[99] Although the treaty circulated through the Senate for another six months, with one amendment or reservation after another being defeated, it failed even in amended form on March 19, 1920. Daniels went down with his president, heading for a decade in the political wilderness.

How cold that wilderness would be was foreshadowed during congressional investigations on the conduct of the war. Daniels's management of the naval war received special scrutiny. For that, history can thank Daniels's subordinate, Admiral William Sims. By war's end, Sims had grown to hate his chief. Some of his animosity was acutely personal. Late in the war, the British proposed making Sims an honorary member of the British admiralty. Daniels (with Wilson's support) had prohibited Sims from receiving the honor.[100] Daniels acted ostensibly on republican grounds, but he might have been disciplining his recalcitrant admiral, who had, in Daniels's view, too frequently sided with the British during the war. After the war, however, Daniels generously reassigned Sims to the naval war college and supported his promotion to four-star rank. Sims was not appeased. To strike back at Daniels, Sims publicly refused to accept his own navy's Distinguished Service Medal, arguing that the honor had been depreciated because promotions and medals had been handed out like political patronage during the war. Republicans in the Senate began a formal investigation of the administration's policies on military promotions and decorations. As a Sims biographer notes, "Sims turned the . . . investigation of the awards matter into a postmortem on the conduct of the war at sea."[101]

Although the subsequent hearings received a good bit of coverage in the press, the affair was soon recognized for the show trial that it was. Daniels understood this game better than Sims. The navy secretary calmly explained his policies, the reasons behind them, and the history of how they were implemented. Conversely, Sims's criticism of the administration's medals and promotions policy looked like a smear of his uniformed colleagues, many of whom were true heroes. As for the criticism of the navy's preparedness, it is true that Daniels had not prepared the navy for the war it would have to fight. The prewar focus on dreadnoughts was misplaced. But in the face of Sims's charges of prewar neglect, Daniels was able to show that Sims had done no better than anyone else in predicting the navy's need to substitute destroyers for dreadnoughts. Even before the investigation was over, the public, perhaps sensing that Wilson's administration was pathetically crawling to the finish line, lost interest. The Republican chair of the House Naval Affairs Committee, Thomas Butler, refused even to hold hearings on the matter.[102] However, one troubling event related to the hearings was Franklin Roosevelt's opportunistic leap onto Sims's antiadministration bandwagon. Promoting his own possibilities in the upcoming elections, FDR publicly claimed to have been more "vigilant" than either Daniels or Wilson. Once the public relations tide turned against Sims, FDR regretted his disloyalty, which temporarily disrupted his relationship with Daniels.[103]

While time consuming, the congressional investigation into the conduct of the war left Daniels politically unharmed. Despite some mishaps, the Germans had been crushed, and the public did not seem to have a taste for the political backstabbing that might tarnish that achievement. More damaging to Daniels was the conduct of U.S. forces in Haiti, which came to light during the postwar hearings. Rumors had reached the press that the marines in Haiti had badly treated, and in some cases murdered, Haitians. Perhaps the marines were angry that they had missed out on the glory in France and that after the war those who had served in Europe got to go home, while they were still stuck in Port-au-Prince or the Haitian outback. Before the details were known, Marine Corps Commandant George Barnett, who had served Daniels faithfully for more than six years, used some ill-chosen words that found their way into print. He supposedly said marines in Haiti had engaged in the "practically indiscriminate habit of killing natives." This did, in fact, turn out to be the case. However, in going on record, Barnett placed himself and Daniels in a difficult situation. As the commandant, he was responsible for his men's behavior. His statement essentially condemned his own leadership as well as his men's conduct. Daniels had little choice but to get rid of Barnett, whom he replaced with John Lejeune in the late summer of 1920. Barnett reverted to his permanent rank of brigadier general and, feeling that he had been made a scapegoat, eventually left the corps with considerable rancor toward his boss.[104] The two men never spoke again.

Despite the mess in Haiti and the loss of the treaty fight, the period between the end of the war and the end of Daniels's term as navy secretary was not without political victories. Indeed, during those years, Daniels saw two of his longtime causes become part of the U.S. Constitution. In January 1919, North Carolina joined thirty-seven other states in ratifying the Eighteenth Amendment, which prohibited "the manufacture, sale, or transportation of intoxicating liquors." The rest of the United States was now as dry as North Carolina had been since 1908. Twenty months later, the Nineteenth Amendment, granting women the right to vote, was ratified. Daniels had supported both prohibition and women's suffrage since he took over the Wilson *Advance* forty years earlier. He had done his own part in promoting equality for women by admitting them into the navy and the Marine Corps for the first time, and more than 11,000 served under Daniels.

Despite these progressive gains, the Democratic Party remained down. That summer, for president the Democrats nominated the innocuous James Cox, governor of Ohio, and as his running mate the dashing Assistant Secretary of the Navy Franklin D. Roosevelt. Daniels was usually an optimist when commencing a political campaign, but following the treaty ratification debacle, he viewed the 1920 race as hopeless. He told Wilson that "Cox and Roosevelt did not have the ghost of a chance."[105] Following the Democratic Party convention in San Francisco, he lamented to his diary, "trying to get into the campaign spirit."[106] Except for Parker's campaign in 1904, that had never been a problem. Daniels blamed the party's sinking chances on Cox, the candidate of the party's northern, urban machines. Going into the convention, Daniels overrated the chances of two of his colleagues—the current attorney general, A. Mitchell Palmer, and former treasury secretary McAdoo—either of whom he would have preferred to Cox. FDR's nomination was the one bright spot for Daniels. Although certain the ticket would sink, Daniels thought it was a good career move for FDR. At the convention in July, Daniels had spoken in support of FDR's candidacy, calling him a "clear-headed and able executive and patriotic citizen."[107] What Daniels did not add was that only days earlier, he had been forced to expel FDR from the USS *New Mexico*, the flagship of the new Pacific fleet.

FDR arrived at the convention before Daniels and requested the commodious stateroom on the *New Mexico*. The Pacific fleet commander, Admiral Hugh Rodman, who had commanded the U.S. battleship squadron in the North Atlantic during the Great War, cared little for Roosevelt. But Rodman understood that he was in no position to reject the request of the politically connected assistant secretary. However, Daniels, as the head of the navy, had the first claim on the flagship's stateroom, and he was probably still unhappy about FDR's unwise public comments during the Sims affair. When Daniels arrived a few days later, he had FDR unceremoniously expelled from the ship, and the future president was forced to set up shop in the older and less spacious USS *New York*.[108]

After receiving the nomination, FDR officially resigned from the Navy

Department on August 6. He handwrote Daniels a heartfelt note, observing, "You have taught me so wisely and kept my feet on the ground when I was about to sky-rocket."[109] What exactly had Daniels taught FDR? In his ever-present broad-brimmed hat, antiquated tie, and three-piece suit (white in the summer, dark the rest of the year), Daniels looked the way FDR imagined a "hillbilly" would look (though he might have noted that the suits were hand tailored). Thus, when they first met, it was natural for men like FDR (and the navy brass) to assume that Daniels could be counted on to do little more than deliver the white vote to the Democratic Party. Generally able to hold his tongue in public and at social functions, though never to the point of shyness, the teetotaling Daniels came across as jovial but somewhat soft-spoken. No backslapper, but comfortably conversant, he was happy to defer to more gregarious guests in social gatherings tinged with politics—and frequently alcohol. Along with his soft, reedy voice and coastal plain accent, these personal traits could easily cause a potential opponent to confuse Daniels's good manners and reserve with an absence of gravitas and thus lead that opponent to underestimate the intelligence and drive, both physical and mental, of the down-home editor. It could be said of Daniels, as was said of Talleyrand, another backstage manipulator, that "many would misjudge him, just as many would underestimate him, and all would be wrong."[110]

Slowly FDR learned that Daniels was not the hick he pretended to be. Time and again, FDR watched Daniels shrewdly maneuver his opponents (including Admirals Fiske and Sims, General Wood, and the Navy League's Thompson) into underestimating him. All the while Daniels would be working diligently on a project—showing an obscure report on naval affairs to a congressman or whispering the right words in Wilson's ear—and then at the right moment he would spring. His opponent would be unprepared for the weight of Daniels's attack. Caught off guard, as Daniels had quietly rallied the support of bigger political guns, the foe was quickly vanquished. By the end of their long tenure together in the Navy Department, FDR would look back and marvel at Daniels's abilities displayed in many situations that arose during their nearly eight years together. Subsequently, FDR cultivated his own false persona, the shallow Ivy Leaguer, whom many a political foe would underestimate. As a historian described FDR after he ascended to the presidency, "As a good politician . . . he masked his [true] character under a carapace of frivolity and banter."[111] Yet behind the jovial facade was a will of steel.

Reflecting on their service together, the night FDR resigned Daniels wrote in his diary, "[FDR] left in the afternoon, but before leaving wrote me a letter most friendly & almost loving, wh[ich] made me glad I had never acted upon my impulse when he seemed to take sides with my critics."[112] Here, then, in a nutshell was the relationship between the two. FDR had been self-seeking and ambitious enough to stab his mentor in the back on more than one occasion; yet he was also introspective enough to understand what he had done, and with maturity and growing confidence he could now look back on their long association and admit that it was from Daniels whom he learned how to play the Washington game. For Daniels's part, he knew FDR's flaws, but he also saw earlier and better than anyone else, probably even better than FDR himself, his subordinate's potential for greatness. Daniels had many opportunities to throw FDR overboard and publicly embarrass him, thus damaging the Roosevelt name when doing so would have benefited Daniels and the Democratic Party. But he did not, because he saw FDR's gifts, his native intelligence and capacity for hard work, his moral and physical courage and simple unaffected patriotism (perhaps the Roosevelt family's greatest attributes), all alloyed with a rare personal magnetism. These gifts, Daniels guessed, correctly as it turned out, would someday be valuable to the Democratic Party.

FDR's gifts did not help in the 1920 election, however, as he and Cox took only ten of the eleven Confederate states plus Kentucky. Neither man carried his home state as they lost to Warren Harding, who if nothing else looked presidential, and the taciturn Calvin Coolidge. The drubbing extended to Congress, where the Republicans added sixty-one seats to their majority in the House and ten in the Senate. The brief era of Democratic suzerainty had ended. What Wilson's rise had given, his fall had taken away.

———

As Daniels's last day in Washington approached, a local newspaperman asked him what he would do upon leaving office. Daniels, taking the question literally, replied, "I'll leave for Raleigh, N.C., the evening of [Saturday] March 5 and arrive there Sunday morning. I'll go home and wash up then to the Methodist church and ask forgiveness of my sins and greet old friends. Monday morning I'll go down to the *News and Observer* office, take off my coat, roll up my sleeves and become an editor again."[113] And that is what he did. Arriving at the train station early on the 6th, he and Addie went to the Bagley home and then parted. Addie attended her family's Presbyterian Church, while Daniels received Holy Communion at the Edenton Street United Methodist Church (where he soon returned to teaching the men's college Bible class, which he had taken over in 1902).[114] However, the day was only beginning. The new governor, Cameron Morrison, organized plans to turn Daniels's homecoming into a Democratic Party pageant. A banquet was prepared in the municipal auditorium, and more than 5,000 people attended. Politicians gave welcome-home speeches, and Daniels was eventually called to the podium. As if to emphasize that he was no longer a public figure, he gave no formal address but said simply, "I have not come from a larger job, but I am back to take up again the greatest work in the world," by which he meant running the *News and Observer*. Then he sat down.[115]

Among the important personal matters to which Josephus and Addie had to attend upon their return to Raleigh was finding a home. Despite being financially well off since early adulthood, Daniels had never acquired that quintessential American asset—a house. As they had since shortly after their wedding in 1888, they lived in Adelaide Worth Bagley's house at the corner of East South and Blount Streets on Raleigh's near south side. By 1921, the once-fashionable neighborhood in which that house stood had become one of Raleigh's poorest. The area had been in decline in the decades since the governor's mansion, which had once stood just two blocks away, was abandoned and the new Queen Anne–style governor's mansion was built on the north side of downtown in 1891. Raleigh's elites gradually migrated north, as newer, larger, and plusher homes were built just beyond downtown, on an arc running from west to east on the north side of town. Never a slave to such social trends, Daniels kept his family in the older neighborhood.[116]

However, at Addie's instigation, Josephus decided to spend his old age in a grander home in a more sedate corner of the city. One gets the impression from his correspondence on the subject that in the absence of Addie's prodding, Josephus would have simply returned to their old home.[117] (Addie's mother and her two unmarried daughters, Belle and Ethel, remained in Washington, where Daniels had secured federal jobs for his sisters-in-law.) Despite the fact that it was his wife's project, Daniels came to love the new home, and building it proved to be a wise personal and financial decision. Following a long-established pattern of suburbanization, Daniels leap-frogged the previous fashionable neighborhoods on the near north side and built "one of the earliest and largest houses" in Raleigh's soon-to-be-most-privileged neighborhood, Hayes Barton, which was named after Sir Walter Raleigh's home.[118]

Even before he left Washington, Daniels discussed the plans for the new house in a letter to his oldest son, Joe Jr., dated April 6, 1920. He informed his son that a navy commander, Lincoln Rogers, described as "a good architect," was going to stop briefly in Raleigh while traveling to Miami on official business. Josephus noted that Rogers had been giving Addie "advice about the house she is going to build out on the hill-top." He went on: "I wish you would go out and take Dan Allen [a Raleigh real estate developer] or somebody else and show [Rogers] where the roads are to be, etc. etc."[119] The use of an on-duty naval officer for this type of personal work would subsequently come to be viewed in Washington as an egregious ethical violation. At the time, Washington officials, particularly those in such rarefied positions as the one Daniels held, typically engaged in much larger abuses of their offices.

By Raleigh standards of those days, the project turned out to be massive. Nearly two years passed between the end of Daniels's term as secretary and the completion of the house on the "hill-top." The couple took up occupancy at the end of 1922 and held a grand housewarming party on New Year's Day 1923. The architect and builder was the locally prominent Howard Satterfield. When the house was completed, Daniels named the large stone structure with its columned facade Wakestone, claiming, "It was built with all the stones that had been hurled at the *News and Observer*."[120] The layout of the house was the classic cross of early nineteenth-century American homes, with an antechamber leading to a great hallway that ran from one end of the house to the other. An airy living room extended down the hallway to the right, and beyond that, to the south facing Raleigh's downtown, was an extensive lawn and garden. The dining room and, beyond that, a vast kitchen were to the left. Daniels's office, his sanctuary away from the *N&O*, was off the antechamber to the left, immediately as one entered the front door. Spacious living quarters for the family occupied the second floor, and the live-in hired help resided on the top floor. Grand in scale but plain by haut bourgeois architectural standards of the day, the home possessed a sturdy elegance that time has not eroded.

In addition to taking charge of the *N&O*, Daniels did a good bit of writing and speaking after his tenure in Washington ended. In his first year back in Raleigh, he published his history of the navy during the Great War, and two years later he published his biography of Woodrow Wilson. Although at the time the biography was the better received of the two volumes, the history of the navy has better stood the test of time. It gives a fairly detailed, albeit understandably biased, account of the activities of the Navy Department during the war, and it remains a good source on the size of the navy, its growth, and its various actions from mining to shipping food and troops. The same cannot be said of Daniels's hagiography of Wilson. Other than for some personal insights concerning Daniels's views of the president and his administration, all of which are favorable and many of which contrast with his diary entries and in some cases his memoirs published two decades later, the book is almost worthless.

Although records of Daniels's royalties from his books have not survived, it is safe to say that during the 1920s, he made much more money from his speeches than he did from his books. In an age before television, public figures could make a decent living on the speaking circuit. At a time when per capita GDP was less than $900, Daniels was earning thousands of dollars a year from his public speaking engagements.[121] He had speeches booked through the Redpath Bureau of Chicago, which billed itself as "Booking Transcontinental Tours of Leading Lecturers, Musical and Dramatic Artists," and the Chautauqau Institution, a Christian foundation with a mission to promote "religion, arts, education, and recreation."[122] During his tours, he spoke as often as five nights a week all over the country, though mainly in the South (arranged through Redpath) and the upper Midwest (through Chautauqua). (In one of Daniels's regular speeches, he publicly came out against the Versailles Treaty, excoriating the authors, including the now dead Woodrow Wilson, for imposing a "Carthaginian Peace" on Germany.)[123] One can trace his travels by his correspondence with Addie, which was often written on hotel stationary. His stops included such out-of-the way places as Ashtabula, Ohio; Norton, Kansas; Yuma, Colorado; and Kearney, Nebraska, where the Hotel Midway advertised itself as being exactly 1,733 miles from San Francisco *and* Boston.

After several years of this grind, Daniels began to slow down, and by the fall of 1927, at age sixty-five, he had cut back drastically the number of speeches he gave each year. A week on the road was now followed by more extended time back in Raleigh or a week of vacation, typically at a Methodist retreat at Lake Junaluska in North Carolina's Great Smoky Mountains. On the eve of the Great Crash of 1929, the News and Observer Corporation, which was now entirely owned by Daniels (except for two shares of stock, one owned by his oldest son and one by Addie), was assessed for tax purposes at $275,000. Summing the value of Josephus and Addie's investments with Herbert Jackson, their other real estate holdings, bank deposits, and so forth yields a figure of almost equal value.[124] Thus they probably had a net worth of approximately half a million dollars, which was 500 times per capita income. A similar multiple today would put their wealth at well over

$20 million, small by the standards of a Duke or a Rockefeller but large by almost any other standard. Daniels's annual income was probably in the neighborhood of $50,000, roughly $2.5 million in today's money.[125] With three of his sons working at the *N&O*, Daniels could have retired and enjoyed a leisurely and financially comfortable old age. But the crash foreshadowed the Great Depression, the Depression brought Franklin Roosevelt to the White House, and Franklin Roosevelt brought Josephus Daniels back into the service of his country.

10. Mexican Sunset

*The Democratic Party is composed of Irishmen, Southerners and
Jews, none of whom can hope to be elected President.*

—JOSEPHUS DANIELS

In the winter of 1865, a small group of young, reasonably well-heeled Confederate veterans from Pulaski, Tennessee, created a fraternal organization that took its name from the Greek word *kuklos*, meaning circle, group, or assembly. Thus the *kuklos* clan, which soon became the Ku Klux Klan, represented an inane redundancy, meaning literally group group or clan clan. Although the educated young men who founded the Klan might have appreciated the mockery of its double name, such ironies were largely lost on subsequent generations of Klansmen. As one historian of the organization puts it, "The Knights of the Ku Klux Klan have not been noted for their sense of humor."[1] The original members adopted wild-sounding titles and secret initiation rites and rode through Pulaski and the surrounding countryside in hooded costumes. Justifiably, local blacks—only recently freed from bondage and still uncertain about their new social, political, and economic rights and roles—quickly developed reservations about these nightriders.

But in the 1870s the fire of the Klan burned out with the return of white Democratic rule across the South. There was no longer any need to don hoods and work from the shadows—literally or metaphorically. Klan members could now take off their costumes and openly run for county sheriff. In North Carolina, the racist Home Rule laws allowed the white Democrats who controlled the state legislature to appoint their supporters to political office in black-majority areas of the state. Once Reconstruction ended, the white power structure in the South preferred African American labor in the fields rather than hanging from a tree. And thus the "first" Ku Klux Klan passed into the history books, where it remained for more than forty years.

Then the Klan came back. It would have been difficult for a prominent southerner of Josephus Daniels's generation to avoid being entangled in

373

one way or another with the Ku Klux Klan after its rebirth, and in fact, Daniels maintained a complex relationship with the Klan. His first mentor, Cousin Ed Nadal, had been a prominent member of the Wilson County Klan during Daniels's boyhood, and Daniels always gave the Klan credit for helping "redeem" the state from its carpetbagger overlords. But when the Klan came back in the 1920s, Daniels saw it as an impediment to southern economic and social progress. The change in Daniels's view reflected both the changing nature of the Klan and the earlier success of the white supremacy movement. In Daniels's view, the Klan brought the "Negro question" back to the forefront of southern politics, where "progressive" white supremacists such as Daniels did not want it. Given Daniels's view, it is ironic that he played a pivotal role in the Klan's revival.

Daniels got mixed up with the Klan's rebirth through his association with fellow Tar Heel Thomas Dixon. A once-prosperous slave-owning family, the Dixons fell on hard times after the Civil War, as, like many landed southern families, they failed to adapt to the new economic realities of the postwar era. Rather than enjoying a life of plantation luxury, young Thomas grew up in the hardscrabble fields of a Cleveland County dirt farm.[2] Despite the economic and social hardships attending such a life, Dixon showed academic promise, and his parents, ardent Baptists, managed to send the boy to Wake Forest College, where he did well. He subsequently earned a scholarship to Johns Hopkins University, at the time arguably the nation's leading institution of higher learning. Although blessed with a good head, Dixon had a hard time settling into adult life, but he eventually turned to writing and there found his calling. After seeing a performance of *Uncle Tom's Cabin*, which he considered a libelously inaccurate characterization of his native region, he determined to set the narrative record straight and thus spent the next four years writing and promoting a trilogy of novels that served as his reply to the popular antislavery play.

Dixon titled his first novel, which he finished in 1902, *The Leopard's Spots*. Described by a critic as "a lurid tale of Negro bestiality curbed by white men resorting to violence and political repression," it was an apologia for Klan violence.[3] Seeking a publisher, Dixon turned to another native Tar Heel, Walter Hines Page, whose name by now graced the New York publishing firm of Doubleday, Page and Company. Although Page was nominally a defender of the downtrodden, his biographer notes, "Commercialism undermined Page's principles more than finickiness about subjects."[4] Page knew the publishing business, and he guessed correctly that Dixon was onto something with his race-baiting work. *The Leopard's Spots* became an immediate best seller, and over the next five years Page published the rest of the trilogy, which included *The Clansman* and *The Traitor*. (The prolific Dixon completed, during the same period, another work, titled *The One Woman*, which was part of yet another trilogy; this one was an attack on socialism.)

Of Dixon's growing body of work, *The Clansman*, published in 1905, proved the most enduring. It became a successful stage production, and just as it reached the peak of its success, a new medium swept rapidly across the country: the moving picture show. Most of the early films, the so-called one-reel photoplays and the slightly more substantial two-reelers, were short by subsequent standards, lasting only twenty-five or perhaps thirty minutes. Costing a nickel, they added to the lexicon the term "nickelodeon." The early films were most notable for creating a generation of film professionals who strove to elevate the medium to a higher intellectual and artistic plane. Among these was D. W. Griffith.

Unfortunately for the history of race relations, Griffith chose as the vehicle for his cinematic masterpiece Dixon's scandalous *The Clansman*, renamed *The Birth of a Nation*. Artistically the film was everything Griffith wanted it to be, and it remains a landmark in cinematic history. Costing a record $110,000, a fortune at the time, with a score written for a thirty-piece orchestra and using the latest in cinematography, *The Birth of a Nation* ran for nearly three hours. Admission cost an incredible $2, which, adjusted for inflation in the intervening years, would equal roughly $30 a century later.[5] And yet in the first four years after the film's release, customers bought 25 million tickets, which represents a box office take of over $700 million in 2012 dollars, making *The Birth of a Nation* an overwhelming financial success by any standard.[6]

Despite the film's artistic achievements, when it was released its financial success was very much an open question. Griffith knew his business well enough to suspect that he had created a potential blockbuster; however, even before its Los Angeles premier the film was enveloped in controversy. The National Association for the Advancement of Colored People officially condemned it, and spontaneous protests erupted in many northern cities. The NAACP leadership quickly recognized the raw emotional response the film engendered—on both sides of the racial divide—and the organization soon began formally coordinating protests against the film. All sides understood that a key battle would be fought in New York at the National Board of Censorship. Created in 1909 to police the film industry, the board reviewed films destined for wide distribution. Its view carried much weight in molding official public opinion concerning the acceptability of a particular film. A negative vote from the board provided ammunition to local public officials and activists who opposed the showing of the film in their communities. Such a vote might not have meant the financial death of Griffith's masterpiece, but it would have certainly been costly. With a fortune invested in getting Dixon's novel on film, Griffith's backers could not afford to the let the board condemn it. Dixon came up with a strategy to win the board's approval. Despite its claims of independence, the board was subject to political influence, and here Daniels entered the picture.

Dixon and Daniels had known each other for years, and Daniels was the first big name Dixon looked up in Washington. Daniels loved the picture show almost as much as he loved baseball. Other than reading, they were his two primary forms of entertainment, and he gladly arranged a showing of the film in the central post office building in Washington. It was a hit. Although one of Daniels's sons claimed that the film premiered "with all the dignitaries present," two key officials were missing: President Woodrow Wilson and Supreme Court Chief Justice Edward D. White. Hoping to include Wilson and White in the list of prominent supporters, Dixon went back to Daniels, who then arranged for Wilson and his family to see the film in a separate showing.[7] The president was pleased with the product. Whether Wilson's famous description of the film—"like writing history with lightning"—is fact or fiction remains the subject of debate, but he was clearly impressed and gave it his approval.[8] With Wilson's consent, Griffith prepared to show the film one more time, in the ballroom of Washington's Raleigh Hotel. He hoped Chief Justice White, a former Confederate soldier from Louisiana and a former member of the New Orleans chapter of the Ku Klux Klan, would see the film. By his own admission, however, White had never witnessed a performance of a moving picture show, and he considered it a vulgar medium beneath the dignity of a gentleman from Lafourche Parish. Hearing of White's stubbornness, Daniels personally arranged "within minutes" for Dixon to be granted an audience with the august jurist, and Dixon persuaded White to view the film later that evening.

As Dixon predicted, the reviews from Washington were overwhelmingly positive. The next day, Dixon and Griffith were in New York showing the film to the Censorship Board. After reviewing the film—and the endorsements of such luminaries as Wilson, Daniels, and White—the board gave its approval by an underwhelming vote of 15 to 8. One can only guess what the vote might have been had Dixon and Griffith not successfully secured their political flank before showing the film to the board. In this Daniels's assistance was crucial.

As a cultural event, there was little to which *The Birth of a Nation* could be compared at the time. Although it inspired protests here and there, the film established artistic and financial standards for all subsequent cinematic success. By the standards of historical scholarship, however, it was arguably less successful. But on a cultural front it was accorded more power than any of the parties at the time might have imagined. Various histories of the Ku Klux Klan allocate a key role to the movie in reviving the moribund organization.[9] Daniels's assistance in getting the film approved by the Censorship Board helped it achieve a wide distribution (and much profit), and the overwhelming popularity of *The Birth of a Nation* subsequently contributed to an interest and increase in Klan membership. If Daniels ever put all of those pieces of the puzzle together, he might have regretted aiding Dixon.

To be sure, *The Clansman* was no manifesto. White supremacists already controlled the South at the time of the book's publication. Dixon aimed at correcting the record of the past, not the social situation of the present. Furthermore, he did not possess the personal constitution required to create or lead a national organization based on the racist doctrines of his novels. Dixon may have written the score for the Klan's revival, but it took a more visionary soul to create the orchestra that would play it. William Simmons was such a man. Simmons grew up in rural Alabama, the son of country doctor. After duty in the Spanish-American War, he had knocked about the South doing a variety of jobs, from preaching the gospel to selling memberships in fraternal organizations, a task at which he supposedly earned the then-enormous sum of $15,000 a year. Simmons decided to use the early success and controversy of *The Birth of a Nation* as a platform for re-creating the Klan, expecting to make money by selling Klan memberships. An entrepreneur at heart, Simmons copyrighted an outline of the Klan's organizational structure, and in November 1915, just before the film's much-advertised Atlanta premier, at an elaborate ceremony at nearby Stone Mountain, Simmons resurrected the Ku Klux Klan.

Southern writer W. J. Cash, who knew the Klan well, observed that "in its essence the thing was an authentic folk movement."[10] As such, its creation myth was *The Birth of a Nation*, and the organization grew steadily over the next few years. The new Klan came to be defined by what its members hated: "the Negro, Jew, Oriental, Roman Catholic, and alien . . . dope, boot-

legging, graft, night clubs and road houses, violation of the Sabbath, unfair business dealing, sex, marital 'goings-on,' and scandalous behavior."[11] In
small towns and rural areas, especially across the South and the Midwest,
these proved to be popular things to be against.

Although soon buffeted by scandal, internal squabbling, and violent excess, all of which would ultimately contribute to the organization's demise,
the Klan would reach its political and cultural apogee in the 1920s, just as
Daniels returned to Raleigh and entered the national political wilderness.
To those, such as Daniels, who could otherwise be described as pillars of
white society and who coexisted with the Klan through its various manifestations, the organization proved to be a double-edged sword. With the help
of lower-class whites, who would later form the bulk of the Klan's membership, the white supremacy movement had removed African Americans
from any meaningful political role in the South. The objective of the white
supremacy movement had been to keep blacks out of politics, resulting in
a coerced social harmony that brought order and economic growth—the
ultimate progressive objectives of the movement. The chaos of the Klan
threatened that order as much as the Fusionists had. Daniels and the white
supremacists had sown the whirlwind of resentment among lower-class
whites to ensure white power. That process continued to yield resentment
and hate even after blacks were disenfranchised, until it spilled over violently through the ideological and organizational structure found in the
resurgent Klan.

The connection between men like Daniels and the Klan was well understood by observers at the time. Cash wrote that the Klan's "body was made
up of common whites, industrial and rural. But . . . people of great prominence in industry and business, indeed, were often, though not always,
chary about actually belonging to it, but they usually maintained liaison
with it through their underlings and politicians."[12] Always a bit too nostal-
gic about the old Klan, Daniels remained "chary" of the new version. Despite the unintended role he played in the Klan's resurgence, his view of and
relationship with it was always ambivalent. He viewed Klan members and
supporters, as any politico might, as potential allies at the polls. And as we
have seen with respect to his battles during the Fusion movement, he was
not above using race to achieve political objectives. Moreover, the Klan's
membership was filled with southerners who were susceptible to racial
demagoguery of the type practiced in the pages of the *N&O*. These were
the people whose racial animosity Daniels had fueled during the Fusionist
era. The Klan contained all of the same forces, with the addition of religious

bigotry, that had made the white supremacy campaigns successful. And perhaps it was here that Daniels drew the line. The racial divide was one thing; carving up society along religious lines was something altogether different. Daniels welcomed into his party the poorest, meanest white elements of white society, but only on his terms.

Although, like the Klan's membership, Daniels was a white supremacist and a devout Protestant, he was also a proponent of religious freedom. He rejected the Klan's anti-Catholic and anti-Semitic platform. Furthermore, as a supporter of public order (at least when his party was in power), Daniels aligned against the Klan's extralegal strategies, especially violence. Thus during the Klan's resurgence in the 1920s, Daniels found himself in a difficult situation, because to be a leader of the Democratic Party in the 1920s required one to take a position on the Klan. The event that proved to be Daniels's Rubicon was the 1924 Democratic Party Convention.

As the national election approached, the Democratic Party had no clear presidential front-runner—or at least no front-runner with a chance of being elected. Among the names thrown around as potential candidates was that of Josephus Daniels. While traveling earlier in the year, Daniels's son Jonathan became aware of a national "Draft Daniels" sentiment. "The politicians have begun to gather for the convention tomorrow," he wrote to his mother. "The plan is to have the [state] convention 'present Josephus Daniels to the country.'" Among the state's leading politicians who pushed Daniels's candidacy were longtime congressman Robert Doughton and future governor O. Max Gardner.[13]

Some observers attributed this movement to the positive publicity surrounding Daniels's role in the recent Teapot Dome scandal, which had just been investigated with much public fanfare and which had favorably put Daniels back in the national spotlight. During his tenure as secretary of the navy, Daniels had fought to keep the government's Teapot Dome petroleum field as a strategic reserve for the navy, which had been converting the fleet from coal to fuel oil. The reserve had been transferred to the Interior Department during the Harding administration, and oilman Harry Sinclair subsequently bribed Interior Secretary Albert Fall for the right to lease the field. The congressional investigation that followed made Daniels look like a paragon of public virtue.[14] It also made him look good compared with several leading Democrats, including at least four other members of Wilson's cabinet (one of whom was another presidential candidate, William Gibbs McAdoo) who had accepted money from one of Fall's co-conspirators.[15]

One major problem confronting Daniels's run for president was that progressivism as a national movement was all but dead, killed by, among other things, the factionalism within the Democratic Party. Also, Daniels's appeal was strictly regional. Daniels himself recognized this all too clearly. According to his son Jonathan, whenever the Old Man was mentioned as a candidate, he would grin and say, "The Democratic party is composed of Irishmen, Southerners and Jews, none of whom can hope to be elected President."[16] Daniels was not being coy when downplaying his candidacy. During his long life he adopted any number of lost causes, but one gets the impression that even if somewhere in the far reaches of his ego he might have enjoyed the thought of being president, he perceived clearly enough that it would never happen. Thus the battle for the 1924 Democratic ticket would not be waged over a "Daniels for President" cry.

Disaster, or perhaps tragedy, remains the kindest description of the 1924 Democratic National Convention, held at Madison Square Garden in late June and early July. Battles over control of the party occurred at many margins: wet and dry, urban and rural, industrial and agricultural, Roman Catholic and Protestant, immigrants and nativists, and the Klan and nearly everyone else. A coalition emerged behind the "Happy Warrior," New York's Alfred E. Smith. About as wet, urban, and Catholic as they came, Smith, a product of New York City's Irish-dominated machine, had strong northern support within the party, but McAdoo was an early front-runner. Protestant and dry, with southern roots but broad (though, as it turned out, not deep) support, McAdoo seemed like a good antidote to Smith. Daniels, who did not think a Catholic could win, placed himself in McAdoo's corner despite the taint of Teapot Dome. (Earlier in the year, Daniels predicted in print that McAdoo would be the party's 1924 nominee and that he would beat the incumbent, Calvin Coolidge, who had become president following Warren Harding's death.)[17]

Even before the balloting for the presidential nominee, battles over the Klan tore the party apart. Since the silver battles more than a quarter of a century earlier, the Democratic Party had changed. Along with the country in general, it had become more urban, industrial, and ethnically and religiously diverse than it had been when Daniels first joined the national committee in 1896. These newer elements of the party resented the strong Klan presence at the convention. Accordingly, there arose a movement to include explicit anti-Klan language in the party's platform. Daniels recognized that the day of the angry white southerner had passed, and he supported the anti-Klan plank. It is possible that if the Klan had been voted down, the outcome of the convention would have been radically different, but before the vote was taken, onto the public stage strode William Jennings Bryan, "like a veteran actor performing an old-fashioned play for precisely the wrong audience."[18]

Bryan had taken a long time to recover from his fall from grace as Wilson's secretary of state. In fact, he never recovered anything like his former prestige. Exactly what role he hoped to play at the convention remains a puzzle even to his biographers.[19] Bryan clearly objected to Smith, but he refused to endorse McAdoo. Perhaps he sought the nomination himself. He came with a prepackaged platform, which he told the press had McAdoo's support, perhaps as a way of subordinating McAdoo. Daniels greeted Bryan warmly, even though the two had never renewed the close relationship they had shared before Bryan's resignation. But then Bryan, bumbling into the Klan debate, committed an act that can only be described as political self-immolation. The resulting sparks set off the whole convention. Siding with the Klan, Bryan pooh-poohed concerns about the organization. In his speech, he asked rhetorically why "the Catholic Church, with its legacy of martyr's blood and . . . its long line of missionaries," and the Jews, who "have Moses . . . and Elijah . . . need a great party to protect [them] from a million Klansmen." He concluded his pro-Klan address with a perverse call for party unity. "It requires more courage to fight the Republican Party than to fight the KKK—more courage to save a nation than throw a brick."[20]

Daniels watched in horror. He had planned to address the convention, hoping to persuade the delegates to vote for the anti-Klan plank. However, following Bryan's disastrous speech, he chose not to. He justified his decision by arguing that Bryan had made such a hash of the affair that his own words were now pointless. When the ballot was taken, the Klan managed to defeat the plank by a single vote. Daniels, in the minority among the North Carolina delegation, voted against the Klan. If Daniels had spoken out against Bryan and the Klan, he might have produced the votes needed to swing the decision in the other direction.

It is hard to say whom Bryan hurt more, McAdoo or Smith. The forces behind each hardened. Bryan might have sought this deadlock hoping that the convention would then turn to him as a compromise candidate. If that were the case, then Bryan's political judgment had slipped badly since his earlier days of orchestrating party affairs. After his pro-Klan address, he became persona non grata to roughly half of the party. Bryan would have one more great moment on the national stage, but his political influence ended at the 1924 convention. Daniels now surveyed the collateral damage. McAdoo had stronger support among the Klan than Smith, who had no Klan support and was, in fact, the organization's main target at the convention; but neither candidate could achieve the party's two-thirds requirement, and the ordeal continued through 103 ballots. Finally, John Davis, a respected New York lawyer and former U.S. solicitor general during Wilson's administration, won the nomination as the party's compromise candidate. The election turned out as badly as the convention. Davis won only the eleven former Confederate states and Oklahoma. Coolidge got the rest and remained in the White House.

Now Daniels fully appreciated the destructive power of the Klan, and back in North Carolina, he increased his previously tepid efforts against the state organization. The upsurge in Klan membership and power at the state and local levels across the country emboldened the Klan's national leadership. Taking the fight to the states, Klan Imperial Wizard Hiram Wesley Evans attempted to push through the North Carolina General Assembly a set of bills that included an antimiscegenation act and others containing strictures on religious education, banishment of the Knights of Columbus, and the establishment of speech codes to be applied to Roman Catholics.[21] The national leadership insisted that Henry Grady, a distinguished jurist and North Carolina's Klan leader, see that the bills were introduced in the legislature. Grady, who saw the Klan as an instrument of social bonhomie rather than of racial or religious terror, refused. North Carolina already had antimiscegenation legislation, and Grady opposed the other bills on both principle and legal grounds. After hearing of Grady's objections, Evans removed the jurist from the state's leadership, an act to which Grady responded, "You can't fire me, I quit."[22]

This split presented Daniels with an excellent opportunity to wound the North Carolina Klan. By this time, the organization's membership had reached between 25,000 and 55,000.[23] Grady was respected throughout the state, and his disaffection with the Klan's national leaders lent credibility to an attack on the organization. Daniels cleverly played up the split as a states' rights issue, recognizing that if he could sell the dispute as a case of national meddling in state affairs—an action that unfavorably reminded many Tar Heels of Reconstruction and, later, Lodge's Force Bill—he could split the membership over the issue. A master at this type of wedge politics, Daniels did exactly that, filling the *N&O*'s front page with articles on Klan outrages. For four consecutive days prior to a vote on the bills, the paper led with an anti-Klan piece. First, an article covered the flogging of an African American postman; then the paper reported that a married couple seeking a separation had been flogged; the next day, the Wake County sheriff was accused of inactivity in investigating local Klan activities; and on the fourth day, the front page reported on a Klan trial in a neighboring county. On the same day, in an editorial, Daniels decried the "recent outrageous floggings" and attacked members of the local law enforcement community who were openly Klan members. "No public officer ought to belong to the Klan," Daniels declared.[24]

As Daniels predicted, the national Klan's meddling in state affairs angered some key legislators. Senator Rivers Johnson, a former Grady opponent, responded to the outrage Daniels had generated by switching sides. He introduced anti-Klan legislation banning masked parades and requiring the Klan to formally register its membership. Daniels supported the legislation, correctly calculating that many of North Carolina's leading citizens who might otherwise maintain Klan ties would be less inclined to do so if prohibited from marching incognito. Although the bill died, so did the Klan's racist and anti-Catholic bills. Despite this, the affair was more than a draw. Leveraged by the *N&O*'s unfavorable coverage, Klan support irrevocably began to erode in North Carolina. By the end of the year, membership had fallen below 8,000, and it never recovered. For Daniels, who in addition to his public stand in the *N&O* lobbied legislators behind the scenes, the Klan wars were over. The Klan ceased to be an important player in state politics.

———

For Daniels, the climax of the North Carolina Klan wars coincided with another messy battle, one from which he would have preferred to remain aloof. Following his disgraceful performance in Madison Square Garden, Bryan did not slink off into a quiet retirement. Rather, he continued to seek the light of public fame while playing the role of the godly hero. Bryan joined the effort to recapture the public school curricula from the clutches of Charles Darwin's theories. By the 1920s, Darwin's ideas on natural selection had found their way into biology classes around the country. In many regions, particularly in small towns and rural areas of the South, the spread of Darwinism caused a backlash, often led by the same white Protestant elements that supplied Bryan (as well as the Klan) with supporters. Bryan decided to create a political movement out of anti-Darwin sentiment, and he attempted to enlist Daniels as a fellow crusader.

Although the 1925 legal case *State of Tennessee v. John Thomas Scopes* (the so-called Scopes Monkey Trial) became a metaphor for the battle over Darwin in the classroom, a year before the trial, the North Carolina State Board of Education had already banned textbooks that favorably presented Darwin's theory of evolution.[25] Bryan sought to follow up that effort by persuading the state assembly to formally ban Darwin's teachings from the classroom. Daniels had his qualms about the theological implications of Darwin's work, but he thought that the matter should be settled in the forum of scholarly ideas, not in the state legislature. Bryan, hoping to persuade his old friend to change his position, came to Raleigh and stayed at Wakestone as the matter formally circulated in the 1925 session of the legislature. Bryan and Daniels spent an entire day discussing the topic. Exactly what was said between them is not known, but it could not have been pleasant for Daniels. He liked and admired Bryan, but when committed, Daniels could be as stubborn as the Commoner. Cloistered in Daniels's office at Wakestone, the two giants went at one another until, finally, "at dusk the Commoner stalked out grim and silent."[26] The two men never saw each other again.

Bryan held the more popular position among the state's political leaders, most of whom, including former governor Cameron Morrison, were Daniels's allies on other issues. But Charles Brantley Aycock had put Daniels on the board of trustees of the University of North Carolina in 1901 (a position he held until his death), and even if he sympathized with the concerns about the implications of social Darwinism, Daniels understood the cost to the educational system from a precedent of legislative micromanagement of the state's public institutions. If Darwin could be politicized, then so could many other topics. He considered the resulting gridlock of the state's educational system to be more costly than the benefit from prohibiting a controversial issue.

The North Carolina House Education Committee conducted hearings on the anti-Darwin bill in early February. Through Daniels's behind-the-scenes lobbying, the measure was defeated by a single vote, but on the strength of the minority report, the bill went to the House floor. Daniels now waged a full battle in the *N&O*. On the 12th he wrote an editorial defending academic freedom and criticizing the meddling legislators. "Teachers and matriculates . . . cannot be denied the right to examine for themselves the arguments and evidences pro and con which great divines and great scientists have put on paper. Discussion and differences cannot be silenced by legislative act."[27] After much further behind-the-scenes give-and-take, the anti-Darwin bill went down in a vote of 67 to 46. Thanks to Daniels's efforts, Darwin's theories could be safely taught in the North

Carolina public schools.[28] There would be no monkey trials in the Tar Heel State.

———

The state faced other political issues in the 1920s and early 1930s. Among the most important was the role of the state government in promoting economic growth. The Roaring Twenties generated a boom in three of the state's leading industries: textiles, tobacco, and furniture production. However, as the decade began, North Carolina's public infrastructure was still geared toward the plantations and sharecropping plots of the nineteenth century. In that world a graded road to the nearest town at a railroad stop served much of the state just fine. Since at least 1912, once the automobile proved to be more than a passing fad, Daniels had called in vain for a massive public-spending project on the state's roads (even though Daniels himself never learned to drive).[29] In 1920, Cameron Morrison, a product of the Furnifold Simmons machine, was elected governor. There was no reason to think he would be much of a progressive, and on social issues he generally was not. (Morrison's primary campaign strategy was to attack women's suffrage.) However, when it came to promoting economic growth, Morrison was a fanatical proponent of what one political writer subsequently called "business progressivism."[30]

Though Daniels had split with Simmons over the tariff during the previous decade, and although he had many disputes with Morrison, including Morrison's objections to women's suffrage and his opposition to a ban on child labor, the *N&O* generally maintained a favorable view of Morrison's business progressivism. The most important of Morrison's economic policies was a bond issue for state roads, $50 million in the 1921 legislative session and $15 million in 1923. These were enormous expenditures by the standards of the time, only $10 million less than the highway construction expenditures of the federal government. As a result, North Carolina would come out of the decade with the nickname "The Good Roads State," but roads were not the only public expenditures promoted in the *N&O* or supported by Morrison. During his term in office, the legislature also approved a $20 million bond issue for the state universities, created a $10 million local-school building fund, and funded an $8.5 million construction and renovation project for the state's ports.[31] Overall, the state's bonded debt increased from $12 million to more than $100 million in four years.

There were few voices against building a network of state roads (or schools or ports). However, there were many loud voices against raising the taxes necessary to pay for those roads, schools, and ports. The public expenditures were expected to generate more economic activity than would be lost as a result of the negative impact of the taxes required to pay for the infrastructure. But there was also a distributional issue. The rich, on whom the required taxes disproportionately fell, especially those who remained in agriculture in the state's rural areas, did not always want to pay for public infrastructure projects that disproportionately benefited New South industries located in urban areas. Nor did they care to finance an expansion of the state's educational programs, which would only increase the probability that their poor and largely illiterate farm workforce would leave the land.[32]

Daniels had long supported expenditures for public infrastructure, and he advocated an increase in the state's tax revenues as well as a shift from the state property tax to a system of corporate and personal income taxes, though he objected to the state sales tax, arguing that it was too regressive.[33] (A critical editorial from an Elizabeth City newspaper noted that Daniels "would be willing to tax industry and industrial workers almost out of existence.")[34] Overall during the period, the state's annual expenditures were growing at roughly 25 percent per year, an enormous rate, and while much of the state's agricultural sector suffered during the decade (cotton growers, who had been hard hit by the boll weevil, suffered through an especially trying period), industry boomed. Of course, there were other difficulties associated with these public expenditures. As one critic noted, "Responsibility for the highways was situated at the county level, and the quality of roads varied accordingly. In many cases, the construction of roads was determined on the basis of political patronage rather than economic necessity."[35] Despite these negative aspects of the public spending associated with business progressivism, overall the decade was one of prosperity for the state's rapidly growing industries and urban areas. Daniels and the *N&O* strongly and consistently supported these changes.

THE BOYS

After returning full time to the management of the *N&O* in the spring of 1921, Daniels found more time for his family than he had during his years at the helm of the navy. His four sons—Josephus Jr., Worth Bagley, Jonathan Worth, and Frank Arthur—all reached manhood before or by the end of the decade, and all except Worth joined the family business in some capacity. Jonathan, who of the four left the most voluminous paper trail, observed that his father was never "austerely separated from [his sons] in any sense," but Frank noted that only after he reached manhood and joined the family business in the 1920s did he get to know his father as a person.[36] Despite their father's perpetually long hours and frequent absences, none of Daniels's sons ever doubted his love. An early biographer referred to Daniels as "a devoted, indeed, a sentimental family man."[37] It was an accurate description.

Although a classic Victorian in other regards, Daniels never displayed any reserve in showing affection for his boys or his wife. (Indeed, Jonathan speculated that his parents had "a very adequate sex life.")[38] Daniels kissed and hugged his sons openly and unselfconsciously. If anything, he was an overindulgent parent, and as the boys reached adulthood, he could be especially generous in financial matters. Two generations of Danielses noted that in his heart the Old Man probably wanted to treat the boys equally, and there can be little doubt that at some level he tried to do so; but Daniels's sons were so different in temperament, tastes, and aptitudes that treating them equally proved impossible.[39]

Of the four boys, the most enigmatic was and remains, even after much scrutiny, the oldest, Josephus Jr. Although nominally affiliated with the *N&O* throughout most of his adult life, including stints as business manager and president, Joe Jr.—as he was known in the family, except to his father, who usually referred to him by his full name—generally did not play a leading role in either the day-to-day business operation or editorial policies of the paper. The extent to which this resulted from his interests or his abilities, or some combination of the two, remains unknown. Surviving family members hesitate to speculate openly—though it is clear that when it came to running the family business, Joe Jr. was moved aside to make room for his two youngest brothers. Generally regarded as a kindly man with an easygoing, unassuming manner, Joe Jr. did not inherit his father's indomitable physical energy. Plagued by poor eyesight, he experienced periods of indifferent health throughout much of his life. Still, despite this physical frailty and a reticent nature in the shadow of his father's imposing reputation, Joe Jr. did not lack redeeming traits. He received his secondary education at a private military academy in Oxford, North Carolina. After working at the *N&O* from 1912 to the spring of 1917, he enlisted in the Marine Corps, where by all accounts this sickly lad proved to be an outstanding marine.

Whether Joe Jr. really wanted to go into the newspaper business is difficult to say. His father certainly thought that he wanted to run the *N&O* someday, but when given the opportunity to play a dominant role at the paper, Joe Jr. never did much with the chance. Furthermore, in business and in politics, Joe Jr. never possessed either the ambition or the drive of his father. His reticence may have derived partly from the timing of his birth. He was born the year after his parents had lost their first child, one-year-old Adelaide (d. July 1893). This was a time when both parents were highly protective and perhaps even overly solicitous of their first son's well-being. His birth also coincided with his father's acquisition of the *N&O*. At the time, turning around the new business and influencing the great political questions of the day occupied a good bit of the Old Man's attention. Furthermore, Joe Jr.'s emotional growth may have been affected by an overly protective mother. Addie was prone to worry excessively about the boy, even fretting when Joe Jr. traveled by train.[40]

Regarding Joe Jr.'s failings, his younger brothers Jonathan and Frank often displayed less sympathy than their parents. The characterization of Joe Jr. as a slacker in the family business emerges clearly from the correspondence between the two youngest sons and their father. Jonathan in particular made a point of keeping his father abreast of Joe Jr.'s failings as a businessman. Shortly after he became ambassador to Mexico in 1933, the Old Man received a letter from Jonathan, who wrote, "It is irritating to do all the work [at the paper] and have Joe do none but I suppose that's that and nothing can be done about it. I think Joe means to do what he can and he plans to do it but he never gets around to doing anything." Jonathan observed that this was nothing new. "It is really not any worse than it has been I suppose," suggesting that his father must have been familiar with Joe Jr.'s professional shortcomings.[41] In an interview years after Joe Jr.'s death, Jonathan said, "I don't like to color my statements about Joe too much, but he just didn't have it." When asked by the interviewer if the Old Man (and Addie) recognized as much, Jonathan replied, "Oh, they were aware of it, yes."[42]

Jonathan's opinions concerning Joe Jr.'s faults as a businessman, though harsh, were not indicative of the personal relationship between the three sons who remained in Raleigh. In fact, the brothers became neighbors and constant social companions. The Old Man owned a large tract of property around Wakestone and divided some of it into lots for his sons. Frank and Joe Jr. lived next door to each other just north of Wakestone, while Jonathan's family lived around the corner on Caswell Street.[43] Despite their professional differences, Jonathan and Joe Jr. got along well when they were away from the newspaper. Their personal correspondence and the accounts of their children verify that the brothers and their wives socialized together, along with younger brother Frank and his wife, Ruth, frequently and harmoniously from the time Jonathan and Frank reached adulthood until their father's death and beyond.[44] Joe Jr. was also personally close to both of his parents. Their extensive correspondence is warm and familiar. The Old Man addressed his eldest son as "Dear Blessed Boy" and, after the younger boys came along, as "Dear Blessed Big Boy."[45] In general, the picture of Joe Jr. one receives from the family's correspondence from the 1920s and 1930s is of a man somewhat at loose ends, occasionally in poor health, a bit melancholy perhaps, but generally content, traveling and entertaining frequently with his wife, Evelina, and later with their adopted son, Edgar. Increasingly distant, Joe Jr. appears to have been rapidly approaching middle age while making the best of having been overshadowed by a famous father and then passed over in the family business by his younger brothers.

The second boy, Worth, born in 1899, shunned the family business altogether—at least until he became a major stockholder after his father's death. The Old Man's relationship with Worth, although excellent by most father-son standards, was arguably more strained than it was with the other boys. In part, this was the result of Worth's geographical distance throughout his adult life. And in part, it was the result of Worth's hardheaded independence, which he displayed from an early age. After graduating from St. Albans School in 1916, Worth matriculated at the University of North Carolina at Chapel Hill in the fall of that year. Once there, he began to exercise his freedom. His relative estrangement from his father's control is revealingly captured in the first volume of the Old Man's memoirs. There, the only mention of Worth is in a passage discussing his younger brother Jonathan's decision to join the Delta Kappa Epsilon social fraternity at Chapel Hill, which Worth had joined earlier. Jonathan had consulted the Old Man on the wisdom of such a move. The father advised against it, noting that the only two organizations to which he ever belonged were the Democratic Party and the Methodist Church, and he only belonged to them because anyone could join or leave as they chose. (This was, of course, false—Daniels belonged to a number of social and professional organizations.) Daniels respected Jonathan for his reflection on the subject and for discussing it with him. As for Worth, the Old Man simply noted that he "had joined [the fraternity], not asking my advice or acquainting me with his purpose!"[46] In this brief passage, one can sense both Worth's independence and the Old Man's consternation at it.

Worth left Chapel Hill to enter the naval academy after the United States entered the Great War; he resigned from the academy, much to his father's displeasure, soon after the war ended. On the day Worth resigned, the Old Man tersely summarized what happened: "Worth came home. Fight."[47] Over his father's protests but perhaps with his mother's support, Worth got his way and reenrolled at Chapel Hill for the spring term of 1919. While he was there, he maintained a steady correspondence with his mother. He was particularly keen to keep her informed of his academic progress, as if he sought his mother's approval to make up for his father's disapproval. He was a good and persistent student and graduated in the spring of 1920. During his final term at Carolina, he and his father investigated medical schools and finally settled on Johns Hopkins. With the Old Man picking up the tab, Worth entered in the fall of 1920 and graduated in 1924. He spent a brief term at Bellevue in New York City and then moved back to the Washington, D.C., area. Except for his military service as an army doctor in World War II, he spent the remainder of his life in Washington. A handsome man in a distinguished way that owed more to manner and bearing than classically chiseled features, Worth also inherited his father's twinkling eyes.

Over time, in adulthood the frequency of Worth's correspondence with his parents declined. With his wife, Josie, also a physician, and two sons, Worthie and Derick—the former a future doctor like his parents and the latter a future president of Playboy Enterprises—Worth settled into a successful medical career. He served forty years on the faculty at the Georgetown University Medical School and ultimately published more than two dozen scholarly articles on a variety of medical topics. All the while, he lived a relatively quiet life away from the frequently rough-and-tumble world of Raleigh politics and the *N&O*.

Joe Jr. was passed over in the family business, and Worth took himself out of contention for control of the newspaper; but in his two youngest boys, Daniels found his equals when it came to a love of politics and devotion to the *N&O*. Both Jonathan and Frank joined the paper as young men in the 1920s. After the Old Man's death, they would run it until they reached old age themselves; Jonathan retired as editor in 1968 and Frank as publisher in 1971. Although they shared their father's interest in the family business, they were in many ways, personally, the most different of the four boys.

Whereas Jonathan was ambitious, often flamboyant, egotistical, mercurial, politically conscious, and a gifted writer, Frank was quieter, self-effacing, more reflective, steady, and businesslike. They were not without their similarities. Both were extremely intelligent and strong willed, and both possessed a well-honed sense of humor in addition to enjoying the

Raleigh social scene. Unlike their father and older brother Worth, both of whom preferred baseball, Jonathan and Frank closely followed the football fortunes of their alma mater, the University of North Carolina. More than anything else, they were dedicated to perpetuating their father's publishing legacy. For better or worse, they would work closely together at that task for nearly fifty years.

Some family members claim that Jonathan was the favorite son; others claim it was Frank.[48] Still others claim the Old Man had no favorite. In any case, one would be hard pressed to find or support claims that either Joe Jr. or Worth was the favored son.[49] If the volume and detail of the surviving correspondence indicates the extent of the relationship, then Jonathan was the closest to the Old Man. Born in 1902, Jonathan attended grammar school in Raleigh. After his father moved to Washington to become secretary of the navy, Jonathan continued his studies at John Eaton School, and later he followed Worth at St. Albans. At age sixteen, he spent the last summer of the Great War undergoing military training in a program at Camp Bingham, near Asheville, sponsored by the University of North Carolina. He then matriculated at Chapel Hill in the fall of 1918. A big man on campus from the time he arrived, he soon joined Delta Kappa Epsilon (against his father's advice). Witty and charming when he chose to be, Jonathan also pursued journalistic and literary aspirations at Chapel Hill. He edited the school paper, the *Daily Tar Heel*, and joined the theater company, Carolina Playmakers.[50] Jonathan graduated with the class of 1921 and remained in Chapel Hill and earned a master's degree the following year. He then set out to make his way in the world, first as a cub reporter at the Louisville *Times*, which was owned by Robert Bingham, his mother's cousin.[51] After a brief apprenticeship in Louisville, he attended the Columbia University Law School, where he either dropped out or flunked out, depending on who is telling the story.

Although Jonathan was by his own admission a failure at studying law, he nonetheless passed the bar exam, like his father, and also like his father, he never practiced a day of law in his life—at least not in any remunerative sense. After leaving Columbia, he returned to the *N&O*. Some biographers describe him as a "reporter" or even "police reporter," and he did do some actual reporting during this period. But his father forced him to start at the bottom of the firm. Daniels made Jonathan the *N&O*'s "bill collector," collecting from advertisers and distributors, a position he had apparently held from time to time while still in college.[52] (It was also the first job Joe Jr. and Frank had at the newspaper.) The Old Man had similarly begun at the bottom of the industry's ladder, collecting money from Wilson County subscribers to the Raleigh newspapers, which he had distributed fifty years earlier.

Once on his own, Jonathan quickly revealed some of his weaker personal traits. Among these was a dangerous combination: profligacy and carousing. On more than one occasion, the Old Man scolded is son, albeit mildly, and then bailed him out of trouble. Their correspondence reveals a caring, perhaps overindulgent father who was capable of confronting his children with their shortcomings but who was also reluctant to let them sink as a result of those shortcomings.

Despite Jonathan's personal foibles, he was a gifted writer of both fact and fiction. He worked at the *N&O* off and on during the 1920s, and between 1925 and 1928 he was the paper's correspondent in Washington, D.C. He married Elizabeth Bridgers, an attractive and vivacious woman, in September 1923, and by all accounts theirs was a true love affair that produced a daughter, Adelaide. However, Elizabeth died suddenly in December 1929, and it is possible Jonathan never fully recovered psychologically from the loss of his first wife.[53] He subsequently changed the name of their daughter to Elizabeth[54] and went into intellectual exile. In the Josephus Daniels papers at the Library of Congress, there is a gap in the correspondence with Jonathan following his wife's death. Their letters did not resume until well into the following year. No doubt seeking a change of pace that might help him put his wife's death behind him, by the spring of 1930, Jonathan was in New York writing for *Fortune* magazine, and his professional fortunes at least were about to improve.

Jonathan had finished the manuscript of his first novel in 1929, and early in 1930 it was published as *Clash of Angels*. A heavily metaphorical account of heaven before the creation of humans, the book draws from Judeo-Christian theological and cultural traditions, but it also included elements of Islam, the pre-Christian Greeks, and even Zoroastrianism. Erudite and intellectually challenging yet also comedic, the book was written in a style *Time* magazine described as "satirico-parabolic."[55] It possesses a self-consciously ironic tone that in some ways probably plays better in the twenty-first century than it did in its own time. Still, *Clash of Angels* was received well enough in literary circles, and it earned Jonathan a Guggenheim Fellowship worth $2,500, which allowed him to travel and write in Europe later in 1930 and into 1931.

While traveling through Europe, Jonathan spent considerable time in France, Italy, and Switzerland. None of his correspondence from those months, however, resonates through the years like his summary of the attitudes he encountered in Germany during the summer of 1930. A decade earlier, Josephus Daniels had confided to his diary concerns about a resurgent Germany, and in speeches during the 1920s he had criticized the Versailles Treaty's indemnity clause, calling it a "Carthaginian Peace." In Germany, Jonathan witnessed the sprouts of the next great war. In a letter to his father from Munich, Jonathan described a visit to the Hofbrau Haus, which Adolf Hitler frequented. Jonathan enjoyed the plebian bonhomie of the German beer hall: "On the first floor the poor people drink. There are no waiters and they get their beer for a few cents by serving themselves." Of the Germans he was fond, but wary. Displaying remarkable journalistic insight, two years before Hitler came to power—a time when Germany had no air force, virtually no navy, and an army that served as little more than a border guard—Jonathan predicted that "if there was another War between France and Germany and the rest of the world stayed out of it, it would take more than Joan of Arc to save France."[56]

After returning to New York and *Fortune* in 1932, Jonathan married again in April, and he returned to Raleigh to work once again for the *N&O*. The following year, he became the paper's associate editor. To those who knew him in Raleigh after his return in the early 1930s, Jonathan could appear larger than life. A successful and well-traveled man of letters and an outstanding newspaper editor, he gave the *N&O* a more liberal voice than it had previously possessed, a voice of racial tolerance and reason. In addition, Jonathan, a heavy drinker, opposed prohibition, and his experiences in Europe led him to look favorably on socialism. While the Old Man disagreed with these positions, in their correspondence his tone was mild and instructive. For example, editorially Jonathan pushed equal treatment before the law for African Americans—so much so that he felt he needed to apologize to his father. After publishing an editorial on the subject, he wrote, "Dear Father: I hope I am not making your newspaper too much the colored boy's friend." Later, in response to statements of this type, the Old Man wrote, "You have sometimes felt that I was too strong in my opposition to the recognition of the negro in politics in our State. But I lived through the days of when they all had the ballot and I observed that 90% of them could be used to their own hurt and to the hurt of the better class of people."[57]

Similarly, although Josephus Daniels supported government regulation of big business, and many of his positions in the 1890s could be described as socialistic, over time he had grown suspicious of the government's direct ownership of capital. In another letter to Jonathan, he chided his son, "When the government goes into the business all the employees feel that their wages and salaries must continue to increase and thus far the government has found no way to operate large enterprises successfully."[58] With respect to alcohol, after prohibition was repealed, Jonathan and Frank agonized over running beer ads in the *N&O*. After deciding to do so, Jonathan wrote sheepishly to his father explaining the decision. In his reply, the Old Man refused to rebuke the boys or to micromanage the firm in his absence. He merely wrote, "As to what you will do in the offices, why you can work that out. . . . I will leave that all to you [and Frank]. . . . You can handle it better in Raleigh than I could."[59]

Jonathan left an impression on everyone with whom he came in contact. Something of a polymath who may have been the last man in Raleigh to know everything and everyone worth knowing, at least by Daniels family standards, Jonathan could seem like a character straight out of an F. Scott Fitzgerald novel—and that's the way he wanted it. During those years, Jonathan and his second wife, Lucy Cathcart, with whom he had three daughters, were at or near the top of Raleigh's social hierarchy. Of course the opinions expressed in the *N&O* offended many leading citizens, and that would always keep Jonathan and Lucy at arm's length from some social circles. Still, they were leading members of Raleigh's elite Carolina Country Club, and their home was a hub for Raleigh's fashionable set. Despite their recognized leadership in these circles, according to their oldest daughter, also named Lucy, Jonathan and Lucy Cathcart considered themselves "Bohemian," and they always looked critically upon their social peers at the country club.[60]

An attractive woman in a formal, icy way, Lucy Cathcart was the daughter of a New York chemist credited with inventing Wesson Oil. She was educated in Germany, but the family was originally from Charleston, South Carolina, which in some southern circles was (and still is) spoken of as if it were the Paris of the New World. Lucy Cathcart's maternal ancestors came from Montgomery, Alabama, the first capital of the Confederacy, a point of pride among some southerners. According to her daughters, Lucy always flaunted her New York upbringing and her Charleston and Montgomery roots; she considered Raleigh hopelessly provincial and the Danielses "nouveau riche" and "common."[61] Jonathan tolerated his wife's condescension well enough. One suspects that he was enough of an intuitive psychologist to recognize that much of Lucy Cathcart's animosity toward their life in Raleigh was a reflection of her own personal insecurities. A daughter later commented on how badly her mother would treat individuals of lower socioeconomic status, especially waiters, railroad porters, and hotel staff. Another daughter recalled that if you were among a group talking to Lucy Cathcart, you did not want to be the first to leave, because she would lead the group in a discussion of your faults the moment you were gone.[62] Of this behavior Jonathan was known to say with good, though typically biting, humor, There are only two kinds of women from South Carolina—those who never owned a pair of shoes and those who treat you as if you never owned a pair. It seemed to be his way of saying that he understood his wife better than she understood herself, and indeed, despite their heavy drinking and often-violent arguments, the couple maintained a genuine affection for each other.

In spite of his national reputation as a writer and his recognized success in several different professional spheres, Jonathan often seemed to wrestle with his father's considerable eminence. Although Jonathan possessed many of his father's talents, some who knew him felt that the Old Man's reputation "formed a shadow which [Jonathan] struggled to escape by being its opposite." Where the Old Man was a warm, gentle, considerate teetotaler, Jonathan, in an effort to be his opposite, "was driven to drink and smoke heavily, and he took pride in expressing anger cruelly and in not appearing cautious or diligent."[63] Both men had large egos, but although he explicitly renounced the title, Josephus Daniels was by any reasonable standard a self-made man. Knowing his true strengths and ever confident of his own abilities, he was always comfortable to appear to be less than he actually was. Jonathan's ego, on the other hand, "needed to be stroked," but unlike his father, he seemed incapable of having it stroked through his own considerable accomplishments.[64] He always needed to appear to be more than he actually was.

Perhaps, as family members and acquaintances suggest, Jonathan's troubled psyche resulted from his insecurities in the shadow of a greater and better man who happened to be his father. Perhaps it was because he worked with the Old Man more closely than the other sons on the editorial policies of the *N&O*. Or perhaps it was something altogether more subtle that we will never be able to understand. Jonathan's daughter Lucy, herself a successful writer and psychologist, clearly felt that the failings of both of her parents were at least partly a response to "very successful teetotaling fathers, who were worshipped by and absent for their wives." She claimed that "rebellions against these controlling, righteous, and/or perfectionistic parents were the bedrock of our household. Both my parents drank too much," with Jonathan "smoking, drinking, and never shying away from risks" to compensate for feelings of inadequacy when compared with such a respected father.[65]

Still, Lucy makes the case that Jonathan was his father's "favorite child," a point with which Jonathan agreed.[66] The two were the most prominent men of letters in the family, and Josephus clearly had a special relationship with Jonathan. He was openly proud of Jonathan's many literary and journalistic accomplishments, which trumped those of the other boys put together, and his correspondence with Jonathan often opened with "My Dear Partner." It is clear from the primary documents that have survived that the Old Man had great confidence in Jonathan. Josephus never relied on his other sons in personal and professional ways as he did with Jonathan.

Despite the Old Man's closeness to Jonathan, in many ways the son with whom Daniels, and Addie especially, shared the best relationship over the longest period of time was the youngest boy, Frank. Quieter, or at least a less public figure, than Jonathan; more competent around the shop than Joe Jr.; and more of a homebody than Worth, Frank remained physically and emotionally close to his parents his entire life. Unlike his three older brothers, he never performed military service; unlike Worth and Jonathan, he never left Raleigh for any substantial length of time to seek his fortune in the wider world. As the baby of the family, he certainly held a special place in his mother's heart. A warmhearted and generally good-humored man who shared his father's considerable intelligence and capacity for work, Frank by and large shunned the political stage, and he was never in the public eye in the way that Jonathan was. Focusing on the business side of the *N&O*, more than any other person Frank was responsible for perpetuating the paper's financial success into the next generation.

Born in 1904, in appearance Frank was more Bagley than Daniels. Broad-shouldered and possessing a thick head of dark hair, Frank was more classically handsome than the other males in the Daniels family, all of whom had the slightly feminine features of their father. Named after his father's oldest brother, Frank was still just a boy when Josephus became secretary of the navy early in 1913. Whereas Joe Jr. could be intimidated by his father's stature, Worth chafed at the Old Man's control, and Jonathan viewed his father as a journalistic and literary peer and competitor, as the years went by, Frank, although the youngest, took on a somewhat paternalistic role with respect to his parents. Even as a young man, he handled the family's business and personal financial affairs, which despite the legal fiction of incorporation, were really one and the same. He eventually replaced Herbert

Jackson in these roles. In both personal and financial matters, Frank's counsel was mature beyond his years. When, during the 1930s, Josephus's brother Charles found himself mired in his own personal financial disaster, from Mexico the Old Man directed Frank to straighten out Charles's finances. Writing to Charles, Josephus noted that Frank had "the best business head in the Daniels family. I don't think much of your business judgment or mine."[67] (The last sentence was, of course, only half correct. The Old Man's business judgment was excellent.) Frank quietly tidied up the mess that was Charles's finances. (Frank also handled some financial problems in which Jonathan managed to become entangled, including unpaid tax liabilities.)[68]

Frank's wisdom and his father's confidence in it extended beyond financial matters. Friends, neighbors, relatives, and longtime, recent, and distant North Carolina acquaintances perpetually sought the family's political patronage. Although it possessed considerable influence, the Daniels family could never meet the nearly unlimited demand for its influence, and even if it could have, there were many supplicants whom Frank wisely kept at arm's length. As time went by, Frank became the paterfamilias of the clan.[69] Neither as reticent as Joe Jr. nor as prickly and flamboyant as Jonathan, Frank often served as the final arbiter of disputes at the *N&O*. He became the pillar of both the family business and Raleigh society. His brother, partner, and frequent combatant Jonathan said of him, "Frank is a solid citizen. He keeps all the rest of us in bread and butter. He's been a very able newspaper publisher. . . . Frank is the Establishment."[70] (Coming from Jonathan, who was often critical of "the Establishment," this can be interpreted as both a compliment and an insult.) Prudent in business as well as his personal life, he was the type of man to whom others turned for counsel of all types. For fifty years, Frank and his wife, Ruth, and their children Frank Jr. and Patricia, served as the embodiment of mid-twentieth-century bourgeois respectability in Raleigh. With Jonathan, he perpetuated and expanded the Old Man's legacy at the *N&O*, taking over the newspaper in the spring of 1933 when their father left Raleigh for Mexico City, where, once again, he found himself in public service.

HEALING OLD WOUNDS

By the time the 1932 presidential election came around, the economic downturn that began in the summer of 1929 had turned into the worst economic crisis in the nation's history. As had happened in 1912, Daniels found himself conflicted over the state-level candidates. For the first time in his life, he seriously considered running for public office. He had his sights set on the governor's mansion and almost certainly would have won the nomination and the election. However, in January he was in an automobile accident in Atlanta while returning from a speaking engagement. His injuries were not life threatening, but he was laid up during the primary season. In the race for the Democratic nomination for governor, the machine candidate, J. C. B. Ehringhaus, defeated reformer Richard Fountain. Daniels sympathized with Fountain, but not enough to buck the machine. In the senatorial race, Robert "Our Bob" Reynolds defeated the incumbent, Cameron Morrison, in the Democratic primary. Morrison, a former governor and Daniels's preference for the Senate, had been appointed to the seat following the death of Daniels's old friend Lee Overman. Daniels liked "Our Bob" personally; but he never took him seriously as a politician, and he expended no effort campaigning on Reynolds's behalf.[71] Rather, as he had done when Woodrow Wilson ran for president twenty years earlier, Daniels shunned the state races and focused on getting Franklin Roosevelt nominated and elected that year.

Initially, Daniels had supported his old cabinet colleague Newton Baker over FDR, thinking the older man would be more electable; but Baker's candidacy never caught fire, and during the primary season, Daniels happily switched to his former subordinate. Arriving in Chicago just before the opening of the Democratic National Convention on June 27, Daniels was still a major player in the party, and he made a splash by announcing that he would not object to a prohibition-repeal plank in the party platform. (He had earlier forced repeal on his fellow Tar Heel delegates.) As he had done with Wilson and his pro-British policy in the run up to the 1916 campaign, Daniels was willing to surrender a policy he supported in return for the chance at victory. And victory it was. FDR was close to winning on the first ballot and did so on the fourth. A grueling campaign followed. On two extended trips, seventy-year-old Daniels traveled to and spoke in Oregon, California, Nevada, Utah, Nebraska, Iowa, Indiana, and Ohio. In September, the *Saturday Evening Post* ran a hagiography of FDR penned by Daniels under the headline "Franklin Roosevelt As I Know Him." The effort paid off. FDR beat the incumbent, Daniels's old colleague from the Great War, Herbert Hoover, by a count of 472 to 59 electoral votes.

Following the election, FDR began assembling his administration. He tagged Daniels for a post but wavered on exactly which one. Finally, he settled on a new position. Before the inauguration, the president-elect asked Daniels to take over the coordination of the nation's railroads and its international shipping, essentially asking him to become the "transportation czar." (Although the U.S. Department of Transportation did not exist at the time, it is clear from their discussion that FDR imagined Daniels as a de facto secretary of transportation with broader powers than Congress would ultimately vest in that office.) According to Daniels, FDR envisioned nationalizing the management and coordination of the country's shipping and hauling businesses, if not their actual ownership. Knowing firsthand Daniels's capacity for organization, FDR tapped the right man. But Daniels did not want the job. He was willing to serve but thought he had enough seniority within, and had spilled enough blood for, the Democratic Party that he could be selective about the position he accepted. (Daniels coveted a return to the Navy Department, but FDR was too shrewd a politician to have his former boss, and an old bull of such standing in the party, in the cabinet.)[72] Daniels never said whether he turned down the transportation post because he did not want the job or because he did not think it was important enough for him. But after he did turn it down, it was not clear he would receive anything from the new administration, and apparently that was fine with him.[73]

Daniels attended the inauguration on March 4 and then returned to Raleigh to continue his chores as publisher of the *N&O*. However, a few days later he received a letter from Cordell Hull, the secretary of state designee and a Daniels associate of long standing. (Hull had been a leading Democratic member of the U.S. House during Daniels's tenure in the Wilson administration.) Hull noted that the president wanted Daniels to serve as ambassador to Mexico. Daniels accepted the appointment and on March 18, 1933, took the oath of office. Two weeks later he and Addie traveled to Mexico City, where a new stage of their lives would begin.

The timing of the position worked well for the family business. Joe Jr., Jonathan, and Frank all now worked at the *N&O*, and it was getting crowded at the top of the firm. Joe Jr., in his late thirties, had proved inadequate. It was time for the two younger boys to get their shot. In the two weeks between taking the oath of office and leaving on the train to Mexico City, the Old Man rearranged the firm's organizational chart. When Daniels had left the *N&O* to take up the position of navy secretary in 1913, he had left three men in charge—Henry Bagley (business), Lee Alford (printing), and Edward Britton (editing)—with his brother Charles and Joe Jr. also playing poorly defined roles. Five chiefs turned out to be a disaster, and only Alford remained throughout Daniels's absence. Having learned his lesson, this time there were only two chiefs: Frank and Jonathan. Jonathan would be the editor. Frank would handle the printing and distribution and serve as business manager. Joe Jr., who had taken the title of secretary-treasurer and business manager when Henry Bagley left the firm late in 1916, was dropped from the letterhead and would henceforth play no important role at the paper.[74]

Daniels's arrival in Mexico did not go smoothly. Many Mexicans remembered the U.S. landing at Veracruz, which Daniels had ordered in 1914, and the resulting casualties, which numbered in the hundreds. As recently as 1928, the Mexican government had rejected the U.S. military attaché in Mexico City, a marine officer, because he had served at Veracruz. When the Roosevelt administration announced that Daniels had been nominated for the ambassadorship, riots broke out in Mexico City, and the U.S. Embassy was stoned. The protestors were an unusual alliance of left-wing Marxists and right-wing ultranationalists. Both groups were offended by Daniels's gunboat diplomacy years earlier.[75]

At the time of the appointment, it was not known how the Mexican government would respond or if Mexican president Abelardo L. Rodríguez would even receive Daniels. However, several factors helped smooth Daniels's path to the post. One of these was FDR's personal letter to Rodríguez in which he noted that Daniels was "an old and trusted friend and that the selection of so distinguished a national personage and close associate of the President [i.e., FDR] is for the purpose of indicating the deep and friendly interest which this administration has in maintaining the present excellent relations which now so happily exist between the two countries."[76] Another factor in Daniels's favor was the goodwill displayed by the Mexican press at what it saw as the elevation of a fellow newspaperman. Although mostly under the control of the Rodríguez regime, the press still influenced the local populace. In the event, despite some vocal protests in the streets, the Mexican newspaper coverage was quite favorable.[77] However, the most important factor was the turn taken by Mexican politics in the years just prior to Daniels's appointment.

When Daniels left office as secretary of the navy in the spring of 1921, Mexico was in its tenth year of revolution. Venustiano Carranza, formally recognized by the Wilson administration following the turmoil of 1914, had tried to stabilize the country, but his fellow revolutionaries Pancho Villa and Emiliano Zapata proved better at making war than making peace. Villa remained at large until 1923, but Carranza eventually had Zapata assassinated in 1919. The following year, as Carranza prepared to step down, he fell afoul of the army in choosing a successor, and he was assassinated by forces loyal to the military. Following a brief regency, General Álvaro Obregón assumed the office of president on December 1, 1920. Although no democrat, at least not by Josephus Daniels's definition, Obregón pulled off a feat no Mexican president had managed in recent memory: a legal and reasonably peaceful transition to the next regime.[78]

Obregón passed the baton to another former revolutionary, General Plutarco Elías Calles, whom Daniels variously referred to as Mexico's *Jefe Máximo* (Supreme Chief) or Strong Man.[79] Like Daniels, Calles had been born into destitution; unlike Daniels, Calles had little opportunity to rise in business. But as a political street brawler, Calles found legitimacy in the way that many impoverished American boys of his generation did: He became a police officer. Getting paid regularly while avoiding field work on a hacienda was a big step up the socioeconomic ladder, and eventually Calles hired out his gun to a series of strongmen during the revolution. Along the way, Calles became embittered toward the Catholic Church and the conservative ruling classes that had traditionally dominated Mexican society. Upon becoming president, he waged a war of expropriation against the church, a war that by some estimates led to the deaths of thousands of church supporters.[80]

When Calles left office in 1928, he was to be succeeded by his predecessor Obregón, who supported Calles's policies, including his persecution of the church. However, this led to Obregón's assassination at the hands of a Catholic fanatic and Calles's return to power. However, to maintain at least the illusion of democracy, the *Jefe Máximo* placed a series of puppets in the presidential palace. Thus when Daniels arrived, Mexico was run by an authoritarian regime, but one with unambiguous populist leanings. Calles remained the power behind the throne; Rodríguez, another former soldier, resided in the presidential palace with the *Jefe*'s blessing. Rodríguez did what Calles told him, and Calles's opinion of Daniels was formed with the help of the foreign minister, Dr. J. M. Puig Casauranc. Puig had read Daniels's *Life of Woodrow Wilson* and was familiar with Daniels's other writings. He became convinced that Daniels was a true progressive who would support the populist strain in Mexico's authoritarian government. Accordingly, Puig persuaded the *Jefe* to take the same view.[81]

The first major domestic issue in which Daniels became entangled involved the relationship between the Mexican government and the Catholic Church. Calles was an avowed atheist, and he oversaw an explicitly anti-church regime. To say that he persecuted the church would not be an overstatement. Because the church sided politically with Mexico's most conservative elements, Calles and his political progeny saw the church as an opponent. While his handpicked successors stuck to the populist, secular trend in the *Jefe*'s policies, some were decidedly less anticlerical in their personal outlook and policies. Thus Daniels had an opportunity to broker a rapprochement between church and state. Politically, Daniels sided with the progressives against the conservatives; therefore he was castigated in the conservative press in both Mexico and the United States for being anti-Catholic. This was unfair. In a quiet and diplomatic way, throughout his tenure, Daniels cultivated better relations between the Mexican government and the Catholic Church. Ignoring the personal attacks on him for treating with the government while it persecuted the church, Daniels worked quietly behind the scenes. His primary objective was simple; he sought the reopening of churches across the country. Rural areas in Mexico had often gone without a priest even when the church possessed considerable power. By the time Daniels was posted to Mexico City, after years of Calles's rule, many Catholics in medium-sized and even larger cities had no regular access to the sacraments. Daniels appealed to national and local Mexican politicians and persuaded one political leader after another to permit the reopening of local churches. This reflected U.S. commitment to freedom of worship, but it also reflected Daniels's own, sincerely held convictions. In Daniels's view, access to the sacraments administered by a Mexican priest might not have been as good for the people as Methodism, but it was better than no access at all.[82]

———

Although Daniels took the church conflict seriously and was responsible for opening dozens of churches across the country, with respect to the importance of U.S. policy in Mexico, the church-state issue paled in comparison with the major economic issues. Daniels explicitly listed five major concerns in his correspondence from this period. Roughly in chronological order, these were (1) a large set of financial claims and counterclaims between Mexico and the United States, and between Mexicans and U.S. citizens, some of which dated back more than a century but most of which were associated with the recent Mexican revolution; (2) water disputes along the Colorado and Rio Grande Rivers; (3) Mexican government debt, which the government had repudiated or on which it had ceased paying interest, and which was held by U.S. investors; (4) disputes over American-owned agricultural land that had been expropriated by the Mexican government; and (5) Mexican oil fields controlled by U.S. firms.[83] From the time he took office in 1933 until war broke out again in Europe in the fall of 1939, most of Daniels's professional time was taken up with these five issues.

Borrowing from Charles Dickens's *Bleak House*, Daniels frequently referred to the claims issue as *Jarndyce v. Jarndyce*. After Daniels settled in at the U.S. Embassy in Mexico City, he found on his desk more than 1,000 claims by U.S. citizens, firms, and the U.S. government against Mexican citizens, firms, and the Mexican government. (These claims excluded those related to water rights, government debt, agricultural land, and oil fields, which Daniels viewed as separate issues.) Counterclaims by Mexicans against various U.S. entities exceeded 600.[84] Converting the claims into dollar amounts, Daniels's staff came up with a figure for both countries: $499,708,539.27 in U.S. claims against Mexico, and $243,894,800.32 in Mexican claims against the United States. Even if the Mexican government had possessed the $250 million difference between the two figures, the disputes could not simply be settled by a lump sum payment, since the plaintiffs in one dispute were not necessarily the defendants in another. Thus each dispute—some as small as $10, others as large as $42 million—had to be addressed case by case. As in *Jarndyce v. Jarndyce*, the costs of litigation were well on their way to eating up the value of many of the original claims.

However, upon Daniels's arrival, Mexican foreign minister Puig, with whom Daniels got on well, offered a means of cutting the Gordian knot of claims. The most direct solution to this costly approach, Puig argued, was for the U.S. government and the Mexican government to serve as trustees of the claims of their respective citizens and/or corporations. Daniels and Puig would agree to a net difference in claims, and the matter would be settled with one lump-sum transfer from the treasury of one country to that of the other. The two treasuries would then disperse monies to settle individual claims. Daniels, a lawyer by training but not mindset, leaped at the transparent logic of the approach. (Not incidentally, he figured that a net $250 million distribution from the Roosevelt administration to various cash-strapped American taxpayers and corporations feeling the brunt of the Depression would be a public relations coup for the Democrats.) Unfortunately, he figured too quickly. Puig had no intention of paying 100 cents on the dollar for the net difference in claims.

U.S. citizens were not the only foreigners seeking relief from damages imposed during that era. Europeans had invested in Mexico as well, and collectively they had already settled for considerably less than 100 cents on the dollar. In fact, the figures Puig shared with Daniels put the total European payment at 2.65 percent of the combined claims. This would knock down to $7 million the lump sum paid by Mexico to settle all of the U.S. claims in question. Daniels was ambivalent. Politically, the amount was too small; however, during the negotiating process Daniels's sympathy had shifted toward the Mexican claimants. His correspondence with wealthy Americans, some of whom had individual claims worth millions of dollars, showed little consideration for their plight.[85] But after considering two facts—the U.S. Treasury was spending millions of dollars on claims commissions that were getting nowhere, and the Mexican Treasury was practically empty—he argued at the State Department and in testimony before Congress that 2.65 percent today was considerably more money than 0 percent in the future. FDR, Hull, and a Democratic majority in the Senate agreed, and a claims treaty was signed in April 1934. All things considered, it was on net a small diplomatic victory for Daniels and a financial windfall for the Mexicans.

Daniels held his head in both hands as he tried to keep it from aching while he went through those disputed claims, on which he worked through much of his first year in Mexico. However, that tale of woe could not compare with those that came next. The first was the dispute over water rights along the Colorado and Rio Grande Rivers. As Daniels humorously described it, "I was almost drowned when I tried to find a landing in the rushing floods of water disputes on the Colorado and Rio Grande."[86] On the Colorado, the major tributaries lay in the United States, and key portions of the river were being dammed for economic development there, including irrigation. The river flows into the Gulf of California, separating the modern Mexican states of Baja California Norte and Sonora. At the time, the Colorado delta was a vibrant Mexican agricultural region, but with the United States holding up the flow of water, it was destined to become a desert. Mexico demanded the flow be maintained. Following the logic of the law of capture, the United States argued that it owned the water in the Colorado. With respect to the Rio Grande, the opposite case held. Major tributaries were in Mexico. Here the United States reversed its argument and noted that under the 1848 Treaty of Guadalupe Hidalgo, which had ended the Mexican-American War, the middle of the Rio Grande separated the United States from Mexico. Thus the United States shared the right of capture with Mexico. Part of the dispute had been subjected to international arbitration, and when the arbitrator (a Canadian) ruled in favor of Mexico, the United States simply rejected the decision. Eventually, both countries agreed to a convention on the Rio Grande, but the Colorado issue was never resolved on Daniels's watch.

After settling the claims case and at least addressing, if not settling, the water disputes, Daniels turned to the issue of Mexican government debt. In terms of value, the claims of Wall Street bondholders against the Mexican government rivaled those of all the other claims described above put together. (Daniels's staff never agreed on a figure, and he simply estimated it in "the hundreds of millions of dollars.")[87] Most of the money had been lent to Mexico's prerevolution government or Mexico's government-sanctioned railroad syndicates. Because of the damage from a decade of revolution and the subsequent nationalization of the roads, the lenders had formed a consortium to retrieve their money. Daniels called the consortium the "Bondholder's Committee." It was chaired by Morgan partner Thomas Lamont. A representative of the committee, along with representatives of other international lenders, visited Daniels in the spring of 1936, and he facilitated a meeting with leaders of the Mexican Treasury. Once the bondholders' envoys began trying to assemble a deal, and talking tough while doing so, Daniels began distancing the embassy, and thus U.S. policy, from Wall Street. When the deal fell through, the representative returned to the United States and placed some of the blame for the failure on Daniels, who was then forced to defend his position to the State Department.[88]

Daniels excelled at this kind of political infighting, and he never backed down from such a fight. In a memorandum to Secretary of State Hull, Daniels explained his position. He again emphasized the near-bankruptcy of the Mexican government. (Recognizing that Mexico could not even pay in a lump sum the $7 million agreed to in the claims treaty of 1934, the U.S. Treasury had accepted annual installments of $500,000. The first payment had only recently been made.) Daniels argued that at least part of any money Wall Street squeezed out of Mexico would come from monies that would otherwise go to meet the claims payments. Daniels would not favor making Wall Street whole, or even partially whole, over the many smaller claimants who had only recently been forced to accept 2.65 cents on the dollar for their claims. In addition, Daniels disputed the net claim that the bondholders presented to the Mexican Treasury (roughly $500 million, though that figure was not substantially larger than the upper bound estimates his own staff had arrived at).[89] Daniels had a long history of anti–Wall Street sentiment. Moreover, he learned that much of the debt originally issued on Wall Street had subsequently been sold to European investors, thus relieving some of the political pressure for a favorable settlement.

To complicate matters, during the negotiations in Mexico, the government debt dispute became inextricably linked with disputes over U.S.-

owned agricultural land that had been expropriated by Mexico's postrevo-
lution governments. The Mexican government viewed these two sets of
claims as part of one big dispute with the United States. For Daniels, the
matter was not so clear. As in the miscellaneous claims dispute, there were
many different U.S. parties involved. But in Mexico City, Daniels found
himself simultaneously negotiating with the Mexicans over the agricultural land and the claims of the Bondholder's Committee. Daniels told
Hull that U.S. claimants could only squeeze so much out of the Mexican
Treasury.[90] Whatever went to one party would not go to another. Not surprisingly, Daniels pushed harder for the landholders than he did for the
bondholders. He could usually be counted on to choose a farmer, even a
large one, over a Wall Street bondholder. The secretary of state supported
his ambassador. The State Department did not force Daniels to press Wall
Street's case in any subsequent negotiations with the Mexicans. In the end,
the bondholders settled for $49.6 million, less than 10 percent of their ini-
tial claim, but it was a better deal than the miscellaneous claims holders
got.[91] As for the agricultural land dispute, like the Rio Grande clash, it was
never satisfactorily settled during Daniels's time in Mexico.

Mexican intransigence on the bondholders' demands and the land dispute foreshadowed a conflict of nearly equal size involving U.S. oil concessions in Mexico. In Daniels's words, he was about to be "troubled with
oil."[92] In the presidential race of 1934, the liberal Lázaro Cárdenas won the
nomination over the conservative Pérez Treviño. Cárdenas's victory proved
to be a watershed in Mexican history. It indicated the declining influence of
the *Jefe Máximo* Calles, who had backed Treviño. The election of 1934 was
the last one Calles would influence in any way. Military and political success had weakened the strongman's commitment to populism. Despite his
leftist rhetoric, Calles had been moving to the right. Although he had not
befriended the church, he had befriended wealthy conservative friends of
the church. Among his other friends were U.S. oilmen. As oil became big
business in the 1920s, disputes between Calles and U.S. petroleum firms
had emerged. Dwight Morrow, the U.S. ambassador at the time (another
House of Morgan man and the father-in-law of Charles Lindbergh), had
worked out a peacekeeping arrangement that permitted enormous U.S. investment to move forward.[93] It was said that the deal included Calles's subsequent enrichment. It was also said that the settlement of other disputes
between the two countries had included a roughly $10 million subvention
for Calles's "support." All the while, in public Calles maintained his popu-

list credentials by continuing to harangue the church and the country's rich conservative leaders. But those in the know understood it was a sham, and among them it was said that in a rich neighborhood of Cuernavaca, Calles lived on the "Street of Millionaire Socialists."[94]

Calles finally gave up the populist rhetoric altogether following Cárdenas's victory. By that time the world had become familiar with the horrors of Soviet communism, and the epithet "communist" carried some weight. Calles began hurling it at Cárdenas. When the *Jefe* did this, he lost the support of Josephus Daniels, the most important American in Mexico. Daniels personally knew well seven men who had been or would someday become president of Mexico. Of those, his correspondence suggests that the one he respected the most was Cárdenas. During his administration, Cárdenas clearly took Mexico down what economists would unambiguously call a socialist path, but Mexican historians emphasize that nationalism, rather than a doctrinaire socialism, was the driving force behind Cárdenas's policies, and he clearly was no communist.[95] Mexico's economy was so tightly bound to mineral and petroleum wealth that socialism, in effect, meant expropriation of the land and capital employed in the mining and oil industries. There simply was not much else worth nationalizing.

The move toward socialism squeezed Calles's rich and generous friends, and it led to the explicit charge that Cárdenas was a front man for communists. Described as "a fervent nationalist as well as a political radical," Cárdenas intended to socialize Mexico's largest industries.[96] He also had experience as a military commander, and he did not intend to be another yes-man for Calles. Again, civil war seemed possible in Mexico. But before the shooting started, Daniels brokered a deal. Perhaps in consultation with Cárdenas (though in his memoirs Daniels recorded only exchanges with Calles), Daniels arranged for Calles to go into a comfortable exile in the United States as a "political refugee."[97]

With Calles out of the way, Cárdenas laid the plans for taking over Mexico's oil industry. The problem was that the vast majority of the capital invested in the industry belonged to privately owned U.S. and European companies. Cárdenas planned to expropriate this wealth and possibly offer a token payment for it. Hundreds of millions of dollars was at stake. By the 1920s, Mexico was the world's second-largest producer of crude petroleum.[98] Although Mexican output slipped in the 1930s, the country was still a major producer. The industry might have served as an engine for economic development. The Mexican Constitution of 1917 vested mineral rights in the national government, but neither the Mexican government nor the country's indigenous companies possessed the capital or the know-how to exploit these vast petroleum reserves. Thus the industry had been dominated by U.S. and European capital, and most of the profits, as well the wages of the highest-paid workers (the managers and technicians), had been repatriated along with the oil itself, which helped fuel economic development in the United States and Europe.

Cárdenas used labor unrest in the oil fields in the spring of 1937 as an excuse to create a commission to recommend reform in the industry.[99] The commission focused on labor reform, with the objective of keeping a larger share of the industry's wage bill in Mexico. To that end, the commission formally recommended a substantial wage increase, including an annual minimum in total wages paid; a forty-hour workweek; mandatory vacation time; a generous pension plan; and the replacement of foreign workers with Mexicans. In short, the commission's recommendations, if accepted by Cárdenas, would have permitted the foreign companies to take the oil and keep their profits, but the majority of the industry's wages would remain in Mexico. Not surprisingly, Cárdenas accepted his commission's recommendations. The oil companies protested and eventually took the case to Mexico's supreme court, which ruled in the government's favor. While continuing to negotiate, the companies threatened to close their Mexican operations. By the spring of 1938, Cárdenas had had enough. He declared the oil companies to be "in rebellion" and "conspiring" against Mexico. On the evening of March 18, at a cabinet meeting, he announced that he was taking over the foreign capital in Mexico's oil industry.[100]

The howl from the U.S. oil companies (and their elected representatives) could be heard from Wall Street (and Washington) to the U.S. Embassy in Mexico City. For five years, economic disputes had dominated Daniels's time as ambassador. Although the dollar value of the expropriated oil assets did not exceed that of the bond claims, the naked exercise of state power in the expropriation added a troubling dimension to the oil company seizure. As a capitalist himself, Daniels could not fully embrace Cárdenas's move. It was theft no matter how hard the president tried to dress it up as a legal response to the oil companies' "rebellion." Still, Daniels felt more sympathy for the Mexican workers than he did for either his fellow capitalists on Wall Street or philosophical notions of the sanctity of private property. In fact, late in 1937 Daniels had pressed a representative of the Sinclair Oil Company to simply accept Cárdenas's demands concerning the labor issues. The oilman rejected the idea out of hand.

Throughout the early months of 1938, Daniels facilitated the ongoing negotiations between the Mexican government and the oil companies. He anticipated some act by Cárdenas, but he was caught off guard by the complete expropriation. He had anticipated that a receiver would be appointed to operate the companies while the terms of a takeover were worked out. The companies and their creditors, represented by a consortium of Wall Street investment banks, put the value of the expropriated capital at $408 million. Mexico countered with a $7 million appraisal. (Given the subsequent output of the fields in question, a claim between $250 and $300 million would not have been outrageous.) Once again, Daniels was placed between American economic interests and the Mexican Treasury. In close contact with Secretary of State Hull and FDR, Daniels counseled the administration to take a circumspect position. Hull issued a stern statement—sterner than Daniels recommended—to the Mexican government on March 26. Daniels, now openly siding with the Mexicans, argued that Cárdenas had not violated Mexican law and that the companies had not been good ambassadors of FDR's version of Wilson's old Good Neighbor policy. On the other side, Daniels counseled Cárdenas to send an explanatory note, essentially a legal brief, to FDR, which Cárdenas did. In response, Daniels then counseled FDR to call for a reasonable "indemnification" for the companies' stock- and bondholders. FDR did so, and the matter was subjected to diplomatic arbitration.

That Hull and FDR quickly came around to Daniels's position on the oil expropriation owed much to the timing of world events. On the day of the takeover, Germany's Foreign Office released the text of the Anschluss Law, which formalized Germany's conquest of Austria.[101] Even before World War I, FDR had been a Germanophobe. As one of his biographers writes, he "recognized from the earliest moments of the Third Reich that Western democracy probably could not coexist with it."[102] Hull felt the same way. Following the Anschluss, the secretary of state complained that Germany was "becoming the colossus of Europe," and in alliance with Japan it would "try to rule the world."[103] Daniels, Hull, and FDR all remembered how the Germans had reached out to Mexico in the previous war. In addition, in the years between the wars, the Great Powers traded their cavalries for tanks, which ran on petroleum. They had built great air forces, which flew on petroleum, and their naval vessels now ran on fuel oil rather than coal. All three U.S. leaders recognized that Mexico and Mexican oil, no matter who owned the capital that brought it out of the ground, would play an important role in the war that was on the horizon in both Europe and the

Far East. They were not going to let Wall Street damage a crucial strategic relationship.

International diplomacy did not interest the oil companies, and they continued to hold out for a favorable settlement. However, after Hitler subsequently invaded Czechoslovakia and then Poland the following year, Daniels declared the oil expropriation issue to be "as dead as Julius Caesar."[104] Still, the negotiations on the dollar amount of the indemnity dragged on for another year and a half. The matter was eventually turned over to a joint U.S.-Mexican commission, which settled on a figure of $30 million in compensation. The companies rejected the amount, but after the United States entered the war, the State Department informed the investors that the deal was now offered on a take-it-or-leave-it basis. They took it. In percentage terms, it was a better deal than the other U.S. claimants got on Daniels's watch.

While Nazism expanded in Central Europe, Daniels achieved the State Department's primary objective during the oil and land negotiations, which was to keep Mexico in the pro-U.S. camp as war approached. Cárdenas's term ended in November 1940. By then, Germany had added Denmark, Norway, the Netherlands, Belgium, and France to its list of conquests. Only Britain, among the European powers, held out. In order to break the British, Hitler launched the Battle of Britain, his attempt to bomb the British into submission, and the Battle of the Atlantic, which was designed to close off the sea lanes. As in 1915, German U-boats would be unleashed to sink U.S. commerce destined for Britain. Mexico was about to become more valuable as a military ally than as a source of revenue for Wall Street or U.S. oil companies.

As a result, Daniels's efforts turning an old enemy into a friend paid off. In 1940, the United State embargoed key industrial goods to Japan; Cárdenas followed suit. In July of the following year, the United States added petroleum to the list of embargoed goods, and Ávila Camacho, the next president, followed suit. Following the attack on Pearl Harbor, Germany and Italy formally joined Japan and declared war on the United States. As Germany then directed its U-boats at the United States, Mexico declared war on the Axis Powers. Furthermore, following passage of the Selective Training and Service Act, millions of Americans were drafted into military service. The resulting decline in the labor force threatened the country's role as the "arsenal of democracy." Rosie the Riveter helped, but so did hundreds of thousands of Mexican workers who were added to the U.S. labor force through the Bracero Program. A potential enemy in the previous world war, Mexico was a staunch and important ally in the next one. As much as anyone, Daniels deserves credit for that turnabout.

———

In the fall of 1941, Daniels, in his eightieth year, remained active as ever. He focused on his memoirs, which eventually ran to five volumes and which he had been working on since the mid-1930s. (George Creel, a member of Wilson's administration during the Great War, reviewed the volume covering the years leading up to the war and noted of Daniels, "No man living is better fitted to write of the years between 1910 and 1917.")[105] While Josephus maintained his vigor, Addie sank into poor health. For nearly fifty years, she had been overweight. Now in her seventies, she was plagued by a number of chronic ailments, including severe arthritis, hypertension, and an accompanying congestive heart condition. She could no longer fulfill her role as hostess at the U.S. Embassy in Mexico City. With war on the horizon, Daniels would not have left his post were it not for his wife's infirmities, but he put her health above his duties. Hoping that she might recover in Raleigh, on October 30 he submitted his letter of resignation to FDR. The president, addressing Daniels as "Chief," wrote a warm thank you to him for his service in Mexico. FDR also granted his old boss an extended vacation before formally accepting his resignation (and thus taking him off the State Department payroll). This was a small financial windfall for Daniels, who had spent from his own pocket to entertain at the embassy in Mexico City. In fact, Frank later told his son, Frank Jr., that if alcohol had been served at the embassy, "it would have probably bankrupted the *N&O*."[106]

After wrapping up matters in Mexico and taking their well-earned vacation, Josephus and Addie arrived back in Raleigh in February 1942. Daniels returned to the *News and Observer* and found that the newspaper was not big enough for him and Jonathan. As one family member put it, "When Josephus came back, Jonathan left."[107] There was no big blowup that led to a break, but it was clear that father and son could no longer work together in a boss-subordinate relationship. Jonathan had run the editorial side of the *N&O* for a decade, and he simply could not go back to being his father's employee. The Roosevelt administration always had a place for men like Jonathan, and with his father's support and blessing, Jonathan became a roving troubleshooter for FDR. Later he served as press secretary, a position he continued to hold after Harry Truman replaced the deceased FDR in 1945.

The move from Mexico City to Raleigh did not improve Addie's condition. By the middle of 1943, she no longer ventured outside the house, and by early December she was bedridden. Daniels continued his work at the newspaper in the mornings and evenings, but he came home for lunch (driven back and forth by his African American driver, Spurgeon Fields; Daniels never learned to drive). He spent every afternoon by his wife's bedside while she maintained consciousness. When she slept, he would slip down to his first-floor office and work on his correspondence. On December 18 she lost consciousness. That day, Daniels wrote a congratulatory message to FDR, who had just returned from his meeting in Tehran with Stalin and Churchill, and informed the president of Addie's plight. That night her condition worsened, and she died the next day. Daniels's grief was palpable. His posthumous gift to her was the dedication of the final volume of his memoirs. The epigraph, a quote from Thackeray, reads, "The truest and tenderest and purest wife ever man was blessed with. To have such a love is the one blessing, in comparison of which all earthly joy is of no value; and to think of her is to praise God."[108]

After Addie died, Josephus continued to work every day, except Sunday, of course. The Daniels clan in Raleigh viewed him with a mixture of awe— as that befitting an old and scarred yet decorated warrior returned from the campaigns—and humor, which stemmed from the Old Man's somewhat eccentric ways. Except for his racist and prohibitionist tendencies, his eccentricities were endearing, mainly because they were so archaic. Among the most notable of these was Daniels's attire, which had been out of date for decades. For his entire adult life, Daniels dressed just as the lawyers, editors, and other professional men of eastern North Carolina had dressed in his youth—in a dark three-piece suit (light in the summer) with a country bow tie. By the 1920s, men's clothiers in Raleigh no longer carried suits of that cut. Addie had a long history in the city, however, and knew Raleigh tailors who handcrafted Daniels's suits. Shortly after Addie's death, Frank's wife, Ruth, took over the task of running Wakestone and purchasing the Old Man's clothes. After some investigation, Ruth discovered that not only did the suits have to be tailor-made, but that they cost several times what the finest gentlemen's stores charged for a contemporary top-of-the-line suit. Daniels himself, usually a frugal man, knew little of the process and had no idea how much his clothes cost, since he had relied for years on Addie to procure them for him.[109]

Josephus Daniels lived long enough to see the end of World War II, and Jonathan finally returned home to relieve his father of the day-to-day editing at the newspaper. The turnover was gradual and took place throughout 1946, as Daniels completed his memoirs, the final volume of which was published in 1947. On May 18, Daniels's eighty-fifth birthday, popular national columnist Drew Pearson saluted him as the last surviving member of Woodrow Wilson's cabinet. By then, the Old Man and Jonathan had worked out a division of labor at the *N&O*. Jonathan supervised the news, and the Old Man saw to the paper's editorial content. Frank continued to handle all of the firm's financial affairs, as well as its day-to-day business matters. After Jonathan took over some of his father's workload, before the year was out Daniels had begun a sixth volume of his memoirs, to be titled "Life Begins at Seventy."

Although the war and its aftermath dominated the newspaper's international coverage, there were always a few domestic and local issues to hold the reader's attention. Daniels continued to fight two old battles: liquor and race. The end of national prohibition had led North Carolina to adopt a local-options system of alcohol sales. Localities that opted to legalize alcohol had their distribution controlled by the Alcoholic Beverage Commission. (Daniels claimed the commission's acronym, ABC, stood for Alcohol Brutalizes Consumers.)[110] Under Jonathan, the *N&O* supported a local option on alcohol and ran ads for brewers, and the members of the staff were known to enjoy a drink or two around the shop.

However, when the Old Man returned to the helm and Jonathan left for Washington, the *N&O* offices went dry again. This policy was not without its inconveniences. A young employee, Baxter Sapp, recalled that the Old Man arranged for movie star Tyrone Power to swing through Raleigh in 1943 for a war bond rally. Daniels might not have been aware of the actor's penchant for carousing, but once Power hit town, escorted by a couple of junior officers, Sapp served as the local escort and *N&O* liaison. While touring the physical plant, one of the officers announced that "Tyrone wants a drink." "Well," Sapp replied, "he's not going to get one here at the *N&O*." But Power's handlers were insistent, and Sapp reluctantly agreed to see what he could do. Eventually, Daniels excused himself to take care of an editorial problem, and Sapp smuggled two six-packs of beer into the photographer's darkroom, where they were quickly consumed by Power and his small entourage.[111] Daniels never revealed whether he knew about Power's escapade at the *N&O*, though he probably would have found it amusing. Still, Daniels's good-natured view of alcohol never stopped him from using it as a political wedge. After the war, he called for a statewide prohibition referendum, which he thought the drys would win. The members of the state assembly disagreed. They recognized that legalized alcohol was a winner at the polls, and they were not going back to prohibition.

As for race, a conflict arose within the family over the *N&O*'s editorial policies following the December 1947 release of the report of President Truman's Committee on Civil Rights. In general, the report recommended an explicitly larger federal effort in the promotion of African American rights. In the years Jonathan ran the paper, its editorials had become increasingly more liberal on racial issues. In practice this meant not so much an explicit renunciation of white supremacy as a less aggressive stand against integration. For example, Jonathan openly challenged the local Protestant bishops to integrate their churches. The Old Man was having none of that. He may have regretted the ferocity of the white supremacy wars, but not their outcome. One of the last editorials he wrote, late in 1947, called for a renewed commitment to the state's segregated public school system. Daniels thought he had solved the "Negro question" almost a half-century earlier, and he would go to his death arguing that the matter not be readdressed. Southern progress, in his view, demanded that African Americans be kept in their place. The alternative, he argued, was the disorder and retrogression of Reconstruction days.

Following his dispute with Jonathan over the civil rights report, the Old Man hosted Christmas at Wakestone. The family custom was to enjoy a huge luncheon in the mansion. Then, as he did every year he was in Raleigh, Daniels proceeded to the Methodist Orphanage, just beyond Wakestone's southern border, with some of his grandchildren in tow. There he dressed up like Santa Claus and gave each of the approximately 300 children a gift at his own expense.[112] On New Year's Day 1948 he came down with a cold. Undaunted, he went into the *N&O* offices the next three days. On Sunday the 4th he received the Eucharist at Edenton Street Church but then returned home and went to bed. After a nap, he felt better, dressed, and came down to dinner. He would not leave Wakestone again.

On Epiphany he was formally diagnosed with pneumonia. He had been sick no more than a handful of days in his adult life, but now he could not rally. His condition steadily worsened. By the end of the week, he could no longer get out of bed. Early the following week he lost consciousness. With his four sons at his side, he died on Thursday, January 15.

With the Old Man gone, ownership of the *N&O* passed to his sons, though Frank and Jonathan remained at the helm. They expanded the company, which eventually owned fifteen newspapers and a radio station. It remained in the family until 1995, when the publisher at the time, Frank's son, Frank Jr., organized its sale to the McClatchy group, 101 years after his grandfather and Julian Shakespeare Carr had purchased the paper on the steps of the Wake County Courthouse. The timing of the sale was fortuitous. The age of the great newspapermen was winding down. Their rise had been witnessed by one of Daniels's heroes, Carlyle, who called them the Fourth Estate.

Daniels had been a leader of the generation of newspapermen who shifted the industry's axis of power. Before Daniels, except for a few big-city publishers such as Pulitzer and Hearst, the politicians controlled the newspaper industry. Daniels's generation turned the newspaper into a true Fourth Estate in smaller cities, such as Raleigh, across the country. The men who controlled the newspaper were now to be feared, for in an age with no radio, television, Internet, or Twitter, they controlled the flow of information. The local newspaper publisher would have a say in how the community developed. Henceforth, politicians would pay a price for ignoring the local editorial page. Of Daniels's generation of newspapermen, it was written, "The qualities that make [such men] appear menacing when they're alive, and admirably larger than life when they're dead, contribute to their ability to constitute a genuine Fourth Estate. A power-hungry newspaperman is an independent social force. . . . That ought to count for something."[113] It did. Sometimes for better, sometimes for worse, Josephus Daniels was one of those men.

Notes

1. Lukas, *Big Trouble*, 649.

2. The U.S. growth rate is calculated from Atack and Passell, *New Economic View*, chap. 1; the growth of Daniels's newspapers is from Deaton, "Analysis of Local Population and Newspaper Circulation," and Morrison, *Josephus Daniels Says . . . .*

3. Black, *Franklin Delano Roosevelt*, 126, 65.

4. Carlton and Coclanis, "Capital Mobilization and Southern Industry," 76.

5. Woodward, *Origins of the New South*, 112.

6. Ibid., 133.

7. Brundage, *Lynching in the New South*; Tolnay and Beck, *Festival of Violence*.

8. Menand, "Lives of Others," 65.

9. Als, "I, Me, Mine," 88.

10. Burleigh, "They All Knew They Were Right," C5.

11. McCloskey, *Bourgeois Virtues*, 57.

CHAPTER 1

1. The quote is from Brands, *Andrew Jackson*, 18.

2. When composing his memoirs in the 1920s and 1930s, Daniels began collecting information on his family's history. The material in this section owes much to that correspondence, found in the Papers of Josephus Daniels in the Library of Congress (hereafter cited as Daniels Papers, LC), containers 22 and 38. Daniels subsequently condensed this material, publishing it in Daniels, "Daniels, Seabrook, and Cleaves Families." It is also referred to in Daniels, *Tar Heel Editor*, 1–46, and Morrison, *Josephus Daniels*, 1–6. Other original documents concerning his family, to which Daniels apparently did not have access, reside in the North Carolina Office of Archives and History. See n. 9 below.

3. Some sources claim members of the family had settled in the area earlier in the century. A William Daniels settled on Roanoke Island as early as 1734; however, no relationship between William and Thomas Daniels could be confirmed by the author.

4. Brands, *Andrew Jackson*, 11.

5. Some sources report Clifford's second wife as "Gilly Jones." See, for example, "Daniel-L Archives," http://listsearches.rootsweb.com/th/read/DANIEL/2000-08/0965953859, September 28, 2009.

6. Daniels, *Tar Heel Editor*, 24.

7. Daniels, "Daniels, Seabrook, and Cleaves Families," 519–20.

8. Ransom, *Conflict and Compromise*, 51.

9. Documents associated with Lois Davis Seabrook's estate have survived and are in the North Carolina Division of Archives and History, C.R.053.508.51. The author thanks Ansley Herring Wegner of the North Carolina Office of Archives and History for her help in locating this source. Daniels briefly mentions the matter in his memoirs; see Daniels, *Tar Heel Editor*, 13, 28.

10. Daniels, "Daniels, Seabrook, and Cleaves Families," 519–20.

11. Current U.S. infant mortality rates are below 10 per thousand; eighteenth- and early nineteenth-century rates ranged from 200 to 300. See Flinn, *European Demographic System*, 16.

12. Thomas, *Confederate Nation*, 152–55, 160–61.

13. Documents explaining these transactions have survived. See Valentine, *Rise of a Southern Town*, 224.

14. Ironically, this transaction was documented by Daniels himself.

15. Daniels, "Daniels, Seabrook, and Cleaves Families," 521.

16. Daniels, *Tar Heel Editor*, 11.

17. Daniels, "Daniels, Seabrook, and Cleaves Families," 522.

18. Daniels, *Tar Heel Editor*, 30.

19. This section owes much to Valentine, *Rise of a Southern Town*; see esp. chaps. 1 and 2.

20. Ibid., 14.

21. Powell, *North Carolina through Four Centuries*, 92.

22. Valentine, *Rise of a Southern Town*, 12.

23. Johnston, "Louis Dicken Wilson," 6:232.

24. Valentine, *Rise of a Southern Town*, 15.

25. Daniels, *Tar Heel Editor*, 151. Also see Daniels's correspondence with one of his editors, Edward Britton, Daniels Papers, LC, container 67.

26. Daniels, "Daniels, Seabrook, and Cleaves Families"; Daniels, *Tar Heel Editor*, 47–51; Valentine, *Rise of a Southern Town*, map among frontispieces.

27. Daniels, *Tar Heel Editor*, 47.

28. Ibid., 113.

29. Though women could not vote, they could nonetheless make known their political allegiances.

30. Interview with Jonathan Worth Daniels, Southern Oral History Program.

31. Daniels, *Tar Heel Editor*, 104.

32. Daniels, "Daniels, Seabrook, and Cleaves Families."

33. Daniels, *Tar Heel Editor*, 52–53; Morrison, *Josephus Daniels*, 9.

34. Daniels explained the details in various correspondences with family members. See Daniels Papers, LC, containers 52 and 53. The transactions are summarized in Daniels, *Tar Heel Editor*, 13.

35. Alas, the house no longer stands, having been replaced by a parking lot for the Wilson County Sheriff's Department.

36. Cronon, *Nature's Metropolis*, 280.

37. Daniels's colorful if somewhat discursive characterization of the Wilson Post Office can be found in Daniels, *Tar Heel Editor*, 98–108.

38. Ibid., 104, 179–80.

39. Interview with Jonathan Worth Daniels, Southern Oral History Program.

40. Daniels's correspondence contains many references to denominational issues, including class distinctions among the members of the mainstream denominations. See, for example, his exchange with a prominent Baptist concerning the expense of Daniels's Raleigh home: Josephus Daniels to Archibald Johnson, January 9, 1920, Daniels Papers, LC, container 54. The quote on predestination is from Daniels, *Tar Heel Editor*, 80.

41. McCloskey, *Bourgeois Virtues*, 78.

42. Cash, *Mind of the South*, 269.

43. Personal correspondence with Frank Daniels Jr., March 31, 2009. Daniels included a version of this story in his memoirs; see Daniels, *Tar Heel Editor*, 99.

44. Author's interview with anonymous Daniels family member.

45. Daniels, *Tar Heel Editor*, 171.

46. Ibid.

47. Ibid., 363; Kousser, *Shaping of Southern Politics*.

48. Daniels, *Editor in Politics*, 134, 251.

49. The literature on the economics of the postbellum South is large and growing. Key sources upon which this material relies are Alston and Kauffman, "Up, Down, and Off the Agricultural Ladder"; Alston and Ferrie, *Southern Paternalism*; Ransom and Sutch, *One Kind of Freedom*; Reid, "Sharecropping"; and Wright, *Old South, New South*.

50. Daniels, *Tar Heel Editor*, 318.

51. Woodward, *Origins of the New South*, 79.

52. Gavins, *Perils and Prospects of Southern Black Leadership*, 6.

53. The material on the boys' lives in Wilson is from Daniels's correspondence with his brothers; see Daniels Papers, LC, containers 12–14. A summary of those years can be found in Daniels, *Tar Heel Editor*, 47–74, as well as the family history in Daniels, "Daniels, Seabrook, and Cleaves Families," 513–24.

54. Author's interview with Patricia Daniels Woronoff.

55. The reference was in a newspaper clipping accompanying a letter from Josephus Daniels to Jonathan Daniels, January 1, 1938, Daniels Papers, LC, container 32.

56. Daniels, *Tar Heel Editor*, 72.

57. Ibid., 64.

58. Ibid., 232.

59. Ibid., 373, 231, respectively.

60. The history of public education in North Carolina in the nineteenth century is covered in detail in Noble, *History of the Public Schools of North Carolina*. For a summary, see Powell, *North Carolina through Four Centuries*, 245–46, 257–58, 290–92, 305–7.

61. Howe, *What Hath God Wrought*, 455.

62. Quoted in Powell, *North Carolina through Four Centuries*, 307.

63. The quote is from Daniels, *Tar Heel Editor*, 55. Valentine, *Rise of a Southern Town*, 48, lists three common (primary) schools, one public high school, and one "charity school."

64. McClure, *Crosley*, 20.

65. Craig, *To Sow One Acre More*, 20.

66. Daniels, *Tar Heel Editor*, 63.

67. Ibid., 56.

68. Ibid., 61; Valentine, *Rise of a Southern Town*, 49.

69. See the discussion in Finke and Starke, *Churching of America*, 156–82. The author thanks Robert Whaples for directing him to this source and related literature.

70. Daniels, *Tar Heel Editor*, 69.

71. Here and below, income figures for the region are inferred from Balke and Gordon, "Estimation of Prewar Gross National Product"; Romer, "Prewar Business Cycle"; and Carlton and Coclanis, "Capital Mobilization and Southern Industry."

72. Daniels, *Tar Heel Editor*, 106.

73. Cohen, "Can You Forgive Him?," 49.

74. Daniels, *Tar Heel Editor*, 69.

75. Ibid., 66.

76. On the Flaglers, see Chernow, *Titan*, 344–46. The quote on Kenan is from Daniels, *Tar Heel Editor*, 68.

77. Daniels, *Tar Heel Editor*, 65.

78. Ibid., 510.

CHAPTER 2

1. Daniels, *Tar Heel Editor*, 75.

2. Ibid., 76–77.

3. Ibid., 80.

4. Ibid.

5. The passage appears in an undated obituary of Daniels written in the 1920s, more than two decades before he died, and apparently written by Daniels himself; see Daniels Papers, LC, container 22.

6. A copy can be found in ibid.

7. Daniels, *Tar Heel Editor*, 86.

8. Valentine, *Rise of a Southern Town*, 60–61; Daniels, *Tar Heel Editor*, 158.

9. Daniels, *Tar Heel Editor*, 142.

10. Much remodeled over the years, the church remains in the same location today.

11. Morrison, *Josephus Daniels*, 9.

12. Daniels, *Tar Heel Editor*, 86.

13. Wilson *Advance*, May 5, 1882, 1.

14. Cottrell's patents are described by Harris; see http://americanhistory.si.edu/about/pubs/harris3.pdf, May 22, 2009.

15. On this characteristic of southern capitalism, see Kuhn, *Contesting the New South Order*.

16. Daniels, *Tar Heel Editor*, 26.

17. Ibid., 88.

18. Cronon, *Nature's Metropolis*, 280.

19. Plesczynski, "Pulitzer."

20. Daniels, *Tar Heel Editor*, 88–90.

21. Nasaw, *Chief*, 102.

22. Ferguson, *Empire*, 213.

23. Nasaw, *Chief*, 102.

24. Ibid., 103.

25. Lepore, "Back Issues," 70, 72.

26. Hamilton, *All the News That's Fit to Sell*, esp. 45.

27. See Carlton and Coclanis, "Capital Mobilization and Southern Industry"; Bateman and Weiss, *Deplorable Scarcity*; and Atack and Passell, *New Economic View*, 457–92.

28. The quote is from Daniels, *Tar Heel Editor*, 193. Daniels discussed prohibition at length in his correspondence. See, for example, his correspondence with Albert Burleson (anti) and Franklin Lane (pro): Josephus Daniels to Albert Burleson, undated, and Josephus Daniels to Franklin Lane, January 19, 1918, Daniels Papers, LC, containers 71 and 87, respectively.

29. Daniels, *Tar Heel Editor*, 196.

30. Ibid., 89, 175–76.

31. Many of Daniels's financial transactions can be found among the documents listed as "Miscellaneous financial papers" in Daniels Papers, LC, container 53. The quote is from Daniels, *Tar Heel Editor*, 210.

32. Daniels, *Tar Heel Editor*, 132.

33. The issue of when newspapers became independent has been explored recently by economists. For a quantitative treatment, see Gentzkow, Glaeser, and Goldin, "Rise of the Fourth Estate," and Hamilton, *All the News That's Fit to Sell*.

34. These figures are from Nasaw, *Chief*, 69, 98.

35. Daniels, *Tar Heel Editor*, 84–85.

36. The house is no longer there, having been replaced at one time by a gasoline station. Daniels's correspondence yields conflicting information about his transactions in Wilson real estate. See Daniels, *Tar Heel Editor*, 151, and the files in "Miscellaneous financial papers," Daniels Papers, LC, containers 52 and 53.

37. Daniels, *Tar Heel Editor*, 108.

38. Ibid., 229.

39. Ibid., 234.

40. Webb, *Jule Carr*, 29.

41. Ibid.

42. Ibid.

43. Speech by William Joseph Peele, August 2, 1888, box 1, folder 1, Peele Papers, Hill Library.

44. Daniels, *Tar Heel Editor*, 229–32.

45. Ibid., 235.

46. The tally is from the account given in ibid., 236.

47. Black, *Franklin Delano Roosevelt*, 68.

48. Daniels, *Tar Heel Editor*, 229.

49. Josephus Daniels to Jonathan Daniels, January 31, 1938, Jonathan Daniels Papers, Wilson Library.

50. Daniels, *Tar Heel Editor*, 234.

51. Author's interview with Frank Daniels Jr., July 12, 2002; Daniels, *Tar Heel Editor*, 249.

52. Morrison, *Josephus Daniels*, 8.

53. Daniels, *Tar Heel Editor*, 94.

54. Cooper, *Walter Hines Page*, 74.

55. Morrison, *Josephus Daniels*, 12.

56. In his memoirs Daniels gives two different dates for the founding of the *Observer*, 1875 and 1876. See Daniels, *Tar Heel Editor*, 344–45.

57. Because the *Observer* had taken over the *Sentinel*, which had been founded in 1865, Daniels always traced the lineage of the *News and Observer* to that date. See Raleigh *News and Observer*, August 14, 1904, 13.

58. Though the timing cannot be confirmed, it appears Daniels continued to serve as the *Observer*'s business agent after Ashe took over the paper.

59. Daniels, *Tar Heel Editor*, 95; Valentine, *Rise of a Southern Town*, 87.

60. This letter is quoted verbatim in Daniels, *Tar Heel Editor*, 95.

61. Ibid.

62. Ibid., 96.

63. Daniels gives various figures for the dollar value of the state contract; however, it ranged from $2,500 to $4,000 annually between 1885 and 1895. See ibid., 437.

64. Cooper, *Walter Hines Page*, 75.

65. Daniels, *Tar Heel Editor*, 95.

66. Morrison, *Josephus Daniels*, 12. Daniels hinted as much in his memoirs; see Daniels, *Tar Heel Editor*, 97.

67. Daniels, *Tar Heel Editor*, 97.

68. Daniels notes that Page sold only "his interest" to Arendell, suggesting that either Arendell already owned part of the paper or someone else did. See ibid., 96–97.

69. The material in this section owes much to Webb, *Jule Carr*, 97–98; Daniels, *Tar Heel Editor*, 247–48; and author's interview with Frank Daniels Jr., July 12, 2002.

70. Wert, "Randolph Abbott Shotwell."

71. The material on Carr's life is from Webb, *Jule Carr*.

72. There are various versions of this story. The one recorded here owes much to Webb, *Jule Carr*, 30–39.

73. Daniels, *Tar Heel Editor*, 151.

74. Webb, *Jule Carr*, 104.

75. Daniels wrote "majority," but in fact Carr owned 100 percent of the business. See Daniels, *Tar Heel Editor*, 247.

76. Ibid. The story is repeated in Webb, *Jule Carr*, 99–100.

77. This version of events can be found in both Daniels, *Tar Heel Editor*, 247–49, and Webb, *Jule Carr*, 97–98.

78. Webb, *Jule Carr*, 98.

79. Daniels, *Tar Heel Editor*, 437.

80. Daniels never explicitly spelled out the terms of this deal. It must be inferred from subsequent transactions. See the correspondence in "Miscellaneous financial papers," Daniels Papers, LC, container 52, and the discussion in Chapter 3.

CHAPTER 3

1. Daniels's extensive correspondence on his years in Raleigh can be found among the papers he collected when he began writing his memoirs and among his correspondence with his son Jonathan. See Daniels Papers, LC, containers 22, 32, and 33. The direct quotes in this and the subsequent paragraph come from the first volume of that effort, Daniels, *Tar Heel Editor*, 229, 260, and 259.

2. Daniels, *Tar Heel Editor*, 265–66.

3. As described to his son Jonathan; see Josephus Daniels to Jonathan Daniels, January 31, 1938, Daniels Papers, LC, container 33, quoted in Daniels, *Tar Heel Editor*, 260.

4. This was from Daniels's correspondence with his mother, May 1887, Jonathan Daniels Papers, Wilson Library. Also see Morrison, *Josephus Daniels*, 15. In his account of Daniels's life, Morrison relied heavily on interviews with, and the personal papers of, Daniels's third son, Jonathan, with whom Morrison was personally acquainted.

5. It was not the first time the two had met. Daniels had been introduced to Addie earlier in the year, when her cousin by marriage, Henry London, was in town giving a speech on Confederate Memorial Day. Daniels made an effort to meet London, a fellow newspaper editor, and they met at the Bagley home.

6. Daniels's correspondence concerning the Bagleys appears throughout his papers. See esp. Daniels Papers, LC, containers 38–40. The quote can be found in Daniels, *Tar Heel Editor*, 262.

7. Jonathan Worth to Zilphia Worth, July 2, 1892, folder 23, Worth Papers, Wilson Library.

8. Herbert Jackson to Adelaide Worth Bagley, July 18, 1887, Bagley Family Papers, Wilson Library.

9. Josephus Daniels to Adelaide Bagley, September 1887, Daniels Papers, LC, container 15.

10. She shared this opinion with one of her younger daughters. See Morrison, *Josephus Daniels*, 17. On Adelaide Worth Bagley's personality, see interview with Jonathan Worth Daniels, Southern Oral History Program.

11. Josephus Daniels to Adelaide Bagley, March 5, 1888, Daniels Papers, LC, container 15.

12. This exchange can be found in Daniels Papers, LC, container 15.

13. Daniels, *Tar Heel Editor*, 270.

14. The documents concerning the description of Daniels's wedding are from correspondence between Daniels and his son Jonathan. See Josephus Daniels to Jonathan Daniels, January 6, 1938, Daniels Papers, LC, container 32.

15. Interestingly, Zilphia took the last name of her employers, becoming known in Raleigh as Zilphia Worth. See Jonathan Worth to Zilphia Worth, July 2, 1892, folder 23, Worth Papers, Wilson Library.

16. Waugh, *Raleigh*, 92.

17. Daniels, *Tar Heel Editor*, 274; Morrison, *Josephus Daniels*, 43. The subsequent description of Daniels's daily diet comes from author's interview with Adelaide Daniels Key.

18. Brands, *Andrew Jackson*, 295.

19. Undated speech, box 1, folder 8, Peele Papers, Hill Library. Daniels gives 1883 as the founding date; other sources list 1884. See, for example, Watauga Club Records, Hill Library.

20. See, for example, Daniels's explication of the state's economic woes in Raleigh *State Chronicle*, November 30, 1888.

21. In August 1904, after Daniels had taken over the *N&O*, the paper published a special edition that included several pieces on the history of the Raleigh newspaper market. The material in this section owes much to that source. See Raleigh *News and Observer*, August 14, 1904. The quote is from Daniels, *Tar Heel Editor*, 434.

22. Daniels, *Tar Heel Editor*, 195, 301–9; "History," http://www.wakeabc.com /history.html, August 27, 2008.

23. Statewide prohibition did not come to North Carolina until 1908; see below.

24. Daniels, *Tar Heel Editor*, 338–43.

25. The figures can be found in Morrison, *Josephus Daniels*, 15.

26. The quote comes from ibid., 17.

27. Daniels variously listed $3,000 or $4,000; see Daniels, *Tar Heel Editor*, 351, 489. However, an earlier biography puts the figure at $1,500 in 1887; see Morrison, *Josephus Daniels*, 15. It is possible the lower figure represents Daniels's net profit from the contract.

28. Clark, Craig, and Wilson, *History of Public Sector Pensions*.

29. Daniels, *Tar Heel Editor*, 351.

30. Ibid. Daniels's research into his father's war record was aimed at deflecting such criticism. His son Jonathan did much of the research. See, for example, Josephus Daniels to Jonathan Daniels, April 12, 1927, Daniels Papers, LC, container 30.

31. Daniels's account of the fight can found in Daniels, *Tar Heel Editor*, 351–52.

32. Ibid., 350.

33. Ibid., 432.

34. Daniels described his plan to take over the *Call* in his memoirs, but the author could find no reference to it in Daniels's correspondence from the period. See Daniels, *Tar Heel Editor*, 437.

35. Josephus Daniels to Adelaide Bagley Daniels, June 7, 1891, Daniels Papers, LC, container 15.

36. Daniels, *Tar Heel Editor*, 434.

37. The *Chronicle*'s nominal capital value had been increased to $2,000 following its merger with the *Call*. Interestingly, this was the price Page had asked for the *Chronicle* by itself, when he had offered it to Daniels in 1885; see above.

38. Daniels, *Tar Heel Editor*, 432–33. In subsequent correspondence with his wife, Daniels put most of the value of the firm down as goodwill; see Josephus Daniels to Adelaide Bagley Daniels, August 6–9, 1894, Daniels Papers, LC, container 15.

39. Examples of this can be found in his papers; see folders 79 and 81, Andrews Papers, Wilson Library.

40. Daniels, *Tar Heel Editor*, 406–7.

41. Daniels did not quantify the amount but refers to the debt in his memoirs. See Daniels, *Tar Heel Editor*, 489–92.

42. Ibid., 489.

43. In fact, Holt and Andrews were regular correspondents. Some of their communication has survived; see folder 80, Andrews Papers, Wilson Library.

44. Daniels, *Tar Heel Editor*, 491.

45. An earlier biography claims that Daniels "kept nothing for himself" from the state contract. This seems implausible, given Daniels's own account of his finances at the time. See Morrison, *Josephus Daniels*, 22.

46. Daniels, *Tar Heel Editor*, 494.

47. Hunt, *Marion Butler*, 45.

48. Daniels, *Tar Heel Editor*, 496. See also the election coverage in the *North Carolinian*.

49. Christensen, *Paradox of Tar Heel Politics*, 37.

50. Daniels, *Tar Heel Editor*, 500.

51. Ibid., 498.

52. Powell, *North Carolina through Four Centuries*, 430.

53. Adjusted for inflation, that figure would be surpassed later in the decade. See Ransom and Sutch, *One Kind of Freedom*, 192.

54. On Hoke's life, see Barefoot, "General Robert F. Hoke." The quotes are from, respectively, Daniels, *Tar Heel Editor*, 508; "General Robert Frederick Hoke: His Life and Campaigns," unpublished manuscript, folder 1, Hoke Papers, Wilson Library; and an undated speech by Daniels in folder 3, Hoke Papers, Wilson Library.

55. Josephus Daniels to Adelaide Bagley Daniels, March 1893, Daniels Papers, LC, container 15.

56. Clark, Craig, and Wilson, *History of Public Sector Pensions*; U.S. Bureau of the Census, *Historical Statistics*, 1140–48.

57. Rockoff, "'Wizard of Oz.'"

58. Daniels, *Editor in Politics*, 49.

59. U.S. Bureau of the Census, *Historical Statistics*, 1122.

60. *McCulloch v. Maryland* decision, March 6, 1819, Minutes of the Supreme Court of the United States, Record Group 267, National Archives.

61. Daniels, *Tar Heel Editor*, 179.

62. Cash, *Mind of the South*, 160.

63. Daniels, *Tar Heel Editor*, 49.

64. U.S. Bureau of the Census, *Historical Statistics*, 888.

65. Lamoreaux, *Great Merger Movement*.

66. Hughes and Cain, *American Economic History*, 359.

67. Business historian Naomi Lamoreaux offers an explanation for this phenomenon in Lamoreaux, *Great Merger Movement*; the argument is summarized in Hughes and Cain, *American Economic History*, 359.

68. *United States of America v. American Tobacco Co.*, 221 U.S. 106 (1911).

69. Daniels, *Tar Heel Editor*, 468, 473–74.

70. Tilley, *Bright Tobacco Industry*, 374.

71. The material on Duke owes much to Durden, *Bold Entrepreneur*.

72. Daniels's personal acquaintance with and characterization of the members of the Duke family comes from *Tar Heel Editor*, 468–79.

73. Durden, "Washington Duke," 2:118.

74. Durden, *Bold Entrepreneur*, 36–67.

75. See, for example, the summaries in Hughes and Cain, *American Economic History*, 327–50, and Walton and Rockoff, *History of the American Economy*, 360–81.

76. Raleigh *State Chronicle*, October 16, 1885, 1.

77. Johnson and Libecap, *Federal Civil Service*, 17.

78. Ibid., 33.

79. Daniels, *Editor in Politics*, 26.

80. Ibid., 21.

81. See the review of the first volume of Daniels's memoirs, at http://www.time .com/time/magazine/article/0,9171,762165,00.html.

82. Daniels, *Editor in Politics*, 21.

CHAPTER 4

1. Although African Americans were overwhelmingly Republican, according to contemporary observers, their votes were often up for sale on Election Day. See Hunt, *Marion Butler*, 56, and Kousser, *Shaping of Southern Politics*.

2. Morrison, *Josephus Daniels*, 25. On the choice between gold and silver, see Friedman, "Bimetallism Revisited"; Friedman and Schwartz, *Monetary History*; and Rockoff, "'Wizard of Oz.'"

3. Josephus Daniels to Adelaide Bagley Daniels, September 23, 1896, Daniels Papers, LC, container 16.

4. Daniels, *Editor in Politics*, 173.

5. Kazin, *Godly Hero*, 61.

6. Daniels, *Editor in Politics*, 49.

7. From the 1890 *Proceedings of the Annual Session of the Supreme Council of the National Farmers' Alliance*, which was chaired by Polk, 33, National Farmers' Alliance Records, Hill Library. The session also condemned "the silver bill" as inadequate to the farmers' needs.

8. Daniels, *Tar Heel Editor*, 484.

9. Ibid., 484–85.

10. Matt Ransom to Bedford Brown, January 1, 1859, Ransom Letters, Rubenstein Library.

11. Daniels, *Tar Heel Editor*, 184.

12. Ibid., 213.

13. Ibid., 450.

14. The material in this section owes much to Daniels's reminiscences in his memoirs. See Daniels, *Editor in Politics*, 49–59, and Friedman and Schwartz, *Monetary History*, 104–11.

15. Parker, *Recollections of Grover Cleveland*, 314.

16. Daniels, *Editor in Politics*, 49.

17. Ibid., 54.

18. Ibid., 55.

19. This was the view of family members as revealed in Morrison, *Josephus Daniels*, 24.

20. Josephus Daniels to Adelaide Bagley Daniels, September 21, 1893, Daniels Papers, LC, container 15.

21. Daniels, *Editor in Politics*, 57.

22. The accounting is from ibid.

23. What follows owes much to Kazin, *Godly Hero*.

24. Ibid.

25. Daniels, *Editor in Politics*, 283–84.

26. Kazin, *Godly Hero*, xiv.

27. The idiosyncratic nature of North Carolina politics during this and subsequent eras is well explained in Christensen, *Paradox of Tar Heel Politics*; for details of the difference between the national political alliances and those at the state level, see Hunt, *Marion Butler*.

28. Author's interview with Patricia Daniels Woronoff.

29. See, for example, *North Carolina Biographical Dictionary*, 59.

30. Daniels, *Editor in Politics*, 85.

31. *North Carolina Biographical Dictionary*, 59.

32. Morrison, *Josephus Daniels*, 24.

33. Ibid., 40.

34. Watson, "Josephus Daniels," 2:13.

35. Webb, *Jule Carr*, 98.

36. Daniels, *Editor in Politics*, 85–101.

37. Ibid., 88 (emphasis added).

38. Josephus Daniels to Adelaide Bagley Daniels, August 6, 1894, Daniels Papers, LC, container 15.

39. This part of the transaction was omitted from Daniels's correspondence but was included in his memoirs.

40. Josephus Daniels to Adelaide Bagley Daniels, August 6, 1894, Daniels Papers, LC, container 15.

41. Chodorov, "Cheers to the Peddler Class," 3.

42. At this stage of his life his aspirations might or might not have included elected office.

43. Daniels Papers, LC, container 24. Daniels reproduced a copy in his memoirs. See Daniels, *Editor in Politics*, 88–89.

44. Daniels, *Editor in Politics*, 88–89.

45. Daniels did not record how he obtained the money to purchase Carr's shares. He might have paid cash, as he was still earning $2,750 a year at the Interior Department, but he might have purchased them with a loan from his banker Brown.

46. Morrison, *Josephus Daniels*, 40, erroneously describes Carr as a major stockholder as late as 1905.

47. Seventy-nine names appear in the document titled "Original News and Observer Stockholders," Daniels Papers, LC, container 24—though it appears that several of these individuals never actually owned a single share of stock. It is possible that they had initially agreed to purchase a share but for some reason never consummated the deal. Approximately twenty-five shareholders owned two shares, though none owned more than two.

48. Daniels, *Tar Heel Editor*, 96.

49. Morrison, *Josephus Daniels*, 40; Webb, *Jule Carr*, 98.

50. Personal correspondence with Frank Daniels Jr., October 2, 2002.

51. At least that was Daniels's claim; see Daniels, *Editor in Politics*, 99.

52. Daniels continually upgraded the machines as newer technologies emerged. See, for example, his correspondence concerning the next generation of Mergenthalers, Josephus Daniels to Josephus Daniels Jr., September 30, 1919, Daniels Papers, LC, container 23. Daniels's correspondence on this issue runs into the next year.

53. Daniels, *Editor in Politics*, 93.

54. Ibid.

55. Ibid., 96.

56. The peak circulation of the *State Chronicle* had surpassed that of the *N&O* earlier in the decade.

57. Daniels, *Tar Heel Editor*, 439.

58. Some scholars hesitate to label the Fusionist coalition as a political party. See, for example, Hunt, *Marion Butler*, 6–7. I use the term here because that was how Daniels perceived it.

59. Woodward, *Strange Career of Jim Crow*, 54.

60. Crow, Escott, and Hatley, *History of African Americans*, 87, 209–11.

61. Quoted in Woodward, *Origins of the New South*, 55.

62. This is essentially the point made in Woodward, *Strange Career of Jim Crow*, 3–109.

63. Ibid., 53–54.

64. Kazin, *Godly Hero*, 39.

65. For the details on Butler's life, see Hunt, *Marion Butler*. The quote is from Daniels, *Tar Heel Editor*, 385.

66. Daniels, *Editor in Politics*, 123.

67. Recent scholarship on the politics of the era questions this view. See the detailed description in Hunt, *Marion Butler*, 51–185. It is possible Daniels empha-

sized the role of Grant because of his carpetbagger background, which made the movement seem all the more evil.

68. Daniels, *Editor in Politics*, 123.

69. The material on Butler's life is from Hunt, *Marion Butler*, and Durden, "Marion Butler."

70. Following the election of 1894, the contrast between their positions was summarized in a series of articles in the *N&O* and Butler's *Caucasian*. For a summary, see Hunt, *Marion Butler*, 73–74.

71. Daniels, *Editor in Politics*, 123. This view is not shared by Butler's biographer; see Hunt, *Marion Butler*, 67.

72. This figure is from Powell, *North Carolina through Four Centuries*, 46.

73. Hunt, *Marion Butler*, 64–65.

74. Raleigh *News and Observer*, November 7–9, 1894, 1. Also see the discussion in Daniels, *Editor in Politics*, 124.

75. Daniels, *Editor in Politics*, 124.

76. This is a vast and ever-expanding literature. The seminal work is Woodward, *Origins of the New South*. For a more recent analysis, see Kousser, *Shaping of Southern Politics*.

77. Woodward, *Origins of the New South*, 209. See also Alston and Ferrie, *Southern Paternalism*.

78. Woodward, *Origins of the New South*, 210–11.

79. Crow, Escott, and Hatley, *History of African Americans*, 95; see also Woodward, *Origins of the New South*.

80. The exact figure is in dispute, as the race of some postbellum legislators has not been determined. See the figures in Powell, *North Carolina through Four Centuries*, 431, and Crow, Escott, and Hatley, *History of African Americans*, 209–11.

81. Daniels, *Editor in Politics*, 133.

82. Cash, *Mind of the South*, 318.

83. Powell, *North Carolina through Four Centuries*, 405.

84. Ibid., 430.

85. Young's home has not survived, though a state historical marker indicates where it stood.

86. Daniels, *Tar Heel Editor*, 134.

87. The legislation also called for the election of justices of the peace.

88. Woodward, *Origins of the New South*, 277.

89. On the complications surrounding African American support for the Fusionists, see Edmonds, *The Negro and Fusion Politics*.

90. Daniels, *Editor in Politics*, 133.

91. Ibid.

92. Cash, *Mind of the South*, 169.

93. Daniels, *Editor in Politics*, 133.

94. Tilley, *Bright Tobacco Industry*, 273–74; Hunt, *Marion Butler*, 79–80.

95. Daniels, *Editor in Politics*, 220.

96. Raleigh *News and Observer*, March 19, 1895, 1; Daniels, *Editor in Politics*, 134.

97. The material on Russell's life is from Daniels, *Editor in Politics*, and Evans,

"Daniel Lindsay Russell." With respect to North Carolina's rice production, see Coclanis, *Shadow of a Dream*, 142.

98. Evans, "Daniel Lindsay Russell," 2:272. African Americans did not always vote Republican, however; see Kousser, *Shaping of Southern Politics*.

99. Daniels was so proud of this characterization of Butler that he included it in his memoirs. See Daniels, *Editor in Politics*, 152.

CHAPTER 5

1. This range of figures is consistent with the average annual rate of return Daniels earned on his earlier papers (30 to 40 percent) and the capital value of the *N&O*, $20,000. Furthermore, Daniels soon began placing large investments with his financier Herbert Jackson. See below.

2. Just over 900 voting delegates would attend the 1896 convention. There were more than 4,000 at the 2008 convention.

3. Daniels, *Editor in Politics*, 158–59.

4. In addition to several supernumeraries, a delegate would be chosen for each congressional district.

5. Daniels, *Editor in Politics*, 159.

6. Jarvis and Ransom had been rivals for years. See Daniels, *Tar Heel Editor*, 506–7, and Daniels, *Editor in Politics*, 160.

7. Daniels, *Editor in Politics*, 164.

8. Ibid., 161.

9. Morrison, *Josephus Daniels*, 76.

10. Daniels, *Editor in Politics*, 157. Much of the material in this section is taken from Kazin, *Godly Hero*, 45–79, and Daniels's firsthand account of the 1896 convention. For the latter, see Daniels's correspondence with his wife, who remained in Raleigh, Daniels Papers, LC, container 16. The account is summarized in Daniels, *Editor in Politics*, 157–70.

11. Kazin, *Godly Hero*, 56.

12. Daniels had initially supported Hoke Smith; but Smith, following his leader Cleveland, supported gold over silver, and his candidacy went nowhere. See Hunt, *Marion Butler*, 85. The quotes are from Daniels, *Editor in Politics*, 157.

13. Kazin, *Godly Hero*, 58.

14. Daniels, *Editor in Politics*, 164.

15. Kazin, *Godly Hero*, 59.

16. Ibid., 60.

17. Daniels, *Editor in Politics*, 164.

18. Kazin, *Godly Hero*, 61.

19. Daniels, *Editor in Politics*, 165.

20. Ibid., 176. The material in this section owes much to Daniels's eyewitness account of these events.

21. Hunt, *Marion Butler*, 98–99.

22. Daniels, *Editor in Politics*, 172. This is not the view of Butler's biographer,

who argues persuasively that Butler and Watson fell out only later, during the campaign. See Hunt, *Marion Butler*, 112–14.

23. This interpretation of events follows from Daniels's memoirs. Butler's biographer offers a simpler explanation of Butler's behavior in St. Louis, arguing that Butler went with Watson over Sewall to keep the Populists from splintering. See Hunt, *Marion Butler*, 102.

24. Daniels, *Editor in Politics*, 176.

25. Ibid., 172, 176.

26. Indeed, at one point Butler had even reached out to the Democrats, proposing cooperation on state elections, a point Daniels did not mention in his correspondence or memoirs. See Hunt, *Marion Butler*, 108.

27. The accounting is Daniels's. See Daniels, *Editor in Politics*, 198.

28. Ibid., 254.

29. On TR's role in pushing for war with Spain, see Evans, *War Lovers*.

30. Brands, *TR*, 325.

31. Daniels, *Editor in Politics*, 61.

32. Ibid., 264.

33. Kazin, *Godly Hero*, 89.

34. Daniels, *Editor in Politics*, 279.

35. This correspondence survives in Daniels Papers, LC, container 43. Other sources, including a Daniels biography, list Worth Bagley as the first U.S. officer killed in the war. See Morrison, *Josephus Daniels*, 32.

36. Daniels, *Editor in Politics*, 281–82.

37. Ibid., 283. See also Daniels's correspondence with his third son, Jonathan, who aided in the compilation and editing of Daniels's memoirs, Daniels Papers, LC, containers 29–32.

38. Daniels, *Editor in Politics*, 153.

39. Cash, *Mind of the South*, 66.

40. Branch, *Pillar of Fire*, 146.

41. As a student at the University of North Carolina, Henry Zaytoun, later a prominent Raleigh orthodontist, heard Daniels speak on campus. "He waived his arms about, trying to arouse the crowd," Zaytoun remembered. When asked if, overall, Daniels was an effective public speaker, Zaytoun hesitated and charitably replied, "He tried to be" (author's interview with Henry Zaytoun).

42. Daniels, *Editor in Politics*, 284.

43. Ibid., 286.

44. Ibid., 421.

45. Meehan, "Locke Craig," 1:452.

46. Daniels, *Editor in Politics*, 297.

47. Ibid.

48. Ibid., 293.

49. Daniels summarized his newspaper's coverage of the campaign in Daniels, *Editor in Politics*, 283–312. The interested reader should also consult the *News and Observer* from the summer and fall of 1898.

50. Other white-owned papers, often repeating charges from the *News and Observer*, published similar observations. See Daniels, *Editor in Politics*, 283–312.

51. Daniels, *Editor in Politics*, 289.

52. Tyson, *Blood Done Sign My Name*, 38.

53. Raleigh *Caucasian*, November 5, 1898, 1.

54. Cash, *Mind of the South*, 86.

55. Woodward, *Origins of the New South*, 254.

56. Hunt, *Marion Butler*, 7, 54. The description of Butler on the stump is from contemporary reports in the *Progressive Farmer*.

57. 1898 Wilmington Race Riot Commission, "1898 Wilmington Race Report," 39–40, which can be found at http://www.ah.dcr.state.nc.us/1898-wrrc/report /report.htm.

58. Daniels, *Editor in Politics*, 284.

59. In fairness to Daniels, it should be noted that the state-created Police Board that was now running Wilmington had been a mixed success at best. See 1898 Wilmington Race Riot Commission, "1898 Wilmington Race Report," 40–41.

60. Manly was described as a "mixed-race descendant of Charles Manly, governor of the state from 1849–51" (Tyson, "Ghosts of 1898," 4).

61. Raleigh *News and Observer*, October 18, 1898, 1.

62. Daniels, *Editor in Politics*, 286.

63. Ibid., 286–87.

64. Charlotte *Observer*, November 5, 1898, 1.

65. Daniels, *Editor in Politics*, 292.

66. Tyson, "Ghosts of 1898," 8.

67. Daniels, *Editor in Politics*, 300.

68. Ibid., 301.

69. Branch, *Parting the Waters*, 631.

70. The accounting is Daniels's. It is difficult to confirm, because there were swing voters among the Populists in the Fusionist camp. See Daniels, *Editor in Politics*, 307.

71. The material on the Wilmington race riot is from Daniels, *Editor in Politics*, 307–9; the pieces in Cecelski and Tyson, *Democracy Betrayed*; and 1898 Wilmington Race Riot Commission, "1898 Wilmington Race Report."

72. 1898 Wilmington Race Riot Commission, "1898 Wilmington Race Report," 1, 177–79.

73. Raleigh *News and Observer*, November 11, 1898, 1.

74. Daniels, *Editor in Politics*, 307.

75. Interview with Jonathan Worth Daniels, Southern Oral History Program.

76. Daniels, *Editor in Politics*, 308.

77. Interview with Frank Daniels Jr., Southern Oral History Program.

78. Daniels, *Editor in Politics*, 145.

79. Folder 1, Carr Papers, Wilson Library.

80. Emerson, "What the Pols Should Read."

81. Daniels, *Editor in Politics*, 382.

82. Branch, *Parting the Waters*, 31.

83. Woodward, *Origins of the New South*, 28.

84. Woodward, *Strange Career of Jim Crow*, 91.

85. Howe, *What Hath God Wrought*, 480–81.

86. Cash, *Mind of the South*, 128.

87. Woodward, *Origins of the New South*, 327.

88. Woodward, *Strange Career of Jim Crow*, 83.

89. Daniels, *Editor in Politics*, 324–26.

90. "To Exclude Negro Voters," *New York Times*, 19 March 1899, 8. The idea was to discourage voting; thus, no one in North Carolina was ever prosecuted for not paying the poll tax. See Kousser, *Shaping of Southern Politics*, 63.

91. Daniels, *Editor in Politics*, 326. The Fifteenth Amendment to the U.S. Constitution guaranteed the voting rights of African Americans. The U.S. Supreme Court ultimately found the grandfather clauses, like North Carolina's, to be unconstitutional in *Guinn v. United States* (1915), but there was no effective federal enforcement of black voting rights in the South until the civil rights acts of the 1960s.

92. Daniels, *Editor in Politics*, 336.

93. The information on the business side of the *N&O* during these years comes from Morrison, *Josephus Daniels Says . . .* , 185–222, and correspondence in Daniels Papers, LC, esp. the correspondence with Herbert Jackson in containers 40 and 41. It appears that the News and Observer Publishing Company paid no regular dividend, and Daniels himself was the residual claimant on the firm's profits.

94. Morrison, *Josephus Daniels*, 43.

95. Daniels Papers, LC, containers 40 and 41.

96. Herwig and Heyman, "Josephus Daniels."

97. Bassett, "Stirring Up the Fires of Race Antipathy," 199.

98. The material on the Bassett case comes from Daniels, *Editor in Politics*, 427–38, and Morrison, *Josephus Daniels Says . . .* , 121–48.

99. These ran, respectively, on November 1 and 2. See Daniels, *Editor in Politics*, 428–29.

100. Hunt, *Marion Butler*, 80.

101. Interview with Jonathan Worth Daniels, Southern Oral History Program.

102. Daniels, *Editor in Politics*, 431.

103. The animosity Kilgo generated among the state's white Democrats would have kept him from the bishopric had it not been for Daniels's support. See Daniels, *Editor in Politics*, 489–91.

104. Ibid., 357.

105. Ibid., 494.

106. Ibid., 435.

107. Ibid., 469.

108. Craig, *Memoirs and Speeches*, 53–54.

109. Daniels, *Editor in Politics*, 360.

110. Maupin, "Armistead Jones." An earlier biography lists Armistead Jones's son, Buck, as Daniels's antagonist during this period, but Buck was only ten years old at the time. See Morrison, *Josephus Daniels*, 42.

111. Daniels, *Editor in Politics*, 362.

112. Ibid., 441.

113. Cash, *Mind of the South*, 227.

114. Daniels, *Editor in Politics*, 422. The material in this section owes much to this source; see esp. 422–23, 440–42.

115. Ibid., 422–23.

116. Kousser, *Shaping of Southern Politics*, 61. The tally of the votes is from Daniels, *Editor in Politics*, 440.

117. Daniels, *Editor in Politics*, 441.

118. Ibid., 520.

119. Ibid., 521.

120. Hughes, *Vital Few*, 208.

121. Howe, *What Hath God Wrought*, 288.

122. Daniels, *Editor in Politics*, 102.

123. Ibid., 102–3.

124. Ibid., 106.

125. Ibid., 108.

126. Daniels, *Tar Heel Editor*, 70–71.

127. Wright, *Old South, New South*, 80. Also see Margo, *Race and Schooling*, 6–32.

128. Leloudis, *Schooling the New South*, 115.

129. Christensen, *Paradox of Tar Heel Politics*, 42.

130. The ratio fell from around 1 in 1890 to 0.54 in 1910. The figures are from ibid., 42–45, and Margo, *Race and Schooling*, 21.

131. Wright, *Old South, New South*, 123.

132. Daniels, *Editor in Politics*, 539.

CHAPTER 6

1. Daniels, *Editor in Politics*, 420.

2. Ibid., 591–93.

3. Ibid., 609.

4. Daniels, *Tar Heel Editor*, 303; Daniels, *Editor in Politics*, 610.

5. Daniels, *Editor in Politics*, 527–29.

6. Meehan, "Locke Craig," 1:453.

7. Years later Daniels candidly confessed that he sat out the campaign; see Daniels, *Editor in Politics*, 607–15.

8. Cooper, *Woodrow Wilson*, 39.

9. There is no shortage of biographies of Wilson. Among those on which this summary is based are Cooper, *Warrior and the Priest*; Cooper, *Woodrow Wilson*; Daniels, *Life of Woodrow Wilson*; and Link, *Woodrow Wilson*.

10. Although ostensibly a comprehensive analysis of the operation of the legislative branch of the U.S. government, *Congressional Government*, which remains in print to this day, was largely an indictment of the workings of the U.S. Con-

gress, particularly the seniority rules and cronyism of the committee system at the time. As of December 2010, the book was still available from Dover Publications through Amazon.com.

11. Brendon, *Dark Valley*, 15.

12. Fleming, *Illusion of Victory*, 363.

13. Ibid., 345.

14. Daniels, *Wilson Era: Years of Peace*, 17.

15. Ibid., 7.

16. Cooper, *Warrior and the Priest*, 121.

17. Ibid., 129.

18. Josephus Daniels to Woodrow Wilson, November 30, 1910, in Link, *Papers of Woodrow Wilson*, 22:121.

19. Daniels, *Wilson Era: Years of Peace*, 16–17.

20. Cooper, *Warrior and the Priest*, 175.

21. Daniels, *Wilson Era: Years of Peace*, 28. More generally, the material on Daniels's relationship with Harvey comes from ibid., 19–30.

22. This version of events is consistent with though not identical to that found in Baker, *Woodrow Wilson*, 3:256–59; Cooper, *Woodrow Wilson*, 92, 148; Daniels, *Wilson Era: Years of Peace*, 31–35; and Heckscher, *Woodrow Wilson*, 242.

23. Heckscher, *Woodrow Wilson*, 242; Daniels, *Wilson Era: Years of Peace*, 32–35.

24. Daniels, *Wilson Era: Years of Peace*, 33.

25. Heckscher, *Woodrow Wilson*, 242.

26. Daniels, *Wilson Era: Years of Peace*, 58–59. Another of Wilson's biographers emphasizes the role of William Gibbs McAdoo in keeping Wilson in the race; see Cooper, *Woodrow Wilson*, 157.

27. Cooper, *Warrior and the Priest*, 157.

28. Daniels placed this coup after the nomination; see Daniels, *Life of Woodrow Wilson*, 136. However, a recent biography puts McAdoo's elevation before the convention; see Cooper, *Woodrow Wilson*, 145–46.

29. Daniels, *Wilson Era: Years of Peace*, 115.

30. Ibid., 68–69.

31. Burleson and Daniels maintained an extensive correspondence that continued through Wilson's second administration. See Daniels Papers, LC, containers 70 and 71. Daniels summarized their relationship in Daniels, *Wilson Era: Years of Peace*, 47–67.

32. Josephus Daniels to Newton Baker, February 2, 1936, Daniels Papers, LC, container 62.

33. The quotes from these meetings are from Daniels, *Wilson Era: Years of Peace*, 75–76.

34. Baker, *Woodrow Wilson*, 3:418.

35. Cooper, *Woodrow Wilson*, 190.

36. Cooper, *Walter Hines Page*, 63–64.

37. Daniels, *Wilson Era: Years of Peace*, 94–99.

38. Cooper, *Walter Hines Page*, 215.

39. Ibid., 243–46.

40. Daniels strongly pushed the view that Page sought a cabinet position; see Daniels, *Wilson Era: Years of Peace*, 94–99.

41. Daniels, *Life of Woodrow Wilson*, 136.

42. Daniels, *Wilson Era: Years of Peace*, 114.

43. The quote is from Baer, *One Hundred Years of Sea Power*, 55. The most comprehensive indictment of Daniels's tenure as secretary is Kittredge, *Naval Lessons of the Great War.*

44. Daniels, *Wilson Era: Years of Peace*, 273.

45. Miller, *U.S. Navy*, 174.

46. Meyer is credited with creating the "Aides" system; see Kittredge, *Naval Lessons of the Great War*, 21. See also Daniels, *Wilson Era: Years of Peace*, 239.

47. Baer, *One Hundred Years of Sea Power*, 56; Miller, *U.S. Navy*, 101. Originally, there were only five bureaus.

48. On the bureau system, see McBride, *Technological Change*, 38–63.

49. For a summary of Mahan and his impact, see Roland, Bolster, and Keyssar, *Way of the Ship*, 255–74, and Miller, *U.S. Navy*, 152–53.

50. Boot, *Savage Wars of Peace*, 62.

51. Concerning the importance of Cannae in the imagination of subsequent generations of generals, see Manchester, *Arms of Krupp*; as for the extension of the metaphor to sea battles, as captured by Mahan, see Baer, *One Hundred Years of Sea Power*, 20.

52. Ferguson, *Empire*, 210–11.

53. See Baer, *One Hundred Years of Sea Power*, 9–26; Miller, *U.S. Navy*, 34–54, 143–65.

54. Economic output figures are from Craig and Fisher, *Integration of the European Economy*, 44. Naval size is from Baer, *One Hundred Years of Sea Power*, 9.

55. Brands, *TR*, 236.

56. Baer, *One Hundred Years of Sea Power*, 12.

57. Daniels, *Wilson Era: Years of Peace*, 132.

58. Miller, *U.S. Navy*, 143–65.

59. Ironically, for arcane technological reasons, Mahan was critical of the *Dreadnought*'s design. See McBride, *Technological Change*, 72–74.

60. Daniels, *Wilson Era: Years of Peace*, 326. For a complete accounting of Daniels's program, see Besch, *Navy Second to None*, 1–7.

61. Massie, *Dreadnought*, 468–97. The material in this section owes much to this volume.

62. Although only slightly larger, by 1,400 tons, than the last of the British pre-dreadnoughts, the *Lord Nelson* and *Agamemnon*, these behemoths exceeded their predecessors by 3,000 tons. The arithmetic here and below is based on the figures in Massie, *Dreadnought*, 477, 485, and Miller, *U.S. Navy*, 171. A nautical mile, or knot, is roughly one minute of latitude, or roughly 1.15 "land" miles.

63. Massie, *Dreadnought*, 485.

64. In fact, Congress had authorized the construction of two large battleships even before the British began construction on the *Dreadnought.*

65. The tonnage figures are from Kennedy, *Rise and Fall of the Great Powers*, 203. Such gross figures tend to compress key issues in naval warfare revolving around technology. These issues include speed; armor plate; the number, size, and accuracy of guns; and so forth, and these items say nothing of the competence of the officers or seamen manning the vessels. Although naval historians tend to pay more attention to these issues than other scholars, when comparative naval strengths are tallied, it is not always clear exactly at what stage of a ship's construction the ship enters the tally or whether there is any consistency across time or countries.

66. The accounts here are based on those in Dupuy and Dupuy, *Encyclopedia of Military History*, 934; Kemp, "Balance of Naval Power"; and Kennedy, *Rise and Fall of the Great Powers*, 203.

67. Preston, *Lusitania*, 38.

68. Kittredge, *Naval Lesson of the Great War*, 211.

69. Ibid., 27.

70. Ibid., 223–24.

71. Interview with Jonathan Worth Daniels, Southern Oral History Program.

72. Kittredge, *Naval Lessons of the Great War*, 27.

73. The memo is dated September 11, 1914, and can be found in Kittredge, *Naval Lessons of the Great War*, 224.

74. Ibid.

75. Howard Banks to Josephus Daniels, October 29, 1914, Daniels Papers, LC, container 62.

76. Benjamin Tillman to Josephus Daniels, March 24, 1913, folder 1, Josephus Daniels Papers, Wilson Library.

77. Besch, *Navy Second to None*, 16. Fiske's supporters gave him the credit for the creation of the CNO "against the opposition of the Secretary." See Kittredge, *Naval Lessons of the Great War*, 28.

78. "Navy League," http://www.navyleague.org, February 3, 2009.

79. Daniels, *Wilson Era: Years of Peace*, 340–41.

80. Creel, review of *Wilson Era: Years of Peace*, 577.

81. Baer, *One Hundred Years of Sea Power*, 52.

82. Quoted in Cashman, *America in the Age of the Titans*, 441.

83. Daniels, *Wilson Era: Years of Peace*, 170, 159.

84. Kennedy, *Rise and Fall of the Great Powers*, 247.

85. Black, *Franklin Delano Roosevelt*, 79.

86. Daniels, *Wilson Era: Years of Peace*, 326–36.

87. Besch, *Navy Second to None*, 1–7.

88. This material comes from Daniels, *Wilson Era: Years of War*, 234, 458–59, 629; Morrison, *Josephus Daniels*, 50–83; and author's interview with Frank Daniels Jr., July 9, 2002. Morrison was able to interview all four of Daniels's sons.

89. Gordon, *Hamilton's Blessing*, 209.

90. Daniels told this story to Franklin Roosevelt, who enjoyed repeating it. See Morrison, *Josephus Daniels*, 87.

91. Webb, *Jule Carr*, 187.

92. Quoted in Morrison, *Josephus Daniels*, 60.

93. McKenna, *Sand Pebbles*, 60.

94. Daniels, *Wilson Era: Years of Peace*, 274.

95. Ibid., 200–201.

96. Ibid., 131, 199–200.

97. Daniels proudly published the order verbatim in his memoirs. See ibid., 386.

98. It is often, though erroneously, thought that Daniels ended the ancient practice of distributing to the seamen a daily "rum ration." Gideon Welles had done this, as Lincoln's navy secretary, during the Civil War.

99. Daniels, *Wilson Era: Years of Peace*, 386.

CHAPTER 7

1. Boot, *Savage Wars of Peace*, 102–3.

2. This list does not include army expeditions in Mexico and elsewhere, since the War Department administered the army's activities.

3. Cooper, *Woodrow Wilson*, 75.

4. The material below owes much to, among others, Black, *Franklin Delano Roosevelt*, and Leuchtenberg, *Franklin Delano Roosevelt and the New Deal*.

5. Black, *Franklin Delano Roosevelt*, 126.

6. FDR's father, James Roosevelt, had another son from an earlier marriage, FDR's half-brother also named James but called "Rosy."

7. Daniels later claimed rather incongruously that their acquaintance was "a case of love at first sight" (Daniels, *Wilson Era: Years of Peace*, 125).

8. Interview with Jonathan Worth Daniels, Southern Oral History Program.

9. Black, *Franklin Delano Roosevelt*, 85.

10. Morrison, *Josephus Daniels*, 61.

11. Ibid., 48; Black, *Franklin Delano Roosevelt*, 65.

12. Daniels, *Wilson Era: Years of Peace*, 124.

13. Brendon, *Dark Valley*, 341.

14. Daniels, *Wilson Era: Years of Peace*, 129.

15. Daniels, *Cabinet Diaries*, 10; Daniels Papers, LC, container 1. After Daniels's death, the diaries were edited by E. David Cronon and published as a single volume.

16. Daniels, *Wilson Era: Years of Peace*, 126.

17. Black, *Franklin Delano Roosevelt*, 65.

18. Daniels, *Wilson Era: Years of Peace*, 128.

19. The original source of this quote seems to have been Daniels himself in Daniels, *Wilson Era: Years of Peace*, 126, which was published posthumously; however, it was antedated in press by Daniels's son Jonathan, in Daniels, *End of Innocence*, 54. It is repeated in, among other places, Morrison, *Josephus Daniels*, 49, and Miller, *U.S. Navy*, 178.

20. Daniels, *Tar Heel Editor*, 129.

21. Black, *Franklin Delano Roosevelt*, 68.

22. Morrison, *Josephus Daniels*, 77.

23. Wilson included Daniels in the discussions with Bryan because the navy would be required to execute any military orders issued for the Far East. What follows owes much to Cooper, *Woodrow Wilson*, 211–12; Daniels, *Cabinet Diaries*, 7–29; Daniels, *Wilson Era: Years of Peace*, 157–60; and Daniels's personal correspondence, Daniels Papers, LC, containers 59–102, which is organized by correspondent rather than by date or topic.

24. Daniels, *Cabinet Diaries*, 7.

25. Daniels, *Wilson Era: Years of Peace*, 160.

26. Weidenmier and Mitchener, "Empire, Public Goods, and the Roosevelt Corollary."

27. Daniels, *Wilson Era: Years of Peace*, 157.

28. At that time, this program was referred to as "rural credits." See Cooper, *Woodrow Wilson*, 222, 253–54.

29. Reed, "American Foreign Policy," 231.

30. Halberstam, *Coldest Winter*, 62.

31. Hastings, *Retribution*, 120.

32. Daniels, *Wilson Era: Years of Peace*, 161–62.

33. See Daniels's correspondence with Herbert Jackson, Daniels Papers, LC, containers 40 and 41. Unfortunately, the financial records of the News and Observer Publishing Company were lost to the fire.

34. Daniels, *Cabinet Diaries*, 54.

35. Ibid., 53–54.

36. Daniels, *Wilson Era: Years of Peace*, 163.

37. Given the events that followed, it is difficult to believe Fiske would have handed Daniels all of the details at this stage if he did not expect the navy secretary to present the plan in an unbiased fashion.

38. Daniels, *Cabinet Diaries*, 54.

39. In his diary, Daniels places this fatal meeting of the Joint Board on May 14. It is possible that there was a meeting of the Joint Board on the 14th; however, on that day, Fiske gave Daniels a five-page, single-spaced memorandum supporting the one he presented the day before. It seems unlikely that a second lengthy document was discussed, formalized by the board, and presented to Daniels all in the same day. Furthermore, as Daniels noted elsewhere, the New York papers published the details of the dispute on the 14th. See Daniels, *Wilson Era: Years of Peace*, 163.

40. Daniels, *Cabinet Diaries*, 66–68.

41. Ibid., 69–70; Daniels, *Wilson Era: Years of Peace*, 167–68.

42. Daniels, *Life of Woodrow Wilson*, 194.

43. Waller's exploits in the Philippines are summarized in Boot, *Savage Wars of Peace*, 120–22.

44. Daniels, *Wilson Years: Years of Peace*, 323.

45. A notable exception is Boot, *Savage Wars of Peace*.

46. Ibid., 132.

47. On U.S. military intervention in the Caribbean and Mexico, see ibid., 129–204; for the diplomatic side of the intervention, see Herring, *From Colony to Superpower*, 378–98.

48. As cited in Nasaw, *Chief*, 229 (emphasis in original).

49. Daniels, *Wilson Era: Years of War*, 522; Daniels, *Cabinet Diaries*, 30–31.

50. Daniels, *Cabinet Diaries*, 42–43.

51. Ibid.; Daniels, *Wilson Era: Years of Peace*, 180.

52. Daniels, *Cabinet Diaries*, 43.

53. Ibid.

54. The figure is from Boot, *Savage Wars of Peace*, 150; Daniels put it at eight; see Daniels, *Wilson Era: Years of Peace*, 186.

55. Daniels, *Wilson Era: Years of Peace*, 185–87.

56. The conquest of Veracruz is covered in Daniels, *Wilson Era: Years of Peace*, 180–207; Boot, *Savage Wars of Peace*, 149–55; and Herring, *From Colony to Superpower*, 378–98.

57. Boot, *Savage Wars of Peace*, 153.

58. Daniels, *Wilson Era: Years of Peace*, 178.

59. Boot, *Savage Wars of Peace*, 159; Herring, *From Colony to Superpower*, 378–98.

60. Daniels, *Wilson Era: Years of Peace*, 178.

61. Boot, *Savage Wars of Peace*, 160.

62. Daniels, *Wilson Era: Years of Peace*, 178.

63. Ibid.

64. Versions of this legend can be found in Boot, *Savage Wars of Peace*, 161–62, and Daniels, *Wilson Era: Years of Peace*, 178–79. The quote is from Daniels, *Wilson Era: Years of Peace*, 179.

65. Boot, *Savage Wars of Peace*, 141.

66. Baer, *One Hundred Years of Sea Power*, 41.

67. Herring, *From Colony to Superpower*, 389.

68. Ibid.

69. Interview with Jonathan Worth Daniels, Southern Oral History Program.

70. Daniels, *Recollections*, 4. The author thanks Patricia Daniels Woronoff for sharing the source via personal correspondence.

71. The material in this section owes much to the personal correspondence between Josephus Daniels and his brother Charles C. Daniels. The originals are in Daniels Papers, LC, containers 12–14.

72. Daniels, *Cabinet Diaries*, 51.

73. Josephus Daniels to C. C. Daniels, August 6, 1913, Daniels Papers, LC, container 12.

74. Daniels's letter to his brother is quoted in C. C. Daniels to Josephus Daniels, April 17, 1913, Daniels Papers, LC, container 12.

75. Ibid.

76. Ibid.

77. The relevant correspondence runs over several years. See Daniels Papers, LC, containers 12 and 13.

78. C. C. Daniels to Josephus Daniels, March 9, 1916, Daniels Papers, LC, container 13.

79. Ibid., December 7, 1916.

80. Morrison, *Josephus Daniels*, 195.

81. Ibid., 45.

82. See the miscellaneous correspondence between Henry Bagley and Josephus Daniels, Daniels Papers, LC, container 43.

83. Henry Bagley to Josephus Daniels, August 18, 1913, Daniels Papers, LC, container 43.

84. The figures in this section concerning the *N&O*'s balance sheet are from a series of written exchanges between Henry Bagley and Josephus Daniels. See Daniels Papers, LC, containers 43 and 44.

85. Memo dated 1924, Brown Funeral Home, Raleigh, N.C., Daniels Papers, LC, container 55.

86. Henry Bagley to Josephus Daniels, February 10, 1914, Daniels Papers, LC, container 43.

87. Josephus Daniels to Adelaide Bagley Daniels, November 15, 1915, Daniels Papers, LC, container 17.

88. Josephus Daniels to Herbert Jackson, January 31, 1914, Daniels Papers, LC, container 41.

89. Morrison, *Josephus Daniels*, 72.

90. See their correspondence in Daniels Papers, LC, containers 41 and 45.

CHAPTER 8

1. Raleigh *News and Observer*, June 28, 1914, 1; June 29, 1914, 1.

2. Ibid., June 30, 1914, 1.

3. This version of the oft-cited quote can be found in Herwig and Heyman, "Origins," 3, and Tuchman, *Guns of August*, 71.

4. Daniels, *Wilson Era: Years of Peace*, 568.

5. Herwig and Heyman, "Origins," 6.

6. Cooper, *Warrior and the Priest*, 221.

7. Daniels, *Wilson Era: Years of Peace*, 569.

8. Cooper, *Warrior and the Priest*, 273.

9. Herwig and Heyman, "Origins," 9.

10. Raleigh *News and Observer*, August 2, 1914, 1.

11. Daniels, *Cabinet Diaries*, 340. Although the actual quote came from an *N&O* article, had Daniels disagreed, it would not have been published.

12. Ferguson, *Empire*, 242.

13. The kaiser's younger brother, Prince Heinrich, also held the exalted rank of grand admiral.

14. Daniels, *Wilson Era: Years of Peace*, 565.

15. Raleigh *News and Observer*, August 3, 1914, 4; the language followed more closely that of Daniels rather than Britton.

16. Kazin, *Godly Hero*, 233.

17. Daniels, *Wilson Era: Years of Peace*, 566.

18. The quote is from ibid., 574. For an example of the criticism Daniels received for censoring the service, see Kittredge, *Naval Lessons of the Great War*.

19. Daniels, *Wilson Era: Years of Peace*, 565–66.

20. These are from Daniels's figures in ibid., 425.

21. Ibid., 566.

22. Ibid., 425.

23. Stevenson, *With Our Backs to the Wall*, 311–49; Strachan, *First World War*.

24. The metaphor is from Massie, *Castles of Steel*.

25. Daniels, *Cabinet Diaries*, 116–17.

26. Cicero, *Fifth Philippic*.

27. See Kittredge, *Naval Lessons of the Great War*, 97–116.

28. Daniels, *Cabinet Diaries*, 91.

29. Kemp, "Balance of Naval Power."

30. Daniels, *Cabinet Diaries*, 97.

31. These are spelled out variously in Daniels, *Cabinet Diaries*, 97; Massie, *Castles of Steel*, 504–6; and Preston, *Lusitania*, 70.

32. Preston, *Lusitania*, 70.

33. Daniels, *Wilson Era: Years of War*, 29.

34. For an elaboration, see Massie, *Castles of Steel*, 504–6. Although the Declaration of London was a major step in the application of the rule of law to war at sea, neither the British Parliament nor the U.S. Congress formally ratified it before the Great War began—though, more generally, the Cruiser Rules continued to be the recognized law of war at sea.

35. The figures are from Massie, *Castles of Steel*, 507.

36. Ibid.

37. Daniels, *Life of Woodrow Wilson*, 250.

38. Kazin, *Godly Hero*, 233.

39. Preston, *Lusitania*, 72.

40. Massie, *Castles of Steel*, 517.

41. Daniels, *Life of Woodrow Wilson*, 250. Daniels had the date wrong. The proclamation was signed by the kaiser on February 4.

42. On German naval strategy, see Halpern, *Naval History of World War I*, 287–334.

43. Kazin, *Godly Hero*, 233.

44. Daniels, *Life of Woodrow Wilson*, 251.

45. In correspondence with the author, Wilson's biographer John Milton Cooper argues that Wilson wanted to follow a neutral path but simply could not find a way to do so.

46. Kazin, *Godly Hero*, 233–36. This is not the view of Wilson's biographer; see Cooper, *Woodrow Wilson*, 292.

47. Daniels, *Life of Woodrow Wilson*, 252.

48. Ibid., 253.

49. Raleigh *News and Observer*, May 5, 1915, 1; Daniels, *Wilson Era: Years of Peace*, 579.

50. Kazin, *Godly Hero*, 235.

51. Black, *Franklin Delano Roosevelt*, 73.

52. Daniels, *Life of Woodrow Wilson*, 253.

53. Daniels, *Wilson Era: Years of Peace*, 428; see also Black, *Franklin Delano Roosevelt*, 74–81.

54. Preston, *Lusitania*.

55. Daniels, *Life of Woodrow Wilson*, 254.

56. Daniels, *Wilson Era: Years of Peace*, 427–35 (emphasis added).

57. Ibid., 427.

58. Ibid.

59. Ibid., 428.

60. Ibid., 142–43.

61. Massie, *Castles of Steel*, 536.

62. William Jennings Bryan open letter, July 2, 1915, Daniels Papers, LC, container 70. A version of this letter was eventually released to the public.

63. Massie, *Castles of Steel*, 540.

64. Ibid., 542.

65. Ibid.

66. Preston, *Lusitania*, 410.

67. Daniels, *Life of Woodrow Wilson*, 255.

68. Massie, *Castles of Steel*, 545.

69. Stevenson, *With Our Backs to the Wall*, 312, 336–37; Massie, *Castles of Steel*, 547.

70. Daniels, *Wilson Era: Years of Peace*, 439.

71. Daniels, *Life of Woodrow Wilson*, 259; Daniels, *Wilson Era: Years of Peace*, 439.

72. Massie, *Castles of Steel*, 549.

73. See Daniels's correspondence with Benson on the naval building program, Daniels Papers, LC, container 66; also see McBride, *Technological Change*, 118.

74. Cooper, *Woodrow Wilson*, 339.

75. In Wilson's defense, the court already had two Catholic justices, including Chief Justice Edward Douglass White.

76. Daniels, *Wilson Era: Years of Peace*, 583.

77. Massie, *Castles of Steel*, 691–700; for a more detailed account of the events leading up to the armistice, see Stevenson, *With Our Backs to the Wall*, 509–45.

78. On the German response, see Cooper, *Woodrow Wilson*, 372–74, and Stevenson, *With Our Backs to the Wall*, 15.

79. Daniels, *Wilson Era: Years of Peace*, 583.

80. Massie, *Castles of Steel*, 704–5.

81. Daniels, *Wilson Era: Years of War*, 96, 92.

82. Massie, *Castles of Steel*, 709.

83. Ibid., 712.

84. Daniels, *Cabinet Diaries*, 106.

85. Daniels, *Wilson Era: Years of War*, 19.

86. The material here is from ibid., 22–30, and Daniels, *Cabinet Diaries*, 119–20.

87. Cooper, *Woodrow Wilson*, 81.

88. Daniels, *Wilson Era: Years of War*, 33.

89. Ibid.

90. The figures are based on average monthly deaths and a total of roughly 20 million deaths.

91. Daniels, *Our Navy at War*; Daniels, *Wilson Era: Years of War*.

92. Analysis of the naval spending programs is complicated by the federal budget process. Daniels drew up a proposal in year one, to be approved by Congress in year two, to go into effect in year three.

93. The most searing indictment is Kittredge, *Naval Lessons of the Great War*.

94. Ibid., 22.

95. Daniels, *Wilson Era: Years of War*, 24.

96. Ibid., 95.

97. Daniels, *Wilson Era: Years of Peace*, 570.

98. Ibid., 584–85.

99. Ibid.

100. Cooper, *Woodrow Wilson*, 5.

101. Daniels, *Cabinet Diaries*, 190.

102. Ibid., 133.

CHAPTER 9

1. Daniels, *Cabinet Diaries*, 139, 143.

2. Ibid., 163, 165.

3. Smedley Butler to Adelaide Bagley Daniels, September 28, 1918, Daniels Papers, LC, container 26. It is interesting that this letter is among the Worth Daniels papers in the Josephus Daniels collection at the Library of Congress.

4. Daniels, *Cabinet Diaries*, 262.

5. Ibid., 357.

6. Ibid., 356–57.

7. Daniels Papers, LC, container 66.

8. Massie, *Castles of Steel*, 140.

9. Daniels, *Cabinet Diaries*, 228.

10. Daniels, *Wilson Era: Years of War*, 89. The efficacy of the mine barrage has been questioned by some historians of the war; see, for example, Stevenson, *With Our Backs to the Wall*, 321.

11. Daniels Papers, LC, container 66; Herwig and Heyman, "Henry Thomas Mayo"; Halpern, *Naval History of World War I*, 362.

12. Dupuy and Dupuy, *Encyclopedia of Military History*, 975.

13. Daniels, *Wilson Era: Years of War*, 69–70.

14. For a concise summary of the war at sea, see Strachan, *First World War*, 201–30. For a more comprehensive treatment, see Halpern, *Naval History of World War I*, and Massie, *Castles of Steel*.

15. Daniels, *Cabinet Diaries*, 120.

16. Dupuy and Dupuy, *Encyclopedia of Military History*, 968. Though slated to

lead the AEF, Pershing was not formally named its commander until after the conscription act passed. See Herwig and Heyman, "John Joseph Pershing," 277.

17. Daniels, *Our Navy at War*, 70.

18. Cooper, *Walter Hines Page*, 375.

19. Strachan, *First World War*, 228.

20. Ibid., 291.

21. The Fourteen Points were (1) open covenants, openly arrived at; (2) freedom of the seas in war and peace; (3) removal of trade barriers; (4) national armament reductions; (5) impartial adjustment of colonial claims; (6) evacuation of Russian territory and independent solution by Russia of its political development and national policy; (7) evacuation and restoration of Belgium; (8) evacuation and restoration of all occupied French territory and return of Alsace-Lorraine; (9) readjustment of Italian frontiers on lines of nationality; (10) autonomy for the peoples of Austria-Hungary; (11) evacuation of Romania, Serbia, and Montenegro, restoration of occupied territories, and Serbian access to the sea; (12) Turkish portions of the Ottoman Empire to be assured secure sovereignty, but other nationalities under Turkish domination to be freed; (13) independence of Poland, to include territories with predominantly Polish population, with free Polish access to the sea; (14) formation of an association of nations ensuring liberty and territorial integrity of great and small alike.

22. Daniels, *Life of Woodrow Wilson*, 291.

23. Daniels, *Cabinet Diaries*, 264.

24. Daniels, *Our Navy at War*, 209, 211; Strachan, *First World War*, 297–99.

25. Massie, *Castles of Steel*, 772.

26. Daniels, *Wilson Era: Years of War*, 335.

27. Daniels, *Cabinet Diaries*, 339.

28. Ibid.

29. Ibid., 343.

30. Massie, *Castles of Steel*, 771.

31. Daniels, *Cabinet Diaries*, 340.

32. Massie, *Castles of Steel*, 772.

33. Daniels, *Cabinet Diaries*, 343.

34. Ibid., 348.

35. Daniels, *Wilson Era: Years of War*, 335.

36. Dupuy and Dupuy, *Encyclopedia of Military History*, 990.

37. Barry, *Great Influenza*.

38. Morrison, *Josephus Daniels*, 103.

39. The expression comes from Fleming, *Illusion of Victory*.

40. Ferguson, *House of Rothschild*, 215.

41. This tally includes the British dominions of Australia, Canada, New Zealand, Newfoundland, and South Africa as independent states.

42. Daniels, *Cabinet Diaries*, 342.

43. Daniels, *Wilson Era: Years of War*, 351.

44. Ibid., 392.

45. Ibid., 476–78.

46. Ibid., 478.

47. Fleming, *Illusion of Victory*, 175.

48. Daniels, *Wilson Era: Years of War*, 285.

49. Fleming, *Illusion of Victory*, 241.

50. Daniels, *Wilson Era: Years of War*, 285.

51. MacMillan, *Paris, 1919*, 6.

52. See Heckscher quoted at http://www.johnreilly.info/wowi.htm, August 14, 2008.

53. Daniels, *Wilson Era: Years of War*, 310.

54. Ibid., 354–55.

55. MacMillan, *Paris, 1919*, 5. What follows in this section owes much to this excellent source.

56. Herring, *From Colony to Superpower*, 381.

57. Quoted in Cooper, *Woodrow Wilson*, 556.

58. Daniels, *Wilson Era: Years of War*, 316–17.

59. On Hurley and the shipping board, see Roland, Bolster, and Keyssar, *Way of the Ship*, 270–74.

60. Daniels, *Our Navy at War*, 306. Benson objected to extending the building program, Daniels Papers, LC, container 66.

61. Quoted in Boot, *War Made New*, 251.

62. McBride, *Technological Change*, 128–30.

63. Daniels, *Wilson Era: Years of War*, 568.

64. Daniels, *Cabinet Diaries*, 375.

65. Ibid., 371.

66. MacMillan, *Paris, 1919*, 143.

67. Daniels, *Wilson Era: Years of War*, 451.

68. Ibid., 369.

69. MacMillan, *Paris, 1919*, 179.

70. Daniels, *Wilson Era: Years of War*, 371.

71. Quoted in Roland, Bolster, and Keyssar, *Way of the Ship*, 274.

72. Daniels, *Cabinet Diaries*, 380.

73. The issue was not simply one of who had the most ships. Daniels and Lloyd George went over the details of ship numbers, tonnage, and armaments in Paris, and there was no question that although the British had more ships and more tonnage, America would have the newer, stronger navy. See Daniels, *Wilson Era: Years of War*, 377.

74. Daniels, *Cabinet Diaries*, 381.

75. Ibid., 388.

76. Interview with Jonathan Worth Daniels, Southern Oral History Program.

77. Cohen, "Can You Forgive Him?," 50.

78. Daniels, *Cabinet Diaries*, 405.

79. Woodrow Wilson to Josephus Daniels, July 2, 1917, in Link, *Papers of Woodrow Wilson*, 43:71–72.

80. Daniels, *Wilson Era: Years of War*, 571.

81. Baer, *One Hundred Years of Sea Power*, 91.

82. The details of House's role in the naval disputes are captured in the footnotes of Daniels's diary during his time in Europe, and in Daniels's postwar memoirs. See Daniels, *Cabinet Diaries*, and Daniels, *Wilson Era: Years of War*, 380–83.

83. Daniels, *Wilson Era: Years of War*, 381.

84. MacMillan, *Paris, 1919*, 274.

85. Ibid., 316.

86. Ibid., 322.

87. Ibid., 310–16.

88. The figure, which can be bumped up or down depending on one's definition of a "war," was compiled by Wilson's press secretary Ray Stannard Baker and is reported in Fleming, *Illusion of Victory*, 373.

89. Daniels, *Wilson Era: Years of War*, 405–6.

90. MacMillan, *Paris, 1919*, 285.

91. Daniels, *Cabinet Diaries*, 386.

92. Daniels, *Wilson Era: Years of War*, 405.

93. The figure was roughly $550 per person, which was roughly the U.S. dollar equivalent of German per capita income at the time, approximately $40,000 today.

94. Daniels, *Cabinet Diaries*, 426.

95. MacMillan, *Paris, 1919*, 465.

96. Quoted in Cooper, *Woodrow Wilson*, 558.

97. Josephus Daniels to Woodrow Wilson, July 30, 1919, in Link, *Papers of Woodrow Wilson*, 62:45.

98. Daniels, *Wilson Era: Years of War*, 479; Daniels, *Cabinet Diaries*, 443.

99. Daniels, *Wilson Era: Years of War*, 464.

100. Baker, *Woodrow Wilson*, 7:514.

101. Herwig and Heyman, "William Snowden Sims," 318. For an extensive account of the hearings, see Kittredge, *Naval Lessons of the Great War*.

102. Although both Daniels and an earlier biographer spent considerable time explaining the hearings, in the end their historical significance was almost nil. See Daniels, *Wilson Era: Years of War*, 492–507.

103. Morrison, *Josephus Daniels*, 128–29.

104. The details can be found in the correspondence between Daniels and Barnett in Daniels Papers, LC, container 64.

105. Daniels, *Wilson Era: Years of War*, 561.

106. Daniels, *Cabinet Diaries*, 551.

107. Daniels, *Wilson Era: Years of War*, 554–55.

108. Black, *Franklin Delano Roosevelt*, 120–21.

109. Ibid., 126.

110. Winik, *Great Upheaval*, 523.

111. McLynn, *Burma Campaign*, 46.

112. Daniels, *Cabinet Diaries*, 543–44.

113. This passage appeared in Daniels's correspondence with Newton Baker; see Josephus Daniels to Newton Baker, February 16, 1921, Daniels Papers, LC, container 58.

114. Later in life they often attended services together, alternating churches; see interview with Jonathan Worth Daniels, Southern Oral History Program. The author thanks Sue McDowell for information concerning Daniels's activities at the Edenton Street United Methodist Church.

115. Quoted in Raleigh *News and Observer*, March 7, 1921.

116. Bishir and Southern, *Guide to the Historic Architecture of Piedmont North Carolina*, 114.

117. Josephus Daniels to Josephus Daniels Jr., April 6, 1920, Daniels Papers, LC, container 23.

118. Bishir and Southern, *Guide to the Historic Architecture of Piedmont North Carolina*, 130–31.

119. Josephus Daniels to Josephus Daniels Jr., April 6, 1920, Daniels Papers, LC, container 23.

120. Author's interview with Frank Daniels Jr., July 9, 2002. Sometimes the story has it that Wakestone was built with all the stones hurled at Daniels, rather than the *N&O*. (The home still stands today, though parts of it were extensively remodeled during the years in which it served as a Masonic temple.)

121. This money showed up in his investments with Herbert Jackson, who was at the Virginia Trust Company. See Daniels Papers, LC, container 18.

122. Spiegelman, "Chautauqua."

123. Undated newspaper clipping, Daniels Papers, LC, container 18.

124. A figure in this neighborhood can be obtained by summing the transactions Daniels conducted with Herbert Jackson between 1894 and 1929, adjusting for interest, repayment, and so forth. See Daniels Papers, LC.

125. An earlier biography puts the figure at $25,000, but that excludes profits from the *N&O* and some of Daniels's writing contracts. With a paid-in capital of $100,000, even a 20 percent return, half of what Daniels had earned on his paper in earlier years, would have yielded another $20,000. See Morrison, *Josephus Daniels*, 151.

CHAPTER 10

1. Chalmers, *Hooded Americanism*, 2. See also Wade, *Fiery Cross*.

2. Cooper, *Walter Hines Page*, 70.

3. Ibid., 168.

4. Ibid.

5. Inflation figures are from Clark, Craig, and Wilson, *History of Public Sector Pensions*, 226.

6. The details concerning Griffith and his masterpiece are from Barry, *Rising Tide*, 141–42; Chalmers, *Hooded Americanism*, 22–27; and Wade, *Fiery Cross*, 119–39.

7. Interview with Jonathan Worth Daniels, Southern Oral History Program.

On Daniels's role in distributing the film, see Steelwater, *Hangman's Knot*. Some evidence suggests that Dixon himself approached Wilson and asked him to view the film. Wilson's papers contain direct correspondence from Dixon and Griffith. See Wade, *Fiery Cross*, 470.

8. Wade, *Fiery Cross*, 470.

9. Two well-known histories of the Klan include an entire chapter covering the role of *The Birth of a Nation* in resurrecting the organization. See Chalmers, *Hooded Americanism*, and Wade, *Fiery Cross*.

10. Cash, *Mind of the South*, 335.

11. Chalmers, *Hooded Americanism*, 33.

12. Cash, *Mind of the South*, 336.

13. Jonathan Daniels to Adelaide Bagley Daniels, April 19, 1924, Daniels Papers, LC, container 30.

14. McCartney, *Teapot Dome Scandal*.

15. Morrison, *Josephus Daniels*, 148. Although in McAdoo's case, the funds were for legal services.

16. Ibid., 152.

17. From a Daniels speech in Baton Rouge, found in an undated newspaper clipping in Daniels Papers, LC, container 18.

18. Kazin, *Godly Hero*, 283.

19. See, for example, the discussion in ibid., 282–85.

20. This version of Bryan's speech is taken from ibid., 284.

21. The antimiscegenation bill focused specifically on intermarriage between "whites and blacks," and the speech codes focused on "derogatory remarks made by Roman Catholics about non-Catholic marriages" (Chalmers, *Hooded Americanism*, 95).

22. Ibid.

23. These figures are from ibid., 92–97.

24. Raleigh *News and Observer*, January 11–14, 1927, 1, 4.

25. On the controversy in North Carolina and Daniels's role in it, see Christensen, *Paradox of Tar Heel Politics*, 55–56; Kazin, *Godly Hero*, 285–95; Morrison, *Josephus Daniels*, 153; and Powell, *North Carolina through Four Centuries*, 464–66.

26. Morrison, *Josephus Daniels*, 153.

27. Raleigh *News and Observer*, February 12, 1925, 4.

28. Though Daniels never took credit for the effort, an early biographer who interviewed surviving witnesses to the fight, including Daniels's sons, gave him credit. See Morrison, *Josephus Daniels*, 153.

29. C. C. Daniels to Josephus Daniels, April 17, 1913, Daniels Papers, LC, container 12.

30. Christensen, *Paradox of Tar Heel Politics*, 50–56; also see Magruder, *Cameron Morrison*.

31. The port project was ultimately defeated in a statewide referendum.

32. Wood, *Southern Capitalism*, 125.

33. Josephus Daniels to Jonathan Daniels, March 22, 1935, Daniels Papers, LC, container 32.

34. Undated newspaper clipping, Daniels Papers, LC, container 18.

35. Wood, *Southern Capitalism*, 125.

36. Author's interview with Patricia Daniels Woronoff; interview with Jonathan Worth Daniels, Southern Oral History Program.

37. Watson, "Josephus Daniels," 2:14.

38. Interview with Jonathan Worth Daniels, Southern Oral History Program.

39. Author's interviews with Frank Daniels Jr., July 9, 2002; Adelaide Daniels Key; and Patricia Daniels Woronoff.

40. Josephus Daniels to Josephus Daniels Jr., August 22, 1914, Daniels Papers, LC, container 23. Also see interview with Jonathan Worth Daniels, Southern Oral History Program, and author's interviews with Adelaide Daniels Key and Patricia Daniels Woronoff.

41. Jonathan Daniels to Josephus Daniels, September 18, 1933, Daniels Papers, LC, container 31.

42. Interview with Jonathan Worth Daniels, Southern Oral History Program.

43. These homes are still there.

44. Daniels Papers, LC, containers 30 and 31; author's interview with Patricia Daniels Woronoff.

45. Daniels Papers, LC, container 23.

46. Daniels, *Tar Heel Editor*, 242.

47. Daniels, *Cabinet Diaries*, 356–57.

48. The former view is explicitly stated by Jonathan's daughter, Lucy Daniels, in her autobiography, *With a Woman's Voice.* The latter view is implicit in Adelaide Daniels Key's claim that Frank's special status in the family derived from the fact that he was the baby. See author's interview with Adelaide Daniels Key.

49. Author's interview with Patricia Daniels Woronoff.

50. For a summary of Jonathan's life, see Eagles, "Jonathan Daniels"; for a more in-depth and personal, though darker, view, see his daughter's autobiography, Daniels, *With a Woman's Voice.*

51. Interview with Jonathan Worth Daniels, Southern Oral History Program; see also Chandler, *Binghams of Louisville.*

52. Jonathan Daniels to Adelaide Bagley Daniels, April 19, 1924, Daniels Papers, LC, container 30.

53. Daniels, *With a Woman's Voice.*

54. Elizabeth Daniels Squire was the author of the popular Peaches Dann mystery series. She died in February 2001.

55. *Time*, April 21, 1930, 80.

56. Jonathan Daniels to Josephus Daniels, September 7, 1930, Daniels Papers, LC, container 31.

57. Jonathan Daniels to Josephus Daniels, July 1, 1933, and Josephus Daniels to Jonathan Daniels, March 22, 1935, Daniels Papers, LC, containers 31 and 32, respectively.

58. Josephus Daniels to Jonathan Daniels, undated, Daniels Papers, LC, container 35.

59. Josephus Daniels to Jonathan Daniels, August 28, 1933, Daniels Papers, LC,

container 31. Jonathan's liberalism at the time must be considered relative to that of his father. For a more complete treatment of Jonathan's position on race, see Eagles, *Jonathan Daniels*.

60. Daniels, *With a Woman's Voice*, 48.

61. Author's interview with Adelaide Daniels Key; Daniels, *With a Woman's Voice*, 8.

62. Author's interview with Adelaide Daniels Key; Daniels, *With a Woman's Voice*.

63. Daniels, *With a Woman's Voice*, 48–49.

64. Author's interview with Frank Daniels Jr., July 9, 2002.

65. Daniels, *With a Woman's Voice*, 48–49.

66. Interview with Jonathan Worth Daniels, Southern Oral History Program.

67. Josephus Daniels to C. C. Daniels, October 10, 1940, Daniels Papers, LC, container 14.

68. Frank did this at his father's request. Jonathan had originally asked the Old Man for help. It is not clear from the surviving correspondence that Jonathan knew Frank handled the matter. See Daniels Papers, LC, container 30.

69. See the correspondence in Daniels Papers, LC, container 36.

70. Interview with Jonathan Worth Daniels, Southern Oral History Program.

71. The state's other Senate seat was now held by Josiah Bailey, who had defeated the longtime incumbent Furnifold Simmons in the 1930 Democratic primary. Daniels had remained neutral in the Bailey-Simmons fight; see Simmons Papers, Wilson Library. For an excellent account of North Carolina politics during this era, see Christensen, *Paradox of Tar Heel Politics*; on Daniels's relationship with Reynolds, see Daniels, *Shirt-Sleeve Diplomat*, 362–64.

72. Herwig and Heyman, "Josephus Daniels," 125.

73. Daniels, *Shirt-Sleeve Diplomat*, 16–17, 22.

74. Managing editor Frank Smethurst now served as the senior nonfamily member at the firm. He had replaced Britton, who had joined Daniels in Washington in 1918. As editor, Smethurst hired the first female journalist, Nell Battle Lewis, at the *N&O*. In the 1920s Lewis led the paper's attack on the Klan and later gave the paper a fervent pro-labor voice. See Leidholt, *Battling Nell*.

75. Moreno, *Yankee Don't Go Home!*, 52–53.

76. Daniels, *Shirt-Sleeve Diplomat*, 9.

77. Moreno, *Yankee Don't Go Home!*, 52–53.

78. Herring, *From Colony to Superpower*, 474–77.

79. Daniels, *Shirt-Sleeve Diplomat*, 54, 55; Herring, *From Colony to Superpower*, 474–77.

80. Herring, *From Colony to Superpower*, 475.

81. See Daniels, *Shirt-Sleeve Diplomat*, 3–56, 99, and Moreno, *Yankee Don't Go Home!*, 52–53.

82. Daniels discussed the attacks against him in a letter to his son Jonathan; see Josephus Daniels to Jonathan Daniels, January 5, 1935, Daniels Papers, LC, container 32.

83. Daniels reported this list in his memoirs, and the individual items show up

in his correspondence during this period. See Daniels, *Shirt-Sleeve Diplomat*, 23, and Daniels Papers, LC, container 82.

84. Daniels reports the figures in Daniels, *Shirt-Sleeve Diplomat*, 106, 115. What follows owes much to this source and Daniels extensive correspondence on the subject; see Daniels Papers, LC.

85. See, for example, his correspondence with the State Department concerning the claims of a U.S. meatpacker whose Mexican firm had been nationalized: Josephus Daniels to Herbert Bursley, October 8, 1941, Daniels Papers, Rubenstein Library, container 2.

86. Daniels, *Shirt-Sleeve Diplomat*, 116.

87. Ibid., 121.

88. Chernow, *House of Morgan*, 299.

89. Ibid.

90. This communication is summarized in Daniels, *Shirt-Sleeve Diplomat*, 121–22.

91. Chernow, *House of Morgan*, 299.

92. Daniels, *Shirt-Sleeve Diplomat*, 23.

93. Herring, *From Colony to Superpower*, 474–75.

94. Daniels, *Shirt-Sleeve Diplomat*, 60, 122–23.

95. Moreno, *Yankee Don't Go Home!*, 41.

96. Yergin, *Prize*, 273.

97. Daniels, *Shirt-Sleeve Diplomat*, 64–65.

98. Yergin, *Prize*, 231.

99. Accounts of Mexico's oil industry expropriation can be found in Daniels, *Shirt-Sleeve Diplomat*, 217–54, and Yergin, *Prize*, 271–79.

100. Yergin, *Prize*, 271–79.

101. "Chronology," http://www.ibiblio.org/pha/events/events.html, May 28, 2009.

102. Black, *Franklin Delano Roosevelt*, 504.

103. Ibid., 446.

104. Yergin, *Prize*, 278.

105. Creel, review of *Wilson Era: Years of Peace*, 576.

106. Personal correspondence with Frank Daniels Jr., July 6, 2010.

107. Author's interview with Frank Daniels Jr., July 9, 2002.

108. Daniels, *Shirt-Sleeve Diplomat*, epigraph.

109. Author's interviews with Frank Daniels Jr., July 9, 2002, and Adelaide Daniels Key.

110. Morrison, *Josephus Daniels*, 254.

111. Author's interview with Baxter Sapp.

112. Author's interview with Patricia Daniels Woronoff.

113. Lehmann, "Paper Tigers," 77.

References

ARCHIVAL MANUSCRIPT COLLECTIONS

North Carolina

D. H. Hill Library, North Carolina State University, Raleigh

    Special Collections Research Center

        National Farmers' Alliance, Records, 1887–1892

        William Joseph Peele, Papers, 1888–1923

        Watauga Club Records, 1884–2000

North Carolina Division of Archives and History, Raleigh

    Estate of Lois Davis Seabrook, Papers

Rubenstein Rare Book and Manuscript Library, Duke University, Durham

    Josephus Daniels, Papers

    Matt W. Ransom, Letters

Wilson Library, University of North Carolina, Chapel Hill

    Southern Historical Collection

        Alexander Boyd Andrews Papers, 1859–1891

        Bagley Family Papers, 1848–1939

        Julian Shakespeare Carr Papers, 1892–1923

        Jonathan Daniels Papers, 1865–1982

        Josephus Daniels Papers, 1863–1947

        Robert F. Hoke Papers, 1865–1943

        Furnifold M. Simmons Papers, 1930–1933

        Jonathan Worth Papers, 1798–1899

Washington, D.C.

Library of Congress

    Papers of Josephus Daniels

        Correspondence, 1878–1948

        Diaries, 1913–1948

        Family Papers, 1855–1948

PERSONAL CORRESPONDENCE

Daniels, Frank, Jr., to author, October 2, 2002; March 31, 2009; July 6, 2010

Woronoff, Patricia Daniels, to author, January 29, 2003

References

AUTHOR'S INTERVIEWS

Anonymous Daniels family member, Raleigh, N.C., February 20, 2004
Daniels, Frank, Jr., Raleigh, N.C., July 9, 12, 2002
Daniels, Lucy, Raleigh, N.C., November 15, 2004
Key, Adelaide Daniels, Mackinac City, Mich., September 7, 2002
Sapp, Baxter, Durham, N.C., December 2, 2003
Woronoff, Patricia Daniels, Durham, N.C., February 21, 2003
Zaytoun, Henry, Raleigh, N.C., November 21, 2007

ORAL HISTORIES

Interview with Frank Daniels Jr., February 13, 2007. Interview R-0508. South-
ern Oral History Program Collection (#4007), University of North Carolina,
Chapel Hill.
Interview with Jonathan Worth Daniels, March 9–11, 1977. Interview A-0313.
Southern Oral History Program Collection (#4007), University of North
Carolina, Chapel Hill.

NEWSPAPERS AND PERIODICALS

Charlotte *Observer*
Clinton (Goldsboro and Raleigh)
  Caucasian
Greensboro *News*
New York Times
Progressive Farmer

Raleigh *News and Observer*
Raleigh *North Carolinian*
Raleigh *State Chronicle*
Time
Wall Street Journal
Wilson *Advance*

WEBSITES

1898 Wilmington Race Riot Commission. "1898 Wilmington Race Riot Report." *North Carolina Department of Cultural Resources* (31 May 2006). LaRae
Umfleet, Principal Researcher. http://www.history.ncdcr.gov/1898-wrrc
/report/report.htm. November 7, 2008.
"Chronology of International Events, March 1938 to December 1941." *The Public's Library and Digital Archive*. Department of State. http://www.ibiblio.org
/pha/events/events.html. June 5, 2009.
"Daniel-L Archives." *Rootsweb*. http://listsearches.rootsweb.com/th/read
/DANIEL/2000-08/0965953859. September 28, 2009.
Harris, Elizabeth. "Patent Models in the Graphic Arts Collection." *National Mu-
seum of American History*. http://americanhistory.si.edu/about/pubs
/harris3.pdf. May 22, 2009.
Heckscher, August. "Woodrow Wilson: A Biography." *John Reilly*. http://www
.johnreilly.info/wowi.htm. June 5, 2009.

"History." *Wake County Board of Alcoholic Control.* http://www.wakeabc.com
/history.html. August 27, 2008.

"Navy League." *Navy League of the United States.* http://www.navyleague.org.
February 3, 2009.

"Thumbprint of the South: A Review of *Tar Heel Editor.*" *Time,* December 25,
1939. http://www.time.com/time/magazine/article/0,9171,762165,00.html.
June 1, 2009.

BOOKS, ARTICLES, AND PAPERS

Als, Hilton. "I, Me, Mine: A New Biography of Christopher Isherwood." *New
Yorker,* January 17, 2005, 87–90.

Alston, Lee J., and Joseph Ferrie. *Southern Paternalism and the American Welfare
State: Economics, Politics, and Institutions in the U.S. South, 1865–1965.* New
York: Cambridge University Press, 1999.

Alston, Lee J., and Kyle D. Kauffman. "Up, Down, and Off the Agricultural Ladder: New Evidence and Implications of Agricultural Mobility for Blacks in the
Postbellum South." *Agricultural History* 72 (Spring 1998): 263–79.

Atack, Jeremy, and Peter Passell. *A New Economic View of American History from
Colonial Times to 1940.* New York: Norton, 1994.

Baer, George W. *One Hundred Years of Sea Power: The U.S. Navy, 1890–1990.* Stanford, Calif.: Stanford University Press, 1994.

Baker, Ray Stannard. *Woodrow Wilson: Life and Letters.* Vol. 3, *Governor, 1910–
1913.* Garden City, N.Y.: Doubleday, Doran, 1931.

———. *Woodrow Wilson: Life and Letters.* Vol. 7, *War Leader, 1917–1918.* Garden
City, N.Y.: Doubleday, Doran, 1931.

Balke, Nathan S., and Robert J. Gordon. "The Estimation of Prewar Gross National Product: Methodology and New Evidence." *Journal of Political Economy*
97 (February 1989): 38–92.

Barry, John. *The Great Influenza: The Epic Story of the Deadliest Plague in History.*
New York: Penguin, 2004.

———. *Rising Tide: The Great Mississippi Flood of 1927 and How It Changed
America.* New York: Touchstone, 1997.

Bassett, John S. "Stirring Up the Fires of Race Antipathy." *South Atlantic Quarterly* 2 (October 1903): 298–99.

Bateman, Fred, and Thomas Weiss. *A Deplorable Scarcity: The Failure of Industrialization in the Slave Economy.* Chapel Hill: University of North Carolina
Press, 1981.

Besch, Michael D. *A Navy Second to None: The History of U.S. Naval Training in
World War I.* Westport, Conn.: Greenwood Press, 2002.

Bishir, Catherine W., and Michael T. Southern. *A Guide to the Historic Architecture of Piedmont North Carolina.* Chapel Hill: University of North Carolina
Press, 2003.

Black, Conrad. *Franklin Delano Roosevelt: Champion of Freedom.* New York: Public Affairs, 2003.

Boot, Max. *The Savage Wars of Peace: Small Wars and the Rise of American Power.* New York: Basic Books, 2002.

———. *War Made New: Technology, Warfare, and the Course of History, 1500 to Today.* New York: Penguin, 2006.

Branch, Taylor. *Parting the Waters: America in the King Years, 1954–63.* New York: Touchstone, 1988.

———. *Pillar of Fire: America in the King Years, 1963–65.* New York: Touchstone, 1998.

Brands, H. W. *Andrew Jackson: His Life and Times.* New York: Doubleday, 2005.

———. *TR.* New York: Basic Books, 1997.

Brendon, Piers. *The Dark Valley.* New York: Vintage, 2000.

Brundage, William Fitzhugh. *Lynching in the New South: Georgia and Virginia, 1880–1930.* Urbana: University of Illinois Press, 1993.

Burleigh, Michael. "They All Knew They Were Right." *Wall Street Journal*, 16 April 2011, C5–C6.

Carlton, David L., and Peter A. Coclanis. "Capital Mobilization and Southern Industry, 1880–1905: The Case of the Carolina Piedmont." *Journal of Economic History* 49 (March 1989): 73–94.

Cash, W. J. *The Mind of the South.* New York: Vintage, 1941.

Cashman, Sean Dennis. *America in the Age of the Titans: The Progressive Era and World War I.* New York: New York University Press, 1988.

Cecelski, David S., and Timothy B. Tyson, eds. *Democracy Betrayed: The Wilmington Race Riot of 1898 and Its Legacy.* Chapel Hill: University of North Carolina Press, 1998.

Chalmers, David M. *Hooded Americanism: The History of the Ku Klux Klan.* New York: New Viewpoints, 1951.

Chandler, David Leon. *The Binghams of Louisville: The Dark History behind One of America's Great Fortunes.* New York: Crown, 1989.

Chernow, Ron. *The House of Morgan: An American Banking Dynasty and the Rise of Modern Finance.* New York: Atlantic Monthly Press, 1990.

———. *Titan: The Life of John D. Rockefeller, Sr.* New York: Random House, 1998.

Chodorov, Frank. "Cheers to the Peddler Class." *Free Market: Newsletter of the Ludwig von Mises Institute* 25 (2007): 1–6.

Christensen, Rob. *The Paradox of Tar Heel Politics: The Personalities, Elections, and Events That Shaped Modern North Carolina.* Chapel Hill: University of North Carolina Press, 2008.

Cicero, Marcus Tullius. *The Fifth Philippic.* Cambridge: Cambridge University Press, 2003.

Clark, Robert L., Lee A. Craig, and Jack Wilson. *A History of Public Sector Pensions in the United States.* Philadelphia: University of Pennsylvania Press, 2003.

Coclanis, Peter. *The Shadow of a Dream: Economic Life and Death in the South Carolina Low Country, 1670–1920.* New York: Oxford University Press, 1989.

Cohen, Rachel. "Can You Forgive Him?" *New Yorker*, November 8, 2004, 48–65.

Cooper, John Milton, Jr. *Walter Hines Page: The Southerner as American, 1855–1918.* Chapel Hill: University of North Carolina Press, 1977.

———. *The Warrior and the Priest: Woodrow Wilson and Theodore Roosevelt.* Cambridge: Belknap Press of Harvard University Press, 1983.

———. *Woodrow Wilson: A Biography.* New York: Vintage, 2011.

Craig, Lee A. *To Sow One Acre More: Childbearing and Farm Productivity in the Antebellum North.* Baltimore: Johns Hopkins University Press, 1993.

Craig, Lee A., and Douglas Fisher. *The Integration of the European Economy, 1850–1913.* London: Macmillan, 1997.

Craig, Locke. *Memoirs and Speeches.* Edited by Mary Jones. Asheville, N.C.: Hackney and Moale, 1923.

Creel, George. Review of *The Wilson Era: Years of Peace 1910–1917. American Historical Review* 50 (April 1945): 576–77.

Cronon, William. *Nature's Metropolis: Chicago and the Great West.* New York: Norton, 1991.

Crow, Jeffrey J., Paul D. Escott, and Flora J. Hatley. *A History of African Americans in North Carolina.* Raleigh: North Carolina Department of Cultural Resources, 1992.

Daniels, Adelaide. *Recollections of a Cabinet Minister's Wife.* Raleigh: Mitchell Printing, 1945.

Daniels, Judge Frank Arthur. "The Daniels, Seabrook, and Cleaves Families." Appendix in *Tar Heel Editor*, by Josephus Daniels, 513–26. Chapel Hill: University of North Carolina Press, 1939.

Daniels, Jonathan. *The End of Innocence.* Philadelphia: Lippincott, 1954.

Daniels, Josephus. *The Cabinet Diaries of Josephus Daniels: 1913–1921.* Edited by E. David Cronon. Lincoln: University of Nebraska Press, 1963.

———. *Editor in Politics.* Chapel Hill: University of North Carolina Press, 1941.

———. *The Life of Woodrow Wilson, 1856–1924.* N.p.: Will H. Johnson, 1924.

———. *Our Navy at War.* Washington, D.C.: Pictorial Bureau, 1922.

———. *Shirt-Sleeve Diplomat.* Chapel Hill: University of North Carolina Press, 1947.

———. *Tar Heel Editor.* Chapel Hill: University of North Carolina Press, 1939.

———. *The Wilson Era: Years of Peace, 1910–1917.* Chapel Hill: University of North Carolina Press, 1944.

———. *The Wilson Era: Years of War and After, 1917–1923.* Chapel Hill: University of North Carolina Press, 1946.

Daniels, Lucy. *With a Woman's Voice: A Writer's Struggle for Emotional Freedom.* Toronto: Madison Books, 2002.

Deaton, Brian. "Analysis of Local Population and Newspaper Circulation." Unpublished manuscript, North Carolina State University, 2005.

Dupuy, R. Ernest, and Trevor N. Dupuy. *The Encyclopedia of Military History from 3500 B.C. to the Present.* 2nd rev. ed. New York: Harper and Row, 1986.

Durden, Robert F. *Bold Entrepreneur: A Life of James B. Duke.* Durham, N.C.: Carolina Academic Press, 2003.

———. "Marion Butler." In *Dictionary of North Carolina Biography*, edited by William S. Powell, 1:291–92. Chapel Hill: University of North Carolina Press, 1979.

———. "Washington Duke." In *Dictionary of North Carolina Biography*, edited by William S. Powell, 2:117–18. Chapel Hill: University of North Carolina Press, 1986.

Eagles, Charles. "Jonathan Daniels." In *Dictionary of North Carolina Biography*, edited by William S. Powell, 2:12–13. Chapel Hill: University of North Carolina Press, 1986.

———. *Jonathan Daniels and Race Relations: The Evolution of a Southern Liberal*. Knoxville: University of Tennessee Press, 1982.

Edmonds, Helen G. *The Negro and Fusion Politics in North Carolina, 1894–1901*. Chapel Hill: University of North Carolina Press, 1951.

Emerson, Ken. "What the Pols Should Read." *Wall Street Journal*, August 18–19, 2007.

Evans, Thomas. *The War Lovers: Roosevelt, Lodge, Hearst, and the Rush to Empire, 1898*. New York: Little, Brown, 2010.

Evans, William. "Daniel Lindsay Russell." In *Dictionary of North Carolina Biography*, edited by William S. Powell, 5:271–73. Chapel Hill: University of North Carolina Press, 1994.

Ferguson, Niall. *Empire: The Rise and Demise of the British World Order and the Lessons for Global Power*. New York: Basic Books, 2002.

———. *The House of Rothschild: Money's Prophets, 1798–1848*. New York: Penguin, 1998.

Finke, Roger, and Rodney Starke. *The Churching of America, 1776–2005*. New Brunswick, N.J.: Rutgers University Press, 2005.

Fleming, Thomas. *The Illusion of Victory: America in World War I*. New York: Basic Books, 2003.

Flinn, Michael W. *The European Demographic System, 1500–1820*. Baltimore: Johns Hopkins University Press, 1981.

Friedman, Milton. "Bimetallism Revisited." *Journal of Economic Perspectives* 4 (Fall 1990): 85–104.

Friedman, Milton, and Anna Schwartz. *A Monetary History of the United States*. Princeton: Princeton University Press, 1963.

Gavins, Raymond. *The Perils and Prospects of Southern Black Leadership*. Durham, N.C.: Duke University Press, 1977.

Gentzkow, Matthew, Edward L. Glaeser, and Claudia Goldin. "The Rise of the Fourth Estate: How Newspapers Became Informative and Why It Mattered." National Bureau of Economic Research Working Paper No. 10791, September 2004.

Gordon, John Steele. *Hamilton's Blessing: The Extraordinary Life and Times of Our National Debt*. New York: Walker and Co., 1997.

Haines, Michael, Lee A. Craig, and Thomas Weiss. U.S. Censuses of Agriculture, by County, 1840–1880. Colgate University, computer files, 2000.

Halberstam, David. *The Coldest Winter: America and the Korean War*. New York: Hyperion, 2007.

Halpern, Paul G. *A Naval History of World War I*. Annapolis, Md.: United States Naval Institute, 1994.

Hamilton, James. *All the News That's Fit to Sell: How the Market Transforms Information*. Princeton: Princeton University Press, 2004.

Hastings, Max. *Retribution: The Battle for Japan, 1944–45*. New York: Random House, 2007.

Heckscher, August. *Woodrow Wilson*. New York: Charles Scribner's Sons, 1991.

Herring, George C. *From Colony to Superpower: U.S. Foreign Relations since 1776*. Oxford: Oxford University Press, 2008.

Herwig, Holger H., and Neil M. Heyman. "Henry Thomas Mayo." In *Biographical Dictionary of World War I*, edited by Holger Herwig and Neil M. Heyman, 247–48. Westport, Conn.: Greenwood Press, 1982.

———. "John Joseph Pershing." In *Biographical Dictionary of World War I*, edited by Holger Herwig and Neil M. Heyman, 276–77. Westport, Conn.: Greenwood Press, 1982.

———. "Josephus Daniels." In *Biographical Dictionary of World War I*, edited by Holger Herwig and Neil M. Heyman, 125. Westport, Conn.: Greenwood Press, 1982.

———. "Origins." In *Biographical Dictionary of World War I*, edited by Holger Herwig and Neil M. Heyman, 3–10. Westport, Conn.: Greenwood Press, 1982.

———. "William Snowden Sims." In *Biographical Dictionary of World War I*, edited by Holger Herwig and Neil M. Heyman, 318–19. Westport, Conn.: Greenwood Press, 1982.

Howe, Daniel Walker. *What Hath God Wrought: The Transformation of America, 1815–1848*. Oxford: Oxford University Press, 2007.

Hughes, Jonathan. *The Vital Few: The Entrepreneur and American Economic Progress*. Oxford: Oxford University Press, 1986.

Hughes, Jonathan, and Louis Cain. *American Economic History*. Boston: Addison Wesley, 2003.

Hunt, James L. *Marion Butler and American Populism*. Chapel Hill: University of North Carolina Press, 2003.

Johnson, Ronald, and Gary Libecap. *The Federal Civil Service and the Problem of Bureaucracy*. Chicago: University of Chicago Press, 1994.

Johnston, Hugh Buckner. "Louis Dicken Wilson." In *Dictionary of North Carolina Biography*, edited by William S. Powell, 6:232–33. Chapel Hill: University of North Carolina Press, 1996.

Kazin, Michael. *A Godly Hero: The Life of William Jennings Bryan*. New York: Random House, 2006.

Kemp, Peter. "Balance of Naval Power, August 1914." In *World War I*, edited by Peter Young. New York: Marshall Cavendish, 1984.

Kennedy, Paul. *The Rise and Fall of the Great Powers: Economic Change and Military Conflict, 1500 to 2000*. New York: Random House, 1987.

Kittredge, Tracy Barrett. *Naval Lessons of the Great War*. Garden City, N.Y.: Doubleday, Page, 1921.

Kousser, J. Morgan. *The Shaping of Southern Politics: Suffrage Restrictions and the Establishment of the One-Party South, 1880–1910*. New Haven, Conn.: Yale University Press, 1974.

Kuhn, Clifford M. *Contesting the New South Order: The 1914–1915 Strike at Atlanta's Fulton Mills*. Chapel Hill: University of North Carolina Press, 2001.

Lamoreaux, Naomi. *The Great Merger Movement in American Business, 1895–1904*. New York: Cambridge University Press, 1985.

Lehmann, Nicholas. "Paper Tigers." *New Yorker*, April 13, 2009, 72–77.

Leidholt, Alexander. *Battling Nell: The Life of Southern Journalist Cornelia Battle Lewis*. Baton Rouge: Louisiana State University Press, 2009.

Leloudis, James. *Schooling the New South: Pedagogy, Self, and Society in North Carolina, 1880–1920*. Chapel Hill: University of North Carolina Press, 1996.

Lepore, Jill. "Back Issues." *New Yorker*, January 26, 2009, 68–72.

Leuchtenberg, William E. *Franklin Delano Roosevelt and the New Deal*. New York: Harper and Row, 1965.

Link, Arthur S., ed. *Papers of Woodrow Wilson*. 69 vols. Woodrow Wilson Foundation. Princeton: Princeton University Press.

———. *Woodrow Wilson: A Brief Biography*. Cleveland, Ohio: World Pub. Co., 1963.

Lukas, J. Anthony. *Big Trouble*. New York: Simon and Schuster, 1997.

MacMillan, Margaret. *Paris, 1919*. New York: Random House, 2003.

Magruder, Nathaniel F. "Cameron Morrison." In *Dictionary of North Carolina Biography*, edited by William S. Powell, 4:328–30. Chapel Hill: University of North Carolina Press, 1991.

Manchester, William. *The Arms of Krupp, 1587–1968: The Rise and Fall of the Industrial Dynasty That Armed Germany at War*. Toronto: Little, Brown, 1968.

Margo, Robert A. *Race and Schooling in the South, 1880–1950*. Chicago: University of Chicago Press, 1990.

Massie, Robert K. *Castles of Steel: Britain, Germany, and the Winning of the Great War at Sea*. New York: Random House, 2003.

———. *Dreadnought: Britain, Germany, and the Coming of the Great War*. New York: Random House, 1991.

Maupin, Armistead Jones. "Armistead Jones." In *Dictionary of North Carolina Biography*, edited by William S. Powell, 3:314–15. Chapel Hill: University of North Carolina Press, 1988.

McBride, William M. *Technological Change and the United States Navy, 1865–1945*. Baltimore: Johns Hopkins University Press, 2000.

McCartney, Laton. *The Teapot Dome Scandal*. New York: Random House, 2008.

McCloskey, Deirdre N. *The Bourgeois Virtues: Ethics for an Age of Commerce*. Chicago: University of Chicago Press, 2006.

McClure, Rusty. *Crosley: Two Brothers and a Business Empire That Transformed the Nation*. Cincinnati: Clerisy Press, 2006.

McKenna, Richard. *The Sand Pebbles*. Greenwich, Conn.: Crest, 1962.

McLynn, Frank. *The Burma Campaign: Disaster into Triumph*. New Haven, Conn.: Yale University Press, 2010.

Meehan, James. "Locke Craig." In *Dictionary of North Carolina Biography*, edited by William S. Powell, 1:452–53. Chapel Hill: University of North Carolina Press, 1979.

Menand, Louis. "Lives of Others: The Biography Business." *New Yorker*, August 7, 2007, 64–66.

Miller, Nathan. *The U.S. Navy: A History.* Annapolis, Md.: Naval Institute Press, 1977.

Moreno, Julio. *Yankee Don't Go Home! Mexican Nationalism, American Business Culture, and the Shaping of Modern Mexico, 1920–1950.* Chapel Hill: University of North Carolina Press, 2003.

Morrison, Joseph L. *Josephus Daniels: The Small-d Democrat.* Chapel Hill: University of North Carolina Press, 1966.

———. *Josephus Daniels Says . . . : An Editor's Political Odyssey from Bryan to Wilson and F.D.R., 1894–1913.* Chapel Hill: University of North Carolina Press, 1962.

Nasaw, David. *The Chief: The Life of William Randolph Hearst.* New York: Houghton Mifflin, 2000.

Noble, M. C. S. *A History of the Public Schools of North Carolina.* Chapel Hill: University of North Carolina Press, 1930.

North Carolina Biographical Dictionary. 2nd ed. New York: Somerset, 1999.

Parker, George F. *Recollections of Grover Cleveland.* New York: Century, 1909.

Pleszczynski, Wladyslaw. "Pulitzer." *Wall Street Journal*, January 30, 2002, A16.

Powell, William S., ed. *Dictionary of North Carolina Biography.* 6 vols. Chapel Hill: University of North Carolina Press, 1979–96.

———. *North Carolina through Four Centuries.* Chapel Hill: University of North Carolina Press, 1989.

Preston, Diana. *Lusitania: An Epic Tragedy.* New York: Walker & Co., 2002.

Ransom, Roger L. *Conflict and Compromise: The Political Economy of Slavery, Emancipation, and the American Civil War.* Cambridge: Cambridge University Press, 1989.

Ransom, Roger L., and Richard Sutch. *One Kind of Freedom: The Economic Consequences of Emancipation.* Cambridge: Cambridge University Press, 1977.

Reed, James. "American Foreign Policy: The Politics of Missions and Josiah Strong, 1890–1900." *Church History* 41 (1972): 230–45.

Reid, Joseph D., Jr. "Sharecropping as an Understandable Market Response: The Post-Bellum South." *Journal of Economic History* 33 (March 1973): 106–30.

Rockoff, Hugh. "'The Wizard of Oz' as a Monetary Allegory." *Journal of Political Economy* 98 (August 1990): 739–60.

Roland, Alex, W. J. Bolster, and Alexander Keyssar. *The Way of the Ship: American Maritime History Revisited, 1600–2000.* Hoboken, N.J.: Wiley, 2008.

Romer, Christina D. "The Prewar Business Cycle Reconsidered: New Estimates of Gross National Product, 1869–1908." *Journal of Political Economy* 97 (February 1989): 1–37.

Spiegelman, Willard. "Chautauqua: Exercise for Active Minds." *Wall Street Journal*, July 20, 2006, D8.

Steelwater, Eliza. *Hangman's Knot: Lynching, Legal Execution, and America's Struggle with the Death Penalty.* Boulder, Colo.: Westview Press, 2003.

Stevenson, David. *With Our Backs to the Wall: Victory and Defeat in 1918*. Cambridge: Belknap Press of Harvard University Press, 2011.

Strachan, Hew. *The First World War*. New York: Viking/Penguin, 2003.

Thomas, Emory M. *The Confederate Nation, 1861–1865*. New York: Harper and Row, 1979.

Tilley, Nannie M. *The Bright Tobacco Industry, 1860–1929*. Chapel Hill: University of North Carolina Press, 1948.

Tolnay, Stewart E., and Beck, E. M. *A Festival of Violence: An Analysis of Southern Lynchings, 1882–1930*. Urbana: University of Illinois Press, 1992.

Tuchman, Barbara W. *Guns of August*. New York: Bonanza Books, 1982.

Tyson, Timothy. *Blood Done Sign My Name*. New York: Three Rivers Press, 2004.

———. "The Ghosts of 1898: Wilmington's Race Riot and the Rise of White Supremacy." *Raleigh News and Observer*, November 17, 2006.

U.S. Bureau of the Census. *Historical Statistics of the United States, Colonial Times to 1970*. Bicentennials ed. Washington, D.C., 1975.

Valentine, Patrick M. *The Rise of a Southern Town: Wilson, North Carolina, 1849–1920*. Baltimore, Md.: Gateway Press, 2002.

Wade, Wyn Craig. *The Fiery Cross: The Ku Klux Klan in America*. New York: Simon and Schuster, 1987.

Walton, Gary, and Hugh Rockoff. *History of the American Economy*. Fort Worth: Dryden Press, 1998.

Watson, Richard L. "Josephus Daniels." In *Dictionary of North Carolina Biography*, edited by William Powell, 2:13–14. Chapel Hill: University of North Carolina Press, 1986.

Waugh, Elizabeth Culbertson. *Raleigh: North Carolina's Capital*. Raleigh: Junior League, 1967.

Webb, Mena. *Jule Carr: General without an Army*. Chapel Hill: University of North Carolina Press, 1987.

Weidenmier, Marc D., and Kris James Mitchener. "Empire, Public Goods, and the Roosevelt Corollary." National Bureau of Economic Research Working Paper No. 10729, August 2004.

Wert, Jeffry D. "Randolph Abbott Shotwell." In Dictionary of North Carolina Biography, edited by William S. Powell, 5:342. Chapel Hill: University of North Carolina Press, 1994.

Winik, Jay. *The Great Upheaval*. New York: Harper Collins, 2007.

Wood, Phillip J. *Southern Capitalism: The Political Economy of North Carolina, 1880–1980*. Durham, N.C.: Duke University Press, 1986.

Woodward, C. Vann. *Origins of the New South, 1877–1913*. Baton Rouge: Louisiana State University Press, 1951.

———. *The Strange Career of Jim Crow*. Oxford: Oxford University Press, 2002.

Wright, Gavin. *Old South, New South: Revolutions in the Southern Economy since the Civil War*. New York: Basic Books, 1986.

Yergin, Daniel. *The Prize: The Epic Quest for Oil, Money, and Power*. New York: Simon and Schuster, 1992.

Index

Adams, Spencer, 191

Advance (Wilson, N.C.), 42–61 passim, 68, 70, 79–80, 93, 127, 144, 279, 322, 366; JD becomes owner of, 45–47; profitability of under JD's management, 54–55

Alford, L. F., 142–43, 279–80, 286, 399

Allen, Dan, 370

American Expeditionary Force, 336, 339, 444–45 (n. 16)

American Tobacco Company, x, 116–19

Andrews, A. B., 102, 141, 425 (n. 43)

Arendell, F. B. "Falc," 72–73, 144, 182, 184, 422 (n. 68)

Arthur, Chester, 57

Arthur, John A., 3, 8, 11, 13

Ashe, Samuel D., 25, 27, 67–69, 71, 77, 80, 87, 89, 133, 140, 146; and state printing contract, 91–98

Asquith, H. H., 327

Austria: Serbian crisis, role in, 289–92

Ávila Camacho, Manuel, 410

Aycock, Charles Brantley, 38, 108–9, 140, 146–47, 193, 198, 214, 278, 283, 384; white supremacy campaign, role in, 180–83; as governor, 196–97, 205; and 1912 U.S. Senate campaign, 207–9; death of, 209

Baden, Prince Max von, 339–42

Bagley, Adelaide Ann Worth (mother-in-law), 66, 83–86, 88, 96

Bagley, Belle (sister-in-law), 369

Bagley, Ethel (sister-in-law), 369

Bagley, Henry (brother-in-law), 278, 280, 399–400; as *N&O* business manager, 283–87, 441 (n. 84); fired by JD, 287

Bagley, W. H. (father-in-law), 65–67, 83, 85–86

Bagley, Worth (brother-in-law): death of, 177, 431 (n. 35)

Bailey, Josiah, 451 (n. 71)

Baker, Newton, 221, 315, 345–46

Baker, Ray Stannard, 447 (n. 88)

Banks, Howard, 235

Barnett, George: becomes commandant of the Marine Corps, 262–63; retirement of, 365

Baruch, Bernard, 283

Bassett, John Spencer, 192–94

Battle, Richard, 109

Beauregard, P. G. T., 53

Bell, John, 4, 6

Belleau Wood, Battle of, 338

Benson, William Shepherd, 334, 353, 357; becomes first chief of naval operations, 236

Bethmann-Hollweg, Theobald von, 290, 308, 312, 315–16, 321

Beveridge, Albert, 256

Biddle, William Phillips, 262

Big Five, 344, 350, 357

Big Three, 361

Bingham, Robert, 391

Birth of a Nation, The (Griffith), 375–77

Bismark, Otto von, 290

Blackstone, William, 63–64, 212

Blackwell, W. T. "Buck," 74–75

Bliss, Tasker, 348

Bourbons, 22–26, 68, 77, 89, 91–93, 106, 146, 148–49

Bowers, Annie, 31, 36

Branch, Alpheus, 45–46

Branch Banking Company (later BB&T), 46